Semi-Nomadic Anecdotes

HOWARD BALLOCH

ISBN: 978-1-4834-0620-6 (sc)
ISBN: 978-1-4834-0509-4 (hc)
ISBN: 978-1-4834-0508-7 (e)

Lulu Publishing Services rev. date: 12/12/2013

For Liani,
who sailed most of this voyage with me,
And in memory of my parents Maisie and Tony Balloch,
who launched me on it

CONTENTS

FOREWORD

When I first came onto this earthly scene, Joseph Stalin was ruling both the Soviet Union and the countries east of the Iron Curtain that had fallen along the line agreed at Yalta. Mao Zedong was in his second year in power in Beijing, and was already deep in ideological and military conflict with the West on the Korean Peninsula, in a war ostensibly between the DPRK and the UN. King George VI was ruling Britain, "Uncle Louis" St. Laurent was half-way through his tenure as Canada's quiet post-war leader, and Joey Smallwood, St. Laurent's co-conspirator in the confederate cause, was only in his early years as the dictator of Newfoundland. Although I did not think much about any of these men for years and years, and even though none of them ever asked for my advice or permission to do what they did, much of my life ended up being influenced by the world they created.

I have never been a diarist, but for as long as my parents were alive I was a regular letter-writer, and some if not all of my letters survived from my student years in Paris and from my postings in Jakarta and Prague. I also kept copies of my letters from the first few years serving in China as Ambassador, but after my father's death in the late 1990s and my mother's encroaching dementia I no longer had an audience for the detailed accounts of my life and so my letter-writing dried up. Throughout my various positions in Ottawa I kept notebooks in which I recorded things to do and brief shorthand-like notes from meetings, and these have been a great source of memory-triggers, even if putting them in chronological order (I had a terrible habit of not dating either the notebooks or the pages) took some help from old friends and colleagues. And in the end there are spaces in my story where notebooks and letters are missing, and all I have been able to rely on is my memory, which is vivid in places and foggy in others.

The story that follows is mostly but not entirely chronological, and I have tried to keep events more or less in the order in which they happened, which in the case of my time as Ambassador to China has been a little tricky given my imperfect memory. I write separately and not chronologically about Mongolia and North Korea, countries to which I was also accredited during my assignment as Ambassador to the Middle Kingdom.

I would also like to thank a number of former colleagues and current friends, especially Jeremy Kinsman, Bruce Jutzi, Gordon Houlden, Guy Saint-Jacques, Bernie Frolic and Marc Dupont for reading parts of this in draft and for suggesting corrections and overlooked events, as well as my wife Liani for doing the same. I am also very grateful to my daughter Cynthia for proof-reading an early version and making both stylistic and substantive suggestions. Also a special thanks to a couple of friends from the world of politics who gave me access to their papers and some who read chapters covering events in which they played a part. Any errors in facts or timing are of course my own.

This is, therefore, not an autobiography, nor a carefully recorded chronological history of my past sixty-two years. It is simply my story as and where I remember it, anecdotes from my passage (so far) through a semi-nomadic life.

BOOK I:

GROWING UP AND FOOLING AROUND

CHAPTER 1

THE EARLY YEARS

· · · · · · · · · · · ·

My father, Tony Balloch, emigrated from Britain to Newfoundland before World War II, returned to fight in the Royal Artillery during the war and then dragged his American bride, Maisie Howard, met during a mid-war visit to Washington, back to Corner Brook. It was there that our family was living both when my eldest sister Pat and younger brother Hugh were born and where my first memories were etched. My sister Joy and I were both born in England during my father's three-year management training assignment to the Bowater Paper Company mill in Cheshire, but we moved back before my first birthday and it was in Newfoundland that my siblings and I spent our most formative years.

Newfoundland was a very good place to grow up, especially with educated parents "from away" who ensured that we learned to appreciate all that was a good about the land and the people around us, without being held back by all the limitations and deprivations that were unavoidably part of the lives of so many of our childhood friends. And Newfoundland in the 1950s was very poor. On non-winter weekends we would almost always go on some sort of excursion, sometimes going out on an old company trawler called the "Grand Lake" to the outports in the Bay of Islands. There, at hamlets like Lark Harbour and Frenchman's Cove we would tie up at the wharfs and wander around and have picnics which we would share with local children, some of whom had clothes made from potato sacks and whose homes were little more than tar-paper shacks.

Back in the 1950s, no one in Western Newfoundland had much money, but my father's salary as a junior manager at the mill was plenty for us to live on and placed us at the upper end of the local wealth scale, along with the few doctors, lawyers the owners of stores and car dealerships. Most importantly, my father's job came with a company house, which changed as he climbed up the management ladder. The first house we had when we returned from England was a half-house at 8 Marcelle Avenue, which had two bedrooms on the second floor, where my parents and sisters slept, and Nurse Plunkett, a nanny who had come over with us from England and who earned little more than her keep, and I shared an attic room at the top of a steep set of stairs. A promotion for my father resulted in us moving across the street to a stand-alone house at 5 Marcelle, and a later advancement to Assistant Mill Manager led us further up the hill to quite a lovely house named "Hookers" at 14 Cobb Lane, which had a large lawn and even its own greenhouse. My parents used to joke that we were guaranteed God's protection at Hookers, as it was sandwiched between the respective homes of the Anglican and Roman Catholic bishops of Western Newfoundland, the latter being the far fancier house of the two. The Anglican was Bishop Seaborn, brother to J. Blair Seaborn who was the Canadian diplomat who brokered the Vietnam peace accord in 1973, an agreement which saw the creation of an international peacekeeping force that allowed the US to withdraw from its terrible southeast Asian entanglement "with honor". At the end of his career and in his retirement, I met Blair Seaborn several times and heard first hand about his involvement not only in the early 1970s but also in the mid-1960s, when he went frequently to Hanoi in a secret US-approved effort to find the forever elusive path towards de-escalation of the war. Bishop Seaborn's son also joined External Affairs, some years before I did, although our paths would seldom cross. The only other neighbour who would reappear in my life was Terry Poole, who was a few years older than I and whose brother and my sister Pat would hang out together in the same crowd. Terry became an accountant and then went into the chemical industry, and we would later in life serve together on the board of Vancouver-based Methanex. Terry reminded me of the nickname he and other boys had for my father, which was "Bean-pole Balloch", and of the general low regard they held for the littler boys of my age.

The division between Protestants and Roman Catholics in Newfoundland was deep when we were growing up; all schools were either one or the other. The sectarian school structure was guaranteed by the 1949 Terms of Union between Newfoundland and Canada, and it would take a constitutional amendment forty years later to fully establish a secular educational system. Protestant children and Catholic children generally didn't mix, and would get into fights whenever we met in groups. My best boyhood friend, Michael Huck, who lived directly across from us next to Bishop Seaborn, was Catholic. Although Michael and I would play together on weekends and skate together on our backyard rink in the winter, if we passed on the street with other friends during the week we would ignore each other completely. My first school was Fern Street School, which began at the first grade and was a single story structure that lacked a real foundation and was so cold on windy winter days that we had to keep our boots and jackets on.

At some point in the 1950s television reached Corner Brook, but we were late in buying a receiver, and the first program I remember was a thirty-minute Friday afternoon cartoon show I occasionally watched at Michael Huck's house. When my parents did finally buy a square black and white set we were limited to an hour a week, but because there was not much choice in programs and only one or two channels, we never felt deprived. The radio, on the other hand, brought Hockey Night in Canada every Saturday evening. The broadcast was from Montreal or Toronto and always featured either the Canadiens or the Maple Leafs, and for some reason would always begin at the end of the first period. I loved listening to the broadcasts, became a firm Canadiens fan, and could watch every play and goal in my mind, courtesy of the colourful language of Danny Gallivan, the English-language play-by-play reporter.

There was a local semi-pro hockey team, the Corner Brook Royals, that was part of one of the NHL feeder organizations, and one year the Boston Bruins came on a pre-season tour of Newfoundland. Of course we all went to the stadium to watch our local team play the pros and it started, as expected, as a hopelessly lop-sided match with the Bruins way out ahead after the first period. Between the first and second periods, the Bruins coach offered to mix up the teams, and when the game resumed with jerseys and players exchanged we were treated to a much more entertaining and balanced match.

Much of my Newfoundland childhood was spent outdoors. Hockey was played on backyard rinks built by us all at the beginning of winter and cleared of heavy snow by my father, whose skating skills were very rudimentary and who never let a chronically bad back interfere with his rink-tending responsibilities. In the mid-1950s a stadium was built and the organized junior hockey program was moved indoors. We used to walk to and from the stadium, sometimes in our skates with skate guards on, which must have helped strengthen our ankles. Skiing was also a regular family activity, although this was long before Marble Mountain was built, the modern ski resort with mechanical lifts just north of Corner Brook. There was a small nine-hole golf club just at the edge of town and we would cross-country ski there almost every winter weekend, and the local Rod and Gun Club would hold ski races for children, organized by age group. These were what now would be called *randonée*, and consisted of skiing across a frozen lake, climbing a hill, skiing along a trail through the woods, down a slalom course and over a small ski-jump and then along the flat again to a finish line. Our bindings clasped our boots at the toe and had a cable around the heel, which could be hooked down for going downhill and unhooked for climbing or racing across the flats. Our skis were simple wooden slats and in the late 1950s we chiselled notches along their length and screwed thin "steel edges" onto them and thought we had become very fancy and modern. One winter the owner of the local Chevy dealership bought a Snow-cat, which was an early predecessor of the snowmobile, a tracked vehicle about the size of a small car, and he would sometimes tow a rope behind it to pull us children uphill, but this was as close we ever got to a modern ski-lift. Electricity for Corner Brook and its paper mill was provided by a hydroelectric power plant fed from a dam well out of town and as a family we would ski from the dam along the penstocks to the plant and from the plant along the transmission lines into town. I have a very clear memory of once doing so with just my father. After my mother dropped us off at the dam I confessed that I had forgotten my hat; my father was quite angry at my carelessness and as it was bitterly cold we had to swap his hat back and forth every ten minutes as we skied back into town.

The winters were long then and for many they were very hard. The houses in our neighbourhood were decently built and had central heating, but across the valley in Curling and further out the Bay of Islands people did not have insulation or furnaces and had to keep their fires and stoves lit pretty well from October though April. This meant that house fires were very common. There was a boy from my class at school who came from a family of thirteen whose entire family died when their house burned down. This was sadly not very unusual.

The ocean froze solid in the bays and along the coast of Newfoundland in those days, most years stretching for a mile or two seaward. There were winter roads across the Bay of Islands that shortened trucking distances by scores of kilometres; in the summer what remained of these roads looked strange, descending to the water's edge on one side of the bay and rising up on the other side as if the trucks could go right across along the bottom.

In 1958 my father was sent to a three-month management-training course at Harvard University in Boston. Rather than returning without him to Corner Brook after our summer vacation in Jamestown, my mother took us four children to Washington where we lived with her parents and went to local schools. I went to Public School 160 on 34th Street, about a twenty-minute walk from my grandparents' home on 36th Place. It was my first experience as an outsider, for my accent and vocabulary and spelling were different from those of local children, and I was teased by my classmates. Every morning before our studies began, all the children would stand, face the American flag, place their right hands over their hearts and recite the American Oath of Allegiance. I objected and refused to do so, staying seated at my desk when others stood up. Not surprisingly, this was treated as a disciplinary matter and my teacher called my mother. My grandfather was a retired US Admiral and very patriotic, but respected the fact that we were being brought up as Canadians, and he came to the school and worked out a compromise. I would respectfully stand up and face the flag with the other children but did not need to place my hand over my heart or recite the oath. Even though I remained silent the daily repetition of the oath seared the words into my young mind and I can still repeat it today.

Spending an autumn in Washington was a great experience for a boy of seven years old. My grandfather, Admiral Herbert Seymour Howard, took me to the David Taylor Model Basin where he had been the Director during World War II, designing warships for the Navy. Watching three and four-foot long models of destroyers and aircraft carriers being towed in the testing tanks was fascinating, and it was thrilling to see the respect given my grandfather as the former head of US Naval Design. This also carried over to summers in Jamestown, for Newport was still a very significant naval base for the US Atlantic Fleet. My grandfather was always well treated when he went to the base or to the then headquarters of the Atlantic carrier fleet across the bay at Quonset Point. He took me on a tour of the USS Midway when it was stationed there, and another outing on the destroyer USS Forest Sherman when it was in Newport, under the command of an officer who had once worked for him. The best of all was a day out on the *Barbara Anne*, the President's motor-yacht, for Dwight Eisenhower and my grandfather had been military colleagues and my grandfather brought me along when invited to spend a quiet summer's day with his old friend. Eisenhower was to me just a nice old man, who put me in the hands of a much more interesting young lieutenant who arranged for me to steer the boat from the bridge and took me down below to see the engine room, which was so clean and polished that there was not even a spot of oil on the floor. The *Barbara-Anne* became the *Honey-Fitz* when John F. Kennedy became President, and we would still see it around Narragansett Bay when the Kennedys were in residence at Hammersmith Farms, but Lyndon Johnson used it little and Richard Nixon quietly disposed of it.

At the end of my father's program at Harvard, he came down to Washington to pick us up and we headed back to Corner Brook on the *Margaret Bowater*, one of the Bowater ships from Baltimore. Bowater was the major supplier of newsprint to both the New York Times and the Washington Post and ran its own small fleet of freighters, each named after one of Sir Eric Bowater's children or other female relatives. As children we loved traveling by sea on the Bowater ships, each of which was fitted out with a few staterooms. The food was, at least to a child's palate, terrific with fresh bread made daily and at every meal there was a printed menu printed on formal little cards with the Bowater crest on the top. We thought these menus were fantastic and we collected them. My little brother Hugh thought they were so valuable that he once tried to sell them. My mother received a telephone call from an older lady who lived down the street, who said that cute little Hugh had offered her his collection of menus, which she had been preparing to buy for a penny apiece when he named his price of five dollars each!

The winter of 1958-59 was a harsh winter in the western Atlantic, and when we were en route back to Corner Brook after Christmas and approaching the Bay of Islands up Newfoundland's west coast, the *Margaret Bowater* got trapped in the pack ice. Once the ship was immobilized the ice thickened and then there was nothing to do except to wait for a Canadian Coast Guard icebreaker, which did not arrive for a day or two. In the meantime we enjoyed ourselves on board, and men from the outport at Bottle Cove came out across the ice and sold fish and other supplies to the vessel's quartermaster. Once the icebreaker arrived it carved a passage for us all the way from the outer roads of the Bay of Islands to Corner Brook, a distance of some thirty nautical miles. My sisters and I were days late for the start of our winter term at school, but we had a wonderful tale to tell to excuse ourselves.

In Newfoundland, once the spring came we would go fishing a lot, both inland on the rivers for trout and salmon and out on the bay for cod and flounder. Bowaters kept a fishing lodge at a place called Taylor's Brook as well as *Strawberry Hill,* a very fancy country house up the Serpentine River where visiting luminaries would come for salmon fishing. We would stay at the former but never at the latter, and learned to fly-fish and tie our own flies at a very young age. The salmon were plentiful, and I do not know whether it was for reasons of conservation or simply to avoid having too many fish that that we as children were allowed to fish only part of the day, generally only until breakfast time. There was a full time cook at the fishing camp at Taylor's Brook called Duff, and he was a real old-style logging camp cook. He was great with basics but could not read, and one time my mother brought up with us a packaged mix for lemon meringue pie and asked him to serve it to us for dessert. Duff looked at the picture on the package and just guessed at how to prepared the filling. It looked fine but the texture was like hard rubber and it was really inedible. To avoid hurting Duff's feelings, my mother took her piece of pie and hid it in her waders and we all followed suit. After lunch we threw our pie into the river. It got caught in a back eddy near the dock and wouldn't go downstream until we were sent out in a rowboat to push it into the current, all to ensure that Duff would not discover that we had tossed away his lovely pie.

When we went out on the bay we would jig for cod without bait, using lines with three or four big lead three-hook jiggers on them every meter or so. We would sometimes catch fish too big for us as children to lift over the gunwales, and if we allowed our jigs to drag near the bottom we would sometimes catch flounder, or flatfish as we called them. We would also go up to Bonne Bay when the capelin were running and walk out into the frigid shallows and catch the little fish in our hands or in buckets and throw them up on the shore. Our parents found the water dreadfully cold and would never swim, and we children would have contests to see who could stay longest in the water, with a minute being quite a feat. Icebergs being carried down the west coast on the Labrador Current would be visible in the distance as we played in the waves.

Although Newfoundland had been part of Canada since 1949, if someone had asked who were the most important world leaders, we probably would have ranked the Premier of Newfoundland, Joey Smallwood, as number one, followed by the Queen of England and then the President of the United States. God might have slipped into that list somewhere, but I am not sure we even knew the name of the Canadian Prime Minister. In 1959, Corner Brook was graced with a visit by the top two, with Joey Smallwood accompanying Queen Elizabeth II at the start of her Royal Tour of Canada. I took part in lining the streets for the parade with all my Boy Scout and Girl Guide colleagues as the Queen's motorcade went slowly down Park Street in front of the middle school, and afterwards I even shook hands with both the Queen and the Premier, who came to a garden party at Corner Brook House which included my parents and other mill managers and their families.

Being a Boy Scout in those days was a great part of childhood. We would really rough it camping in the woods and learned lots of survival skills. We were also given the opportunity to collectively participate in events that came from time to time to Corner Brook. One was the visit of a Canadian submarine, which took us on board for a trip out the bay and even for a brief dive. It was terribly small inside but a tremendous thrill for us young boys. Another much earlier event for the Girl Guides and Boy Scouts, probably around 1956 or 1957, was a visit by Lady Baden-Powell, widow of the founder of the modern scouting movement, Robert Baden-Powell. Lady Baden-Powell came to Corner Brook and we had a big jamboree of all the Guides and Scouts of Western Newfoundland up on the baseball field between our home and the Armoury. At night there was a big sing-along to honour Lady Baden-Powell and the Guides led in the singing of one of their songs which was meant to include the word Amsterdam, avoiding the last syllable as "damn" was then considered a curse word. When they got to that part of the song I yelled out "Damn" at the top of my voice and thoroughly embarrassed my sisters and parents!

Once we moved to Hookers, my parents began a tradition of hosting a dance every New Year's Eve. The party would start quite late, and as children we would not participate, but we would sit behind the railings at the top of the stairs to the second floor and watch the dancers. There were many such events in our childhood where we were expected "to be seen but not heard". One year my father decided on the afternoon of the dance to burn in the living room fireplace all the pine boughs that had been used as Christmas decorations. The boughs burned easily but as they burned, they started to float up the chimney and the soot coating the flue caught fire. They also blocked the flue and the house quickly filled with thick and acrid smoke. We were all rushed out of the house and the fire department was called, and we stood on the lawn watch great flames shooting out of the top of the chimney. It was as entertaining as fireworks on the first of July! The fire department said that there was not much they could or needed to do as long as the chimney fire just burned itself out, which it did after an hour or so. My parents opened all the doors and windows to try to get rid of the smoke and the dance went ahead as planned, but it was months and months before the smell of burning pine had completely dissipated. Hosting a New Year's dance meant that my father had to save up and use many months of his liquor rations, for there was still a monthly limit on how much alcohol an individual could buy. One year, when my father had stocked up for the party, we awoke one morning to find all the booze stolen, along with a hand of bananas that had been sitting on the sideboard where the bottles had been stored. My father called the police and they came and said they would be unlikely to find the thief and recover the alcohol. So my father went back to the liquor store and got a special dispensation to buy more, and brought it home, only to have it stolen that very night. This time the police said that enough was enough, guessed who the felon was and went out and recovered all the booze.

We never had any doubt about the importance of the paper mill to the community in which we lived. My father did his best to make us aware of what papermaking entailed and the large number of people the mill relied upon, and who in turn relied upon the mill. He would take us out to the woodland operations to see the wood being harvested and hauled. There was one woodland railway that was named Howard's Brook where I enjoyed being pushed on a sidecar along what I thought was my very own railway. We would also go to the mill itself on Sunday afternoons as my father liked to make a point of wandering along the paper machines and around the groundwood digesters to chat with the men who were working the Sunday shifts rather than being at home with their families. We would collect handfuls of pulp from the front ends of the long paper machines and take it home and make coarse paper in our bathtub, drying it on wire screens and then using it for hobbies or drawings.

Growing up without television had many advantages. Winter evenings would involve us children putting on plays for our parents or building things. My father was a big fan of Meccano and the engineering skills a young mind could learn from it, and we built lift bridges and huge cranes expressly made too tall or wide to be moved to the basement on Sunday nights, which was one of my mother's house rules. It was wonderfully sturdy and far more durable than the American knock-off toy Erector Sets. The small electric motors that drove our machines were actually the same as the ones used in British military during World War II and they could withstand enormous abuse. I managed to keep my Meccano set long enough to share it with my children, all of who would become engineers, and it is now put away once again awaiting still another generation.

In the early summer of one of our later years in Corner Brook, my father came home one day and told me that Danny Gallivan and the immortal Rocket, Maurice Richard, were staying for a couple of days at the Glynmill Inn at the bottom of Cobb Lane prior to heading up the Humber River for salmon fishing. I instantly stopped what I was doing and ran down the hill to find two men sitting on the veranda at the inn. I went straight up to the older looking of the two, because I knew that the Rocket was "old" since there was already radio speculation about his retirement and said "Mr. Richard?" Gallivan laughed and pointed to his companion with his thumb. I then proceeded to impress them by recounting many of the Rocket's great goals of the previous season and by clearly knowing just about every NHL player and relevant hockey statistic. The following morning I brought my hockey stick down to the Glynmill Inn and the

13

Rocket not only autographed it but he even taped it for me. That stick gave me special status the next winter hockey season, and was, I was completely convinced, the entire reason why I scored more goals than ever before.

Almost a decade later, just after my parents moved to Montreal, I decided I wanted to buy my father a birthday present in the form of tickets to a Canadiens game during the Stanley Cup playoffs. Of course tickets to the playoffs were harder to find than ten-carat diamonds. After countless dead ends, I cold-called Danny Gallivan and reminded him of our conversations on the veranda of the Glynmill Inn and asked if he could help. Not only did he remember, but without any hesitation whatsoever he gave me two tickets for free, and my father and brother got to see a playoff game. Much, much later, in another century, I ran into Danny Gallivan's daughter, who was working for Methanex in Vancouver and told her this story. She appreciated hearing just another confirmation of what a classy guy her father was.

From Newfoundland to Nova Scotia

In the early 1960s, my father was promoted to be the Manager at the Bowater paper mill in Liverpool, Nova Scotia, so we packed everything onto one of the Bowater ships and headed down there in time for me to start Grade 6. My sisters were off at boarding school and the house my father bought was still being renovated, so my parents and my brother Hugh and I lived for three months in a tiny garage apartment behind the house of the previous mill manager, Mowbray Jones. It was a special time being in a new town and living in a very small place, and we had a lot of fun as a little foursome. Not only did we have in Liverpool the first house my parents actually owned, we now had two cars, one my mother's Chevy station-wagon and one a little Vauxhall that my father drove to and from work. One day shortly after moving into our house, my friends and I found my father's car parked in the back in front of a basketball net that we had hung on the garage. Wanting to play with my friends, I said that

I would go and look for my father to get him to move the car. Seven-year old Hugh simply jumped inside, put the car in neutral and rolled it down to the bottom of the garden. My father was more bemused than angry as no harm was done, and I was admonished as much as Hugh was for letting him do it.

Our own house at 49 Main Street was an old nineteenth century sea captain's house with wrap-around porches and a widow's walk on top. Part of the renovations that were completed before we moved in was to finish what had earlier been an attic, out of which was carved a room for my brother and me. Behind the eaves there were many crawl spaces and secret passages, and in one of them Hugh and I later installed our very first darkroom where we could develop and print our own photographs. Hugh and I also built a fabulous tree house in an old oak tree behind the house, expanding it again and again until it had rooms on three levels and entry points both via a ladder near the trunk and a secret entrance off one of the branches. We even camped out overnight in it from time to time.

Liverpool was a much older and smaller town than Corner Brook, dating back to before the American Revolution. It had received many loyalists, both white and black, in the flood of those who moved to Nova Scotia's south shore from New England, and it had long lost the hard edge that was still very much part of life in western Newfoundland. In addition to the paper mill there was a small shipbuilding and repair industry, a tannery and some tourism. Liverpool was also just one of many towns along the coast half way between Halifax and Yarmouth, smaller than a few and, at about three thousand souls, bigger than many. As a family we explored all along the coast, and spent time inland up the Mersey River at friends' cabins on Lake Rossignol and at Bowater's "Mersey Lodge", a lovely and well equipped fishing cabin, where we learned to shoot both rifles and shotguns.

Liverpool left fewer impressions and influence on me than Newfoundland had, since I spent only a year and a half at school there before being shipped off to boarding school, and summers were spent largely in Jamestown. I did all the things that normal boys of my age did and made some good friends. I learned to drive on the sand at Crescent Beach where there were no cars or hydrants to run into, and played hockey on the bog behind our house and in a loosely organized league that still played outdoors on ponds and lakes. I caddied at the golf course at White Point Lodge, a lovely seaside hotel that we went back and stayed in when our first two children were small, and picked up golf while there. I also started to misbehave, hitchhiking up to nearby Bridgewater with friends and sneaking beers and the occasional cigarette. I was growing up pretty normally.

It was during this time in my life that I started to get fanatical about sailing. In the 1950s we had a little rowboat named *Blomidon* (which we pronounced "Blow Me Down") after the range of mountains in western Newfoundland. *Blomidon* had a mast and a single sail and a short centreboard and even thought it was only seven or eight feet long, my grandfather used it to teach me the rudiments of sailing at a very young age. Then I took lessons from the local Conanicut Yacht Club in Jamestown and began racing, and I talked my parents into buying us a little "Blue Jay" class sloop, which was thirteen feet long, so I could race in the local club and in the Narragansett Bay competitions. Rather than a new boat, my father insisted on spending a minimum amount and bought us a very dilapidated old boat, the third or fourth oldest on the bay, and one that required a huge amount of work before it would even float. We named it *Evangeline* after the heroine in Longfellow's epic poem about the Acadians. The refurbishing of its hull and deck was a project I took on with my brother Hugh, who was a tireless sander even at the age of eight or nine, and we spent hundreds of hours getting our *Evangeline* seaworthy. We succeeded and proceeded to participate in many races and became proficient not only as young sailors but also in caring for a boat, something that our friends with fancy new boats did not have the same chance to learn.

Off to Boarding School

My parents had decided when we were still in Corner Brook that we should all go off to boarding schools in central Canada or New England, and by the time we moved to Nova Scotia my sisters were already both at King's Hall, an all-girls school in Compton, Québec. I was given the choice of going to the all-boys school nearby called Bishops College School (which was the all boy's partner school to King's Hall, and which eventually absorbed it in the general move to coeducation in the 1970s), to Trinity College School in Port Hope, Ontario, or to St. George's School in Newport, Rhode Island, across the bay from our summer house in Jamestown and the school my mother's brother Seymour had attended from 1929 to 1933. Since only the last of these three had a sailing program, the choice for me was a no-brainer, and so as our Jamestown summer of 1964 wound down I stayed behind, crossed the bay and settled in as a Second Former (eighth-grader) for a five-year sojourn at an all-boys New England prep school.

St. George's School was probably not much better and not much worse than most of the New England private boarding schools of that time, with most of the relatively wealthy boys drawn from the Boston-NYC-Washington corridor. There were a few from more distant US cities, including Chicago and San Francisco, a token black or two in every graduating class (our year had two, the year before us none), usually one or two exchange students from Britain or Scandinavia, and one Canadian, me. The New Yorkers and the Bostonians were very cliquish, and outsiders were razzed and generally made to be very conscious of any differences in their upbringing or accents. I cannot say that I enjoyed my time there, but I stayed busy and survived, and gradually emerged with at least a few friends.

The academics at St. George's were, I suspect, pretty average, although I had a few teachers that in memory stand out, either because of how good they were or how bad I was. In the latter category was a Latin teacher I had in my first year, Mr. Watt, who had come over from Scotland for a two-year stint after retiring as headmaster of the Edinburgh Academy. Mr.

Watt was a delightful man with a lovely wife who would invite students to dinner from time to time. He seemed ancient to us then but I suspect that he was probably in his mid-sixties at most. At the end of my first term of Latin he wrote in my report card "If Balloch would make an effort to learn the rudiments of the language, he might make some progress. If not, not". This would become part of family lore and my father would delight in finding opportunities to use the "If not, not" phrase.

Another memorable teacher was Dr. Norry Hoyt, or Norris Dresser Hoyt, who had a Ph.D. in English from Yale and who was also a good photographer and sailor and who wrote articles for Yachting magazine. All his articles were published as having been written by N. Dresser Hoyt III, because when he was first given an assignment the magazine had sent him a sample they wished him to emulate, it had been written by someone who had used his first initial, his middle name in full and the suffix "III". Norry, who had a great sense of humour, sent in his first article following the sample all the way down to changing his name, and he published sailing stories as N. Dresser Hoyt III for the rest of his life. Dr. Hoyt was a great teacher in the sense of bringing to life whatever we were learning about, and he was also the faculty advisor both for the Photography Club and the *Lance*, the school's yearbook. He and his wife Kitty were very kind and generous people and they kept their door open to any student who wanted to drop in. In my second year at St. George's my interest in photography started to take off and during one of the long weekends I spent with my cousins outside New York, my uncle Seymour gave me an old pre-war camera of his. It was a terrible old camera with a bellows lens, and when I started using it around the school, much to the mockery of other boys, Dr. Hoyt took me under his wing and taught me not only how to process pictures but how to think and compose. He also lent me a used camera of his, and I was truly smitten, and I then saved up enough to buy a used Nikkormat FT, the starter Nikon SLR.

The only real outlet for aspiring photographers at St. George's, as I suspect at most similar schools, was the yearbook, which was basically a photographic record of the year, all the sports teams and their triumphs or failures, the school plays and traditional events, and an extended section for the graduating class. By my third and middle year at the school I was one of the principle photographers, and started working on editing and layout as well. Dr. Hoyt would spend hundreds of hours with us teaching us the basics of journalism, creative writing and layout, and by the end of the year when we started sending sections off to the publishers and receiving proofs, it was a most fulfilling activity. By my last year I had become Editor-in-Chief of the *Lance*, and so spent an even greater amount of time focused on the yearbook, working with Dr. Hoyt and lounging around his main floor. As the deadline for publishing approached, his home became a messy extension of our workroom, as we would bring layout ideas and photos and proofs over to get his advice, and they would end up spread all over the Hoyt's living room.

Sports were an important part of my St. George's life. In the autumns I played football, moving from the junior "Middler" team in my first year gradually up to Varsity in my last two, playing guard and linebacker. We never had a championship team but seemed to win more than we lost, and would as often as not beat our arch-rival Middlesex from southern Massachusetts. In winter I naturally played hockey, which was still an outdoor sport in those days played on a rink that in spite of being open had proper chilling facilities. We would "put the rink in" just after Thanksgiving, staying up all night using big hoses to sprinkle down very thin layers of ice until it was about three inches thick. The wives of our coaches would bring us hot chocolate and cookies and I loved staying up all night to be part of this annual kick-off of skating and hockey. As in football I started at the bottom but spent the last three years on the varsity team, and although we again were never a great team in the New England leagues, I loved the game and the winter afternoons in the open air.

My spring sport was of course sailing, for which we had a terrific coach, Jeff Spranger, who taught English and went on to be editor of Sail magazine. As soon as we arrived back from Easter vacation in April we would be out on the water. Our boats were British-built Fireflys when I started, fast little planing racers with sharp bows and flat sterns. They were sufficiently unstable that we would occasionally capsize, which meant being dunked in the very cold early-spring water of Narragansett Bay. Coach Spranger decided that the Firefly could be improved upon and one of the most fun projects I was to be involved with during my years at St. George's was modifying an old Firefly hull into a plug for a new fibreglass class, which we called the Dragonfly. I and one or two other sailing team members worked with Spranger to plan and then execute this project, and in our last year we sailed in a brand new class of boats that we had helped create. The Dragonfly was clearly superior to the Firefly, faster and when righted after a capsize was virtually empty of water, and Spranger began selling the class to other schools and clubs. Although a few fleets sold, it was almost at the same time of the introduction of the 420s, very similar in conception and design but produced in much larger numbers and very well-marketed. The result was that the Dragonfly class never caught on and disappeared forever when the St. George's fleet was retired some twenty years later. Our inter-scholastic sailing competitions were team racing, with four boats from one school pitted against four from the other around tight little Olympic-style courses. The winner of a race would receive a half-point, second-place would receive two points, third-place three and so on, with the team with the lowest points winning. This meant that sometimes a team member could make as significant a contribution to victory by chasing a competitor off the course to let two team-mates pass ahead, as finishing first. We were a good team and won the New England championships twice when I was there.

During my five years traipsing back and forth between boarding school and home, home life was also changing. When the family was still in Nova Scotia, my sister Pat was at Dalhousie in nearby Halifax and Joy finished up at King's Hall and went off to Smith College in Northampton, western Massachusetts. In our house at 49 Main Street, bedrooms were re-arranged to accommodate regular visits, including all major holidays, of the new "almost-family-member", Tim Tuff, who was the son of an army friend of my father's and a student at Dalhousie with Pat. Tim and I shared a third-floor room during our Christmases and other holidays together and became, in spite of our age difference, quite good friends. At the time I never would have imagined then that he would later marry my sister Pat and that we would become uncles to our respective children, and own adjacent summer homes almost a half-century later. Tim will reappear in these anecdotes as my story unfolds.

When I arrived at St. George's in the autumn of 1964, I did not consider myself particularly more Canadian than American, given my mixed parentage and the fact that Newfoundland had not in any case seemed very Canadian. But as schoolboys do, upperclassmen and even my own classmates instantly pigeon-holed me as the Canadian and teased me about my accent, different spelling and for simply not being one of them. As a result, my attachment to Canada grew, as it often does among those living outside their own countries, and being Canadian became part of my persona. It did not hurt that my favourite hockey team was *Les Canadiens* from Montreal and that they were having a good decade. With most of the school supporting the Boston Bruins or the New York Rangers (the league was still only six teams when I arrived in Newport, stepping into its first expansion while I was there), I could respond to the teasing about my country by boasting about *Les Canadiens*. We had a physics teacher and track-and-field coach named Dr. Hersey, who was an ardent hockey and Bruins fan, and he arranged a group of us to go up to Boston to watch a game at least once a year, and I actually caught a misdirected puck on two different occasions, once in a game between Boston and Montreal. Dr. Hersey was a great sport and I would pound on the door of his house whenever Montreal beat Boston in a critical game, which we would of course listen to on the radio, even after "lights-out".

At our little church in Nova Scotia I had learned to sing as a chorister and so at St. George's I joined the chapel choir. During my first year my voice had not yet broken so I was one of a small group of sopranos, and then after some time off to allow my voice to mature I spent the last three years as a baritone. We were a good choir and ended up travelling and recording. The best trip of all was in my senior year, when we were invited to sing the Easter services at the National Cathedral, which was quite prestigious and gave us a fun weekend in Washington. Being seniors, the weekend was a mix of singing heavenly songs and looking like angels in the cathedral, and behaving rather like devils the rest of the time. Because I was billeted along with a couple of friends with my grandparents, just a short walk away from the cathedral, I was not able to fall to any external temptations, but several of my classmates were not so fortunate and ended up getting caught having a Saturday night party with lots of alcohol and marijuana in the garden of one of the local families who had put them up. The ring-leaders were two senior students, each of whom was completing his fifth year, having joined with me as second formers in 1964. Nonetheless, they were expelled to make a very clear statement that drugs and alcohol were not acceptable, although we learned after the school year had ended that they were both allowed to finish their courses and home and were given their diplomas two months later.

By the end of my Fourth Form (Grade 10) in the summer of 1967, our family had already moved to Montreal, which was the host of Expo67, one of the World Exhibitions which are held no more frequently than every five years under the auspices of the Paris-based International Exhibitions Bureau. Although I was not there all summer (I had a job teaching junior sailing at the Conanicut Yacht Club in Jamestown), my parents had bought both Hugh and I full summer passes, and I spent every day I could touring the pavilions and enjoying the Expo. Hugh managed to go and see absolutely every exhibit and filled his Expo Passport with stamps to prove it. It was both a very educational process, going into the pavilions of distant countries and learning about them, and it was also a pride-building event for a young Canadian. I came away from my times at Expo67 determined to become as bilingual as all the attractive university-aged hosts and guides who were omnipresent on the site, creating the image of a very young, hip and multilingual Canada.

Summers during my boarding school years were spent teaching sailing up through 1967, and then in 1968 I was offered a job as a boat-boy on the gorgeous 80-foot sailboat of John Nicholas Brown, patron of St. George's School (he gave the funds that were used to build its beautiful chapel) and one of Rhode Island's wealthiest men. Brown's house in Newport harbour would eventually become the New York Yacht Club. My father thought me working on a wealthy man's boat and spending the summer in Newport with rich kids was a terrible idea and nixed it. Instead, he arranged for me to work in the woods of Nova Scotia on a team from the Bowater Paper Company surveying the property lines between company land and Crown land. While I would spend weekends in Liverpool and have the opportunity to connect with my old friends, the weeks were quite brutal, slogging through marshy forests or up the mountains bordering Annapolis Valley, working with axes and power-saws to clear and re-stake the property lines. The air was so thick with mosquitoes and black flies that we had no hope of not being heavily bitten and I like others gradually got used to the discomfort. During the weeks we would either sleep at a rented and ramshackle house at the edge of the Valley or stay in the woods in a makeshift camp wherever we were. The team I worked with was a typical hardy group of woodsmen, although there was one fellow who was very well-read and something of a recluse. He alone would not go back to Liverpool on the weekends, preferring to remain at the camp house and read on his own. One of our mates told me that he had suffered some sort of family tragedy, and lost his wife and child, and now preferred to stay away from society as much as he could. He was a very soft-spoken man and loved to talk about philosophy and history, and in the evenings he and I would play chess together on a little plastic portable set he carried. Although I cannot say that I became a great woodsman, the experience of working that summer was infinitely more valuable than a summer spent polishing brass and drinking beer in Newport would have been. And I have never been particularly bothered by mosquitos or blackflies since.

During the latter part of our Fifth Form (Grade 11) and the autumn of our Sixth Form, an important focus of our lives became university entrance. By this time I had slowly worked my way up onto the school's "Honor Roll" and was encouraged by my teachers to apply to a top tier of Ivy League universities in the United States. But I was now determined to go back to Canada and study there, become bilingual and re-root myself north of the border.

And so I applied to McGill, Bishops University and the University of Toronto, was accepted by all three and decided without much hesitation to go to McGill. First, however, I wanted to improve my French, so took the summer semester of 1969 at l'Université Laval in Québec City.

On to University

My summer semester at Laval in Québec City was great experience. I had a French tutor, took French courses and also took an introductory economics course, taught of course in French. My tutor was so appalled at the poor quality of my French that he suggested we pretend I had never learned the language at all, and start again at the beginning. I worked very hard at it and really started to make some progress, helped by finding some local friends who accepted my insistence that they never, ever, speak English with me. One of them was Claire Trépanier, daughter of a senior judge in the federal court and my not-very-serious girlfriend for the summer. She would spend hours with me just talking and helping me develop the beginnings of comfort in the language, and it was with her and her friends that I learned not to be embarrassed by mistakes. It was a lesson well learned for I was to subsequently learn other languages, almost always reaching a level of fluency vastly out of kilter with my level of grammatical accuracy.

For my eighteenth birthday, just before heading to Québec City, my family gave me a little gas-fired red motorbike that required pedalling uphill but which would tootle along on the flat at about twenty kilometres an hour. L'Université Laval had moved only a half dozen years earlier from its ancient home inside the city walls to suburban Ste. Foy and the motorbike gave me welcome mobility to go in and out of town on my own schedule rather than that of the public bus system. One of my challenges in improving my French was that local people were very friendly and welcoming to English Canadians and other tourists, and would switch out of French as soon as they realized one was not a native French-speaker. To avoid this, as soon as anyone spoke to me in English I would explain that I was actually a student from Germany and could not speak English, in in this way keeping the exchange going in French. One day I was in a drug store and, when the clerk switched to English upon hearing my horrid French, I used my spiel, only to have a great hand come down on my shoulder and a German tourist begin blabbering at me in his native tongue, of which I did not speak a word. I signalled him aside and explained what I was doing. He was so entertained that a young Canadian would pretend to be a German in his own country, with memories of the second war not having fully faded, that he bought me a beer and a sandwich and we had a very nice chat, in English of course.

Before arriving in Québec City, I had arranged to live with a family in a residential area not far from the university, hoping that my exchanges with family members would also help my French. In fact, the notion of a "family stay" was quite fraudulent, for the family had turned their basement into three tiny bedrooms and a little kitchenette. They rented the rooms to three students, none of whom were francophone, and we shared the kitchenette and a tiny bathroom and virtually never saw the family. My bedroom did not even have a window. On the day of my French exams (one language and one literature), I woke up as planned, showered and had breakfast, and was about half way to the university when I noticed it was still dark out. I looked at my watch and saw that it was only 0330; my nervous concentration had simply blacked out reality! But I did pass all my courses, which gave me some additional credits which were recognized by McGill and helped get myself well launched on my desired path of becoming truly bilingual.

My next stop was McGill University, beginning in the autumn of 1969 at a time of general student radicalism and the beginnings of an aggressive Québec separatist movement, with post-box bombings and the violent acts of the Front de Libération du Québec, the FLQ who would in my second autumn kidnap both the then British Consul General, James Cross, and the Québec provincial Minister of Labour, Pierre Laporte, whom they not only kidnapped but murdered. In general, however, the McGill campus was more infected by the broader left-wing and anti-war radicalism of the overall North American student movement than by Québec nationalism. And at the beginning of my time at McGill I was too busy sopping up my new and freer university life, and getting involved in debates about global politics, to take much interest in provincial politics.

My years at university were, like most everyone's, a time of freedom and experimentation in ideas and life. In part because of the tenor of the times, we all fashioned ourselves as radicals and went to anti-war rallies and sat up late at night discussing the political theories of Marcuse and Fanon or the poetry of Sylvia Path. We smoked marijuana and drank terrible wine, and discussed world affairs with intense earnestness. In my first year I played on McGill's junior varsity hockey team, and was called up to the varsity Redmen for a few games midway through the season, where I mostly sat on the bench except when filling in for an injured starter or being used as a penalty killer, which for some reason was one of my strengths. It was clear to me, however, that my talent was simply not at the level needed to be a regular linesman at the varsity level, and so in my last two undergraduate years I gave up hockey and concentrated on my studies and other dimensions of university life.

My first year at McGill I lived at home with my parents, which after five years at boarding school was a bit of a mistake, but students with homes in Montreal were not allowed to apply to live in university residences due to a shortage of rooms. I moved out for my second year. My parents in any case moved to Connecticut at the end of 1970 when Bowaters North America was listed on the New York Stock Exchange and it headquarters established in Stamford. I lived first in a fraternity house and then in a series of apartments around the student ghetto, learning to cook and clean, or not, and manage my own daily life. My roommate in all of the apartments was Peter Jacobsen, and we used to joke that whenever there were too many dirty dishes in the sink, we would change apartments. Peter was a philosophy and political science student and was a terrific debater. He went on to get a law degree, and became a litigator and eventually one of Canada's leading libel lawyers.

In the spring of 1970, after the US extended the Vietnam War into Cambodia with the bombing of Phnom Penh, campuses across America erupted in protests and strikes, and four unarmed students were killed at Kent Sate by National Guardsmen. I went down to Harvard University to join the protests and stayed with my high school roommate Hugh Bowen. We went to a huge rally in Harvard Square during which the students announced that they were going on strike in opposition to the government's expansion of the war, and I was called up on the stage to speak to the rally on behalf of Canadian students, which I did, promising (with absolutely no mandate to do so) that students in Canada would support their American brethren by boycotting exams as well. Because the Canadian university year ended a couple of weeks before the American one, we had effectively finished all our exams, which meant that the promise was completely irrelevant, but I was still wildly cheered. Later in the rally, a vice-provost of Harvard College came and asked to speak to the students and was first drowned out by the booing crowd who did not want to hear from "the establishment", as we called all authority in those days. Finally the student leaders managed to quiet the unruly crowd enough to let the vice-provost be heard. He announced that the university's Administration would not penalize students for boycotting exams, and that the Administration itself was now officially coming out in opposition to the war. This of course electrified the crowd, and proved the beginning of a nationwide shift in attitudes that saw the anti-war movement transformed from a liberal student movement to a very broad-based opposition, eventually pushing the Nixon presidency into withdrawing from Vietnam in 1973.

We all fashioned ourselves as radicals in those days, even if we worked hard to do well in our university courses and become doctors or lawyers or business leaders or academics. There was then a national CBC television show, produced weekly, called *Under Attack*, in which a panel of students would challenge some public figure to a debate. *Under Attack* came to McGill at least once or twice a year, and once brought William Kunstler, the New York ACLU lawyer and defender of the "Chicago Eight" organizers of the protests at the 1968 Democratic National Convention. Peter Jacobsen and I were both chosen as student panellists and of course we ended up creating arguments that attacked him from the left, even though there was really no room to do so, but it was a highly entertaining show and afterwards Kunstler came back to our apartment and held court with about twenty-five of political science students and faculty in rapt audience.

In spite of our recently adopted clothing as political radicals, most of us were fairly conventional in our lives. During my first university summer I headed out west along with most of my friends. After staying with pregnant sister Pat and her first husband David in Vancouver and pumping gas and doing other odd menial jobs, I moved up to Windermere and taught sailing for two months at the Rocky Mountain Boys Camp. In another summer, I did research work at an economic consultancy, working on the planning of a "New Town" around the intended new international Toronto airport in Pickering. Even though neither the airport nor the new town were ever built, the work was really interesting, trying to apply theoretical sociological structures on the layout of a planned community, something that had been done extensively in post-war Britain and a little in France as well, but rarely tried in North America.

At McGill I kept up my sailing and joined the sailing team. We practiced out of a club in Beaconsfield at the edge of Lac des Deux Montagnes and sometimes at the Royal Military College in Kingston. We raced in 420s and 470s and turned out to be a pretty good team. In my first year, one of our members was Peter Hall, who went on to be a member of Canada's Olympic team for many years, and who had a sister, Ingrid, who I would later work with in the Foreign Service. In the spring of 1972, when I was captain of the sailing team, I became eastern Canadian collegiate champion and was invited myself to try out for the national team heading for the Olympics in Kiel, Germany. (The main Olympics were held in Munich, but the sailing was sensibly situated in the North Sea.) The trials were held in Kingston in breathlessly light air, never my strength, and I unfortunately placed third behind two sailors from Vancouver, both of whom seemed to be able to propel their boats simply by dreaming of wind. I was named an alternative member of the national team, which meant that if one of the chosen 470 skippers had been unable to go to Kiel I would have been called up, but that did not happen. I also continued to sail with the family when I could in the summers and occasionally in the autumns, taking jobs helping deliver boats from Narragansett Bay to their winter homes at the end of the season. One boat I helped sail back to Lunenburg, Nova Scotia one summer was the schooner *Atlantica*, which had been built at Expo67 as the Atlantic Provinces' exhibition in lieu of a pavilion. *Atlantica* was a lovely boat, just short of 60-feet long, which had been sold to a Toronto businessman, Blane Bowen, after she was launched on the last day of Expo67. Blane had been given my name by a mutual friend in Toronto and the trip resulted in a friendship that lasted a long time. It was the first time that I had sailed a traditional schooner with its many sails and without modern winches, and after sailing her back to Nova Scotia two autumns in a row, I was sufficiently in love with *Atlantica* to ask Blane to give me a first option to buy her if ever he should sell.

In my last year at McGill we were expected to write some sort of extended essay, and I and fellow student Jim Wright decided to do research on the issue of Chinese representation at the United Nations. By this time Canada, now with Pierre Trudeau as Prime Minister, had recognized China and a number of other western countries were leaning towards following suit, but the US was putting lots of pressure on any countries they could to remain faithful to the regime in Taiwan. Jim and I designed a research plan, which included interviewing the representatives of many countries to the UN, largely to justify spending time in New York City, and off we went. We interviewed many diplomats, including some third world ambassadors who were quite frank with us in saying that they felt fully at ease shifting their votes back and forth on the issue depending on how they felt their vote would be helpful in extracting support for issues of importance to them from the Americans and others. Our research also brought us to Ottawa, where a relatively junior officer of the Department of External Affairs invited us into his office to discuss how Canada, then a major proponent of Beijing's assumption of the UN seat, was approaching its pro-Beijing campaign. The officer was Jeremy Kinsman, whose bilingualism impressed me enormously when taking a call in the middle of our meeting and communicating in French quite heatedly with someone at our mission in New York. Jeremy would rise to the highest levels of Government and serve as Ambassador to several major countries, including Russia, Italy and the UK, and Jim, who joined the Foreign Service in the same year as I, would end his career as Head of Mission in London. Both Jeremy and Jim have remained close friends over the ensuing decades.

In the gap between my Bachelor's degree and my Master's, I worked at the National Institute of Economic and Social Research in London, which was a wonderful professional and personal experience. I sublet a room in Clapham South from Barry Glynn, a commercial artist who painted covers for romantic novels and commercials. I paid five pounds out of my weekly paycheck of sixteen pounds (delivered weekly in cash in a brown envelope) for the room. Barry was a delightful cockney with a working class background, and was the total antithesis of many of the other young people I met through my workmates and through Tim Tuff, who was then living in Deddington in Oxfordshire. Tim had a tiny and very old home, with a front door lintel that was so low that even short people had to duck to enter. I spent quite a number of weekends with Tim and what seemed like a constantly shifting circle of other visitors in Deddington, having Sunday brunch at the local Unicorn and wandering around the countryside. I also spent a weekend in a coal mining town in Wales with the family of a fellow junior economist at NIESR, which was like going back to pre-war years; the small one-story stone houses and the blackened miners coming up through the town at the end of a shift was right out of an old black and white newsreel.

I was one of the two most junior assistant economists at NIESR, but I worked on two quite interesting projects. The first was helping with a study on he likely impact on the British economy of joining the European Common Market. Because I was very inexperienced and not very knowledgeable, I was kept away from the core economic analysis involved. My central task instead was to do a comparison of the detailed definition of comparative statistics between Britain and the continental members of the Common Market. This was intensely boring, so I tried to find interesting statistical definitions to share with my colleagues. Among the more interesting ones I found I discovered when exploring why Belgium had so few highway deaths, when at the time driving in Belgium was reputed to be very dangerous, with far too many big American cars being sold into the second hand car market by the large number of NATO troops and officials from the US and Canada. I discovered that to count as a highway death in Belgium, one had to die at the scene of an accident; if the paramedics rushed someone to a local hospital where he or she expired, this counted as a "hospital death by trauma" and was not related to fatalities on the highway. When I told my colleagues about this, it led to a rash of jokes about Belgium police being instructed to toss dying motorists off the highways to keep their record of highway deaths low, and gave me momentary fame in the institute. When the Director passed by our office one day and was introduced to me, his only remark was "Oh, yes, the Belgian highway death fellow", before moving on to meet the next young economist.

The second task with which I was charged was doing econometric modelling in support of the institute's quarterly economic forecasts, which in those days when published were market-moving events. We were primarily using regression analysis, which in laymen's terms is trying to find an equation in which a number (sometimes a rather large number) of independent variables can be used to predict a particular dependent variable, like economic growth or the volume of coal imports. It was the very early days of computerized analysis, and the PC was more than a decade still unborn. NIESR did not even have its own computer. We did have card-punching machines and would prepare our programs on batches of rectangular cards about the shape and size of airplane boarding passes. We would take shoeboxes of these cards over to the government's computing centre next to New Scotland Yard, and hand them through a bank-like wicket so that our programs could be put in the queue for processing. This we would always do shortly after lunch and then pick up our results before work the following morning, taking the afternoon off in between. When we went back to the office with our thick accordions of paper output under our arms, the older economists like George Ray and Laslow Campbell-Boroz would look at our red eyes and thick piles of computer paper and say "Oh dear, you must have been up all night". We would respond in the affirmative, failing of course to mention that we had been partying until the wee hours while the government computer was doing our work.

My Masters year was a combination of taking more difficult graduate courses, working as a teaching assistant in an introductory course in international relations and beginning to outline my thesis. The early 1970s represented the height of empiricism in political science, and I was encouraged by my advisor Professor Janice Stein to use empirical content analysis to support my principle theories in the thesis I was trying to write on *Chinese Support for Revolutionary Movements in the Third World*. I ended up doing so, and received a Master's degree for my efforts, but I became quite disillusioned with the relevance of what I was doing and sceptical of the pretences of the political science community and its preoccupation with the scientific method and empirical methods. I had also taken two riveting courses from a visiting professor named Henry Ehrmann, who was in the closing years of a long career spent mostly at Dartmouth in Hanover, New Hampshire. Ehrmann taught European political economy and comparative politics, and was a most fascinating man. He had left Germany as a young and outspoken anti-Nazi in the 1930s, and eventually was put in charge of designing the political re-education of German prisoners of war in camps in the United States and Canada. Largely enticed by Ehrmann's broad vision of the inextricable links between politics and economics, I decided that I wanted to pick up again the economic side of my undergraduate time and do a doctorate in political economy. By this time there were very few universities left in North America that had schools of political economy. The University of Toronto had the last political economy program in Canada, so it was there that I decided to go to do my doctoral courses.

I only spent one academic year in Toronto, completed all my required doctoral courses and took what comprehensive exams I needed to, but I never really enjoyed either my personal or academic life there. Coming into the school of political economy with a Master's degree and a determination to pursue a doctorate degree, I was unaware that the faculty was already tearing itself in half over internal arguments that would see it divided in separate faculties of economics and political science within two years of my arrival, rendering irrelevant my purpose in having chosen Toronto in the first place. There were only one or two professors who welcomed my desire to go back in time and treat the two disciplines really as one, and one, Ian Drummond, was happy to serve as my faculty advisor. At the personal level, I moved into an apartment on Markham Street just south of the "Honest Ed's" discount store, sharing digs with Ross Baker, who had also done his undergraduate work at McGill and would eventually become a Professor at the University of Toronto and a great expert on Canadian health care management, and a budding radical lawyer named Jim Fish who would become principal lawyer for some of Canada's largest unions.

It was in Toronto that I took up running. After leaving McGill's hockey program, my fitness had deteriorated and I was determined to do something about it before too late, so I started running around the very short second-floor track in the 100-year old Hart House gymnasium at the University of Toronto, and tried to push myself for slightly longer distances every few days. By the end of the year I was effectively addicted to it and running at least several miles every day, a habit that became a regular part of my life for the next forty years.

My year in Toronto coincided with my sister Joy and her husband Chip living in Ann Arbor, Michigan, where Chip was completing his law degree following his stint in the US Navy, which he had joined to avoid the draft. We spent many weekends together either in Ann Arbor or Toronto, since the two were only a four-hour drive apart. At the time I had a little bright red BMW 2002 (referring to the engine capacity, not the year, since it was still the early 1970s), and I would simply fly down Highway 401 to Detroit, and then out Interstate 94 to Ann Arbor. Joy and Chip had their first child when I was in Toronto, so spending time with them in their little farmhouse in Michigan was very special family time. I had also driven my BMW non-stop out to Vancouver the year before (with a co-driving hitchhiking companion I had picked up in Ann Arbor) when my sister Pat's first husband David died, and after several months with Pat and her two small children, had driven it back to the east by myself. It was probably the most peppy and fun-to-drive car I ever owned, even though it was a boxy and virtually unknown brand in those days.

As soon as my courses and comprehensive exams were done in Toronto, I sold my little red BMW and headed off to Paris, where I would pursue my doctoral research.

On board ship en route to Newfoundland at age 1,
with mother and sisters Patsy and Joy

On "my own" forestry railroad at Howard's Brook

Spring ice in the Bay of Islands

With sister Pat at Lark Harbour, Bay of Islands

Age 5 or 6, saluting my grandfather,
Admiral Herbert S. Howard

With Maurice Richard (The
Rocket) and Danny Gallivan
at the Glynmill Inn, 1960

Ready for hockey practice, dressed
of course as a member of the
Montreal Canadiens

Learning to use a compass
on one of the Bowater ships,
age 11

Family, 1967, Grandparents, AEB and MCB and Pat, Joy, Howard and Hugh

Canoeing with MCB

With AEB and surrogate mother
"Cheech" who had brought him up
after his mother's departure and his
father's death

Graduating from St. George's
School, June, 1969

Sailing with Hugh and MCB, Summer 1970

Cousins' land at Gordes, Provence

Luc Colin's mill in Chanpagne

Sailing in the Med, 1975

CHAPTER 2

PARIS AND THE
BOHEMIAN LIFE

• • • • • • • • • • •

I arrived in Paris in the late spring of 1974, having completed all my
course work and my comprehensives for my doctorate at the University of
Toronto. At that time air travel was a tightly regulated industry and the
only fares that were not regulated and very expensive were those for charter
flights. As students we would all join some ersatz organization and then
fly to Europe as part of a charter with only members of that organization
on board. In order to save money, I joined the "Scottish Terrier Breeding
Association of America", took a bus down to New York, stayed with my
parents for a few days and flew to Paris via Iceland on an old Boeing 707,
for the price of about $200.

As an additional advisor for my PhD thesis, I added Professor Georges
Lavau of the Fondation nationale des Sciences politiques, to complement
Ian Drummond, the political economist from the University of Toronto.
Lavau, who had been introduced to me by Henry Ehrmann, my former
McGill professor, arranged for me to be "apparenté", or seconded, to
"Sciences Po" as it was commonly called. Sciences Po actually referred to
both the Fondation nationale des Sciences politiques and one of France's
Grandes Écoles, l'Institut des Etudes politiques, with which it was physically
co-located and largely intertwined, although the students of the IEP were
destined for senior levels in the French public service, while others were
aimed at academic or other careers.

Before I left Canada my dear friends Irène and Robert Rigal had introduced
me to a French graduate student at l'Université de Montréal who rented

to me her small flat in northern Paris near the Porte de Clichy. I took it for three months, hoping to move closer downtown once I got the lay of the land. The apartment was really very small, just one bedroom with a squat toilet and separate shower room shared by three other apartments down the hall. The area around Porte de Clichy was then very heavily peopled from Algeria and other former French colonies in North Africa. As I settled in and started to frequent the local stores and cafés, I found everyone extremely friendly, always offering to help out with one thing or another. There was also the Porte de Clichy metro stop just a block away, and I could get to Sciences Po, which was in the 6ième Arrondissement on Rue Guillaume just next to the Rue du Bac metro stop, with only one transfer at Saint-Lazarre.

My first days at Sciences Po served as a real eye-opener to French higher education in the 1970s. As a foreign doctoral student, I was given the same treatment as the advanced post graduate students from France, and I had such extraordinary benefits as being permitted to borrow up to three books at any given time from the library. I still could not enter the stacks to browse the collections, however, and had to wait in line to hand my withdrawal forms to harassed librarians, and then come back hours later to pick up the requested books, assuming they had been found. Given my experiences with my own carrel and endless borrowing privileges right in the stacks of the Robarts Library at the University of Toronto, this was very frustrating. In doing my research for university papers, I had never been very methodological in selecting source material, preferring to sift through collections to find interesting and sometimes less well-known works on any given subject. I used to pretend this was a function of my creative nature, when really it was probably more due to intellectual laziness and lack of rigour!

I had chosen for my thesis topic "The Relationship between Economic Planning and the Social Structure of France", which was intended to be very much in the old space of political economy, not quantitative at all and almost closer to a cross between structural economics and political sociology. I intended to show that in post-war France the process of planning and budgeting in five-year cycles reinforced the existence of a socio-economic elite that both governed the country and dominated industry. I had written a paper on the subject in my Master's year at McGill in a course I took with Henry Ehrmann, who had encouraged me in my interest in European affairs and had introduced me to Professor Lavau. I found Lavau terribly boring as a lecturer, but an absolute delight in person, and he was fantastically helpful to me in sending me off to meet fascinating people who had played key political and administrative roles in the early years of post-war France. As it turned out, meeting these people was really the only part of my doctoral studies that I really enjoyed. The premise of my thesis was treated as blatantly obvious to every French person I met, both inside and outside the elite, and over time I was to grow very bored with all the research and writing that was needed to complete a thesis. I likened it to a scientist re-proving Galileo's theorems a hundred years after they had become assumed truths.

However, Paris was of course more than my studies, and indeed I knew in my heart that I had chosen my thesis topic as much to enable me to live in France as to satisfy my interest in the topic itself. At the beginning I was astounded at how far my budget could be stretched, and I had a very good budget, being the lucky recipient of a Canada Council Fellowship for three full years of graduate study. The stipend was $5500 for the first year and $6,000 for each of the next two, which now does not sound like much, but living the way I did I even managed to save enough to eventually buy a little car. As I gradually began to meet new friends, first at Sciences Po and then through various connections from university days in North America, I started to get to know my way around the city, which included learning how to get super-cheap seats for the opera and musical events, and which earthy restaurants north of Montmartre had fixed fare meals which included all the wine you wished to drink, filled up by the customers themselves from great oak barrels stacked against the back wall.

After a few weeks living in Porte de Clichy and taking the metro back and forth to Rue Gillaume, I decided that I should buy a bicycle not only to commute to school but also to get to know the city better. Paris within its ring road, the Périphérique, is really not that big a city and I found that I could get almost anywhere on two wheels almost as fast as I could by metro. I set an objective of exploring a new arrondissement every weekend, and over the next year I am sure I bicycled thousands of kilometers within the Périphérique, and in doing so really did get to know Paris quite well. I learned that there were many cities in Paris, and that whole worlds existed, and whole lives were lived, in very small neighbourhoods. The tourist's Paris was largely limited to an extraordinarily handsome centre with a few outlying "musts", like Montmartre, but you could get off the beaten track quite easily and find a friendliness completely absent from the fancy shops and expensive restaurants of the Paris most visitors saw.

One of my early sojourns on my bicycle was a visit to the studio of a Canadian artist, introduced by a friend of mine who had studied fine art at McGill. This artist, who was of Japanese origin and had grown up in Vancouver, told me of another artist friend of his who had a flat to let near the Jardin de Luxembourg. The flat owner was a fellow British Columbian named Henry Boyer, who was a professor and Artist-in-Residence at the University of Verona in Italy, and who would be in Paris the following week.

I met Henry Boyer and his lovely and much younger Alsatian wife, Annie, for an afternoon coffee in a café near the Rodin Museum, and hit it off fabulously with both of them. Our afternoon stretched into the evening and we retreated to a nearby restaurant and talked for hours and hours. Henry had grown up as Henry Boyer in Prince George, British Columbia, but his father was the first of his family to come to Canada. The family was of minor French aristocratic stock, who had left France for Mauritius sometime in the late 18th or early 19th century. His grandfather had also been an artist. Through the vagaries of local upheaval and a desire for greener pastures, the family had wended their way to Canada and settled in Prince George. Henry, who had been born around the end of the First World War, went to Paris to study art in the late 1930s, left after a short time for Canada as the clouds of war gathered, and returned in the early post-war years to continue his studies and pursue his vocation. In Paris, he re-assumed his old family name and became Henry Boyer de la Giroday and over time became an artist of some repute. (At the Emily Carr University of Art and Design in Vancouver, there is now a scholarship named after him.) But by the mid-1960s he could not live on the sale of his work and so he took up teaching, ending up at the University of Verona. At some point he had come into a small inheritance, which he spent buying a pied-à-terre on Rue Bréa between the Raspail-Montparnasse intersection and the southwest corner of the Jardin de Luxembourg. This was to be my home for the remainder of my time in Paris.

The apartment was very small, built on the fifth floor of an eighteenth century walk-up, renovated to create a tiny bed-room on a sixth-floor loggia with a little but modern bathroom behind it under the eaves. On the main floor I had a kitchen measuring perhaps three square meters, and a southern exposed living room with full-length French windows overlooking Rue Bréa, with the stairs to the loggia running up the eastern wall. It was simply furnished with lots of cushions and perfect for a bachelor's life in Paris. The sun would stream in most of the day, and I would leave the tall windows wide open during all but the most inclement weather. Over time as I was to make more friends, there were people constantly dropping by, bringing wine and food, sometimes staying over. This was Paris as it was meant to be. I have lived in many places since, but none has surpassed, in terms of being appropriate for the setting and the particular time of my life, my little aerie at Rue Bréa.

The first evening after moving into my new apartment (it was a pretty easy move, one subway trip with two suitcases and then a second trip on my bicycle with a back-pack), I went to Café de la Rotonde, the café on the corner of Boulevard de Montparnasse that had been a favourite of Pablo Picasso and made famous in one of Hemingway's novels. I ordered a coffee, saying to the waiter "Puis-je avoir un café, s'il vous plait". He grunted and said "un quoi?". After a couple more efforts, he appeared to understand and turned to his colleague behind the bar, calling out "un expresse". Ok, I thought, so here we call coffee "expresse" as the word "café" must simply be too general a term. A night or two later I was back at La Rotonde, and asked the same waiter for "un expresse". He glared at me and said "un quoi?" and I repeated myself. He turned to the bar and called out "un café". I grabbed him by the sleeve and asked him, in perfectly understandable French, what the hell he was doing. I told him that he had served me a few days before and done the reverse "café-expresse" thing on me. I said that I had just moved next door and if he wanted me as a regular customer he would have to do away with the bullshit. He blushed and confessed that he enjoyed messing around with tourists trying to speak French, and knew from my accent and my clothes that I wasn't local. He was typical of so many Parisian waiters and store clerks who treated anybody not from Paris as if they were of a lower species, but he actually was forever thereafter very friendly to me and would always find room for me and my friends whenever we appeared, even during the crowded summer afternoons when La Rotonde would be full of Picasso or Hemingway buffs from California or Cologne.

On one of my frequent visits the previous winter to Ann Arbour, Michigan, where my sister and brother-in-law, Joy and Chip, were living while Chip was at law school, they had introduced me to friends of theirs, François Bancilhon and his wife Chantal. François was doing graduate work in computer science and had in turn introduced me to his Paris-based sister Christiane and her husband Yves Raynouard. Christiane was a school teacher and Yves worked in tourism for one of those many para-statal agencies that existed in France at the time, his having to do with the establishment of "villagéatures", or vacation resorts organized for the unions. I got in touch with Yves and Christiane shortly after my arrival and they invited me out to their home in a southwestern suburb of Paris near the end of the RER commuting line. They lived in a huge apartment complex in a flat that as a North American I found rather small, but it was typical for the French middle class and they had made it into a very nice home for themselves and their three children. They welcomed me with open arms and became very good friends, and whenever I tired of the city or felt lonely, I always knew that I could take the RER out and invade their home for an evening. As is often the way, through them I met more local friends and doing so made a huge difference in helping me settle down and begin to enjoy life in Paris. The following winter Yves arranged a good deal at a ski resort in the French Alps, and about ten of us spent a fantastic week skiing near Chamonix. The mother of Francois and Chantal also had a summer house at a place called Asnières-sur-Oise and I spent a couple of weekends there as well. Asnières-sur-Oise was about 60 or so kilometers north of the northern gates of Paris and on one hot weekend I decided to bicycle all the way there from my flat in the 6ième. I left early in the morning and arrived before noon, having gotten a bit lost part way there, and then about 3 or 4 kilometers from their home I blew a tire and had to walk the last bit, carrying my bike. I was exhausted and thirsty when I arrived, and a swim in their pool and a cold beer were very welcome restoratives. I also happily accepted Yves' offer of a ride back to Paris at the end of that weekend! Yves and Christiane remained friends forever, as did Francois and Chantal, although Christiane was to sadly die of lung cancer (she was a terrible chain smoker when I was living in Paris) in her early fifties.

I also had a few other contacts in Paris from friends and family, some were students and some were in business there. Betsy and Mal Robinson were introduced to me by my parents were from Wilton, Connecticut, and lived in the western suburb of St. Cloud where their two children went to the American School of Paris. They invited me out to dinner from time to time, and for a real American Thanksgiving when November rolled around, and we always ended up talking politics and drinking too much cognac or armagnac, and I would generally end up sleeping over rather than struggling unsteadily back into town. Through the Robinsons I heard that the American school needed a hockey coach, and I ended up coaching a very mediocre and unenthusiastic bunch of spoiled kids during my first Parisian winter. As soon as I could I found a replacement and quit. Mal Robinson worked for IBM in Paris and later introduced me to Frank Commiskey, who was head of IBM Europe and a great sailor, who asked me to crew on his beautiful 45-foot Swan in a couple of races in the English Channel, which was fun, but as I was unwilling to commit all my weekends to crewing I lost my place rather quickly to a more reliable deck-hand.

At the beginning of my university years in Montreal I had decided to start learning music again and I had taken up the flute. I had earlier learned to read music as a member of the St. George's School choir, but had never played an instrument (if we forget about, as we should, a very unsuccessful effort at the piano at age six or seven). In Paris it did not take me long to find a flute teacher, Patricia Nagel, who herself was a student but far more advanced than I and actually studying with Maxence Larrieu and Michel Debost, two of the pre-eminent flutists of the day. Through Patricia I met a whole bunch of other young flutists, almost all destined to professional careers. (Patricia ended up as first flutist with the Toulouse Symphony). Paris was very much the centre of the flute world in those years. I worked very hard at my flute, and much preferred spending time practicing Telemann or Mozart or even scales than slogging through post-war French documents for my thesis. I was to gradually get reasonably proficient at the flute, and actually attended a couple of master classes with both Larrieu and Jean-Pierre Rampal. However, the raw talent of a true musician was really not there in me and I found it took me much longer to learn a new piece than it did the other truly gifted flutists that I hung out with at master classes and in get-togethers when we would play as trios or quartets. One spring afternoon I was practicing a piece in my apartment with the tall windows wide open to let in the fresh air, thinking that my lilting Mozart concerto was a very appropriate and romantic contribution to my little corner of Paris. I heard a little voice calling out "monsieur". At first I assumed it had nothing to do with me, but the calling persisted and so I went to the french windows and looked around. Across the narrow Rue Bréa and just ten meters down the street, there was a lad of ten or twelve years old or so waving at me. He was clearly trying to get my attention, and I waited for the compliment that was sure to come. He then called out, quite politely "Monsieur, est-ce que vous pouvez fermer votre fenêtre; la musique dérange ma grand-mère" ("Sir, could you close your window; the music is disturbing my grandmother"). A deranged grandmother thus dashed my ambitions to join some great philharmonic orchestra and my dreams of having all the pretty young flutists fawn all over me! But I did enjoy the music world a lot, and even as a lark one night "busked" with a violin-playing friend of mine in the subway at Montparnasse, making so little money that we decided we would not try it again. I kept playing well after Paris, right into the early 1980s until the arrival of our children and new pleasures and pressures gradually squeezed my flute out of my daily life. My silver flute itself rested a decade or so in its case, much to the relief of grandmothers and other music lovers on many continents, and then was adopted by our daughter Cynthia.

Rue Bréa was a wonderful place to live, a real Paris neighbourhood with the cafés of Boulevard du Montparnasse just down the street and the southwest gate of the Jardin de Luxembourg a few hundred meters away. There were the usual little stores and there was also a restaurant called Chez Dominique, which had long been a hangout for the White Russian crowd. Many of the wealthier émigrés from Moscow and St. Petersburg had settled in Paris after the Russian revolution, and it was at Chez Dominique that they would meet and plot their return and argue about aristocratic titles. One night, just after going to sleep in my little loft, I was jarred awake by gunfire and the sound of ricocheting bullets, followed shortly by the iconic pulsing sirens of the Parisian police. I was to learn later that some simmering feud had finally crossed into violence, to be settled with the death of some Count or Grand Prince. There were, in fact, huge numbers of titled aristocrats in Paris from almost every corner of Europe, both east and west of the Iron Curtain. There was a professor at Sciences Po who claimed to have done a study of the Paris telephone directory and said that there were fifteen thousand listings of royalty or titled gentry, of which he estimated less than five percent had a legitimate claim to their alleged title.

Because Rue Bréa was, like so many streets of Paris, very narrow, it was easy to follow, intentionally or inadvertently, the lives of neighbours across the street. After I had been in my apartment for a few months, almost directly across from me into a flat that had been previously vacant moved a very handsome couple perhaps ten years older than I. Once established they seemed to be present on a cycle of a week or two, interspersed with longer absences. He was a very well-dressed and well-groomed dark-haired man and she was a tall and shapely brunette. My drifting in-and-out friends and I watched this stunning pair from the vantage of my little living room, and created an imagined life for them, seeing in two of them a British spy and his paramour, living glamorous and dangerous lives. On a lovely evening some months after they had taken up residence, the fellow saw me in my window and singled to me to come over and so I did. He introduced himself simply as Roger and said he was a writer, and he invited me to come to a party a day or two hence. I did, bringing a Swedish girl named Camilla that I was seeing at the time. When we entered Roger's flat we found ourselves surrounded by an international crowd of very well dressed and beautiful people. In meeting Camilla, Roger added the surname of Salloch to himself, which we found interestingly coincidental given its similarity to mine. It was a typical noisy and liquid Parisian evening and soon it was done. Not more than a few days later, I looked over to Roger's apartment and noticed that not only were there no signs of life, but that that there was no longer any furniture; the flat had been completely vacated and Roger Salloch and his beautiful girlfriend had disappeared. This of course completely cemented our belief that he was actually a spy, the name of Salloch clearly invented on the spur of the moment, rather awkwardly and thoughtlessly mimicking my own which he had just heard for the first time. Camilla and I and other friends subsequently wove a fabulous existence for him, creating fictional forays for him from Moscow to Madrid and Montevideo. Roger stayed for many years in my mind firmly fixed as a dashing member of the clandestine service, and it was not until about twenty years later that I came across his name as the screenwriter of an obscure avant-guard movie. He turned out in fact to be exactly who he pretended to be, and made some sort of life as a not very successful writer, and the similarity of our surnames was simply coincidental. But for a while, and although he surely never knew it, he was a skillful and danger-seeking James Bond, slipping in and out of strange countries and extraordinary adventures.

Around Christmas of my first year in Paris I received a letter from Blane Bowen, owner of the schooner *Atlantica*, asking if I would like to help fit-up a sailboat and then deliver it in the early spring from Malta to Dubrovnik in what was then Yugoslavia, now Croatia. I instantly accepted and when the time came I took a train down through Italy to Sicily and a ferry across to Malta. Malta was fascinating, with its Phoenician looking people and fabulously colourful fishing boats and tiny coastal villages. I arrived well in advance of the planned sailing trip, for the boat, a heavy 45-foot Hilyard ketch called *Thyatera*, was still up on the hard and there was much work to do to get her into the water and ready for the trip. As much of the work was the boatyard's to do and not mine, I had plenty of time to wander about the island, out to the village of Marsaxlokk in the east and to the ancient capital of Mdina at Rabat in the south, where in 1565 a small group of soldiers of the Knights of St. John of Jerusalem had marched round and round the parapets, fooling the invading Ottoman Admiral, Dragut, into avoiding what he saw as a heavily fortified city and proceeding north to the better defended St. Angelo. I also went out to the bay in the northeast where Saint Paul was shipwrecked in the decades after the death of Christ. I had read several books about Maltese history and found that it was easy to slip back in time and find the past just oozing out of the land and the cities. Joy and Chip had also spent some weeks in Malta when Chip was in the US Navy on board a supply vessel stationed there, and they had given me lots of advice of things to see.

I planned also to go to Malta's second island, the smaller Gozo to the northeast. Nicholas Monsarrat, a Canadian author, was living there and he had written some wonderful books about Malta, like the *Capilan of Malta*, a tale about the Nazi bombardment of the city when the citizens of Valetta took refuge in the huge network of catacombs built after the defeat of the Ottomans four centuries earlier. I had been given Monsarrat's telephone number by his first wife, who lived in Toronto. I called him to see if I could come by and he was friendly and quite welcoming until the end of our conversation, when he asked, almost as an afterthought, how I had gotten his number. When I told him that his ex-wife had given it to me, he bluntly said: "oh, then don't come", and hung up.

Once *Thyatera* was in the water I started provisioning her for the coming season generally and our upcoming trip particularly, and I lived on board for four or five days. Moored next to *Thyatera* was a lovely old wooden boat, maybe seventy or eighty feet long with a professional skipper on board, a Briton of perhaps fifty years old. He had been sailing and looking after boats all his life. In the evening he would invite me over and we would sit on deck drinking local wine and the very distinct and very delicious local bread, cooked in big stone ovens heated from wood and containing a little potato flour as well as wheat. This old British fellow (for fifty was old to me then) absolutely entranced me with his stories of life at sea and in harbours all over the world. But I was there one day too long, and on the fifth night his stories started to repeat themselves, and I went to bed thinking that maybe a life spent on boats would not be the life for me, for if everything came down to only enough stories for four evenings, then maybe the excitement would pale.

For the trip itself, Blane Bowen and I were really the crew of Tony and Kitty Griffin and their niece Ginny, a girl a year or two younger than I. Tony was a very successful Toronto businessman and a friend of *Thyatera's* owner, Sir Michael Clapham, then the Chairman of the Confederation of British Industry. Tony and Kitty's commitment was to leave *Thyatera* in Dubrovnik where the owner would pick her up for a cruise along the Dalmatian coast. Our trip started well, with a steady northeasterly breeze of maybe 15 knots, and we just flew for the first many hours sighting the southern coast of Sicily in daytime and coming up to the heel of the Italian peninsula at dawn the next morning. We had no intention of stopping anywhere and turned northward into the Adriatic with the wind gradually climbing into what was to be a real *Bora*, a furious northern wind whose western counterpart is known as a *Mistral* in Marseille and whose eastern counterpart in the Aegean as a *Meltemi*. Back in the 1970s weather forecasting was much less accurate and no storm had been foreseen. With the *Bora* coming straight down the Adriatic we had to beat into it and a very deep and sharp sea the whole way, and as the wind started to increase to 25 knots and beyond we decided to shorten sail and take down the main, and to continue on storm jib and mizzen alone. Unfortunately, the main halyard jumped its shiv as we started to take down the sail, and try as we might we could not free it. So up I went to the top of the mast in a bosun's chair to cut the halyard with a knife. I have never been a great lover of heights and although it only took about 15 minutes, it felt like an hour, pitching wildly back and forth, and I was very glad to get back on deck. We also had to turn quickly away from the Albanian coast to which we were getting too close, for in those days Albania was the hermit dictatorship of the communist world, and yachts that came within 12 miles of its coast were arrested and impounded, with their crew unceremoniously deposited at a Yugoslav border post after several weeks in an Albanian jail.

We finally made landfall back on the Italian coast in a lovely protected harbour at Porto di Castro. We bought fish over the gunwale from a local fisherman and had a dinner made all the more delicious by the tension of the day, and spent the night at restful anchor. The next morning we restrung the halyard and continued our way north in lighter winds, and ended the voyage with a few days to spare and visited the fascinating and history-rich islands of Vis and Split before mooring in Dubrovnik.

As my circle of friends in Paris grew I ended up meeting a few famous people. Though one of Yves Raynouard's colleagues, one of the founders of the still very young Club Med invited me to a party at his very beautiful flat near Les Invalides, where there was a crowd of "beautiful people", many of them actors. I struck up a conversation with one stunning young blond woman, who I thought was about my own age, who effused over Canada and its natural beauty and seemed as simple and open and pleasant as could be. She turned out to be Catherine Deneuve, just at the beginning of a tremendously successful screen career, who was (unfortunately) attached at least for the evening to some middle-aged producer who had parked his Ferrari next to the same lamp-post to which I had locked my bicycle. At least I had a nice chat with her that evening, and was to meet her again from time to time during the following few months. Somewhere during that same time I also met Keith Carradine, then simply the brother of David Carradine who was still alive and a superstar actor. Keith was a good musician and was part of a small group of us who played together from time to time, and his acting career was still at its earliest stage, shortly to take off. The circle of my acquaintances seemed to be in a constant shift, as if I was being carried along by a great ocean current, connecting loosely to one set of people and then through them passing on to new scenes and other people, some very transient.

It was not long after my arrival in Paris that I took a train south to Marseilles to stay with my mother's elder brother, Herbert Seymour Howard Jr. and his French wife Fernande and their youngest child, Catherine, who was then just coming to the end of her secondary school years. Seymour was a fine and well-known architect, who had met Fernande during the war. They had lived in New York for many years, first in a little home north of the city in Croton-on-Hudson and then in Oyster Bay in a modern home Seymour had designed and which was featured on the cover of Architectural Digest in the mid-1960s. Seymour was then teaching at the Pratt Institute, a fine architectural school and became its director, but found the politics of academia in the highly charged 1960s no longer to his liking, and so they moved to France in 1969, leaving their two elder daughters behind, one studying with me at McGill and the eldest working in the Widener Library at Harvard. Fernande had very much wanted to return to her native land, having never really enjoyed life in America, and also deeply offended by an attempt by some to besmirch Seymour, who was quite left-leaning but far from a communist, during the McCarthy excesses of the 1950s. By the mid-1970s, Seymour and Fernande had an apartment just west of Marseilles in *l'Unité d'Habitation*, an iconic modernist complex designed by the great Le Corbusier and built just after World War II. Seymour was a great fan of Le Corbusier and considered himself an architect of the same school of letting grand structures and concepts lead detailed design, and wrote a book in the mid 1960s called "Structure: An Architect's Approach". *L'Unité d'Habitation* was one of Le Corbusier's more modest works and had a multicoloured façade composed of apartment balconies on the southern side facing the sea. The ground floor was intended to be a community area with small shops and cafés, but the demand was not sufficient to support them and it was mostly empty. I had developed an interest in architecture when I was in my teens courtesy of Seymour, for he had introduced a lot of ideas and styles to me when I visited them in Oyster Bay on holiday weekends away from St. George's in the 1960's. I had taken a multidisciplinary course in urban planning at university, and had worked one summer at a planning consultancy on the Ontario Government's plans to build a New Town of the sterile British variety in Pickering, near a planned new international airport that was never to be built. I found many of Le Corbusier's works lacking a sense of human scale, and I would argue with Seymour about Chandigargh and Brazilia. Seymour and Fernande's apartment in *l'Unité d'Habitation* was not very large but was multi-story and allowed an inhabitant to move many of the internal walls, so the actual layout of rooms was flexible. I stayed there on long summer weekends and found it easy to imagine a long life drinking coffee and eating fresh baguettes on their balcony looking out over the Mediterranean. In the afternoons we would go to the rocky shore at Sormieux, and we would swim and picnic at "les calanques". We would also go to their olive grove in the very beautiful valley across from Gordes, where they had a tiny shepherd's hut built of rough stone. There was only one bedroom on a tiny second floor, so Catherine and I would sleep in the living room, her on a sofa and me on the floor and I would wake up and creep outside and take photographs of the beautiful valley as the earliest rays of light came across the mountains to the east.

In the Jardin de Luxembourg there were two tennis courts that were open to the public and which one could rent for fifty centimes an hour.

I had met somewhere an Italian fellow called Dominique Dacunto with whom I started to occasionally play. Dominique was a banker and offered to introduce me to a friend of his, Keith Payne, who worked for the Parisian office of the Royal Bank of Canada and who played hockey with a group of Canadians. I met Keith and his lovely Dutch wife Elizabeth, and through a travelling acquaintance of my parents managed to get my hockey brought to Paris, and joined "Les Canadiens de Paris". Although we were just a random group, we were in fact quite good, everyone having played at either the university or Junior A or B level at home. One fellow, a tough defenseman with very limited vision in one of his eyes, had played a year in the NHL with the Atlanta Flames (later to become the Calgary Flames) and was to dislocate my shoulder with a ferocious but clean check late one season. I played most of the time on a line with Keith Payne, the banker, at centre and Yves Moquin, a schoolteacher from Montreal who was a fabulous right wing. We practiced once or twice or week, either at a rink at Meudon, which was our "home' rink in the southwest of the city or at a rink at Neuilly-sur-Marne in the western suburbs. On the weekends we toured around the country and played exhibition games against the top tier of the Federation Francaise de Hockey sur Glace. We went to Rouen, Tours, Chamonix, Grenoble, and other cities and the games were almost always great fun. The local teams saw us as a big challenge and we won most of our games, but not all. Our biggest problem was that our games were generally on Sundays in the late morning, and we would have driven from Paris on Friday night or Saturday, and gone out on the town on Saturday night. So on Sunday morning the team was generally in pretty bad shape for at least the first period. Keith or Yves or Jacques Cloutier, a young married student from St. Jean up in the Saguenay, always brought some beer, so after a couple of "hair-of-the-dog" restoratives between periods, we generally felt looser and played better. Our dressing rooms were like the stories one heard about the NHL teams in the 1940s and 50s, when half the players smoked and drank beer in the dressing rooms.

Our games would generally draw a small local crowd of hockey enthusiasts, but there was one game where we filled the small stadium. It was at Caen in the north, and the local town council really put on a show, flying Canadian flags at the city hall and at the arena. The elderly mayor himself came out and made a speech after a very friendly game which we won rather handily. The mayor said that this was the second time in his memory Canadians had bombarded his city, and both times they had been most welcome. The first of course was the liberation of Caen by the Canadian First Army Corps after the landings in Normandy in June of 1944. We all felt very touched and proud.

Another game at which we pulled a large crowd was in Geneva, which was the farthest we ever went for a game and where we had been invited by the Geneva Canadiens, a team made of expatriates like ourselves. Many local Swiss came out to watch what was billed as a championship game of Canadian teams in Europe, which was clearly an overstatement since we had invited no other team to play, but we did expect a close match as we had heard that the Geneva Canadiens had beaten all the local teams they had played. Most of the players on the Geneva team were working in banks or international organizations or at the Canadian mission, but in spite of the billing of two tightly matched Canadian teams, they were hopelessly outmatched. At the end of the first period we were leading seven or eight to nil, and had stopped pushing very hard after ten minutes or so. Remembering another hopelessly one-sided game when the Boston Bruins were touring Newfoundland and came to play the Corner Brook Royals, I suggested that we go to our opponents' dressing room and mix up the teams. The local team thought that was a great idea, so we swapped players and jerseys and went out on the ice much more balanced for the second and third periods. Of course all the family members and friends of the players caught on quickly to our ruse, and the word passed through the crowd, but it was a much more even and entertaining game afterwards.

On our hockey team were a few regulars from the Canadian Embassy and the Canadian mission to the OECD. Glen Carr was the ex-Atlanta Flame who had joined the Canadian forces after his short NHL career and was a cypher clerk at the Embassy, Reg Pruneau was a big tough RCMP liaison officer, and Gilles Gingras and one or two other political or trade officers would come out at least from time to time. Paul Heinbecker, who will feature later in this story, was senior economist and number two at the OECD mission and was a strong if irregular player on the team my first year but left before the second. It was chatting with Gilles and Paul that made me think about the foreign service as a career, and they encouraged me to write the exam the following September, which was held at embassies all around the world as well as at universities across Canada. I told them that as long as the day of the exam was rainy and I was not losing a beautiful day in the parks or on my bike, I would do it.

One of our better hockey players was a fellow named Ian Hunt who had been a star on Queen's University team and who arrived late in the summer of 1975. He had left Queen's more than a year earlier and had been playing professionally in Eindhoven in the Netherlands, which he did not like very much. He found a job in Paris as a filing clerk at the Canadian mission to the OECD. The mission mainly dealt with economic research and policy coordination among western countries and was not nearly as concerned about security as the much larger Embassy. Ian was very industrious about his job and offered to take on the role of opening up the mission and closing it down every day, which the officers of the mission welcomed. What they did not know, or if they did they turned a blind eye, was that Ian was actually sleeping in the mission at night and thus saving money by not having to rent a flat! There was another Canadian friend of mine, Phillippe Leblanc, who came over one summer to travel and who stayed with me and other friends for a few nights until we made clear that there was a limit to our hospitality. He then bought a EurailPass which allowed young people to travel anywhere on European trains for a period of three or six months. After he bought his train pass we would see Phillippe only occasionally, as he spent every night of his remaining time in Europe on a train going somewhere or coming back.

In today's world of instant communications, mobile phones, e-mail and Skype, the world of 1970s communications were ancient times. And

France was an age behind North America. Not only did mobile phones not yet exist, but fixed phones were administratively difficult to acquire in Paris, and calls were very expensive. I never did get a phone for my little apartment at Rue Bréa, even though I applied. My application languished for months in some bureaucracy and then I was told I would have to get my landlord to sign half his life away on ten different documents, and even that for local service only, so I let it drop. For local calls one would buy tokens from a bartender at a café and use a booth in the back, but for long distance calls one had to go to a post office and telecommunications centre (known as a "PTT"). There you had to line up and give the number you wished to call to a generally grumpy middle-aged matronly telephonist, and when it was your turn you would be directed to a booth to pick up the call, and the telephonist would interrupt from time to time to tell you that the prepaid time was coming close to running out. So I almost never called home, and communicated with family and friends by letter. Half way through my time in Paris, a telecommunications revolution struck, and around the city started to appear caller-operated public telephone booths, all silver coloured and very modern looking, which could be operated simply by depositing coins in the appropriate slots. North America had arrived. Long distance calls were still, however, very expensive, but the new coin-operated phones had a habit of occasionally breaking down and allowing callers to place calls for free. Whenever this happened, the word would spread quickly from mouth-to-mouth, and the expatriate young would jump on subways or bikes and head up to the broken phone in Montmartre or wherever and join a long line. The rule was two-minutes a call, strictly enforced by the people waiting, and you hoped you would get your turn before the telephone company came and shut down the phone booth for repair.

Everyone who visited loved my apartment at Rue Bréa. This included Prunella Tuff, my "sister-out-law", a term we invented to describe the relationship between us as she was the sister of my brother in-law, Tim Tuff. I stayed in London with Prunella and her architect husband Chris Scarlett in their little house on Markham Street in South Kensington, and I agreed to let them borrow my Paris flat in return. Chris was a pilot and had his own plane, and he and Prunella would come to the continent often. We eventually set up an arrangement with a third couple, Wiya Waworunto and his wife Judith, who I had met through their daughter who was living in Paris and with whom I played tennis at the Jardin de Luxembourg. In the small world department, it turned out that Wiya, a Balinese, and Chris were already good friends, having worked on design projects together. Wiya and Judith had an apartment in Rome, and we agreed to play "musical homes", allowing me to spend a weekend in Rome while Prunella and Chris were in Paris and Wiya and Judith in London. A few years later I would reconnect with Wiya in Indonesia, but when we met each other first in Europe I had not even begun to contemplate a foreign service career.

I was very careful in the way I spent my money and managed to save enough from my handsome Canada Council Fellowship to buy a car in the middle of 1975, and this was to completely transform my life. It was a little dark blue Fiat-124, very spartan with a radio being the only item added to the absolute minimum. The floors were even uncarpeted metal and the windows of course hand operated. But its simplicity did not matter, for all of a sudden I could go anywhere anytime, and I did. One of my first trips was over to England on the channel ferry from Calais to Dover, and I drove up to see Pat and Tim and their growing family. They were the living at Fenny Compton in Oxfordshire on a beautiful little estate, in a lovely home with a great Aga oven in the kitchen and a garden full of flowering bushes. Getting off the ferry in Dover I had to remind myself continuously to drive on the left, and I did not seem to have any difficulty remembering. I would say "left" aloud to myself whenever I got on or off a highway or started the car for the beginning of an errand. On the way back to France, I got off the ferry in Calais and started to relax, and headed immediately down the left side of the road, until the air-horn of a large truck made me realize my error. I went to England several times with my little car, and also did a tour of the great chateaux south of Paris and down through the Loire Valley, which was very beautiful. Having a car and an interest in going places also greatly added to my popularity. I would grab friends on weekends and go anywhere and everywhere, north to the coast at Mont St. Michel, to Tours and Nantes, even to Grenoble where I stayed with a schoolmate of my sister Joy, Sarah Collins, who lived there with her boyfriend, a nuclear scientist at France's central research laboratories. He showed me pictures using latest nuclear pulse imagery in which you could see sideways through a locomotive showing all its mechanisms more clearly than an x-ray showed a human's skeleton.

In the early spring of one of my Paris years my brother Hugh came to Europe and stayed with me in Paris for a while before we wandered off to Italy and Greece, where we were planning to meet our parents for a sailing trip in the Aegean Islands and a subsequent car trip through the Peloponnesian peninsula. Before we went south, we went to Belgium for a weekend. A student artist from Canada by the name of Lynne Hart had moved to Paris a few months earlier to study engraving at the studio of some famous artist. Lynne was the girlfriend of a graduate student I had gotten to know in Toronto and didn't know many people in Paris. When she heard that we were going to Belgium she invited herself along, so the three of us piled into my car and headed up to Bruges and Ghent, to see galleries and canals and old towns. She was a tall pretty blond girl and one day while we were picnicking in a charming park next to a canal in Ghent, a bee flew into the bottle of wine we were sharing. As Hugh and I watched, Lynne took the end of a thin knife and tried to extract the bee from the bottle, tilting it a little, and then a little more and then, *whoosh*, down she poured the red wine over the front of her stylish, and completely white, blouse and slacks. Hugh roared with laughter and I joined in, and Lynne naturally got furiously angry at us. She eventually forgave us, and we went back to Paris as friends once more.

On our way south, Hugh and I went first by train to Verona and saw Henry Boyer, from whom I rented my flat in Paris, and his family and spent a few days there. Henry himself took us around the city and showed us all the city sights and was clearly a well-known character, for he would stop and chat with everyone, from street cleaners to university professors. Henry and his wife Annie had us to dinner at their home, which was an apartment on the top floor in a courtyard off Via Capello. Across the courtyard we could see a balcony on which the famous dialogue between Juliet and Roméo allegedly took place. Henry assured us that what we were looking at was absolutely the original balcony, and he said he knew this because he had watched it being built for the very first time a couple of decades earlier. Apparently the city had been so anxious to provide tourists with as many attractions as they could that they built onto a credible looking house in a credible looking courtyard a real stone setting for a fictional dialogue.

From Verona, Hugh and I went on to Venice and wandered around as good tourists do, and then down to Rome, where we did not stay long, and then off to the east coast to catch a boat to Greece. We went through Bari, which is where our father had been briefly headquartered during the march up Italy in 1943 when he was serving as a liaison officer between the British 5th Army and the American 8th Army. His billet had been a villa near the coast, right beside one occupied by Josef Broz (better known as Tito) and other Yugoslav freedom fighters who would cross the Adriatic for raids on German installations. That is all part of my father's story, not mine, but Hugh and I were interested in it. We arrived in Brindisi far too early for the boat to Greece, and spent wandering one of the most boring seaports either of us had ever visited.

We arrived in Athens a few days before our parents and explored Athens and its environs. Knowing that we needed some sort of skipper's certificate to charter a boat without a crew, we also went to the office of the Honorary Consul of Togo, where for $35 in cash we bought Masters Papers certifying that the Minister of Merchant Marine Affairs of the Government of Togo had ensured that one "H. Balloch" had passed all the necessary courses allowing him to captain vessels of up to 60,000 tons. We avoid using a first name as we could subsequently share the use of these official Masters Papers when either of us needed them.

In Glifada, we rented a 35-foot Swedish built sloop for our trip through the northern Aegean, and spent a lovely week with our parents, Maisie and Tony, wandering from Hydra to Milos and back up to Kea. It was the first time Hugh and I had travelled as adults with our parents and it was a new and very enjoyable experience, and our evenings were full of interesting talks about history over local Greek food and resinated wine. Mum painted lots of paintings, some of which hang in the homes of her children still today, and Pop and Hugh and I took lots of photographs. The following week, after leaving the boat, we toured down the eastern Peloponnese coast to Epidaurus and then back up to Corinth and Olympia, before going our separate ways again. The fellow we had rented the boat from was Greek with a girlfriend from Montreal, and he asked me before I left whether I would be willing to act as a charter skipper if he had groups that needed an experienced hand. Never to say no to a sailing opportunity, I agreed and went back a few months later to sign on as the skipper for a British couple and their daughter who followed almost the same route that we had followed en famille.

My good friends from Montreal, Irène and Robert Rigal, returned to France for the summer to visit their families in Strasbourg and Asson, near Pau in the Pyrenées, respectively. They invited me to come down to Asson in August where Robert's family still farmed. I went down and lived there for about two weeks, working in the fields alongside Robert and his brothers and cousins. It was harvest season and while the skilled hands worked with scythes, the unskilled, including me, pitched the hay up on horse-drawn carts. It was heavy work and we would start at five in the morning, return to the farmhouse at about nine for our first main meal, work again until another meal just after noon, and then would knock off work at about three. We would stop occasionally at the end of the long hillside fields before turning and heading back in the opposite direction, and Irene and the other ladies would bring bread and watered-down wine out for us. It was truly bucolic. I had difficult at first understanding the local accent, which was influenced by nearby Spain, and in which the French words for axes and beans and others beginning with "h" would all be aspirated, although my name was not. I visited the Rigal farm one last time just before leaving France in 1976, and I left two cases of reasonably good wine there since it was too administratively complicated and bureaucratic to import it to Canada. Robert's family encouraged me to return and Robert told me that every summer I did not come to visit he would take a tithe of one bottle. I never did return and when I saw Robert many years later in Montreal he told me, alas, that all my wine had been consumed.

Perhaps a good way to describe what my life was like in those days is to quote myself, writing at the time in a letter to my parents in 1976:

"On Easter weekend I went with a bunch of friends to the champagne district in the Haute Marne, to a little town called Blaise, next door to Colombey-de-deux-Eglises of the late lamented general's fame (DeGaulle). A friend of mine named Luc has an old water-mill which he is (very slowly) restoring-retrofitting – not completely as it was at the time when it was most active five centuries ago, but a compromise with some parts restored and some parts modernized. It is really a most beautiful spot, the rolling hills of the upper Marne with hundreds of little villages tucked into every nook and cranny, all built of gray stone, the oldest without cement and many still with thatch instead of the more common red-tile roofs. (Seeing so many little hamlets helps me understand how there can be 38 thousand communes in this country – until now I have been baffled by this number.) The mill is a big affair, built first in the fourteenth century, stretching right over the creek which for so long gave sense to its existence, with a living room inside at one end, then the milling room, and the work and storage rooms above and beyond the water. On the far side of the stream the building was added onto in the seventeenth century, with a little pointed tower and a square building with crooked walls and windows. Beyond still are the woods, full of birds and flowers. The whole pace of the place is so tempered that one is easily teased back in time.

"*Our complement was ten in all, and we slept hither and thither on floors, beds, and whatever else was handy. As we did not do much sleeping, lack of sleeping amenities was not hard to bear! Saturday we spent most of the day digging up an old sixteenth-century millstone we found buried in the garden, fishing for trout in the stream, basking in the glorious sun and generally being pleasure-oriented. We had a huge dinner that night which saw a case of wine disappear, and after singing songs and sitting around the fireplace exchanging stories of every imaginable sort, we all flaked out at sometime well into the wee hours of the morning. Nonetheless, I got up pretty early and wandered about the surrounding woods watching for animals and birds and along the stream looking for trout (of which there were many – Saturday night's dinner was trout). By noon all the world was up and as the sun was unquestionably over some yard-arm or other, we broke open the red martini and began a second day. We ate at about three o'clock our Easter fare, consisting of paté, poulet, confit d'oie and cheese, all in the bright outside, where the food and wine and sun had us all prostrate in pleasurable siesta before the evening twilight. At some point a neighbouring 70-year old inn-owner dropped over, established himself with a glass and recounted endlessly of Africa and big-game hunting and of other times in France when the Third Republic was optimistic and then when he fought in the Résistance and of many other things. An old fellow with but a single leg and a coarse but charming manner, making flattering if ridiculous propositions to all the girls of our group. As there were three Canadians amongst us, we broke out a bottle of Black Velvet Rye so that the old fellow could try something new, and he did exactly that for two or three hours until only a quarter of the bottle was left. But he was highly entertaining and I am sure he would have continued forever had his wife not sent two of his grandchildren up the road to the rescue, to drag him off to supper and to leave us to try to cleanse our brains by leaping into the little stream, still only a springtime cold of 45 or 50 degrees.*

"*The next morning we were up by nine-ish. Even if there was no earthly excuse for being so, we were all peckish again so I made a giant batch of super thin crepes with fromage et jambon, and we all stuffed ourselves silly again, washing our meal down with a third case of wine. Our host, Luc, had to drink extra, for just before dinner he had been exercising his authority as Deputy Fishing warden only to receive a black eye from a truculent and permit-less angler a half mile upstream from the mill. The poor and well-known local fellow had not even caught anything, and it was no wonder he gave Luc a good clout – after all, who should have to have a license to catch nothing? By the time our seamless meal and multitudinous crepes were all finished, Easter had slipped away and Monday had already arrived so off to bed we went. That morning when we had all dragged ourselves up, cleaned up the mill, went down the road to have a drink and a light lunch of mostly champagne (this was the champagne district after all), at the inn owned by our elderly one-legged friend of the day before, who got a great kick of showing us his big-game trophies and his small arsenal of deadly weapons and who started to get going again on his stories, so it was mid-afternoon before we got on the road for Paris, arriving late in the afternoon, tired, wine-logged but suntanned and happy."*

Thus was my life in Paris when there was no such thing as responsibility or tomorrow. And of course as any young man in Paris at almost any time in history, I fell in and out of love as fast as the weather changed. But as Bohemian and delightful as the life was, I knew it was not forever, and much to the surprise of most of my friends I started to yearn for a more serious path.

When the day of the Foreign Service exam rolled around it was a gorgeous day, and in spite of my promise to take the exam only in the case of inclement weather, by that time I had talked myself into a real interest in a diplomatic career. So I spent the six hours required in an embassy function room writing both the general civil service exam in the morning and the more specific Foreign Service exam in the afternoon. Several months later I was told I had done sufficiently well on the exam to merit an interview, and was asked to come to the Embassy on a Monday morning some weeks thereafter. The interview team was sent out from Canada to meet with selected candidates from Britain and Europe, with the latter being interviewed in Paris after the British-based had been met in London. Courtesy of a name beginning with "B", I was the first interviewee, and as I walked into the room I could see that the interview team had clearly been out late on the town and was suffering from hangovers measured somewhere between severe and deadly. After meeting each of them and storing their names in my head so I could answer each one of them by name, I couldn't resist saying "Well, gentlemen, it is clear I am going to have to go easy on you this morning." Alan Sullivan, later to become a friend and our Consul General in New York, could not resist laughing and I realized that the interview might be as much about comportment as substance. Half of the interview was spent trying to upset me, with one panel member asking me what I would say if someone suggested that a person who played a lot with hockey sticks and flutes and other long things had something of a subconscious phallic preoccupation, to which I laughed out loud and said that I would say that the person so suggesting must have some sort of problem of his own, possibly not even a subconscious one. Then I was asked what a young embassy officer in an Eastern bloc country should do if he was at a dance and the wife of an important local Minister started to make it clear that she would like to have more than a simple dance. I answered that it depended entirely on three things: how beautiful the lady, how large the husband, and whether the officer in question had or had not already been thinking about a career as a second level but very happy used car salesman. This brought a second laugh from Alan Sullivan, and this time Bernard Giroux, the Trade Commissioner on the interview team, joined in. Alan later told me that from this point on I was a complete shoo-in. I was to receive my offer to join the service a few weeks after the interview, with a suggested reporting date in early June. I immediately appealed on the basis that I needed the summer to finish my thesis, and was granted a late entry date of September 6th. I then turned to my thesis for at least two days of concentrated work, realized that I might spend the rest of my life enchained, threw all my notes and drafts into a cardboard box and spent the next four months thoroughly enjoying Paris and the Mediterranean.

My last trip across the English Channel in my little Fiat was a trip all the way to Edinburgh where I met with my thesis advisor, Ian Drummond, who was teaching at the University of Edinburgh during a two-year break from the University of Toronto. I saw my cousins, the Aglen family when I was there; by this time my cousin Edward (middle son of Sir Frank Aglen, successor to Sir Robert Hart and the last British Inspector General of China Customs) had knocked down half of the family house to save on heating bills, and made it quite clear that there was no room to put me up. So I stayed in a hostel, and got together with cousins Selma and Brigid who were both in Edinburgh at the time and very nice and friendly. I also took advantage of being in Edinburgh to have tea with my old Latin teacher from St. George's, Mr. Watt and his wife. By this time they were getting on in years, probably around 80, but Mr. Watt was still very sharp, not surprised that I had not stayed with Latin and pleasantly surprised that I had ended up doing well academically both at school and at university. He also thought my newfound choice of career to be well suited to the character he had known a dozen years earlier. I told Professor Drummond that I was heading back to Canada to join the Foreign Service and would try to finish my thesis over the coming year. He said that he thought I was making a good move and not to worry too much about the thesis; he expressed doubt that I was in fact made of academic cloth and said that I would be one of many at "External" whose PhDs died unfinished. He was in that respect at least, prescient, and somewhere en route to and from Ottawa and Jakarta and Prague the cardboard box with all my notes and a hastily written first chapter disappeared forever.

And so I closed up my lovely little flat on Rue Bréa, arranged for the Fiat and my boxes of thesis notes and books and records to be shipped to Canada, and closed the Bohemian chapter of my life, at least the figurative one.

BOOK II:

EARLY YEARS IN GOVERNMENT

CHAPTER 3

FIRST YEAR IN OTTAWA

• • • • • • • • • • • •

Leaving Paris behind was not nearly as difficult as I thought it would be, mostly because joining External Affairs turned out to be both busy and exciting. Arriving in early September, I was part of the second contingent of the "Class of '76", the others having arrived in June and already at work. We were gathered together in a conference room and given a rudimentary briefing and then a single piece of paper with a list of departmental divisions that we had to individually visit to complete our entry formalities. These included the Personnel Security Division in the basement for an oath of secrecy, a security briefing and the issuance of a building pass, followed by several personnel divisions for setting up pensions and other administrative arrangements, and the most important of all, the Assignment Officer who would be in charge of looking after us and guiding our training and development.

The Department of External Affairs in the 1970s was still a stand-alone foreign office and the rotational professional staff, the diplomats, were all called political officers even if the corps was made up of lawyers, economists, social scientists, cultural experts and others. External, as it was simply known, had moved into the Lester B Pearson Building, its new headquarters on Sussex Drive, a couple of years before I joined, and it seemed a very modern and professional complex.

The incoming Class of '76 was as diverse as any. One or two were entering immediately following completion of their first university degree, but they were the exceptions, for most of us had either done more advanced academic work or been out in the real economy for a while. We had several lawyers who had completed law school, passed the bar and spent a couple of years in big Toronto or Montreal firms, we had a fellow who had completed a PhD in Hegelian philosophy at Oxford, and we had a former actor, a journalist, and a Greek philologist. Our roots were in all corners of the country. We were all pretty smart, we knew it, and we were all intensely competitive while pretending to be blasé and laid-back.

At our initial briefing we were told that we actually were not real Foreign Service Officers yet, and that twenty percent of us would probably never become ones. We were the lowest of the low, probationary officers with the designation of FS1Ds, meaning Developmental Foreign Service Officers Level-1. We were to be trained and tested during our first year and then either passed into the ranks of the full service as FS1s or let go. (At that time there were five levels in the service, with only a very small handful of FS-5s serving as Ambassadors in the most important capitals or in top two or three positions in headquarters.) We all looked around at each other and wondered who would not make it; as we chatted over coffee in the cafeteria everyone tried their best, and generally succeeded, to seem incredibly brilliant and worldly.

My assignment officer, an experienced FS2 with perhaps ten years or so experience, was Jean-Paul Hubert, and I found him personable and sympathetic. When I told him that I thought the $11,000 entry-level salary that I had been offered had not taken into consideration my post-graduate education or some of my experience, he impressed me by agreeing on the spot that I could start at $14,000 per year. He also told me that I would likely have four three-month assignments during my training year and we discussed the fields in which I was interested. Many of the FS1Ds would spend the autumn on temporary assignment at our mission to the United Nations in New York as staffers for more senior officers caught up in the business of the General Assembly and the myriad of UN committees and meetings that run from September through December every year, and this was a greatly coveted training assignment. As a late entrant I was not eligible for the UN assignment, however, and I was sent to the East Asia Division. This was in the Asia Bureau on the fifth floor of Tower A. I was to spend many years of my professional life on A-5, but of course I did not yet know that.

I reported as instructed to the East Asia Division and as there were no free desks in the Division itself, I was assigned to an office shared with other Asian divisions for temporary assignments or officers visiting from abroad. I found, to my great surprise as I walked into the office, my old university mate Jim Wright already working there. He and I had been great friends at McGill but had not stayed in touch afterwards. He had completed a Masters Degree and had joined External in the June cohort and was now assigned to the Japan Division, although he was shortly to move to another lap of his training. Even though we were never assigned to the same mission and our times in Ottawa were to rarely overlap, Jim and I have remained close friends our whole lives. He was to complete his very successful career thirty years later with five years as Head of Mission in London. He will reappear later in these sketches of mine.

My first boss in the East Asia Division was Deputy Director Peter Hancock, not an Asian specialist but an expert on communist regimes and a Russian speaker with several overseas assignments under his belt. The other Deputy Director was John Higginbotham, a China specialist and a fluent Mandarin speaker. The Director was a man named Douglas Small, who was probably at the peak of his career and seemed to my inexperienced eyes and ears to be hopelessly outclassed by two brilliant deputies. Hancock was terrific to me, and within a week or two I was acting desk officer for Vietnam. My predecessor, a fellow called Chris Malone, had been reassigned somewhere else in the department. There were two positive sides to this, the first being that I would have some real responsibilities and answer directly to a more senior officer than some of my colleagues working for FS1s just back from their first overseas assignments. The second advantage was that I would get an office to myself, although when I moved in it took me several late nights and a whole Saturday sorting through a most disorganized mess of filing cabinets and drawers. Hancock had told me to sort the mess into some semblance of order by subject matter, and then to ship the whole amount to Records, the department's central registry. As I was going through the mess I came across correspondence that my predecessor had been having with one of the leading politicians of the Parti Québécois, the separatist provincial party that would come to power for the first time in November of that year. The correspondence concerned the foreign policy positions the PQ wanted to take in preparation for creating the separate country of Québec, with Malone providing background taken from material circulating inside External, some of it classified. This was clearly improper if not treasonous communications for an officer who had sworn allegiance to Canada and taken an oath of secrecy. I showed the material to Peter Hancock, who sent me off with it to Graham Mitchell, our then Coordinator for Federal-Provincial Relations. Graham took it from me and told me to speak no further about the matter. Within a week or two the word spread in the cafeteria (which served better rumours than food) that Chris Malone had precipitously left the service. He was to re-emerge as a senior person in Québec's Ministry of Intergovernmental and International Affairs a year or two later when the PQ was firmly entrenched in power, but he did not seem to survive the return to power of the federalist liberals.

Although most of my work was related to Vietnam, Laos and Cambodia, all still relatively "hot" following the fall of Saigon the previous year, I ended up pitching in on some China files as well. Joe Maken was another FS1D assigned to the division and he and I were given the job of writing any and all letters in reply to those written by Canadians to the Prime Minister, the Secretary of State for External Affairs (or the SSEA as he was called in government), or senior officials on any matter having to do with our part of the world. It was government policy that no letter would go without a formal response, and all but crank letters would receive a response signed by the person to whom the original letter had been addressed. Crank or form letters would be answered at the divisional level, with the Director beginning the letter with "The Secretary of State for External Affairs has asked me to respond to your letter of . . .". At that time there were no word processors or computers, so every letter had to be typed separately and there was a convention that wherever possible personalized.

In every division of the department this job fell on the most junior officer. I was asked to help Joe work his way out from under a pile of literally thousands of letters written to the government criticizing the exclusion of Taiwanese athletes from the 1976 Olympic Games in Montreal. Although Canada had recognized the People's Republic six years earlier, it was not until after China took its rightful seat at the UN did Olympic participation switch, and many Canadians were unhappy that we had not found a way to allow athletes from Taiwan to participate. John Higginbotham had made a heroic effort right up until a few weeks before the Olympics to find a solution, and even had proposed the eventual solution of having the Taiwanese compete under the name of Chinese Taipei and a flag composed of the five Olympic rings, but regimes on both sides of the Taiwan Strait were rigid and obdurate then and there were no Taiwanese athletes in Montreal.

I had rented a little apartment at 53 Crichton Street in New Edinburgh, just a ten minute walk from the Pearson Building across the handsome little cantilever Minto bridges, which had been built in the middle of the 19th century as the northern-most crossing of the Rideau River before it runs over the Canadian Shield to join the Ottawa.

As FS1Ds we tended to stick pretty close together, and we would often eat dinner together and then play Risk or Diplomacy or other board games late at night when we finished our long days.

We lost our first colleague fairly quickly. One of the June intake was a well-travelled actor, a little older than our average, by the name of Ralph (pronounced Rafe) Lamoureux, who spoke with a bit of an Irish accent. Rafe had a very sharp wit and was always an entertaining fellow to be around. In the departmental cafeteria on the main floor of the Pearson Building, there was a very clear pecking order and hierarchy, although none of it was ever explicit. Very senior people sat at small tables along the eastern and southern windows, which had a view of the Rideau River. Assuming we were not lunching with more senior people in our divisions, which was in any case rare (middle-level officers would never be seen with FS1Ds), we always lunched at two large tables in the centre of the cafeteria. Rafe Lamoureux could generally be relied on to be at one of the two tables recounting some fascinating experience or other in some corner of the world. Until one day he simply was not there. It turned out that he was not who he had pretended to be, that his background was a carefully constructed lie, which it would have had to be to get by the initial security checks. But someone pulled a thread somewhere and his story started to unravel, and he was quietly and efficient excised. None of us ever heard from or of him again.

FS1Ds also had responsibility for the production of a daily report called POPSUM. Each of us would join four colleagues on a two-week-on four-week-off rotation, and go into the Operations Centre at about 0400 in the morning and produce for the SSEA and senior staff a summary of all the important telegrams coming in from posts around the world. This was actually both very interesting and a lot of fun, for it gave us an insight into how the service really worked. It was substantively fascinating because we would be reading about political and economic developments in every corner of the globe more or less as they were happening. This was still before live global broadcasting or all-news television channels like CNN. POPSUM was supposed to be limited to four pages, and our job was to both select the most important messages and to produce a précis for each one as short and informative as possible, allowing a maximum of reports to be summarized. Coming in very early did not absolve us from desk work or permit shortened afternoons, so while on POPSUM duty we would be living on caffeine and adrenaline.

POPSUM would be on every senior officer's desk by eight o'clock every morning, and would also be circulated more broadly during the day, and then out to missions in weekly diplomatic bags, so that Ambassadors and other senior field officers could stay up to date with developments and their colleagues' analyses in areas of the world for which they were not responsible but might have a general interest. (In the Canadian system, telegrams would as a matter of course be copied electronically by instruction of the drafter to all posts having a direct involvement in the subject matter.) There was one FS1D in our group by the name of Peter Jenkins who had been a journalist before joining External, and he had fixed views about many developments happening in various parts of the world. At this time Bill Bauer, a tough anti-communist curmudgeon was our Ambassador in Bangkok and his Deputy Chief of Mission was Manfred Von Nostitz, also a veteran of the southeast Asian conflicts. Bangkok had been made responsible for Laos and Cambodia when we closed all our Indochinese offices following the collapse of the 1973 peace accord. Ambassador Bauer and Manfred sent in a telegram about North Vietnamese infiltration into Laos and its efforts to destabilize Thailand. Jenkins summarized the message in a few sentences for POPSUM, but in doing so both changed the substance and made the authors sound like they were soft on communism. That edition of POPSUM was published and about a week later, when the diplomatic bag was opened in Bangkok, Ambassador Bauer went ballistic. Shortly thereafter Peter Jenkins slipped away, the second casualty of our group.

Training in External was not formal or codified. You learned on the job. Shortly after my arrival in the East Asia Division, Peter Hancock asked me to prepare a memorandum for the minister on some subject relating to our policy towards the Hanoi government. I did just that, and returned to his office with a short memorandum which began "Dear Minister . . .", causing Peter to roar with laughter. A Memorandum to the SSEA was a very serious and formalized document, prepared on specially coloured legal-length paper, with strict formatting and gating requirements. In order to actually reach the SSEA, a memo had to be initialed by a Director and Director General, and depending on the subject matter, signed by the Under-Secretary or at least one of the Deputy Under-Secretaries. It ensured careful decision-making, but it was quite tedious and not very useful when dealing with fast moving international events. At a later time in my career I would effectively blow it up.

When I entered the service in 1976, Don Jamieson was Secretary of State for External Affairs, having been named to the position by Prime Minister Trudeau earlier in the year. Jamieson was not a natural diplomat but a natural raconteur. He was a delightful and funny Newfoundlander, representing Burin-Burgeo, and he had been a radio journalist for many years before entering federal politics. At the provincial level in the two 1948 referenda on the constitutional future of Newfoundland and Labrador, Jamieson had campaigned vigorously against joining Canada and was known as "the voice" of the Economic Union Party which favoured joining the United States. The EUP, which was of course disbanded after Confederation, had been led by St. John's businessman Ches Crosbie, father of John Crosbie, Minister of Trade under Brian Mulroney and later Lieutenant-Governor of Newfoundland. Ches Crosbie was well known as a heavy drinker and came to dinner at our home in Corner Brook a few times; my mother said that he once fell asleep during the soup before the dinner had hardly begun.

One of my first substantive responsibilities as acting desk officer for Vietnam was to organize the visit of a Vice Minister of Foreign Affairs from Hanoi. Although we had full diplomatic relations with Vietnam, bilateral relations between most western countries and Vietnam had been somewhat tense, and this visit was the highest level visit to take place in either direction since the fall of Saigon. Organizing the visit was terrific experience. Peter Hancock guided me gently through the process and was a tremendous help, and he even suggested that I travel with the Vice Minister as the liaison officer throughout the trip. On the first day, the Vice Minister, who was a very small thin man with a wide grin always pasted on his face, had a meeting with Don Jamieson, which gave the Vietnamese much face due to their different levels. During our advance briefing of the Minister, he asked me where I had grown up, and when I told him Corner Brook he was more interested in that than the briefing, asking me about where we had lived and what other Newfoundlanders I knew in Ottawa. Just after the meeting with the Vice Minister began, Jamieson said to him "well, Vice Minister, what you have in this here department is a Newfoundland sandwich – there's me at the top and Balloch there at the bottom, and everyone else is stuck in-between." The interpreter had no idea what to do with that, all the Canadian officials laughed, and the Vietnamese delegation sat stone-faced until our Under-Secretary (the Vice-Minister's real counterpart) cleared his throat and suggested we turn to bilateral economic relations.

The fall of Saigon having been only eighteen months earlier, and the Vietnamese community in Canada being very anti-North, the visit of the Vice Minister from the communist regime was given full security, which meant RCMP officers were assigned to the delegation at all times, with six motorcycle outriders when in transit between meetings and when we travelled by car from Ottawa to Montreal. We also knew from intelligence that the Vice Minister had served as an interrogator of both captured American and South Vietnamese officers, and we did not know whether this might not also be known in the community. The Vice Minister was very appreciative of the security and the RCMP officers were extremely professional and polite, as always. When the time came for his departure from Mirabel Airport in Montreal, the Vice Minister asked me to gather the security detail together so that he could thank them. I did, so, bringing the six Mounties into the VIP room where we were awaiting the flight. The Vice Minister lined up the six Mounties and made a little speech, in French, about how he had enjoyed his trip in Canada and how much he appreciated the security he had been offered. He then reached into his pocket and took out a small felt drawstring sack, and proceeded to take out and give to each officer a small silver-coloured ring, which looked rather like a Canadian engineer's ring. As he handed them out he explained that these were gifts from the hearts of the Vietnamese people and carried special meaning, because they had been made from the fuselage of a shot-down American bomber. The Mounties, hardly left-wing and all very large, bristled and I was sure that they were all thinking that they should either refuse the rings or pick up this little commie and toss him through the window. I was standing behind the Vietnamese, and I signaled furiously to the officers to take the rings and just suck it up, which of course they did. However, once the flight had left, they cornered me and made me by them all a beer as payment for not opting for the homicide option.

A few weeks later I attended a weekly staff meeting of the Asia Bureau, chaired by our Director General, Louis Rogers. Rogers was a very tall, thin man in his late 50s or early 60s and a very formal old-style diplomat, having served as Head of Mission in India and Israel. He wore half-glasses over which he would stare down junior officers, was known for his temper and his eccentricities. He used to take an afternoon nap in his office, closing his door and simply lying flat on his back on the floor. If we needed something from him in the early afternoon, we would approach his secretary who would peek under his door before knocking. We were all quite scared of him. At the bureau meeting in question, held around a long conference table with officers of all levels seated more or less by division, Louis Rogers said that among the administrative matters he wished to deal with was the language of written material. He stated that francophone officers were free to write all their correspondence in French if they so wished, even formal Memoranda to the SSEA, who, Rogers assured us, could read French even if he didn't speak it. From my distant corner I couldn't help piping up with my own comment, saying "Yup, Jamieson reads French all right, but he doesn't understand a word he reads!" Total silence as everyone in the bureau turned to me waiting for the Rogers ax to fall. Louis Rogers glared over his half-glasses at me and said, a little acidly "And who are YOU?". "Howard Balloch, Sir" I answered in my best Newfoundland accent, "lowest man on this here External Affairs totem pole and a Newfie to boot, just like the Minister". At this point, most people started to laugh and even Rogers smiled. He harrumphed and turned back to weightier matters and I escaped execution.

All Foreign Service officers were expected to have a level of proficiency in both official languages of Canada before they were assigned abroad. In reality this only meant that those anglophones who did not speak sufficient French had to go off on language training at some point during their first year, since it was unthinkable that a francophone officer with advanced education would not already be fluent in English. Proficiency was tested formally with both a written and oral exam. When I went for my exam it turned out that I was marked to be tested for my English proficiency. Since I had been hired in Paris and been studying in French, someone had inadvertently lumped me in with others hired out of French language institutions. Tempted as I was to take the English test, I pointed out the error and took the French test, happily passing with perfect marks and a life-long exemption from further testing or training.

Security was taken quite seriously at External Affairs, which I suppose was a very important and good thing. Security staff would go through offices every night and if we had left a classified document on our desks or in wastebaskets, or left our file cabinets unlocked, yellow Security Infraction forms would be left on our desks. Off to the basement we would go to collect the offending document, confessing our guilt with a signature at the bottom of the forms. If we received too many we would be summoned to the basement for an interview with a Security Officer, and a black mark would appear in our personnel file. In 1971 journalist Daniel Ellsberg had published in the New York Times classified US government documents that he was given by a deep source in the Department of Defense. This led to the famous "Pentagon Papers" case, which was a very important First Amendment case fought between the New York Times and the US Government in front of the US Supreme Court. Five years later, in the autumn of 1976, US News and World Report published a whole edition focused on the case. The magazine had as its front cover a full size photograph of one of the key CIA documents, with a label in large red letters across it saying "Top Secret". Peter Hancock and I decided to leave the magazine on my desk overnight to see what would happen. Sure enough, the next morning I had a dreaded Security Infraction. After chuckling over this with Peter, I went down to the Internal Security Division in the basement to retrieve my magazine and get the infraction annulled. The security officer on duty was smarter than I, however, and when I said that the offending item was just a magazine photograph of a classified document he simply said, "Then it should have been downgraded, shouldn't it?" Try as I might, I could not get him to accept that this was a simple prank, and I am sure to this day somewhere in the bowels of the Lester B. Pearson building is my security file, with an infraction duly noting that I had threatened western security by leaving a Secret CIA document unprotected on my desk.

In November of 1976 the political situation in Canada entered a new stage in its history with the election of the Parti Québécois as the first separatist government of Québec. I watched the election results at the apartment of Jacqueline Caron, also a junior officer from my class and a lawyer from Québec City. We must have been about twenty there that night, with myself and a couple of others being the only anglophones, but we were functionally bilingual so the evening was all in French. Although most of the francophones were in the federal public service, there were a number whose sympathies clearly lay with the PQ, and I sensed among all of them a real pride that René Levesque, the journalist and former liberal and now a fierce Québec nationalist, had won the election. The reaction in the Montreal business community was negative, and an exodus of corporate headquarters began virtually immediately. In a highly publicized move that took place actually before the election, the huge SunLife Insurance company had moved all the gold in its vaults in the SunLife Building on Dominion Square into a caravan of Brinks Armoured trucks and taken it all down the road to Toronto.

Not everyone in Jacqueline's apartment was working for the government, but all were friends of someone who was. Jacqueline introduced me to a friend of hers, Marie Lajoie, who came from Baie Comeau and whose brother Jacques had been in the service until he died of leukemia the previous summer. Marie was a certified nurse, very pretty and a real charmer. She had been in a bad bus accident a few years earlier and suffered serious damage to one of her legs and walked with a limp and couldn't run or play tennis, but she was a great swimmer and biker. We saw quite a bit of each other over the months to come.

Late in the calendar year I had my first opportunity to travel abroad as part of an External delegation. Our Director General Louis Rogers was planning a trip to Japan and China and Vietnam and both Doug Small, our Director, and Peter Hancock were meant to join him after the Japan portion of the visit, but at the last minute Small got sick and so Peter bumped himself up a notch and added me to the delegation as note-taker for the latter half of the tour. We arrived in Beijing in early December and met with Arthur Menzies, who had taken up his post in June, in the middle of one of China's most turbulent years. The Tangshan earthquake in the early summer had left almost 300,000 dead in Eastern Hebei and even damaged significant parts of Beijing, but more important was the political earthquake that had seen Zhou Enlai, General Zhu De and Mao Zedong all die. After Mao's death the dreaded Gang-of-Four were arrested and the final vestiges of the Cultural Revolution were washed away. The purpose of the visit was a general one; it had been more than three years since Prime Minister Pierre Trudeau had visited and more than six since we had established diplomatic relations, and the government wanted to keep up a regular pattern of discussions between foreign ministries. There wasn't much to the relationship at this stage beyond some very modest trade, mostly in wheat, and cultural exchanges that had seen the Canadian Brass travel around China and the Cultural Revolutionary operas like "The White Haired Girl" travel around Canada, but we sensed that an inflection point was being reached and that the years ahead could see a much fuller bilateral agenda.

In Beijing we stayed in the new tall eastern tower of the Beijing Hotel, the tallest building in the country at something like 24 stories, and even though it was only 30 months old it already smelled of mold and stale tea. The Beijing Hotel was the only hotel I stayed at in Beijing until I was running the Asia Branch a decade and a half later, and I and other visiting Canadian diplomats were always put in rooms on the 12th floor, presumably because the listening systems were well installed there. I came out of the front of the hotel on my first morning and watched the two-way sea of bicyclists pedaling east and west along the hugely broad Changan

Jie. A single black Red Flag car went by, presumably carrying some official, and about two minutes later another one went by in the opposite direction. I thought to myself that it was preposterous of Mao to have built Changan Jie with such grandeur when a boulevard a quarter the width would have clearly met Beijing's transportation needs. Thirty years later I would sit in my car in horrible traffic jams on the same road in front of the same hotel, and ask my driver why the city government had built such a narrow east-west thoroughfare!

Because the East Asia Division was somewhat short-staffed, my time there was doubled from the normal three-month training period to a full six months and I remained there until the late winter. Eventually, however, I had to move on to my second training assignment, and for this I was assigned to the Defense Relations Division. I had been warned by colleagues who had already served part of their training year in defense relations that it was not very exciting work, but nothing prepared me for the extent of the agony. The rank and file of the people in the division and in the Department of National Defense, with whom we dealt daily, were either military or of a military mind-cast. To them, probationary Foreign Service officers were the equivalent of military-grade lieutenants awaiting their commissions, and we were absolutely excluded from all interesting work. I was assigned to be the External liaison with Emergency Preparedness Canada (EPC), an organization loosely connected to the Department of National Defence (DND), a Canadian FEMA of sorts, charged with coordinating the civil response to external aggression or natural disaster. I had to do such enormously important tasks as to update the cross-country list of emergency contacts at the provincial and municipal level. EPC was made up mostly of retired middle-level military officers and bureaucrats that had failed to advance their careers in any real department, and I quickly came to the conclusion that if we were indeed ever attacked by the Soviets, our only hope would be that the fist bomb would wipe out EPC headquarters and all their senior staff. Within our own External hierarchy, there were some very sympathetic and supportive managers. The Divisional Director, David Rose, probably then in his early forties, knew that most of the work we had to do was not terribly challenging and did his best to include junior officers in matters relatively more interesting. The Director General, Angus Matheson, was a lovely older man closing in on retirement and had a lot of time for juniors. During a chat one day we discovered that my mother had gone to school at Elmwood in Ottawa with one of his sisters in the 1930s, and that I had gotten to know her and her children when I was at the University of Toronto in 1973. When my time in Defence Relations was drawing to a close in the spring of 1977, I was invited out to the his farm, set in the rolling hills west of Arnprior, and spent a lovely day with the Matheson family walking in the woods and across the fields and listening to Matheson's stories of his experiences in government service.

Just about the only enjoyable part of my time in the Defense Relations Division, or DFR as it was called, was participating in military simulations. There were two when I was there. The first was a NORAD (North American Air Defence) simulation of a surprise attack across the Arctic by the Soviet Union, an exercise run out of NORAD headquarters and involving DND and External in Ottawa and the Department of Defense (DOD) and the State Department in Washington. The second was a NATO wide simulation of a gradually escalating series of clashes between NATO and Warsaw Pact land forces along the Iron Curtain. Both were fun, involving spending 24 hours or so in the very impressive DND operations centre, with its huge wall of electronic maps and tracking systems. In one of the simulations I was given the role of the Secretary of State for External Affairs, and had to speak on special secure telephones with other actors playing both other Canadian leaders and foreign leaders as well. Because the defence departments took these exercises very seriously, and because we were situated in the real high-tech operations centres where Soviet air and military movements were being constantly monitored, the scenarios felt very real and it was natural to take the exercises very seriously.

Most of my time in DFR was spent reading hopelessly uninteresting reports from what seemed to me to be marginally relevant NATO committees, and I vowed that I would do my best to avoid the whole sub-world of the military and East-West relations for as long as I worked in government. It was a vow I was to partially break twice in my career, once when I served in Prague and once during the first Gulf War at the beginning of the 1990s, and in both cases the circumstances and my role in things made the issues much more interesting than I would have expected. In retrospect, I suspect I was simply not yet knowledgeable enough, or attuned enough to the real threat of the underlying tensions of the cold war to recognize that a lot of the work being done in the world of defense relations was really very important. I was young and champing at the bit to get my career going.

Throughout the winter on 1977 the biggest issue for all of us plebian FS1Ds was where we would be posted. In the autumn the Personnel Department would publish for internal service circulation the Posting List of available positions for the coming summer, for virtually all rotations were done during the summer school break to limit the impact on Foreign Service families. As soon as the list was posted we talked of almost nothing else, and would bombard our assignment officers with questions and arguments why we would be perfect for this job or that. By sometime in January we had to submit our Posting Preference Forms, with no less than five choices and a brief summary of why we were interested in each. Perhaps not surprisingly, there was some competition for certain positions, although we were a sufficiently diverse group to ensure there was interest in almost every part of the world. Some of us would defer substantive work for a year or two to learn difficult languages, and the Posting List contained positions in Moscow and Ryadh and Beijing and other distant foreign capitals that would not be open for one or two more years. Personnel had a complex balancing task in selecting junior officers for language training in the most complex foreign languages because the officers concerned would likely be making a career-long choice. Most Chinese or Russian or Arabic speakers would spend half or more of their career in positions abroad or at home where their language was needed. The thought of going off on Chinese language training crossed my mind, but I had spent too much of my still young life studying and I was impatient to head off somewhere exotic and get started on real work.

All first assignments in those days were for two years, with extensions very rarely granted, which meant that fifty percent of the junior positions all over the world were available each year. Although some of us, like the international lawyers, focused immediately on a few positions that fit closely with their professional qualifications, most of us looked first for an exciting place and then focused secondarily on the substance of the position. We were also wisely advised by more experienced officers that the quality of a posting depended heavily on the character of the Head of Mission, who could make or break careers, so we also started to share rumours and service stories about great and terrible ambassadors. I had no interest in any position in Western Europe, having just lived there, and Eastern Europe seemed dreary and too related to east-west and defence related issues which did not interest me at the time. I really wanted to go somewhere interesting in the developing world and if possible to a good position with economic analysis and reporting responsibilities. At the top of my list I put a political-economic position in Dar-es-Salaam, Tanzania, followed by positions in Thailand and Ghana and a couple of other African and Asian places that have slipped from memory. But I was most interested in Tanzania and thought the position there really seemed perfect for me.

Early in the spring my assignment officer, Jean-Paul Hubert, asked me to come to his office, and told me that Andrew McAlister would be going to Tanzania instead of me. I was quite disappointed. Jean-Paul told me that he thought I should consider a new position that had just been added to Jakarta as a result of the annual resource allocation process. Following the federal budget and the approval by Parliament of Main Estimates (which gave External Affairs and all other departments their annual appropriations), the department would review branch requests for new positions or relocations, and a supplemental Posting List would come out. In some years this resulted in positions that officers had set their hearts on actually disappearing. The new position in Jakarta sounded very interesting, responsible for economic analysis and reporting, with a small consular component at least for the first year.

I took the Jakarta Post Report and some briefing material from Personnel home and spent a weekend trying to learn as much as I could about Indonesia and decided to try for the job. Jean-Paul Hubert had told me that the current Head of Mission, Tom Delworth, was leaving and would be replaced by a younger man on his first ambassadorial assignment, Glen Shortliffe. A key step in a posting process was always a telegram from Personnel to the Head of Mission concerned nominating the individual involved, but Delworth deflected the approvals to Shortliffe, who interviewed me in Ottawa and pronounced me acceptable. I also liked what I had seen of him in the interview, and what I had heard from colleagues about him. Young, a very hard worker, he was also a big supporter of juniors who worked with him.

The fact that I lost the competition for the Tanzanian assignment to Andrew McAlister is one of those little forks in life that have enormous consequences as the years unfold. Andrew had a great first assignment in Dar, met a young Danish aid worker called Binte who he would marry. He had a very successful Foreign Service career, his last two assignments being as Ambassador to Thailand and then, entirely in keeping with his wish to return to where he started, as Ambassador to Tanzania. I went off to Jakarta, married Liani, cemented my interest in Asia and lived the life I have lived. Liani and I stayed friends with Andrew and Binte over the years, and Cynthia stayed with them at the Ambassadorial Residence in Bangkok when she was travelling through during her university years. And just shortly before I began to write these memoirs Liani and I dined with them and we joked about what might have happened to Andrew and to me had I gone to Dar and he to Jakarta. Chance and happenstance play a huge role in determining the direction and speed of one's voyage through life, and downright good luck has certainly been a reliable fellow traveler of mine.

The release of a formal "Posting Confirmation Form", or the PCF as it was known, followed the approval of the Head of Mission and set in train the pre-posting rounds of medical exams and tropical vaccinations, meetings with relocation companies (although I was shipping only some books and records and a minimum amount of personal effects) and the division responsible for overseas accommodations where I learned which house I was being assigned in Jakarta. The Foreign Service provided furnished housing for all its overseas staff and mission management would decide which home to allocate to which incoming staff member depending on family size and seniority. Because Jakarta was a difficult city to find adequate apartments for single people, almost all the housing was sufficient for families with at least a couple of children, and when I saw pictures of my large three bedroom home I wondered what on earth I would do with all that space.

The pre-posting arrangements went by in a whirlwind, the FS1Ds went out on a series of good-bye drink-ups as each one of us left, so we all spent many mornings nursing hangovers. Some romances cemented quickly into marriages that resulted in a couple rather than a single officer being posted, while others, including mine, downshifted out of gear. The posting and disengagement process for me was quickly over as my posting was to start early in the posting season. I packed up and released my apartment, sent furniture and everything I was not taking to Jakarta off to long-term storage in External's warehouses, and sold my little Blue Fiat to my colleague Gary Soroka, who took it with him when he and his wife Joanne were posted to Washington. I then flew down to New York to spend a few days with my parents in Wilton, Connecticut before setting out on the next big chapter of my then young life.

CHAPTER 4

TO THE EXOTIC EAST

• • • • • • • • • • •

Because my position was a newly established one, and because the incoming Ambassador wanted his full team in place from the moment of his arrival, my departure for Indonesia was in early July, a little in advance of most of the rest of the "Class of '76". For most, they had to await the departure of a predecessor, sometimes needing to await in turn the end of children's school terms or other obligations, making August the standard time for transfer.

In Connecticut, my parents, and especially my father, were almost as excited as I was that my real Foreign Service career was starting off with a posting to the Far East. They had not been very enamoured of my bohemian and clearly not too serious life as a student in Paris and were pleased that I was not only embarked on a serious career, but also heading to Asia where my father's father, Gideon, had spent his entire working life. They drove me to JFK Airport from Wilton to see me off. Given that it was the rainy season in Southeast Asia, they gave me a new umbrella as a good-by present. Unfortunately, after passing through whatever counted for security in those days, I looked back through the glass barrier to see my mother waving good-bye and my father holding up the errant brolly, which I had duly forgotten.

My first stop in Asia was Tokyo. On the long descent to Narita I noted how from the air the countryside appeared very pastoral and beautiful, looking not surprisingly Japanese with endless little hills and ridges shaped like the concave roofs of traditional homes, with lots of pretty little towns in a very wet land rather lower than I had expected.

The trip was quite circuitous and I had a long layover in Tokyo. There I formed my first impressions of the interface between west and east, and noted in a letter home how all Westerners and Asians seemed to move differently in the crowded airport, with the former avoiding as much human contact as they could and looking hot and frustrated, many repeatedly going up to harried airline staff to ask questions, while the Asians travelers took the crowds all in stride, and even if clearly waiting a long time masked their impatience. I made a promise to myself that I would try to deeply understand the cultural differences, and the behavioural implications of those differences, over the next few years. Forty years later I am still trying.

My flight out of Tokyo had technical problems an hour or two after takeoff and we ended up having to route through Taipei, where my Canadian diplomatic passport kept me on board while others deplaned and engineering staff repaired the plane. After several hours we got airborne again, and I eventually arrived in Hong Kong and finally checked in at the Sheraton at about 0130 local time, some seven hours later than scheduled. I could not really sleep that first night, probably half from excitement and half from jet-lag. I got up anyway at 0700, figuring that I had to force myself onto new days and nights. After playing my flute to remind me that I was still me even if the world had changed, off I wandered to begin exploring what I then thought to be one of the most extraordinary cities imaginable, with endless waves of Chinese, Caucasians and South Asians rushing this way and that, local hawkers selling newspapers and street food and an almost overpowering array of smells. It was a very hot day, 38°C and intensely humid, for a taiphoon named Thelma was sending great wafts of heavy air over the area. I shopped for a sound system for my home in Jakarta, and for some shirts and a tropical suit, having dropped into the Canadian Commission for advice on where to find things.

In the late afternoon of my first day I was met by American friends of my parents, Howard and Ruth Heinz, who had lived there for several years managing the far eastern division of the Heinz's eponymous family food business. They were a charming couple and took me along with their college-age son Chris, visiting from America, over to the old Repulse Bay Hotel for dinner. We ate on the open porch looking out over the fishing boats and the sea with great punka fans slowly keeping the air moving above our heads. The Repulse Bay Hotel was one of the last vestiges of the old Hong Kong. It was torn down and replaced several years later, but in the 1970s there was still nothing modern in it, and even the punka fans were kept working by turbaned South Asians pulling on long ropes at the edges of the veranda. By the time we sat down for dinner I was feeling the impact of jet lag very deeply, and I remember looking down at my steak and wondering whether I could possibly eat without throwing up. Had I been able to see myself thirty-five or forty years later, I would have marveled at the ease with which I would travel back and forth across the Pacific.

The following morning I took a pre-dawn trip to Aberdeen with Chris Heinz to see the fishing boat village and the boisterous open markets, sights and sounds and smells that were all new to me then. Following that, I went to meet with the senior very stuffy British general manager of the Hong Kong and Shanghai Bank in its old office east of where the modern iconic headquarters stands. My father had decided that he would like to have two nineteenth century drawings of the Hong Kong waterfront painted by George Chinnery given to the bank in memory of his father Gideon, who had spent his working life in Asia and had served as the bank's non-executive Chairman on two brief occasions. The bank was of course thrilled to be given the drawings and added them to their Chinnery collection, which I was shown and which contained other drawings similar to those of my grandfather, as well as some fabulous little oils of everyday life in the streets of Macau, Canton and Hong Kong. Today, the decision of my father to give quite valuable drawings to a giant bank that would simply swallow them up seems a strange one, but it seemed logical at the time and was to serve me as an entry key to senior levels of the bank in the years to come, although at the time I obviously did not anticipate that.

After a fitting for my light tropical suit, whose sleeves were forever to be of a slightly different length and which would be sent on to me in Jakarta, I flew to Singapore, where our mission was a large central mission for Southeast Asia, where I received my final training and briefings from non-External Affairs program heads. These were principally immigration and the RCMP. Jakarta had no immigration program of its own and was for immigrant and student visas serviced by Singapore. In between the three or four visits a year that Singapore-based immigration officers would make to Indonesia, all immigration and short-term visitor visa work was handled by a junior political officer of the Jakarta Embassy. As the most junior officer coming in to take up a new position, all the least interesting tasks were dumped into my lap along with my main responsibility for economic analysis. The incidental immigration and visa work I was to do would rarely be interesting, the far less frequent RCMP work much more so.

I remember on my first morning in Singapore sitting in a hanging chair overlooking a tropical garden at the Goodwood Park Hotel. There was a chatter of birds which seemed to come in waves, birds with long and busy voices although I could not see them yet for there was not even the slightest light. And as I sat there, the tropical summer day emerged, from darkness to sunlight in a transition unimaginably brief for someone used to more northern spheres. I was to end up loving the quick transformation of night into day and day into night in the tropics, generally trying to start a run in the darkness and have the sun come up before its end.

Briefings complete, I was then off to Indonesia and a new adventure.

Jakarta – Settling In

Landing at the old Jakarta airport for the first time was an instant immersion into an atmosphere unlike any other. The rich sweet clove smell of the pervasive "kretek" cigarettes interlaced with that of heavy earth and rotting vegetation and sweating people, the hot and humid air seemed almost tangible, and people shouting and talking and shoving created the sense of a rich and fertile cacophony, a chaos both offensive to the senses and strangely attractive. If you were to return me from a future life a thousand years hence and drop me down for three seconds each in random airports of the 1970s world, I would know in an instant when I touched down in Jakarta.

Steve Woolcombe, the Chargé d'Affaires ad interim and my immediate supervisor as Political Counselor kindly met me at the airport and brought me directly to the Embassy, then located at Budi Kemuliaan a hundred or so meters off Merdeka Square which fronts the Presidential Palace and the tall monument to the independence movement (sometimes rudely referred to as Sukarno's last erection). Canada had been using the Embassy's central building, the chancery, since 1948, and it was in my view everything a tropical embassy should be. A colonial Dutch building with very high ceilings, it was all on one floor with smaller buildings out back used by embassy drivers and maintenance staff. It was white stone but well weathered with climbing mold at the ground level on the outer walls. Inside, the offices were all quite large, with tall French windows looking out onto small gardens of palms and other tropical plants with huge fronds or wide leaves. I was immediately struck with the earthy fecundity of the place, and was to later learn that when I planted a small mango sapling in my garden I could expect to harvest mangos within a year.

The chancery at Budi Kemuliaan was unfortunately on its last legs. The Indonesian government wanted all the diplomatic missions to be further away from Merdeka Square, and wanted to rehabilitate our building for some unit of the Ministry of National Defence. And it certainly needed rehabilitation. A few days after my arrival, Jakarta had a day of torrential rains and almost instantly we had an embassy flood. Built directly on the clay ground that underpinned the whole city, the chancery had no basement or anywhere for the water to go when the roads filled, so the water simply came in under the doors and through the floor and all of a sudden we had either inches or feet of water to deal with. The chancery was also not the most secure building. Going there with a colleague late one night to pick up some work, we realized that neither of us had remembered to bring our keys. The local night watchman, who himself had no authority to enter the mission unless accompanied by a Canadian, told us not to worry, climbed up on the roof, removed a panel next to a skylight in a reception room, dropped down inside and then opened up the embassy for us from the inside. In fact, by the time I arrived in Jakarta, it had been long decided to move from our lovely old if somewhat dilapidated building to a modern office tower, Wisma Metropolitan, in the southern business district of the city.

After touring me around the Embassy to meet colleagues and staff and see my office, Steve took me to the Hotel Indonesia on Jalan Thamrin where I was to spend a few days before moving into my own house. He then brought me to his club for a swim and a drink and then to his home for supper with him and his wife, Anne. She was German and some years older than Steve, who was probably less than forty at the time, and was a constant complainer, and spent the entire meal comparing Jakarta to Paris from whence they had been cross-posted at the beginning of the year. Poor Steve having to put up with that, I thought, and I escaped to the hotel as soon as I could. Steve was a smart fellow, and will feature further in the story of my time in Indonesia, but was never confident enough to be given much higher levels of responsibility. (I think he reached Director level in the department, but never Director General. Years later when I was an Assistant Deputy Minister, he came to my office looking for an assignment somewhere in the Asian orbit, and I had to gently suggest that perhaps he should seek a teaching job instead. But that is another story . . .)

Staying at Hotel Indonesia and being downtown for a few days was a good way to begin. I found the sound of the city almost solid, touchable. Car horns of every pitch, grinding gears, old diesel engines with their straining tired efforts at picking up speed to piggy-back the buses ahead and grab waiting passengers, jackhammers, the clicking cartwheels of square little wheelbarrow stores being pushed or pulled, the cries of peddlers hawking every imaginable merchandise, an occasional cry rising above the cacophony. Yet I immediately fell in love with it, for the sound was right for the place. Everywhere there were vast numbers of people. Some were jumping in and out of Bajajs, the tiny three-wheeled Jakarta taxis either powered by pedals or motored by a belching two-stroke engine, driven by drivers outside and behind the cabins in which the passengers sat. There were people hanging on the outside of buses and sitting on the top of overloaded trucks, children playing pick-up soccer on the sidewalks or flying kites, lots of chatter and laughter. Poor young women with children strapped to their bosoms or their backs, pleading for money, street urchins offering shoe shines, legless beggars with their hands out for alms.

The setting for the all the noise and the masses of people was the physical city of Jakarta, a strange amalgam of the low and stately colonial, modern hotels and office buildings some twenty or thirty stories high, and key squares and rotaries graced with dramatic monuments in the exaggerated socialist realist style to heroic freedom fighters or model peasants or workers. All about youth and strength and vision, and legacies of the then not too distant time of Sukarno and his Soviet friends. Outside the Hotel Indonesia there was one such statue a hundred feet high of a young couple and their child called "Ibu, Bapak, Anak, Keluarga Indonesia" (Mother, Father, Child, Indonesian Family) with the young man looking like a weight-lifter on steroids and the young mother like a busty Russian call-girl with Asian eyes.

Off the central arteries in the older part of the city, I found green streets graced with towering flame trees and flowering bushes and mangoes, with stately high-ceilinged homes of the colonial era, now belonging to the wealthy generals, the Chinese and local businessmen, and diplomats. Other streets, making up the bulk of the city by far, were unpaved, unplanned and narrow, with red-tiled houses and commercial establishments of all sizes and shapes massed hodge-podge into neighbourhoods which seem like rural towns uprooted and dropped between the thoroughfares of modern times.

I started work in earnest the following week, and by the time the new Ambassador and his family (two boys, aged ten and twelve) arrived on the Thursday I had been in country a week and felt almost like an old hand. The evening of his arrival, Ambassador Glenn Shortliffe invite the officers who had met him and his family back to the residence for an informal get together. The Official Residence was a lovely old colonial home in Menteng, with high ceilings and large French doors that opened onto a patio and a large and handsome back lawn. When someone mentioned to the Ambassador that there had once been a swimming pool in the residence garden, but a former Head of Mission had decided to fill it in to increase the size of the lawn, Shortliffe joked that he would order us all back with picks and shovels to unearth it.

Ambassador's Gopher

With Glenn Shortliffe's arrival, I realized that my working life would largely orbit around his. I had been interviewed by him in Ottawa prior to having the posting confirmed, and it was clear that among my responsibilities would be to serve as what we called the Ambassador's "gopher", effectively a cross between his executive assistant, the embassy's protocol officer and the ambassador's hit-man. Whenever he left the city to visit the provinces or went to high level meetings, I would accompany him. I served as the secretary to the CPM, the Committee on Post Management, which was terrific for learning about how an embassy really worked and also for knowing what was going on right across the mission at any given time. I was to learn that the position also gave me the power of access control and led section heads to try to use me to obtain ambassadorial agreement to whatever they were pushing or promoting, without having to use up their own credit directly with Shortliffe.

One of the first events that I attended that came with the gopher role was Shortliffe's presentation of credentials about two weeks after his arrival. At 0830 on the appointed day a small fleet of limousines from the Presidential

Palace arrived at the Official Residence, along with 24 ferocious looking soldiers on motorcycles. After a five-minute discussion with the President's Aide-de-Camp and the Indonesian Chief of Protocol, we got in the cars and roared off to the Palace. Just before nine in the morning was about the busiest time on Jakarta roads, so it was quite a thrill to charge along the busy boulevards down a cleared lane where the motorcycles had carved a swath, with pushed aside but fascinated motorists watching the show. We drew up in front of the palace where a guard of honour was waiting. I thought the palace magnificent, with splendid porches and reception rooms, wide-open spaces and columned entrances designed to impress in a style that combined both Indonesian and European motifs. After being greeted by the Secretary to the President, Shortliffe formally inspected the Guard of Honour and the Canadian national anthem was played, a little ponderously. I had reviewed a version the day before and, finding it dreadfully slow, encouraged the band to play a little faster, which they did and got almost all the notes correct. Then we went inside the Palace and upstairs to a special reception room where President Soeharto and his foreign Minister, Adam Malik, and lots of other highly paid help stood awaiting us. The Ambassador handed over his letters, made a short speech to which the President replied. Each of us were individually introduced to the President and to the accompanying Ministers and then out came the "Bren", a local sparkling drink, presumably non-alcoholic, made from the roots of some Balinese vegetable. After a ten-minute informal chat between the Ambassador and the President, the national anthems were replayed and out we were turfed to head back to the Residence for real champagne. It was all rather grand for a young officer and a great way to start a posting, and I was to recall this ceremony much later in life when presenting my own credentials far to the north.

The following weeks and months were a period of finding a new rhythm, moving into my own house, trying to balance my reporting responsibilities with those of ambassadorial gopher and getting around to meet colleagues in other embassies and friends outside the diplomatic service. My letters home from the time tell of an almost endless series of dinners, formal and informal, with interesting and boring counterparts and food exotic, generally hot and sometimes toxic! But I was settling in.

Sailing and the Second Evangeline

Almost immediately after arriving in Jakarta I hunted down the tiny foreign community that sailed out of Tanjung Priok, a filthy industrial harbour north of the city. Within a week or two I had found an oil company representative from New York who raced every Sunday in a mixed group of 25-40 foot boats, mostly owned by Australians and Americans. I went out racing a couple of times, became a little frustrated with the limited experience and seamanship of the skippers, although one had a charming wife who prepared the greatest lunches, so I gravitated more to that boat than others. I decided to see if I could find my own boat.

Among the other young officers of the mission was the junior-most trade commissioner who had arrived about six months before me. From the Eastern townships in Quebec, Pierre Pichette was athletic and game for almost any adventure, and I talked him into buying a sailboat together. I had hunted for one at the docks and in the creeks up near the port and found a very old open gaff-rigged sloop, built many decades earlier to an eighty-year old "Nord Neerdlinger" design. It was a great heavy nineteen-foot boat, seven feet broad in the beam, rather similar to the old New England catboats with a long boom and big gaff, and a very small jib. It had an outboard motor that could be hung over the stern, and no cabin or shade protection at all. Pierre came with me to see it and we bought it on the spot. We renamed it *Evangeline* which has been the name of all the boats I have ever owned (only three) and we began using our free time to meander up through the islands north of Jakarta, generally leaving in the early morning and coming back at dusk, bringing friends and lunch and lots of Bintang beer along for the day. We would head out to the closest little island called Pulau Adam or further to the many islands of Kepulauan Seribu (the "Thousand Islands") where we would anchor and snorkle to see the coral and the tropical fish, and there would be local fishermen in their little sailing boats and dugout canoes and mangroves and great palms along the shores.

I wrote then that I wanted to have a painting made of us in Evangeline done in the style of Winslow Homer's "Breezing Up", for the style of the boat was quite similar and the afternoon winds generally very strong. The only change from "Breezing Up" would be that the crew of nineteenth century New England boys would be replaced by two curley-headed bearded youths and two pretty local girls in batik skirts. Unfortunately I never did get a painting made, and the only pictures that remain of that Evangeline are a photograph in my father's family album from a visit in 1979, and a picture of me as a sunburned skipper that Liani keeps somewhere. In fact, while sometimes we did invite pretty girls along, most of the time we had a gaggle of friends, sometimes families from the Embassy, sometimes couples from the expatriate community. For much of the year, the early evening in Jakarta would bring a thunder storm or two, and many was the day when we fought our way back to harbour in torrential rain and heavy winds. But even then I recognized that it was the stuff of dreams. And it certainly put an end to my racing with other expatriates.

Evangeline and the handful of modern sailboats owned by expatriates were by no means the only sailing boats to be found in the waters north of Jakarta. In fact, the area was teeming with "Bugis Schooners" as they were called in English, although half most of them were single-masted sloops rather than true schooners. In Indonesian, they were called "Perahu Bugis", which literally meant "Buginese boat", the Buginese people being from the coast of southwest Sulawesi. The boats were generally between 70 and 120 feet in length, with deeply bowed decks and huge bowsprits made like tripods, great brown sails and masts and gaffs that were imperfectly straight as they were made directly from the trunks of trees and trimmed logs. They would rarely have motors, and after dropping their sails would pole their way to the wharves and dock bow-to. Arriving in Jakarta they would be heavily laden with exotic hardwood from Kalimantan and Sulawesi, or with copra or tea or spices from the Moluccas and Nusa Tengara, the eastern islands of Lombok, Sumba, Sumbawa and Flores. Leaving Tanjung Priok on their return voyages, they would carry manufactured goods and general cargo as supply for the outer islands. These great workhorses of the islands, or sailing vessels just like them, had been plying the trade routes of the East Indies for hundreds of years. Generally their sails were made from canvas or heavy cotton, some beige and some dark brown from being tarred for durability, like the sailors who sailed them, who were deeply weathered and darkened by the tropical sun. While the sailors often looked as fierce as pirates, whenever we passed by them at sea they would hail us in a friendly way, and we would try to get close enough to ask them where they were coming from and how long they had taken to reach Jakarta. Some worked long routes from the east and took up to two months for a round trip, and they would tie up in the harbour at Tanjung Priok especially reserved for them. When friends or family from outside Indonesia came to visit, the Bugis Schooners at the sailing port were a mandatory visit, and it was always fun to watch these great beasts of the sea as they unloaded their teak or other cargo, and to see the sailors stitch new sails on the wharf. The whole scene was a bustling, dynamic scene that could have been set at any time within the previous thousand years of active inter-island trade.

Settling into my own house was easy. It was a comfortable three-bedroom bungalow much too large for a bachelor, fully furnished by the Embassy and taken care of by a wonderful houseboy and cook, Rachmat. It had an air conditioning unit for each area of the house, but the machines were terribly noisy and very hard to regulate. Once I became acclimated to the tropical temperatures I ended up turning off all the air conditioners except the one in my study, where I kept my books and records and stereo set. Over time I found that I caught fewer colds than colleagues who lived in fully air conditioned surroundings, and I rarely felt more than modestly uncomfortable in the tropical heat. Rachmat was a charming young man, probably around 20 years old when I arrived (he claimed not to know how old he was), and he stayed with me and my successors in the house for at least a couple of decades after I left. We last met him in the 1990s, then with a lovely young wife and two beautiful children. Also resident in the house were lots of cicaks (pronounced "cheechaks"), cute little lizards that could be anywhere from one to 15 centimeters in length, and they would keep the house free of insects and were considered very much welcome. There were larger lizards too, "tokays", who lived outside or under the floors and could be heard at night calling "tOkéé . . . tOkéé". They were considered very good luck to have under a home, and they would never be hunted or harmed.

Among the personal challenges to getting set up was the process of clearing my goods through customs. As a means of eliminating illegal payments and avoiding any chance of corruption, the Embassy had determined that all Canadian staff would have to personally clear their own goods, as local staff would not be able to do so without the payment of bribes to local port and customs officials. Luckily local staff helped fill out the eight copies of each of the six or seven required forms, and drove us around to all the departments and agencies that had to stamp them. The process of clearing my car, ordered from Japan, took two full days of my time, fifteen hours in total, bowing obsequiously to 53 separate bureaucrats from whom I needed separate signatures. Along the way I spent many hours sitting in one anteroom or another waiting for some petty official to demonstrate his importance while he "finished something off" for an extra ten minutes. I was ready to either kill someone, or toss our anti-corruption policies in the wastebasket by the time I finished! Apparently the Australians also had similarly frustrating "do-it-yourself" guidelines, while all the European diplomats, from both east and west, paid the roughly $1000 in bribes required and got their cars in a half a day.

A New Chancery

The move to a new chancery took place a few months after my arrival and created all sorts of challenges and problems for which we were not prepared, and for whatever reason some fell on me to solve. In an embassy building it is normal for the registry and communications centres to be housed in very secure facilities, effectively vaults. The new vault doors had been brought in from Canada and installed on the fifth floor of this modern office building. Just as the construction of the concrete walls surrounding the doors was to begin by a construction team over a long weekend, we discovered that the doors were locked and nobody seemed to have the combinations. Telegrams were sent off to Ottawa and in due course we received an answer with the manufacturer's initial combinations which were meant to be changed once we were actually using the vaults. As no one else was around, I called the contractor and met him and his team of workers at the building. Wrong combinations! And there went not only a long weekend of work but the scheduled moving date. We eventually moved in October rather than in August as planned, and I was to learn the Indonesian expression of "jam karet" or "rubber time".

When we finally got to the actual move of the chancery, we were already in Ramadan, the Muslim fasting month, when workers were not allowed to eat or drink between sunrise and sunset. This generally led to either shorter working days, workers with limited energy or both. Junior officers joined our Canadian administrative staff in supervising the move in three-man shifts, with one staff member at each site at all times and another in any vehicle moving between the two, since there could never be confidential material or secure equipment left without Canadian oversight. I was in charge of one shift at the new embassy building when we moved the two large internal safes for the registry and communications centres, where the most secure material and communications were kept. These safes were really old, dating almost certainly from the interwar years, and were basically six-foot tall blocks of virtually solid steel, weighing almost a ton each. They looked like the safes one sees in bank-robbing scenes in movies set in the late 1800s. The first safe was brought over to Wisma Metropolitan and put in the service elevators, which promptly went down to the basement rather than up since the weight surpassed the elevator's design capacity. I realized that the only way we were going to get the safe up the now six floors, was to carry it by hand. The local workers started to manhandle the safe up the stairs, but only got up about a floor and a half before giving up, claiming that the safe was too heavy given that the day was a day of fasting and they did not have the energy to carry on. The local foreman told me we would have to leave one safe in the stairwell and one in the delivery truck until after Ramadan ended the following week. This was a non-starter so I called Ron Ellis, our burly property clerk, and my friends Pierre Pichette and Harold McNairney from the trade section. Together we muscled the safes all the way to the fifth floor and their new homes, while the local foreman and his team of workers watched in total amazement. There are some things you do for your country that are neither recognized nor rewarded!

Strains of Islam

Living in a Muslim country was obviously a new experience for me. It did not take long to get used to the fact that the Muslim day was all around us, and I grew to love the sound of the pre-dawn call for prayers, often happening as I would be getting back to my home from a morning run begun in the pitch black night. My early morning runs were wonderful as I ran almost every morning along only a couple of different routes. I would run past shopkeepers and food sellers getting set for the day, some with little children who recognized me and would run alongside me for a few meters, calling me "Boulet" or "Blonde person" and chatting away as if I was a long-lost friend. The tukangs (a word which is derived from the Chinese words for "push" and "box") would be pushing their carts or carrying their goods suspended from evenly balanced shoulder rods. There were food stalls with open woks already frying wonderfully smelling food, and so the whole experience was very rich – and I would try to time my runs so I would be just arriving back at home as the sun rose. It was a wonderful way to start the day.

In Indonesia, as elsewhere, Ramadan is brought to a close 29 or 30 days after it begins (depending on the sighting of the crescent moon), and the final prayers and fasting are followed by great celebration, fireworks and feasting. In Arabic this is Eid Ul-Fitri, but in Indonesia it is called Lebaran. Watching the beginning of Lebaran near the national mosque on the night of September 14th, 1977, I wrote a free-form poem, and I reprint it here:

Lebaran in Jakarta

Wailing pierces almost to the marrow,
And in the milling mob which crowds the portals of the mosque
You sense a change, a shifting of the ether.
Bowed and covered heads remain unmoving,
And yet the noisy silence warns
Of that which is to come as year gives way to year.

Gone tonight (this single night alone)
The bobbing rhythmic movement of the tukangs,
Half trotting with their casks of oil or stacks of meagre ware
Balanced on rods across their stooping shoulders;
Even their hopeful cries and special drums are silenced,
Their splayed and broken feet cruel witness to their lives.

Old and wrinkled covered heads turn westward
Bowed low beneath unseeing eyes they cower,
Bodies crouched on knees as curved and trembling backs repent
And gathered hands and mumbling chines atone the selves inside,
Towards a Mecca which has drawn its power from the season,
As if it were an autumn moon, those heads a darkened formless tide.

Children's faces burn with failing patience –
Anticipation stored too long begins to overcome
The fragile firmament which has been their control;
Belief derived from order not conviction,
Prescribed by meaning which they cannot share
Except by innocence transformed in rite-inspired hope.

Along a ways we walk beside a stream,
Whose walls of darkened red and ruddy clay reach out
Through giant reeds and trees which cast their eerie shadows.
And from the stream we hear the pulsing cries of crickets and of
landtoads,
Whose voices seem an odd and irreflective counter
To the eighty million faithful cowed in fervent prayer.

A moment then of quiet and entrancing tension,
The wailing slows and echoes die as for a second time is frozen.
The night absorbs all light, all sound, impenetrably rich.
And then as if it were the movement of another world
A tempo starts to build, at first confused, disordered,
And then begins to find its human warmth and cadence.

The children are the first to bridle and break forth,
Their solemn world transformed from subdued eyes and humbling
rules.
Their feet cannot resist the growing essence of new night
Which carries chanting dancing groups of youthful effervescence
With heads tossed back and laughter leaping from the very soul
Until the moment, repressed, held back, and now released alive.

The heavens are alight and filled with colourful designs
Of fireworks, whose deafening pulses from all sides offend.
The night bursts forth and voices grow alive rearmed with spirit,
Charged with all the triumph of Lebaran –
End of Ramadan, the fasting and the prayer
The year begins anew; the past forgotten, forgiven and reborn.

Provincial Visits

Ambassador Shortliffe was soon to begin his required visits to major provincial capitals, and of course I always accompanied him. One of the first such visits was to Bandung, capital of West Java and a beautiful city set in the cooler hills high above the Javanese lowlands. Glenn's wife, Sylvia, joined us for the drive up through Bogor, through the Puncak Pass and across the West Java plains. There were no big freeways at this time and the drive took almost five hours, but it was very beautiful and a far better way to see the country than by super-highway. We passed through freshly planted rice padis with their seedlings an iridescent shade of green unimaginable in temperate climates. The padis carpeted the lowland plains, and were terraced into the hillsides like intricate pieces of lace. Above them on the steeper hills that bordered the plain were deep green tapestries of tea plantations, with the bushes standing in oblique symmetrical patterns. Images flashed by and repeated themselves: water buffalo plodding through flooded fields, driven by headless farmers hidden beneath huge straw sun-hats shaped like inverted saucers; streams running down half hidden gorges, crisscrossed with bamboo and wicker bridges, beneath which laughing children played and saronged women washed their family's clothes; bananas of all kinds (Liani and I were later to count 27 different varieties), papaya and jackfruit trees, yellow-green pomelos hanging from citrus trees like huge limes for giants, the lush crowns of the hairy rambutan and an endless variety of other vegetation in one of the most fertile places on earth. And people everywhere. This was Java, the most crowded island in the world with a population density you could see and sense everywhere.

As we approached the city of Bandung and the road became more crowded, we were met at the city's formal boundary by a police escort. With a police car and motorcycle outriders, we roared into town and traffic parted like the Red Sea at the hand of Moses. Bandung was, and still is, a very beautiful and semi-colonial city, with a population of only about 1.5 million then, the centre of Indonesian intellectualism and the highest concentration of universities and institutes of higher learning, and a city with a very interesting history. It was the final redoubt in the resistance to the Japanese in 1941, and it was the final redoubt again for the Dutch in the Indonesian war of independence after World War II. It was also the site of the seminal 1955 Bandung Conference, where Julius Nyrere of Tanzania, Kwame Nkrumah of Ghana, Zhou Enlai of China and Indonesia's Sukarno were the stars, creating the concept of the "Third World" and beginning a movement that later (in Belgrade in 1961) adopted the formal title of the Non-Aligned Movement, opposing the hegemonic aspirations of both America and Russia. An interesting footnote to that meeting, which was to have relevance for my own dealings with the Chinese over the decades to follow, was the formal recognition by Zhou Enlai at the Conference that the first allegiance of all overseas Chinese should be their adopted countries, not China, a statement which allowed China to be a welcomed part of the movement. Bandung had by the 1970s also become the centre of Indonesian engineering and the site of Indonesia's fledgling aerospace industry.

We had a series of required meetings in Bandung, some pro forma for a foreign ambassador and some actually interesting. The mayor was local and deeply proud of his city's history and noted to the Ambassador during our meeting that, "I am not interested in producing industrial goods for Indonesia; my job is to produce tomorrow's leaders." And indeed at the time the Bandung Institute of Technology was probably the leading engineering and technological university anywhere in the Third World. Our meeting with the local Governor was formalistic but our meeting with the Security Chief of the province was particularly memorable. He believed that he could speak English and refused the use of an interpreter. Almost nothing of what he said, however, was understandable. Shortliffe and I just nodded sagely whenever he came to a stop that implied he had finished making a point. At one stage he seemed to describe some dimension of activity in which West Java was unsurpassed, and Shortliffe made the seemingly safe comment of "Congratulations". I realized and whispered to Shortliffe that the Security Chief had just said that West

Java had the highest consumption of illicit drugs in the country, with most brought in from Aceh and Thailand. At the end of our meeting, our host stood up, looked Shortliffe deeply in the eyes and said in English; "Sweet Memories", at which Sylvia Shortliffe dissolved into a coughing fit and I rushed everyone into the limousine where we could give freedom to our laughter. This was the first of many provincial visits. We travelled back to Jakarta by train, and if there is any single result of the trip that seems important it is that it was during this trip that my personal relationship with Shortliffe really began.

As the junior member of the political-economic team at the mission, my day-to-day boss was Steve Woolcombe, who began to resent my close relationship with the Ambassador. He would send back drafts of my economic analyses to me with caustic comments and requests for revisions, and I would toil late into the nights trying to improve them. In the 1970s this was real work, since we did not have PCs or even word processors yet, so any report that had to be revised had to be rewritten and retyped from the beginning. And the worst part was that I really did think my reports were well done, with (like Mozart in the movie *Amadeus*) neither too many nor too few notes. I was also circulating drafts to the section heads of the aid and trade divisions, since they had their own perspectives on local economic developments and trends, and their comments were always more positive than Woolcombe's. At a certain stage, I realized that his criticism had little to do with the real substance of my reports and more to prove a point about who was whose boss. I modified my strategy and started to include the Ambassador in the circulation of my draft reports, telling Woolcombe that the Ambassador had asked me to do so. When Shortliffe commented that he thought a report was fine, Steve no longer had any choice except to dial back on his efforts to hold me down.

Ambassador Shortliffe was, however, not an easy Head of Mission. He turned 40 only in the November following his arrival, and was at the time the youngest Canadian Ambassador anywhere. As many Heads of Mission do, he caught the "ambassadoritis" virus, and saw himself as more important and more beyond criticism than he merited. Among his heads of section, only Head of Aid Lorne Heuckroth had the fortitude and intellectual strength to stand up to him, with both Steve Woolcombe and Head of Trade, David Armour, completely cowed. The result was that there was really no one who was willing to prevent him from intemperate behaviour, which sometimes was just putting his own reputation in danger but sometimes threatening the credibility of the whole mission. He got into a particularly useless battle with the then Director General responsible for Southeast Asia in External Affairs, who was his ambassadorial predecessor in Indonesia, Tom Delworth. Delworth was senior to Shortliffe in the system and an older-style Ambassador, a prickler for correctness and detail, and he would sometimes send back to Jakarta by diplomatic bag copies of Shortliffe's reports with the grammar or facts corrected in red pen. This would drive Shortliffe around the bend, and after reading one such report, he went back to the Residence in a foul temper for what turned out to be clearly liquid lunch. He returned to the office afterwards and dictated a most intemperate response to Delworth, and told his secretary, Mickey Jeffrey, to type it up in final and take it to the communications centre for encryption and dispatch. Mickey, a delightful lady in her mid-50s and the epitome of a special breed of Head of Mission Secretaries (who always knew What Needed to Be Done), came to see me and showed me the proposed missive. She was completely right in seeing it as a potential detonator for a nuclear war between the mission and Ottawa. I figured that life was long and I had nothing to lose. So I went to see Shortliffe to advise him against sending Delworth the message. We had an unholy row, with him turning bright red and asking me "who the fuck" did I think I was telling him what to do, and me responding that I was completely aware that I was beneath the lowest of all animal matter but I still thought his message provocative, unnecessary and dangerous for his and the mission's credibility. It was fifteen minutes of vituperative exchange, the tone and volume if not all the substance of which were audible in the anti-room to the Head of Mission's office where Woolcombe, Heuckroth and Armour were waiting for the start of a management meeting. Eventually, Shortliffe calmed down, asked me to redraft the message in gentler tones and called for the heads of section to be brought in to start the planned meeting. I remember clearly the glances I received from Woolcombe and the other heads of division, each pitying me and wondering whether I would be on a flight back to Canada the next morning, or simply thrown into a Jakarta canal. In fact, it was the beginning of a long and deep and mutually respectful relationship I was to have with Glenn Shortliffe that ended only with his departure as Clerk of the Privy Council in the early months of the Chrétien government many, many, years later.

Although Ambassador Shortliffe generated a lot of heat in the embassy with his driving personality, high expectations and frequent outbursts, a real feeling of common purpose and camaraderie developed. As we approached the November weekend when our young Ambassador was to celebrate his fortieth birthday, nobody mentioned anything about it or wished him well. Then on the Saturday night the entire Canadian staff of the embassy gathered outside the Residence. Bob Cullen, our communicator knocked on the Residence door while the rest of us hid out of site behind trees and bushes. When Shortliffe came to the door, Bob excused himself for intruding but said that he had just received a "Flash" telegram for the Ambassador's eyes only and handed over a sealed "Crypto-Custodian" envelope, from which one could only infer something terribly serious. Bob was deadpan, and Shortliffe opened the envelope to find a birthday card, at which point we all emerged from hiding, armed with a case of champagne. It had of course all been arranged with the connivance of Sylvia Shortliffe (there are limits to "surprises"), who had even brought their sons Newton and Scott into the plot; Glenn later admitted to me that he had been feeling rather down that no one had remembered his birthday.

From early in the 1950s, the Embassy had maintained a small hill station in the hills just west of Puncak Pass, just beyond Bogor. Popular in the Dutch era and among the military and other elite in the post-independence period, the "Puncak" was a cool and bucolic farming region dotted with cottages and pools. The Embassy's two bungalows stood side by side on the side of a south-facing valley, and were staffed by a family that would provide cooking and cleaning. Access to the cottages, one slightly larger than the other, was by rotation and ignored rank or status among Canada-based staff such that a secretary would have as regular access as a Counselor. Of course, the professional obligations of diplomatic staff frequently meant that allocated weekends would prove inconvenient, and there was an active cashless exchange market for Puncak time. As soon as Ambassador Shortliffe arrived he realised that his participation in the rotational pool could only cause resentment, and so he consequently rented on his personal account a separate bungalow for his family a few kilometers distant.

Given that there were roughly twenty-five Canada-based staff at the mission, and the fact that there were two bungalows at our Puncak station, we would each get weekend access to a cottage about once every three months. Part of the trading was aimed at being there when friends would have the second cottage, since a weekend could turn painful if one cottage was used by a young family seeking peace and quiet and the other by a rowdy group of singles looking for dancing and a good time. It generally worked out fairly well, and although personally I enjoyed it immensely when I used it, the existence of *Evangeline* and my frequent travels out of Jakarta made it less important to me than others. But it was still fun to be there, and at the end of my posting was one of the places Liani was to visit with me as we were falling in love.

Relatively early in the posting I began to get to know other Canadians in Indonesia working for Canadian companies. Among these was the representative of the Bank of Montreal, Toby Price. Toby, who was maybe eight or ten years my elder, came from one of the principal families of the very old and rather small Quebec City anglophone community, and had started his professional life with brief stints in the Navy and then in the Foreign Service before escaping to banking. Toby and his Dutch wife Eliane were lovely people and became very close friends of mine, and later of Liani's as well. Toby was a great art collector and he and Eliane had both a cute little villa at the edge of Menteng in Jakarta and their own rented bungalow in the Puncak. Many was the evening I spent at Toby and Eliane's home, usually drinking too much cognac late in the night, and I invited them a couple of times to come with their little girl and boy out in Evangeline with me. It was Toby who was to get me interested in Indonesian Art and it was he who introduced me to Alex Papadimitriou.

Alex Papadimitrou was born late in the 1920s of a wealthy Greek father and a Dutch-Indonesian mother. Educated in Europe and one of the few discerning art collectors in Indonesia in the 1950s and 1960s (President Sukarno was another), Alex was not only an extraordinary expert on Indonesian art but an erudite and delightful companion whenever we were together. He and his gorgeous wife Caecilia (of Chinese-Indonesian descent) had a bevy of children, at least four or five, and their estate south of Jakarta was always full of people and laughter. When I was first introduced to Alex, he most patiently described for me the main threads of modern Indonesian art, and it was he who recommended that I buy both the fabulous painting of Roedyat entitled "Kampung" and the works of Rudipradjaya, and sold to Toby Price a gorgeous painting by Afandi of a hill cottage that Toby and Eliane gave Liani and me for a wedding present. We still have all of those paintings today. But Alex and Caecelia were more than art dealers or advisors, they provided a welcoming place where I could drop by and chat, stay over for dinner without any warning, play a game of chess, and generally feel at home. I stayed in contact with them over the years, and Liani and I brought our four children out to their estate in 1993 during a visit to Indonesia. Alex was aging then and would die a few years later, but he lives on in the annals of Indonesian art and in our hearts.

The Mystical Island of Bali

Somehow we were always finding good reasons to go to the magical island of Bali, a tourist destination even then but not nearly as over-run as it was to later become. There were a few hotels at Sanur, and lots of little inns at Kuta, but Nusa Dua did not yet exist and the island seemed able to absorb the tourists without changing its essence. I am sure I was there at least once a quarter. On one visit, David Armour and his young and second wife Ruth and I decided to drive to Singaraja from Denpasar by crossing over the mountains of the interior of the island where tourists were not encouraged to go, rather than via the eastern coastal road and around the top of the island. We hired a little "jeep", which in spite of its squared shape and non-optional open cabin (its removable top had long since disappeared), it was simply a Volkswagen Beetle with a jeep-like body, but still with an air-cooled engine and minimal power.

Bali is a volcanic island, and there is in the North still an active volcano, Mount Batur, which steams and bubbles constantly, and occasionally disgorges a stream of lava. The soil of Bali is therefore very rich, but it is also very fine and dusty. As the three of us worked our way north from Denpasar along the forest roads, the little VW engine became less and less happy, as the dusty soil started to clog its cooling system and its carburetor. The little villages we passed through were just collection of huts clustered together in the Balinese forest, and they were also not very friendly looking, and people stopped and stared at us as we went by. All the men carried big curved knives, which started to look quite menacing. At one point a young man tried to jump into the back of the jeep, but failed when I floored the accelerator and pulled away too quickly for him. We were forced to stop in the middle of the next little village because there was a tree down across the road. The men chopping it looked up and glared at us as if we were an apparition, then went back to their work slowly and methodically and made no haste to clear a space for us to pass through. A group of boys approached us and watched us silently, their long curved knives held loosely at their sides. My attempt to communicate in Indonesian produced no reaction in blank faces; it was clear that the national language was as foreign to them as English would have been. Finally the road was clear enough and we passed through, and climbed higher and higher on the two-track road. An effort to ask directions from a wizened old lady produced a beetle-nut spit and a blank stare. Up and up and up and the ashdust just got deeper. I drove as fast as possible just to keep going. Up to the axles, and skidding and sliding perilously close to where the track wasn't, but I knew I could not stop on the rise. And then we went over a crest and steeply down into a little valley, forcing me to downshift quickly into first gear which pulled a great gulp of dust into the engine which instantly stalled. We got it going again, progressed another few hundred yards and then the little car died forever. So we set out on foot, with no idea how far we still had to go before we hit the northern road. Ruth was almost rigid with fear, and the long-curved knives had really spooked both her and David. It started to rain, but it turned out only to be about forty-five more minutes of walking before we saw a town in front of us, which turned out to be Kintamani, on the east-west road south of Lake Batur. We must have been a very strange site, covered in mud from the rain and the dust, and the locals looked at us as though we were from another planet. We took a "bimo", which was a tiny unstable minibus, back to Denpasar, and gave the keys to an unhappy car rental agent with a vague description of where his jeep had broken down. I suspect he never found it.

Christmas in the Tropics

The final months of 1977 rushed by with provincial visits, general embassy work, sailing on the weekends and gradually building a life outside the mission. There was a weekend in November when several of us headed west to the Sunda Straits and spent an overnight at a very simple resort at Cerita beach in Anyer, facing Anak Karakatoa (literally the "child of Krakatoa"), the 300 meter high volcanic accretion still growing from the water-level stub of the great August 1883 eruption of Krakatoa, the largest and most destructive volcanic explosion in recorded history. I had a particular interest in Anak Krakatoa, for my grandfather Gideon Balloch, en route to China from England, had written of the inexplicable extended darkened skies and the apparent end of daylight while at anchor in the Bay of Bengal. Gideon's ship was delayed a week before it could weigh anchor, and it was literally decades before the world was to piece together how serious the eruption of Krakatoa had actually been. But by the 1970s the coast of Java on the Sunda Strait was very beautiful, with lovely western sunsets and calm waters, and I decided to organize Christmas there for myself and friends stranded far from families.

But before Christmas there was still work to do in Jakarta, and a year-end cycle to go through on the diplomatic circuit. Thursday the 22nd of December was the Ambassador's Christmas party for the embassy staff and for all the Canadians in country who could make it to Jakarta for the event. As guests entered the official residence they were greeted by Christmas music played by me on flute and Janice Sutton on piano. Janice was a political officer married to our head of administration. We had practiced a bit in advance, but it did not really matter because the music was pretty hard to mess up and people were not paying enough attention to notice when we did. The residence was nicely decorated and the atmosphere was very Christmassy, even though many guests were arriving in a pool of sweat after a hot and sultry Jakarta day. Ninety-five percent of the guests were non-embassy types and many had not yet met Ambassador Shortliffe and his wife, so most of the introductions were done at the door. That was fine, almost. After a little while it was clear that something was wrong. First, there seemed to be too many people whom no one from the mission knew and second there were some very un-Canadian accents. After a few years in Canada even the strongest Scots brogue or Texan drawl is tempered somewhat. Nobody, however, seemed particularly perturbed - it was a fine and friendly bunch – until Sylvia Shortliffe was called to the telephone. Sweet and vacuous Lady Ford, wife of the British Ambassador, was on the phone with a story that two Canadians were on the way over having arrived first at the wrong party. A few minutes later someone with a strong southern US accent asked David Armour if he could point out the head of the embassy's Oil and Gas Division, which did not exist, and we all began to realize what had happened. Imam Bonjol was Residence Row, with the Canadian Residence separated from the British only by the Saudi Residence, and the American Residence across the street only fifty meters further along. Numbers for houses in Menteng were not well displayed, and the whole street was ill-lit, and as hundreds of Canadians, Americans and Britons arrived in the same area and saw people who looked more or less like them exiting their vehicles and going into well-lit Residences, minds turned more towards food and drink than to the flag only vaguely visible high above the entrance. So there we were. Three Residences filled with some of the right guests and some of the wrong ones. Faced with this complex gaff, the three hostesses conferred and agreed there was only one thing to do: Nothing. A little more effort was made to identify new arrivals, and everyone else was wished a Merry Christmas and included in the revelry. We never did come up with an estimate of how many were where they ought not to have been, but once the singing began (again to flute and piano accompaniment), and the Christmas grog poured, no one seemed to mind. And we admired those who actually realized their error, took advantage of the situation and went to two and maybe even three Christmas parties on a single night.

Cerita Beach was of course a terrifically unwintery setting for a Canadian Christmas, but somehow we turned on the Christmas spirit and had lot of fun. Bob Gibbons, who worked for the railway consulting firm CNCP on a CIDA-funded project rehabilitating and modernizing the Indonesian rail system, and his wife Sam (a nickname for Helen, somehow) came down from Bandung to join about ten of us from Jakarta. Sam and Bob were going through a bit of a rough patch in their marriage, and I spent some time talking to Sam trying to encourage her. I was later to hear from other friends that I had not helped much, and might have done more harm than good; I was never much of an amateur psychiatrist! The local Toronto Dominion Bank representative, Paul Skerman, an Australian, and his Canadian wife Vicki also joined us and they were a lot of fun. We decorated a bush outside our thatch cabins and all brought one present for one other member of the group, chosen randomly, with the limitation being that the total cost of the gift could not be more than 1000 Rupiah, or about $2.50. For our Christmas dinner I brought an already cooked turkey and a Christmas pudding, and of course the requisite cognac with which to light it, and we spent two days swimming and playing volleyball during the day and playing charades at night around a bonfire.

Sulawesi and Soroako

Although the occasional senior-level visit was a lot of work, we did not have too many of them and I spent a lot of time travelling. Some were trips with the Ambassador to provincial capitals. We went to Ujung Pandang in Sulawesi fairly early in our time there, since Sulawesi was the site of several of our aid projects and also of the giant Inco nickel project. During our first trip there, Shortliffe thought we should have a reception in the provincial capital for all the Canadian residents in the province and the local government leaders. Somehow I was charged with making it happen (the second line of my job description was, after all, "protocol officer"). When we got to the hotel in Ujung Pandang after being up-country at an aid project, I discovered that the hotel had no idea what we had meant when we faxed through our request for a reception to be prepared for a hundred guests. So I dispatched two staffers to buy soft-drinks, beer and as much Australian wine as they could find and I went into the hotel kitchen and taught the staff to make canapés from bread and tinned fish and eggs and pretty well anything we could lay our hands on. It was not the fanciest fare, but the reception went off fine. Afterwards, Ambassador Shortliffe looked at me and said "good job, but whoever was in charge of the crappy food should be fired". I agreed.

Seeing the big Inco nickel mine in Soroako was also a great experience. We flew up to the site, substantially north and east of Ujung Pandang, in deHavilland Twin Otters. Coming in to land we saw the village built for engineers and international workers and as I looked at it from the plane I thought that it looked exactly like a specially built mining site town in Canada, with neat little rows of bungalows and a couple of larger buildings that were clearly schools or clinics or community centres, although there was something a bit weird about it. It turned out that it was indeed exactly like a Canadian mining site town, but with every building on stilts with the main floor three meters above the ground and open space underneath, built that way to ensure that snakes and other wildlife would not be able to enter. At the time of our visit, Inco had completed one production line and was starting to mine the ore, and while we were there we participated in the inauguration of a 135MW dedicated hydro power plant that would allow the mine to be expanded to two more lines. We were hosted there by the head of Inco Indonesia, Phil Jessup, an extremely polished and charming New Yorker, son of the well-known American jurist of the same name who was for many years the US representative on the UN Security Council and later a judge with the International Court of Justice in The Hague. I was to get to know Phil much better during our time together in Jakarta, and saw him occasionally back in North America in the years that followed.

Another Inco manager was Tim Babcock, an anthropologist who was charged with ensuring that the company's relationship with the local community and their whole approach to project development took into account local sensitivities and needs. Tim was later recognized by both CIDA and the World Bank as having done a model job in positioning Inco in the local community. Tim was from Corner Brook, Newfoundland, and remembered both of my sisters, Pat and Joy, and I had been at school with his younger sister Christine. His father ran the local flower shop when we were little, and I was to see Tim and his wife Helen several more times when they passed through Jakarta. Small world.

During a provincial visit to East Java, we were taken to visit a sugar plantation out on the plains west of Surabaya after our formal government meetings. The setting was very beautiful, with vast fields of maturing sugar cane glistening in the tropical sun, the little villages beehives of lively activity with children playing in the streams while their mothers beat clothes against the rocks. The sugar mill was a different story and was like going back in time. Huge flywheels driving the Dutch-built mill were powered by direct-drive steam engines that dated back to the 19th century. And the heat and the steam were more oppressive than any other place I have been before or since. The workers wore shorts and no shirts and nothing on their feet, and looked like they were all about to expire. When we asked the mill manager what his accident rate was, he smiled happily and said "Tidak apa apa, there are always lots of workers wanting jobs". It could have been a scene right out of the worst of the industrial revolution.

Visit of HMB and other Friends

My brother Hugh was, at the time of my departure for Indonesia, finishing his investment banking training program at Chase Manhattan Bank in New York, and shortly thereafter heard that his first overseas assignment would be in Bahrain. Since this was only a quarter of the world away rather than half, I invited him to come to Jakarta at his first convenient opportunity and he did. We met up in Singapore where we explored the city and justified spending large amounts of money on stereo equipment by turning our purchases into late Christmas gifts for each other. As usual, we stayed at the Goodwood Park, which I am still convinced is one of the finest understated hotels in the world. I tied my trip into consultations with the regional head of the immigration program, Ian Hamilton, for whom I worked when overseeing the issuance of visas, and he and his wife Donna very generously invited Hugh and I to dinner. Ian was an Asiaphile, and had served in several places in the region. He eventually retired fairly young and became a novelist, writing a series of books with Asian themes like *The Water Rat of Wanchai* and *The Wild Beasts of Wuhan*. After our time in Singapore, Hugh came down to Jakarta for a few days of sailing and mucking about both in the city and up in the hills at the Puncak. In Jakarta, Hugh had a contact in the Chase office by the name of Ron Freed, who had just moved there with his stunning Vietnamese wife Hoa and a gorgeous little two-year old toddler named Jennifer. Ron had been in the US military during the last days of Vietnam, had fallen in love with Hoa there, but they had been separated when Ron's unit was moved to Thailand with the 1973 withdrawal of US forces. Just before the fall of Saigon, as Northern forces closed on the final redoubts of the South, Ron commandeered a helicopter in Thailand and personally flew to Vietnam to exfiltrate Hoa and her family. Dinner with the Freeds at their house was the first of many for me and began for me a friendship with Rod and Hoa that was to last many years, a friendship that slipped away only as their marriage sadly fell apart fifteen or twenty years later.

Hugh and I agreed that I should pay a return visit the following year, but by the time I did Hugh had decided that Bahrain was not worth visiting, so we met in Zermatt and spent a fabulous week skiing in the Swiss Alps together.

Consular Work

During my first year in Jakarta and until a more junior person arrived in the summer of 1978, I also served as the mission's consular and visa officer. Generally this meant very little work. The issuance of visitor visas was managed by the two front office receptionists, Nettie and Nancy, who checked names against a control list sent to us by our mission in Singapore, and all I did was sign them when they were brought to me. This probably took about ten minutes a week. Generally, visitor visa applicants were not interviewed, and immigrant and student applicants were interviewed by Singapore-based officers during regular visits to Jakarta. On occasion I would be asked by the Singapore office to meet with an applicant. During one such interview, the candidate in front of me suspected that my questions implied that I was simply waiting to be bribed, and he pulled out a little felt bag and poured onto my desk a small pile of diamonds, that looked both very real and very valuable to my totally untrained eye. When I waved my hand to indicate he should put them away, he interpreted this to mean that the initial offer was insufficient, and he then poured more diamonds onto the desk. Of course I sent him packing, explaining that no matter what his offer was, I simply did not have the authority to issue an immigrant visa, nor the skills to forge one!

In the 1970s, Canada did not charge for visitor visas, although Indonesians did not know this. Nettie and Nancy were a very efficient pair and every junior consular officer who worked with them appreciated the effort they put into their work. What we did not know is that they had a great racket going. A year or two after I had left Jakarta to return to Ottawa, an Indonesian mentioned in passing to an embassy officer that he found our $25 visa fee quite reasonable relative to higher fees at certain other embassies. Surprised and a bit confused, the officer investigated, and he found that Nettie and Nancy had for the better part of ten years been charging all visitor applicants a $25 visa fee, which went right into their pockets! They were of course fired, but those of us who had served at the embassy during their time there all secretly admired them for their ability to run their highly profitable scheme for so long.

There were less pleasant aspects to consular work. In one case I had to arrange the identification and burial of a young Canadian killed in a terrible car crash, which meant dealing with a horribly mangled body and having to arrange on behalf of the aggrieved family a cremation and funeral ceremony. We also had the normal flow of general cases, of thefts and lost passports and quite a lot of drug-related cases. I was lucky to have supporting me a superb consular clerk, Cary Dark, who loved the work and had the ideal sympathetic disposition to do the job well. He also intensely hated having to do clerical work in the office, so when a call came in about another drug case in Bali or a poor Canadian caught in some mess in a distant city or town, Cary was more than ready to jump on a plane or train and head out to provide succour and usually solutions. Cary was a delightful character, a couple of years younger than I, and lived very close to my own home in Bangka Barat. His home saw a constant flow of pretty Gulf Air flight attendants as Cary's houseguests and he often had fun parties. Because we were relatively short of clerical hands at the Embassy, he was supposed to do the filing as well as the consular work, but he always found a good reason to avoid the former.

About a year after I arrived in Jakarta we started another cycle of normal post rotations and new people came in from Canada and other posts. As was our practice, we were all assigned "buddies" among incoming staff, and it was our job to help them settle down, learn where stores and other places were, how to get around before they received their cars and so on. I

123

had two buddies coming in over a single weekend and so stocked up a bit on cash to help them with early purchases of foodstuffs and the like. When parked in an older part of town called Glodok, my car was broken into and my wallet with several hundred dollars in it was stolen along with all my credit cards, driver's license and other key documents. I went to the local police station and made a big scene. Having thought it through in advance, I decided to make a point of emphasizing that I had no concern about the "small amount" of cash in the wallet, and that I would offer a substantial reward for the return of everything else. Two days later I received a local registered letter from the police station with the wallet and all its contents, minus the cash of course. The police graciously refused the reward, having presumably shaken down the local thief for their share of the cash!

I was able to drop my consular responsibilities with the arrival of a more junior officer, and I volunteered to help out in the development division which was experiencing a rapid increase in the number of aid projects without a commensurate increase in staff. Ambassador Shortliffe was very interested in development and felt that the aid projects we were managing were much more important than the traditional reporting done by political/economic officers. He was sympathetic when Lorne Heuckroth, our very experienced Head of Aid, asked to borrow about 30% of my time. I was given a mix of power and industrial projects which increased my opportunities to travel other than simply with the Ambassador, and I loved it.

One of my aid projects was a joint CIDA-USAID affair, where we set up three experimental rural electricity cooperatives in very poor districts of Sumatra, Sulawesi and Lombok. We provided the generation and transformer systems, the Americans the transmission lines and the cooperative design and training. It was an interesting project and I learned a lot, both about power but also about the tensions one could create in bringing inexpensive power to some people (even if in need) while the national energy company, PLN, was charging higher rates to other people. I had two other power projects, both still at the proposal stage, one for a model mini-hydro project in Sumatra (where a regional grid was still light years away), and a larger 45MW conventional power plant to be built in Cilcap in South Java.

My last aid project, already in the implementation stage was a fertilizer distribution project, providing railway cars, inland storage depots, trucks and commodity handling equipment. I was also part of a cross-division team designing an "industrial cooperation" program, where Canada's development dollars would be spent to allow Indonesian concerns to draw upon the expertise of the Canadian private sector, universities and not-for profit institutions like hospitals. At the beginning I was quite excited by this program, trying to set up training programs, scholarships, apprenticeships and institutional exchanges, but from the beginning there were too many chiefs given the participation of all section heads. We never got the chiefs to Indians ratio to a fraction of less than one, so not a single real industrial cooperation project was launched during the whole time I was in Indonesia.

Visit of AEB and MCB

My parents came for a two week visit late in the first half of 1978, and I managed to get almost ten days off to travel with them. After a few days in Jakarta, during which I even managed to get my father (difficult) as well as my mother (easy) out sailing on *Evangeline*, we headed eastward by train to Bandung. After a day in Bandung, we took a night train to Jogjakarta. It was a lovely way to see the country, and the fact that the train was old and the speed slow may have made it a better trip than had it been fast and modern. We click-clacked our way through tiny one-light hamlets over the mountains and across the southern alluvial plain. When in Jogjakarta, we visited the mighty Borobodur temple, with its wonderful transition in friezes from a lusty and bacchanalian foundation level rising both skyward and behaviourally to the triumph of pure spirit at the apex. From the Borobudur we wandered around the other temples of the district, all smaller but many as moving, somehow more magical when still unrestored, emerging out of the trees or the bushes as we bumped along primitive country roads. There was one evening we ate at a lovely little outdoor restaurant at the old Puri Artha in Jogjakarta, with the light provided by perimeter torches and tabletop hurricane lanterns, and a five or six person gamelan orchestra playing the lilting sonorous cycles of Javanese music. The gentleness of Central Java seeped into our souls. My parents understood then how attractive Java could be. We went from there on to Bali, where we stayed at Batu Jimbar, part of Tanjung Sari, a magical thatch-roofed resort in the centre of the Sanur beach.

Tanjung Sari was owned by Wiya Waworunto, a descendent of a high-born Balinese family who long owned the land bordering on the Sanur beaches southeast of Denpasar. Wiya has already appeared briefly in this story, for he was the friend of Chris and Pru Scarlett's who owned the Rome apartment that he and his wife Judith would swap for weekends for the Markham Street house of Chris and Pru in London and for my little Rue Bréa apartment in Paris. In the early 1960s, Wiya had developed the two ends of the beach into resort complexes in which he kept a small equity but which were largely owned and managed by professional hotel chains. One was the Bali Beach and the other the Bali Hyatt. But Wiya kept the centre of the beach for himself where he built the Tanjung Sari (where I always stayed) with its twenty or so thatched cabins, each with one or two bedrooms and a modern bath. The hotel also had a lovely pool, an outdoor bar and restaurant, and an atmosphere infinitely more Balinese than the large hotels at the beach's northern and southern ends. The Tanjung Sari over the years was to become a very popular place for famous people seeking to flee the public eye; Yuko Ono and Mick Jagger both stayed there at one time or another.

In "the world is definitely small" department, during its effort to diversify away from making paper, my father's company, Bowaters, had bought a small Singapore investment firm in the middle of the 1970s, and in so doing had acquired an interest in a real estate project in Bali. That project's local partner was Wiya, and the project was to develop the land behind Tanjung Sari in a complex of very beautiful villas designed to be luxurious but to retain a traditional Balinese style. The project was named Batu Jimbar. Playing on his role as a corporate director of Bowaters, my father managed to get Bowaters to pay for his trip to Asia with the justification of learning more about their Singapore subsidiary, and this of course also allowed him to secure use of a two-bedroom villa at Batu Jimbar. It was only after he had done so that we put two-and two together and realized that this was a complex controlled by my friend Wiya.

Needless to say, given our multiple connections with him, Wiya ensured that we were treated royally during our stay in Bali. We toured around the south of the island, getting as far west as Tanah Lot, a beautifully proportioned Hindu temple set on a rocky outcropping in the sea, an island at high tide and a peninsula when the tide was out. My mother fell in love with Tanah Lot and made several sketches and a beautiful oil painting of it. In fact, she painted a lot of scenes in Bali, and was very much in her element there. At one point she realized that she was running out of some paints and of fixative for her water-colours, which needed to be stabilized before being prepared for travel. Wiya told us that Donald Friend, a famous Australian painter, was a long-time resident of Batu Jimbar in a house just a hundred meters south of ours. So my mother, unabashed, led us over to Friend's villa to ask to borrow artist's supplies. Donald Friend could not have been more gracious, not only giving my mother the products she needed, but inviting us for a lovely lunch on the third floor of his villa, a floor without walls looking out over the turquoise sea. Donald Friend was not to spend much longer in Bali before returning to Australia for the last years of his life, but he had been at Batu Jimbar for ten years by the time we visited, and was very well-established. He had a huge retinue of beautiful young Balinese, of both genders, running his household and meeting his and his guests' every need. They all had one of four names, of course, Wayan, Made, Nyoman and Ketut, simply indicating whether they were the first, second, third or fourth born. (At the fifth child the cycle would begin again.) This has been the centuries long tradition of the

Sudras, Bali's largest Hindu caste, that of the farmers and fishers. Unlike in India, there is less hierarchy among the castes, with the royal, warrior and intellectual castes consider gentry and higher than the Sudras, which make up some 90% of the population.

On our last evening in Bali I took my parents to a performance of the traditional Kecak dance. The setting was a beach set about with bonfires and the surf in the distance, and it was as entrancing as it could ever be. More than a hundred dancers performed in perfect unison, chanting and swaying in trancelike rhythm, throwing their arms skyward in perfect unison as the bats swept overhead. For my parents (as for me always) the dances of Bali were something special and another clearly distinguishing feature of this magic island. My parents were to come again in early 1979 for a very quick visit during a business trip to the region. On the second visit the only sojourn we managed outside of Jakarta was to Carita Beach for a couple of days. From there we hired a local boat to take us out to the fuming Anak Krakatoa, which was interesting but on the way back the sea got stormy and the boat began to leak badly. We were tossed about on the short sharp waves of the Sunda Strait, the engine kept sounding as if was on its last breath, and even we as passengers had to help with bailing. When we finally reached terra firma I think my father was ready to give up going out in small boats, never his favourite pastime, forever.

New Colleagues and the Rotational Life

Among the new arrivals in the summer of 1978 was Peter Oldham, accompanied by his wife Margaret and three sons from about four to eight years old. They moved into a house next door to me and over time would become good friends. Peter was a bit older than I and was senior political analyst, cross posted from Wellington. He and I made common cause in managing our difficult and hard-to-please boss, Steve Woolcombe, but Peter did not have a close ambassadorial function to protect him as I did, although his greater service experience made it easier for him to push back.

During the autumn of every year, thousands of diplomats pour into New York City to attend the annual UN General Assembly session and the vast number of meetings of special committees and agencies. Prior to those meetings it is normal for foreign ministries to reach out though their embassies to contacts in other foreign ministries to plan and prepare for what will transpire in New York. In Jakarta, we received a telegram of instruction from Ottawa, asking us to see if two delegates from the Indonesian Foreign Ministry, Mssrs Soefardi and Effendi, would be attending the 1978 session of the UN's special committee on the peaceful use of outer space. I trotted off to the Departemen Luar Negri (foreign office), to find out. After returning to the Embassy, I prepared a responding telegram, which said "Soefardi has been moved to a different department and will not participate, and Effendi is dead" and then I looked at this terse message and could not resist adding "which counts him out too, even for a UN discussion." I sent the message off, and later was told by Jeremy Kinsman that he read my answer in New York while sitting behind Canada's flag in the General Assembly, pretending to listen to the rambling speech of some tinpot dictator from Nowheresland and reading the thick morning "In-Pack" folder of overnight messages. When he got to my message, he was so tickled by it that he pulled it out of the pack and passed it to members of the delegations nearby. Pretty soon, a whole section of the early alphabet country delegates were laughing, leaving the speaker uncertain whether there had been a mistranslation of his very serious speech or whether he had buttons or zippers undone! Jeremy was later to become a very dear friend of mine and one of Canada's most brilliant diplomats.

During the summer of 1978, Steve Woolcombe heard that his assignment was to be shortened and that he was being cross-posted to the economic division of the embassy in Washington. Steve was very pleased as the job was an interesting one, and his wife Anne was ecstatic with the prospect of leaving Jakarta. By this time I had more or less gotten used to Steve and with my role and relationship with the Ambassador largely meant that I was immune from any impact of his curious supervisory skills, but it would mean a new boss for me. Several months later, in came Terrence Lonergan with wife Iris and baby boy, cross-posted from our little Embassy in Tananarive in Madagascar. Terrence was, in spite of his good Irish name, a francophone and had worked mostly in French-speaking countries until arriving in Jakarta. The immediate impact of this was that he did not attempt to redraft or edit reports that were written by Peter Oldham, who headed up the two-person political division or by me, a tendency that some more senior officers adopted to underscore that they were in charge even when they could find no really substantive problems in draft reports. This had been a Woolcombe special. Terrence was also bearded, which meant that fully half of the accredited diplomats of the mission were now wearing beards. Abusing my position as gopher, I put through to the Ambassador a memorandum to all male staff making beards mandatory, burying it under a bunch of routine documents he needed to sign, figuring he might not be reading everything in his signature pack. An hour later I hear a loud "BALLOCH" from Shortliffe's office and when I went in he said "nice try!" with a laugh and dropped the memo into his wastebasket.

Law of the Sea Consultations

During the 1970s the Trudeau government put an enormous effort into advancing a number of international legal efforts. None was given higher priority than negotiating a treaty to codify international maritime law. With the support of the United Nations, the new Law of the Sea was to deal with everything from adopting common definitions for territorial waters (expanding them from three to twelve nautical miles from the coast) to the definition of the wider "exclusive economic zones" extending certain coastal state responsibilities and rights to 200 miles or to the end of the continental shelf, to the resolution of maritime boundaries to the exploitation of minerals in international waters. In the way of the UN, the law of the sea negotiations would adopt a moniker drawn from the initial meeting, the United Nations Convention on the Law of the Seas, UNCLOS. It was a huge endeavour and the three-ocean Canada had been a leading proponent of more formalized governance for the world's oceans, in part because it believed its own interest would be better protected than in a world where right was simply a function of might and the reach of one's navy, as indeed it had been for the previous thousand years. By mid-1978, much of the work on the new Law of the Sea treaty had been completed, but the talks had become stuck, as they normally do, when the national interests of big players emerged at stake.

Canada had been very skillfully led in the multi-year negotiations by Allen Beesley, an international lawyer who had been Legal Advisor in External Affairs when the talks began, but who was now our head of mission in Australia. When named as High Commissioner to Australia he retained his role as our chief negotiator at UNCLOS. A brilliant but paranoid diplomat, Beesley came to Indonesia in September 1978 to make common cause with his Indonesian counterpart prior to an upcoming seventh session of the multilateral negotiations somewhat later in the year. Canada and Indonesia were part of a group of what were called "Like-Minded Countries", because of their extensive seacoasts, unresolved maritime borders with neighbours, and because the potential seabed mining of nickel modules was seen, if unregulated, as threatening the nickel industries of both countries.

Ambassador Beesley flew to Indonesia for the bilateral two-day meeting without any staff, and asked Ambassador Shortliffe to provide him support. Having taken precisely one course in International Law at university, and having been sent into the Indonesian foreign ministry on a couple of occasions to seek their views or support on some arcane legal issue relating to the UNCLOS talks, I was selected as the logical officer to support Beesley. The Indonesian lead negotiator was Mochtar Kusumaatmadja, a career diplomat who had just been named foreign minister by Soeharto to replace the ailing Adam Malik. He was supported by a deputy negotiator named Halim and a junior note-taker. Because the two governments wanted the meeting to be totally confidential for fear of irritating countries unsupportive of a universal governing law, especially the United States, it was decided to meet at a secluded hotel in Bali. When Shortliffe learned that the new Foreign Minister himself was going to attend, he decided to come along as well, which Beesley immediately opposed, as he did not wish to have to share the spotlight. They finally agreed that he would come for the final dinner, where he could pursue with Mochtar issues other than those of UNCLOS.

So off I went to Bali. I went a day early because I wanted to be there ahead of Beesley, but the more important reason was that a group of my friends were there already, staying in Kuta, the "hippy" town where you could rent little rooms for a few dollars a night and eat omelets made with gently psychedelic mushrooms. The beach at Kuta, complete with a topless area up at its northern end, was clearly favoured by the young over the pricier and more staid beach at Sanur on the eastern side.

Landing in Denpasar in those days was special. Sweeping in above the sandy beaches of the western side of Bali's southern teardrop, we descended to the Nguruh Rai airport over the asymmetrical sand dunes and the soft beaches and the breakers rolling in from the southwest. For me, arriving in Bali was always like arriving home, to see the smiling faces and to banter with friendly if cocky porters and taxi drivers. But Allan Beesley's arrival was not smooth and his luggage was lost en route from Australia. The fact that baggage officials and airline personnel did not seem to treat this as an important or rare occurrence frustrated an already angry Beesley even further. In those days at least, average Balinese still seemed deeply rooted in their own Hindu culture. As in other non-material societies, the concept of strict personal ownership seemed a little foreign to the Balinese, and if things they owned were not very important to them, they could not really understand why anyone would care much about a couple of pieces of luggage that would probably turn up the next day. It wasn't until I had plied him with a few drinks at the poolside bar of our hotel did Beesley's black mood begin to lift. I was to learn how mercurial he was as the two days progressed.

The bilateral talks went very well, and I found Beesley, who was a complete master of the international legal issues involved in the UNCLOS process, and indeed of the negotiating dynamics and individuals involved, a very impressive negotiator and, at least in his interaction with our Indonesian counterparts, fantastically charming. We sent many messages off to Ottawa and Geneva and New York, and all were identified as having been sent from "Denpasar", since we feared that anyone seeing messages referring to our setting as "Bali" would simply not believe we were engaged in very serious discussions. Had anyone seen us in our shorts and sandals and sitting around a table by a beautiful beach, we would have been doubly doubted.

After the talks we gathered for dinner, and Ambassador Shortliffe joined us. Having a secluded and private dinner with Foreign Minister Mochtar was too good an opportunity for Shortliffe to miss, and so he turned the conversation away from the law of the sea and began to focus on bilateral and other matters. I could see Beesley, no longer centre stage, starting to fume. After fifteen minutes of discussion between Mochtar and Shortliffe on bilateral matters, Beesley got up from the table and left the room, without saying anything. Knowing that something was wrong, I followed. Beesley turned to me and said that he would not be ignored like a piece of furniture by an upstart like Shortliffe, who was ten years his junior, and that he would leave immediately. He ordered me to arrange an earlier flight and a car to take him to the airport. I told him there was no flight out of Denpasar that evening and I would not in any case assist in him in ruining not only two good days of talks but the mission's relationship with our local foreign minister. I finally got him to return to the dinner table by telling him that he risked undoing the masterful job he had done in bringing Mochtar very far forward on critical UNCLOS matters, but he continued to pout until the dinner was over. Afterwards, when the Foreign Minister and his team had left, he blew up at Shortliffe for ignoring him, and Shortliffe, no shrinking violet himself, exploded in return and called Beesley a self-aggrandizing egomaniac. As the two titans went at each other, I put a bottle of Hennessey VSOP Cognac and some glasses on the table and then yelled STOP loud enough to actually make them shut up for a moment. I said that they sounded like schoolboys and that the cognac and glasses were there to allow them to start acting like mature adults and at least enjoy their fight. While each of them looked like they wanted to kill me, Glenn poured Beesley a cognac, Beesley accepted, and the venom seemed to leave the room. Somehow out of this small act of defusing what was at best a silly argument, I earned a place in Beesley's firmament, and from that time until he retired from the service many years later would reach out to me with personal pleas for support on one matter or another, on most of which I had no influence whatsoever.

Visit of Jack Horner

In the early part of 1979, we had a rare but welcome high-level visit from Ottawa. Jack Horner was a life-long Progressive Conservative who had recently crossed the floor to the Liberals and been immediately appointed by Trudeau as Minister of Industry Trade and Commerce. He was on a multi-country tour of Asia, and arrived in Jakarta after a formal visit to Beijing, leading Canada's first minister-level trade mission to China since the death of Mao. Deng Xiaoping had over the previous year consolidated his control over the Party and just in December of 1978 had launched his policy of "Reform and Opening Up". Governments around the world, and particularly those in Asia, were watching and trying to discern what this meant. Indonesia, with its own substantial and influential Chinese population, had enjoyed a very rocky relationship with China in the 1960s and early 1970s, and believed with some justification that domestic instability had been fanned by Beijing. The Soeharto government was also doing quite well in the 1970s, and was enjoying a period of substantial support and attention from the west, and it did not wish to see a strong and resurgent China emerge to steal the spotlight. Horner had been a very successful farmer before entering politics, and was not a natural politician or diplomat. He was a straight shooter who disliked both the artful constructs of diplomatic discourse and the practice of his handlers to try to straightjacket him in his interaction with foreign counterparts and leaders.

When we took Minister Horner to see President Soeharto, the latter was really not at all interested in talking about the bilateral trade and investment relationship between Canada and Indonesia. All he wanted to hear about was Horner's evaluation of developments in China, and his impression of Deng Xiaoping, who had received Horner, and others in the new Beijing leadership. We had known that this would be of interest to the Indonesian President, and we had briefed Horner carefully to be circumspect in his responses because of the Indonesian sensitivity towards China. In response to Soeharto's questions, Horner began with a carefully composed and well-nuanced comment from his briefing note, before turning to the President and saying: "Mr. President, I am a farmer, not a diplomat. The Ambassador and all those officials", waving his hands towards the line of us sitting to his right, "want me to tell you all sorts of stuff that doesn't make any sense to me. All I know is what I saw and heard with my own eyes and I can tell you that China is a real mess. You don't have to worry about them catching up with you for a hundred years." Soeharto beamed and engaged in a way we had never seen before, and was for the rest of my time in Jakarta especially friendly and open towards high-level visitors from Canada. Horner had hit a home-run.

Horner was clearly not a stupid man, but he was not in his element dealing with foreign interlocutors or in being a Minister on a foreign tour. He insisted in bringing his confidential briefing books with him to every meeting, even though as far as we could tell he never referred to or used a single brief. After the call on the President we were all back at the Ambassador's Residence for lunch, when we realized that the Minister's briefing books were missing. Realizing where they must have been, I jumped in the Ambassador's car and got the driver to take me back to the Presidential Palace on Merdeka Square. A young protocol officer met me on the steps with the books in his arms. As he gave them to me he assured me with a perfectly straight face that he had seen the books when they were left behind and that he had made sure that no one had looked at their contents. Right. I assured the Minister, of course, that the books had been found where he had left them and that there was no damage done. And at the Ambassador's instruction, no report of the briefly missing briefs was ever filed with Ottawa.

Minister Horner's visit was substantively relevant for the relationship, for he signed on behalf of the Canadian Government several important bilateral agreements. One of these was a new double taxation agreement, very much welcomed by our business community. It was formally entitled a "Convention on the Avoidance of Double Taxation and the Prevention of Fiscal Evasion with Respect to Levies on Income and Capital". The ceremony was televised, and the two Ministers were to sign all twelve copies (four copies in each of Indonesian, English and French) in front of bright lights and whirring cameras. Just before the ceremony, a local Foreign Affairs official advised me that the Ministers were to sign above and not below the phrase "FOR THE GOVERNMENT OF . . ." and despite my pleas that this was not normal, he insisted and I gave in. As the signing began, I leant over Minister's shoulder as he started to sign his pile of treaties, beginning with one of the French versions, and told him to sign just above the prescribed phrase and he signed. Someone did the same for the Indonesian Minister of Foreign Affairs, Mochtar Kusumaatmadja, who was about to sign an Indonesian version when he said "No, that's not right. I am supposed to sign below the line", and then proceeded to do so. With my straightest face I walked over to Mochtar and told him that it was Canadian treaty practice to sign above the line in French and below in English. He looked at me quizzically, glanced over to see where Horner had signed, and said: "That is rubbish, but it was quick thinking so that is how we shall do it." No harm done. Later, someone put up in the embassy a photograph of the signing with me leaning over Horner's shoulder pointing to the document. The caption added at the bottom of the mounted picture was "Balloch to Minister, 'It is spelt 'H-O-R-N-E-R'". It was funny but a little unfair.

Trade Adventures and a Swimming Grizzly

Aside from the visit of Minister Horner, I did not have much to do with the trade program while in Jakarta, except through my responsibility for the industrial cooperation program. For quite a long time the Indonesian government had been wrestling with how best to renovate and enlarge some of its major Sumatran coal mines, originally developed by the Dutch in the 19th century, and how to finance the associated infrastructure. The largest of these mines was called Bukit Assam, and the World Bank offered to get involved. Ambassador Shortliffe, Lorne Heuckroth and Bob Brown from our Trade Division dreamt up a very creative approach to the project, putting together a billion-dollar Canadian consortium that would finance and develop the entire package of mines, railways and port facilities. This took pulling together a number of major mining, engineering and infrastructure equipment firms, financing from both CIDA and the Export Development Corporation and Canadian commercial banks, and it was a very major undertaking. I was drawn in largely because of my role as Shortliffe's shadow. I ended up writing a lot of the documentation that had to be prepared for Ottawa and for the Indonesian government to sell the comprehensive Canadian package rather than a piecemeal approach being proposed by the World Bank. In the end, we were not successful in winning the whole integrated deal, as the Indonesians decided to proceed with smaller discrete projects, but it was an exciting experience to be involved in something so large, taught me a lot about project financing, and Canadian firms eventually did quite well in winning associated contracts.

Beyond the NATO-wide defence products sharing agreements, Canada has never been a significant player in the global weapons market. Nonetheless, some of the equipment produced for the Canadian Armed Forces become export products. In the 1970s, one such piece of military kit was the "Grizzly", a very versatile 6X6 armoured personnel carrier built by GMDD (later EDD) in Windsor, Ontario. The Indonesian army was modernizing and looking for a new APC and had selected three potential vehicles, Canada's Grizzly and its American and French equivalents. Generally the way that Canadian military products are marketed is with the strong support of the government and the direct involvement of the Canadian Commercial Corporation, a crown corporation created for this purpose, and while the companies that manufacture the equipment pay for the shipping of samples and related costs, the Canadian military provide the personnel involved in demonstrations.

For the Embassy in Jakarta, getting involved in a military export was novel. The trade division was of course in charge, but others of us were interested. The first series of tests that the Indonesians put the three contestants through were conducted at a military base in West Java, where the APCs were driven up and down incredibly steep and heavily vegetated hills to prove their dexterity. They were also shot at with live ammunition to test their armour; and they shot at other things to demonstrate their firepower. Bob Brown, one of the Trade Commissioners, attended all these tests and told my friend Pierre Pichette and me about them. He invited us to accompany him for the final test, which was to be launched off a landing craft to prove that the Grizzly was amphibious.

To avoid attracting unwanted public attention, the amphibious tests were carried out before dawn. The Grizzly was loaded on an old and rather wobbly-looking Indonesian landing craft in the harbour in Jakarta the evening before the test, to be taken to a lightly inhabited shoreline east of the city. Just after midnight, we boarded a small coastal patrol vessel and motored alongside the landing craft for the couple of hours it took us to get to the testing area. There was a northerly breeze of about 15 knots and the seas were running with waves of maybe a meter and a half or two, breaking as they approached the shore. When we arrived at the prescribed place and were about two hundred meters from shore in relatively shallow water, the test began. The Grizzly powered up, the front ramp of the landing craft was lowered, and with one of the three crew members (one being an invited Indonesian) standing in the open hatch on the little turret, roared its engine and powered into the water. Just as the vehicle left the ramp, the landing craft was caught by a cross wave and heeled sharply to starboard.

The Grizzly entered the sea at a 30 degree angle instead of on the level and kept on going, straight to the bottom, five meters down. We were all stunned and watched for the crew to appear. One of the Canadians and the Indonesian appeared on the surface quickly and were immediately thrown rescue ropes. Then followed an increasingly worrying four or five minutes before the third man popped up. He was Sergeant Legault, the vehicle's driver and a very tough Canadian Non-Commissioned Officer with a crew cut and the arms of a lumberjack. When brought on board and asked why it took him so long to get out, he said in a very nonchalant tone that he had had to shut the vehicle down properly and close all its plugs and valves.

The Grizzly sat on the bottom for a day before being pulled out, and it was cleaned up quickly and was apparently fully functional. The embassy line was that the Grizzly had passed the "24-hour submersion test" with flying colours! It was generally agreed that the age and quality of the landing craft and its instability were the cause of the mis-launch, and the trade division and the GMDD representatives hoped that the sale was not lost. When one of our friends in the Indonesian Ministry of Defense said that the French were circulating photographs of the disaster, having clearly had a spy on board our coastal patrol vessel, one the GMDD fellows shrugged and pulled out of his briefcase photographs of the windows of the French APC being blown out during the live-fire tests. Everyone had agents everywhere.

Mountain Climbing

Ever since my friend Pierre Pichette and I had started going to the Puncak to stay at the embassy's bungalows, we had chatted about climbing the mountains that soar out of the valley at its western end, beyond the lush green of the padi fields and the jumbled red-tiles of the village roofs. Puncak Pass was at an altitude of about 800 meters, from which the mountain peaks above rose another 2500 meters. Around Christmas of 1978, Pierre and I and a friend from the US Embassy, David Refus, began to plan our assault, and by the time we got around to doing it a couple of months later our group had grown to ten. The idea was to climb overnight, reaching one of the two peaks in time for sunrise. The two mountains were called Gedé and Pangrango, the latter being a hundred meters higher, but Gedé having a much better vantage point from which to watch the dawn stream across the plains of Java east of Puncak Pass.

On the afternoon of a full-moon Friday, we gathered at the embassy bungalow in the village of Megamandung. Although the weather was generally clear, the mountains themselves were wreathed in cloud, which was completely normal for the mountains would always be clear at sunrise and then cloud over at about seven or eight in the morning. It had been decided to eat prior to departure, taking snacks as energy food and enough sandwiches and fruit for one proper meal. We estimated that it would take us about six and a half hours to reach the peak, and we planned to begin at nine in the evening to give ourselves plenty of time to reach the peak well before five in the morning, when the first light of the new day would start to appear in the east. The climb was not very steep and we needed no special equipment; it was really just a steep walk of about 16 kilometers. We brought warm clothing, for although we would begin on a tropical evening at only 800 meters of elevation, as we climbed through the night it was bound to get cold. Supplies and clothing were distributed among the men, the women not asked to carry anything. After an early dinner, we set of for our takeoff base at the botanical gardens at Cibodas, on the far side of the pass, where we left our cars. We were all set and loaded up about fifteen minutes ahead of schedule, and we slung our packs up, checked our flashlights, matches and odds and ends, took a head count and set off, beginning with David Refus in the lead and me trailing to ensure we lost no one as we ascended.

Although it was not very steep and although we were all fresh the beginning was not very easy. The path was rocky and quite wide, but no one was used to walking uphill, and we naturally started too fast and did not think about the gradual strain on our legs and lungs. We had planned to limit our rests to once an hour, but we were not twenty minutes into the climb when the first tired voice called for a break. We did not permit it immediately, but shortened our climb-rest cycle to forty minutes. The first couple of hours were boisterous and fun, and we did a bit of singing in spite of the heavy breathing. When the singing subsided, Peter Oldham and I carried on a dialogue of philosophy and geometry and literature, which led to groans and mockery from those above. And as we climbed and climbed, the rocky path gave way to forest humus and our straight line upwards shifted to the gradual incline of a great circle around the mountain's base. The moon was brilliantly full, and people learned that they saw better without artificial light, so flashlights were stored away. After several hours we broke into a little clearing at the end of which was a hot spring on the left and an eerie waterfall on the right, with steam spewing upwards, murky and haunting in the moonlight. The waterfall fell away just an arm's length to our immediate right, plummeting scores of metres to an area below as black as pitch, and the whole scene was about as inviting as the hollows of a Goya hell. We had to cross the waterfall by walking across large stones close to its crest, and the steam was so hot and thick that we were instantly drenched and could barely see our feet and the stone in front of us. There were several among us who needed much encouragement to cross. The third or fourth person to cross got the shock of their lives when, half way across, out of the hot and swirling mist of the hot spring to the left emerged a human form on a rock, crouched low, head thrown back and swaying from side to side. Seemingly in a trance, it was a pilgrim taking some sort of a cure, and his strange performance certainly added to the eeriness of the place.

We climbed and rested, climbed and rested. At about 2300 meters, where the two peaks divide, we crossed a flat savannah with three-meter tall grass and bogs and marshlands, and then started up the final ascent, in some sections passing through steep parts where we had to pull ourselves up with our hands and provide boosts for the weaker among us. Pierre, David, our official supplier of instant energy in the form of American jelly beans, and I rotated positions, and finally split the group into faster and slower, with Pierre volunteering to stay with the stragglers and urge them on. Because the mountainside was treed, we could not see through to the peak, and we had to just keep climbing on faith, which at times left some of the group and left others joking about climbing to heaven. Time went by almost unnoticed, we gave up stopping entirely, trying instead to regain energy by pausing for ten seconds or so before each major effort to pull ourselves another meter peakward. Finally, off to the east a horizon began to appear and the first pinkness of dawn spurred us forward. Wanting to be at the summit when the sun emerged, we pulled ourselves together for a final assault and charged up the last seventy or so metres, breaking out onto the paths at the peak. Instead of the great broken away crater of Genung Gedé that we expected to find at the mountain's top, we found a pleasant meadow in a slight cone about one hundred and seventy metres across. The meadow was covered with grass and what we christened "sheep-trees", dense little white bushes that looked in the pre-dawn light just like sheep. As we looked around and waited for the sun to rise, the slower group arrived and Pierre exclaimed: "Tabernac, on a monté la mauvaise caulisse de montagne!". He was right, we had climbed the higher Pangrango and walked not 16 kilometres but 25. It was pretty funny, and we wondered how many other groups could set out at the base of one mountain and end up at the peak of another.

On the way down we made better time, but our legs were tired and some, like Pierre, had old joint injuries acting up. Half way down we stopped above the falls we had crossed the night before and bathed in the beautiful hot spring, no longer eerie. Then it poured with tropical rain for the rest of the day and it was four in the afternoon by the time the last of our group got back to our cars at the Cibodas botanical gardens. We drove back to the embassy bungalows, had hot showers and strong drinks, and all went to bed. I slept twelve hours straight. A couple of others slept sixteen and two of the group did not go back to work for a week. No permanent damage was done, and although everyone had vowed in the pouring rain on the way down that they would never climb another mountain, by the next evening some of us were already talking about having another go at Gedé itself.

HRB as Undercover Drug Officer

Drugs from Southeast Asia were making their way into Canada in the 1970s in surprisingly large volumes, and the RCMP had established a drug interdiction team in Singapore. This did not seem to have much relevance for us in Jakarta, since the major provenance of the drugs was the "golden triangle" in the area where Thailand, Myanmar and Laos come together. Bangkok was the major consolidation centre and shipping port and it was there that most international interdiction efforts were concentrated. The drug smugglers were constantly trying to find new and creative routes out of the region, and the RCMP picked up a tip about a Canadian gang smuggling heroin through Bali. The heroin was liquefied and put in bottles of scotch or cognac, and then smuggled as duty-free alcohol into Canada. A favourite ruse was to have an innocent looking young Canadian or American approach middle-aged tourists in the departure lounge of an airport with a sob-story about missing a father's or grandfather's birthday and wanting to send home a small gift, the gift being a bottle of booze. The young person would say that they had been planning to go back to Canada themselves, but had to head somewhere else in Asia for one reason or another. Kind middle-aged people always fell for the story, and when they landed in Vancouver they would be met by a "brother" or "sister" of the person who had given them the bottles and relieved of their package, never knowing that they had just served as an unwitting mule. The bottles were perfectly resealed and completely indistinguishable from the real thing, so that upon arrival in North America they passed easily through customs, and the mules were not the slightest bit nervous since they thought they were carrying an innocent gift for a family celebration of some sort. When the RCMP found out that Bali was being used as an easy transshipment centre precisely because it was far from Bangkok and local officials unconcerned about drugs being exported, they decided to set up a trap for the smugglers, aiming not at the tourist mules but at the actual gang members. I was roped in given my language skills and the need for cooperation from the local authorities. When an informer in Thailand indicated that there was about to be some shipments made through Denpasar, we spent several days staking out the airport in Bali and watching for the transfers. I was given the role of a young traveler and told to try to mix with other young, hoping to discover those passing bottles to the unwitting mules. It was a titillating mix of boredom and excitement, although during my efforts unfortunately no transaction was uncovered, no chases initiated or gunfights held, and no one was arrested. Later, the RCMP and their local colleagues caught two young gang members carrying a half dozen duty free bottles of liquefied heroin each as they were leaving Singapore for Bali, and that eventually helped bring down a smuggling ring masterminded by a man from Calgary. He was eventually arrested in Bangkok and spent the rest of his life in a Thai jail.

Visit of CIDA President

One of the last high level visits we had during my time in Jakarta was the visit in March of 1979 of the President of CIDA, Michel Dupuy. Dupuy was an old-style diplomat who was to later become a member of parliament and a Minister in the Liberal government in the early 1990s, and eventually a French language novelist. He came for ten days fairly early in his tenure and wanted a very full program; at the end of the 1970s one of Canada's largest aid programs in the world was in Indonesia. The development section was as large as any in the Embassy, and we had so much going on that the CIDA officers were overwhelmed. As the embassy's economic officer, I was drafted to help with the overflow, and I had been given three small projects to manage along with my economic reporting responsibilities and my general responsibilities in support of the Head of Mission.

Ambassador Shortliffe, determined to impress Dupuy, put together a very demanding program that, after two days of intense meetings in Jakarta, included visits to aid projects in Java, Sulawesi and Lombok. Our intent was to have our wrap-up meetings at a hotel in Sanur on the southwest coast of Bali, just west of Lombok, where we could, at taxpayers' expense of course, have a reasonably relaxing couple of days. Both the project in

Sulawesi and the project in Lombok were far from the nearest airports, and we spent hours and hours in four-wheel drive vehicles wending our way to and from projects. When we arrived in Bali we again drove for many hours, visiting a potential agricultural project in the northwest corner of the island, before finally arriving late on the first of April at the Bali Beach Hotel. It was an idyllic setting in fading light of the late afternoon, with a local gamalan player and the frangipani blossoms adding Balinese sounds and scents. Everyone went to their rooms, changed into shorts and sandals, and gathered in a group near the pool and ordered beers or other evening cocktails. We all started to relax, particularly Shortliffe, for whom the visit had gone very well. We were sitting in a group near the pool, chatting about our intense week, when a waiter came over with an envelope and asked whether one of us was the Canadian Ambassador. Shortliffe identified himself and took the letter, opened it, extracted an embassy telex, and just about dissolved in a mixture of frustration and fury. Passing it to Dupuy he explained to the rest of us that we had just been invited by the Vice-President of the Republic to join him in North Sumatra the following day to participate in the opening ceremony of a Canada World Youth project. As Shortliffe and Dupuy put their heads together and tried to figure out how we could politely decline, Lorne Heuckroth and I argued persuasively that we would simply have to accept the invitation as any other response would be interpreted as insulting. I went to the front desk to use the telephone and came back to say that the embassy had worked out how we could get to where we needed to go, which was to fly back to Jakarta on a commercial flight almost immediately, and take a chartered Twin Otter (a small twin-propeller bush plane) north. The distances were long and we could expect, I explained, to land at about four in the morning. The gloom set in quite heavily, and Shortliffe ordered a last scotch. Then the waiter returned with another telex, which said "April Fools: The Phantom Strikes Again". Lorne Heuckroth and I had set up the whole charade, complete with fraudulent government telexes, with support from Mickey Jeffrey and our communicator Bob Cullen in Jakarta. Dupuy, having watched Shortliffe try to contain his shock, anger and disappointment when reading the telegram, found it very funny which helped Shortliffe to gradually come down from a mountain of fury, promising to ensure that my next assignment would be in Detroit (a much more terrifying and career-destroying threat in those days to a young foreign service officer than the worst war-torn third world hell-hole). A footnote to our trip was that Dupuy asked Shortliffe to return to Canada as Vice-President of Policy in CIDA, which Glenn accepted, leaving Indonesia less than two years after he had arrived.

Liani

The story of my time in Indonesia would not be complete without some greater explanation of how it transpired that Liani and I ended up together. I had dated a number of young women during my time in Jakarta, a Canadian aid worker who accompanied me to Bali with my parents, a Dutch lady who turned out to be already married (this I discovered when I went to pick her up for a date at the Hotel Indonesia, only to meet her irate husband who had just arrived from their home in Surabaja), and a number of others. When Liani was going out with my good friend Pierre, she even tried to set me up with friends of hers, and I remember one very lovely girl named Mimi, who came sailing with us, and who was charming and beautiful but a bit timid and not very international. Liani and I saw a lot of each other over my last year in Jakarta, and by the time of our great mountain climbing expedition, I was very much captivated. It was shortly after that that I realized that my feelings were not entirely unreciprocated, and then began a very intense several months. We spent time at the Puncak, went back to Carita Beach (having borrowed and smashed up Peter Oldham's car, mine having been already sold in preparation for my imminent departure), ate at delightful little restaurants around Jakarta, and worked on setting up her new apartment. I tried to get Ottawa to agree to allow me to stay another year, but extensions were rare and I had begun this effort too late and so I had no choice except to leave in mid-summer. By that time, we had grown very close, and we agreed to write regularly and try to meet before the year ended in Canada.

CHAPTER 5

BACK TO THE MOTHER HOUSE

• • • • • • • • • • • •

Some weeks before I left Jakarta I began to think that I should explore an alternative career, not so much because I hadn't enjoyed my first posting but more because I found what my banking friends Toby Price and Paul Skerman were doing was pretty interesting. Furthermore, I knew that the Foreign Service could throw a lot of rocks in one's path and movement up the system was normally slow and unpredictable. I also had really enjoyed my time in Southeast Asia and wanted to think through whether staying in the Foreign Service, with no certainty of being able to return regularly to Asia, or moving to a banking career in Asia, would over the long term be a more satisfying path. As Liani was now working in the TD bank and enjoying it, I have to admit that thoughts of being together in Asia also factored into my thinking. So I got in touch with both the Bank of Montreal and the Toronto Dominion Bank through Toby and Paul, and wrote to the manager of the HSBC that I had met en route to Jakarta before my posting began. TD and HSBC both invited me to come to Hong Kong for interviews, and the Bank of Montreal told me that they would be in touch with me when I was back in Canada.

The TD interview with two mid-level investment bankers was very friendly and they said that with my background they would welcome me as part of their HK team, but I would still have to apply through their normal recruitment process in Canada and do the normal training in Toronto. The HSBC interview was very serious, and the fellow I met seemed quite positive about my chances, but he made it clear that all bankers in HSBC had to start in commercial banking and serve for a period at the branch level, and that a move into investment banking would by no means be certain. So I just parked what I had learned in the back of my head as worth pondering in the months to come, and headed back to Canada by a rather indirect route.

For years I had wished to visit the Soviet Union to see what it was really like. I had studied a bit of Russian history and read Russian novels, had taken a course in East-West Relations at McGill and spent a very boring few months in the Defence Relations Division before my Jakarta posting, but I still could not imagine the place. How could more than two hundred million people live there and be as oppressed and mindless and backward as we were led to believe? My friends Jim and Donna Wright were there half-way through their first posting, having gone on Russian language training for a year after our first year together in Ottawa, and they had invited me to come to Moscow on my way home. I picked up an Aeroflot flight out of Bangkok, stopped in Tashkent for a day and then flew into Moscow for a ten-day visit.

Moscow was fascinating, and not at all grim in the summer. Jim and Donna were lovely hosts and took me around in the evenings and on the weekend, and gave me ideas of where to wander during their working days. I rode the subway, took local buses and tried to get a sense of the place. I had learned a few words and phrases in Russian, and studied the Cyrillic alphabet to be able to read signs, and so managed to find my way around. I went up to the Lenin Hills where the University of Moscow and various other Soviet institutes of higher learning were located and walked among students dressed differently than their western counterparts, but behaving much the same, kicking soccer balls or sitting in the parks or walking hand-in-hand. Jim and Donna took me out into the countryside where we visited a beautiful old cemetery where many famous Russians were buried, and one evening to a cute little restaurant on the Arbat, which had an extensive and very impressive menu. When we tried to order, however, our waiter (whose cooperation could apparently only be obtained if we buttered him up by asking where he was a student, since being in a lowly service job was considered humiliating) told us that there only beef, potatoes, tomatoes and cucumbers were available, so we could have them done up one way for our appetizer and one way for our main course. We did.

My visit coincided with the Moscow Universiade, the global university-level sporting competition, held one year before the Olympic Games. While the Moscow Olympics in 1980 were to be marred by a western boycott in reaction to the Soviet invasion of Afghanistan, in 1979 all the Olympic venues were ready and student athletes from around the world were descending on the city. Jim had the official responsibility to look after Canadian participation and athletes, and I went with him and Donna to the opening ceremony, which was very grand even if it was thick with Soviet propaganda. At the opening ceremony, the students in the stands across from the press box displayed cards which, when held over their heads, said "No Neutron Bomb", which was the then rumoured weapon of the Americans that would leap them distantly forward of the USSR in the arms race.

In the end I left Moscow with an image of a poor place with a people simply trying to get along with their lives. Men laughed in the pubs, grandmothers delighted in the bubbling life of grandchildren in the parks, everyone followed sports. And, although it seems a silly conclusion to have reached, I found the people more Russian than Soviet or communist. The durability of cultural origins was a theme that was to return to me later in my professional life, in both Prague and Beijing.

From Moscow I went to Paris and saw some of my old Paris friends for a few days. I spent a night with François Bancilhon and two of his little daughters, and we visited Chantal and days-old newborn daughter number three at a nearby clinic. François and I went for a long run in the western hills; he had just stopped smoking and was taking up running seriously. I felt I could run forever in the cooler climate of the northern hemisphere after my tropical training.

Then it was across the Atlantic and back to Canada to take up new responsibilities in External Affairs headquarters, commonly referred to in the Service as the Mother House. I had pretty well used up all my vacation time so could not spend the weeks in Jamestown I would have liked, but I did manage to get a long weekend there en route to Ottawa, and several more weekends before the autumn cold set in. It was then that I told my parents that Liani and I had fallen in love and that we were thinking of getting married. They had met Liani during their visit to Indonesia and both liked her, but they had not seen her as a future daughter-in-law, and I did not know how they would react to an inter-racial marriage. I told my mother first since I wanted her as an ally with my father, unquestionably the more conservative of the two. In the end they both seemed thrilled and were pleased that I had invited her for Christmas.

After bunking with Gary and Joanne Soroka for a week at their home near the Rideau Canal, I found a nice little two-bedroom apartment or Rue Marguerite, a working-class neighbourhood east of the Rideau River and the west of the Vanier Parkway. I bought a brand new car, a bright red Pontiac Phoenix, a GM "K" car, which the dealer promised was the latest and greatest vehicle and which would never need rustproofing. When we sold it five years later in 1984, it had rusted so badly that we could see through to the road on the front passenger's side, and in order to get a safety certificate we had to have aluminum sheets welded to the floor. My shipment from Indonesia arrived, my sparse furniture was taken out of long-term storage and I settled back into Ottawa and the life of a junior public servant. I threw myself into my new responsibilities with energy and enthusiasm, and outside of work did little else other than write letters to Liani, literally half a world away, and run between five and eight miles every morning. Long distance telephone calls were very expensive, and Liani did not have a telephone in her flat. When I did call, I would have to dial the number of the owner of her house on Jusuf Adinawata, which would waste expensive minutes until Liani got to the phone. We thus spoke only about once a month, but we wrote to each other almost every day. She agreed to to arrange her annual vacation at Christmas and come to North America.

When Liani came in December, she flew across Europe to Montreal and landed at Mirabel, the large international airport built well north of the city on the multiple assumptions that Montreal would not be dragged into relative decline by its dalliance with separatism, that high speed rail links would be built to downtown terminals in both Montreal and Ottawa, and that technological advances would not permit larger aircraft to land and take off with greater frequency and manageable noise at airports in built-up areas. I drove to Mirabel from Ottawa and arrived very early, and was pretty tight inside. I hadn't seen Liani in almost six months and was not sure whether any of this was going to work. What would we do over the following three weeks if it turned out we did not really have such deep feelings for each other? When I saw her coming through the arrivals door, however, I think that all these thoughts were washed aside.

Liani spent a week with me in Ottawa as I was still working, and being Liani, she spent the time not only walking around but sewing curtains for my little apartment and rearranging things to make it a much nicer home. We then drove down to Maine and stayed with Joy and Chip for a couple of days, drove through Jamestown so Liani could see a place that was clearly an important part of my life, and we walked on the beach and at Beavertail and visited "Mist", our old family home then closed-up for the winter. (I wonder what we would have thought at that time if a little voice had approached us to tell us that a third of a century later we would be renovating our own home just a few hundred meters away for our four children and another new generation just beginning!) Then it was on to Wilton, Connecticut, where we spent Christmas with my parents and Hugh. My parents bought us tickets to see the Messiah performed at Carnegie Hall in New York, where we also spent a day with Karl and Theresa Sweger and their children, a Swedish family with whom Liani had worked and traveled as an au-paire when she first moved to Europe in 1973. Karl was in the Swedish Foreign Service and was sent to Geneva after Jakarta, and ended up in 1979 being reassigned to the Swedish mission in New York.

Liani seemed to have a wonderful time in Wilton over Christmas, sharing in the cooking and in all our old traditions, meeting my parents' friends, walking the dogs in the woods, and being part of the family.

On the way back to Canada, it seemed to me that the world was unfolding as it should, and when I asked Liani to marry me she said that if she could stand me during a Canadian winter at minus twenty degrees, she figured she could probably put up with me during the summers as well. And so we began planning her permanent move to join me in the spring, which of course entailed not only being apart for a few more months but all the bureaucratic formality of sponsoring her immigration. Parting at Mirabel was tough, but we were both happy that things had gone so well and that our whirlwind romance of the year before had grown deeper and apparently durable roots. So we said good-bye for a time and I went back to work.

Earlier in the autumn I had completed my dalliance with departure from the Foreign Service in an exchange of meetings and letters with the Bank of Montreal. In September I took a day off for unstated personal reasons and went to Toronto for an interview, during which we talked a lot about Asia and political stability and shifting economic balances and my experience in Indonesia. Two weeks later I received a letter from the bank's personnel department offering me a position heading up a risk analysis team focused on Latin America, about which I knew absolutely nothing. Nor did I speak Spanish or Portuguese. Thinking that this was an error of the personnel people and that the bank had really intended to offer me a position focused on Asia, I called up the fellow who had interviewed me and told him of the amusing mistake. He told me that there was in fact no mistake, and that he and others who met me felt that I had the requisite economic and analytical skills to deal with any part of the world, and that I would learn quickly about Latin America, where the bank felt its greatest medium term vulnerabilities lay. I was flabbergasted that my Asian knowledge and experience seemed to be largely irrelevant, and after a few days called back to decline the offer. Had it been an Asia-focused position I might have been more tempted to accept it, but in reality I was beginning to settle into a substantive position in External and probably would have declined in any case. Sometime in the following year a periodic Latin American sovereign debt crisis occurred, and the Bank of Montreal and other Canadian banks were heavily impacted, resulting in them pulling substantially back from exposure to the region. I learned from Toby Price that the unit I was to have headed was wound up and its members looking for new jobs. Good choice, Howard.

As the focus and substance of my work over the three years between the summer of 1979 and the summer of 1982 was to have some consistent themes, before I describe them let me stay on the story of my personal life at least through the summer of 1980.

The winter went by quickly, I completed all the formal requirements to sponsor Liani to immigrate to Canada as my fiancée, and she arrived on May 13th, a Friday. Some believe that Friday the 13th is a bad luck day, but my mother Maisie was born in 1920 on Friday the 13th of January, so for our family any Friday the 13th has always been a good-luck day. We had already decided to try to find a better place to live than Rue Marguerite, and so almost as soon as she touched down we started looking for a home. Our budget was quite tight but we really wanted a free standing home if we could find one, and we did not want to be out in the suburbs. We looked around the area where our apartment was located, and across the Rideau River in Sandy Hill as well as in New Edinburgh. It did not take us too long to find a little house on Wayling Avenue with a little garden in the Kingsview Park area of Vanier, a block from the river. Vanier was then a separate primarily working-class and francophone municipality, surrounded on all sides by Ottawa, and Wayling Avenue was in the nicest part of the town created as a cul-de-sac when the Vanier Parkway was built, making the area accessible only from Montreal Road. It was a cute little home of about 1200 square feet, completely square, with a very small one-car garage alongside. However small, it was perfect for us and we were to have lots of fun with Cynthia and Caleb when they arrived, expanding it once before we left for Prague in 1984.

We bought the Wayling Avenue house from an old couple, Monsieur et Madame Béland, who had been the owners since the war. It was designed in the 1930s by the Dominion Housing Authority, precursor to CMHC, as part of a federal effort to get housing construction going, and the Bélands still had the original plans, which told a builder how to build the house in whatever building material might be available, from concrete block to solid brick to wood. Ours was built in concrete block, and although there was no fireplace visible in the house, the plans showed one in the logical place in the centre of the living room wall. Furthermore, there was a chimney with two flues, and when I inspected it from the roof it was evident from the soot that both flues had been used, one presumably for the furnace and one for the fireplace.

We moved into the house quickly, taking it over on June 1st, and spent all our spare time painting and refinishing things ourselves. Every room needed repainting, the kitchen needed modernizing and we turned an unfounded porch in the back into a little eating area. As we very much wanted a fireplace, as soon as we owned the house I took a pick to the wall in question and started chopping away everything that wasn't a fireplace. I pretty soon hit the brick of the chimney and gradually cleared away all the plaster and finally discovered only a very small opening, bricked in on all sides, with an old wire extruding from the side. We discovered that the original owners of the house had installed an "electric fire" on the main floor, just an early form of the convex reflecting heaters common until the 1970s, and had put a real fireplace in the basement, where we did not want it. So that began the biggest project I was to undertake. As Liani continued with the sanding and painting, I hollowed out the chimney, closed off the basement fireplace, reinforced the floor of the living room with reinforced concrete and built a new fireplace, complete with a proper smoke-trap. And aside a small house fire that it caused during a visit of Joy and Chip the following year through compressing old wiring together, it was a great fireplace and we spent many long cold winter evenings in its physical and psychological aura of warmth. During the time when we were working on the house, Liani and I would finish very late in the evenings, and end our long days by swimming in the old quarry pond which had been renamed MacKay Lake in Rockcliffe. To this day it is one of our favourite swimming places, on all but one side now surrounded by homes while then it was completely in the woods.

As we were settling down in Ottawa we also began planning our wedding for later in the summer. We did not want a large or commercial affair and decided to have it in Jamestown at the end of August. In the end it was a very special low-key wedding, just perfect for us.

To our wedding we invited close Jamestown friends and a few from Canada: Glenn and Sylvia Shortliffe, Toby and Eliane Price, my old college mate Peter Jacobsen and his girlfriend of the day. We rented Brushwood from the Chews, which lies between the old family home of "Mist" and "Green Chimneys", the new family home of our own we were to acquire a third of a century later, with the land sister Pat was to buy and build "Spyglass" on in between. Our bridal dinner was a barbeque picnic at Green's Pier with everyone in shorts and relaxed summer attire. The wedding itself was in the chapel at St. Matthews Episcopal Church on Narragansett Avenue and the music was provided by the local organist and a flutist who taught music at URI in Kingston. Liani wore a beautiful but simple white silk dress, which she made herself, and I wore a white silk Chinese-style shirt that she also made. My sister Joy served as Liani's maid-of-honour and wore a multi-colour hippy-style skirt, and my ten-year old nephew and godson Geoffrey served as ring-boy. After the ceremony we went back to Mist for our wedding reception, where all the food and even the wedding cake was homemade by Maisie, Joy and Liani herself. The next day we invited all who were still around to a picnic at Beavertail. Even after all these years I cannot imagine a more perfect wedding.

But back to the working side of my life . . .

CHAPTER 6

TRANSPORTATION POLICY AND ECONOMIC NEGOTIATIONS

• • • • • • • • • • •

As I had hoped, on my return from Jakarta I had been assigned to one of the several economic divisions in External Affairs. The Science, Environment and Transportation Policy Division carried the departmental acronym of EST and was further subdivided into three sections implied in its title. I was in the last of these three and the junior man in a totem pole of three, with Ingrid Hall and Jean-Pierre Gombay both older and senior to me. Our collective responsibility was to support Canada's Chief Air Negotiator and manage all of Canada's involvement in international civil aviation and maritime transportation issues. These latter roles meant that we managed Canada's relations with the US on matters relating to the Great Lakes and the St. Lawrence Seaway as well as our participation in The International Civil Aviation Organization (ICAO) and the International Maritime Organization (IMCO, later to become IMO). In everything we did we had to work closely with Transport Canada and other domestic departments responsible for the management of domestic policies and programs related to the issues we dealt with at the international level, and I was soon to learn that interdepartmental negotiations and relations were every bit as challenging as international negotiations and relations.

Our Divisional Director was Peter Walker, an experienced officer who was later to become Ambassador to Austria and High Commissioner to India. Ingrid Hall, our Deputy Director and my initial boss, was an economist and sister to the very talented Olympic sailor Peter Hall with whom I had sailed from time to time at regattas and at the Olympic trials in 1972. Ingrid was smart and tough, but fair and patient and always willing to spend a little extra time explaining issues that were arcane and complicated. She was married and was at that time just back from maternity leave, happy to have a pair of hands to take over files and reduce the pressure on her. She was to leave the division less than a year after I joined, and went on to a very good career, serving in Indonesia as Ambassador in the 1990s when I was running the Asia branch, and retiring after serving as our Ambassador to Austria and Chair of the International Atomic Energy Agency Board of Governors. Jean-Pierre Gombay had immigrated as a youth to Canada from France with his family, studied at the elite College Brébeuf in Montreal and the Université de Montréal, and was cartesian and a little bombastic. He was one of those mid-level officers who pretentiously smoked a pipe and tried to push junior officers around. He was also the most disorganized officer I think I ever came across during my career, his office being a complete shambles of documents piled hither and thither in three-foot tall stacks. Although he claimed he always knew where anything was, he could never find a critical document when we needed it, and I learned to never let him have the original copy of anything. He disappeared to an economic job in Washington at some point during my tenure in the division, and once I received my first promotion to FS2, I became the senior officer of the section as new juniors arrived. But I am getting a little ahead of myself.

As the junior member of the transportation group, I was charged with the maritime transport files, considered less sexy than the air negotiations since Canada's merchant marine industry was small and the international negotiations rather slow arcane processes. I actually enjoyed the IMCO work, however, both because the issues realting to maritime safety and environmental protection interested me and because it allowed me to go with reasonably frequency to London where IMCO was headquartered. Furthermore, the IMCO general assembly was chaired at that time by Canadian Bill O'Neil, then Commissioner of the Canadian Coast Guard and former head of the St. Lawrence Seaway. Bill, while a good bit older than I, was a delight to work with.

Issues at IMCO that preoccupied us in those days were divided between substantive issues of maritime safety and environment on one hand, and Canada's role as an IMO Council member and leading player in the organization on the other. Environmental matters were still preoccupied with tightening regulations on shipbuilding following the disastrous grounding of the large Liberian-flagged crude carrier, Amoco Cadiz, off the coast of Brittany in 1978. The major impact of that disaster, which saw more than a million and a half barrels of crude oil disgorged onto the northwestern French shoreline, was a strengthening of navigational requirements for large commodity carriers, and a codified requirement that all vessels carrying crude oil would after a relatively short period have to be built with a "double hull", such that a piercing of the outer skin of a vessel would not also result in a rupturing of the vessel's large crude-containing tanks. As it turned out, negotiations on the substantive issues seemed easy for me, because our objectives were clear and I found many sympathetic ears among all but the most intransigent flag-country delegations.

Our delegations to IMCO meetings always had only a single External officer on them and that was me, and I was expected to strategize and implement all the negotiations with other delegations and on the assembly floor, based of course on positions crafted by the technical members of the delegation. During my first autumn we had the biannual IMCO assembly meeting and Canada was up for re-election to the governing Council which met four or five times a year in regular session and occasionally in emergency session, rather like the UN. Prior to the assembly we sent out telegrams to overseas embassies instructing them to lobby on behalf of Canada's re-election, which they all dutifully did, reporting back on promises of support, some truthful and some not, and a more standard reply suggesting that respective delegations meet during the assembly to finalize arrangements of mutual interest. This meant lots of horse-trading at the London sessions, either direct vote trading or trading votes for support on positions of substance; the Japanese, for example, would try to persuade us to soften our anti-whaling position. We were successful in getting Canada re-elected to the IMCO Council both years that I was involved, and as a result I would also go to London for most Council meetings in support of Bill O'Neil, who remained our representative for many years beyond my involvement. When he later approached retirement age as a Canadian public servant, he ran in the IMCO election to become its Secretary General. With very wide support among all types of countries, he was elected, moved to London for a very happy final chapter to his professional career.

One of the best things about being the External Affairs officer responsible for IMCO was that it took me to London on a fairly regular basis. IMCO at that time was in Piccadilly in an old building which now serves as the Japanese Embassy, directly across from Green Park. While sometimes I would stay in a nearby hotel, whenever the visit was long enough to permit it (and a working week of meetings was) I adopted the practice of renting a short-term furnished flat somewhere in the South Kensington area. This allowed me to live a little more independently during my stay. I still had a few friends there from my time at NIESR in 1971, and I had some friends serving at the High Commission. I would also have dinner almost every visit with Prunella and Chris Scarlett, assuming Pru was not off someplace exotic in her role as Director of the Commonwealth Society. I had always gotten on well with Pru, and seen a lot of her when in London in 1971, and then more of both her and Chris when I was living in Paris. Our friendship was of course strengthened by Pat and Tim's marriage, shortly after which Pru and I decided that we should introduce ourselves to other as brother and sister-out-law, since having our respective brother and sister married did not quite make us in-laws. Pru and I had many similar intellectual interests in Asia and Africa and third world development, and Chris had become a great fan of Indonesian art and architecture and was involved in a variety of architectural projects blending east and west. I would generally invite myself over to their cute little multiple-story Markham Street rowhouse, and we would talk long into the night over many bottles of good wine.

The most interesting policy issue facing the country in the maritime transport area at that time was whether or not Canada would change its long-standing open approach to the use of foreign-built and foreign-flagged vessels. Just before my departure from Indonesia, thirty-nine year-old Joe Clark and the Progressive Conservative Party had narrowly defeated the Liberals in the May 1979 federal election and formed a minority government, having won more seats than the Liberals but not enough for a majority. In their election campaign the PCs had promised many policy changes after 16 years of Liberal rule. One policy that the PCs had promised to review was Canada's shipping and shipbuilding policies. At the end of World War II, Canada's merchant marine had been the third largest in the world, but it had shrunk to almost nothing with the emergence of flags of convenience. Canadian flagged vessels had to hire Canadian crews and pay Canadian labour rates, and except for shipping in the Great Lakes, which required Canadian-flagged but not necessarily Canadian-built vessels, there were no restrictions on the use of foreign-built and foreign-flagged ships to or between Canadian ports (unlike in the US, where the Jones Act makes it impossible for a foreign-built or foreign-flagged vessel to carry freight between two US ports). The shipbuilding and shipping industries in Canada were strong supporters of legislative change and encouraged the Conservative government to follow-through on its election promise. Not that I mattered a hoot, but I was a strong proponent of the proposed change in hopes that it would revive Canada's proud merchant marine tradition. Don Mazankowski was the Minister of Transport in the Joe Clark government, and he was invited to a seminar and reception hosted at a hotel in Hull on a snowy February afternoon in 1980 on the future of Canada's shipbuilding industry, hosted and organized by the industry. There were about thirty industry representatives and about the same number of civil servants and parliamentarians. Mazankowski was scheduled to make some remarks at the reception and everyone was eagerly anticipating that he would be outlining a major and more supportive policy shift. Just as he was about to speak, there was a flurry of activity around the Minister, and he and all the Members of Parliament rushed away without saying anything. As we all stood around wondering what happened, the word spread that there was a vote of confidence in the House of Commons and that there were somehow not enough conservative members on duty to defeat it. Well, in spite of rallying all the members present in the Ottawa area, the PCs lost the vote, the government fell, Trudeau came back from a brief retirement to lead the Liberals back to power, and that was the end of a new maritime transport policy.

Shortly after the fall of the Clark government there was a scheduled IMCO Council meeting in London, and Liani came with me and we stayed in my brother Hugh's flat and went to the theatre and generally enjoyed London. We also went sailing in the Solent with Hugh and Paul and Theresa Monk, co-owners of Hugh's boat, Duellist II. Hugh's girlfriend of the moment was a beautiful English red-head, whose temper was as hot as her red hair, and who was soon to pass into history and be replaced by a lovely young investment banker, Susan Vorhiss, who I met on my next trip to London and who was to become our sister-in-law and mother to all of Hugh's children. The last time we were to sail with Hugh and Susan and Paul and Theresa Monk was thirty-one years later in the New York Yacht Club's annual cruise in the summer of 2011.

Air Negotiations

International civil air relations in the late 1970s were still firmly stuck in the mercantilist era. They were and are still all about the trading of economic interests in one particular sector of global trade ungoverned by the GATT (the General Agreement on Tariffs and Trade, the WTO's predecessor). So instead of being generally open under the governing principles of a multilateral regime to which all countries subscribe, the right to have a country's airlines operate scheduled flights to carry passengers to and from another country, and in some cases beyond that country, depends entirely on what were known as "Air Agreements" between those two countries. When I took up my position in EST in 1979, Canada had something like 75 bilateral Air Agreements. And they were all structured on the theory that because there would be a relatively finite number of people travelling between Canada and France, for example, every passenger travelling on a Canadian carrier would not be travelling on a French carrier, and vice versa. The result of this 'zero-sum" presumption underlying civil aviation, the bilateral agreements established which city pairs could be served, how often carriers could fly, and what fares could be charged. Before Air Canada could start a new service between Toronto and Las Vegas, for example, the US State Department would have to agree to an amendment to the route list annexed to the bilateral civil aviation agreement, and Air Canada would have to file a route application, detailing frequencies and fares, with the aeronautical authorities of both countries (the FAA in the US and the Canadian Transport Commission or CTC in Canada) awaiting approval from both agencies before initiating the proposed services.

When I began working on transportation issues, Ambassador Ralph Collins was our Chief Air Negotiator, a position generally reserved for a senior diplomat with substantial experience and a certain amount of gravitas, needed not just to deal with foreign counterparts but also with the powerful lobbyists from the airline industry. Ralph was in his sixties and not well at this stage, having smoked very heavily throughout his life and now suffering serious arterial issues. I did not have a chance to support him on any active negotiations before he left at the end of the year as Ingrid Hall was his primary assistant. Furthermore his general approach to requests by other countries for negotiations on either amendments to existing agreements or for new agreements entirely, was simply to defer or deflect the proposed talks. The word in the bureau was that Collins' favourite word was "no", no to new rights, no to new talks, no to even meetings with foreign embassy representatives pushing talks. But I did have a chance to talk to him about his career, which was very interesting. Collins was a mandarin speaker and had had served in Beijing and he encouraged me to rekindle my interest in Asia. He told me that the most fulfilling Foreign Service careers were built around getting to know one part of the world really well. I listened carefully, but did not then imagine that I would end up taking his advice and spend more than a third of my working life in China.

On civil aviation files, most of the autumn of 1979 was spent learning from Ingrid and doing economic analyses of the value of various routes and rights that would be negotiated with other countries. The interdepartmental group involved in air negotiations was an interesting group of older professionals with whom I got on very well. Transport Canada was in those days divided into three almost separate entities named the Air, Maritime and Surface Administrations. The Air Administration was led by the "Air Transport Administrator", Walter McLeish, an elderly official who had worked his way up the ranks over the prior thirty years to become a very powerful bureaucrat. The Chief Air Negotiator was formally the joint appointment of the Minister of Transport and the Secretary of State for External Affairs on the recommendation of the Air Transport Administrator. As a general rule, McLeish would not get involved in any except the highest profile negotiations (like those with the US), but it was he who the CEOs of the airlines would call if they felt the Chief Air Negotiator was not listening sufficiently to their views. The international group at Transport Canada under McLeish was led by Ray Yang, who had moved to Canada from Taiwan twenty-five years earlier. Formerly a pilot in the Republic of China's Air Force, Ray had flown the last of the Nationalist controlled squadrons down the gorges of the Yangtze River from Chongqing all the way to Taiwan in late 1949 as the Nationalist forces escaped the communists and fled the mainland. Ray was a delightful man and told wonderful stories of his time with the Guomingdang. Bill Gerwin and Joe Ledbetter were the other two members of the Transport Canada team, both middle-aged experts who had been involved in air negotiations for more than ten years. They knew all the files and were tremendously kind to me in helping me learn my way around. I respected them a lot and did not adopt what I was to learn was a common attribute of External types, that we were generally smarter and more worldly than our colleagues in domestic departments. As time went by, especially after travelling together to far-off places, we all became good friends. Bill, a tall and completely bald former Air Force

Transport Squadron pilot, invited Liani and I to dinner with him and his wife at their modest home in the western part of Ottawa, and recounted great stories both of flying in the Far North and of earlier civil aviation negotiations. With Joe Ledbetter we were to become particularly close. Joe was originally from Kentucky and had served in the US Air Force at the end of World War II and in Korea, and had immigrated to Canada after falling in love with a woman from Ottawa with whom he had two children. His wife was an artist and after their children had grown she divorced Joe and went off to do her own thing. Joe remained at Transport Canada several years after I had moved on from the transportation job and then retired, but we stayed in touch and he became "Uncle Joe" to our children. He bought a farming property in Prince Edward County on Picton Island in Lake Ontario and grew walnut trees. He had a little catamaran there, which was great fun to sail, and tractors and all sorts of farming machinery, on which our children loved to play. The last time we stayed with him our twins were five years old, fifteen years after Joe and I had started to work together. Joe loved the peacefulness of his walnut farm and of the changing seasons of Prince Edward County, and he died there just a few years ago.

The third leg of the interdepartmental team was the CTC, which regulated all air transport issues, from safety to fares and frequencies. In retrospect, having CTC part of the negotiating team may have been bad public policy, since regulators should in principle have no interest in policy making or in determining how to balance the interests of consumers and industry, but they were part of the team. The person mostly involved in the actual negotiations was another "Joe", Joseph Gertzler, a Viennese who had fled to Canada at the time of the Anschluss, Hitler's takeover of Austria. Like Joe Ledbetter, Gertzler was a fierce anti-communist and hated any accommodation we entered into with Aeroflot or other Eastern European carrier. Any and every fare, whether part of a regular seasonal fare structure, an advance booking or promotional fare, and even the fares offered by the charter companies, had to be specifically approved by the CTC as part of its regulatory mandate. CTC worked with Statistics

Canada to gather all the statistics necessary to understand the market, and knew, for example, not just how many passengers travelled between Toronto and London, but where their ultimate origin and destination were, perhaps justifying a direct route between Calgary and London or between Toronto and Manchester. They also tracked the purpose of travel, whether business, tourism or family reunification. To analyze this vast data, they had a substantial analytical capacity and ran models to determine the likely impact both on the market and on carriers of any route or fare proposal. In preparing for negotiations, and in reacting to proposals from other countries, CTC would take charge of the modeling, which was a crucial part of our knowledge base and gave us an advantage in negotiations over almost all other countries, except perhaps the US, whose Department of Transportation also had built quite complex models to support their negotiations with both their own carriers and foreign governments. At one point when the Soviet Union proposed an increase in frequencies for Aeroflot's Moscow to Montreal service, we ran the CTC model and discovered that an Ilyushin 62 (the old Soviet airliner with four engines attached to the rear fuselage, copied inexactly from the British Vickers VC-10) needed to have a load factor of 120% to break even at the fares Aeroflot was offering!

Managing our air relations with the Soviet Union and other east-block countries was complicated by the fact that, following the Soviet invasion of Afghanistan, the US had suspended Aeroflot rights to serve New York, so Montreal and Gander became the only points they could serve in continental North America. Gander was also a necessary stop on all flights between Moscow and Havana or other cities in Latin America, since no Soviet plane of the day had the range to fly all the way, and both scheduled passenger flights and occasional all-cargo flights would have to stop and refuel. Not surprisingly, our intelligence community was very interested in who and what was travelling from and to Moscow, and there were many refueling or maintenance staff in Gander, and at Mirabel, who had somewhat more shadowy tasks to perform than their surface employment suggested. A further problem at both Gander and Mirabel was that during the stopovers of Aeroflot, LOT and other Soviet-bloc carriers, passengers not scheduled for Canadian disembarkation would get off the planes and refuse to re-board, declaring themselves political refugees and asking for asylum. Sometimes these airlines would park their planes far from the terminal and refuel without allowing passengers off, but even then we had a few cases of passengers who would open emergency doors and jump out, generally breaking legs or ankles in the process. Aeroflot also had to pick up and drop off passengers in Gander because the Soviet fishing fleet used St. John's for repair and replenishment and for rotational crew changes. Soviet research vessels also called at East coast ports and all of this maritime traffic was under our management. A specific visit authority had to be granted diplomatically for research vessels, while the use of Canadian ports by the Soviet fishing fleet was governed by a bilateral agreement. This work was very "intelligence" rich, for our intelligence community would try to glean whatever they could from not only the continuous trickle of defectors that came off Soviet vessels, but they would also run operations targeting both ships and planes, and as a matter of course I would consult with an appropriate contact in our intelligence division before granting permission for a vessel or plane to use Canadian ports or airports. After the Soviet invasion of Afghanistan we imposed some restrictive measures on Soviet vessels, and this meant more interchange with the local Soviet Embassy, not less, and at one point I went to Moscow to try to iron out some irritations in all of these understandings.

As was customary in those days, any visit behind the Iron Curtain would be preceded and followed by sessions in the basement with one of our intelligence divisions. Before I went to Moscow to discuss transportation issues, I had a briefing with Major MacKay, an old Scot who had spent his entire life in the world of the shadows, and was at the tail end of his working life and in charge of counter-intelligence briefings. All of the junior officers loved his stories, and we would try to turn him from giving us the standard briefings to recounting his experiences. On this occasion, knowing that I was going to Moscow and would be staying at the Mezdanarodnaya Hotel, Major MacKay warned me against sexual entrapment. He told me in his heavy Scottish brogue that in the past officers had been approached in their rooms late at night by extraordinarily beautiful women and that I should have no doubt for whom they were really working. I took all this with good humour, and subsequently at lunch in the departmental cafeteria regaled my colleagues with an imitation of his warning, using my best Scottish accent. And then I headed off to Moscow.

The Mezdanarodnaya Hotel was a relatively modern hotel down at the edge of the river, with a giant and ugly brass rooster in the centre of the lobby that would crow out the hours, and a bar that was always full of pretty young women, who clearly were out-of-bounds for us. On my second night in the hotel, just after I had fallen asleep, I received a knock on the door. When I opened it there was a beautiful blond girl, clad only in a flimsy nightie and holding a light bulb. "I am Swedish and staying in the room next door" she said in a lilting and very convincing Swedish accent, "and I need some help in changing my light bulb". I looked at this gorgeous woman, tried and failed to suppress a memory of Major MacKay's warning, and wondered for a moment whether I really cared about a career in the Foreign Service! Sighing inside, I mumbled a ridiculous excuse about not being able to help due to a sore leg and closed the door.

The other special file I managed in those days was the establishment of what was a virtual airline bringing Vietnamese "boat people" to Canada from the camps in Southeast Asia and Hong Kong. After the fall of Saigon in April of 1975, large numbers of South Vietnamese had fled their country in small boats and made their way to Thailand and Malaysia and other countries. Some also made thrie way to Hong Kong although in much smaller numbers. Throughout the region these refugees were put into camps managed by the United Nations High Commission for Refugees, and Canada, the US and Australia agreed to resettle most of them. After they were interviewed and selected and processed by teams of immigration officials, getting them to Canada was done by charter aircraft, leased by the government from commercial carriers WardAir, Ontario Worldair and CPAir. At the height of this movement we were flying at least one flight a day. I was put in charge of making sure all the service rights were obtained from the countries where the camps were located and over-flight rights obtained from the countries in between the camps and Canada. I was also part of a three-person team that negotiated with the carriers. This was very satisfying work, because we all felt we were part of a truly humanitarian exercise, and my own little achievement in improving the efficiency and reducing the cost of the airlift was successfully negotiating over-flight rights from Vietnam itself, initially vehemently opposed to western resettlement of the "traitors" who had fled communist liberation.

Ralph Collins retired late in 1979, and was replaced early in the new year by the very senior Harry Jay, who had returned from a four-year assignment as Ambassador in Geneva. Jay was an old multilateral negotiator, skilled in the art of finding words to paper over differences and to bring the conflicting views of many different parties to some sort of compromise. In a multilateral forum, lengthy eloquence frequently trumps substance. These are not skills useful in bilateral economic negotiations, which while not always zero-sum generally involve the divvying up of limited economic rights and benefits. Harry Jay was a very nice man but a hopeless economic negotiator. Ingrid Hall spent the first few months of Jay's tenure as his principal assistant before heading off on another assignment and leaving that role to me. We were at the time embarked in three tiers of negotiations: a complex series of negotiations with a number of countries in an effort to obtain round-the-world rights for Canadian carriers; a number of more limited negotiations with Caribbean and European countries seeking greater access to the Canadian market; and a fundamental renegotiation of the transborder agreements with the United States. Although the three sets of negotiations were intertwined in terms of timing, with months between rounds with the Europeans being filled with talks with India or Trinidad, and the very political talks with the US being held frequently, in this story I will deal with them one by one.

Canada's overall international aviation policy of the late 1970s was the result of a Cabinet decision in the middle of the decade which made Air Canada, still a Crown Corporation, Canada's designated carrier for all transatlantic, Caribbean and eastern US services. CPAir was our designated carrier for transpacific, South American and west coast US routes. The competition between the two was intense, reinforced by both east-west and private-government divides and suspicions. The "Division of the World" policy, as it was known, was coming apart with the desire of the two carriers to serve long-haul routes from eastern Canada to the western US and from Vancouver and Calgary to major cities in the American east. Compounding this was a plan Air Canada had for an around-the-world service, initially with an all-cargo service using its old fleet of DC-8 freighters and then with more modern "Combo" 747s which carried passengers in the forward 60% of the aircraft and all cargo in the rear. CPAir bitterly opposed the extension of Air Canada's route rights across Europe and down to India and Singapore and then up to Hong Kong and back to Canada. However, seeing the writing of policy changes on the wall, CPAir themselves were lobbying for Toronto-New York and the right to fly to any European city that Air Canada did not serve. Not only did this make coming up with negotiating strategies very difficult, since the airlines were strong and effective lobbyists, it also meant that the actual negotiations were carefully scrutinized, with representatives of the two major airlines sitting in on all bilateral sessions as observers.

Putting together all the rights for an around the world service was complicated but rather fun. With India and Singapore we had to negotiate new agreements, which meant travelling there. The negotiations were fine and businesslike and successful, and gave me the opportunity to visit India for the first time. While in Delhi, Joe Ledbetter and I did some exploring of Old Delhi and the Red Fort, and we took a weekend night to go down to Acra, visited at dawn the lustrously haunting Taj Mahal, probably the world's most perfectly proportioned and beautiful shrine. The evening before we left Delhi to return to Canada, we all went out to eat genuine Indian curry, which I had always loved. Our Indian counterparts very kindly invited us out to a restaurant called the Moti Mahal, which means Pink Pearl in Hindi. I ordered my curry "medium hot", the second highest of about five choices, believing that such a category would fit my capacity for the hottest curries served in the west. It was blisteringly hot but there was no way I was going to admit being a western weakling in front of colleagues and local hosts, so I pretended it was fine and, with plenty of local beer as coolant, washed it down where it turned my insides into a nuclear calandra in meltdown phase. I spent so much of the flight back to Canada, via London, in that very special room in the jetliner with all the fixtures appropriate to my condition, that I wondered why I had bothered to buy a regular seat. Even after arriving back in Ottawa, it took me days to want to eat anything more than plain rice or bread. I was to go back to the Moti Mahal on later visits to Delhi, and the curry was always terrific, but I always ordered a mild curry and never again pretended to play in the local league of spice levels.

With Ingrid Hall's departure and my elevation to Head of Transportation Policy came new-found professional responsibilities and a degree of freedom which I really enjoyed. The divisional Director, Peter Walker, left and was replaced by Stephen Heeney, an Asianist educated at Oxford and a thoughtful executive whose general approach to management and supervision reminded me of a shepherd; as long as you were moving in the right direction he would leave you alone, and when he thought you needed a course correction he would gently nudge you in the correct direction. He spoke Japanese and served there twice in his career, once after our time together in the Economic Bureau as Deputy Chief of Mission when I was Director in the Asia Branch, and later was appointed Ambassador to the Philippines. Also joining the division in the summer of 1980 was an officer a year junior to me, Guy Saint-Jacques, who would work on a mix of files in both the science and transportation sections, in the latter as terrific help to me. Meticulous, thoughtful, and industrious, Guy was the antithesis of the "yes man", his advice was always based on thorough analysis even if it went against the prevailing wind. Guy went off on Chinese language training during the same summer that I left the Economic Bureau, but our paths were to cross again and again, most valuably for me when he served as my Political Minister in Beijing two decades later. He is now, as I write this, our Ambassador to China.

About a year into our efforts to knit together the fabric of rights that would permit around-the-world service and at most a year after he had taken up the Chief Air Negotiator's position, Harry Jay retired. The airlines had not been happy with him and he himself clearly felt out of place in the focused world of mercantilist negotiating. He was replaced by a very different character, Gary Harmon, who was also nearing the end of his career and who had just returned to Ottawa from four years as Ambassador to Cuba. Gary was about the most modest and least flamboyant negotiator imaginable, but he was thorough and effective. When he did not completely understand something or fully appreciate the implications of a foreign counterparty's proposal, he would say so and break from the negotiating table, and huddle with me and other Canadian officials for an explanation, going over it as many times as needed for him to be fully at ease. Gary was also a delightful character with a lovely wife, Margaret, with grown children about the same age as Liani and I, and we were to become close to them, seeing them often even long after I had moved on from the transportation desk.

With Gary as our leader, we went to European capitals and obtained the rights to allow Canadian carriers the ability to carry local passengers, not originating in or destined to Canada, on flight segments between London, Frankfurt and Zurich on one hand, and points in Asia on the other. For these rights we had to trade away to British and European carriers the right to integrate their Canadian flights with flights to the US or elsewhere in the Americas, picking up and dropping off local passengers during Canadian stopovers. We negotiated similar rights with Singapore and Hong Kong, and also secured an even more open environment for all-cargo services. Over time, especially as the passenger levels grew and the advantage of point-to-point service became clearly apparent relative to multi-stop flights, most of these rights that we had given away were to prove of little value. The only service I know of today that is a legacy of those agreements is a

Cathay Pacific service between Hong Kong and New York that stops in Vancouver, open to passengers travelling between Vancouver and New York, and Vancouver and Hong Kong. Once we had obtained all the route rights needed, Air Canada established services over Europe all the way to Delhi and Singapore. Unfortunately the service was never extended all the way around the world, and within a few years Air Canada sold its aging fleet of cargo planes and retreated completely from the all-cargo business, rendering rather useless the complex of agreements we had negotiated.

During my three years on the transportation desk we conducted no negotiations with South American countries, services to and from which were dominated by CPAir, but we did have a few rounds of talks with the smaller Caribbean countries served by Air Canada and Eastern Caribbean Airways (ECA), an airline based in Barbados and shared by a number of the island countries. The multi-national negotiating team across the table from us was led by a man who we referred to as Bob the Mouse, not due to stature but in reference to Peter Sellers in the movie "The Mouse That Roared", a cute comedy about a dictator from a tiny country who decides that the only way to prosperity is to fight, and quickly lose, a war with the United States. In the movie Peter Sellers bumbles his way to victory, which of course messes up his plans. In our battle with Bob the Mouse, who had decided to go to war with Canada, we had to deal with requests for outrageously generous rights for ECA, including the right to pick up and drop off local passengers between any Canadian and US cities on routes between the Caribbean and Canada. His declaration of war was expressed in having local Caribbean aeronautical authorities consistently turn down Air Canada's requests for fare or frequency adjustments on routes already being operated under existing bilateral agreements. Bob the Mouse had lived in Ottawa for fifteen years, was a dual Canadian-Trinidadian citizen, and unfortunately had worked in CTC so knew all about both the capacity of regulatory authorities to be disruptive. In our negotiations we would be faced one minute with threats of service reductions and the next with the pleas of a developing nation partner to which big and generous Canada should be sympathetic. And the following week Air Canada would have its filing for a coming seasonal schedule rejected without reason, and we would have to get our local embassy to intervene at a political level, usually with the local Minister of Tourism. It was enormously frustrating and rather funny at the same time. Although we must have had five or six rounds of negotiation over my three years, we never did succeed in making significant changes to Canada – Caribbean services, which was fine as far as the dominating Air Canada was concerned, but I remember that my Barbados file was thicker than that for any other country! Another Caribbean file was Jamaica, whose government wanted to obtain permission to increase Air Jamaica's frequencies to Toronto. At my suggestion we made it clear that if they started up a Kingston-Montreal service, and thereby helped out the struggling Mirabel airport, we would look at their request sympathetically. And so it was done.

At the end of the 1970s, deregulation had become a major objective of the US Government in its domestic aviation market, freeing up new companies to compete with the huge legacy carriers of Eastern, TWA, PanAm, American and United. New entrants like Braniff and US Airlines and Continental wanted to compete head to head with the majors and the view of the US government was that they should be allowed to do so. The Canada-US civil aviation was at the time governed by four distinct agreements: the main Air Services Agreement, which contained the crucial Annex listing every route pair available to a single carrier of each country, at that time some 45 routes in total. The second agreement was the Local and Regional Air Services Agreement covering short-haul services between city pairs close to the border (Winnipeg-Fargo, Halifax-Portland, etc.) open to smaller and sometimes seasonal airlines. The third agreement covered charter services and the fourth was the Pre-Clearance Agreement that allowed each country to establish customs and immigration processing centres in the airports of the other. This latter arrangement was loved by travelers of both countries since they could avoid crowded immigration and customs lines at US airports, and by Canadian airlines which could operate services to a broad range of US cities, including those without border clearance facilities.

In the negotiations of 1980-82, the US government wanted to deregulate the transborder market. American airlines not yet operating wanted multi-carrier access to the market, for routes like Toronto-New York were high-volume routes with a large component of business travelers, and therefore high-yield (producing higher per-passenger mile revenues). Canadian carriers were not desirous of seeing increased competition on existing routes, all listed in the route Annex and limited in all cases to one airline from each country. What Air Canada and CP Air, our two major international carriers, wanted was the addition of new routes to reflect the changing economics of the continent and the rise of the American southwest and of Canada's west. Routes from Toronto to Texas and California and Nevada were high on the carriers' wish-lists, as were routes from Calgary and Vancouver to both these same regions and to eastern US hubs like Chicago and New York. The negotiations began with a meeting in Washington in which Canada pushed an updating of the existing route annex with the addition of dozens of new city pairs, while the US countered with a proposal to scrap the old approach entirely and establish an open market for any carrier that wanted to fly between any city-pair. Under the US proposal, fares and the frequency of service would be left entirely up to the airlines, and government regulation would be reduced to safety issues and to limiting of anti-competitive or market disruptive practices.

The first formal round of the bilateral talks with the US took place at the end of Harry Jay's short tenure, was probably partly the cause of his departure, and was like two ships passing in the night. The US negotiator was a very sharp negotiator named Jim Ferrer, who made a cogent case for a new deregulated approach to the mature transborder market, with open access to routes and the end of fare regulation. The negotiations took place in Washington, and the airlines of both countries had representatives there as observers, in the case of the US this meant representatives of the American Airline Association, and in the case of Canada a representative of the regional carriers (then Eastern Provincial Airways, Québecair and Pacific Western Airlines) joined our regular duo of Air Canada and

CPAir. Ambassador Jay initially simply ignored the US proposals and put Canada's desire for an expanded route Annex, with no changes to the underlying agreement. However, Ambassador Jay had the multilateralist nose, always trying to sniff out a compromise and did not seem to our airline representatives to grasp how serious the issue of deregulation was to them. Vlad Slivitsky and Glen Hutchins, vice presidents at Air Canada and CPAir respectively, were regularly on the phone with their headquarters and if they were unhappy with something Jay had said or was proposing their CEOs would call Walter McLeish or the Minister of Transport and Harry Jay would be in turn called to account to them.

No progress was made and the talks were suspended for several months. Harry Jay slipped into retirement and the unflappable Gary Harmon took over. In the ensuing many rounds, we offered some compromises, with greater access to a limited number of high-volume city pairs by additional carriers, and a looser form of fare regulation in which fare bands would be established within which carriers would be free to price their offerings. Ray Yang also retired and was replaced by a tall Dutch Canadian called Hans Lovink, part of a new breed of officials in Transport Canada, smart and career focused, but without the military background or historical perspective that made the older generation so enriching to work with. The frequent meetings in Washington were fun, because I was able to not only see friends at the Embassy but a couple of schoolmates from St. George's who were working there, and I would eat occasionally with my uncle and aunt, Mac and Mary Howard and with cousins Laura and Murray Belman. One early morning during a set of negotiations there, I twisted my ankle very badly while running in Rock Creek Park. After being tended to by an old family friend and doctor, Neville Connolly, I was on crutches by the time the talks began in the morning, leading American negotiator Jim Ferrer to quip that "it's clear that the Canadian position is so weak it needs crutches". But we still did not manage to close the gap; Canadian airlines believed that an "open skies" regime across the border would allow the larger American airlines to dominate as they had more extensive route systems that would permit more efficient integration. And the Americans would simply not agree to a simple extension of the old system of named routes, especially as they had deregulated their domestic market completely, and managed to negotiate a deregulated regime with the UK and were trying to do so with a couple of other European countries. I finally persuaded our side to leap-frog the US position and propose a truly open North American aviation market, allowing Canadian carriers to carry local traffic between American cities (a right called "cabotage") and vice versa, which would have created a truly even playing field. The US negotiators were stunned and intrigued, but the American carriers were vehemently opposed to permitting cabotage and the proposal died a quick death, but at least we had taken an initiative we could present to the public as being pro-consumer. Canada and the United States eventually agreed on a fully deregulated transborder aviation system without cabotage, but it was not concluded until more than a year after I had moved on to another job.

One issue that absorbed a substantial amount of my time between 1980 and 1982 related to the National Energy Program conceived of by Minister of Energy, Mines and Resources Marc Lalonde and introduced in the autumn 1980 budget of then Minister of Finance, Allan MacEachen. The objective of the NEP, as it was known, was to impose a domestic pricing system for oil and petroleum products that would be substantially lower than international prices, driven up by the 1978 oil crisis. It was also a revenue grab by the federal government in a sector of the economy constitutionally under the responsibility of the provinces. Among its many components, the NEP imposed a tax on aviation fuel for international carriers, which were assured tax-free treatment by international treaty law and by Canada's many bilateral civil aviation agreements. During the pre-budget interdepartmental consultations, I was invited to a meeting hosted by an Assistant Deputy Minister of Finance, Sid Rubinoff, and I pointed out that the proposed measure would constitute an export tax on fuel and therefore violate Canada's international undertakings. No one was very interested in the views of a junior officer from External Affairs, especially as my voice was only one of many in government warning against elements of the proposed NEP, which had the backing of the Prime Minister and enormous support in Cabinet. Hal Caloff, a senior official from the Department of Justice assured everyone that the fuel tax could be re-packaged as a subsidy recovery, and in the budget it was introduced as the "Transportation Fuel Cost Recovery Charge" shortened to TFCRC. Unfortunately, Minister MacEachen's speech-writers had found the construct too cumbersome for the budget speech, and the Minister said explicitly that the government was imposing a new export tax on aviation fuel that would generate hundreds of millions of dollars in federal revenue over the ensuing years. The day after the budget, we received a formal complaint from the US Embassy, and within the next few weeks almost every other country followed suit. Of course we did our best to defend the TFCRC as not being a tax, but the Minister's speech and the facts both undermined our position, and eventually Canada had to cancel the tax and refund international airlines literally hundreds of millions of dollars.

During one of the last rounds of bilateral air negotiations with the US in which I participated in the spring of 1982, Liani, then pregnant with our first child, came to Washington with me. We stayed with my grandmother at 2807 36th Place, where my mother had grown up and where we had all lived for a time in 1958 when my father was at Harvard for an AMP program. It was blossom season and my parents came down from Wilton, and we had a lovely time walking through the gardens at the National Cathedral and along the Potomac River, and saw Mac and Mary and cousins Laura and Murray Belman.

As Liani's pregnancy advanced, I realized that we were approaching a time when I would wish to travel less, and I had been in the transportation job for three years in any case, so I asked for a re-assignment to a less peripatetic position. So in August, just after our little Cynthia was born, I moved to the Officer Assignments Division of Personnel.

CHAPTER 7

PERSONNEL

· · · · · · · · · · · ·

The move to Personnel was a shift into the inner workings of the Foreign Service. Rod Irwin was my immediate boss as Deputy Director and Craig MacDonald was Director. Rod was an old personnel hand, having served in the division as a more junior officer a decade earlier, and was to replace Craig in the following summer as Director. Rod was a delightful and helpful colleague and guided me well during my time in Personnel. Over the years he and his wife Penny became very family good friends.

Personnel was always considered a plum assignment, and officers who served there were generally "high flyers", as I was apparently emerging to be. I had received my promotion to the FS2 level half way through my time on the transportation desk and was made the Assignment Officer for the approximately 190 FS1 officers in what was called the "Political Economic Stream", the officers of the old External Affairs. In 1980 and 1981 the Foreign Service had been consolidated, the old Department of Industry Trade and Commerce divided in half, with the domestic side becoming the Department of Industry and the foreign trade bureau and the Trade Commissioner Service transferred to External, which was renamed the Department of External Affairs and International Trade. The immigration service was also transferred to the Department, as was the foreign branch of CIDA, the Canadian International Development Agency, with the intention that its corps of development officers would convert to the Foreign Service group, making four rotational groups of officers, the Political Economic, Trade, Immigration, and Aid Streams. Each of the four had a separate assignments group.

The job of an assignments officer was much more complicated than simply slotting people into positions. It involved getting to know the officers for whom one was responsible, which meant meeting all of those who were serving in Ottawa and writing back and forth to those posted abroad. In the case of the FS1s, somewhere between thirty and forty percent would move every summer, and this meant understanding the interests, strengths and weaknesses of those on the move as well as the requirements of every position at home and abroad likely to become open. Every proposed overseas assignment had to be cleared with Security and approved by the relevant Head of Mission, and every assignment in Headquarters had to be approved by the receiving bureau or division's management. Striking a complete equilibrium in supply and demand was the ultimate objective, since no positions were meant to be left vacant and no officers left without jobs. Every job abroad had a fixed term of either two, three or four years, the shorter terms applying to hardship posts and the longer terms to missions in the developed world. Extensions were frequently encouraged and sought, especially in posts for which specialized language skills were needed, since it made little sense to send someone off to learn Chinese for two years and then have them serve only two years in Beijing. Theoretically, an officer's first assignment abroad was always a two-year assignment, as it was really considered part of one's training and development. Secondments to and from other departments could be used to perfect the balance, and indeed were always part of the mix, with a few positions in the Foreign and Defence Secretariat of the Privy Council office (PCO) and a number of positions in the intelligence world, always filled with Foreign Service officers. In counterbalance, a few specialized positions in the larger embassies and high commissions were usually filled with experts from domestic departments like Finance, Agriculture and the Bank of Canada.

The job was like playing with a giant puzzle. Once I had interviewed all the HQ officers at the FS1 level eligible for overseas assignment, communicated with those abroad scheduled to be moved, I then received a "Posting Preference Form" from each of the officers potentially on the move, containing five positions in which he or she was interested. This was before computerized spreadsheets so we had to organize the material by hand in a kind of double book-keeping, with a list of positions and a list of officers, both constantly adjusted to ensure the equilibrium we sought could be achieved. Many officers of course tried to game the system, putting on their list one fantastic position they really wanted and four positions for which they would be deemed unqualified, and in those cases we would go back to them and squeeze out a more realistic list using the threat of sending them to some place they really did not want to go. I worked very hard at finding a "best fit" model for the coming summer posting season, and actually tried but failed to develop a mathematical formula for measuring how close the assignment model was to having every position filled with officers of the right skill-sets in missions where they wanted to go. In the end, filling about eighty percent of positions with competent officers happy to be so assigned took less than half of our efforts, and then dealing with the twenty percent remainders of both officers and jobs took our remaining time. We were also constantly providing career counseling relating to professional development, and dealing with personal and administrative problems such as alcoholism or family breakdown or security breaches. Like other assignment officers, I occasionally had to tell an officer that his Foreign Service career was being brought to a premature end for some reason or another, which was always very difficult.

In my first year in the Assignments Division I began serving on personnel boards, the first being an Appraisal Review Committee, which looked at all the written employee appraisal reports to ensure that consistent standards were being applied, returning outliers to supervisors for revision when the widespread inflation (accepted to a degree because of the highly competitive nature of the promotion system) was simply over the top, and made recommendations on performance pay, the service's form of annual bonuses. I also served as the voting secretary for the FS1 to FS2 promotion board, which was that year chaired by a senior Ambassador, Louis Delvoie. The promotion boards were a huge undertaking, and required very careful record-keeping, for promotions were appealable to Appeal Boards run by the Public Service Commission, and if an appeal was upheld the entire promotion list would be thrown out and the process restarted. On my first board there were something like 150 officers eligible for promotion and only 22 openings. In each officers file there would be at least four years of appraisal reports, each report being five or six pages long and some with many annexes of letters of commendation and the like. A promotion board was charged with producing a ranking of eligible officers and was composed of four officers, one from Personnel and at least one from outside the core stream of the officers being considered. The board was not supposed to know how many officers would be promoted. The process would generally take three or four weeks and would only be completed when the board, like a jury, had reached unanimity on ranking all the officers under consideration. Even though formal eligibility was reached after four years in grade, the average length of time officers spent as an FS1 before being promoted was somewhere between six and seven years, which meant that officers not promoted would immediately ask where in the ranking they had been placed, taking solace if they were close to the cut-off line, or despairing if they had fallen down the list from the year before. I was lucky in my career to be move upward through every level as fast as theoretically possible, except from FS1 to FS2, when in my first year of eligibility no one with a minimum time in grade was promoted.

In my second year in Personnel, Rod Irwin moved up to replace Craig MacDonald as Director and I replaced Rod as Head of Assignments, although I was not given the Deputy Director title due to the fact that I still relatively junior. Marc Perron, a feisty Québécois with a delightful sense of humour and just back from his first Ambassadorial post in Gabon, became Director General. Working with Rod and Marc was a real pleasure; they were both very approachable, consummate professionals and neither took themselves too seriously. Rod was to end his career as Ambassador to Russia and Marc, after a very successful time as Ambassador to Egypt would end his career as Ambassador to Mexico, a posting from which he departed in 1997 after undiplomatically and publicly decrying the level of corruption in his host country, along with the lack of seriousness with which the Mexican Government was pursuing its war on drugs. In the early 1990s Marc and I were to serve together on the department's executive committee, he as ADM for Africa and the Middle East and I as ADM for Asia Pacific.

As I became more experienced in personnel matters, I also was given the opportunity to become involved in other departmental management issues. The department always had a senior officer designated as Inspector General, who would draw together teams composed of officials both from the department and other departments with representation abroad and conduct "inspections", which were a combination of a financial audit and a critical review of position strength and staffing. In the early 1980s the largest of Canada's overseas missions was still London, which had a huge Canada-based establishment from National Defence as well as many other departments, and almost 500 locally-engaged staff. I was assigned to the Inspection Team whose not very well hidden agenda was to substantially reduce the size and cost of the London mission. It was fun to be back in London again I managed to spend an evening with Chris and Pru Scarlett at their Markham Street home. My brother Hugh was still in London, and I extended my stay by a long weekend and went for a very cold autumn sail in the Solent on his "Duelist II", a 24-foot sturdy little sloop that he was racing regularly.

Although the trade function had been transferred from ITC to the Department in 1981, the units involved had been left in the C.D.Howe building in downtown Ottawa and the prevailing sense was that they were still closer to the Department of Industry (then renamed Industry Canada), than to their new brethren at External Affairs. The Under-Secretary struck a task force to rectify this, and to deal in detail with a gaping inconsistency between the authorized personnel strength levels of the combined department (as determined by parliamentary appropriation in the annual "Main Estimates"), and the department's position structure and number of staff at senior executive levels. I was assigned as Personnel's representative on the task force, and participated in the decisions on how to better integrate the trade and immigration functions into the department.

In the end the task force did not pursue radical change, and most of the trade-related divisions and bureaus were moved more or less as-is to the Pearson Building. Further structural change was to follow somewhat later, which is part of another chapter of this story.

In the lore of the Foreign Service, the greatest advantage of serving in Personnel was that you could choose your own next assignment. While there was undoubtedly some truth to this, there were enough checks and balances to prevent too much abuse. As I would have been five years in Ottawa by the summer of 1984 an assignment abroad was logical in my own case, and Liani and I talked a lot about where we might go. My first preference was to spend a year at l'Ecole Nationale d'Administration (ENA) in Paris and then move in 1985 to the senior economist's position in the embassy in Paris. This was a position I felt particularly qualified for, given my time at Sciences Po and my knowledge of and interest in the French economy. But it was not to be. The Deputy Chief of Mission in Paris was at that time Fred Bild, who was later to become our Ambassador to Thailand and then to China. Fred and his wife Eva were both Auschwitz children, survivors of the Nazi genocide that murdered their parents and other family members. At this time the Ambassador to France was Michel Dupuy, with whom I had toured around Indonesia when he was President of CIDA. Fred had the full confidence of Ambassador Dupuy in managing personnel matters at the Embassy and wrote a private message to Rod Irwin to say that while they were happy to have me come to ENA and be considered for the embassy's economic job the following year, they really did not want to offer a guarantee to the follow-on assignment. For Liani and me this was not enough, and the last thing we wanted was to spend a year settling down in Paris only to be re-assigned the following year to somewhere in francophone Africa, so I declined the ENA position, and chose instead the job of Deputy Chief of Mission and Head of Chancery in Prague, Czechoslovakia. Prague was not a very important post, but the position was reasonably senior and the setting looked fascinating. Rod Irwin sent the required request for confirmation to Ambassador David Peel in Prague, who accepted my appointment, and we were soon embarked on another adventure.

The year before we left for Prague we had knocked down the garage on our little Wayling Avenue property and built an extension, with a garage below and a new master bedroom and bath on the second floor. We also added a beautiful little sunroom behind the garage looking out into the back garden, which by this time was half planted with vegetables. In the autumn of 1983 we had harvested more than 150 pounds of tomatoes, lots of broccoli and cauliflower and beans and even cantaloupe melons, although the raccoons or squirrels got more of our melons than we did. The extension made the house, while still small at about 1600 square feet, much more livable and also easier to rent. It did not take us long to find a tenant, an architect from Montreal who had taken some sort of airport construction oversight job with Transport Canada. He and his family seemed nice enough and so we left our little home in their hands and took off for Frankfurt.

CHAPTER 8

PRAGUE

● ● ● ● ● ● ● ● ● ● ●

Before we left Ottawa we had ordered a new car, a brown Volvo station-wagon, for delivery in Frankfurt, so it was there Liani and I and our little two-year old Cynthia flew in the early summer of 1984. We stayed at a Kempinski Hotel outside of Frankfurt, which Cynthia loved because they had huge fluffy duvets she could play in, and then took a week driving down the Romantic Road from Wurtzburg, where we stayed on a hilltop in the guesthouse of a winery, to Augsburg, stopping in the restored medieval towns of Rothenburg, Dinkelsbuhl, and Nordlingen. We then zipped through Munich and ended up for our last two days in Garmisch-Partenkirchen in the Bavarian Alps and walked in the gorgeous mountains, eating heavy Bavarian food, and preparing ourselves psychologically for crossing into communist Czechoslovakia.

Our final overnight stop in West Germany was Regensburg, another very pretty old town, and then we took country roads to all little town called Furth im Vald and from there to the border. Crossing the border was a laborious affair, even with diplomatic passports and all the required papers that the Embassy had sent us, and the sense of hostility was palpable. On the west side we could see lots of evidence of NATO ground forces, with trucks of soldiers and heavy equipment on the roads and in the towns, and once across the border we would catch glimpses through the trees of Warsaw Pact tanks and heavy guns. The massed armies of West and East were literally only a few kilometers apart, separated by a border that was actually three separate lines, an armed West German border post, the border itself which had a double line of 10-metre high fencing with coiled razor wire in between, and then the inner Eastern line, several hundred metres inside Czechoslovakia. The inner line, also made of a tall fence, was where incoming traffic was inspected for contraband or illegal propaganda and where outgoing traffic was stopped, and cars and trucks inspected for hideaways. Between the inner line and the actual border is where the border police would roam with dogs, and where frantic escapees would more often than not be caught and shot.

In the mid-1980s there was no divided highway between West Germany and Czechoslovakia; in fact there were no such highways at all in Czechoslovakia. Once we had cleared the border, we proceeded towards Pilsn (where Pilsner beer and the original Budweiser brand originated) on the rural highway, driving through the middle of towns and villages and frequently having to slow or stop for farm vehicles and other local traffic. The comparison with the tidy, clean and modern West Germany was immediate and radical, and was like being thrown back in time. The towns were tattered and the houses and storefronts dirty, the carts and trucks and tractors looking twenty-five years or more out of date. We entered Pilsn, a substantial industrial city with tall smokestacks spewing grey filth into the skies, on a secondary road, got lost and had to ask for directions as to how to get through the city to the main road. Our Czech at this stage was not very good, but somehow we made ourselves understood and got back on the highway to Prague.

Prague is a city built around five hills on the Vltava River, a tributary of the Elbe that provides most of the latter's volume. Entering the city on the main road from Pilsn, we came between two of the hills and saw this old and extraordinary city emerge before us. Even though in disrepair and not very clean in those days, Prague was breathtakingly beautiful, with no modern office towers to mar a cityscape unchanged in hundreds of years.

The house assigned to us in Prague had been the Deputy Chief of Mission's house for as long as anyone could remember and was at 2, Za Hanspaulkou, high on the Dejvice hill. It was an art deco house built in Czechoslovakia's most flourishing period, between the end of World War I and the 1938 Munich Agreement, which effectively gave Hitler a green light to annex the country. The entrance was on the ground floor, from which a staircase led to the main receiving rooms on the second floor with natural light in the hallway provided by most beautiful etched glass windows. The bedrooms and a family room were on the third floor, along with a balcony with a gorgeous view across the valley towards Hradçany Castle and St. Vitus Cathedral. There was also an apartment on the ground floor that was lived in by our "watcher", an older very stout lady named Pané Kourkova, who reported on our comings and goings and on our visitors to the Czechoslovakian police. Pané Kourkova had a daughter and grandchildren who would come around to visit her, and she would feed both them and Cynthia rich kolaček and bobovkas and other fatty pastries, and her grandchildren would play with Cynthia. We did not mind being watched and bore Pané Kourkova no ill-will; she was doing what she had to do and was always charming towards us. We had a garden as well, perhaps thirty meters square, with fruit trees and currant and berry bushes that provided a lovely harvest in the autumn.

Ambassador David Peel and his wife Diana were just finishing up the last of their three years in Prague, and were very gracious to us in the few weeks we were together. Their daughter Anne was a race-walking member of Canada's Olympic team, and back in Ottawa in later years we were to end up living just up the hill from them in Rockcliffe. The Ambassador's residence was an extraordinary old home called Hadovka, on the main thoroughfare between the airport and the city, then called Leninova and now Europska. Hadovka was the old manor house for that part of Dejvice with foundations that dated back to the 11th century and a basic structure built in the 16th. It had two wings and crenellated walls and a central courtyard reached through a main floor arch under the receiving rooms, and had vegetable and fruit gardens extensive enough to provision all of the residence's needs. It also had its own tennis court where Liani and I would play, and even take lessons from Jiri Vranek, an eighty year old who stumbled about the court on long broken knees but whose strokes still showed his form as a national champion back in the 1930s.

When the Peels departed in early July, I was named Chargé d'Affaires ad interim until Terry Bacon arrived in September, and as Acting Head of Mission borrowed Hadovka for a few events that needed more or fancier space than we had in our own home. One such event was the visit of Canada's co-commissioners for Expo 86, Patrick Reid and Jimmy Pattison. Two more different people would be almost impossible to imagine. Patty Reid was an Irish born graduate of Sandhurst who had emigrated to Canada after the Second World War, and a somewhat specialized diplomat who had spent many years involved in Canadian participation in international exhibitions. He was well over six feet tall and had adopted an air more pompous than patrician and very much liked to be fawned over. Jimmy Pattison was at that point only part way on his path to become one of the world's wealthiest people, and was short, feisty, witty and very direct. The two of them came to Prague to encourage Czechoslovak participation in Expo 86, which was a BIE-blessed international exposition of a second tier, and not a full "universal exposition" like Expo67 in Montreal or Expo 2010 in Shanghai. Its theme was modern transportation and by mid-1984 there were quite a number of countries normally active in the international exhibition business that had not committed to participate. Czechoslovakia was one of these, so I took Pattison and Reid around to meet the key officials responsible for the decision of whether or not to participate, and then hosted a reception at Hadovka. To the reception we invited as many of the Czechs that we could find that had been involved in past expositions, including of course Expo67. One man I invited to the event was Miroslav Galuška, a man in his early sixties who had seventeen years earlier been Commissioner-General of the Czechoslovak Pavilion at Expo67, one of the most popular of all the international exhibition halls in Montreal due to its wizardry in design and presentation.

Miroslav Galuška had lived a most interesting life. Born in 1922 he was just a teen-ager when the Nazis marched into Prague. He worked in a forced labour factory in Berlin during the war and became a journalist thereafter, covering the Nuremberg trials of the Nazi leaders on behalf of a Prague newspaper. After the Soviet-backed communist coup in 1948, he became a diplomat and served in the late 1950s as Ambassador to Britain. Along with many of his compatriots he became increasingly disillusioned with communism and after his very successful time in Montreal at Expo67, where he had promoted and supported young Czechoslovak artists and intellectuals as they became engaged with their counterparts from Canada and elsewhere, was named Minister of Culture by Alexander Dubcek. As the "Prague Spring" unfolded and Dubcek pursued political reforms, Galuška opened wide the freedoms on cultural expression. After the Soviet invasion crushed the Prague Spring in August 1968, he like all of Dubcek's ministers was sidelined from decision-making and then replaced with a Soviet puppet.

Following what the Soviets called the "normalization" in Prague, in an effort to persuade the outside world that not all liberals had been purged, the puppet leaders allowed Galuška to serve as the Commissioner-General of the Czechoslovak pavilion at the themed exposition in Osaka in 1970. He again gave the artists and designers working on the pavilion complete freedom, with the result that the exhibits exuded an evident anti-Soviet bias. This was too much for the regime and he was formally ousted from the Communist Party and never allowed to hold office again. Instead he became a private teacher and a secret supporter of the intellectuals who opposed the regime, writing illegally produced manuscripts and pamphlets of everything from simple poetry to radically anti-regime political tracts. These were called "samizdat", reproduced secretly and circulated at substantial risk.

One story I had been briefed about before I had left Ottawa was an aborted defection by Galuška in Osaka in the summer of 1970. Before the Japanese event had begun, Galuška had been approached in Prague by a predecessor of mine with an offer to bring him and his wife to Canada, and he had agreed. A complex operation was mounted in which he would be whisked away during an off-site dinner in Osaka and taken by private plane to Vancouver. The defection would be timed to coincide with a visit to West Germany by his wife so she could not be held behind as leverage against him. Everything had gone according to plan until the very last moment, when Galuška himself decided that he would not defect, with the excuse that his elderly mother, still in Czechoslovakia, needed his support. The real reason, he told me much later, was that he just could not bear leaving the country he loved, irrespective of how awful the regime.

During the reception for Jimmy Pattison and Patty Reid, I was careful not to spend more than a moment of greeting with Galuška, but I had a junior officer give him a note suggesting that I wanted to meet more privately. This turned out to be an unnecessary caution, and without being asked he sent me a proposed schedule of Czech language lessons along with a description of his fees. Teaching foreigners Czech was something he was allowed to do, and so he became absolutely the worst teacher I was to ever have in any language. He did become a fabulous companion and a good friend. At every lesson he would come to our house, and after twenty minutes or so pretending to study the outrageous declensions of Czech nouns, we would then go outside for a walk. There we would talk openly and I would really learn what I wished to learn. Through Galuška I was to meet many interesting people, sometimes in parks or down by the river late in the evening, and from them I was able to collect samizdat and other material. He was a wonderful man, very cultured and completely fluent in English, the only language we ever used together except when we were putting on the teacher-student act. When Barbara Frum, the long-serving host of CBC Radio's evening show "As It Happens" and the nightly television interview program "The Journal", came to Prague with her dentist husband Murray Frum, I took them on a long walk in Šarka Valley with Galuška. Barbara Frum told me later that listening to Galuška was the most moving and elucidating discussion she had ever had with anyone from Eastern Europe. Even long after both I and the communist regime were gone from Prague, Galuška and I stayed in touch. (Barbara and Murray Frum were the parents of conservative columnist David Frum, George W. Bush's one-time speechwriter and the pen behind the latter's famous "Axis of Evil" speech.)

The mission in Prague was not a large one. It had a small three-person political-economic division, which I headed as well as being Head of Chancery and Post Security Officer. The trade division consisted of a single Canadian trade commissioner and one or two local staff. When we arrived the outgoing trade commissioner was Rob MacKenzie. Rob and his wife Sandy had a girl almost exactly Cynthia's age, and even though we only overlapped briefly we got on very well. The Mackenzies subsequently had two boys roughly the same age as ours, and twenty-five years later we went on family vacations together in Yunnan and Hebei, after I brought him to China as my Commercial Minister in Beijing. Colonel Ken Mitchell was our military attaché, who had a staff of two, and there was a small administrative section and the usual security contingent of five military police. Hana Gregorova served as Ken's translator but was also available for broader embassy work. Hana was a lovely lady then in her late thirties, who later defected and moved to Ottawa. There in the she met, quite randomly, and then married my dear friend Jeremy Kinsman, but all that happened much later.

Our Chancery (the main Embassy office) was an old large three-floor home located on a short street called Mickiewiczova just north of the park Chotkovy Sady on the steep Bruskou hill above Mala Strana. When I arrived there was no safe-speech room, which greatly hampered what we were trying to do in our political program. While the British allowed us to use theirs when needed, this was less than ideal, and I made a successful case to Ottawa that we should install one. After several months a specialized team arrived with a prefabricated kit specially designed to fit under the edge of the roof on the third floor, and after that we were able to have conversations and meetings on which the Czechoslovak listening services could not eavesdrop, a particulalry appropriate expression since we had literally built our room under the eaves.

Being constantly watched and listened to was a fact of life behind the Iron Curtain in those days, and we were always aware of this. People who came to dinner would be circumspect around the dinner table and then speak more openly when we walked in the garden. It was often that a half sentence would be ended with "chapeté . . ." or "you understand", which required no further explanation. We had been well briefed in Ottawa and knew that everyone who came to our house would be noticed and their names and quite likely our conversations recorded, but they knew that too, so as outsiders we really had to rely on the judgment of those we invited as to whether meeting with us in the open would cause them unwanted grief. Even though we would have the Chancery "swept" on a regular basis, we still knew that the only place we could discuss things confidentially was inside the safe speech room, and the residences were never swept at all.

There was a time late in our posting that we received a phone call from my father after we had been away for a weekend. My father said that he had called us repeatedly on the Saturday to wish Liani a happy birthday, and finally "a nice young man with quite good English" had answered and told him that we were away. My father could hear a televised hockey game in the background when the young man answered. We could only conclude that one of our "listeners" had found the unanswered calls were interrupting his concentration on the game and so had intercepted the call from his listening post. We would also occasionally be left "calling cards" which were obvious signs that we were being closely watched. Once, after a series of dinner parties to which we had invited some sympathetic locals, we found that Liani's dinner and menu planning diary had been taken apart and the pages put back in an impossibly random order. As the diary had a tightly bound metal binding, not loose-leaf, this was clearly done professionally. The watchers were simply telling us that they were watching closely and had, of course, copied all of our dinner lists.

Playing spy versus spy was not always as innocent as having lists of dinner guests purloined. Shortly after our arrival at a time when I was Chargé d'Affaires, the embassy's Military Attaché, Ken Mitchell, was out taking photographs in the countryside with his British counterpart when they were caught by the Czech military, and taken off and held in custody for almost a whole day before being released with a threat of expulsion for spying. They claimed they were in a public place not marked as restricted, but this carried no weight with their hosts. Mitchell came to me and proposed that we formally protest their arrest. At the British Embassy, both the Ambassador John Rich and the Head of Chancery, a lovely man named Peter Smart, were away and the Chargé d'Affaires was a young officer on his first posting, a rather blueblood sort of fellow from Cambridge, Richard Makepeace. Makepeace thought we should make a big stink about the affair and have the Czechoslovak envoys in London and Ottawa called in, while I thought a modest protest would be more appropriate given that two NATO colonels running around photographing in the Czech countryside was rather inviting an incident. Makepeace in the end got quite huffy, but the two colonels realized that we did not want to set off a chain reaction the end of which could easily result in their removal, so we all agreed to protest formally with a diplomatic note, but not to escalate the matter. (Richard Makepeace and his beautiful Nepalese wife Rupa were to leave Prague the following spring. He went on to learn Arabic and become a specialist on Middle Eastern affairs, ending his career as Consul General in Jerusalem where he made international news in 2007 when negotiating the release of a journalist taken hostage by Hamas.)

The diplomatic community in Prague was not very big, and of course we had no contact at all with the Soviets or other east-block representatives. The NATO embassies stayed quite close together, but even within that community there was an inner core with the Americans, Canadians, British, French, Austrians and West Germans in and out of our respective missions on a regular basis. And it was only with the Americans and British that we had a fully open intelligence sharing relationship. Initially I tried to meet diplomats in other friendly and in some not-so-friendly embassies to see if there were particularly well informed or interesting people around. I even tried to reach out to the Chinese and called on the Deputy Chief of Mission, a man well into his 50s. When I asked him if he was a specialist on Czechoslovakia, he said no, since although he had studied Czech in Beijing, only two of his four postings had been to Prague! In the end, no one seemed as well informed as the leading NATO countries, and so I ended up sticking pretty close to our home diplomatic circle and trying to build my own network among local elites and intellectuals.

There was at that time an ongoing debate in the community of Czech-watchers and Czechoslovak expatriates about the future of not only the country but of Czech culture. Largely led by the brilliant novelist Milan Kundera, in exile since 1968 in Paris, the pessimistic group argued that the heavy Soviet hand was squeezing dead everything that made the people of Bohemia and Moravia (the Czech lands) special, and this "Slavification" or "de-europeanization" was beyond the point of no return. Others, like the banned novelist Josef Skvorecky and perhaps the greatest modern historian of Czechoslovakia, Canadian Gordon Skilling, whose wife was Czech, argued that the Czech spirit could never be extinguished. I knew of this debate before I went to Prague, as I had spent time in Toronto with Skilling, whose long "History of Czechoslovakia" and shorter "Czechoslovakia's Interrupted Revolution" had been the first books I read before the posting. I had also met Skvorecky and his wife Anna, who together ran the Toronto-based "68 Publishers", publishing all the banned novels and other books that were not permitted inside Czechoslovakia. Some of these had been written in 1968 or before and had subsequently been banned, some had been written by émigrés, and others still had been written inside Czechoslovakia and smuggled out. There was a small network of diplomats who aided and abetted the smuggling, even if it was officially frowned upon and the use of the diplomatic bag for such purposes strictly forbidden. I also bought hundreds of books from 68 Publishers and ran a little lending library out of our house in Prague for our local friends. The borrowing terms were that no one could keep the books permanently, and borrowers could either return them or pass them along to others. None in the end ever found their way back to our home at Za Hanspaulkou. It was a practice that probably could have been easily brought to an end by the authorities had they really wished to, and we speculated why we got away with it. We concluded that either the government felt that to take action would create more problems than it would solve, or those making the decision not to do anything simply turned a blind eye, secretly sympathizing with those who were trying to keep the great traditions of Czech writing and literature alive.

In the diplomatic community, we were also divided between optimists and pessimists. The US Ambassador Bill Luers and his wife Wendy were optimists as were we, although most of his staff was not. Our second Ambassador, Terry Bacon, was also a pessimist about the future of the Czech culture along with the French, who seemed heavily tainted by the views of Kundera and his band of Paris-based exiles. My father had gone to the New York's World' Fair in 1939 as the clouds of war were forming. The Czechoslovak pavilion, under construction the year before when Hitler's armies occupied the country, had been left unfinished. My father took a photograph of the Jan Huss quotation that was put up in large letters across the unfinished building, saying: "When the tempest of wrath hath past, the rule of thy country will return to thee, O Czech people". I had him produce many copies for me and I gave them to local friends and contacts, who greatly appreciated the gesture and the implied understanding behind it. Just as the words had comforted the Czechs during the Nazi occupation, so did they again during the long years of communism and Soviet domination.

One of the best ways to get to know a bit more about what was going on behind the grim grip of the communist regime was through music and art. Liani and I started going regularly to concerts and art exhibitions, and gradually began to build a network of contacts of musicians and artists, and even some very sympathetic people in the Ministry of Culture. During our first autumn, we hosted a dinner for a touring Canadian pianist, Jane Coop, then at the beginning of what was to become quite a successful professional career. We invited several musicians as well as a particularly charming Director General from the Ministry of Culture, Lubos Travnicek, who when we walked in the garden told me which artists were worth getting to know and which were effectively the lackeys of a state that he despised but had no choice but to serve.

Before going to Prague I had read the novel, *The Good Soldier Svejk* by Jaroslav Hasek, the dark comedy about a Czech soldier in the Austro-Hungarian army during World War I. In the novel, Svejk stumbles from crisis to crisis, constantly undermining the war effort through a mixture of sheer idiocy and excessive enthusiasm, and effectively becomes a force of passive resistance. On many, many occasions, Czechs would ask whether we had read the book, and nod knowingly when they received an answer in the affirmative. Czechoslovakia had been deserted by the western democracies at Munich in 1938, ignored again during the communist takeover in 1948, and a third time when crushed by Russian tanks in 1968. The Czechs faced such outrageously uneven odds as a small satrapy in the massively powerful Soviet empire that the only rational path was to get on with their lives as best they could, protect their culture and bend but not break with the prevailing wind, just like the good soldier Svejk.

We met a lot of interesting artists and performers in Prague. We were invited to the studio of Ota Janacek, who livelihood was as an illustrator of children's books, and he gave us a lovely book of fables for Cynthia, and he overlayered the printed illustrations, his own, with additional watercolour figures and comments. We also bought from him an oil painting, which was the other half of his passion, a gorgeous semi-figurative scene with a European sky and on the land beneath a whole egg, breaking forth from a broken egg, a symbol for the hardiness of the Czech people who would survive whole when they broke through the shell of Soviet communism. We went to the country studio of Olbram Zoubek, the great sculptor and designer, who was when we met him already almost sixty years old and whose work always skirted the edge of censorship. Zoubek's studio was always full of artists and sculptors who were more radical than he and whose works were more blatantly challenging to the regime. But generally the artists, often with the quiet connivance or support of sympathizers in the Ministry of Culture, managed to push the boundaries of what was allowed. We went to one exhibition sponsored by the Ministry at a small gallery next on a boat in the river downstream from the city centre. All the work was very modern and some was subtly anti-state, but because the artists had entitled the exhibition something like "Commemoration of the 35th Anniversary of the Glorious Communist Revolution", the exhibition was not only permitted but sponsored by the state. The censors had never even bothered to look at any of the individual works displayed. Works of both Janacek and Zoubek (still alive as I write these words in 2013) have graced our homes throughout our subsequent life, reminding us of the time that their creators were quietly trying to find their own paths between creativity and submission.

I had two junior officers during my time in Prague, Jill Sinclair, who had already been there for some time when we arrived, and Don MacKay, who arrived some time after us. Jill was fluent in Czech and had wonderful contacts throughout the dissident community and was our major contact with them. I was careful not to crowd Jill or horn-in on her work, although through her I did meet both Jiri Dientsbier and Ivan Havel, brother of Vaçlav Havel. Dientsbier was then working as a night watchman and coal-stoker, having been stripped of his journalist credentials after the crushing of the Prague Spring (he had worked as Radio Prague's foreign correspondent in the Far East and in the USA in the late 1950s and early 1960s). Dientsbier was also the spokesman of the Charter 77, and he would make public statements to western journalists from time to time, even knowing that each time he did the result would be a return to prison or to an effective house arrest that would leave him for another protracted period without contact with the outside world.

Meetings with any of the dissidents had to be carefully arranged, and I was very conscious of the fact that Jim Bonthron, a predecessor of mine had been caught exchanging documents in a park with domestic "enemies of the regime" and had been unceremoniously expelled from the country. Although I would always take measures to be reasonably satisfied that I was not being followed, in the end we relied on the dissidents themselves to make the critical judgment on whether it was safe to meet or not. I would go to a place designated by our contacts, such as a church in the old part of town, and be met there by someone entirely innocent in the eyes of the authorities, such as a tour guide or a priest. They would take me through some old building or another and we would usually end up in a private flat of a sympathizer. There I would wait until it was judged safe for others to come, and then when they did we would be able to exchange books and samizdat and chat about how the world was unfolding. I met Vaçlav Havel only once, arranged by his brother Ivan, late one night down on a park bench on Kampa Island. He was a very impressive man even when dressed as a street sweeper. My successor's successor, Rob McRae, became truly close to him and proved to be a vital supporter during the 1989 Velvet Revolution. Rob built a whole support system for Havel and the dissidents, and actually rented an apartment on Vaçlavske Namesti (Wenceslaus Square) for the revolutionaries to use as a headquarters during those tumultuous final days of communism. Havel, as President, awarded McRae the highest honour the Czechs ever awarded to a foreigner.

It was not only the highly visible dissident signatories to Charter 77 who were oppressed by the regime. We met many creative people from musical composers to artists to photographers who had had their work or personal lives affected negatively by the heavy hand of the state. One such couple, Jiri and Hana Kučera, became quite close friends of ours. He was a photographer who had worked with more famous dissidents and also had tried to publish his own creative and modern work, only to be stymied and threatened by the police. One of the regime's favourite threats was that the children of those refusing to toe the party line would be denied schooling beyond a certain age, a very powerful threat in a society that treasured learning and culture. The Kučeras had been assigned a most miserable basement apartment in an uninteresting part of town, and would come over to our home in Dejvice where their children, Pavel and Hanička, would play in our garden and on our children's swing set with Cynthia. A few years later they obtained permission to go on a vacation to Yugoslavia, and from there they escaped to the west. They eventually settled in Vancouver, where we would occasionally see them, and brought their children up as Canadians.

The second junior officer I had was Don MacKay, who as a young boy in the early 1960s had lived in Prague when his father was serving on the security side of the embassy. Don and his young wife Kathy were fun and party-loving people. He brought his fancy sports car, a Camaro Z28, into Czechoslovakia and wherever he went he would get a lot of attention from local youths. Sports cars were very rare behind the Iron Curtain and Don loved the attention. Just after Don arrived, Liani and I decided that we would buy a second car for me to zip around in, something inconspicuous and smaller than our Volvo station wagon that she in any case needed most of the days. So we bought the smallest VW then on the market, a simple Golf, a model that was already finding its way into Czechoslovakia. We ordered it from a dealer in Weiden, just across the border in West Germany, a place where many western diplomats would go out on weekends to buy supplies hard to find behind the iron curtain. Don and Kathy were heading to Weiden to do just that, so Liani and I and Cynthia crammed into the back of the Camaro for the free ride. It was very uncomfortable on the bumpy Czech roads in a car not ever intended for long distance riding in its tiny back seat, and poor little two-year old Cynthia, crammed in the middle on the hard drive-shaft hump, did not enjoy it at all. When she needed to go to the bathroom we would stop and she could get out, and we soon heard a frantic "pee pee pee" every five minutes as she had learned how to seek at least temporary relief from the discomfort of the middle back seat. After several hundred stops we finally made it to Weiden. While I would not suggest a direct causal relationship, Don and Kathy's marriage did not last and it was twenty-eight years before Don was to finally father a child of his own, when living with his second wife, working as an economic officer at our Embassy in Washington.

In spite of the oppressive system of government and the general atmosphere of east-west hostility that pervaded my working life, living in Prague was wonderful from a personal standpoint. We had a lovely house in a beautiful city, which we spent a lot of time exploring. We would wander through the back streets of the Old Town and visit charming little churches and other buildings. We would go to concerts at the ornate nineteenth century

Narodni Divadlo (National Theatre) and at little concert halls or on the grass up above the city near Hradçany. We would take Cynthia and go down to the open "Bull Market", where people could sell their produce privately. Cynthia would go on the very simply children's rides there, and we would eat delicious local sausages and ice cream in the summer.

We also spent many weekends travelling to cities and towns outside of Prague, from the hot springs of Karlovy Vary, known as Karlsbad during the Austro-Hungarian Empire, to the medieval Moravian town of Telč with its central square surrounded with rows of homes each with a unique and colorful façade, to the 15th century gothic cathedral of St. Barbara's with its double row of flying buttresses in Kutna Hora. St. Barbara's was so beautiful that we took my parents there when they visited in the spring, and it was there that while swinging Cynthia between them, they inadvertently let her go. She flew high in the air and did a complete summersault before landing flat on her front. Aside from a scrape or two, there was no real damage. We also took my parents on one of our day outings to near-by Karlstejn with its extremely well-preserved castle, built by the greatest of the Bohemian kings, Charles IV, in the mid-14th century, with a central tower that surely has inspired as many children's fantasies as any building in the world. As we traveled around the countryside we would eat at little restaurants with their local beer and sausages and knedlike and other heavy Czech food. Everywhere we went we found people to be extremely friendly and not wary of foreigners. Our pretty little Cynthia of course won over the heart of every waiter and barmaid and tour guide we met.

As we travelled around the countryside, as long as we stayed well away from the border, we were only occasionally reminded of Europe's great divide. One weekend Liani and I and Cynthia got in our Volvo and headed out of Prague to the northeast, rather vaguely on the hunt for some minor castles and manor houses. At one point we came out of a little valley onto a plateau and could see many flags fluttering in the distance off to the right. As we approached we could make out that there were also many military vehicles and we deduced that it was some sort of Warsaw Pact exercise.

Knowing that we would not be permitted to get too close, I decided to see whether we could at least get in range of my camera, so I drove along the road we were on, parallel to the maneuvers, and then turned right towards the exercises down a very small country road that led into and presumably through a copse of oak and birch trees. As I proceeded into the woods at a very modest speed, all of a sudden out from behind the trees about fifty metres in front of us appeared soldiers carrying an iron pole to block our way. Not surprised, I stopped and started to back up, at which point another group of soldiers with another iron pole blocked our way from behind. Young soldiers with patches of the CSSR Army on their uniforms surrounded the car, armed with AK-47 automatic rifles. When I started to open the door the nearest soldier raised his rifle and told me to stay in the car. And so we sat for more than two hours, unable of course to contact anyone in this time before mobile phones. Finally another group of soldiers arrived and put up behind us some large signs which, as we saw on our eventual retreat, forbade passage into what was all of a sudden a very clearly marked restricted military area. Once the signs were up and photographs taken of our car on the wrong signs of the signs, an officer came up to us, copied all the information from our passports and other documents, and brusquely told us to back up and leave. We did, rather relieved not to have had the car impounded. When I complained about this treatment on the following Monday to the Foreign Ministry, I was simply shown photographs of our car well passed the signs clearly establishing a restricted area, and of course I could do nothing further. While there was probably no real danger to us during the incident, it was a little unnerving having teenage soldiers pointing automatic weapons at not just me but at Liani and our little daughter.

Forays for us out of the country included a number of weekends to Vienna, first out of interest and later in our posting for doctor's appointments for Liani's pregnancy and to arrange for her to give birth to our second child there. Vienna was architecturally beautiful and very clean, and free of the inconveniencies of life in a communist country, but both Liani and I found the Viennese a little stand-offish, and we never developed a desire to live or spend much time there. We also took our rotational weekend once at the embassy flat in the Bavarian Forest in Freiburg, and spent another quiet weekend in Nuremburg, both in clean and free West Germany, but we generally did not feel the need to leave Czechoslovakia as regularly as some of our diplomatic colleagues seemed to.

Just after our first Christmas in Prague we took a longer trip to Indonesia to see Liani's family, and stopped in Goa in India on the way. In Goa, we stayed at the Fort Aguada Hotel, which had been recently spruced up for the 1982 Commonwealth Heads of Government meeting. We had fun touring old Goanese ruins and the local markets and Cynthia acted a ball-girl as we played tennis in between times on the beach, and it was a very pleasant family break. And being in Indonesia was special as well, for it was the last time Liani was to be able to spend time with her father and grandfather, and the first time the family there met Cynthia. We were there for a week, and then back to Czechoslovakia.

Prague was not exactly on the beaten path for high level visits from Canada. In our time there we only had two. The first was by John Bosley, then Speaker of the House of Commons, who was invited by the President of the Czechoslovak rubber-stamp parliament. Although the visit was entirely without substance, there was lots of protocol to work out and I was in charge. It went off fine although Bosley almost tore his hair out at the vapid level of the exchanges he had not just with his hosts but with the quisling General Secretary Husak and other members of the government, and when he was given a Czech vase as a gift upon departure, he was so glad to be leaving that he told me to keep it. It is actually a very handsome piece of traditional porcelain, and it still graces our living room and is known to Liani and me as "The Speaker's Vase".

The other minister we had visit was Otto Jelinek, Minister of Fitness and Amateur Sport in the first Mulroney cabinet. Jelinek and his family were originally from Prague, his father inheriting a successful business in the beverage business, owning bottling plants and cork factories. The family had left Czechoslovakia at the time of the communist coup in 1948 and settled in Southern Ontario. Otto and his sister Maria became great figure skaters and as a pair represented Canada in the Olympics and World Championships in the 1960s. The old Jelinek family home was up near St. Vitus Cathedral on the Hradçany hill, was expropriated by the communists and then rented to the Austrian government as the Austrian Ambassador's Residence. I arranged with the Ambassador for a tour of his home for the Minister, which was much appreciated. After the Velvet Revolution and the fall of communism, Otto Jelinek returned to Prague as a businessman, and is at the time of this writing the Chairman of the Czech committee vying to bring a future Olympic Games to Prague.

While we had no formal sporting events during the visit of our Sports Minister, ice hockey was to become a surprising highlight of the spring of 1985. The World Hockey Championships were hosted in Prague from the middle of April to the beginning of May, and although we very much looked forward to supporting the Canadian team, we did not expect Canada to do very well. The International Ice Hockey Federation was then dominated by the Soviet Union and east-bloc countries, with the Nordics thrown in for good measure. The annual championship always coincided with the NHL playoffs, so the best Canadian players were generally at home, playing for teams contending for the Stanley Cup. There were always enough good players from teams already eliminated for Canada to put together a credible team, but never enough or with enough time to be a serious threat to the Soviets or the Czechs, whose players did nothing but play hockey on teams kept together all year long. In the mid-1980s they were still not allowed to play professionally abroad, so the Soviet and Czech and other East European teams consisted of absolutely the very best hockey players those countries produced. As the initial games of the championship began, a barebones Canadian team arrived, supplemented every couple of days with players from NHL teams just eliminated. In the elimination round, Canada managed to beat the easy teams, but narrowly lost to the USA, which in those days normally fielded a team of well-practiced university all-stars, and got shellacked by the Soviets 9-1.

As the final round of the hockey tournament got under way right at the end of April, a few star players arrived, including Mario Lemieux, then right at the beginning of his professional career. And then the Canadian team started to win. Across the border in West Germany, the 1985 G-7 Summit was simultaneously getting underway, and as is usually the case the parliamentary press gallery was tagging along with Prime Minister Mulroney and his delegation. All of a sudden the hockey championship in Prague looked more interesting than the tightly scripted G-7 Summit, and the journalists decided they all wanted to come across the border to cover the hockey instead. Prime Minister Mulroney said publicly that he not only understood but that if he were given the choice he would rather watch the hockey than attend the summit! Getting the journalists in was not so easy, however, since in those days getting visas, especially for members of the press, was a bureaucratic and excruciatingly long process. Communist regimes were always suspicious of western journalists. I went to see my normal contacts in the Foreign Ministry and asked for special dispensation, this being Canada's national sport and a great opportunity to show Czechoslovakia's friendly side. Much to our surprise, the Foreign Ministry agreed and last minute visas were arranged for the entire list of journalists we presented, although the journalists were not permitted to cross the land border but had to fly in from Frankfurt and pick up their visas upon arrival at the airport in Prague. The next problem was accommodation, of which there was none available, so we distributed the journalists among embassy staff members, and they slept on spare beds or couches. Paul Koring of the Canadian Press slept at our house.

On the ice, things were going well for Canada, beating Sweden and the USA in successive games. Then in the semi-finals the Canadians had to face the powerful Soviets, reigning World Champions and a team to whom they had lost very badly in the opening round. The Canadian team played a dream game, and were fired up and inspired as never before, and beat the Soviets 3-1. The crowd of sixteen thousand was completely behind Canada, since Czechs had always hated their Soviet masters following the 1968 invasion, and the few Canadians in the crowd gradually got the entire stadium chanting "Da da Ca-na-da, Ny-et Ny-et So-vi-et", which was deeply embarrassing for the senior Czechoslovak Ice Hockey Federation officials who were sitting with their Soviet counterparts to watch the game. The gold medal game was a bit of a let-down, with Canada losing 5-3. The game was clean and fair, however, and no one went away terribly disappointed since we had at least beaten the Soviets and taken the Silver Medal. That night Czech radio showed its true colours in announcing the results, stating that Czechoslovakia had won the world championship and that two Russian players were among the three most valuable players of the tournament. The fact that Canada had won the Silver and beaten the Soviets was artfully ignored.

Back before World War II, Prague had been one of the most tolerant European cities with respect to different religious communities, and the Jews, who numbered around 100,000 in Prague alone and perhaps 300,000 in the country as a whole, were fully assimilated into all walks of life. This seemed like the civilized end of an eight hundred year history of cyclical acceptance and persecution. Franz Kafka and other great writers and musicians were part of the Prague Jewish community of the early twentieth century. But the rich intermingling of Jews and Christians, and within the Jewish community itself of German speakers and Czech speakers, and of Zionists and pan-Europeanists (anti-nationalists) was to come to a quick and tragic end. After the Slovak declaration of independence and treaty of subjugation to Germany in early 1939, German troops overran the Czech lands in March and the decimation of the Jewish community both in Prague and throughout Czechoslovakia began. In Slovakia it was actively implemented by local Slovaks, while in Prague and elsewhere in Bohemia and Moravia it was mostly the work of German soldiers. More than 200,000 Czechoslovak Jews, some whose families had lived there since the 12th century, were rounded up and deported to their deaths in Nazi concentration camps of nearby Terezin and more distant Auschwitz. By the time we lived there the community had been reduced to just a few thousand, for of the small numbers who had survived the Holocaust those who could emigrate had done so after the end of the war. Under the communists, state anti-Semitism was interrupted only briefly by Dubcek's democratic reform and the tolerant social policies of the Prague Spring. I made a habit of openly visiting the Jewish community centre and became a great admirer of Dieter Galsky, a lovely Jewish elder and the official head of the community. Galsky had survived the war and all the persecution since, and was determined to protect what he could of both the human community and its tremendous physical legacy, evident in both architectural treasures and artifacts. Liani and I and started eating lunch occasionally at the Jewish community centre. It was there that we learned of the collection of Judaic treasures that was just beginning a tour of the United States, under the name of the "Precious Legacy". The more we learned about it, the more convinced we were that it should also tour Canada and we knew that if it returned to Prague directly from the US, it would be extremely difficult to resuscitate it for another international tour. I spoke with US Ambassador Bill Luers, whose predecessors had worked hard to persuade the Czechoslovak government to let the exhibition be assembled and leave Prague in the first place. He got me in touch with Anna Cohn of the Smithsonian in Washington, who had been project director on the US side. I also called on the Ministry of Culture and the Foreign Ministry. Initially only the Americans were keen on seeing the tour extended to Canada, but we gradually persuaded the Czechs that it would be a good thing for bilateral relations, whatever that meant. Once we had agreement in principle, we had to find sponsoring organizations and exhibition space in Canada. Calgary's Glenbow Museum and Montreal's Musée de Beaux Arts were both enthusiastic, with Toronto's Royal Ontario Museum less so due to an already committed schedule over the ensuing few years. In the end we put it all together, and even managed to add a smaller but deeply moving exhibit of paintings and drawings done by children in the concentration camps, extraordinarily touching pictures of both hope and despair seen through the eyes of children most of whom were to die in the Nazi genocide. It turned out to be a wonderful and successful tour, and Liani and I went to the opening of its Montreal leg the following year.

It was sometime in early July of 1985 that I received a message to call Glenn Shortliffe in Ottawa. Glenn had just taken up a new position, as Assistant Deputy Minister for Administration and Personnel, and the Under-Secretary for External Affairs was Marcel Massé. In its second year in power, the Mulroney cabinet had started to get serious about governmental reform and about reducing the size of the public service. When I called him, Glenn explained that he wanted me to shorten my posting to Prague and come back to Ottawa to work with him to implement fundamental reforms and budget reductions in the department, which was now the Department of External Affairs and International Trade. He offered me a Director-level position, heading up the Resource Management Division. Tempting as this was, I was really not ready to leave Prague. Liani was pregnant with our second child, due in September, and I felt I was really only starting to hit my stride in the Prague position. We had several calls and I finally compromised, agreeing to go back to run a task force of departmental re-organization for six to eight weeks, and then return to Prague until early in 1986 at which time I would return to Ottawa to take up full-time the job as Director of Resource Management.

Liani and I cancelled the arrangements we had made for having our second child born in Vienna. I went back to Ottawa for a two-week session in July, allowing me to take up my role as Chairman of the Reorganization Task Force, kicked out our tenants using the "diplomatic clause" we had included in the lease, and bought a cheap second hand car (a Honda Civic, which turned out to be the worst car we were to ever own). I then returned to Prague to pick up Liani and Cynthia and we all went to back to Canada in late August, and settled temporarily in our old home on Wayling Avenue. The substance of my new job I will pick up in the next chapter, but on the personal level everything was pretty busy. The house had been abused by our tenants and that took some cleaning up, and before we knew it mid-September arrived along with our new little son Caleb, bringing much joy to both his parents and his big sister. In November we went back to Prague for a final six weeks, including a Christmas, which saw my brother Hugh and his wife Susan come to stay. They had accepted our invitation months earlier, long before we knew that our posting would come to an early end. When they realized we would be in pack-up mode they offered to not come, but we insisted and we had a wonderful time with them. We took them to see our favorite haunts, heard the Ryba Mass played at St. Vitus, bought Christmas carp at an outside stand set up by a street-side vendor, and had a very traditional Christmas. The day after Christmas the movers came and there were boxes everywhere, and at the end of that day Cynthia turned to us and declared "Now I know why they call it Boxing Day". We found buyers for both our cars, and Cynthia was very sad to see a German fellow drive the brown Volvo away. A final two weeks of whirlwind good-byes and we were gone, closing somewhat prematurely what had been a short but fascinating and very fulfilling assignment in Prague.

Liani in Indonesia

View from embassy bungalows
towards Genung Pangrango and
Genung Gede, which we climbed
in 1979

Pelabuhan Ratu, Southern Java

Sailors mending sails at the schooner harbour at Tanjuk Priok, Jakarta, 1978

With civil aviation negotiating team in 1981: Left to right, Irene Hart, Ray
Yang, Gary Harmon, Donna Mitchell, HRB, Joe Ledbetter

Wedding, August 29, 1980

HRB and Liani on the day
of our wedding

Prague in winter

Hradçany and St. Vitus Cathedral from our home on the
Dejvice hill in Prague, 1984

Art Deco window in our Prague home

Liani and Cynthia on the Charles Bridge in Prague, 1985

Canadian Embassy to Czechoslovakia, HRB's office behind the flag

All four children in the summer of 1989, unperturbed by events in China!

HRB leading Canada-Korea Joint Economic Commission talks in Seoul, 1993, flanked left by Ken Sunquist and right by Barry Carin

US Secretary of State Jim Baker, Australian Foreign Minister Gareth Evans,
and entertainer HRB at ASEAN dialogue meeting, 1992

Prime Minister Jean Chrétien thanking HRB and National Unity team after
close win in 1995 Québec referendum

BOOK III:

OTTAWA AND MANAGEMENT

CHAPTER 9

DIRECTOR, RESOURCE MANAGEMENT

• • • • • • • • • • •

When I arrived in Ottawa for my first bout of temporary duty as Director of Resource Management, my initial task was to prepare a plan for the Under-Secretary on departmental reorganization, left incomplete following the 1981-82 move of the trade function from the Department of Industry Trade and Commerce to External Affairs. While the formal structure had changed and parliamentary appropriations were now voted on the Main Estimates for the combined department, no one had actually moved from the C.D. Howe Building downtown to the Lester B. Pearson Building and not one senior position, or junior one for that matter, had yet been declared overlapping or redundant. Three years later, everyone was firmly entrenched and even the slightest breath of reductions or reorganization was met with a fierce defence. So Marcel Massé, the Under-Secretary, and my old friend Glenn Shortliffe, who had come back to the department as Associate Under-Secretary (the old name for Assistant Deputy Ministers) after serving as Vice President of Policy at CIDA, decided to prepare a plan in secret, obtain Ministerial agreement to it, and then impose it on the department. There were several other senior officers that Massé and Shortliffe were keeping aware of the plan, but we tried to keep our work as quiet as possible.

I chaired the working-level task force in support of Massé and Shortliffe, but not without some tremendous help. Jim Judd, who had worked with Shortliffe before and like me understood personnel issues from having worked as an assignment officer. Jim was smart and tough and did not mind breaking with tradition. There were a couple of technical people from my new division who understood the budgetary process and knew where the keys to all the hidden little safes of money around the department were hidden. I also had Shortliffe's permission to consult with Treasury Board, the government's central agency overseeing the allocation and management of personnel and financial resources voted to departments by parliament, effectively the governmental comptroller. Treasury Board had an "Analyst" for each department with a small staff sufficient to understand and interface with that department's corporate management staff, and the TB Analyst for our department served as an informal member of our task force. Having some help understanding how funds and people had been distributed under the pre-integration structure, and being advised on what had worked and what had failed in other major reorganizations across the government was extremely helpful. Our initial work was kept so confidential that we did not even use departmental resources for the printing of proposed new organization charts and the like. Instead, I took hand-written proposals to a reliable graphics company, who produced very handsome charts and other presentation material. Nowadays this would all be done by a junior staff member with PowerPoint, but we were still in the pre-computer age then and I learned quickly that having a polished professional presentation with glossy handouts would go a long way in winning over an audience. The graphics company charged us thousands of dollars for their work and I was aghast, but Shortliffe assured me that he could bury the expenses.

The result of our work was a proposal for complete integration and restructuring of the department along geographic lines. We proposed that there be five Geographic Branches for the USA, Europe, Latin America, Asia Pacific, and Africa and the Middle East,. Each of these would be headed by an Assistant Deputy Minister (ADM) who would be charged with overseeing all policies and programs and embassies in his or her region, including political and economic issues, trade policy and trade promotion, consular and immigration. Each would have their own small resource management secretariat (with a "dotted-line" relationship with my division) to give the ADM the flexibility to move money and people around his or her own region with minimal interference from the corporate centre of the Department. These "Geographic Tsars" would be alone in answering to both the Minister of External Affairs and the Minister of International Trade through the separate Deputy Minister dedicated to each (the Foreign Affairs deputy was to keep the Under-Secretary title for another nine years, until the election of the Chrétien government in late 1993). In addition we proposed an Economic and Trade Policy Branch be created from units diverse units distributed in branches of the old ITC and External, and a Trade Promotion Branch be charged with overseeing the promotion of Canadian trade and the department's relations with the private sector at a high level. There would also be International Political Branch, led again by an ADM who would be the equivalent of the European concept of "Political Director", manage Canada's involvement in the UN and other multilateral organizations, and oversee Security and Intelligence. The plumbing of the Department would be structured into Personnel, Corporate Management and Administration Branches, which would be part of the department's "Core", and be overseen by a single very senior officer, who alone would be called Associate Under-Secretary. We did not just propose this broad structure, we took apart budgets and detailed personnel positions and put them together again right down to the lowest level clerk and secretary. Everyone was to be housed in the Lester B. Pearson Building, with each branch given a floor in one of its four towers.

The reorganization proposal was accepted by the deputy ministers and the Ministers, and then announced to the department. One of the biggest issues of working-level concern turned out to be how to fit everyone into the building. While we had proposed a fairly widespread use of open space, this was strongly opposed by the rank and file of the officer corps, and their "union", the Professional Association of Foreign Service Officers (PAFSO), sought and obtained agreement from senior management to replace the planned open open-space layout with a plan which saw almost all line positions given very small offices of about 100 square feet each, less than two-thirds the size of traditional departmental offices.

Once the reorganization was implemented and I had finished shuttling our growing family to and from Prague in January of 1986, I settled down into the more regular job of being the departmental comptroller. My job was to run the department's annual planning and resource allocation process, administer a quarterly corporate management reporting system and make recommendations on quarterly reallocations to meet shifting needs, to manage a small person-year reserve known as the "Under-Secretarial Pool", and the department's contingency financial reserves, and oversee the department's Grants and Contributions, which were divided between the obligatory obligations such as Canada's UN or IMF fees, and discretionary contributions such as support for Canadian non-governmental organizations like the Canadian Institute of International Affairs. In managing these grants and contributions, we simply exercised a control function to ensure that budgets were not overspent or misallocated; the real decision-making was closely held at the level of the Under-Secretary and Ministers, since decisions to increase or decrease grants to Canadian associations and institutions were always very political.

The Resource Management Division was relatively large, with about 15 people, and gave me good experience in managing both people and processes, even if the day-to-day work was not as substantively interesting as the line directorships in the geographic or economic branches of the Department. Although I worked closely with the Under-Secretary and others on "The 8th Floor" as the senior-most team of Associate Under-secretary and ADMs was called, I also had a Director General to report to. In my first year on the job this was Marie-Andrée Beauchemin, a beautiful and stylish but mercurial woman who used to alternate between yelling at and flirting lightly with male subordinates, a really complicated set of signals to receive from a boss. Because I was in place before she arrived and because I was both clearly the master of my files and close to senior management, I had an easier time in my relationship with her than other directors. Her spouse, deMontigny Marchand, would eventually become Under-Secretary, and I ended up in late 1989 working directly for him, but this was still some years away.

By the time I settled back in Ottawa after Christmas, both Glenn Shortliffe and Marcel Massé had moved to PCO, Glenn as a Deputy Secretary under Paul Tellier and Marcel as Secretary to the Cabinet for Federal-Provincial Affairs. Replacing them in the Department were Derek Burney as Associate Under-Secretary and James H. (Si) Taylor as Under-Secretary. Si Taylor was a life-long Kremlinologist and a great expert on East-West issues and was largely uninterested in Departmental management matters, so Derek effectively ran the Department from a management standpoint.

In the 1986 budget, the Mulroney Government announced a further tightening of the budgetary restraint that it had begun with its first budget the year before. Departmental budgets were cut across the board with the objective of saving $500 million from operating expenses, and both inflation and all new initiatives had to be absorbed within existing appropriations. Given that inflation was then running at around 5%, this was a real burden on departments and it was up to me to support senior management in coming up with a rational plan to meet the imposed targets. Derek wanted a series of options developed involving a range of actions from a draconian program of post closures to other less extreme measures, but he was determined that the political level recognize that severe cuts would come with real costs and could not be simply absorbed by having Ambassadors entertain less, which was almost the impression we were getting of the view of Ministerial political staffers. So we produced a few options, only one of which Derek decided to take to Joe Clark, Secretary of State for External Affairs.

The cost reduction scenario that we proposed to Clark involved the closing of twenty-five missions, a mix of embassies and consulates in every region of the world. It was what was to become known as a "Musical Ride" list. Whenever the RCMP was told to reduce costs, the first unit they would propose abolishing was the ceremonial Musical Ride, which was Mounties doing a mix of dressage and equestrian acrobatics, enormously popular among the public and a great Canadian symbol. Politicians loved the Musical Ride and were expected, by refusing its proposed elimination, to exempt the RCMP from any reductions whatsoever. Clark was not easily cowed, however. When he saw our long list of proposed post closures displayed on the screen, he turned to Burney and said "Derek, if we close all those posts, there will be NO room left whatsoever for career appointments". Clark's tongue-in-cheek remark was made in the context to Foreign Service unhappiness with the number of political appointments to Ambassadorial positions made by Prime Minister Mulroney since coming to power in 1984. Clark obviously knew we were gaming him and sent us back to the drawing board, and we eventually got him to agree to a more modest program of five post closures, including Helsinki and Quito and three consulates. In the end the outcry over Helsinki was so strong we did not close it, while the Quito closure proceeded only to be reversed with a reopening two years later.

The mid-1980s was very early in the expansion of the computer era, and the government, and especially those departments where national security was a concern, was well behind the rest of the world in permitting personal or desk-top devices. More importantly, the internet did not yet exist; its first version was to emerge in 1986 when the US National Science Foundation Network provided access to its computing sites electronically by universities and research institutions. Commercial internet service providers were still five years away when I was running the Resource Management Division. Personally interested in computers, I persuaded the department to buy me a "portable" computer, the Compaq Portable, which had a tiny screen, weighed 28 pounds and cost $5,000. I would lug this monster back and forth between home and the office so I could work in the evenings, and the more I got used to doing so, the more I believed that personal and portable computers could revolutionize the way the foreign service functioned.

At this time the Department employed something like 700 "Communicators", a technical corps of cypher clerks who ran a very sophisticated and very secure global communications network in support of the foreign and intelligence services. Every embassy and consulate had at least one or two, and some, like London which served as a relay mode between Ottawa and many of our missions in Europe and Africa, had dozens. The basic way a message went from a desk officer in Ottawa to a colleague sitting in Bonn or Buenos Aires was as follows: the initiating officer would hand-write a message, a secretary would transcribe it into a special "telegram" format, the originator would sign a box in the lower left corner, a supervisor would approve and sign a box in the lower right corner, and then the telegram would be hand-carried to the Communications Centre in a secure area of the second floor of A Tower. There a communicator would re-transcribe the message on a computer console, and produce a paper tape about two centimetres wide with holes punched in it displaying a non-enciphered form of the letters composing the message. This tape would then be fed into an enciphering machine, which had two tape readers, one for the message tape and one for a code tape, and a tape maker which would produce a third tape containing the encrypted form of the message. This tape would then be fed into a telex machine which would transmit over government controlled lines a message that would be an unintelligible series of five letters separated by spaces that looked like this: TYUIP LKJHG DFGHJ MNBVC. At the other end, in the communications crypt of an embassy, a communicator would feed the tape that the receiving telex produced into a similar cypher machine along with the appropriate code tape (which was changed daily) and produced an "au clair" tape that would be fed into a text producing machine that would print a readable message. This message would be either hand carried to the recipient or put in his message box, depending on its urgency.

When brainstorming about how to deal with the pressures being forced on the Department's person-year establishment by government cuts, we looked at the secure communications system and the large corps of communicators and wondered whether we could reduce through the use of modern computers the number of human steps between sender and receiver. How wonderful, we thought, if an officer could input his own message on a desk-top computer and the recipient receive it on a screen at his desk half a world away, without anyone having to re-transcribe or manually operate enciphering or decrypting machines?

I called Doug Woods, who was Director General of Communications and in charge of the whole global communications network. Communicators in posts abroad were under the administrative authority of Heads of Mission, but answered professionally and for appraisal purposes to the Communications establishment in Ottawa. Much to my surprise, Doug was completely at ease with the concept of an automated encrypting and communications system supporting desk-to-desk messaging between officers at home and abroad. He told me that he and another colleague, Paul Dunseath, had along with some other communications specialists been thinking about this, and that they had already automated a couple of the old manual steps within the communications centre. So Doug and Paul and I began to spend hours together, and soon came up with the concept design for the "Canadian Online Secure International Communications System", or "COSICS", and put together sub-teams of technical and security experts to figure out the challenges we needed to overcome. Many professional communicators participated in our work. We also reached out to our closest allies, the Americans and the British, and found out that both of them were toying with similar ideas. The three of us travelled to Washington, and to London and the UK's communications research centre in Cheltenham and met with both foreign affairs units and the more shadowy organizations charged with security and secure communications. We came away deeply convinced that we were on the right track.

As the COSICS program gained steam, we met with the Communicators union and found that they were in general not opposed to the initiative, knowing as technical experts that the systems we were planning to put in place would require higher degrees of professional skills at every mission even if fewer positions would be involved. A new category of employee was created, the "Technical Administrators" (or "TAs") to replace the communicators (or "CMs") and a multi-year transition and training plan was developed. The plan was to put a beta system in place with Washington, the two New York missions (to the UN and the Consulate General) and a dozen headquarter divisions all hooked up to the experimental network. For the desktop units we used early-era personal computers made by

Micron, a Canadian company, with a full keyboard and a little black and white seven-inch screen. One day one of my staff members, Carey Dark, (who I had recruited as I had known of his "techie" interests when he worked with me as consular clerk in Jakarta), came to me and said "colour screens". I asked him what he was talking about, and he explained that he believed that eventually desk-to-desk communications would be done with colour screens and we should privately invest in the development of communications protocols that could take advantage of colour. I told him I thought he was nuts; after all what would be the purpose – would we highlight messages in red or blue? Smart Carey, not-so-smart Howard.

At one point in the autumn of 1986 Doug and I went on a quick tour of the posts to be used in the experimental phase of COSICS to meet with both mission management and the communications staff. When we got to the UN mission in New York, we met with the Committee on Post Management, chaired by Ambassador Stephen Lewis, a former NDP politician, a flowery orator and a fierce defender of the downtrodden. Even before I could open my mouth, Ambassador Lewis lit into me with a speech saying that he had never seen such a nasty, anti-labour and anti-human program and that we should be ashamed at this outrageous attempt to replace hard working employees with machines and so on. I simply could not believe the vitriol, but instead of responding, I got up, left the room and went and asked the head communicator at the mission to come back to the meeting with me. When we walked back in, I asked him to tell the Ambassador what he thought of COSICS. The senior communicator said that he and all his younger colleagues thought the automation of our secure communications system was long overdue and, in spite of the job losses and the many early retirements it might precipitate, it would represent the best possible career opportunity for the those communicators who stayed, helping them to become vanguards of the computer age. Lewis was nailed and embarrassed in front of his own senior employees, who unlike him were all professional Foreign Service types, and it was years before he would again look me in the eye. Lewis always had a tendency to let his prodigious oratory skills get far ahead of ahead of critical thinking.

I remained involved in the COSICS project even after I left the Resource Management Division as Chair of the department's User's Committee and a member of its supervisory board. It made some significant advances over the next year or two, but as the commercial internet industry started to take off, it became increasingly evident that the right solution was not to try to build everything ourselves but to use, to the extent consistent with our security needs, systems and software becoming available in the commercial market. And the result was a successful transformation, over a relatively short period of time, of our old clunky and highly resource-intensive system into a modern foreign service with globally secure desk-to-desk communications.

Aside from the COSICS project, much of my time was spent in simply running the department's resource tracking and allocation system. We would receive monthly reports from the accounts division and prepare quarterly reports for senior management. We also would handle the preparation of the Department's detailed annual budget for approval by the Treasury Board and for eventual inclusion in the detailed appropriations bill, the Main Estimates, that the government would submit to parliament immediately after the higher level Budget Bill was passed. This involved really getting to know the whole department well, how and where managers hid away money or inflated their budgets, how the multi-year capital budget (largely for building new chanceries) fit into the annual appropriation process and how it could be better managed. In an era of restraint and reductions, it was also vital to pick apart operational budgets to ensure that some posts were not starving while others were awash with cash.

During the summer of 1986, Marie-Andrée Beauchemin moved on to become Director General of Cultural and Academic Relations, and my old friend Rod Irwin replaced her. Working with Rod was a joy, he always supported his people and allowed them freedom to fly when they were doing things right. Rod was also a no-nonsense guy who had learned negotiating by dealing with the Soviets in Moscow, and he would never undermine me if I had staked out a tough position on resourcing with a branch ADM or a Head of Mission, so having him as part of my team made life easier than it had been with Beauchemin, who was always interfering in support of someone's special plea to her.

Rod and I obtained from senior management the mandate to conduct a series of "A-Base" analyses of large posts, examining them from the ground up and making the Heads of Mission and their headquarter sponsors justify every position and every dollar of cost. We "A-Based" London and Geneva and Paris, our largest European posts, and precipitated the ire of very senior ambassadors when we made resource reduction recommendations. Having Derek Burney as the senior official in charge of our work made a huge difference, for Derek was a tough manager and was not easily pushed aside when he believed what he was recommending was correct. He would be very tough with us to ensure that what we were recommending was well supported analytically, but once he was satisfied that we were proposing sensible and not system-destructive reductions, he would back us up unequivocally.

Running the annual resource allocation process was easier on the financial budget side than it was on the allocation and utilization of PYs, or "person-years", a unit of account equal to hiring one person full-time for one year. Parliamentary appropriations actually contained both a dollar budget and a set PY establishment for every department of government, and any Minister who allowed his department to exceed either could end up being carpeted by the Public Accounts Committee of the House of Commons.

Most Heads of Mission and headquarters Directors and Directors General were not very attentive to their budgets, and in the past there had been vast variances between budgets and actual spending. Reorganization had created a system of geographic resource management secretariats with professional administrators in them, and they would report monthly to their DGs and ADMs on their budgetary situation, and this was greatly improving financial management. The fight annually for new PYs in the past had been dominated by powerful Heads of Mission lobbying directly with departmental senior management, and so the large posts grew and the little posts tended to stagnate. With our new geographically organized department, we forced the geographic ADMs to try to deal with their own needs first from within their own region. They and the ADM responsible for the multilateral posts, had to produce a list of regional reallocations, a second list of highest priority positions not funded from within, and a third list of lowest priority positions that the branch would give up if its overall PY allocation was reduced. Rod and I would meet with the DGs and ADM of every branch prior to senior management review, so by the time that the triumvirate of Derek Burney, Under-Secretary Si Taylor, and Deputy Minister of Trade Gerry Shannon had to deal with the painful annual process, all but the inter-regional reallocations were resolved.

In February 1987, Derek Burney left the Department to become Chief of Staff to Prime Minister Mulroney and was replaced on an acting basis by Joe Stanford, an older and extremely thoughtful diplomat who had served as our Ambassador to Israel. I knew Stanford would be no Derek Burney and that I had learned just about everything I could about departmental and governmental resources management and appropriations, so I began to plan my exit from the departmental plumbing. I looked around at Director-level positions likely to open up over the next few months, and found one that was of particular interest, Director of North Asia Relations. With the backing of Joe Stanford and Rod Irwin, in early April I sought an interview with the ADM Asia-Pacific, Jean McCloskey, and she agreed to support my transfer.

On a personal level, the years back in Ottawa following our posting in Prague were good years. The Resource Management job involved some but not too much travel, almost never required urgent weekend work, and I could spend a lot of time with Liani and our two little children. In January 1986, just after returning from Prague, we had driven in our second hand Honda Civic to Woodstock, Vermont, to celebrate my parents' fortieth wedding anniversary with our whole family, Pat and Tim and their six children, Joy and Chip and their three, and Hugh and Susan, still without. It was a lovely weekend of cross-country skiing and sleigh-riding and evening feasts and wood fires. It was not a great drive in the Honda and Liani and I made up our minds to get rid of it as fast as we could. Back in Ottawa we found a second-hand Volvo station wagon for sale, in very good condition and exactly the same colour as the one we had owned in Prague. When we brought it home, little three and a-half year-old Cynthia was thrilled that the "German man had given our car back", and we did not disabuse her of that belief for many years.

We would spend our winter weekends skating (by the winter of 1987, Cynthia's skating skills were very strong) and skiing with Caleb on my back, and summers bicycling around Ottawa and sailing in Jamestown. We replanted our vegetable garden, and our flower-filled rack garden outside our little sunroom, both of which our tenants had totally ignored in spite of attestations of being dedicated gardeners.

When I and my brother Hugh had come of age in the early 1970s, my father had told us that he was dividing between us a very small holding he had inherited from his mother in a family company in Australia. It was a dairy enterprise still run by distant cousins, the Morts, in Bodalla, New South Wales, almost due east from Canberra. The company produced a fine cheddar, and the town of Bodalla had at its entrance a five-meter giant statue of a round cheese, whose advertising jingle used to be "Chompa chompa Bodalla". The land and cheese factory had been in the family since my great-great-grandparents settled there early in the early 19th century, and the ownership had been divided *per stirpes* through several generations. The result was a widely distributed ownership, with Hugh and I owning a tiny percentage, from which we derived an annual dividend of a few hundred dollars every year. The largest shareholders were not the Morts still living and working in Bodalla, but a few older descendants of the original owners now back in England. In 1986, Panfida Foods, the Australian subsidiary of a British conglomerate, made an offer to buy Bodalla, an offer the Morts who lived there strongly opposed. They reached out to us and we pledged to fight the offer. Hugh and I tried to find an alternative bidder who would buy the enterprise with the family, and I met with one wealthy self-made man in Britain who was looking to acquire land to hold for future generations who agreed to make a bid. Unfortunately he and other potential bidders all backed away following the stock market crash of October 1987 and the Panfida bid was accepted by a majority of the shareholders, led by the UK-based shareholders no longer close to the family. So Bodalla was lost, but at least we had pushed the Panfida bid price up, and the result was a little windfall for both myself and Hugh. The Morts in Bodalla were terribly disappointed, but a few years later Panfida lost interest in the business, having been unable to complete other acquisitions to create a larger enterprise, and the business was broken up and the lands sold off in an auction. Many local family members and former sharecroppers were able to buy back the land and the business and take it forward, and this time without the burden of an extended network of distant shareholders.

For Liani and me, the money I received from Bodalla meant that we could begin thinking of making a down payment on a larger home, trading up from our tiny Wayling Avenue house.

CHAPTER 10

DIRECTOR, NORTH
ASIA RELATIONS

• • • • • • • • • • •

The Lester B. Pearson Building is a modern looking structure, designed by the Toronto firm of Webb Zerafa Menkes in the late 1960s, and intended to look like an extension of the igneous rock wall which separates the Rideau and Ottawa Rivers at the Rideau Falls, part of the massive Canadian Shield. It is composed of four towers of varying height, the tallest being Tower A, high in which are Canada's state dining rooms where presidents and foreign ministers and provincial premiers are entertained. All but one of the towers are connected up through the fifth floor, and then they divide. The tenth floor of Tower A is the floor of the Minister of Foreign Affairs and his staff, the floor below holds the state dining and reception rooms, and on the 8th floor have always been the Under-Secretary (later the Deputy Minister of Foreign Affairs), and the Deputy Minister of International Trade. Arrayed below them were the Geographic, Multilateral and Economic branches, the heart and soul of External Affairs.

By simple happenstance, the Resource Management Division and the North Asia Relations Division (which was always referred to by its three-letter acronym, PNR) were actually side-by-side on the fifth floor, the former in Tower B and the latter in Tower A. Although I used the inter-tower door (which was supposed to remain permanently locked due to different levels of security) to move all my office and personal paraphenalia from one to the other, in all but geographical proximity the distance between the two was cavernously large.

I arrived in PNR in the early summer of 1987 and started to attend weekly branch meetings chaired by the Assistant Deputy Minister, Jean McCloskey. The three Directors General (one each for the North Asia, Southeast Asia and Oceania, and South Asia Bureaus) and all the Directors attended. At this time, each Bureau had a Relations division, which looked after political matters and what we used to call "general relations" and one or more Trade divisions, which looked after the promotion of Canadian trade. In the case of the North Asia Bureau, there was one Relations Division (mine) and two Trade Divisions, the Japan Trade Division covering only Japan, Canada's second largest trading partner, and the North Asia Trade Division covering China, Korea and Indochina. Immigration matters, originally designed in the 1985 reorganization to have their own division in each bureau, were managed by a single branch-wide division, and administrative and financial management issues were managed by a small secretariat. The handling of economic matters and market access issues was a blurred area, with relations divisions arguing that economic matters could not be separated from broader political relations, and trade divisions arguing that the economic function should be theirs due to the close link to the promotion of Canadian trade and investment. After my very first branch meeting, McCloskey, who came from old ITC and did not seem to have a very high opinion of the "striped-pants" types of old External, called me into her office with Art Perron, the Director General for North Asia and my immediate boss. After perfunctorily welcoming me to the branch, she then quite forcefully said that in her branch, economic issues were the purview of the trade divisions and that she did not want any turf wars between my trade colleagues and me. I had been unaware that there had been such a jurisdictional battle, and I certainly was not going to start one by countering a direct decree from on high, so I assured her that I was fine with whatever separation of responsibilities she deemed proper for the branch. It was, however, not a very friendly start.

Neither geographers nor atlases had been consulted in the geographic separation of the Asian bureaus, for my North Asia Relations Division managed not only the logical countries of Japan, China, Mongolia and the Koreas, but Indochina as well. Given the hostile relations between the ASEAN countries (Malaysia, Singapore, Indonesia, Brunei and the Philippines) and communist Vietnam, Laos and Cambodia, it had been felt that it would be better to keep the management of our relations with separate teams. The bonus for me was that I was responsible for Vietnam, as well as internally riven Cambodia and smaller Laos, which added some very interesting files to my portfolio.

My team in PNR was a top-notch one. My two Deputy Directors, both older than I, were Bruce Jutzi covering China and Indochina, and David Preston covering Japan and the Koreas. Mongolia was at this time still managed by our Eastern European Bureau since it was a controlled satrapy of Moscow, no more independent than the eastern republics of the USSR. Bruce was a mandarin-speaking "old China hand" and would prove a stalwart for me throughout the Tiananmen crisis two years later. He ended his career many years later in 2008 as Director General of Security and Intelligence after several years as Ambassador to the Czech Republic, where he and his wife Pearl had lived in the lovely residence of Hadovka. David Preston had been a predecessor of mine in Jakarta where he had been famous for running to and from work every day, more than 6 kilometres each way in the tropical heat. David was one of the hardest workers I have ever known and a true generalist. After his time with me in PNR, David went on to work on US affairs, and eventually became High Commissioner to Bangladesh and finally Ambassador to the Republic of Poland, retiring in 2009. In addition to my two deputies I had another very talented sinologist and mandarin-speaker in Gordon Houlden, who combined a slightly scattered approach to his work (his office was never neat), with tremendous judgment and a very deep understanding of China. Gordon would have a total of five postings in greater China, lastly as Minister in Beijing and then as head of mission in Taipei, before leaving the service in 2008 to become Director of the China Institute at the University of Alberta, where he is still teaching. On the non-China side, David Preston had Ron Mackintosh, a very able economist working with him. Ron also had responsibility for managing Asia-wide economic issues, and when

APEC was created partway through my time in the division, Ron became APEC desk officer.

A New Emphasis on Asia: Pacific 2000

Prime Minister Mulroney had put a major emphasis on relations with Japan and China after coming to power in 1984. He attended the Economic Summit in Tokyo in the summer of 1986. After the Summit, Mulroney had a formal bilateral visit in Japan, and then went on to Beijing, which was the first state visit of a Canadian Prime Minister in a decade. In Beijing, Mulroney spent substantial time with both Deng Xiaoping and Zhao Ziyang, and was publicly very gracious to the legacy of Pierre Trudeau in establishing diplomatic relations with the PRC and easing China out of its Cultural Revolution exile. He also brought Alvin Hamilton with him, the long-retired Minister of Agriculture from the Diefenbaker government of 1960, which authorized the shipment of a million tons of Canadian wheat to China at the time of the famine created by the Great Leap Forward. Mulroney also met with Hu Yaobang, who was to be purged six months later, allegedly for pushing political liberalization too forcefully. Upon his return to Canada, Mulroney asked that Cabinet be presented with discussion papers on the future of our relationships with each of the two major Asian countries, and in the spring of 1987, before I arrived in the Asia Pacific Branch, Cabinet had considered at two different sessions our relationship with each.

At an early branch management meeting, Jean McCloskey said something about the need to look at how to solve the tight resource situation in both Tokyo and Beijing, and I asked why the Department had not sought incremental funds and PYs (position-years) when it prepared the two Cabinet submissions on Japan and China. She stated that Si Taylor, the Under-Secretary, was opposed to making these thoughtful presentations into a resource grab, and that she had been told that there were no incremental resources to be had for any programs. Having just come out of two years as Director of Resource Management, I had no doubts when I said "Jean, there are always extra resources to be had if you go about it the right way". While she was a little upset that I would imply that the Branch had not done all it could with the Cabinet submissions earlier in the year, she was intrigued and accepted my bet that we could actually go back to Cabinet and get a substantial increase in our resource base as long as we made the argument as part of the substantial global shift in economic power towards Asia.

Although the rise of China was not much in the public consciousness yet, the emergence of Japan certainly was, for 1987-88 were the height of Japanese economic strength, driven not only by two decades of strong export and investment growth but by a massive asset bubble, the unsustainability of which none of us had yet perceived. In addition to the evident economic clout of Japan, this was also the time that Korea and Taiwan broke through to middle-income status, and the OECD coined the term Newly Industrialized Economies (the NIEs). Korea, Taiwan and Singapore were already NIEs, and it appeared that Malaysia and Thailand would likely follow suit in fairly short order. In spite of this, most of Canada's Foreign Service resources were still deployed in Europe, and European and East-West issues still dominated the thinking in Fort Pearson. And so I sat down with my colleagues and started brainstorming how we could not only turn heads in Ottawa towards the implications of an Asia on the rise but how we could help the whole country prepare for the Pacific century. We came up with the title "Pacific 2000".

If it was to gain the approval of Cabinet, or indeed have any relevance for actually changing behaviour and buttressing national preparedness, Pacific 2000 clearly could not be a program limited to External Affairs and International Trade. With McCloskey's blessing, we began a series of consultations with other government departments and confidentially with the Asia Pacific Foundation of Canada, the principal trade associations like the Canada Japan Business Council and the Canada China Trade Council, as well as the major provinces. We first tried to identify what the country, and the government, needed in order to be better prepared for the tectonic shift towards Asia already well underway. We came up with a list of quite disparate needs, from an enhancement of Asian language teaching in our schools, to new programs of educational, scientific and technological cooperation with Asian countries, universities and other institutions, to a increase in media coverage of developments in Japan and China and a broader understanding of Asian cultures among our young, to an expanded array of posts and trade offices in the region to support small and medium size businesses. Obviously, not all of these could be fixed overnight by government programs, but we felt that if we identified the needs we might be able to either kick-start positive change or at least raise awareness among those who could bring that change about. By the time we had a reasonably presentable product, which took almost a year, Pacific 2000 contained proposals costing $120 million over five years. It included: seed funding for a Federal-Provincial effort to increase the teaching of Chinese and Japanese in secondary schools; a youth exchange program with key Asian partners; a media exchange and fellowship program to be managed by the Asia Pacific Foundation to encourage more young Canadian journalists to focus on Asia; funding for enhanced cooperation in science and technology with Asian partners and particularly Japan; and an expansion of Canada's presence in the region with new posts and more people.

Knowing what it took to get something through Cabinet, I had done a lot of work to get the support of other departments and, through them, their Ministers. While some of the incremental funding would come to the Department, other departments would also benefit, and politically it was also attractive because of the support that it would receive from Western politicians and provinces. Our real problem was in our own department, where the highlighting of Asia was virulently opposed by the Latin American and European Branches particularly, and Under-Secretary Si Taylor was an East-West guru and a Europeanist at heart and did not really believe that the world was soon to undergo a fundamental rebalancing. So at a level way above my pay-grade it was decided to make

Pacific 2000 into a broader program called "Going Global" and tack on a bunch of resource requests for Latin America and elsewhere. However, as no one else had done the homework and consensus building that we had, the other resource requests were very minor relative to those built into Pacific 2000. And, when it did finally get approved by Cabinet in 1989, most of the funding approved was for the Asia-focused programs we had designed. Eventually some of the most important programs, including more post openings in Asia, the funding of S&T cooperation with Japan, and the seeding of enhanced Asian language teaching, were implemented. Others were to die on the vine in one round or another of overall government cutbacks, but on balance the effort was worthwhile and helped in the gradual redirection of the Canadian ship of state towards to Asia Pacific region.

We did not wait for final Cabinet funding to get some of our ideas started, however, and I had always believed it was easier to obtain forgiveness than permission. So when it was announced in late 1987 that the new Japanese Prime Minister, Noboru Takeshita, would come to Canada and the United States at the beginning of his mandate, we proposed to the Prime Minister's office the creation of a joint study group to analyze how to enhance bilateral science and technology cooperation. The idea was quickly taken up by Mulroney, with the strong encouragement of his Chief of Staff, Derek Burney, who had served in both Japan and Korea, in the latter as Ambassador, and who was a big believer in the growing importance of Asia. Mulroney raised the "Complementarity Study" proposal with Takeshita, who readily accepted the proposal and the two agreed to each nominate a co-leader for the study within the next month. We chose physicist Professor Geraldine Kenney-Wallace, President of McMaster University and Chair of the Science Council of Canada as our co-chair and Stephen Heeney, who had been Minister and second-in-command at the Embassy in Tokyo was seconded to the Asia Pacific Foundation of Canada to lead the secretariat functions and to keep the study focused and on track. It eventually reported to the two Prime Ministers in 1989, suggesting enhanced cooperation among scientific agencies of government, universities and advanced technology industries in such areas as: biomaterials and biotechnology; oceanography and ocean engineering; space science and cosmology; artificial intelligence, robotics and photonics; and finally sustainable development and environmental management. The Complementarity Study report came out just as Cabinet was considering our funding proposals under Pacific 2000 and was certainly helpful in ensuring a positive review.

The visit of Takeshita was the first of many bilateral high-level visits that I was to be charged with over the years. It was then more or less a pro forma requirement that a Japanese Prime Minister would pay a visit to Washington at the beginning of his mandate, and it was equally normal that a visit to Ottawa would be included to avoid the impression of the trip simply being that of a vassal state to the imperial centre. Takeshita took over as Prime Minister in early November and it was a couple of weeks later that we were given six weeks warning of the visit. This meant negotiations with the Japanese and the PMO on agenda items, a lot of briefs to write, and logistical and security preparations to put in place. Deputy Chief of Mission Stephen Heeney and tireless David Preston, my Deputy Director for Japan, were tremendous colleague to work with. They and I and other colleagues later theorized that six weeks was a perfect amount of lead time for a Prime Ministerial visit in either direction, especially if more than one city was involved. If a visit was announced four months in advance, one would use every minute of that time planning and revising, often unnecessarily, until the very last minute. Less than six weeks really did not allow sufficient time to organize everything needed from hotel accommodations to speech venues to the negotiation of desired outcomes. In any case, the Takeshita visit went off flawlessly. I had my first direct dealings with Prime Minister Mulroney, briefing him in advance in his office with Derek Burney, and then meeting with him prior to the actual sessions with Takeshita. As long as one was well prepared, clear and direct in one's introduction of the planned agenda while being conscious that the Prime Minister had already dealt in depth with many of the issues to be raised and did not need to be spoon-fed, Mulroney was attentive and a pleasure to brief. He was also very gracious with his praise after a successful event, and sent through Derek a personal note of thanks to me once Takeshita had left.

Under Heaven One Family - China and the Taiwan Question

While our relations with China were on a good strong footing following the visit of Prime Minister Mulroney to Beijing in 1986, our relations with Taiwan were not. When Canada recognized China in 1970 it had recognized that the government in Beijing was the legal government of China, but we had also not, explicitly or implicitly, accepted that this gave the People's Republic the right to take Taiwan back by force. We had simply "taken note" of the Chinese re-iteration that Taiwan was an inalienable part of the territory of the People's Republic of China. This obfuscating "Canadian formula" was to pave the way for many other countries to recognize China, but it left our relations with Taiwan in a dark grey zone. In 1970 there was little commercial exchange between Taiwan and Canada, but by the mid-1980s our business community was calling for more support, better visa services, and direct air links. The newly consolidated Canadian Airlines, created by the merger of CPAir and Pacific Western Airlines (the latter actually purchasing its larger rival) was particularly enthusiastic about starting up services between Vancouver and Taipei, but this was very sensitive because air relations were governed by formal bilateral treaties, impossible between Canada and the Republic of China. In 1986 the government had encouraged (and helped fund) the establishment of an office of the Canadian Chamber of Commerce in Taipei, and there was an equivalent non-diplomatic Taiwanese office in Toronto, but neither government was really happy with these offices and the irksome questions of visas and direct air services still had not been addressed. This was to turn out to be a thoroughly fun file.

As I understood the sensitive civil aviation question from my time earlier in the decade as assistant to the Chief Air Negotiator, I knew that the establishment of direct air services between Canada and Taiwan would not be an easy knot to untie. With the help of our legal division, who examined our domestic legislation governing aviation with a fine toothed comb, we found a path forward. We discovered that in the basic laws establishing the Canadian Transport Commission and the role of the Minister of Transport, the latter was given the responsibility to approve international air services as set out in international or bilateral treaties, as well as a never-used residual right, in almost a throw-away phrase, to approve "other such services as may be deemed to be in the public interest" or something along those lines. After getting Transport Canada on board, I went to see Rhys Eyton, then President of Canadian Airlines, and told him of our plan, which was to work out an arrangement under which air services might be permitted "in the public interest" but without any enabling agreement between the two governments. He loved the idea and agreed to keep his people cooperative while we worked out the details. The big problem was that Taiwan would insist on reciprocal rights, which would mean aircraft of China Airlines, with the Republic of China flag on their tail fins, landing in Canada, which the Chinese would vehemently oppose. The Chinese very firm position was that air services were a forbidden sector of economic relations with Taiwan since they clearly implied recognition of the sovereignty of the government of the Republic of China, which is why no country had established air services to Taiwan following recognition of the PRC. Only the US and Japan, both with services to the island prior to establishing diplomatic relations with China, got away with ongoing air services as a "grandfathered" right. Services between Hong Kong and Taipei were conveniently explained away as "domestic" services since both were Chinese territories, even though Chinese sovereignty was exercised over neither at the time.

Starting late in the winter of 1988, I held a series of secret meetings with the Administrative Deputy Minister of Foreign Affairs of the Republic of China, a man who then went under the name of John Chiang, to work out a deal. Chiang Hsiao-Yen was one of the illegitimate twin sons of Chiang Ching-kuo, former President of the Republic of China and son in turn of earlier President and famous Guomingdang leader Chiang Kai-shek. Chiang was a graduate of Georgetown University in Washington and a charming dinner companion, but a very tough negotiator. Sensitive to a Chinese reaction, I insisted that we avoid meeting in either Canada or Taiwan, and we first met in Tokyo to discuss the broad outline of an understanding. On our side we insisted that China Airlines could not serve Canada because it was clearly the state-owned "flag carrier" of the Republic of China, and that if they wished reciprocal rights to flights by Canadian Airlines, which was not state-owned and thus not a "flag carrier", they would have to designate another airline. Initially Chiang suggested that this would make any deal impossible. I also offered a more flexible approach to the Taiwanese representation in Canada, allowing them to open an office in Ottawa and to station foreign ministry diplomats to that office, with diplomatic privileges. This was an important concession which Chiang was more than happy to reciprocate for our office in Taipei, although I said, somewhat disingenuously, that this was of no importance to Canada since we were happy with the existing Chamber of Commerce arrangement.

Following the first round of secret talks in Tokyo, I went on to Beijing and met with the Foreign Ministry and explained that the Canadian Government had been advised by one of its private carriers that it was considering establishing services between Vancouver and Taiwan, and that Canadian law would allow such services without a formal bilateral air services agreement if judged to be in the public interest. The Chinese reaction was predictably negative, and we were warned that the approval of such services would be damaging to the relationship between Canada and China. I left without reaching any sort of understanding. A few months later, after another round with the Taiwanese, we re-engaged again with Beijing but this time I was unable to go and so sent Gordon Houlden instead. Our intent was to reiterate our position and to emphasize that the Canadian Department of External Affairs might be unable to prevent "permitted" air services, quite different from "authorized air services under a bilateral air agreement" from being initiated. All hogwash, of course, but what we were trying to measure was the depth of Chinese concern and whether in reality any Canadian interests would be seriously put in jeopardy. Gordon reported that the Chinese gave not an inch in their sustained insistence that the services should not be allowed and that at risk was "damage to the relationship". Gordon's judgment was that the Chinese were much more concerned about form than substance, and that of we managed the file deftly we would get away with the establishment of air services. We noted that while clearly warned of our intentions, the Chinese Foreign Ministry did not elevate the issue by seeking a meeting for their Ambassador with Minister Clark, nor did they call in Ambassador Earl Drake to read him the riot act.

After several rounds of talks, I reached final agreement with the Taiwan side at a meeting with John Chiang in San Francisco in October 1988. To make it appear non-official, I combined the trip with a family vacation, bringing Liani and our two children, Cynthia and Caleb, along as well. After the talks were over we spent a lovely weekend touring around Carmel and the Monterey Peninsula. The Taiwanese folded on the carrier issue and agreed to create a new carrier called Mandarin Airlines, which was effectively owned by China Airlines but in not too apparent a way. Air services were begun the following spring with services offered by both Canadian Airlines and the new blue-and-white planes of Mandarin Airlines. On the offices issue, we replaced the non-governmental head of the Canadian Trade Office in Taiwan with an experienced diplomat, Trade Commissioner Ron Berlet, brought the office into our global secure governmental communications network, and allowed the office to start offering visa services through a courier system to Hong Kong. In parallel, we allowed Taiwan to upgrade its presence in Canada with a new office in Ottawa to be run by an experienced diplomat of their own, and we each gave each other's representatives full diplomatic cover. The Chinese objected but kept the decibels reasonably low and took no retaliatory action. Everything proceeded happily forward. Once again, Canada had found a solution to a vexatious China-Taiwan issue, and Australia, New

Zealand, Holland and Britain all followed suit, establishing direct air services to Taipei and allowing Mandarin Airlines to reciprocate.

(After Hong Kong retrocession in 1997, China Airlines replaced the ROC flag on the tail of its aircraft with a plum blossom and kept flying to Hong Kong, now part of sovereign Chinese territory. A few years later, it sought and was granted permission to use regular China Airlines planes to fly to Vancouver and elsewhere, and Mandarin Airlines quietly disappeared from the skies. By 2012, scheduled air services between major cities in China and Taipei and Kaohsiung had been established, and the intense political sensitivity of air services passed into history.)

Chancery Redevelopment Projects

When I arrived in PNR in 1987, we had major Chancery redevelopment programs running in both Beijing and Tokyo. In Beijing, we had been at the corner of Dongzhimenwai and San Li Tun in a very small building since the establishment of relations in 1970. By the mid-1980s we had added several temporary buildings and were planning to move to a spacious new lot a few hundred meters to the west. There we were in the midst of planning a compound, which would contain the Chancery and the Ambassador's residence as well as staff quarters for at least half of the Canada-based personnel. In the late 1970s, we had run a nation-wide design competition for the new compound and had selected a Toronto-based group, Nicholson and Associates, to design the project and to oversee its construction.

In Tokyo, the Chancery situation was very different. But first, a little history. When Canada established its first Embassy in Japan in the mid 1920s, as it took responsibility for its own foreign relations after the Statute of Westminster, Prime Minister Mackenzie King appointed as our first Ambassador Herbert Marler, a Montrealer from a business family and subsequently a Member of Parliament. When Marler arrived in Tokyo, he did as Ambassadors do and called on his already-established counterparts from other countries. When he called on the British Ambassador, who had a handsome residence across from the Imperial Palace grounds, the haughty and stout sixty-year old Sir John Tilley, told this colonial upstart, whose country he believed only His Majesty's true envoy should represent, to find a home befitting a colony out in Shubuya or some such distant place. Marler, who was an imposing man well more than six feet tall and a proud Canadian, rankled at the outdated colonial attitude and told his staff as they left the stuffy old Brit to find "a place we can buy that is larger in every dimension" than the British residence. And they did. Across from the Akasaka Palace grounds on Aoyama Dori, they found a beautiful and very large neo-classical residence built during the Meiji restoration, with enough land next door to build a Chancery, which was built and opened in the early 1930s.

By the end of the 1970s it was clear that the forty-year-old Chancery, built for a mission of a dozen people, was woefully insufficient for our modern needs and a decision was made to raze and rebuild. The problem was that the Department's capital budget was very limited and costs in Tokyo were very high. Treasury Board was willing to "top-up" our internal budget to something in the range of $35 million, but for that amount of money we would have been able to build only a very modest building, hardly in line with the image Canada wished to portray in the newly emergent Japan. Our chancery building program was organizationally situated in the Administration Branch, then led by a strutting but not very imaginative former merchant marine captain named Roger Marsham. Roger was the first official I knew to have learned the advantage of the mobile telephone, then carried by virtually no one in the public service. If you called Roger's office on any nice day during the summer, his secretary would tell you that he was in a meeting but would call you back shortly, which he would as soon as he finished the next hole on whatever golf course he was playing that day. Our Ambassador in Tokyo at this time was the larger-than-life Barry Steers, a career Trade Commissioner whose great size at six foot four and equivalent girth were complemented by a commanding take-no-prisoners personality. Steers, who wanted a very grand chancery to be built, was very frustrated by the fact that no progress was being made on the project and asked Jean McCloskey to see if she could bounce Marsham from the project and get directly involved in the interest of our broader objectives in Japan. As ADM, this was hardly something McCloskey could spend time on, so she asked me to see if I could help.

The vision that Ambassador Steers had for the reconstruction project was huge and would cost close to a quarter billion dollars. A national design competition had been run and a gorgeous conceptual design by the Japanese-Canadian architect Raymond Moryama had won, but there was no way the government could afford to build it. While a Japanese builder had offered to finance it with a construction loan, the Department was forbidden to borrow, given that the only entity permitted by law to indebt the Canadian Government was (and still is) the Department of Finance. I called a senior ADM in the Public Works Department, Reg Evans, who I had heard was behind a brilliant financing scheme for the new CBC headquarters in Toronto. He agreed to help out and over the next six months we negotiated a creative deal to build the project. We brought in two partners, Shimizu Corporation (who would build the complex) and Mitsubishi Banking and Trust. The structure of the deal was that we would sell the air rights above 3/7ths of the property to Mitsubishi in return for the commercial revenue from space built in excess of Embassy needs and rented to private businesses, hopefully but not necessarily Canadian companies. The whole complex, which would have separate entrances for the Embassy and the commercial area, would be branded "Canada Place". To ensure we were not permanently alienating Canadian government property, the front-end deal was paralleled with a repurchase agreement that would guarantee that after thirty years the ownership would revert to the government. Shimizu both built the building and purchased from Mitsubishi an investment vehicle in the form of a long-term bond for its pension plan. In the end there were about ten inter-locking legal agreements to make the whole thing work. The negotiations were complicated, and like all negotiations in Japan drawn out and full of posturing. When we finally concluded, Shimizu hosted us at the finest traditional Japanese restaurant at which I have ever eaten, before or since. We all sat on the floor on tatami mats, ate fabulously and drank copious amounts of hot sake, each of us individually attended by a geisha girl, who played drinking games with us and sang and danced for us. The Japanese particularly got roaring drunk, and a couple of the Shimizu types passed out on the floor. My run from the Prince Hotel around the Akasaka Palace the next morning was very painful.

Half way through the chancery project negotiations, we received a letter from Global Capital Corporation of Tokyo offering the Canadian Government $4 billion to purchase, as is, the entire Embassy complex, containing Marler House (the Residence) as well as the entire plot of land. Very nervous that the amount was so high that the Minister of Finance, Michael Wilson, would be tempted to accept the offer as a means of lopping a healthy chunk off the national debt, before we circulated the letter outside the branch I did two things. First, I had someone build a financial model showing that renting a similar property over the next twenty years would put the government at a financial disadvantage relative to a sale, which required a series of very creative assumptions. Second, I called Stephen Heeney at the Embassy in Tokyo to have someone investigate the background of Global Capital, which turned out to be a shell company created by the Yakuza, the Japanese mafia, and laundered money Marcos had embezzled from the Philippines. Luckily, the provenance of the funds was sufficient to dissuade Ministers from pursuing the potential sale, but the would-be buyers did not go-away quietly. The next thing we knew a member of parliament from Southwestern Ontario asked a question in the House of Commons on why we had refused a legitimate offer and suggested that I and others might be on the payroll of Shimizu. The RCMP did a cursory investigation into potential corruption and came to visit me in my office. I asked the two investigators whether they thought that a "commission" of 1% would be normal for such a transaction, and when they answered in the affirmative I asked them if they really thought I would be still sitting in my little office in Tower A of the Lester B. Pearson

Building if I had received a pay-off of something in the neighbourhood of $40 million! The whole affair died a quiet death.

My final coup in the Tokyo chancery project was when the approval of Treasury Board Ministers was sought for the complicated deal, the Secretary of the Treasury Board insisted that I rather than Roger Marsham do the oral presentation because he really had no idea how the details of the multiple agreements all fitted together. We were very lucky to have structured the deal at the height of the Japanese bubble when both the yen and all prices were sky-high (I remember going out to a jazz club in Repongi with Joseph Caron and paying $84 for two whiskys). Two years later real estate prices were way down from their lofty heights and might not have supported the cash flow model that justified the financing on the basis of future rentals from the limited area available for commercial offices. But half of a life's success is a function of timing, and we structured a great deal and the Embassy got a gorgeous new chancery, which was built in record speed and opened in 1991, and it was all done at no cost to the Canadian taxpayer.

Early in 1989, we had a formal groundbreaking for the new chancery during a visit to Tokyo of Joe Clark for a regular bilateral Foreign Ministers meeting. This was combined with a trip to an ASEAN dialogue meeting, that year held in Kuala Lumpur. Joe Clark and Prince Takamado, who lived across Aoyama Dori in the Akasaka Palace and was a great friend of Canada after studying law at Queen's University, led the formal sod turning.

During one of my visits to Japan with Joe Clark, the Japanese had organized a bilateral meeting in Kyoto, and we were scheduled to take a specific Shinkansen bullet train, which of course kept to a very precise timetable. Clark had brought to Japan both his wife Maureen McTeer and their daughter Catherine, and this meant that schedules tended to slip. So we had Clark's program printed with an incorrect departure time for the train, building in an extra fifteen minutes. We arrived at the station almost ten minutes later than planned, but still caught the train, leading Clark to remark that it was kind of the Japanese Rail authorities to delay the bullet train's departure for him. This was the same visit where Ambassador Steers had organized his driver and a junior Embassy officer to take Catherine Clark out to Tokyo Disneyland. They spent longer than intended at the amusement park and on the way back the driver was further delayed in heavy traffic. Joe was beside himself with worry as the hours passed by without any sign of Catherine and no word from the driver. She of course eventually turned up, but we collectively decided to mark down losing a Minister's daughter high on the "career-limiting moves" list.

Asian Multilateralism One

Not all my initiatives were successful. North Korea, or the Democratic People's Republic of Korea as it is formally known, was as much a pariah in the 1980s as it is today. On one of our trips together, the Secretary of State for External Affairs Joe Clark asked me what I thought the international community should do about the threat North Korea posed to regional and potentially global peace. When I responded that part of the problem in Asia was that we had none of the multilateral confidence building institutions or consultative processes that we had across the East-West divide in Europe, he encouraged me to bring him a proposal that he could use to promote the multilateralization of peace-building in North Asia. Professor Paul Evans of the Joint Centre for Asia Pacific Studies University at York University and the University of Toronto had written about the need for greater institutionalization in the north Asian region, so I got together with him and we designed how such a system might work. The result was a proposed "North Pacific Cooperative Security Dialogue" which like the CSCE in Europe would involve both governments and non-governmental actors and contain military conflict-avoidance undertakings and confidence-building measures, political processes and cultural and university exchanges as well. Clark proposed this in a speech and we were sent around to drum up international support. Initially, the Gaimusho

(Foreign Ministry) in Japan expressed support for the initiative, as did South Korea and the Soviet Union. China was non-committal. And then the US weighed in heavily in opposition. The US Navy ruled the Pacific and was deeply opposed to any measures that would require greater American transparency or advance notification of US naval exercises and movements in an ocean completely dominated by the US "boomer" submarines fleet. Furthermore, the US State Department was quite content to be able to control virtually all serious political dialogue in the region through their influence over Japan and South Korea. Under pressure from the US, the Japanese withdrew their support for the inclusion of any military confidence building measures and soon the initiative was pushed increasingly to an academic non-governmental track, which meant that it no longer could fulfill the purpose we had intended. Although it did not die entirely, and indeed was still being championed by Canada through the early 1990s as an effective means of drawing the North Koreans into a multilateral dialogue to reduce their isolation and broaden their contacts and the number and nature of countries with which they were engaged, the NPCSD was effectively dead. In retrospect it was easy to conclude that to propose such an initiative without US support was to tilt at windmills, yet there have been many times since 1988 that I have wondered whether North Korea might have been eased out of its isolation, or at least the whole nuclear issue made easier to manage, had a cooperative security process been put in place.

It was also during my time as Director of North Asia Relations that the Pacific Rim countries began the institutionalization of intra-regional economic dialogue in a forum that could include both clearly sovereign states and other "economies", meaning Hong Kong and Taiwan. Smaller economies of the region wanted a broader dialogue in part to limit growing Japanese influence throughout the region, while each of Taiwan and Hong Kong wanted to have their own place at the economic table. The Pacific Economic Consultative Committee (PECC) had been a lose organization of business leaders from Asia and North America and had conducted annual get-togethers for years, to which governments generally sent observers, but no substantive discussion of trade facilitation or the removal of regional barriers to trade took place at PECC. In January of 1989, then Australian Prime Minister Bob Hawke proposed the formalization of an Asia Pacific Economic Cooperation Forum, with an initial membership of twelve countries (the ASEAN countries, Japan, Korea, Australia, New Zealand, the United States and Canada), and Gareth Evans, Foreign Minister of Australia (after privately dismissing APEC as "four adjectives in search of a noun") hosted the first meeting in Canberra late in the year. China was invited as an observer, but the core group would not agree to it becoming a full member until it also agreed to have Hong Kong and Taiwan admitted as well. I ended up being the chosen official to initially represent Canada at working-level meetings, although Jean McCloskey led our delegation to the November kick-off meeting. Once again thrown into a China-Taiwan issue, my most significant contribution at this time was the brokering of a deal in which all delegations, including the "observer" delegation from Beijing, agreed that APEC membership going forward would refer to "economies" rather than "countries", allowing China, Hong Kong and Taiwan to be brought simultaneously into APEC at the organization's second formal meeting in 1991.

The last active file that I was involved in during this time was the international effort to bring sustainable peace to little Cambodia. Once known as one of the world's most peaceful places, Cambodia was completely torn apart during the Vietnam War following the expansion of the American bombing campaigns across the Vietnam-Cambodia border in the spring of 1970. Cambodians had subsequently suffered horribly under the Khmer Rouge, who the Vietnamese had toppled but not crushed in 1978, and was still caught in what seemed to be an endless civil war ten years later. A series of multilateral meetings began under the auspices of the UN beginning in 1987, and the Paris Peace Talks were kicked off seriously in 1989. I went to one meeting in Paris with Secretary of State Joe Clark as the senior person from the Asia branch. Our main delegates were the very experienced Alan Sullivan and Nick Etheridge, Alan an old and effective multilateralist and Nick an experienced Southeast Asian hand, having served in Indochina as part of Canada's involvement in the peacekeeping force that allowed the US to withdraw its forces in 1973.

At the one Cambodia meeting I went to I got to know the Soviet delegate, Igor Rogachev, with whom I went out drinking one night along with several European delegates. Rogachev was a delightful and heavy-drinking fellow, tough as nails during the meetings but very open and relaxed in a non-official setting. Little did I know that I would reconnect with Rogachev in 1996 when we were both Ambassadors in Beijing. I did not stay involved in the Paris Peace process of 1989 for very long, however, for just as the international community began trying to put a peaceful Cambodia together, a peaceful China began coming apart.

China and the Tiananmen Crisis

By the mid-1980s, the bilateral relationship between Canada and China was becoming very active. Following a 1984 visit to Canada of then Premier Zhao Ziyang and a subsequent 1985 visit of ceremonial President Li Xiannian (Deng Xiaoping was still very much in charge, but had no title) Prime Minister Mulroney made his first visit in 1986. Following the Prime Minister, everyone seemed to go, including the Governor General, the gracious Jeanne Sauvé, in March of 1987, followed by a parliamentary delegation led by the Speakers of both the Commons and the Senate. In the other direction came the old warhorse Yang Shangkun, soon to replace Li Xiannian in the ceremonial position of President, followed by Vice Premier Tian Jiyun in the spring of 1988.

In the autumn of 1988, I accompanied SSEA Joe Clark to Beijing for formal bilateral talks that had been established as annual events the previous year. Visits by foreign Ministers were always taken seriously, and Clark was received not only by his counterpart Qian Qichen but by newly appointed Premier Li Peng as well. During an exchange with Foreign Minister Qian, Joe Clark tried to make a case for changes in the Chinese legal system and argued for a greater respect for the presumption of innocence in criminal trials. Qian turned to Clark with a completely straight face and said of Chinese criminals "Why would we try them if they are not guilty?".

Prior to the great two-way onslaught of bilateral exchanges during the first Mulroney government, ministerial visits in either direction had been relatively rare, and any outgoing delegation had someone from External Affairs included to help guide the group. By the time I arrived in PNR, this was no longer possible. Aside from all the highest level state visits, some thirty ministerial or vice-ministerial working visits took place between 1987 and 1989 in either one direction or the other, and our little China team, composed of China-hands Bruce Jutzi and Gordon Houlden, with the support of a couple of more junior officers, was run off its feet just managing the flow. In fact, we were seeking Ministerial help to manage what we were calling a "traffic problem", and the Prime Minister's office explicitly instructed Cabinet members to get a sign-off from the SSEA before travelling to China. Occasionally, such as in the case of a request to travel to China in early 1988 by Otto Jelinek, the Minister of Amateur Sport, Joe Clark turned down such requests.

The constant flow of high-level visits had two consequences. The first was to lull the government, and indeed the public, into the belief that everything in China was evolving in an irreversibly positive direction, and the second was to keep such a tremendous pressure on the professional China watchers in the Embassy in Beijing and in PNR in Ottawa, that they really had no time for reflective analysis. So much forward movement was being made in bilateral trade, in the overall economic situation, and in the lives of the average Chinese, that we simply did not see the growing public concern, especially among the young, over corruption, over inflation and over the abuse of power by officials. We were thus all caught by surprise when the death of purged reformer Hu Yaobang on April 15, 1989, brought the students to the streets in protest. On April 20th, the night before Hu's funeral, more than 100,000 people, mostly but not exclusively students, appeared in Tiananmen square without any clear demands or focus to their protest, mourning Hu and demanding to meet the country's leaders. Our Embassy began to take notice.

During the early days of the protests, political officers from our Embassy visited Tiananmen regularly and started reporting daily on developments. In PNR, Bruce was the one among us who was initially worried the most, especially after an editorial appeared in the Party's newspaper, Renmin Ribao, on April 26th calling the protests "counter-revolutionary turmoil" aimed at overthrowing the regime. Knowing that such an editorial could have only appeared if authored or blessed by the highest level of the Party, both Bruce and our Ambassador in Beijing, Earl Drake, thought we were in for some real trouble. When the students extended their protest to May 4th, (the anniversary of the 1919 country-wide student uprising to protest the ceding of Qingdao and other former German territories to the Japanese by the Versailles Treaty), we started to map out what we might need to do if the crisis deepened, and we warned the political level that Canadian interests might well be challenged. On May 13th we set up a formal Crisis Management Group, which gave us access to the Department's Operations Centre, with its multiple televisions permitting the monitoring of all available channels, 100 telephone lines and computer terminals and kitchen. It also gave us additional manpower in the form of junior officers temporarily assigned to us, to monitor both the media and incoming reports from Beijing and elsewhere, and to speak to Canadians with children or relatives in China who were starting to call us for information or help in getting in touch with loved ones. The Embassy began verifying its register of Canadian in China, reaching out to as many as they could and establishing "trees" of contacts so that emergency networks could be activated in case of need. We also asked our missions in Washington, Canberra and London, to set us up with direct contacts in the US State Department, the Australian Department of Foreign Affairs and Trade, and the British Foreign Office, so that we could coordinate our responses to the growing crisis.

With CNN reporting hourly on the situation in Tiananmen Square, and our Minister Joe Clark being asked questions in the House and by the media, it was vital that we kept him completely up to date on what was happening in Beijing. The clunky old departmental system of sending memoranda to Ministers was hopelessly slow, for even an urgent "walk-around" document taken by hand through the hierarchy for the requisite signatures of the ADM and the Under-Secretary, and then into the Ministers Registry to be logged in, could take hours before it was in the Minister's hands. In addition, we had the Prime Minister's Office calling at all hours for updates. Because of his personal interest in China, Mulroney wanted a constant feed of accurate information and analysis. To meet this need we created a simple briefing note called the "China Bulletin" and issued an update at least twice a day and sometimes more often. We distributed the China Bulletin to everyone with a need to know, from ADM Jean McCloskey to Under-Secretary Si Taylor, to the Minister and his staff, to the PCO and the PMO, as well as to Ministers and senior officials of other government departments concerned, Defense, CIDA, and Immigration. Initially, Jean McCloskey did not like the fact that we were issuing updates without senior branch sign-off, but when I argued that they did not contain policy prescriptions and that the need for speed was paramount, she relented. I approved the Bulletins and they were then instantly faxed to all recipients. If I wasn't available, Bruce signed them off. Nothing was permitted to block the flow of information. Consequently, neither Joe Clark nor the Prime Minister was once caught flat-footed by the media. We also kept an open dialogue with the reporters of the parliamentary press gallery, sharing whatever basic information we could so that they were not solely reliant on CNN and so that they could see that the government was as on top of the crisis as it could possibly be.

By the time we set up the formal Crisis Management Group, the situation in Beijing was seriously worsening. The students were becoming increasingly radical with the refusal of the government to withdraw the April 26th editorial, and a hunger strike of a core group of 40 or 50 student leaders was begun. Mikhail Gorbachev, who was stunning the world with his reforms in the Soviet Union, was due in Beijing on the 15th for the first state visit of a Soviet leader since the Sino-Soviet rift in 1963. State visits always begin with a review of an Honour Guard, and except in the most inclement winter weather, this takes place on the western edge of Tiananmen Square, just in front of the Great Hall of the People. This was now the site of a series of parked busses that the students were using for meetings and other needs. To have the government unable to use Tiananmen Square during the extremely high profile visit of Gorbachev was humiliating for the Chinese leadership. By the time the Soviet leader arrived in Beijing, our Embassy was corroborating media reports that the crowd in the square had grown to well over a quarter of a million people, with the students now joined by workers and others from all walks of life. Gorbachev's welcome was held at the airport and a planned visit to the Forbidden City had to be cancelled.

After failed attempts to persuade the students to leave the square on May 18th by Li Peng and on May 19th by Zhao Ziyang (accompanied by an aid named Wen Jiabao), we began to treat the possibility of a violent confrontation and military intervention as increasingly likely. Protests had now spread to Shanghai and many other cities; Tibet was already under martial law, which was declared in Beijing on the 20th. A curfew was established, only to be ignored by the students. The broadcast facilities used by international media were all shut down, although journalists still snuck into the square and managed to surreptitiously smuggle both short TV footage and photographs out of the country. After a series of telephone conversations between Ottawa and the Embassy in Beijing on the 20th, we moved to full contingency mode that evening.

Following the declaration of martial law and the evident increase in tensions, on May 20th I called the Chinese Ambassador in Ottawa and told him that the Secretary of State for External Affairs wished to see him. Zhang Wenpu was a charming, erudite man, originally educated in a western missionary school in Beijing in the 1930s. In the spring of 1989, he was allowing his Embassy to be used to pass information to Chinese students in Canada and it was evident that a number of the Embassy staff, and probably the Ambassador Zhang himself, were fundamentally pro-student. He came in to meet Clark, who was very polite and began by saying "Ambassador, you must be as profoundly worried about what is happening in Beijing as any of us", and then asked him to convey to the Chinese government Canada's friendly concern and deep hope that matters could be resolved in a peaceful way. Zhang had little to say, but assured the Minister that the views of Canada would be passed along to the authorities in Beijing. The main purpose of calling in the Ambassador was simply to be able to say publicly that we had done so; no one had any illusions about somebody in Beijing caring at this stage what western governments thought. In fact, our Embassy was telling us that the Ministry of Foreign Affairs was completely in the dark about what was happening, and that a number of its younger officers were in fact in the square with the students.

As the crisis deepened in the third week of May, we authorized the sending to Beijing of special emergency communications equipment that would allow radio communications both locally and with headquarters and would not rely on local or international telecommunications infrastructure. The Embassy was initially dismissive; they had already sent someone to Hong Kong to buy scores of walkie-talkies, which they shared not only internally but with "wardens" among the Canadian community in the city and also with the US, Australian and British embassies. In Beijing, the Embassy was in constant contact with those three and the German Embassy, while from headquarters we were finding useful the connections we had established with both the American and Australian task forces (like our crisis management group), while the Foreign Office in London seemed totally preoccupied with the implications of the crisis for the situation in Hong Kong, part way along the path from the 1984 agreement to the 1997 return of the colony to China.

As events in Beijing were unfolding and the Chinese government looking increasingly hardline, Chinese students in Canada were also holding their own supportive protests on university campuses across the country. When martial law was declared in Beijing, the Chairman of the National People's

Congress, Wan Li, was in the middle of a Canadian tour, having visited Victoria and Vancouver. He proceeded to Calgary and then to Ottawa, where he gave a speech that talked about the student movement. His speech was a careful balance, expressing understanding for the student movement but not endorsing it. However the press interpreted it otherwise and the public reports were that Wan Li had come out clearly on the side of the students. Gordon Houlden, who was travelling with the NPC Chairman and his group, told us that Wan Li was "fence-sitting", but that was not at all the way the press decided to portray him. From Ottawa the delegation went on to Toronto, where a piano player stole the limelight. He was a young Chinese studying in Canada, engaged to play during an evening event. According to Gordon, he transitioned almost seamlessly from the "Ode to the Yellow River" to the "Internationale" and pandemonium ensued, with the musician being eventually unceremoniously hustled out of the room while shouting slogans in support of the student movement. Houlden, who spoke fluent Chinese, was present for otherwise private but vehement debates among the delegation members about the crisis and whether Wan Li and other leaders should be more sympathetic and supportive of the students. Houlden reported that even when Wan Li was in their presence, the delegation members kept up their fierce and open debate. Wan Li, while personally cautious in his comments, did not try to shut down the discussion or prevent pro-student voices from expressing themselves.

From Toronto, Wan Li went on to Boston. There he cancelled all his US engagements, which had included stops in New York and Washington, and basically laid low until after the crackdown. After about a week, he returned to China, going first to Shanghai "for medical treatment" and disappeared for several weeks during which time he was effectively being detained. He did not publicly reappear until well into July and when he did was quoted as being fully in support of the crackdown. Wan Li, like others, had clearly been brought back into line, even if his departure from the government's position had never been as far as the Canadian press had reported.

There were about 4500 Chinese students at Canadian universities and colleges in 1989, and the scholastic year either had already or was about to come its normal close. Most of these students wanted to defer their return to China until matters clarified, and we learned that although the Chinese Embassy and the Consulate General in Toronto were publicly saying that the crisis was winding down and the number of the students in the square diminishing, they were privately advising their students to remain in Canada as long as possible. Some of the Chinese diplomats were telling our officials privately that they feared that the country could break down in civil war.

Once martial law had been declared and the students' hunger strikes sustained, we realized that force to clear the square was a very real possibility, so Bruce and Gordon and I, along with Gar Pardy, who was Director General of the Consular Bureau, started mapping out the actions that we would have to take if military force was used. Protecting Canadians was obviously a high priority, so evacuation plans were dusted off, reviewed and refined. We discussed with Ambassador Drake who he considered to be essential Embassy staff, and recommended that he encourage families and non-essential staff to be prepared to leave. While he did not fully implement the staff reduction to essential levels, he did encouraged all the trade officers and other staff with summer leave plans to advance those plans and leave right away, and many did. I contacted National Defence headquarters to see if we could borrow a couple of 707s normally used for troop transport, and they readily agreed, going so far as to conduct a "training" flight to Japan on June 1st, leaving one transporter at Tokyo's Haneda airport ready for further deployment. And we outlined the political steps that we could take, limited really to ministerial statements and carpeting the Chinese Ambassador for a formal protest. All that we could do then was watch and wait.

The last days of May and the first day of June were very tense. Our Embassy was reporting substantial military movements around Beijing and the gathering of mobile forces in key locations. In the square, unarmed soldiers had entered and tried to persuade the students to leave, but the protesters turned them away. On June 2nd several platoons of foot soldiers were turned back by angry public crowds on roads leading towards the centre of the city. The Embassy reported to us that the General of the 38th Army Group had refused the order to move towards the square and was immediately replaced. By late afternoon on June 3rd the square was surrounded. The tanks and a full battalion of infantry rolled eastward along Chang'an Jie and entered the square shortly after midnight, Beijing time, on Sunday, June 4th.

We had done everything we could think of to prepare for whatever might happen, and were keeping a rotating shift, with either myself, Bruce or Gordon in the office or Operations Centre on a 24-hour basis. I was weeding half-heartedly in my garden on the afternoon of June 3rd, a beautiful late spring day, when the telephone rang and my seven-year old daughter Cynthia called me from the deck to say that the call was for me. It was Bruce, who simply said "It is happening". He had just been on the phone with Dan Dhavernas, Deputy Chief of Mission at the Beijing Embassy, who had described to Bruce the view from his window in his apartment on Jianguomenwai Avenue, the eastern extension of Chang'an Jie, the great east-west thoroughfare that separates the Forbidden City from Tiananmen Square. Dhavernas had described the very beginning of the violence, with armoured vehicles firing on demonstrators just prior to the assault on the main square. I yelled to Liani, who was upstairs tending to our five-week old twins, that the military crackdown was starting, grabbed the car keys and drove the short two kilometers to the Pearson Building. When I arrived at the office Bruce was back on the telephone with Dhavernas in Beijing, who was simply corroborating what we were seeing on CNN. The killing had started and we went to work.

We quickly advised Joe Clark and the PMO, and sent Clark's office a draft press statement condemning the use of force that we had prepared the day before, suggesting that it be immediately issued. Clark came almost immediately into the office for a fuller briefing, which we gave him in his office. He approved the statement, which hit the press just before five in the afternoon. The statement was very brief, noting that protesters were being "killed in substantial numbers" and called on the Chinese Government to "cease its military action and return to peaceful methods to resolve the current crisis". In one of the little quirks of time zones, students of history may someday be curious to see that the Secretary of State for External Affairs statement on the June 4th use of force in Tiananmen Square was time dated June 3rd.

As the statement was being issued, we stayed in contact with Beijing, trying to learn more, calling back and forth every hour or two or whenever anything new developed. Lines to China became harder to access as tens of thousands of people with family members in China tried to call them, worried how they might be affected by the spiraling crisis. At a certain point I took the decision to keep one line open all the time. Fearful that we would lose the line if not in constant use as operators were trying to free up lines to satisfy a huge public demand, we had junior staff members in Ottawa and Beijing talking on it non-stop, reading hockey scores, articles out of the newspapers and even telephone directories.

At Clark's request we called in a visibly shaken Ambassador Zhang Wenpu on the morning of the 4th to underscore the depth of Canada's dismay at the killing still going on and to encourage restraint. The meeting, which was hosted on our side by Jean McCloskey as the "Acting Under-Secretary", was short and to the point, and the Ambassador made no response to our protests. We also issued another statement immediately after the meeting using tougher language than they afternoon before, "condemning" the Chinese crackdown and expressing "horror and outrage at the ongoing killing" which Canadians had been watching on their televisions. After the meeting I walked Zhang back to his car and he turned to me and said that this was one of the saddest days of his life. The crisis was eventually to end his upward movement in the Chinese Foreign Service. Bruce and Pearl Jutzi had some weeks earlier organized a June 5th dinner with Zhang and his wife along with former Ambassador John and Jean Small, with whom

Bruce had served when on his first China assignment. Bruce did not expect Zhang and his wife to show up, but they did, and Bruce described him as sad and very subdued. In the months that followed and internal Chinese investigations carried out, investigators discovered what we already knew, that Zhang Wenpu had been vocally in support of political liberalization in discussions in the Embassy, had allowed his staff to communicate that support openly to Chinese students in Canada, and had turned a complete blind eye to the decision made by 11 of his staff to "go over the wall" and seek political asylum in Canada. Removed from Ottawa about nine months later and replaced with a conservative hard-liner, Zhang Wenpu would never serve abroad again. And it wasn't until late in my time as Ambassador that even private contact with us was again permitted.

The evacuation plan to assist Canadians to leave China was also immediately activated. Canadian Airlines had a regularly scheduled flight due to fly to Beijing on Monday the 5th and were planning to cancel it due to the unrest. I called CEO Rys Eyton and asked him not only to maintain the schedule but also to be prepared to charter further planes to us. We sought from the Chinese Foreign Affairs Ministry authority to fly into China the government Boeing 707 then parked conveniently at Haneda in Japan, but our request was immediately turned down. Instead we chartered two additional Canadian Airlines planes, and began on June 7th to ferry people to Japan and Hong Kong, where they could find commercial flights home. Although we were not able to use the DND 707s to fly to Beijing, we did use them to ferry home from Japan evacuees who had flown into Tokyo on our chartered Canadian Airline flights or on the few JAL flights still operating. The Embassy and the Consular Bureau together did a superb job with the evacuation, getting Canadians to gather at pre-ordained sites, generally at hotels on the northern outskirts, and then moving them on Embassy busses to the airport as planes became available. The Embassy also sent convoys of vehicles draped in Canadian flags through army checkpoints into the university campuses where Canadians were studying, to provide transport for students who otherwise would have been stranded. In Canada, we opened consular "hot lines", manned in the Operations

Centre, for Canadians to call in with any information about their family members in China, and these were almost overwhelmed by the volume of calls. In addition, people were calling their Members of Parliament who in turn were not only calling us but also calling Joe Clark's staff, and it was a tremendous effort not to have our ordered approach to crisis management overturned by some angry MP who wanted a constituent's worry treated as a higher priority than others. There were a few isolated special cases that became a burden for the Embassy, such as a teacher from Ontario who was a visiting professor at Southwest Teacher's University in Chengdu. The university administration were refusing to return her Canadian passport to her, and thus preventing her from travelling. Luckily the university authorities relented just before the political pressure forced the Embassy to dispatch a junior consular staff member from Beijing to Chengdu with an emergency passport.

The 600 or so Canadians registered at the Embassy turned out to be less than half of the Canadians actually in China, and by the end of the evacuation we had relocated more than 800 people and accounted for more than 1400 passport holders who had managed to leave the country one way or another. There were stories later about confusion at the Beijing Airport, and one story in particular from an academic who alleged that he witnessed three self-absorbed and almost hysterical Embassy staff members frantic about getting their pet cats on the plane, and disinterested in helping non-diplomatic evacuees, but none of us believed the story since we had no record of anyone trying to move pets, and we had moved most non-essential staff out of Beijing in the lead up to June 4th. Many months later, the US Congress reviewed the performance of the US Government in reacting to the crisis, and admonished the State Department for not having done as good a job as Canada in rounding up and evacuating its citizens.

The public reaction in Canada to the use of force by the Chinese state was immediate and visceral. Canadians were outraged and individuals and commentators called on the Canadian Government to take the most extreme measures we could, from breaking off diplomatic relations to suspending commercial flights to abolishing the aid program. Editorials in newspapers across the country, irrespective of their political biases, called for firm measures, with the Financial Post stating that Canada should no longer provide export credit from EDC for exports to China, and that Canada should henceforth oppose China's efforts to accede to the GATT. The Chinese Canadian National Council, a coalition of community, business and cultural associations, issued a statement calling for extensive sanctions, the recall of our Ambassador and the cutting off of all development assistance. On Monday, June 5th and the first day of Parliament since the crackdown began, there was an emergency debate in the House of Commons on the crisis in China, and politicians of every stripe were unified in their denunciation of Chinese actions. We set out the Government's position in an extensive statement made by Joe Clark, in which we laid out all issues, from outrage at the killings to concern over Canadians to the risks of a China in chaos, but we did not yet attempt to define what overall policy adjustments might be required in the relationship. It was simply too early to see beyond the immediate violence and confusion. Although part of the public record in any case, we released Clark's House of Commons statement in a public press release, and began a practice which went on for a week or so of also releasing a daily "Situation Report" in a formal press release every morning. It was in the "Situation Report" of June 6th that we repeated and strengthened our consular advice and recommended that all Canadians leave China.

As the days passed and the actual killing stopped, it was clear that the Government needed to be seen to take action in response to the Tiananmen crisis, and probably would have to fundamentally reset Canada's relationship with China. My concern, and that of Bruce and Gordon and Ambassador Drake and other professionals was that we had spent twenty years building the relationship, which had begun during a period of frightful Chinese behaviour during the Cultural Revolution, and we did not want to see all that effort thrown away. This was especially true in the academic and cultural fields, where the relationships our governmental programs had fostered were with more open and liberal Chinese individuals and institutions, hardly supporters of the vicious military crackdown we had just witnessed. I was meeting at this time at least once daily with Joe Clark and I suggested that we draw a line between short-term measures and longer term ones, and that we find a way to build a national consensus over the latter. He readily agreed.

There were several immediate issues that we had to deal with. The first issue was whether or not to recall Earl Drake, which not only parliamentarians but also advisors to the Prime Minister were calling for. Recalling an Ambassador in the world of diplomacy is a step not taken lightly and usually signifies a very serious problem in the relationship between two countries. Our concern was that if we recalled Drake there would be a significant risk we would end up without an Ambassador in Beijing for some time during a period when we would need him there, since it was unlikely that the political situation would improve or the Chinese Government issue an apology that we could point to as a change for the better justifying the Ambassador's return. Not recalling Drake was clearly unacceptable to the PMO, and so we recommended that in the press release announcing that the Ambassador was being brought to Ottawa for consultation with the Government and the Foreign Affairs and Defence Committee of the House of Commons, we would explicitly say that he would then immediately return to Beijing to continue monitoring the situation and to do everything possible to protect Canadian interests still at risk. The Prime Minister approved this formulation, and whenever we spoke with the press afterwards we repeated that Drake's return to Ottawa would be brief.

Another major issue to deal with was the large community of Chinese students in Canada, many of whom were due to leave at the end of their studies and whose visas were running out (or already had in some cases). This was easy. Joe Clark called Barbara McDougall, then Minister of Manpower and Immigration and obtained instant agreement for an amnesty, allowing all Chinese students in Canada to remain until the situation in the own country stabilized. Many would never go back.

And the last group of immediate measures was simply to suspend any consideration of any new aid projects and all planned bilateral visits and activities until the situation in China became clearer and a longer-term policy response developed.

We then turned our attention to the development of that longer-term policy response. With emotions running high among the general public and within all the communities involved with one aspect or another of the bilateral relationship, the challenge was clearly going to be not just to come up with sensible policy but to build a national consensus around that policy. I proposed the idea of a "National Round Table" which Clark himself should chair, inviting representatives of the full range of interested groups, from exporters to Amnesty International, from universities to cultural groups to various factions within the Chinese-Canadian community. We suggested to Clark that the objective should be to have our policy well articulated prior to the G-7 Summit scheduled for mid-July in Paris, since we did not wish to have the future of our important relationship with China, however damaged it might be, to be directed by some irrational compromise reached for the purposes of a G-7 consensus. So we invited forty people to Ottawa on June 22nd, just eighteen days after the Tiananmen massacre, for the National Round Table. The forty were intended to represent five broad groups: business; the Chinese Canadian community; universities, professional media watchers from the media and cultural organizations; and aid organizations and other NGOs. The invitations were ad hominem and offered in a letter signed by Joe Clark; we absolutely did not want unpredictable interventions from unknown directions. We tried to limit participation from the Government, but naturally invited Minister of International Trade John Crosbie. Crosbie's predecessor, Pat Carney, who had not run again in the 1988 election, called Clark to ask if she could come and Monique Landry, the junior cabinet minister responsible for CIDA was pushed by her officials to request a place at the table as well. Naturally, dozens of senior and middle level officials also expected to be able to represent their departments or agencies. Clark was terrifically firm about this, saying that the round table was only to listen to those outside of government, and while Crosbie and Landry were of course welcome, and Carney could come to listen as a private citizen, the only other government representatives at the table would be the Under-Secretary and myself. We knew where we wanted to come out and I personally spent hours either by telephone or in person discussing the issues at stake with almost every one of the participants.

The June 22nd National Round Table was everything we hoped it would be. Clark was a superb chair and said almost nothing, and certainly gave no indication of his own or the government's views. Business representatives spoke of the importance of trade to Canada and of the positive influence more business contacts with the west would have on Chinese attitudes and behaviour, with one western businessman warning that cutting wheat sales would hurt not only western Canadian farmers but the poorest segments of the Chinese population. The Chinese Community representatives, who were not in unison, called for sanctions but wanted no measures that would either hurt the average Chinese or upset their own links with their country of origin. NGOs argued for the continuation of certain forms of aid and the elimination of others. The academics, whom we knew intimately since several of them had served as resident sinologists in our Embassy in Beijing, talked of how hard it had been to develop the relationships that Canadian scholars and researchers now had with so many, generally liberal thinking, colleagues in China. I sat next to Clark and passed him notes as to who might call on next as each intervener was wrapping up, trying to keep the tone and thrust of the messaging in balance. And a consensus started to emerge. There would be business, but not "business as usual" at the political level. Certain programs should be cut or scaled back, but linkages should be sustained and nurtured with the forces of positive change and reform. In closing the meeting, Clark articulated this consensus at a very high level, saying that while we could clearly not go forward with business as usual, we also did not wish to either become "anti-China" or throw way decades of building linkages with the forces of reform. He then closed by thanking everyone for coming and promised that the Government would issue a policy statement within the next fortnight.

The next step was to ensure that Cabinet and Prime Minister Mulroney were on board, the latter's views particularly important not just on the substance of the proposed statement but on its timing, since it would obviously guide his hand at the Paris G-7 Summit. I was in almost daily contact with my foreign service colleague Bob Grauer, who was then serving in the PCO, and I made sure he saw no problems in what we were trying to do, and Joe Clark walked Mulroney personally through the elements of our proposed policy before he took them to full Cabinet. The policy, articulated in a formal statement issued by Clark on June 30th, entitled "Canada and China: The Months Ahead", set out on the negative side a series of measures: there would be no high-level visits, Ministerial visits or "celebratory" exchanges like symphony visits for the foreseeable future; all aid projects and export credit applications would be subject to renewed scrutiny and any that supported the propaganda apparatus of the state or the government as it was structured would be turned down. The statement pointed out that several aid projects and one export credit application had already been refused approval on the basis of the new guidelines. The export credit application was one for the provision of communications equipment for a very tall tower being planned for Shanghai; the application had actually been turned down just before the events of June 4th but the decision had not been made public, so we dressed it up as being a result of the new policy. On the positive side, the policy statement also made clear that aid and export credit projects that met the new more stringent criteria would be approved, and that the government would be doing everything it could to preserve all the linkages – business, academic, cultural, personal – that had been built up between Canadians and their Chinese counterparts over the previous twenty years.

The June 30th policy statement worked. Reaction across the country was almost uniformly positive to the message that we would continue doing business with China but not support "business as usual" at the political level. Newspaper editorials welcomed the ban on senior level visits and to the tightened criteria for aid and export credit while trying to sustain the linkages built up over time. Prime Minister Mulroney went to the

G-7 Summit in Paris less than two weeks later and was able to take a real lead in encouraging his counterparts, including the reluctant French and Japanese, to adopt a remarkably similar (although less detailed) collective response in the Summit's communiqué.

We were not completely through the woods yet, however. Conscious that the policy statement made clear that new aid and export credit projects would be approved if they met the more stringent criteria set out in the policy, I was determined to start the flow of new projects again since too long a hiatus would create the impression that we had actually suspended all new projects. At this time the Vice President for Asia at CIDA was David Holdsworth. David was very reluctant to proceed with new project approvals, fearing that CIDA and his Minister would be criticized publicly, irrespective of what the over-arching policy was. Push as I might, I could not get him to move. Then in mid-September, EDC approved a new loan for some commercial telecommunications equipment for Nortel. A number of newspapers and public commentators reacted furiously, accusing the Government of getting soft on China, completely ignoring the fact that we had explicitly said that there would be new projects approved over time. Paul Heinbecker, recently returned from Washington and now serving as the Prime Minister's Foreign Policy Advisor and speech-writer, called me and told me the Prime Minister was concerned about the negative publicity. I got on the telephone and called some friends in the fourth estate, and in the nick of time, on September 21st, the Globe and Mail published an editorial that analyzed the furor over the EDC loan, pointing out that the government was doing exactly what it said on June 30th that it would do. The editorial ended with the pithy phrase "This is good policy". The PMO relaxed and the heat was off.

To go back in time to June and July, we were very sensitive to the Chinese diplomats leaving their Embassy and seeking to stay in Canada. For many there was no issue, either they were single or they came out as a couple, but in one case we were not quite sure what was happening. A young married female diplomat, whose husband also worked at the Embassy, sought medical care at the Riverside Hospital, complaining of exhaustion and massive headaches. The Embassy's security office sought to intervene and wanted to move her immediately back to the Embassy, and we suspected that she was actually trying to seek asylum, possibly without her husband. When the RCMP watching service brought this to our attention, I got in touch with one of the senior doctors at the Riverside, Dennis Pitt, who with his family were personal friends of Liani and mine. I explained to him in strict confidence what was going on, and he agreed to let me plant a mandarin-speaking person in the hospital to monitor things. Bruce Jutzi and I then contacted Gilliane Lapointe, who had served in Beijing a number of years earlier and who was now working in the cultural bureau in External. The hospital found her a uniform that fit, and she became a "nurse" for a few days. The woman's husband and other members of the Embassy would come to the hospital and speak freely to the woman and to each other, without it ever occurring to them that the attending nurse, a 40-year old Caucasian, was a fluent mandarin speaker actually working for External Affairs. It turned out that we were right that the woman was considering seeking asylum, but in the end she decided by herself to go back to the Embassy so we did not need to take any action.

As the post-crisis weeks passed, Bruce Jutzi prepared to leave the division to take up his assignment as Minister-Counselor in Beijing, replacing Dan Dhavernas. At first he thought he would have to leave his wife Pearl and their two children behind, which would have been a great pity as Pearl, a mental health expert, had just given up her job with the Ottawa School Board. By late August the situation in China's capital was sufficiently stable, in part because of martial law, and the whole Jutzi family went ahead and moved to Beijing, where they stayed several years. Having Bruce in Beijing was a very good thing during the difficult time in our relationship that followed, for he was patient and thoughtful and immune to the excessive swings between blind optimism and despair that seemed to be so common among many China observers. Back in the headquarters division, Gordon Houlden stepped into Bruce's shoes as Deputy Director, so we had superb talent and excellent judgment at both ends of the line, and when I left to go to Policy Planning at the end of the year I knew that management of the China relationship was still in as good a set of hands as I could have wished.

Hong Kong Jitters

The Tiananmen crisis certainly exacerbated nervousness in Hong Kong about the Chinese attitude towards the freedoms and civil liberties that the People of the British territory had been guaranteed in principle, under the handover agreement signed in 1984. The handover agreement established that there would be a "Basic Law", effectively a mini-constitution for Hong Kong, promulgated well in advance of the 1997 transfer of sovereignty, and at the time of Tiananmen the Chinese and British authorities were deeply mired in the negotiation of what that Basic Law would contain. The question of how the UK would treat its Hong Kong subjects was still unclear, but it was perfectly clear that open access to Britain would not be in the cards. The pool of Hong Kong residents interested in immigrating to Canada had grown very substantially after 1984, and the use of military force to crush a non-violent protest movement was like dropping a super-heated rock into that pool. Now it seemed that everyone in the British colony wanted to come to Canada, and to come soon. Our "Commission" in Hong Kong (it would only become a Consulate General in 1997) was flooded with applications, and anyone who could started buying up property in Vancouver.

It was against this backdrop that a real estate development on the old Expo86 land in Vancouver's False Creek came on the market. Developed by Victor Li, son of Li Kashing (both Victor and his brother Richard had studied in Canada, and both spent some time working in Toronto to learn some business skills before returning to Hong Kong), the condominiums in the Concord Pacific complex were put on sale before the buildings were completed. This type of "pre-sales" of new apartment complexes is very common in Hong Kong (and in China today) but virtually unheard of in

Vancouver, at least in the 1980s. It was mid-autumn of 1989 when news hit the Vancouver streets that Victor Li's project had sold out entirely in the space of one or two days in a Hong Kong pre-sale program, and there were no more apartments in the complex available for local Vancouver buyers. The public reaction was immediate and very angry, as the clear inference drawn was that a Hong Kong developer was giving unfair advantage to his offshore compatriots to the disadvantage of local Vancouverites. British Columbia Premier Bill Vander Zalm, unpredictable at the best of times, made a public statement implying that he would not only limit access to the Vancouver real estate market by people in Hong Kong but would also look at taking away permits from projects already approved. His comments were top news in Hong Kong, and our Commissioner (Consul General equivalent) there, Anne-Marie Doyle, had to deal with an extremely upset business community and public more broadly. She even received a request from the Governor's office to issue some sort of statement calming the waters. First, however, we had to get Vander Zalm under control. I discussed the matter with Joe Clark and he suggested that Anne-Marie and I sit down directly with the BC Premier. I called Anne-Marie and we each jumped on flights to the west coast and met Vander Zalm in his Victoria office. Initially unapologetic, he eventually agreed to issue a "clarification", stating that immigrants from Hong Kong would always be welcome in British Columbia and to become homeowners there, but that developers would be encouraged to ensure that the local community was never denied the opportunity to buy into local projects. We also arranged a meeting for Victor Li with Vander Zalm, and the young but very polished Victor spoke to the press afterwards, apologizing for the oversight in the Concord Pacific sales, saying simply that he had never imagined them to sell out so quickly and that he would ensure that Vancouverites could participate in any future pre-sale programs.

Woven through all the tumultuous events in China during the spring and summer of 1989 was also a complex family situation. Liani had become pregnant during the autumn of 1988 and we discovered just before Christmas that she was going to have twins. Caleb, then three years old, was the first to call the double pregnancy, telling his mother that there were two babies "in there" a week or so before the doctor confirmed it. In anticipation of going from a family of four to a family of six, we decided to expand our house at 155 Acacia Avenue, adding a new master bedroom and bath on the third floor, and replacing an old one-story garage with a better built garage and a study on the second floor above. The house project was due to be completed in April and the twins were due at the beginning of June. As the early stages of the China crisis emerged at the end of April, I was in my office one day when the telephone rang and Liani mumbled something about water and breaking. Having had experienced lots of problems with the home's old iron pipes as we were getting the third floor bathroom put in, I wasn't surprised and simply answered "Well, call the plumber"! Not that kind of water, it turned out, and I rushed home to bring her to the Montfort hospital, where our twins were born on April 25th. As I left the house, there was no roof, and the workers all stood on the half-finished third floor to cheer us as we drove away. What with new twins and two other children seven and under, and the China crisis, I am sure that I did not sleep between May and September, and I certainly did not provide the level of support that Liani had every right to expect. But we made it through.

On my final day as Director of North Asia Relations at the end of the year, the bureau had a good-bye party for me. My gift from the officers and staff of the division was a large mayonnaise jar filled with staples, paper clips, rubber bands, short lengths of chain and other assorted items used to hold things together. A label on the jar said "China Linkages; To be Preserved at All Costs", a deeply appreciated tribute to my determination through the dramatic events of 1989.

CHAPTER 11

DIRECTOR GENERAL, POLICY PLANNING

• • • • • • • • • • •

Luck in life comes in many forms. Being Director of North Asia Relations at the time of the Tiananmen crisis resulted in me getting unheard of exposure for someone of my level with Joe Clark and even the Prime Minister. Having had the courage to simply ignore departmental procedures that were established long before 24-hour news channels, and do what needed to be done certainly helped us perform as well as we did, but if I had been still hidden away in the resource management job or away in some quiet posting, I would never have received the career boost that the crisis in China gave me. And it did not take long.

Although my team and I were completely absorbed by the events in China during most of 1989, there was a lot else happening in the world. Most dramatically, Mikhail Gorbachev was slowly dismantling the seventy-year old Soviet empire, loosening the straightjacket of control imposed on Poland, East Germany and Czechoslovakia, allowing the evident will of the people to over-ride the preferences of quisling dictatorships to maintain the status quo. One-by-one the local communist parties were to be ousted as the intravenous drip of power from the Kremlin was cut off, and requests by puppet regimes for Soviet intervention refused. With the announcement on the 9th of November by the new East German leader Egon Krenz that East Germans were now free to visit West Berlin unimpeded, the Berlin Wall had begun to crumble both figuratively and literally.

The raising of the Iron Curtain was earth-tilting change, and very difficult for many of our older colleagues to fully understand, given that they had spent their entire lives working a world governed by the East-West paradigm. The politicians actually understood it better than many of the older officials and diplomats, for politicians deal in change all the time. Prime Minister Mulroney intuitively understood the gravity of the tectonic shift taking place, as did Joe Clark, and while they deeply admired the wisdom that Si Taylor, our Under-Secretary, brought to everything he did, they found him somewhat deferential and not as action oriented as they would like. Mulroney in particular liked to have initiatives proposed to him where Canada could show leadership. And so Si Taylor stepped aside and headed off to Japan as Ambassador and was replaced by deMontigny Marchand.

As 1989 drew to a close, I had settled back to a post-crisis management of issues in our relationships with Japan and Korea and Indochina. China had retreated to a watching brief and an occasional issue to manage, but there were no high-level visits to organize, no bilateral talks to prepare for. Canada's relationship with the world's most populous country had moved into hibernation.

One December afternoon I was in my office and received a call from the new Under-Secretary's executive assistant asking me to come up to meet with Mr. Marchand. Having no idea what was happening, I of course went up to the 8th floor for what seemed to me a rather unfocused thirty minute chat about the state of the world, starting with China and Asia and then moving to the Soviet Union and Czechoslovakia, which was that very month in the throes of its dramatic Velvet Revolution. DeMontigny knew I had served in Prague and was clearly testing me to see whether I stayed current with matters outside of Asia. At the conclusion of our chat he told me that he would like me to become Director General of the Policy Development Bureau, the bureaucratic title for the Head of the Policy Planning Staff. My departmental initials would be CPD. He told me that he saw the job as a principle pillar of support for him in thinking about big issues, in helping pull disparate parts of the department together in making coherent multi-dimensional policy recommendations, and in keeping an eye over the horizon for matters likely to surface over the medium term. Of course I accepted.

My first two objectives as CPD in taking over the Policy Planning Staff was to figure out what it was supposed to do and then to build out a team to do it. I sat down with a number of senior officers of the Department whose views I respected, and got a wide range of advice on how to make the bureau relevant. Aside from preparing briefing notes for Ministers on Cabinet matters, and managing administratively all Cabinet submissions made by the Department, the unit had a rather vague mandate, along the lines of something like "to analyze emerging global political and economic issues and provide advice as required to the Under-Secretary of State and the Deputy Minister of International Trade". Whatever that was supposed to mean . . . I did read George F. Kennan's book on the creation of the Bretton Woods institutions at the end of World War II, when he took his role as head of Policy Planning at the State Department to guide the structuring of the post-war world order, and I talked with many predecessors, including Jeremy Kinsman, Paul Heinbecker, George Haynal and John Higginbotham. The more I heard of past experiences, the more I realized that to do this job well I would have to get involved in all sorts of files that officers senior to me would feel were theirs alone to manage. This would obviously create a lot of friction; the question was whether that friction would create more light than heat. Both survival and relevance seemed historically to boil down to one essential ingredient, the policy planner's relationship with the Under-Secretary.

In this I was very lucky. DeMontigny Marchand clearly saw me as part of his immediate staff, and going forward from the day I took on my new role, I would meet with him in his office every morning between 0800 and 0845 to review the day ahead. There were generally three or four of us in addition to the Under-Secretary at these morning meetings: Jeremy Kinsman, then Assistant Deputy Minister for International Political and Multilateral Affairs, effectively Canada's "Political Director"; myself; deMontigny's executive assistant; and often but not always Don Campbell, Deputy

Minister of International Trade. As Head of Policy Planning, I also became a member of the Department's Executive Committee for the first time.

Woody Allen once said, "Eighty percent of success is just showing up". If that had been true for me by being Director of PNR during the Tiananmen crisis, it was to be doubly true as head of Policy Planning. The following two years were to prove extraordinarily rich in terms of global challenges and change.

The Policy Planning Bureau had grown from simply a political think tank in the old External Affairs to a regular bureau with three divisions, a Political and Strategic Analysis Division, a Trade Policy and Economic Analysis Division and a Cabinet Secretariat Division. The first two were traditional policy planning units, the first focused on global political issues, the second on international trade policy and economic change, and the third a rather bureaucratic unit responsible for managing the briefing process for the Secretary of State for External Affairs and the Minister of International Trade on non-departmental Cabinet issues about which the Department had concerns. The bureau acted as a central clearinghouse and traffic policeman for Cabinet and House committees. We would receive all Cabinet Committee or full Cabinet documents, and ensure briefing notes were prepared by whatever line division was dealing with the matter at hand. Similarly, we were also responsible for all departmental preparation for the appearance of Ministers or officials before the Standing Committee on External Affairs and International Trade of the House of Commons and, needed much more rarely, its Senate counterpart.

My first objective in forming my new team was to find people smarter than I was to head up the two critical policy divisions. The Secretariat Division appeared to be already in the thorough if workmanlike hands of Rick Belliveau (later our Consul General in Shanghai and Ambassador to Algeria). For the trade and economic division, the smartest person I could think of was Michael Hart, a completely irreverent iconoclast who had been involved in the negotiation of the Canada-US Free Trade

Agreement. Michael had originally been in the trade policy branch of old IT&C, and was now serving in an ill-defined position in the US Branch while simultaneously teaching international trade on a part time basis at Carleton University. I invited Michael, who had a big bushy beard, out to lunch and as we sat down he immediately said: "I should have been offered your job. Why on earth would I want to work for you?" This was the best opening line at a job interview I have ever heard, before or since, but by the end of the lunch, after realizing that not only had I no intention to stifle him but actually wanted him to get his elbows up and upset some apple carts, he agreed to come on board. On the political side I selected Claude Boucher, who had been running the Federal-Provincial Coordination Division, a background that I did not know at the time would prove very useful. Claude was the antithesis to Michael Hart, soft-spoken and a quietly effective negotiator who never seemed to ruffle anyone's feathers.

Although I seemed to rub some of the ADMs the wrong way as I started to get involved in files for which they had primary responsibility, I hit it off tremendously well with Jeremy Kinsman, even though his responsibility for all multilateral and defence related issues had me rubbing elbows with him almost constantly. With the East-West divide in huge flux, the future of Canadian forces in Europe and indeed the whole repurposing of NATO were very much key issues, and Jeremy and I spent many hours brainstorming about them. Jeremy was also a runner, with whom I had occasionally run when still in the Asia branch if the two of us happened to be leaving the departmental changing rooms at the same time, and this now became a habit almost every lunchtime. We would use our runs to discuss both substantive issues and the tactics we needed to use to bring about attitudinal change. Two of Jeremy's Directors General, Mark Moher and Jon Noble, were much less welcoming as they saw me arrogate to the Policy Planning staff commentary on matters they felt were their responsibility. That I was junior to them in the service, and the only Director General level officer on the Executive Committee, must have also rankled.

My close relationship with both Under Secretary Marchand and Political Director Jeremy Kinsman made it natural that I would be involved in the G-7 process, which for Prime Minister Mulroney was always a major priority. Mulroney was a natural consensus-builder, and his warm and outgoing personality and his complete fluency in both French and English made him a very effective player at G-7 summits. And he seemed to love the summits, in part no doubt because of his ability to forge common positions between leaders who did not really see eye to eye and who did not share a common language. And for those of us who were supporting him, it was clear that he was very talented at this extraordinarily high-level game of global multilateralism.

At the Houston G-7 Summit in July of 1990, the major pre-occupation of the leaders was naturally the changes in eastern Europe and in the Soviet Union and the desire to support Gorbachev with a substantive economic olive branch. The political communiqué of the Summit, was, like that from most Summits, largely negotiated by officials in advance and simply blessed rather quickly by leaders. The 1990 communiqué covered a number of issues not discussed at length, including the situation in China. A year after Tiananmen, the leadership in Beijing still completely unapologetic for the event, and the human rights situation inside the country had in no way begun to improve. So the reference in the communiqué remained critical and suggested that real change was needed before the G-7 countries would normalize their relationships with China. The political communiqué staed that: "We acknowledge some of the recent developments in China, but believe that the prospects for closer cooperation will be enhanced by renewed political and economic reform, particularly in the field of human rights. We agree to maintain the measures put into place at last year's Summit, as modified over the course of this year. We will keep them under review for future adjustments to respond to further positive developments in China."

In fact, there was growing disarray in the alleged consensus on not re-engaging with China at a high political level. President Bush had already authorized confidential talks led by National Security Advisor Brent Scrowcroft and Assistant Under Secretary of State Lawrence Eagleburger, and both the Japanese and French were champing at the bitt to have their political ties re-established. At this stage Canada was somewhat behind others, and while I knew that the Prime Minister felt that Canadian public opinion would not support a resumption of high-level visits, I did not want us to slip completely off the Chinese radar. After consulting with our Chargé d'Affaires in Beijing, my old friend Bruce Jutzi (we were between Ambassadors, Earl Drake having just retired and Fred Bild not yet having arrived), I suggested to Under Secretary deMontigny Marchand that he and I go to China right after the Summit to debrief the Chinese leadership on what had transpired in Houston, given that China was interested both in the treatment of China and in the evolution of western relations with the rapidly changing Soviet Union. DeMontigny agreed and ran the idea past SSEA Joe Clark and Prime Minister Mulroney, both of whom thought that this was a perfectly acceptable step to take.

Marchand and I flew on to Beijing just about as fast as we thought we could after the Houston Summit, arriving about four days later. Our first meeting was with Vice Minister Liu Huaqui who welcomed us as the most senior Canadian delegation to visit since the June 4th incident, and it was a reasonably civil discussion, although the Vice Minister made it quite clear that the Chinese leadership had taken note that Canada was slower that other countries in resuming high-level contacts. The only issue which really seemed to irritate Liu and this was to become a constant refrain over the next year or so, was that Canada was "hi-jacking" Chinese students but allowing them to stay indefinitely in Canada. There was some truth to this, since we not only allowed the 4500 students who had already been in Canada before the Tiananmen crackdown, but applied the open stay policy to all those who arrived over the following year, eventually covering almost 10,000 students. Three months earlier, in April, the Asia Pacific Branch had proposed that the policy be reversed and no new students be allowed to take advantage of it, and we had gotten SSEA Joe Clark to write a formal letter to the minister responsible, Barbara McDougall, but she took no action and allowed the program to continue.

After our meeting with Liu Huaqui, were then received very graciously by Qian Qichen, then foreign minister and later to become a State Counselor and Vice Premier. As we began the meeting, Qian said to deMontigny, "Yesterday I received the Japanese Prime Minister's Personal Representative to the Summit and he told me that Japan fought to exclude any reference to China in the communiqué, but all the Europeans and North Americans insisted on harsh language so Japan could not win. And yesterday the French Ambassador called on our Vice Minister and told him that France had wanted the language to welcome recent change in China and propose a shift towards more normal relations, but that all the other G-7 countries had opposed the French position so France could not win. Mr. Vice Minister, what really did happen at the G-7 Summit?" Without missing a beat, deMontigny explained, "Mr. Minister, every country at the meeting except Canada wanted softer language on China, but Canada wanted the language that is actually in the communiqué. As Canada is such a large and powerful country, all the others had no choice but to agree!" Qian laughed heartedly and the meeting went on very smoothly from there. As the years went by, my respect for Qian Qichen continued to grow, and I always found him extraordinarily well-informed, deeply respectful of western perspectives and in many ways an updated version of Zhou Enlai., managing as he did his country's relationship with the outside world during a difficult and occasionally confrontational time.

The Raising of the Iron Curtain and the End of the Soviet Union

The most immediate global issue facing NATO and Canada in early 1990 was the re-alignment of Europe and what it would mean for everything from German membership in NATO, to institutional structures of the European Economic Community to our individual relations with the bruised but still extant Soviet Union. Almost immediately after I started in Policy Planning there was a joint meeting of all the NATO and Warsaw Foreign Ministers in Ottawa. The stated purpose was to advance the Open Skies Treaty, a radical step forward in the de-escalation of cold war rigidities as it would allow unrestricted unarmed surveillance flights by NATO over Warsaw Pact countries and vice versa. The Ottawa meetings were more than that, however, for they allowed both Prime Minister Mulroney and Joe Clark extended sessions with Soviet Foreign Minister Eduard Shevardnadze, and both Jeremy and I attended the latter meeting. Shevardnadze was extraordinarily gripping, speaking so softly one could barely hear him but by doing so commanding total silence in the room. The discussion went way beyond the Open Skies treaty and touched on Soviet worries about a unified Germany, which Shevardnadze treated as inevitable but candidly said was still seen in Moscow as threatening to peace over time given history, and also to short-term stability in Moscow, where conservative forces were increasingly unhappy with Gorbachev's "concessions" to the West. Shevardnadze was accompanied by several officials, including his Policy Planner and long-time strategic advisor, Sergei Tarasenko, roughly my equivalent. I was to get to know Tarasenko better over the next couple of years.

Change in Europe, so fundamental to world peace, was a hugely preoccupying foreign policy priority between 1989 and 1992, and it is almost hard to recall how uncertain was the outcome of all the local turmoil, nationalist pressure and military and communist backlash. Poland and Czechoslovakia and Hungary were already flaunting their history as "Central Europe" a term forgotten for a half century, reminding themselves and others of their historic connections to the mainline countries of Western Europe. Could these countries someday become part of the European Community? What about NATO? There was to be a NATO Ministerial meeting on April 18th, and the Prime Minister wanted a good Cabinet discussion beforehand. Logically, Jeremy was asked to prepare the Cabinet Memorandum and he turned to me to work with him and his team on both the background and some of the issues that would need to be addressed. The memo tried to look both at the future of NATO and the CSCE (the Conference on Security and Cooperation in Europe, which was started in 1973 and had resulted in the "Helsinki process" of confidence building measures between East and West), and to define where Canada could and would wish to be active. Jeremy and I did our best to ensure that the issues to be discussed by Cabinet focused on actions which Canada could take to improve the chances we would achieve our national objectives, not always consistent with those of our European partners. We identified that Canadian influence in Europe was bound to diminish, that a Europe dominated by Germany would not be in our national interest, and that we needed to ensure our institutions were strong enough to deal with the likely rise in unconventional threats to security, such as civil disorder, environmental devastation and terrorism. Clark was very active at the various NATO meetings, and Mulroney, having acted as a father figure at the joint NATO-Warsaw Pact foreign ministers' meeting in Ottawa, during which he had met separately with Shevardnadze, Genscher, Jim Baker and others, was regularly on the phone with Presidents George H. Bush and Francois Mitterand.

Jeremy Kinsman came back from the NATO Foreign Ministers meeting in April frustrated. The meeting had not gone very well, no one was willing to think outside the box or be able to conceive of where we all wanted to end up by the end of the century, which is the question Jeremy thought we should be posing. I then received an invitation from the Institute for East-West Security Studies to come to a confidential meeting in May with other policy planners at a place called Krottorf Castle in West Germany. John Edwin Mroz and Peter Voltren of the institute had been quietly approached by the West German government to try to get a quiet dialogue going among all the major countries involved, without any press whatsoever, to see what institutional structures might assist a smooth German re-unification process. The purported theme was "What would be the ideal Europe at the end of the 1990s?", with the unstated required elements being a unified Germany and a transformed and non-threatening Soviet Union.

Krottorf Castle was a fantastic old manor house near Groningen in Rhine-Westphalia, surrounded by a double moat and in a gentle state of decay. There were thirteen of us there for three days and there was no formal agenda beyond the basic question. The policy planners from all major West European countries were there: Robert Cooper of the UK, Jean-Marie Guéhenno from France, Klaus Citron of West Germany, Piet Dankert from the Netherlands and his Italian counterpart Fransesco Bascone. Also attending Sergei Tarasenko of the Soviet Union and several very high level people from the newly emerging non-communist regimes of Central Europe: Zdenek Metejka, Deputy Minister of the Czechoslovak Foreign Ministry, Ferenc Somogyi who was a State Secretary from Hungary, and Thomas Nowotny from Poland. Dennis Ross, the US Policy Planner was invited but as he was not involved in East-West issues, being almost permanently focused on Middle East issues, so Jim Dobbins, Assistant Secretary for European and Canadian Affairs, attended. It was a very high-intellect group and our exchanges were informal and very instructive on what the hot buttons would likely be in the immediate future, which was to say in the months and year or two to come.

As important as our collective discussions were, just or more vital were the many walks that we took with each other around the moats and across the bridges into the beautiful countryside nearby. Krottorf Castle is set in the middle of a wooded area, but it was early spring and the leaves were not fully out. There were neighbouring fields freshly planted and the smell of the earth and the warmth of the sun made a very special setting. At one point I walked across a bridge and into the nearby fields with Czech Deputy Minister Matejka, and tried to resurrect my rapidly disappearing Czech. Matejka said as we walked that in the past he could have never believed that the day would come when he would be realistically talking about his country becoming a member of NATO or the European Community.

We collectively left Krottorf with a number of agreed messages. First, it was time to turn off the Western rhetoric about who won and who lost the cold war; which was making Gorbachev's domestic situation in Moscow much more difficult. Second, a balance had to be found between offering an economic hand to the Soviet Union and the gradual standing down of deployed forces across the old divide; President Bush particularly opposed the granting of assistance until the Soviets had made real movements to reduce their threatening missile force. This was to mean that the first economic peace offerings would simply be the opening up of markets and the removal of trade restrictions. Third, North American military presence in Europe could be reduced but not eliminated – it was interesting that Tarasenko was adamant that this was the only way a visceral Russian fear of a strong and unified Germany could be tempered. Fourth, NATO would have to be "re-purposed" and we could probably get rid of some other organizations like the CSCE. (Unfortunately, the bureaucratic reality turned out that, international organizations being always difficult to euthanise, the CSCE ended up being maintained in the form of the OSCE in Vienna, although it is hard to argue that it has ever contributed anything positive to peace or stability in Europe, just as the difficult-to-negotiate Open Skies Treaty was both politically and technologically rendered irrelevant even before it came into force.)

Among my own suggestions at the Krottorf gathering was that we should encourage our leaders to focus on individuals and not on organizations, because when average people everywhere turned on their televisions they did not see NATO or the CSCE or the Warsaw Pact, they saw Gorbachev and Havel and Bush and Kohl. I said that we had to start treating Gorbachev as a winner and as someone protecting his people's interests when engaged in discussions with the West. And I suggested that we invite Gorbachev to the upcoming G-7 Summit, which was to take place in Houston in July. Jim Dobbins and all the European policy planners thought this idea was a very good one. When I got back to Ottawa I shared our thinking with Jeremy Kinsman, and he ran the idea of a Summit invitation up the line. I was later told that Mulroney loved the idea and discussed it with President Bush during one of their regular telephone calls. Bush, however, did not like the idea primarily because he believed the Soviet Union was not yet militarily de-fanged, and as he was the host of the Houston Summit an invitation to Gorbachev was not issued until the following Summit in 1991.

A great deal happened in East-West affairs in the year that followed, and by the time Prime Minister John Major hosted his G-7 colleagues and special guest Mikhail Gorbachev at Lancaster House in London for the 1991 Summit, Germany was united, the first Gulf War had been fought and won, Lithuania's independence had been recognized and Latvia and Estonia were on the cusp of formal declarations of independence. Gorbachev came to Ottawa in the late winter of 1991 for a bilateral visit, and brought Shevardnadze who had meetings with Clark just before the latter was reassigned to become Minister of Constitutional Affairs. I attended the meetings during that visit and also attended the G-7 Summit in London. Just after the formal photograph was taken of Gorbachev with the western leaders on the steps of Lancaster House, with many of the G-7 officials watching from the sidelines, Prime Minister Mulroney brought Gorbachev over to briefly chat with Jeremy Kinsman and me, telling Gorbachev that we were the ones who had been pushing for his invitation to the G-7 gathering for more than a year.

Economic and Trade Issues

International political issues clearly preoccupied my time as head of Policy Planning, but not exclusively so. Very early in 1990, the Mexican government proposed to enter into negotiations on a free trade agreement with the United States. At this time John Crosbie was Minister of International Trade, and although the 1988 election had been fought and won on the issue of bilateral free trade with the United States, we were now in a period where any and every economic problem across Canada was being blamed on free trade, from the closing of a local business to a decision of a Japanese automaker to locate in the Ohio instead of Ontario. The first reaction of the staff in Crosbie's office, and indeed in most political offices around town, to the public news that Mexico and the US might start their own free trade negotiations was to let it happen and keep Canada out of another bruising public issue.

When Michael Hart heard that there was a chance we might voluntarily stand aside from the free trade negotiations between the United States and Mexico, he suggested that we should prepare an analysis for our Ministers showing what a stupid decision this would be. I agreed and he prepared and I approved a brief and very cogent argument as to why it would be to Canada's enormous disbenefit to allow the US to negotiate other free trade agreements in a kind of hub-and-spoke network, with the United States always at the hub and other countries, including Canada, stuck out on the spokes. Our core case was based on the flow of foreign direct investment. We used as an example a Japanese company looking at competitive investment locations for the establishment of a major North American manufacturing facility. If the US had a series of "hub-and-spoke" agreements, the only way the Japanese firm could gain duty-free access to all the markets would be to situate in the United States, since to situate in Canada would ensure access to the US market but not to Mexico. Michael and I were asked to come and discuss the matter further with Minister Crosbie, which we did, and he in his usual humourous way said that he had been really looking forward to "being ridiculed and vilified once again not only by his cabinet colleagues but by every Canadian from coast to coast", but that he bought our argument. He subsequently made the case to Prime Minister Mulroney, who was hearing the same argument from a trusted and very powerful source, Derek Burney, who had moved to Washington as Ambassador several months after Mulroney's second election victory. Mulroney was completely on side that the NAFTA could not proceed without Canada, and after some effective lobbying with Jim Baker by both he and Derek Burney, and a tough Cabinet session to get all the doubting thomases in line, the trilateral process was assured.

At this early stage in the opening up of the Canadian economy to the increased competition resulting from the bilateral FTA with the United States, senior Canadian business leaders were worried about the level of competitiveness of Canadian firms and the Canadian economy generally. The Business Council on National Issues (the BCNI, later to become the Canadian Council of Chief Executives), hired Michael Porter and his Boston-based Monitor Group to conduct a study on Canadian Competitiveness and to make recommendations on policy changes that would improve the ability of Canadian firms to compete internationally. Porter had done a similar, seminal study on the Swedish economy. BCNI asked the government to nominate up to three government advisors to join a steering group with their executives to interact with the study team. At this time, Finance Minister Michael Wilson had already commissioned an internal government report on productivity, with ADM Kevin Lynch leading a group of senior officials to work on various dimensions of the problem. From our department, the brilliant economist Barry Carin and I were involved in that group, which also included Andrei Sulzenko, Alan Nymark, George Anderson and Bob Blackburn from various other departments. In response to the BCNI request, it was decided that myself, Bob Blackburn and Kevin Lynch would be the representatives to the BCNI process. The first substantive meeting of the steering group followed six months work and the submission of an initial draft by Monitor. When Kevin, Bob and I reviewed the draft we were aghast at the sloppiness of the work and simplistic level of both the analysis and the recommendations, and we found that the private sector members of the steering group had reached the same conclusions. It appeared that Porter had handed off the study to junior analysts, and could not have spent any time reviewing the draft report, which simply seemed to be the report on Sweden all over again, with the word "Canada" occasionally patched in. BCNI invited Porter and his team to a meeting in Toronto where we all tore the draft report to shreds. Tom d'Aquino, head of the BCNI Secretariat, told Porter he had three months to redo the report in its entirety or to face the public humiliation of having Monitor fired by BCNI. The final report was an improvement over the draft, but its recommendations were largely self-evident and it never had much of an impact on either industry or government policy. At the time I had no idea that my nephew Geoffrey Tuff would one day become a full partner at Monitor.

The First Gulf War

On the 2nd of August, 1990, Iraqi forces invaded Kuwait in a lightning strike and occupied its little southern neighbour. Our Under-Secretary deMontigny Marchand, Jeremy Kinsman and I were all on vacation and the acting Under-Secretary was Raymond Chrétien, nephew of Jean Chrétien, who had won back the leadership of the Liberal Party that year, having lost it to John Turner prior to the 1984 election and having spent the intervening time working on Bay Street.

When the Iraqi invasion hit the news, I called both Jeremy and deMontigny by telephone from our summer home in Jamestown, Rhode Island. Our Ambassador to the UN, Bob Fowler, then sitting on the Security Council, had helped convene an emergency meeting which passed a Resolution, the first of many, demanding an immediate withdrawal, but no one believed words from the UN were likely to quickly dislodge Iraq. Jeremy suggested we all foreshorten our holidays and return to Ottawa. Luckily, our planned family vacation was already on its final day, so we drove back to Ottawa listening to as much news on the radio as we could, knowing that I would be involved in a new crisis. By the time I got back on the evening of the 3rd, Prime Minister Mulroney had been back and forth to Washington to meet privately with President Bush and National Security Advisor Brent Scowcroft, and pledged Canadian support to whatever US-led multilateral effort might be required to force an Iraqi withdrawal. When Mulroney returned he made clear both directly to Clark, and to us through the PCO, that he wanted to pursue a two-pronged policy: robust support for Kuwait and the US on one hand, and a firm insistence that any action taken be taken by as broad an international coalition as possible with a clear UN blessing.

On the morning of August 4th, the Department's Executive Committee met and struck a crisis management group, known simply as the "Task Force" chaired by Andrew Robinson, Director of the Middle East Division. There was also to be a higher-level coordinating committee, in which

Andrew would participate, but this took a few days to get coordinated. Andrew asked me to share with him my experience the year before during the Tiananmen crisis. I sat down with him and explained all the things I thought we had gotten right and also the things we could have done better. I particularly recommended that he create a briefing instrument that would avoid departmental hierarchy, which he immediately did, issuing a "Gulf Crisis SITREP" at least once a day. He also had one of his deputies take charge of constant communications with outside stakeholders and interest groups, including the diverse network of Arab Canadian groups. (Andrew was terrific officer and after several more years deeply involved in Middle Eastern matters, eventually ended his career as Ambassador to the Ukraine during the Orange Revolution.)

The autumn of 1990 was substantially a diplomatic autumn, during which we were very active in coalition consultation and building as strong a united front against Iraq as possible, hoping that if bereft even of Arab support, Saddam Hussein would eventually back out of Kuwait. Michael Shenstone, one of our great Middle East experts and a former Ambassador to Israel as well as to some Arab countries, was then in a pre-retirement position in my Policy Planning bureau, doing a study on the long-term security threats of water and environment. Pulled from that, he became a roving Ambassador for us, shuttling around the Middle East and the Maghreb, trying to simultaneously build pressure on Iraq and reinforce the cohesion of the growing coalition. He even went to Baghdad and met with both Foreign Minister Tariq Aziz and Saddam Hussein. In New York and Washington and London, we (then a member of the Security Council) tried to constantly pull the US and the UK back to the United Nations to ensure that whatever action was eventually required would carry the weight of international law.

Given my role as the Under-Secretary's "hit-man" on all kinds of global issues that involved many branches and bureaus, I was deeply involved in the day to day coordination of our response to the crisis. Jeremy Kinsman ended up as Chair of the Interdepartmental Crisis Coordinating Committee and I became its Deputy Chair. We also had a Co-Chair, who was in theory Chief of the Defence Staff General John de Chastelain, although he virtually never attended, usually sending one of his senior generals instead. As the autumn progressed the importance of the military side of our operations increased, and once the Security Council's Resolution 678 was passed on November 27th, most of us were convinced that it would take military force, and not just the threat of it, to oust Saddam from Kuwait. By this time Canada had the fifth largest military contingent in the coalition, after Saudi Arabia, the US, the UK and France. We had four ships, two squadrons of CF-18 Hornets, a helicopter support squadron, and in all approximately 3500 men and women of the Canadian Forces in theatre.

After the war in late-1991, I wrote an article on "The Crisis as Superstar in the World According to CNN", and in it I described a typical day of that time. It was set sometime late in the crisis, probably in either late December or early January as the January 15th deadline for Iraqi withdrawal approached (the attack on Iraq by the coalition began on January 17th). I repeat it here:

0330: Two intelligence analysts arrive in the Task Force Operations Centre on the second floor of the Pearson Building. The "Ops Centre" as it is known, smells of coffee and stale pizza. Banks of televisions are broadcasting a series of channels. Two or three people are watching, one occasionally changing channels of all but one television, that one broadcasting CNN. A bank of VCRs stands ready for recordings, although none is now operating. The clatter of teletype machines can be faintly heard from a small room next door, as the Reuters, AFP, AP and CP wires spew their unending fare. Periodically someone brings a sheath of long strips from the teletype room and pins them to a board on the wall.

The two intelligence analysts receive from the senior watch officer, a Deputy Director of the Middle East Division, the first draft of the morning "SITREP" composed entirely on the basis of news stories and incoming telex traffic from our missions.

The "SITREP" contains a number of fixed headings including: "Diplomatic Developments", "Military Developments", "Refugees and Humanitarian Assistance", "Economic Assistance", "Baghdad Embassy", and "Consular Situation". The "SITREP" is in bullet form and is never more than two pages in length.

The analysts go through a code-controlled inner door at the back of the Ops Centre to review "special" traffic (highly classified intelligence), and to prepare packages of special material for the PM and Ministers, and for senior Crisis Committee members, and to recommend changes or additions to the more widely circulated "SITREP".

0420: One of the two intelligence analysts passes back through the Ops centre, giving the senior watch officer his suggested changes to the "SITREP" and then leaves for the daily 0430 briefing at National Defence headquarters.

0545: I get out of bed, stubbing my toe on a chair and knocking the laundry basket down the stairs, waking my five-year old son. We have a quick grown-up conversation about the crisis, before I hear my morning cab roll up outside. About a dozen other officials from the department and from PCO are similarly fighting their way out of sleep and into transport.

0615: The Crisis Coordinating Committee meets in the Ops Centre Conference Room, windowless and sealed but for one door as it is a "clean" room, and swept from time to time. Senior departmental officials, including Jeremy Kinsman (Committee Chair), myself, Andrew Robinson (Task Force Head and Director, Middle East), Marc Perron (ADM Middle East and Africa), Louise Fréchette (ADM Economic Affairs), Gavin Stewart (ADM Consular and Immigration), Peter Daniel (head of Press and Communications), Admiral Larry Murray from the Defence Staff and Bob Grauer from the Prime Minister's Office are at the table. Several briefers and staff members are also in attendance.

The "SITREP" is circulated, and Andrew Robinson as Head of the Task Force, orally briefs the committee on developments. The senior intelligence analyst who participated in the National Defence Headquarters briefing gives an update from his perspective and shares written material with some but not all the people around the table. The "SITREP" is at the same time being distributed all over town to Ministers and Deputies, having been signed off by Andrew Robinson as head of the Task Force, and subject to no further hierarchical clearance.

After Andrew's briefing and a few questions, the discussion turns to the day ahead. Two other pieces of paper, one entitled "Diplomatic Agenda" and the other a proposed text for the SSEA to use at an afternoon session of the Joint Parliamentary Committee, are circulated. The "Diplomatic Agenda" is a point-form two-page sheet summarizing what the Prime Minister, the SSEA and our diplomatic missions would or should be doing in the ensuing few days, listing head-of-government and foreign minister telephone calls that might be made, international meetings to be attended, a mid-day round table for the SSEA with Arab Canadians, speeches to be made and themes to be stressed.

0700: A further official enters the room, arriving from the PCO Communications Committee held in the Langevin Block. Another piece of paper, entitled "24 and 48 Hour Communications Strategy" is circulated, along with a "Media Analysis" containing a brief summary of all the major Canadian newspaper and electronic media coverage of the past day. The discussion then focuses on what the media stories are, how various observers are playing our very active diplomatic efforts, how they are playing the Israeli angle and so on. We talk for a few minutes on whether we should be doing more in briefing the media. Someone flags a concern of Canadian media in theatre about not being included in closely controlled American, British or French media pools as ground forces gradually move into position.

0730: Four of us brief Under-Secretary deMontigny Marchand, whose EA is watching CNN as we enter the office, keeping the points to the minimum that he will wish to discuss with the SSEA or his colleagues at subsequent meetings. He is given copies of the "Diplomatic Agenda" and the notes for the Parliamentary Committee, but there is no sense that they are being submitted for review or clearance.

0900: The Under-Secretary, Jeremy, Andrew Robinson and I brief SSEA Joe Clark, as usual at his East Block Office on Parliament Hill, with his Chief of Staff Roy Norton and his Press Spokesperson in attendance as well. We focus on whether the Cabinet should be authorizing the Canadian CF-18 fighters to train over the desert in a "sweep and escort" mode with American bombers, which would imply a willingness to take on such an aggressive role if conflict proves necessary. The Clerk of the Privy Council, Paul Tellier and Chief of Staff Stanley Hart are simultaneously briefing the PM, just as the Chief of the Defence Staff John de Chastelain and Admiral Murray are briefing their Minister, Bill McKnight.

0930: The Ad Hoc Cabinet Meeting begins, chaired by the Prime Minister. This is a very small meeting, comprising the PM, the SSEA, the Minister of National Defence and the Ministers of Energy, Mines and Resources and Transport, really an "inner cabinet". The Under-Secretary sits in on the meeting and briefs us afterwards that the entire discussion is focused on the change in Canada's role, moving to "sweep and escort" will mean an aggressive role for Canada for the first time since the Korean War, and the reality that Canadian lives will be at risk.

1030: I wander back to the Ops Centre just to see how things are going and to see if there any last minute messages from regional posts. Operators of the "1-800" consular lines are busy; families of Canadians still in countries neighbouring Iraq are worrying that something serious may indeed be happening and want everything from the details of our emergency evacuation plans (we had been advising people to leave by commercial means weeks before) to message-passing services to knowledge of their elderly relatives back in their countries of origin. Andrew Robinson, indefatigable, is on the telephone with our Deputy Permanent Representative to the UN in New York, having a heated conversation about something to do with Jordan. The Ops Centre is a bee-hive. A brief message comes in and is circulated from Larry Dickenson, our Ambassador to Kuwait now stationed in Bahrain, who has just spent a half-day in Taif with the Kuwaiti Emir.

1145: The SSEA calls from his Hill office with some changes to his remarks to the Parliamentary Committee. Translations are also changed.

1215: The SSEA and Andrew Robinson attend the Round Table with representatives of the Arab-Canadian community. Jeremy Kinsman and I head down to the locker room for a mid-day run out to the Aviation Museum and back.

1345: Back in the office, I take advantage of a lull in the day to look through papers, read the mail, discuss non-Gulf issues with Claude Boucher and a couple of other staff members not caught in the Gulf vortex.

1530: At the Parliamentary Committee in the Railway Room of Centre Block, chosen for its size and media-friendliness", the SSEA, flanked by Jeremy and myself, makes his twenty-five minute statement and answers questions. The Liberal Foreign Affairs critic, Lloyd Axworthy, repeatedly accuses the Government of a lack of action to find a peaceful way out of the crisis; the SSEA parries fairly easily but does let the critic get a little under his skin – it is evident that he is tired. Other questions are largely predictable and the hearing winds up just after 1630, which was the time limit established.

1640: The SSEA is scrummed as we come out of the parliamentary hearing; reporters try to stop Jeremy and me for quotable quotes but we spar, (knowing many of them) and walk through.

1715: Kinsman and I arrive back at the Department, slightly late for the standard afternoon meeting of the Crisis Coordination Committee. A new "SITREP" has been distributed, a new shift of watch officers and intelligence analysts are now on duty, the shift in place in the wee hours of the morning now gone. The afternoon meeting is a much larger than the morning one, and most of the ADM-level committee members are not present. The afternoon meetings are more or less "open", much less disciplined and allow up to thirty or thirty-five mid-level officials from the Department, from DND, CIDA, EM&R, Transport and PCO to participate. Although somewhat frustrating because of the familiarity of the ground being retraced, this meeting is useful in diffusing knowledge and helping the larger team stay up to date with unfolding developments.

1830: The meeting is over. We all head back to our respective offices to clean up whatever has collected during the day. CNN is still on my TV, one staff member sitting on the couch catching night scenes from Israel as I enter. I answer about a third of my telephone messages, including two from journalists with whom I have good and safe relations. One is chasing the CF-18 role story (it is starting to leak out and I know it will be well known in a day or two, but I refuse to be drawn even on an unattributable basis) and the other is just fishing, so we talk for a bit about the growing tension and the stakes involved and possible outcomes. I meet briefly with staff to discuss the next "Analysis and Outlook" theme.

1945: I head home, taking a taxi in hopes of catching the twins before they go to bed. I miss, again, but catch the older children.

2130: Andrew Robinson, still at the office, telephones me to discuss the SSEA's plans to talk to a number of G-7 colleagues the following day. If we end up putting young men and women in harm's way in a hot war, it will not because any stone on a possible pathway to peace was left unturned. We agree on a few lines and I agree to run up a note on my PC and bring it to the morning meeting the next day.

This was a typical day during the late phase of the crisis. The Ad Hoc Cabinet Committee met on average twice a week from September through November, three times a week until just before the beginning of the air-war in mid-January, and almost daily thereafter until the end of the military phase of the conflict six weeks later. The Joint Parliamentary Committee was created to allow parliamentary involvement, including questioning by the Opposition Liberals, after Parliament rose for its normal extended Christmas break. It met every day for one hour and was televised on the Parliamentary channel and CBC and CTV frequently picked up its proceedings. The standard practice was for the SSEA and the Minister of National Defence to each appear once a week, and officials or outside experts on other days. Not surprisingly, the media followed Ministerial appearances closely and turned them into nightly news stories, while the appearance of officials was watched for anything new and occasionally chosen for quick clips on CBC Newsworld but rarely brought to centre stage. I appeared twice when Jeremy was unavailable. During one of those appearances, Lloyd Axworthy got quite aggressive about the Government's "hawkish" policy being out of keeping with Canada's peacekeeping traditions. I answered with what I thought was a pretty emotionless explanation of the reasons behind what we were doing. When I got back to my office I received a telephone call from the PMO switchboard, who connected me with the gravelly voice of Prime Minister Mulroney, who said "Good job today, Howard, you really gave Axworthy a good right hook!" It was then I knew that I had probably stepped beyond the proper limits for an official. In retrospect, the openness of the Government in having these daily public Parliamentary Committee meetings undoubtedly helped build the national consensus which backed the Government's position to participate in the coalition and to put Canadian forces personnel in harm's way.

During the entire Gulf crisis, Jeremy Kinsman and I never missed more than two consecutive days for our runs. For most of the crisis we kept them secret, as there was no reason to have the Under-Secretary or the SSEA or the PMO start wondering about our sense of priority. All confidentiality fell apart, however, on January 16th, when we were called in (we always ran with one of us carrying a then rather bulky cellular phone) from our run some ten hours before the beginning of the air war. We were forced to respond to a simple "get back" order, which we understood for the early warning that it in fact turned out to be. There followed a very fast return run from well out towards the Aviation Museum, and a direct elevator ride to the 8th and 10th floors (those of the Under-Secretary and the SSEA respectively) where we wandered in and out of meetings in steaming and sweaty winter running gear for the next two hours. Gone forever was any secrecy to our mid-day runs, leading the SSEA to subsequently choose around 1300 to call us to ask about some trifling matter or another, always ready to tease us about our heavy breathing!

Watching participants in the decision-making process during the Gulf War told me a lot about their underlying characters. The Prime Minister, focused and stalwart throughout, was determined that Canada play its full and proper role, both militarily and diplomatically, and he never erred off the path that it was Canada's responsibility to ensure that both the role of the UN was respected and that every effort be made to avoid a military solution if possible. SSEA Joe Clark initially did not like the notion of committing the Canadian military to a potential conflict in which we had little influence and not, in his view, terribly much interest. But once the collective decision was made, he threw himself into the business of ensuring what we did was done well. When the question of Canada's role in the hot war came up for consideration and some were arguing to keep Canadian aircraft in support roles well to the rear of the conflict, he came out in clear support for the more aggressive "sweep and escort" role. When one of the other Ministers said that Canadian support would waver "as soon as Canadians started coming home in body bags", Clark countered by saying that he initially had been opposed to military involvement but once it had been decided to participate, he believed we should participate fully. Canadians, he said in response to the remark about public support wavering, were made of "stronger stuff" and they would be ashamed if once committed to a conflict we hid our soldiers and airmen in the shadows. The Canadian Forces were phenomenally lucky, and also obviously very skilled, and avoid any fatality during the air war and thus Clark's thesis would go untested. However, two decades later the early years of the Afghan conflict were to prove him right.

The final chapter of the Gulf War was a rather sorry matter, when a senior Iraqi diplomat sought and received landed immigrant status and entered Canada in late March. Mohammed Al Mashat had been the Iraqi Ambassador to the US and a frequent apologist in television interviews and press conferences for Saddam and his brutal regime. Internally, the matter was handled on a need-to-know basis by Associate Under-Secretary Raymond Chrétien, who for some extraordinary reason decided not even to advise the Under-Secretary or any of the senior officials involved in managing the crisis. When the story broke publicly, all of us were caught completely off guard and no one was very happy with Raymond. But the most sorry part of the affair was that a number of Ministers, including the newly appointed Secretary of State for External Affairs, Barbara McDougall, and Minister of Employment and Immigration Bernard Valcourt (who had replaced McDougall in that portfolio on April 21st) tried to dodge any responsibility for the decision and instead hung Raymond personally out to dry. It turned out that the offices of both ministers had been advised of the intended approval, and the Ministers themselves were either left uninformed or conveniently forgot that they had been. The case was later held up as a sad abrogation of Canada's long tradition of Ministerial responsibility and official anonymity. Inside the Department, the fact that Raymond Chrétien had kept the whole affair away from the team managing the Gulf crisis smacked of somewhere between negligence and revenge for not having been part of that process after the initial few days the summer before. Relations between him and deMontigny Marchand, never warm, became very frosty and were never to recover. Chrétien was sent shortly thereafter off into exile as Ambassador to Belgium and Luxembourg, where he languished in a position less important than his previous job as head of mission in Mexico, until three years later when Jean Chrétien rescued him and appointed him Ambassador to the United States.

Pacific "Quad" and "Quint"

Some time late in my first winter in Policy Planning I tried to break the eurocentric habits of the Department's cerebral cortex and bring some focus on major change in Asia. There were regular meetings of NATO policy planners, and a reasonable cadence of regular bilateral meetings with major European foreign ministries, but there was no such interchange across the Pacific. Having just served as Director of North Asia and having been the principal architect of the Government's Pacific 2000 program, I was struck by how little attention was paid to large issues in Asia, from the risks implicit in having no dialogue with the rogue state of North Korea, to an evidently still unpredictable China, to the lack of institutional structures in the trans-Pacific community, with ASEAN and APEC still very much entities in early and fluid evolution.

I initially reached out to my Japanese counterpart through our Embassy in Tokyo, suggesting that we collectively approach the Americans and the Australians to see if they would be interested in have periodic quadrilateral meetings to discuss long-term Asia Pacific issues. Both thought the idea was a good one, and American Policy Planner Dennis Ross suggested that we hold the first such meeting in Alaska at the Elmendorf Air Force Base, which we did. The meeting was a good exchange of views, and it was especially good having an Australian perspective at the table. We also received a briefing by the base commander, whose planes were charged with protecting the northwestern NORAD sectors, and who had kindly put us up in the spartan but adequate housing for visiting air crew. The base itself was a secure area and access was tightly controlled, but once cleared we could wander anywhere. On the couple of mornings I was there I went out for my morning run along the edges of the main runway (called the "flight path" in air force parlance) and it was a real thrill to do so as screaming F-16s took off beside me.

In terms of focus, as policy planners do we pretty well covered the waterfront. I tried to give Joe Clark's North Pacific Cooperative Security

Dialogue one last resuscitation but was roundly beaten back. The only file on which really useful progress was made was on coordinating our approached to Hong Kong, then in a very nervous state still less than a year after the Tiananmen crisis, which had completely destroyed any confidence there might have earlier been in China applying a "light touch" in intervening in the territory's affairs after retrocession in 1997. It was at Elmendorf that we decided that prior to the handover each of our countries should enter into as many agreements as possible with Hong Kong that would apply both before and after the change in sovereignty, thus demonstrating and eventually ensuring that there would be little impact, at least in terms of Hong Kong's foreign economic and trade relations. We individually sold this to those in our governments responsible for relations with the crown colony, and then collectively approached the office of the Hong Kong Governor, still the conservative David Wilson. At this time one of the Governor's policy advisors was Vincent Cheng, on loan from the Hong Kong and Shanghai Banking Corporation, and he thought this "Through Train" policy was a terrific idea and sold it both to his boss and eventually to the Chinese Government, who recognized that it was in their interest to demonstrate that continuity would be assured when the handover eventually took place.

With the outbreak of the Iraq crisis in the summer of 1990, it was more than a year and a half before we had a second meeting of the "Pacific Quad", as we called ourselves, this time meeting in Kyoto in Japan. I am not sure we talked about anything very weighty, but I do remember eating absolutely wonderful local food. At our second meeting, my Australian counterpart suggested that in future we invite New Zealand to join, and as we all agreed the "Quad" became a "Quint", but I was gone from Policy Planning before the first meeting of the enlarged group took place.

The Beginnings of Constitutional Wrangling

When Prime Minister Mulroney moved Joe Clark from the External Affairs portfolio to become Minister of Constitutional Affairs, I was a bit saddened to lose a Minister with whom I had worked very closely since the beginning of the Tiananmen crisis two years earlier and I anticipated not having anything to do with his new files. I was wrong. The Government was facing one of the most acute crises in national unity since the Québec referendum of 1980. The Meech Lake accord had failed in the spring of 1990 and the threat of another referendum was mounting following the January publication of the Allaire Report of the Québec Liberal Party, which recommended a massive devolution of power from Ottawa to Québec City, and the April report of the multi-party Bélanger-Campeau Commission, which recommended that the Québec government hold a referendum in 1992 on either sovereignty or renewed federalism.

Joe Clark threw himself into his new responsibilities with the thoroughness and vigour that he applied to everything he did. He crisscrossed the country and consulted widely. Inside the government, he had PCO build out a substantial secretariat and commissioned a vast number of studies on federal-provincial issues. He asked deMontigny Marchand to prepare a study on the concept of sovereignty and the essential powers of a modern state and deMontigny naturally turned to his internal think tank, Policy Planning. I decided that this was not something that my group should do alone, so I pulled together a group of officers whose intellect and professional background represented the most thoughtful perspectives External Affairs could bring to bear. Not everyone I approached could afford the time, but in the end the group was pretty impressive. Claude Boucher, my Director of Political and Strategic Analysis, helped run the process but was also a well-read thinker in his own right. Ferry de Kherkhove (who had replaced Michael Hart in the summer of 1991), Ian MacLean, George Haynal, Jim Mitchell (then working in PCO), Joseph Caron (who had replaced me as Director of North Asia), and our great Hegelian scholar Gary Soroka all agreed to work with us. In the end we drafted a multi-volume report covering the kinds of powers a national government really had to wield in the modern world, while identifying the implications of the emergence of such super-national entities like the European Union. Our report would have been very unpopular had the Liberals been in power, because it was relatively decentralist, but strongly protective of federal powers in the foreign, defence and trade policy areas. Although we fed our report into PCO as requested, I bootlegged a copy directly to Clark, who invited me out to lunch to discuss it. He liked the report and later told me that it was the most helpful of all the multiple reports prepared for the new round of constitutional talks. The Charlottetown Accord was to eventually fail in the national referendum in the autumn of 1992, and its death helped set the scene for the return to power in Québec of the Parti Québécois and the referendum of 1995, which had a big impact on my life, but that is part of another story.

Speechwriting and Odds and Ends

There are only a few odds and ends to add about my time in Policy Planning, which was to undergo a fairly significant change in the summer of 1991 when Reid Morden replaced deMontigny Marchand as Under-Secretary. Morden's management style was radically different from Marchand's. Instead of meeting with a small and inner group of close advisors, as deMontigny had done with Jeremy and myself, Reid was very inclusive of all the ADMs. He replaced our morning "USS Meeting" with a daily meeting of the Executive Committee at 0800 in the 8th floor Boardroom. Often these meetings would only last 10 or 15 minutes, but they contributed very positively to team building at the top of the house, and kept everyone aware of all major issues facing the country and the department on a day-to-day basis.

In Policy Planning, one of the roles I was to take on fairly early was as a speechwriter for the SSEA. Normally, a first draft of any speech would be written by the functional division responsible for the event and then reworked by either staff inside the Minister's office or by one of a handful of trusted professional speechwriters around Ottawa. For some reason, I ended up re-writing a speech Clark made in early 1990 to a CIIA event, and his staff got in the habit of asking me to redraft speeches they received from other parts of the department. At this time Paul Heinbecker was serving as Prime Minister Mulroney's Foreign Policy Advisor and his principle speechwriter, at least on international matters, as well. Paul was a great thinker and had a tremendous talent of putting complex ideas into pithy and impactful speeches. And he would sometimes ask me for my thoughts or help. I worked with him on two particularly memorable speeches, one the PM gave in Harare in 1990 on the universality of human rights and the responsibility of civilized nations to breach the wall of sovereignty when necessary to defend those rights, and another in 1991 at Stanford University's 100th anniversary celebration on the expansion of NATO, quite a radical concept at that time. Paul would prepare a first draft of a speech, and circulate it to me for commentary before sharing it with the political staff in Mulroney's office. I would send back a version with my ideas incorporated, and Paul would prepare a further draft and then share it with Mulroney's staff. Every draft would have the draft number printed on the upper right hand corner of every page. Paul would give an early draft to the PM himself, who would make comments which Paul would incorporate before recirculating. Then it would go back and forth with the speech undergoing continuous "improvements", often losing critical ideas and becoming less and less readable. Paul sent me back a Draft 47 version of one of the speeches. As the day of the speech approached, Mulroney reacted to the latest draft quite negatively as lacking punch and focus, at which point Paul pulled out a very early draft, perhaps the fifth version, and sent it in as Draft 48. Mulroney thought it was finally just perfect and that was the version he delivered. Keeping early drafts of speeches was a trick I learned from Paul, and applied later when I was to write speeches for Chrétien, both on national unity issues and later on China.

In November of 1991, there was a shuffle of Deputy Ministers and Jean McCloskey was moved from her position as ADM Asia to become Deputy

Minister of Investment Canada. Reid Morden, the new Under-Secretary, called me and asked if I would like to take the Asia Pacific branch over from Jean. This was brave on Reid's behalf since I was very young for one of the most senior ADM jobs and there would inevitably be a lot of noses out of joint. But I was thrilled.

CHAPTER 12

ASSISTANT DEPUTY MINISTER, ASIA PACIFIC

• • • • • • • • • • •

Reid Morden must not have found it easy to appoint me to take over the Asia Pacific Branch. I presumed that he had been given a short list of qualified candidates by the ADM of Personnel, as blessed by the Public Service Commission, including a number of senior level officers serving as heads of post in the region. The position was an EX-5 level, the highest public service rank below a Deputy Minister, and I was still only an EX-3. I had never run my own mission and had only been a Director General for two years. But Reid knew the team he wanted and I seemed to be part of it, and I was very excited when he approached me. It was, in fact, a great team, and with more than two decades of perspective I still believe, as I did then, that this was historically the best and the smartest executive team ever assembled in the Department, whether at External Affairs by itself or after being combined with International Trade.

Reid Morden's Executive Committee was mixture of those who had served with deMontigny Marchand, but some new faces as well. It was a strong group of talented people with good brains: Reid Morden himself, Don Campbell, Bill Clarke, Louise Fréchette, Marc Perron, Stan Gooch, David Wright, Barry Carin, George Haynal, and of course my great friend and running partner Jeremy Kinsman. Our morning meetings were sharp and focused, but we also got together for more thoughtful dinners or one-day strategic planning retreats, during which there were viniferous benefits. At some early moment in Joe Clark's tenure as SSEA, he had issued a fiat that all banquets and receptions held in the Pearson Building for foreign guests should serve exclusively Canadian wine. This was as it should be, and many a fancy foreign palate was surprised by how good the best wines produced in Canada actually were. A collateral impact was that the Department's very good cellar of French wines, built up over the years by a professional sommelier, now could not be used. As there was no stricture on the provenance of the wine consumed when foreign guests were not present, Reid would arrange to have the Department's fine wines decanted and served to us during our internal dinners and meetings.

One of the realities of running a big branch, which made this wonderful new job of mine both exciting and a little frustrating, was that my agenda was set by events, both scheduled and unexpected, not by planning. The sheer breadth of my geographic responsibilities, stretching from Mauritius to Mongolia and from Afghanistan to the South Pacific meant that I could rarely get very deeply into any single issue or relationship for very long. With China, Japan, India and Pakistan, the ASEAN countries and Indochina, Australia, New Zealand and the burgeoning APEC file all part of my responsibilities, I felt that most of the time I was only skimming along the surface of the waves. Or being rolled by them.

The East Timor Crisis

On November 12th, 1991, a few days before I was to move from Policy Planning to the Asia Branch, Indonesian troops attacked East Timorese protesters in Dili. A small handful of government troops and many protesters were killed. As in the case of the Tiananmen crisis assertions about the numbers killed varied widely between what the protesters claimed and the government admitted, but probably were slightly more than one hundred. The event was not covered live by CNN or any other news service, and details of the massacre filtered out slowly as foreign journalists, a number of whom themselves had been beaten by government forces, managed to smuggle out video footage of the violence. When news of the event broke internationally, the reaction was swift and memories of Tiananmen rekindled. Barbara McDougall, who had been Secretary of

State for External Affairs since the cabinet shuffle of the previous April, immediately announced the suspension of Canadian aid and export credit and the cancellation of high-level visits. She had more or less taken a page out of the Tiananmen manual, but unlike Joe Clark who was scrupulous about consulting with affected stakeholders both inside and outside government, she just made the decision and announced it.

On my second day in my new ADM office in the middle of the northern side of the fifth floor of A-Tower, I received a call from the office of Michael Wilson, the new Minister of International Trade, asking me to come and see the Minister. Wilson was a heavyweight in the Mulroney Government, and after more than six years as Minister of Finance had just moved over to the trade position, serving simultaneously as Minister of Industry. The context of the move had nothing to do with him being ousted from the key Finance role and everything to do with the immediate importance of the trade and industry portfolios given that the trilateral NAFTA talks were entering their most crucial phase. There were simultaneously a number of very contentious bilateral trade issues going on between Canada and the USA, some with a Japanese collateral dimension.

When I arrived in Wilson's office on the top floor of B-Tower, I found a very incensed Minister, furiously angry that he had not been consulted on the McDougall announcement of sanctions against Indonesia. He told me that he wanted to write a confidential "Dear Colleague" letter to McDougall, pointing out that she had gravely ignored his responsibilities, Ministerial solidarity and even the need to consult Cabinet in her hurried announcement. He told me to prepare a tough letter for him to sign. These are the kind of letters one would never pass down the line for drafting, so I wrote it myself and had it hand carried back to Wilson's executive assistant. Again I was called to his office, where Wilson took a pen to my proposed letter and toughened it up to a point where it almost hurt to touch. His secretary retyped it and off it went.

The next morning I was in my office and I received a call from Ruth Archibald, chief of staff to McDougall, telling me to come immediately to the 10th Floor. Rushed immediately into McDougall's office, I saw the Minister standing there holding the letter from Wilson between thumb and forefinger as if it was as toxic to touch as it had been to read. "How dare he write me such a letter" stormed McDougall, "I am foreign minister and I am damned if I am going to run around town begging for permission to do what I have to do". She looked at me and said "Howard, draft me an unapologetic response to this piece of garbage and make it tough". And so I wrote for her signature a very firm response to Michael Wilson, explaining why she had taken the decision, which was hers to take, and why the exigencies of time required immediate action. She signed it and off it went to Wilson's office. Annoyed at McDougall's lack of any sort of apology, Wilson took issue with her excuses and explanations in another firm letter sent back the following day. By the time we were done, there had been an exchange of four or five letters and neither Minister, both of whom saw me (as they were supposed to) as their principal support on Asian issues, ever knew that I was writing letters back and forth to myself.

The East Timor file was to continue absorbing a substantial amount of attention over the coming months. In reaction to the widespread condemnation of the actions of the Indonesian Army, the Government of Indonesia did not try to justify or hide what had taken place. It appointed an investigative commission and expressed regret for the killings, even though it did fall short of criticizing the military's action. After a discussion at Cabinet, we "clarified" the Government's position publicly, taking care not to undermine McDougall's position but rendering the suspension of aid and export credit as "temporary measures" pending the report of the Indonesian investigative commission and further government actions. No other country had taken as significant or precipitate action as we had, and our Ambassador to Indonesia, Ingrid Hall, who had been my boss long before when I came back from Indonesia in 1979, was worried that we were isolating ourselves and by so doing reducing the substantial influence we had built up over many years. This was particularly evident with respect to the attitude of Australia, which then and on many other occasions between the Indonesian invasion of East Timor in 1975 and independence in 1999 almost blindly accepted the Indonesian Government's position, and of the US and Japan as well. It seemed that everyone saw Indonesia as a bulwark against communism and had no real objection to the undemocratic leanings of Suharto's "guided democracy". On the other side of the ledger, Portuguese and other supporters of East Timorese independence held up the Canadian reaction as principled and evidence that the Indonesian Government was clearly behind the killings.

I asked Ingrid Hall to seek a call on the Foreign Minister, Ali Alatas, to explain our, now modified, position more clearly. She told me that Alatas was in Singapore, but that she had sat down with senior officials at the Foreign Ministry, who were all quite upset that Canada, a friend, had reacted precipitously without bothering to uncover either the facts or the Government's position. I had known Alatas from my time dealing with APEC, and in a couple of meetings that he and Joe Clark had held on the Cambodia peace process, where Alatas was the key deal-maker. My first meetings with him had been all the way back in the 1970s in Jakarta, when upon his return to Indonesia from his posting as Ambassador in Geneva, he had become very friendly with Ambassador Shortliffe. I decided to call him directly.

When I reached Alatas in Singapore he was clearly more upset with the incident than with the position being taken by Canada or any other country, and he asked me if I thought it would be useful if he came to Ottawa to meet with McDougall and other Ministers. I told him I thought that this was a wonderful idea, but that I would need to set it up and get back to him. Enlisting the support of PMO as well as Minister Wilson, I persuaded Barbara McDougall that this was a good opportunity to show leadership, allowing any improvement in the relationship to be directly linked to the outcome of the Indonesian official inquiry, which Alatas had told me in confidence would be very critical of the military.

Alatas arrived in Ottawa one cold and snowy day in the middle of February. The Indonesian Government had released their investigation's "Interim Report", which was clearly not a whitewash of the military, putting a certain amount of blame on the soldiers as well as the protesters, although it had not yet announced any decisions as to what to do with the report's findings. I had, without advising McDougall, arranged to have Alatas put up at Rideau Gate, the government guest house, and arranged a private dinner there for Joe Clark, who as Constitutional Affairs Minister had no further responsibilities for foreign affairs but who was both a senior member of the Government and someone who had a real personal affection for Alatas, gleaned from international meetings together. By this time I had received McDougall's sign-off on an adjustment to our hardline policy, allowing new aid projects to again be considered. After his meeting with McDougall we had in fact scheduled a meeting with Monique Landry, Minister responsible for CIDA. The evening with Joe Clark was very informal and very friendly. It was as evident to Clark as it was to me that the Dili massacre had deeply shocked Alatas, and he was trying his best to find a way to manage the diplomatic fallout. Alatas was wonderfully soft-spoken, a truly syncretic Indonesian Hadrami, and came across as both a non-dogmatic Muslim and a traditional Javanese teacher at the same time.

Alatas' meeting with McDougall was scheduled for 0900 the following morning, and I was set to brief McDougall in advance at 0815. I had someone meet Alatas at Rideau Gate to escort him to the Pearson Building, and I went up to McDougall's office to brief her. 0815 came and went, 0830, 0845, 0900 and still no Minister. Finally at about 0910, I left her office and went down to the hall to the Boardroom where Alatas was patiently waiting, and we made small talk. Finally at about 0920, McDougall walked in wearing dark glasses, said to me, *sotto voce,* "I have changed my mind". After a perfunctory introduction, she then launched harshly into the inadequacies of the Indonesian Government's Interim Report, saying we had" hoped for more", and stating that Canada had no intention of yet adjusting its policy. I felt like crawling into the woodwork, since I (with Joe Clark's help) had carefully set up Alatas to expect some positive movement and was astounded and quite frankly humiliated by McDougall's heavy handed presentation and direct language, and she was still wearing sun glasses even though we were in an inside conference room with no windows. Alatas appeared unfazed, however, and calmly outlined the situation, explicitly explained why Western comparisons with Tiananmen were simplistic and completely unfair, stated that the military commander of East Timor had already been replaced, and emphasized how seriously the commission of inquiry was going about its work. He said that he completely recognized the universality of basic human rights, but that observers needed to separate between institutional respect for those rights and incidental crises that everyone abhors. He also cautioned about making relationships "conditional" on specific outcomes, and warned that the international community should "encourage the development of national competences" and not be too intrusive. When McDougall seemed unmoved by what was actually a brilliant peroration, Alatas said very gently that if continuing to give aid to Indonesia caused too much of a problem for the Canadian Government, we should "dispense with it", but that such a move would be a pity since Canadian aid really was helping poor women and others in greatest need.

As an indication of my respect for Alatas, I drove with him to the airport; from Ottawa he was to fly to New York to meet with the UN Secretary General. In the car he patted me on the knee and told me not to worry about my Minister and that it was clear she had had "a more interesting evening last night than you and I and our friend Joe". I guess both my discomfort and McDougall's hangover were easy to discern.

In the end, the Indonesian Government cashiered the two leading generals in charge of the unit stationed in East Timor at the time of the riots, and court-martialed more than dozen others. Ali Alatas did a remarkable job pushing his own Government to come clean, and at the same time in limiting the damage to Indonesia's relations with other countries. He had been at the time mooted as an eventual possible successor to UN Secretary General Boutros Boutros Ghali, largely because of the seminal role he had played in the Cambodia peace process, but the East Timor crisis diminished his global stature somewhat, and by the time Boutros Boutros Ghali was coming to the end of his term, Alatas was no longer really in contention. I was to have a lot to do with him over the next three years, in APEC and in our dealings with ASEAN, and he stayed a friend throughout. Alatas remained Foreign Minister for the remainder of the Soeharto regime and kept his post well into the administration of Jusuf Habibie. In one of those little twists of history, it was Alatas who arranged and oversaw the referendum in 1999 that brought about East Timor's eventual independence.

Hong Kong and the Through Train

Hong Kong was a nervous place in the early 1990s. The core agreement to return Hong Kong to China had been reached while Margaret Thatcher was Prime Minister in 1984, but since then the crisis in Tiananmen had shown a harsher China, and when I took over the Asia branch, the formal date of handover was less than six years in the future. While in policy planning I had participated in thinking through the collective western policy of supporting Hong Kong through a network of international treaties that would remain unaffected by the handover, and we were starting to put it in place. John Higginbotham, a mandarin-speaking China expert with whom I had briefly served during my first assignment in the Department fifteen years earlier was now our Commissioner in Hong Kong, having replaced Anne-Marie Doyle the summer before. John was a very enthusiastic Head of Mission, and encouraged not only the Department of External Affairs and International Trade to be active in engaging with the government of Hong Kong, but many line departments as well. During the three years I spent as ADM, we negotiated a new air service agreement, a foreign investment protection agreement, a police cooperation and anti-fraud agreement and probably a half dozen others, all of which would remain in place after the handover of Hong Kong to China. The Chinese were initially wary of the "Through Train" policy, but gradually saw that it was very much in their interest, and quietly gave Hong Kong their approval. The only treaty that we wanted and could not persuade the Hong Kong authorities to agree to was a double taxation agreement; to which they were ideologically opposed largely because such a treaty by convention also contains anti-tax avoidance measures and Hong Kong saw itself in those days as somewhat of a tax haven.

My two primary counterparts in meetings in Hong Kong were the Governor's policy adviser Vincent Cheng on broad policy matters, and in dealings with the Hong Kong Government on bilateral trade and investment and on APEC matters was the Government's Director of Trade, Tony Miller. Half way through my time as ADM of Asia Pacific, Tony, like most of the senior British in the local administration, was replaced by a local Hong Kong citizen. His successor was Donald Tsang who would go on to become the territory's second Chief Executive after retrocession.

Shortly after I returned to the Asia Branch, Chris Patten was appointed to replace David Wilson as the Governor of Hong Kong. Sir David had been a quiet Foreign Office type while Patten, who was a conservative politician who had failed to win his seat in the previous election and was a much more public figure. Outspoken on matters of civil rights and the rule of law, he pushed the Chinese hard by encouraging public support for more direct local participation in the political process. That the British had studiously ignored basic democratic principles for their one hundred and fifty years of colonial administration in the colony made Patten's push for local enfranchisement ring a little hollow, and it was not welcome in Beijing, but in the end it probably helped ensure that the Chinese would scrupulously respect their undertakings in the Basic Law. Patten came to Canada in 1992 and we treated him very much as if he were the elected leader of a sovereign country. I travelled with him across the country and his message of greater local participation in the political process and sustained civil liberties and an unchanged legal system was welcomed by the large communities of immigrants from Hong Kong in Vancouver and Toronto.

Howard Balloch

Re-Engaging with the Dragon

Between the immediate announcement of our post-Tiananmen policy of a cooler relationship with China and my return to the Asia Branch two and a half years later there had been no high-level visits from China to Canada, and the most senior level visit in the opposite direction had been that of our Under-Secretary deMontigny Marchand when he and I went to Beijing following the Houston Summit in July of 1990. Canada was gradually falling out of step with other G-7 countries. Within six months of Tiananmen, the US had begun secret high-level talks with Beijing in the form of confidential visits by National Security Advisor Brent Scrowcroft and Deputy Secretary of State Larry Eagleburger, although these were kept secret for almost two years. In the autumn of 1990, the Canada China Trade Council (later to change its name to the Canada China Business Council), issued one of its occasional policy position papers, entitled "Special Report: Assessing Canada's China Policy: Is it Time for a Change", based on interviews that it had carried out both with its members as well as with academics and former government officials. The government, preoccupied with the Gulf crisis and the likelihood that Canadians would be soon sent into their first hot war since Korea, did not respond. In January of 1991, my predecessor as ADM for Asia Jean McCloskey and deMontigny Marchand met with Joe Clark to suggest a relaxation in our ban on high-level visits, but the timing was terrible with the Gulf War just about to break out, and even though he had met with his Chinese counterpart during UN Security Council deliberations in New York only a few months before, he dismissed the idea as a distraction and suggested that the matter be reconsidered later in the year. They raised the matter again with Barbara McDougall when she took over as Secretary of State for External Affairs in the April cabinet shuffle of that year, but she was similarly not yet ready to make a move, not as in Clark's case because of more pressing matters but because she was firmly against the lifting of sanctions irrespective of the moves by other countries or public opinion.

In the meantime, the British, who were inevitably engaged at very senior levels on matters relating to Hong Kong, sent Foreign Minister Hurd to Beijing in April, to be quickly followed by both Australian Foreign Minister Evans and French Foreign Minister Dumas. Then the dam seemed to break. Three G-7 heads of government paid official visits to Beijing during the latter half of 1991, in the form of Prime Minister Kaifu of Japan in August, Prime Minister Andreotti of Italy and Prime Minister Major of Britain in September, followed by US Secretary of State Jim Baker in November. The furthest Canada had been willing to go by this time was a visit of Bill McKnight, Minister of Agriculture, who went to China to discuss agricultural trade matters in November, 1991, a trip that Joe Clark and Prime Minister Mulroney both thought would be an appropriate first step and one unlikely to precipitate much negative public reaction, and indeed there was none. Shortly after becoming ADM, I had a day-long strategic retreat with my Directors General and Directors to look at the major challenges facing Canada in Asia Pacific, and none loomed larger than finding a way back to normalcy in the relationship with China. Barbara McDougall had taken over as Secretary of State for External Affairs the previous April, and I knew that she had turned down a recommendation from my predecessor and deMontigny Marchand that she support the renewal of higher-level contacts, including at the foreign minister level, but I hoped that the level of activity pursued in the interim by other G-7 countries would change her mind. However, from my very first meeting with her in the aftermath of the East Timor incident, she made it very clear to me that she was a strong proponent of maintaining sanctions on China.

Barbara McDougall's animus towards the China file was aggravated shortly after the Christmas holidays, when three Members of Parliament, Conservative Geoff Scott, Liberal Beryl Gaffney and New Democrat Svend Robinson, travelled on January 7th to China at the invitation of the Chinese People's Congress (a more or less open invitation that the Chinese were hoping would be taken up by as many parliamentarians as possible, given that no ministers were visiting). Robinson was the mastermind behind the visit, and his intention from the beginning was to create an incident that would draw attention to China's dismal human rights record. Ignoring the schedule organized for them by the NPC, the trio met clandestinely with the wife of one of the jailed organizers of the 1989 student movement, Wang Juntao, visited (but were not allowed inside) a prison, and announced their intention to both lay a wreath in Tiananmen Square to the fallen students and to hold a press conference. This was too much for the Chinese who unceremoniously picked them up, separated them from the Embassy officer travelling with them, and put them on the first flight available to Hong Kong, without allowing Ambassador Bild, who has replaced Earl Drake more than a year earlier, to meet with them. On arrival they did of course hold their press conference, and the news of their expulsion was carried by television and newspapers around the world, exactly the coverage they had been hoping for. Barbara McDougall condemned the treatment of the three is a scrum with the press, using language that I thought a little over-the-top since the whole affair was planned by Robinson to elicit exactly the Chinese reaction they received. She called the affair an "affront to Canada" and to Parliament, and agreed that the latter should conduct a thorough review of our China policy, something that was to take place in March.

In February 1992 I received a request for a meeting from former Saskatchewan Premier Grant Devine, who came to my office with a Canadian of Chinese origin who had worked in the uranium mining industry, Howard Kuang. Devine told me that Howard's contacts in the Chinese nuclear industry had met with him and told him that China was seriously interested in buying Canadian CANDU reactors. My first thought was to wonder what brand of dope former Premiers smoked, since it was initially unimaginable to me that this was really a serious démarche. I listened carefully, however, and suggested that they leave the matter with me and be extremely careful not to socialize the idea more widely, since I knew that it would receive a very negative reaction at the political level. I did gently ask our China team whether they were hearing anything about a renewed Chinese interest in Canadian nuclear technology, but as they were not I more or less parked the thought in the back of my head for a while.

As promised by the government in January, the House of Commons' Standing Committee on External Affairs and International Trade (SCEAIT), convened at the beginning of March to consider Canada's China Policy. Both Svend Robinson and Beryl Gaffney were actually members of the Standing Committee even though they had been the ones who instigated and starred in the January incident. Both representatives for the Government and outside parties were called, the latter a cross-section of business, academic China experts and representatives of the Chinese Canadian community. I was to be the senior spokesperson for the Government, explaining and defending Canada's policies. My problem was that Barbara McDougall's views were not far from those of Robinson and indeed those of the Liberal Party's foreign affairs critic, Lloyd Axworthy, while the Prime Minister was emitting mixed signals, publicly speaking about the need to link human economic policy with human rights while quietly supporting the resumption of higher level ties with China. The approach I adopted was to publicly situate McDougall and her unwillingness to re-engage as an indicator of the seriousness with which the Government treated the human rights question, while positioning our on-going economic engagement as simply protecting Canadian competitive interests. In my opening statement I said, "Where are we now? We are on track . . . Some adjustments have been made, Ministerial visits and meetings have taken place here in Canada, in China, and at international events. China is simply too important internationally to avoid this. Having led the way on our China policy among the G-7 and a couple of other major players in China, we are clearly trailing on the way out". I pointed out that, "Only one other G-7 country has not had its foreign minister in China. We are not uncomfortable with that position, by the way . . . Minister McDougall made this very clear a week or two ago. The foreign minister (of China) is not being invited to Canada and she has absolutely no intention of going to China for the time being". I then added that, "We believe that with trade, with interchange, with the exchange of goods, people, ideas, the pressures for political change must and will follow. There are historical forces at work in China as there are historical forces at work elsewhere." When the Committee later grilled both me and Robert Van Adel, Vice-President of the Export Development Corporation, on the Government's sustained programs of concessional financing for Canadian exports to China, we both robustly defended the policy as necessary to allow Canadian companies to compete on an even playing field with American, European and Japanese competitors. As my time in front of the committee wound down, a very sensible and thoughtful Conservative backbencher from Nova Scotia, Howard Crosby, threw me a soft pitch and asked about the linkage between human rights and our general policy, and I answered, "There are a lot of things we don't want to put up with, but simply wishing it away doesn't make it change. It is a question (of) how we use the levers that are under our control, whether they be bilateral or multilateral, international . . . we use whatever tools we can. Right now we believe that some of the instruments that are at our disposal to improve these things, political dialogue and our development assistance program, can bear fruit, but it isn't easy". The committee also grilled Ambassador Fred Bild, and he defended well the nuanced course we were trying to chart, and in the end the parliamentary hearings and the unceremonious expulsion of Svend Robinson may have slowed but did not stop the gradual re-opening of political relations between Canada and China.

While in Beijing Ambassador Fred Bild was being constantly bombarded with criticisms by his contacts in the Chinese Foreign Ministry that Canada's policy towards China was increasingly out of step with that of others, in Ottawa we were facing parallel criticism, voiced quietly, from Canadian businesses. Powerful companies like Bombardier and Nortel and Manulife and both the Bank of Montreal and the Royal Bank of Canada all had major commercial objectives in China, and they told us that these were being jeopardized by Canada's reluctance to re-engage. André Desmarais, who had become the primary voice of the CCBC (Canada China Business Council, having changed its name just about then from the

Canada China Trade Council) came to Ottawa just around the time of the parliamentary hearings and invited me out to lunch. He pointed out that the CCBC had been formed by his father Paul Desmarais actually before Deng Xiaoping had made his famous speech kicking off China's opening up and reform process ("It does not matter whether a cat is white or black, as long as it catches mice"). Since Tiananmen, André told me, he and his father had been to Beijing on several occasions and they were getting a very clear message that China valued its relationship with Canada and wanted to get back on a path towards normalcy. I told him that Minister McDougall was even more opposed to softening our position since the Standing Committee hearings, and that the Prime Minister and his office were very pre-occupied with domestic constitutional matters and would be difficult to get engaged in the China question. Furthermore, Mulroney had if anything hardened his position on human rights matters because of his interest in bringing an end to apartheid in South Africa, a matter he was now pushing hard through the Commonwealth and in direct engagement with African leaders.

When we agreed that we could not bring a shift in our China policy in through the front door, André and I began to discuss how we could do so through the back. It was at this time that Beijing also handed us a gift in the form of a new Ambassador. The charming Zhang Wenpu had been replaced in 1990 by Wen Yezhan, who had been cross-posted directly from Pyongyang and was a real old hardliner, unapologetically and energetically defending the Tiananmen military crackdown. His no doubt career-protecting habit of simply spouting Chinese propaganda and whatever instructions issued to him by Beijing made him a rather unloved envoy in Ottawa. In late 1991, he himself was replaced as Ambassador by Zhang Yijun, who I had dealt with when I had been Director of North Asia and he Director of North America and Oceania in China's Foreign Ministry.

Zhang Yijun was a soft-spoken and delightful character, who would and did in private let down his hair and engage at a truly human level. Like any diplomat he of course had to follow his instructions, but he did so with a style that made it clear what was serious and what not so serious. In those days, every visit between Canada and Taiwan was watched very carefully by Beijing, and anything that even vaguely smelled of being an "official contact" precipitated an immediate diplomatic protest. And there were many such protests, as Taiwan was trying to exploit this period of coolness in the international treatment of China to advance its own interests. The Taipei government or its front organizations would pay for members of the federal parliament (provincial politicians were not objectionable, since they could be characterized as "province-to-province" contacts) to go to Taiwan on "study tours", and try to get as many senior government officials there for some sort of meeting or conference. Whenever they did, China would protest, and this normally meant an instruction to the Ambassador to seek a meeting at the highest possible level to lodge a formal protest, the words of which were carefully prepared in Beijing. Both Zhang Yijun and I found these constant protests very tiresome and so we worked out an informal agreement where he would call me by telephone to advise me that he had received another such instruction. I would ask him who had transgressed and how, and he would quickly tell me, without reading the propaganda in his instruction about the need to adhere to our "one-China" policy or the "hurt feelings of the Chinese people" or "damage to the bilateral relationship". I would tell him that I would duly record that he had come to see me to register the protest. The calls were over in two or three minutes and we both avoided wasting time trading useless propaganda and diplomatic inanities.

So André Desmarais and I brought Zhang Yijun into our plotting. Given that the Canadian Government was not going to invite a high-level Chinese leader to Canada, we had to figure out how to get the Prime Minister re-engaged in some other way. This was still before APEC Summit meetings, and China was of course not a member of the Commonwealth or the Francophonie, so there was no opportunity for a Prime Ministerial meeting in the corridors of some international gathering of leaders. André and I came up with the idea of an invitation for Vice Premier Zhu Rongji to address some sort of business event, after which a meeting in Ottawa could be worked out. Early in 1992, André approached Prime Minister Mulroney through political channels and proposed that the PM invite Ambassador Zhang to a private chat over lunch at 24 Sussex Drive. I approached Eddie Goodman, the irrepressible founder of the Toronto-based law firm Goodman and Goodman. Eddie, who was already in his 70s, had the energy of a much younger man and had been involved in dealings with China and with the CCBC for a long time. He loved the spotlight, and agreed in principle that he would invite Zhu to "The Annual Goodman Forum", an event featuring an interesting speaker at a gathering of business leaders in Toronto. The fact that there had only been one other such speech in the past was dutifully ignored. Now all we needed was the Prime Minister's sign-off. Ambassador Zhang came to see me before the lunch with Mulroney to discuss the approach he should take. I told him to either say nothing about Tiananmen, or better, if he felt he could, to express personal sadness at what had happened. Most importantly, I told him, he should concentrate on the positive role Canada under Mulroney was playing in the world. At the lunch Zhang was perfect, saying that he had personally found the use of military force in Tiananmen a violation of Chinese traditions and a terrible decision, but that we had to put it behind us. He praised Mulroney's leadership on the South African issue and said that an important member of the G-7 and a permanent member of the UN Security Council simply could not afford not to have a robust relationship, led by dialogue at the highest level of their respective governments. André then mooted the idea of an invitation to Ottawa for a Vice Premier if he happened to be here on a private visit. Mulroney not only agreed, but raised the matter in cabinet by saying that the time had begun to start re-engaging with China. Michael Wilson had a scheduled Asian trip in April of 1992 for an APEC Ministerial meeting and it was agreed that he would swing through Beijing as our first high-level visitor since Tiananmen. Wilson's visit was not widely criticized in the press and at a meeting with Zhu Rongji he said that the Government of Canada would welcome an "unofficial" visit at an appropriate time over the coming year.

Now that the path to the unthawing of the China relationship was clear, the Prime Minister was quite open to adding to the agenda, and approved the idea of Joe Clark, whose job as Minister of Constitutional Affairs was effectively over since the collapse of the Charlottetown agreement, going to Hong Kong and China on an informal visit. Clark had been invited to go to a Williamsburg Conference at a resort hotel outside of Guangzhou, and had had a long-standing invitation to visit India as well, so we crafted a fairly substantial visit for him that included meetings in Hong Kong before the conference and in Delhi and Beijing afterwards.

Joe Clark went to Hong Kong in mid-March, and in Hong Kong met with both Governor Chris Patten and members of the semi-democratic Legco, and then went on to the Williamsburg Conference just across the Pearl River delta in Zhongshan. After the conference and a largely touristic trip to Delhi, where he was accompanied by both Maureen McTeer and their daughter Catherine, he flew back to China. I joined him in Beijing where the government really laid out a red carpet, billing him in the local press as "Deputy Prime Minister". He was received warmly by Foreign Minister Qian Qichen, who he knew well, and also by Minister of Foreign Economic Relations and Trade Li Lanqing, Deputy Premier Zhu Rongji, who would be coming to Canada just a few weeks later, and Premier Li Peng. Clark stressed throughout that his visit was not a "dramatic break" in Canadian policy, but a "step forward in the evolution" of the relationship and that Canadians expected their government to be engaged in China in ways that would support positive change, including in such areas as improvement of the legal system. His message was graciously received by all his interlocutors, except by Premier Li Peng, who was very stiff, and who insisted on repeating that the Tiananmen crackdown had been the government's proper response to an insurrection aimed at bringing down the state. Qian Qichen, on the other hand avoided the propaganda and responded positively to Clark's olive branch on re-engagement in matters such as legal reform, and simply referred to the Tiananmen crisis as the "regrettable events of 1989". While there was clearly not going to be a shift in the official Chinese explanation of the use of force in June of 1989, at least there was a growing body of regret about what had taken place, our high-level exchanges were back in place and we could start moving forward in the relationship.

The next step was the Goodman Forum and the Zhu Rongji visit in May. The luncheon event was hosted at the King Edward Hotel, and the room was only large enough for about three hundred people, composed of mostly business leaders but with a few representatives of the Toronto Chinese community and a number of academics who I had ensured were included. When Zhu was invited to speak, he went to the podium, made a point of setting aside his formal speech notes and proceeded to wow the audience by speaking extemporaneously, in English, for about twenty minutes. Given that this was a private event, no Cabinet members were present and I was the senior representative of the government.

One of the officials travelling with Zhu was a man named Zhang Guobao, listed on the official Chinese delegation list as from being from "Office of the Vice Premier". Ambassador Zhang Yijun approached me and said that Zhang Guobao wished to discuss, on a very informal basis, the question of nuclear cooperation. I arranged a private meeting room at the delegation's hotel that afternoon and met with Zhang, who told me that the Chinese government was indeed serious about the possibility of buying some Canadian heavy-water reactors as part of its mixed-technology approach to nuclear power. After our meeting, I called Reid Morden and told him that I was going to arrange a meeting for Zhang with senior AECL people, on a very informal basis, and hearing no objection from Reid, I then did so. Zhang Guobao was in fact a rising star in the State Planning Commission (he later became Chairman of the successor National Development and Reform Commission), and I was to learn the following year that the Chinese Government had decided that the CANDU purchase was being considered both as an attractive acquisition for technological reasons and as a potential carrot to Canada in the warming up of the relationship. China's nuclear interest was indeed extremely welcome to AECL and to those of us in Ottawa who were supportive of our proprietary heavy water technology, but I suspected that Barbara McDougall, Minister of Foreign Affairs and already uncomfortable about the warming of our relationship with China, might have been opposed, and it was in any case premature to pose a theoretical question until we knew the Chinese were really serious. In collusion with Reid Morden (who curiously would, upon his departure from the public service, later become Chairman of AECL), I ensured that the discussion about potential nuclear cooperation, parallel to the core higher-level Zhu Rongji agenda on generally normalizing the relationship, was never reported formally to her.

After the Goodman Forum, we flew to Ottawa where Zhu was warmly received by Prime Minister Mulroney, but without much fanfare. We avoided anything that could be used by the Opposition to criticize the Government for reversing our China policy; there was no formal meeting with multitudes of ministers present, no state dinner or cultural show, all of which would be normal elements of an official visit. Mulroney did, however, host Zhu for a "private" dinner at 24 Sussex with a few ministers and senior officials present. The dinner was very relaxed and Mulroney told Zhu that we were open to re-engagement at high levels, but that we wished to simultaneously engage in a dialogue on human rights issues. A very important step back to a normalized relationship had been taken.

After the meeting with Prime Minister Mulroney in Ottawa, I traveled with Zhu Rongji to Montreal, where a dinner with a dozen of Canada's most senior business leaders had been arranged. The host was Paul Desmarais and the setting was his beautiful Chinese themed receiving rooms on the top floor of the head office of Power Corporation on Victoria Square. Zhu and his aides were awestruck, as everyone was the first time there, by the beautiful Chinese artifacts and the graceful elegance of the setting. As we sat down for lunch, Paul Desmarais asked each of the businessmen to introduce themselves. A rather typically Canadian competition of modesty followed, with each businessman understating their own personal importance, and each trying to sound less grand than those who had gone before. Of course we had given Zhu Rongji detailed notes on each person and their company and he knew very well what a large segment of the Canadian economy was represented around the table, but it was clear to me from his reaction that he was delighted by the approach and how impactful modesty was. The last two to introduce themselves were Peter Munk and Harrison McCain. Munk stood up and said "I'm Peter Munk, prospector", which had everyone thinking that no one could be more modest than that, but McCain topped him with "I'm Harrison McCain, potato farmer" and sat down. Not bad lines for the founder of the world's largest gold mining company and the chairman of a $20 billion food conglomerate.

Travelling with Zhu Rongji was a delight. Wherever we went he was always interested in learning more about Canada and what he was seeing and the people he was meeting with. At his request I arranged a private breakfast with Alan Taylor, Chairman and CEO of the Royal Bank of Canada, who Zhu had gotten to know as Mayor of Shanghai and with whom he had sustained a close personal relationship. Zhu also had a family connection with Canada, with his daughter Zhu Yanlei completing a Master's degree in Regina, and we quietly arranged for her to join him for part of the trip. Yanlei was to become a personal friend and I saw her many times later when I was living in China. After completing her graduate studies in Canada she moved to Hong Kong and worked her way up to a modestly senior position in Bank of China International; she never fell prey to the temptation of so many "princelings" to set up some sort of business on her own where she could parlay the connection to her father for great wealth. During the 1993 visit, after the Montreal business lunch I went with her father on to Vancouver, where we met with both the Lieutenant Governor and the Premier, and in the end the visit we had billed as "unofficial" visit would be recorded in Chinese records as an "official" four-city visit to Canada.

There was no question that by the time of the Zhu Rongji visit, which was the final ice-breaker in the largely frozen Canada-China bilateral relationship, we had been lagging far behind the warming up in relations between other major countries (we felt our "comparables" were the G-7

Howard Balloch

and Australia) and China. We were held back by a public that had been more involved in and supportive of a warm and robust relationship prior to Tiananmen and that therefore had felt more shocked and betrayed when it happened. When Ambassador Earl Drake was back in Ottawa during his brief recall after the crisis, he commented to the House Standing Committee that "maybe we have been too naïve about China" and was excoriated in the press for saying so. He was, however, largely correct; there was nothing to suggest in the reform and opening up that had taken place between 1978 and 1989 to suggest that a bunch of old generals and party hardliners had become soft democrats who believed in granting their people substantial civil and political rights. After the Zhu visit, and the publicizing of early post-crisis visits to Beijing of US National Security Advisor Brent Scowcroft, I renewed the efforts we were making through our embassies in various capitals to stay very closely on top of where other countries were in their China policies. The only country that I personally made an effort to directly deal with was the United States, and when incoming President Bill Clinton announced his intent to nominate Winston Lord as Assistant Secretary for Asia, I flew to Washington and spent a delightful afternoon and dinner with him. Win (married to the novelist Bette Bao Lord) was an old China hand and had served as Ambassador to China under Jimmy Carter, and he and I hit it off very well, and would continue to informally compare notes on Asian matters for as long as I remained in my position.

The Zhu Rongji visit was followed in 1994, now with the Liberal government of Jean Chrétien in power, by a more formal official visit by another Vice Premier, Zou Jiahua. Zou was in charge of infrastructure development and had a particular interest in nuclear power. Since the discussion with Grant Devine in my office, we had held low-profile discussions on the possibility of a nuclear relationship, including talks between Zhang Guobao of the State Planning Commission and AECL executives during the Zhu Rongji visit of 1993, but we were still treating the file as very sensitive. The public and press were still quite negatively disposed to anything Chinese and to any implication that the Canadian Government was "forgetting" Tiananmen. Every press conference began with questions about what changes since the Tiananmen crisis justified a warming in the relationship, and polls suggested that the deeply negative attitudes towards the Chinese regime among average Canadians had not abated.

A day or two before Zou Jiahua arrived, Ambassador Zhang Yijun asked to see me privately and told me that he had heard from Beijing that the Vice Premier himself would like to visit a Canadian nuclear facility. He said that he understood that this could be quite a sensitive matter so he had avoided having it raised in the normal course of mission planning between Embassy staffers and the visit planning team on our side, which consisted of officers from both the North Asia Relations division and the Office of Protocol. I was pleased with his caution, because I knew if it had been raised officially we would have not been able to keep the matter confidential and we might have been forced to refuse the request. I decided to set up the visit but to do so secretly, and not to advise the Minister of Foreign Affairs, André Ouellet. I went to see Reid Morden, Deputy Minister of Foreign Affairs (the new title of the Under-Secretary following nomenclature changes brought in by the new Chrétien government), and told him of the request. I said that I was thinking of taking the Vice Premier to Darlington early one morning without any press or public knowing about it, and that the visit would not appear on the official program. He concurred with the approach.

On the first morning after Zou Jiahua arrived in Toronto, we left the Four Seasons Hotel at 0500 in a non-descript van with one unmarked RCMP car as security. Zou Jiahua, myself, Ambassador Zhang and just three other Chinese officials went to Darlington, leaving a much larger number of delegation members at the hotel. This latter group left for a visit to a Nortel plant in Bramalea as planned at 0900. The press, always present with such a high-level visitor, watched the motorcade leave on schedule, complete with the car used by the Vice Premier and so suspected nothing. Meanwhile, at Darlington we toured the CANDU reactor and then sat down in a conference room to allow Zou to ask questions of the plant manager and the senior AECL executive who was hosting us. Zou took out a notebook and proceeded to ask a dozen or more highly technical questions, and then a series of questions on both capital and operating costs. The question and answer period lasted almost two full hours, and I knew then that a CANDU deal with China was indeed much more than a mere possibility.

Japan

One of the most enjoyable elements of my time as ADM Asia Pacific was dealing with the Japanese. Japan was then our second largest trading partner and a major investor in Canada, and by in large the relationship was free of any major irritants. But Japan was no longer the Japan I had known as Director of North Asia Relations. The Japanese bubble had burst cataclysmically in 1990 and the economy remained in a deep recession for years. Si Taylor had moved to Japan as Ambassador when deMontigny Marchand replaced him in the autumn of 1989, bring an end to the eight-year reign of the larger-than-life Barry Steers. The change was profound, and the almost constant tension between Steers and headquarters was replaced with a deeply cooperative approach to management of the issues and the relationship.

In May of 1991, Prime Minister Mulroney and Prime Minister Kaifu had established a high-level bilateral panel to examine the future of the relationship, called Canada-Japan Forum 2000, and former Alberta Premier Peter Lougheed had been named as Chair on the Canadian side. I had a lot of interaction with Lougheed and both the Canadian and Japanese panelists as they prepared their report, which was submitted to the leaders of the two countries during the visit of Prime Minister Kiichi Miyazawa in December, 1992. The report contained eighteen proposals for bringing longer-term focus and new energy to the relationship, and I sat in on the meeting with the two Prime Ministers when it was presented. Miyazawa opened his remarks by commenting on how stunning Canada's new Embassy in Tokyo was, and Mulroney pointed to me and told his

Japanese counterpart that I had been responsible for negotiating the deal that got it built. Not a bad start!

I also participated in lots of Ministerial meetings, most of which dealt with the few trade irritants that we had at the time, such as the Japanese bias towards US goods in its trading regime, giving for example a tariff advantage to American soybeans over Canadian rapeseed, and to American wood products over Canadian equivalent products. The Americans of course pressured the Japanese to maintain these preferences, and Japan generally bent to American pressure, and the early 1990s saw a significant rise in US-Japan agreements on sectoral issues that effectively resulted in Japan directing its importers to purchase American products to help reduce growing trade friction between the two countries. The US was also interpreting the "rules of origin" arrangements of the Canada-USA Free Trade Agreement in such a way to disadvantage Japanese autoplants in Canada, but at least on this issue, Canadian and Japanese interests were aligned, so our meetings focused on how we could combine our efforts to influence US lawmakers and trade officials. On bilateral matters, we did finally late in 1993 achieve tariff equivalence on all grains and oilseeds, but did not get better access for wood or food products until the end of the Uruguay round of multilateral trade negotiations. Japan's trade regime was also full of complex non-tariff barriers, from special import price regimes to prohibitively expensive certification and packaging requirements.

One of the most agonizingly boring Ministerial meetings I ever sat through was a bilateral meeting between SSEA Barbara McDougall and the MITI Minister of the day during the 1991 G-7 Summit in London. It was customary in those days for foreign ministers but not trade ministers to attend summits, but the Japanese MITI Minister always tagged along as MITI could never agree to being out of the limelight. In order to keep him busy during the summits, the Japanese would seek meetings with foreign ministers since the counterparts to their Minister were not present. McDougall agreed to meet him and brought me along as note-taker. We had prepared a brief for her containing all the trade irritants but she had not bothered to read it, and the MITI Minister simply wanted the meeting for form's sake and spent most of the meeting boringly reciting his government's plan to breath new vigour into the listless Japanese economy. I was jetlagged and had been for a long morning run around Hyde Park with Jeremy Kinsman and literally fell asleep. At the end of the meeting, McDougall shook my shoulder and woke me up. I was of course embarrassed, but she said, in a whisper loud enough I thought the Japanese to hear "Don't worry about it; if I could have slept I would have too!" As we stood up to leave, the MITI Minister gave McDougall a set of men's cufflinks and tie-clip as a parting gift, further confirming in McDougall's mind of the misogynist nature of Asian politicians.

Other Bilateral Relationships

Our economic relationship with Korea was growing rapidly in the early 1990s, with Korean carmakers beginning to invest in Canada and Korean manufacturers beginning to eat away at Japanese dominance in many electronic sectors. Canadian exports to Korea were also growing, but faced the same sort of pro-American bias that existed in Japan. And the Koreans were always very tough negotiators. We had with Korea a Joint Economic Committee (JEC), which as ADM I chaired (unlike in the Japanese case where it was chaired at the Deputy Minister level), and which met twice-yearly to deal with economic and trade issues between the two countries. As in Japan, one of our major objectives had for some time been to gain better access to the Korean market for canola and canola oil, an increasingly important crop for Western Canada. The Korean tariff on canola oil was twice as high as that on US-produced soybean oil. At one JEC session in Seoul, the Korean negotiators brought in a so-called "independent" expert from some sort of agricultural institute. He spent an hour describing why soybean oil and canola oil were really completely different and why Korea was fully justified in not applying the well-established principle of "equivalence", which we were arguing should apply. That evening, I sent someone from our Embassy out to buy bottles of both soybean oil and canola oil in the local market, each sold in large clear plastic bottles with shrink-wrapped brand and product descriptions. I had the shrink-wrapping outer skins removed and when the JEC meeting started the next morning, we placed both bottles on the conference table. I said to my Korean counterpart that I had not completely understood what their expert had explained the day before, so I would like them to begin by explaining again the difference between the products, surely made easier by having a sample of each product available. Of course no one on the Korean side could identify which bottle was soy and which was canola!

Later in my time as ADM Asia Pacific, the Mulroney Government was trying to get foreign fishing fleets off the Grand Banks to deal with the severe depletion of the cod stocks. Most countries, from the US and the Portuguese to the Russians and Japanese, recognized the severity of the problem and their fleets were withdrawn. The last two holdouts were the Koreans and the Spanish, and both were obdurate. I was tasked with introducing this issue into the Canada-Korea JEC negotiations. The Koreans were totally unmoved by arguments about the fragile state of the cod stock and the need to allow time for them to recover, and unconcerned about the fact that Canadian fishermen had already been forced to stop fishing, devastating hundreds of small poor communities in Newfoundland and Nova Scotia. Knowing that the Koreans would only respond to serious pressure, I advised my Korean counterpart at the JEC that Canada was concerned about the safety of Korean electronic equipment being imported into Canada. I told him that we would henceforth be requiring an inspection of Korean-made microwave ovens and VCR equipment, both flooding into Canada in huge quantities at the time. In case the message was not fully understood, I said that all such equipment would have to be brought into Canada via Gander, Newfoundland, where the single inspection centre with a solitary inspector would be established. The Koreans did not believe we would carry through with this, but we proceeded to prepare the measure and sent an advisory to Canadian importers, who were upset but somewhat understanding. They started advising suppliers that they would switching to non-Korean sources and the suppliers complained to the Korean Government, who finally realized that we were indeed serious. After massive inter-Ministerial bloodshed in Seoul, the Korean President ordered that the Korean fleet be withdrawn from Canadian waters. That left only the Spanish, who were finally forced off the Grand banks in the "Turbot War" involving the arrest by the Canadian Navy of Spanish fishing vessels. Spain threatened war if her fishing vessels were not released, but Canada stood firm under the determined command of my friend Brian Tobin, then Minister of Fisheries, and eventually Spain backed down.

In the early 1990s our relations with Vietnam were becoming more extensive, driven in part by an immigration program focused on family reunification, as the nearly one hundred thousand boat people and other refugees who had been given asylum after the end of the Vietnam War began to sponsor their parents and other relatives to join them in Canada. We had also started a small development program and had a resident diplomat in Hanoi, operating out of a tiny office in an old ramshackle building. Our Ambassador was still cross-accredited from Bangkok. In early 1992 I went to Hanoi with the objective of engaging more fully with the Vietnamese and to support our small but enthusiastic business community there. I was the highest level official from Canada to visit since the 1970s, and I was received by Prime Minister Vo Van Kiet. Our meeting was a leading news item on the state-controlled television and radio. The following morning I left the charming but rather run-down Metropole Hotel (later to be beautifully restored for the filming of *L'Indochine*, starring Catherine Deneuve) and ran around Hanoi's central lake. As I did so, several old men who were sitting by the lake or doing their morning exercise bowed to me as I went by, saying "Bonjour, Monsieur le Ministre . . .". Part of the purpose of my trip was to prepare for the upgrading of our mission to a full Embassy, and our local officer, Marius Grinius (who would later return to Hanoi as Ambassador) took me around to look at possible chancery buildings and residences. Grinius took me to the completely run-down former office of the commercial division of the Soviet Embassy, which had been vacated in such haste that Russian calendars and product brochures were still lying around. It was in a great part of downtown Hanoi, just across and a few hundred meters along a major boulevard from the Ho Chi Minh Mausoleum. The building was filthy, but behind the grime there was a lovely art-deco building, built during the French colonial period between the two World Wars. Grinius told me that he had proposed to acquire the building but that the Administration Branch in Ottawa was taking a lot of time evaluating it, needing to prepare needs analyses and property studies, and that he was very worried we would lose the opportunity to some other country. I told him to arrange a meeting with the officials from the government responsible for diplomatic offices, and I signed the lease then and there on behalf of the government of Canada. Forgiveness, I reminded Marius, was always easier to obtain than permission. And indeed, upon my return to Ottawa, no one seemed too fussed and the property teams eventually did a wonderful job refurbishing the building, and it is still our Embassy to this day.

Before the expansion of the Vietnam War into its western neighbour, National Geographic ran an article entitled "Cambodia, the Peaceful People". Unfortunately, by the late 1960s both the Vietnamese and the Americans were conducting operations there, and they and the Chinese ware backing one Cambodian faction or another. When the US expanded its bombing campaign into Cambodia in 1970 (the expansion of the war into Cambodia was the focus of the students at Kent State University who were killed by the National Guard, which in turn triggered the massive US nation-wide protests and anti-war strike), the country simply imploded into more than two decades of vicious civil war. As part of the final peace settlement reached in the Cambodia peace talks in Paris in the autumn of 1991, a United Nations Transitional Authority in Cambodia, or UNTAC, was established and Canada sent a small military contingent of a few hundred people, whose most important role was to lead the de-mining effort, a huge undertaking. I visited Cambodia in the autumn of 1992 and met with the new co-leaders of the Transitional Government, Hun Sen and Prince Ranariddh, the son of the movie-making monarch, Norodom Sihanouk. I spent an evening with Ranariddh, who was an engaging and modest bon vivant. We had dinner at a small traditional restaurant with a mixed group of Cambodians and foreigners, and went back to his home and listened to old jazz records until very late.

In Cambodia I also met with the commanders of the Canadian military contingent there under UNTAC, as well as a Sergeant in charge of the de-mining team who made an enormous impression on me. I believe his name was George Satropoulos and he was as tough a nail as I ever met, and had earned a reputation in Phnom Penh for fearlessness and hard work that was inspiring both the international and local de-mining teams. I heard later that he had stayed for several tours of duty in Cambodia, and eventually left the Canadian Forces to stay and work in the clearing of the mines from the "killing fields" for more than a decade.

When I visited Cambodia we had no Embassy there, and upon my return to Ottawa I persuaded Reid Morden and eventually Barbara McDougall to approve a new model of representation, a mini-mission which would have basically just an Ambassador, supported by a small local staff and administered by an ally. We entered into discussions with Australia, with whom we had had for some time both a personnel exchange program with one or two officers every year serving inside the other's foreign ministry, as well as a consular service agreement, where Canadian consular services were offered to Australians in countries where Australia had no office, and vice versa. The Australians used to tease us that they were clearly the better negotiators, since they ended up representing us in Bali and Honolulu and we ended up representing them in places like Bamako and Kinshasa. I approached the Australian High Commissioner in Ottawa to ask his ministry to see if they would agree to take this one step further and they agreed in principle to do so. We reached a formal agreement on the arrangement during a trip I took to Canberra later in the year, and the result was that we ended up with one-man missions, led by a fully-accredited Ambassador, in both Cambodia and Brunei, in both cases supported administratively by the local Australian missions.

Being the senior official in charge of all our interests and relations in Asia gave me a wonderful opportunity to see some places for the first time and to visit other places I had been before. I went to India and Pakistan to chair our annual bilateral consultations with each (a Canadian Minister or senior official could not visit Delhi without also going to Islamabad) and to Thailand with senior Bombardier executives in a failed attempt to rescue their contract for Bangkok's light rail system. I went to Wellington for the only time in my life and was struck by how much it and its inhabitants resembled England and the English of an earlier, simpler time – I thought I was in Brighton of the antipodes.

In the winter of 1993 Jeremy Kinsman and I decided to travel together to Tokyo and Canberra. Canada held regular consultations on both bilateral and global political issues with both Japan and Australia. We had good discussions in Tokyo, led on the Japanese side by Vice Minister Saito whose government would be the host of the next G-7 Summit, so our discussions really covered the full global agenda. Saito then hosted us for a fabulous dinner at a restaurant on the top floor of the New Otani Hotel so Jeremy, who did not know Tokyo as well as I, could get a sense of the sheer size of the Japanese capital. I also took Jeremy on my favourite run around both the Imperial and Akasaka Palaces. Jeremy and I were in the middle of writing a book together, *The Globerunners Guide*, offering runners routes in every city that we had visited, which included more than forty capitals and major cities. Jeremy even wrote about running in Kuwait three days after its liberation from Iraqi occupation. Every chapter contained not only information about running and jogging routes, but also frequently suggesting routes that would take a runner by one or two of the best restaurants in the city so that they could come back in the evening to enjoy a nice dinner. We more or less finished the book, whose theme was "We run to eat and we eat to run", and sent it off to publishers in Toronto and New York. Random House offered to publish it but only if we financed the first printing run, which Jeremy and I were not prepared to do, and no other house thought there would be market for the book, so it died on the vine. But *The Globerunners Guide* still was a lot of fun writing.

From Japan, Jeremy and I went on to Canberra for a very interesting set of discussions with Peter Wilenski, Australia's Secretary of Foreign Affairs (deputy Minister) and his senior team. Jeremy was particularly interested in spending some time with Wilenski, who had been a very activist Australian Ambassador to the UN during the tumultuous period of 1989-92 where Jeremy had worked with him on Gulf War issues. This was a time when many of the old paradigms of international relations were being put to the test and found wanting, and new concepts emerging. The limits to sovereignty in cases of severe abuse of human rights and the notion of pre-emptive defence, which really boiled down to justifying an offensive strike in a case of a growing threat, were concepts that Wilenski had been quite articulate about when at the UN. They also were quite similar to principles that Canada had been trying to advance, led by Prime Minister Mulroney both in word in his Harare and Stanford speeches in 1990 and 1991, and in deed in his aggressive approach to apartheid and to the coalition's actions in the Gulf War. Wilenski was joined for our talks by Mike Costello, who was to replace him later that year when Wilenski was diagnosed with cancer. Costello was a smart, tough Asianist who believed in the rise of China and the gradual decline of Europe. In addition to excellent exchanges at a quite high intellectual level, we also codified our understandings on Embassy sharing and the sharing of more political and economic analysis at a global level. We had long shared raw intelligence, but this was something new, sharing the analyses and perspectives of each other's officers and Ambassadors out in the field, and even in the months that followed that this would turn out to be very helpful. The Australian perspectives on developments in places like Indonesia, a country of far greater importance and concentration to Australia than Canada, were inevitably richer and better thought through than our own, and I could only presume and hope that the Canadian reciprocal material was equally valuable.

En route home from Canberra, Jeremy and I went through Melbourne for one day visit. Our primary objective was to eat at what we had heard was the best Greek restaurant in the world, improbably named "Joe's Tavern" on Augusta Street. We found it without difficulty, but when we sat down to order and asked to see the wine list, we were told that the restaurant did not have any wine. Before our hearts sank completely, the waiter told us that we could go and buy our own wine at a nearby "bottle store" and that he would hold our table for us. We did so and ended up having a great meal, concurring with whoever it had been who had recommended the restaurant to us.

Restructuring the Branch

After a year as ADM Asia Pacific, I came to the conclusion that making geographic branches responsible for the full range of Canada's interests in a region had been a smart decision back at the time of the reorganization in the mid-1980s, but that the integration was insufficiently delegated. We still had separate trade and relations divisions and Directors General responsible for each of North, Southeast and South Asia. I decided to seek senior level approval for integrating at one level further down, at the Director level. Directors were senior officers generally ready to become Ambassadors in smaller countries, where they would in any case have to manage all dimensions of a relationship, with officers from a trade background having to deal with political relations and analysis, and traditional External officers having to promote Canadian exports and investment interests. So why not replicate this at headquarters? With the agreement of Under-Secretary Reid Morden and the new Deputy Minister of Trade, Al Kilpatrick, I did just that, creating single divisions for both China and Japan, and multi-country divisions for logical groupings of smaller countries throughout the region. I also had all the new Director-level country heads report directly to me, eliminated one of the three Directors General and had the other two serve as major negotiators and issue or crisis managers on major matters under the Branch's purview. To instill pride in the Asia Pacific Branch I had already had the name of the branch put up in large brass letters in the elevator lobby of the fifth floor of A-Tower, and I had photographs of every Canadian Head of Mission in the region, and all my predecessors, hung in the waiting room outside my office.

Now that I was a senior officer with many people reporting to me, some of my long-held beliefs were being put to the test. Whether or not I would give more junior people the authority and freedom to act that I had always wrestled for was one of the biggest questions. I did not like being bothered by little issues, but I also did not like to not be informed about what was going on. So I did my best to instill in the branch and throughout the region a sense that people were empowered to exercise their best judgment and yet never allowed to leave their seniors in the dark. I even had a sign printed for a branch wall in headquarters that said "Forgiveness is easier to obtain than Permission" and encouraged directors to both believe and live by it, encouraging in turn their own staff in whose judgment they had faith to live by it. It was how I had so far managed both to enjoy a bureaucratic career and to do quite well, and there was no reason for me to change my beliefs now that I was the one who granted forgiveness or permission. I also tried to instill in everyone who worked in the branch, at home or abroad, that it was a privilege to be part of Canada's "Asia Team", and that serving abroad at our posts was not an assignment but a privileged part of a career focused on Asia.

Asian Multilateralism Two

Following the first APEC Ministerial meeting in Canberra in 1989, the fledgling new 12-country organization settled into regular meetings of "Senior Officials" and an annual ministerial meeting to which most APEC members sent both Trade and Foreign Affairs Ministers. During my two years away from the Asia branch, the "three Chinas" had been brought into the organization as we had initially planned, with Taiwan and Hong Kong joining as "economies" rather than countries. Singapore was to be the site of the 1992 ministerial meetings, so we held our quarterly meetings of senior officials there. It was during the June meeting that my Korean counterpart introduced the notion of an APEC leaders' meeting, which immediately caused consternation for the Chinese senior official, Wang Guozhang, because of the implications of having the political leaders of Hong Kong and especially Taiwan present. Being an old hand at managing the sensitive issue of Taiwan, I met privately with Wang and worked out a deal which would see economic ministers attend from Taiwan and Hong Kong while heads of government or state would attend from other members. I also met with Donald Tsang, the new Hong Kong senior official, who I had known when he was working in the Governor's office in 1990 and who had replaced Tony Miller as the territory's Director General of Trade. Tsang thought the arrangement was fine, and would have the added benefit of being part of the "through train" of arrangements which would apply both before and after the 1997 handover of sovereignty.

Donald Tsang eventually was to become Hong Kong's Chief Executive, following Tung Chee-Hwa in 2005. In the early 1990s he was already a devotee of bow ties. Although it was not until after I became Ambassador to China that I began wearing bow ties exclusively, I often wore them at international meetings, including at APEC events, and at one of our meetings in Singapore, Ambassador Wang Guozhang of China joked that the Hong Kong and Canadian representatives, having supported one another on some proposal, were "shuang bow-ties", a bilingual pun on the Chinese word for twins, "shuang bao tai"!

The whole purpose of APEC was to encourage countries of the region to pursue more rapid relaxation of their trading and investment regimes, and to make it easier for private firms to do business through trade facilitation and streamlined and harmonized investment approval processes. In order to do address the real problems that businesses faced, we wanted to have input from real businesses. We proposed the creation of an "Eminent Persons Group" made up of business leaders from each of the economies, with the instruction that they report back to the 1993 ministerial meeting, with the hope that ministers would pass on a series of key recommendations to the APEC leaders. For our eminent person, I nominated John MacDonald, founder and Chairman of MacDonald Detweiler, a choice Trade Minister Michael Wilson wholeheartedly supported. John was a successful and gifted entrepreneur and a delightful companion at meetings and meals, and thought the name of the business leaders' group was amusing. For many years afterwards he would always refer to himself as "eminent", and when I called his office I would always ask for "His Eminence".

The other regular multilateral forum in the region was built around the Association of South East Asian Nations, a body created initially in the 1970s to encourage economic integration among the five major Southeast Asian countries of Malaysia, Singapore, Indonesia, the Philippines and Brunei. Born with grand dreams of building globally competitive regional industries, with each member assured of one or two, ASEAN had in fact never managed to significantly liberalize trade, even among its members. It had, however, served to be an effective body for dealing with regional irritants and conflicts, and for coordinating approaches to matters such as the flood of refugees pouring out of Vietnam and later Cambodia in the late 1970s. In order to support ASEAN and to help deal with some of the issues with which it was dealing but which had more global implications, an "ASEAN Dialogue" had evolved, and at one ASEAN Foreign Ministers' meeting each year the foreign ministers of "Dialogue Partners" would attend. The partners included Canada, the US, Japan, Australia and New Zealand (South Korea, China, India, Russia and the EU would also eventually become dialogue partners, but not until well after my time).

As Secretary of State for External Affairs, Barbara McDougall represented Canada at the ASEAN Dialogue meeting in 1992 in Manila, and I was her principal support. She was very unhappy at the prospect of attending the meeting, initially suggesting that her Parliamentary Secretary go instead. She eventually agreed to attend, but once in Manila was not very happy. On the evening of her arrival, she asked me to organize a discussion with Gareth Evans, Australia's very active Foreign Minister (and the author of the "four adjectives in search of a noun" reference to APEC). I tried to arrange something in the afternoon, but Evans was fully booked with bilateral meetings with regional counterparts, so we finally agreed to get together after the formal evening banquet. Evans and Mike Costello, my counterpart in Australia's Department of Foreign Affairs and Trade, came over to McDougall's suite for an informal chat. Discovering that Evans liked dry martinis apparently as much as she did, I was put in charge of making them and the four of us stayed up talking very late in the night, which meant that I had a foreign minister with dark glasses on all the next day. She then decided to leave a day early, in part because she was getting no coverage at all in the press.

McDougall's departure left me as Canada's representative for the last part of the Dialogue meeting, which was substantively fine since I knew all the regional participants and the issues very well. It also meant that I was on the podium for the press conference of dialogue partners, sitting next to Jim Baker of the US and Gareth Evans of Australia. We all expected that most of the questions from the international press would go to Baker and be about American political issues, since there was very wide speculation that he was about to resign as Secretary of State to manage President George H. W. Bush's re-election campaign. When asked that question, Baker dismissed the speculation as an idle rumour. In fact, the questions were quite evenly distributed and both Evans and I were asked questions. The following day there appeared in the international and local press a photograph of Baker and Evans and me, laughing and clearly enjoying an exchange among ourselves. What actually had happened was a journalist had asked Baker why he had visited Mongolia three times over the past eighteen months and ASEAN only once. He answered that Mongolia was a country with a difficult history, sandwiched between two large neighbours, and that no effort expended by the United States to help it get firmly launched as a successful young democracy could be too much. This was a good and politically correct answer. Then, with his microphone off, he turned to Evans and me and said "Actually the hunting and fishing is so good I just can't keep away! And I am planning to go back again in the autumn". Having dismissed in Manila the possibility of leaving his position to become Bush's campaign chief, he actually did just that a week later, and never made it back to Mongolia while in public office. I did see him in Ulan Bataar some fifteen years later when we were working together on a commercial matter, and he told me that he still regularly came to hunt and fish there.

In June of 1993 Kim Campbell won a tightly fought Progressive Conservative leadership convention against Jean Charest and became Prime Minister just before the annual G-7 Summit in Tokyo. This was obviously her first chance to interact with any of her G-7 counterparts and I went along to be with her for a bilateral meeting with Japanese Prime Minister Kiichi Miyazawa, and for a short bilateral visit to Seoul following the summit. The Japanese bilateral meeting went well, as Miyazawa knew his Canadian files from a spring visit he had made to Canada just before Mulroney's announcement that he would be stepping down, and Campbell spent plenty of time with me and her briefing team in advance to prepare thoroughly. Miyazawa was exceedingly deferential to this beautiful 45-year old blond woman, clearly not his image of a politician, but in a way that flattered rather than offended Campbell, so there was no harm done.

The visit to Korea was brief and the new President and former activist, Kim Young-Sam, very graciously received us, and kindly referred to me as a great friend of Korea during the exchange. I had met with him in 1987 when I was Director of North Asia Relations and he was running for President in the first real democratic election the country ever held. We had been strong supporters of democratization and Kim was to turn out to be a very forceful and effective leader. On the Prime Minister's plane after the visit, one of the journalists circulated a photograph of Kim Young-Sam hosting a banquet for Kim Campbell with the caption "Kim he hosts Kim she for kimchee".

When Kim Campbell became Prime Minister, it was already clear that the Progressive Conservatives would be tossed out on their ears at the next federal election. The economy was sluggish largely due to external factors, but it was publicly and unfairly blamed on the systemically restructuring measures of continental free trade and the GST (Goods and Services Tax) that the Mulroney team had bravely introduced. Added to this was the disastrous constitutional mess left in the wake of the failure of the Charlottetown Accord in the referendum of late 1992. Just before the final cross-Canada vote on the Charlottetown Accord, I was at a dinner in Ottawa for a group of us with Newfoundland links. Craig Dobbins, the founder and CEO of Canadian Helicopters and Vic Young, CEO of Fishery Products International were both there as were a few other senior bureaucrats, but it was a strictly personal and non-political evening. John Crosbie arrived late, having spent the day campaigning to encourage a "Yes" vote in the referendum, as it was definitely an all-hands-on-deck effort by the full cabinet. I had worked with Crosbie when he was Minister of International Trade both when I was Director of North Asia and when in Policy Planning we proposed that he take to Cabinet a recommendation to join the NAFTA negotiations. In part because of those interactions, and in part because of our fathers' relationship back in Newfoundland, we got on very well. He came into the room where the rest of us were gathered and collapsed backwards on a sofa and proceeded to unleash a ten-minute and hilarious diatribe *against* the agreement in favour of which he had spent the day campaigning. He called the agreement a tangled skein of compromises and excessive government that absolutely no-one could understand, and then did impersonations of some of the provincial and federal principal players involved, including some of his cabinet colleagues – it was John Crosbie at his best! We laughed so hard one would have thought that the matter being mocked was not serious. At that time we all believed that a failure of the Charlottetown Accord to be ratified would put the very existence of Canada at risk. In the end, maybe it did, and a direct result was our narrow victory in the Québec referendum three years later in which I was to play my own part. But we could not know that then, and it is in any case a later part of this story.

Although it had nothing to do with my duties in the Department of External Affairs and International Trade, it was during my time as ADM that I became involved in a "skunk works" of senior officials trying to think though how the information age was changing the function and processes of government. The group was organized by a former public servant, Steve Roselle, who by the early 1990s had become a professor out in California and a bit of a guru on the information age. We would meet about once a month late in the afternoon and keep our discussions going over dinner. Other members of the group, mostly ADMs at the time, included: David Dodge, later Deputy Minister of Finance and eventually Governor of the Bank of Canada; Kevin Lynch, who would replace Dodge as Deputy in Finance and much later become Clerk of the Privy Council; Mel Cappe, another future Clerk; Jim Lahey, a senior ADM in Immigration and a great demographer; Bob Blackburn and Jim Lahey from Industry Canada, Moira White who would eventually take over the Royal Mail, and a few others. I am not sure that we had any impact on the way government was evolving, but it was a highly interesting group and a great opportunity for me to get to know some of my senior colleagues from the domestic side of government, relationships that would prove useful when I became Deputy Secretary to the Cabinet for National Unity. Steve Roselle later collected some of the papers we wrote, including my "Managing Crises in a World According to CNN", in a book he edited and published in the US. It was, I suspect, not a bestseller.

Acacia Avenue in Rockcliffe Park is not only the street on which the Balloch clan lived, it was also where the Japanese, Korean, Thai and Indian Ambassadorial Residences were, with most of the other southeast Asian heads of mission also nearby. During the three years of my stewardship of the Asian Branch, Liani and I would be invited frequently to dinners at these residences and sometimes, particularly when Liani had become friends with the wife of an Ambassador, the children would be asked along. In the case of Thai Ambassador Chawat Arthayukti, his lovely wife Savalak would bring trays of delicious Thai spring rolls and other food around to our house when they were preparing major receptions or dinners. Combined of course with Liani's Indonesian and Chinese cooking, our four children became great connoisseurs of a full range of Asian food at a very young age.

In the spring of 1993, Liani and I took the four children to Indonesia, via Tokyo, for the three boys' first trip to Asia and Cynthia's second. In Tokyo we stayed at Marler House at the kind invitation of Ambassador Don Campbell, who had replaced Si Taylor the summer before. In Jakarta we reconnected with our old friends Alex and Caecilia Papadimitriou and spent a day with them at their lovely estate south of the city, and also spent a couple of days in the Embassy hill station bungalow in Puncak Valley near Bogor, where Liani and I had begun our romance fourteen years earlier. The bungalow staff were still the same individuals who had been there in the 1970s, and they were all delighted to see that the young bohemian officer they had known was now a senior government official with four beautiful and partly Indonesian children. Most of the time we spent with Liani's mother and family in Krawang, and the children were delighted by travelling monkey shows and the zoos and parks and earthiness of Java. Seven year-old Caleb had an accident as we left an amusement park at Ancol, north of Jakarta, tearing a gaping hole in his thigh on a unprotected piece of rebar. We rushed him off to a local hospital where his leg was sown up without anesthetic, and I learned as I held him down for the doctor just how strong a child he was becoming. It was a very good visit, and aside from a collective "sit-down strike" in the middle of the Tokyo Airport to protest their fatigue and the length of time between decent meals, the four children all became more comfortable with the crowds and the smells and the cultures of Asia because of it.

Last Months at Foreign Affairs

In the lead up to the general election of early November 1993, it was assumed within government as indeed throughout the country that the Liberal Party would be victorious. Few, however, predicted just how big the landslide would be. The Conservatives were reduced to a two-set rump as the briefly serving and gaff-prone Kim Campbell was swept aside with the more right-wing Reform Party under Preston Manning taking most of the conservative vote in Western Canada and indeed in parts of Ontario. But an almost bigger event was the emergence of the separatist Bloc Québécois as the official opposition, winning virtually all of the seats in Québec under the leadership of the mercurial orator and former Conservative Minister Lucien Bouchard. This was to become personally very relevant for me in the months to come.

A few days after the election came a reasonably big surprise for me when the new Cabinet was named. Trimming the number of full Ministers to a complement somewhat smaller than the outgoing Conservative government, Prime Minister Chrétien announced the creation of a new tier of "Secretaries of State", a couple of whom were appended to the Department of Foreign Affairs and International Trade. Of direct relevance to me was the appointment of Raymond Chan as Secretary of State for Asia Pacific. At the beginning, no one was quite sure what to make of these new positions, and it was evident that the Prime Minister and his team had not really thought through their roles. It soon became apparent that they were to be more like specialized parliamentary secretaries (who assist Ministers in the parliamentary and public duties, but do not get involved in departmental work) than junior ministers since they were never invited to Cabinet meetings and were given no car and driver or other perquisites of ministerial office. They were to have one assistant and an office provided by their respective departments, who were supposed to figure out how to make use of them. As ADM for Asia, I was not very happy about having an extra political appendage to support, but I did my best to help Ray find a role and to come to grips with both his responsibilities and their limitations. Ray was a nice enough fellow, just elected to parliament for the first time, who had been given his position largely due to his stature in the Chinese-Canadian community in Vancouver. But he did not know Ottawa, either literally or its complex political world. We had a coffee on the morning after his appointment and I had to draw him a map of the principal buildings of Ottawa, showing him where the Prime Minister's office was in relation to Parliament, and when he asked my secretary to get the Prime Minister's Chief of Staff on the telephone so he could appeal for car and driver and more extensive support, I had to gently explain to him that in the pecking order of Ottawa, he would have to seek an appointment if he wished to see Chief of Staff Jean Pelletier, who was politically more powerful, and therefore more difficult to access, than all but a very small handful of senior ministers.

Although I was initially worried that the creation of the new position of Secretary of State for Asia Pacific would erode my responsibilities as Canada's senior person on all matters Asian, events were to quickly set those concerns at ease.

During the previous two years, as ADM for Asia Pacific I had been responsible for representing Canada at APEC meetings, and APEC was due to hold its first ever summit meeting in Seattle on November 19th and 20th 1993 at the invitation of President Clinton. This meant the first foreign policy focus for the newly elected Liberal Government would be towards the Pacific rather than either southward towards Washington or towards Canada's traditional European partners. So within days of the election, I was asked to squire Prime Minister Chrétien to Seattle, preceded by a stop-over in Vancouver to meet, in a roundtable format, Canadian business leaders with interests in the Pacific theatre.

I flew out to Vancouver with the Prime Minister and his lovely wife Aline in a government Challenger. The only others on board beyond two security staff were Jean Pelletier, the former Mayor of Québec City and now the Prime Minister's Chief of Staff, and Eddie Goldenberg, the Prime Minister's long-time advisor and friend and now in charge of setting up the policy apparatus of the PMO. As we flew across the country we chatted about the days ahead of us as well as a lot of other things. At some point in the conversation, I must have been hedging my answers in some way, for Jean Pelletier interrupted me to say, in the extraordinarily gentlemanly way he approached everything, something along the lines of: "Monsieur Balloch, we are Liberals, we believe that senior public servants like you are doing your best for the country and we trust you". This loosened me up and began a relationship of openness and frankness with Jean Pelletier, Eddie

Goldenberg and indeed with Prime Minister Chrétien that remained throughout (and indeed beyond) my remaining eight years in government.

We had a very successful and reasonably well scripted Vancouver roundtable with business leaders, who pushed the Prime Minister to recognize the growing importance of Asia, to move trade resources there from Europe and elsewhere, and to personally dedicate his time and attention to building strong links with Asian leaders. Chrétien was open to this advice, assured his audience that it was no coincidence that he had appointed a special junior minister to focus on the region and that his first foreign event was Asian-focused even if it was happening in the United States.

Then off we went to Seattle, to be joined by Foreign Minister André Ouellet, Trade Minister Roy McClaren, Ray Chan and a few officials, mostly from my branch but with Canadian Ambassador to Washington Derek Burney and a couple of senior US-focused Ottawa colleagues also present, since the first bilateral meeting between our new Prime Minister and President Clinton was also scheduled to take place during the visit. Because the PMO was not yet really set up or staffed administratively only two weeks after the election, I had also made arrangements for extra staff to come from the Asia branch to provide support for the PM and his senior team.

For the most part, the non-summit part of the APEC meetings were rather boring, with Trade and Foreign Ministers meeting to go through the motions of discussing and approving texts on regional trade and other issues that had been carefully negotiated and scripted by senior officials. In fact, many of the Ministers did not even attend the ministerial meetings as they were accompanying their Presidents or Prime Ministers in the myriad of bilateral meetings that were taking place all over the city, with every major hotel taken over by one national delegation or another. The only ministerial event that I recall was the reception hosted by US Secretary of State Warren Christopher at the Boeing Museum, where the exhibits of old aircraft were absolutely fascinating. Christopher was so uninterested in APEC that as he read a speech it was clear he had never even read in advance, twice mistakenly referring to OPEC rather than APEC.

Among the most important bilateral meetings arranged for the Prime Minister was with President Jiang Zemin of China. Given his seniority in terms of time in position (at this point no APEC leader was on that scale junior to Canada's, a situation which was to completely turn around during Chrétien's many years in power), the meeting took place in a suite in Jiang Zemin's hotel. André Desmarais, in his role as Chairman of the Canada China Business Council, was invited to join our small group for the meeting. André was also very close to Chrétien, as he was married to his daughter, France, and undoubtedly was a strong behind-the-scenes proponent for making the China relationship a very high priority for the new government. On the Chinese side, Chairman Jiang was joined by my APEC counterpart and long-time friend Liu Huaqiu, now a Vice-Minister, and a few but not many others. I had briefed Chrétien before the meeting on all the major issues, one of which was the requirement to raise the concerns of Canadians about the human rights situation in China. Memories of the Tiananmen incident of 1989 were still very much alive. Chrétien did not like to raise this issue because he felt that China was making substantial progress and whining relatively purposelessly to the Chinese leadership on a subject on which they were quite obdurate seemed quite futile. Nonetheless he reluctantly agreed to raise the matter so that he could say he had done so when questioned later by the press. In the end, the atmosphere during the bilateral was nothing short of terrific. After a slow start when Jiang Zemin was quite wooden, Chrétien's open informality got a parallel response from the Chinese President and the exchange quickly became open and friendly, touching personal family matters as well as matters of state. But the matter of human rights was a subject not raised. As we left the suite and rode down in the elevator, I mentioned to the PM that he had forgotten to raise human rights, but if he agreed, I would see if I could get the Chinese to acknowledge, if asked, that he had done so. Chrétien said fine, and as soon as I could I got Liu Huaqiu on the telephone and asked him to agree to have their spokesman corroborate any statement

Chrétien might make to a press enquiry that human rights were discussed during the bilateral. The last thing I wanted, or Chrétien needed, right at the beginning of his efforts to build a stronger relationship with China was a public outcry that his government did not care about human rights in China. Liu Huaqiu was initially very negative to my request, but gradually came around to realize that a simple acknowledgement that human rights was a subject "touched upon during a wide-ranging discussion" was likely to cause far less controversy than seeing the Canadian Prime Minister embarrassed for not having raised the matter.

The main event in Seattle was of course the first summit of the then 15 APEC heads of government or heads of state. In the preparatory meetings over the prior months, I and a couple of other APEC Senior Officials who had been involved in G-7 or other "summitry" had argued hard for a format that would promote a truly open and informal dialogue, with no preset scripts or lengthy pre-negotiated communiqués. Sandy Kristoff, my American counterpart at the time, was very much of this view and as the Americans were the hosts, she managed to insist on this format over the objections of many of the formalistic Asians. The meeting itself was an all-day affair out on Blake Island in the Seattle harbour, with leaders meeting alone in an improvised meeting room in a log cabin tourist lodge. Every leader was fitted with an earpiece for simultaneous interpretation (the interpreters were housed in a special temporary building and had to handle two-way translation from seven or eight different languages into every other language simultaneously, which was quite complicated, since when the Thai PM was speaking, it had to be interpreted into Japanese and Chinese and Tagalog and Indonesian as well as English). The earpiece also allowed leaders to dialogue with their country's "Senior Official", the only other people allowed to accompany the leaders to Blake Island. For Canada, I was that Senior Official.

Before the leaders meetings began, during the breaks and at the end of the day, I was with the Prime Minister as we wandered around, occasionally speaking with other leaders and officials (there were, by agreement, no sit-down bilaterals during the day on the island) and occasionally chatting à-deux, generally in French. Chrétien was interested in my perspectives on Asian matters, but our conversation also somewhat naturally came back to the national agenda. He was interested in where and when I had mastered the French language and we chatted about the likely national unity challenge looming in 1994, as it was clear to him that the Québec liberals had almost no chance of staying in power and that the ardent separatist Jacques Parizeau would almost certainly become Québec Premier and push quickly for a second referendum on sovereignty. I did not think much more about our conversation after the day ended, but it would later become clear that the Prime Minister would not forget our exchange.

During a pre-lunch break in the formal discussions, when the leaders were still in their isolated conference area chatting among themselves, I wandered with Liu Huaqiu behind the old buildings and the temporary structures built for interpreters, communications and security staff. There we found some chefs preparing planked salmon, with large salmon filets tacked to planks being roasted against open fires, Haida style. I showed this to my friend Vice Minister Liu, and then engaged with one of the cooks in a conversation. It turned out that the State Department had hired Haida cooks from British Columbia to prepare a traditional "Washington State" aboriginal feast. Liu found this enormously amusing, and later teased our American counterpart that the mighty USA had to import even the cooking technology from Canada to host the APEC leaders!

The bilateral meeting between Prime Minister Chrétien and President Clinton took place in Seattle before we moved to Blake Island for the leaders' retreat, and I (quite logically) did not participate. But once on the island, Chrétien and Clinton had several informal exchanges as leaders wandered about, and I was at Chrétien's elbow for most of them. At one point, Clinton and I got into a chat and he asked, as he would, about my background and family, and we had a very personable exchange. Many years later, when I met him again after his presidency, he said to me: "Oh yes, we met in Seattle, and how are your twins?" blowing me away with his prodigious memory.

Career Choices

The APEC summit done, I returned to Ottawa as the Christmas season approached. Just before our trip to Seattle, I had received a call from the then Clerk of the Privy Council, Glenn Shortliffe, with whom I had worked in both Indonesia and Ottawa. He said that he was looking at re-staffing the Deputy Secretary positions at PCO at the beginning of the year and asked me whether I would be interested in taking over the Priorities and Planning secretariat, and he told me that my old friend Jim Judd, later Canada's spy-master, would be likely coming in as Deputy Secretary for Operations. I told Glenn that I would be interested but that I was also seriously considering leaving government sometime during the new year. We agreed to pick up the conversation after the Christmas break. It was not until mid-February that I received another call, but it was not Glenn who called me but Jean Pelletier, the Prime Minister's Chief of Staff, asking me to come over to the Langevin Building to have a chat with him. I of course did so, and he told me that the Prime Minister had enjoyed the time we had spent together in Seattle and that they would like to ask me to come over to the PCO to manage the national unity file.

Pelletier also told me in strictest confidence that the Clerk would be replaced, which meant that the pre-Christmas conversation that I had had with Glenn Shortliffe was now moot. He called Eddie Goldenberg into his office and we chatted together about the unity challenge the country would be facing, and they asked me how I thought the federal government should approach the file. I answered that I thought the government should be directly and deeply involved, that it should try to do a much better job selling Canada in Québec, that it should leave no separatist lie unchallenged, that it should be flexible on contentious issues such as whether the federal or provincial levels should be responsible for manpower training, and if the opportunity arose it should try to seek a constitutional change that would bring Québec permanently into the constitutional family. Pelletier and Goldenberg said they agreed with all but my last point which they thought would be suicidal, and they stressed to me that Prime Minister Chrétien had no intention whatsoever of re-opening the constitutional debate during his time in office.

Pelletier encouraged me to spend more time with Eddie, which I was to do in spades, and also to chat with Paul Tellier, at that time CEO of Canadian National Railways but who had been Deputy Secretary for National Unity during the referendum of 1980, as well as with other veterans of that time. The following week I followed his advice and took a train to Montreal for a good discussion with Paul Tellier on his experience in 1980 and the lessons he thought should be applied for the next referendum.

In December of 1993, I had been approached by a headhunter representing Alcan, wondering whether I would be interested in a senior VP position there, looking after governmental and public affairs. I had said yes and met on a couple of occasions early in the new year with Jacques Bougie, Alcan's CEO. Nothing was finalized by March. So when in Montreal to meet with Tellier, I went to see Jacques Bougie and told him of the offer to take on the PCO unity job, and told him that I thought I could not refuse such an important job even if it was likely to be far from enjoyable! His reaction was that he completely understood why I had to answer the call of my country. He told me that while the job I was being considered for would have to be filled (it was almost immediately filled by Dan Gagnier, an old government friend from years before, and in fact a veteran of the unity wars of the 1980s), I should come back and talk to him once the referendum was over as he was sure there would be a place for me. This he was to reiterate privately to me at a May 1995 meeting of the Business Council on National Issues after I had briefed him and other senior chief executive offices on the Government's analysis of the Québec situation and our planning for the referendum.

The new Clerk, Jocelyne Bourgon, previously Deputy Minister of Transport, took over the PCO from Glenn Shortliffe in late March. In the formal governmental structure I would be working for her, so I had another round of interviews with her and Ron Bilodeau, Deputy Minister to the Minister of Inter-Governmental Affairs and Associate Clerk of the Privy Council. They agreed to my appointment and it was set that I would wrap up my responsibilities at DFAIT and move to PCO in the early summer. I had advised already my two departmental deputy minister bosses, Reid Morden (Foreign Affairs) and Don Campbell (International Trade), and we agreed that I would try to tie up a few loose ends, which included a last trip to China as ADM to accompany Trade Minister for the new government's first ministerial visit to Beijing.

A memorable beginning of my trip with Trade Minister Roy MacLaren to Beijing was our arrival. I had warned him during our flight that the infrastructure in Beijing was still quite rudimentary, and that we could expect a long drive into the city on an old and crowded road, shared with donkey-carts and farm trucks. Instead, after being met by officials of the newly renamed Ministry of Trade and Economic Cooperation (MOFTEC) and Ambassador Fred Bild, we were whisked into town along the brand new airport highway, an astounding change for those of us who were used to the "old China" of carts and herds of sheep slowing down our progress. As we flew down the almost empty highway, McLaren, who had a great sense of humour, turned to me and said he hoped that the remainder of my information about China was as up-to-date as my warning about the old road and the traffic!

Roy MacLaren was a delightful travel companion. Having been a foreign service officer, serving in Hanoi, Saigon and Prague early in his professional career prior to going into business in Toronto, he then had a checkered political career, losing as often as winning his Toronto seat and serving briefly in the Turner cabinet prior to the Mulroney landslide of 1984. He would in the end only serve in the first Chrétien government before being named as High Commissioner in London, but for as long as he was our trade minister he worked hard and effectively. In Beijing, our major meetings were with the "Iron Lady" MOFTEC Minister, Wu Yi, and focused both on bilateral trade issues and on Chinese accession to the WTO. Some months before, Wu Yi had been in Washington for bilateral trade talks with Mickey Kantor, who had been appointed US Trade Representative in 1993. The US was unhappy with a Chinese ban on the import of US wheat due to a widespread infection of the "TCK" fungus commonly found in wheat shipped out of US Gulf ports. During a post negotiation press conference, Kantor had railed publicly against the Chinese ban, and stated that the fungus was also found in Canadian wheat, which China was continuing to import in large quantities. Surprised by the public airing of the issue and the mentioning of Canadian wheat, Wu Yi retorted that Canadian wheat was of the highest quality, and she would personally stake her job on no TCK fungus being found in Chinese grain imports from Canada. This was an extraordinary testimonial to the quality of Canadian wheat and MacLaren led off our bilateral talks with a very effusive appreciation for Wu Yi's support. After his comments were translated, Wu Yi, realizing there was little to be gained by just acknowledging the gratitude, retorted heatedly that while Canadian wheat was high quality it was still far too expensive. Forgetting that there were officials on the Canadian side of the table who understood Chinese, she then turned to her Vice Minister and asked in mandarin whether the Canadian prices were any different than anyone else's! Years later, during a concert to which I had invited Wu Yi, then State Counselor, I reminded her of this and she found it very amusing.

As soon as I returned from the MacLaren trip, it was time to clean out my Asia Branch office and to leave the Lester B. Pearson Building, assuming correctly that I would probably never return to work there again, although I had no idea what roads really lay ahead.

BOOK IV:

NATIONAL UNITY

CHAPTER 13

TO THE PCO

· · · · · · · · · · ·

Arriving at the Privy Council Office, or PCO as it was always called, was rather a rude shock. The Intergovernmental Secretariat I was to take over was being ably run by an Assistant Secretary, Michael Wernick, a constitutional expert who had been deeply involved in the background work done for the failed 1992 Charlottetown Accord. (He was much later to rise to the level of Deputy Minister at Indian and Northern Affairs.) Michael was supported by three or four people and housed in very sub-standard offices at the corner of Elgin and Sparks, with a complex back entry to the Langevin Block, where the Prime Minister's Office and that of the Clerk of the Privy Council are both located. Michael's team was composed of dedicated professionals, largely economists and constitutionalists. There were, however, no communications professionals. Worse, except for some links with academics and the old "constitutional industry", their networks with key communities within Quebec were virtually non-existent. A small office in Montreal existed for this purpose, but proved in the months to come to be somewhat of a gadfly on the political scene, mistrusted by many with whom they had contacts and largely incapable of providing insight or analysis beyond the superficial. The Montreal office also had established itself as a voice for a particular approach to federalism, the public articulation of which (to journalists and opinion-leaders) was to further undermine its credibility, so we closed it.

From the moment I took up my new position as Deputy Secretary, I could sense a huge divide between what was expected of me from the Prime Minister's Office (PMO) and how the Clerk of the Privy Council saw my role. The latter, Jocelyne Bourgon, had been Deputy Secretary for Intergovernmental Affairs in the lead-up to the Charlottetown Accord disaster, and saw herself as still in charge of the unity file. Furthermore, she had brought one of her principal lieutenants from that time, Suzanne Hurtubise, into the PCO in a not very well-defined role, and Suzanne also had a sense of ownership of the national unity file. It did not take long for a conflict to emerge.

The Clerk held morning operations meetings for all Deputy and Assistant Secretaries of the Cabinet, which was normal practice. At one such meeting early in my tenure, Bourgon asked me to summarize what we were doing in my secretariat and what our early thinking on strategy was. My response was apparently unsatisfactory to her and she asked me, Michael Wernick and Suzanne Hurtubise to remain after the meeting, which of course we did. The four of us then spent almost two hours analyzing at a theoretical level the arguments the Parti Québécois would likely be putting forward and the logical federalist counter-arguments. Bourgon wrote extensively on a white board, drawing circles and arrows that struck me as academically distant and dry, and at best only marginally relevant to the political war we about to fight. And Suzanne Hurtubise praised everything that Bourgon said or wrote and told me quite directly that as I learned more she would be there to guide me. That their wonderful theorizing had failed miserably with the defeat of the Charlottetown Accord seemed to have been completely erased from memory. The whole scene was bizarre, and completely at odds with the meetings that I was having on a daily basis with Eddie Goldenberg of the PMO and on a less frequent basis with the PM's Chief of Staff, Jean Pelletier. These latter meetings were focused, intensely political, and all about dealing with a knowable enemy about to unleash on the political scene a potentially mortal threat to the country. There was nothing theoretical or academic in the minds of Goldenberg or Pelletier. We would be fighting for our country and it would be a political and very intense fight. Our opponents would not be trying to put logical arguments in front of the electorate; they would be using every ruse and dirty trick imaginable to persuade fifty percent of the population, plus one critical vote, to give them a mandate to destroy one of the oldest and most successful democracies on the planet. The good news was that not only my PMO friends but also Ron Bilodeau, Associate Clerk and substantially older than Bourgon, told me to focus on the political battle ahead and take direction from the political side when and if there was a clash between what I was hearing from PMO and from the Clerk. Ron, a veteran of three decades of bureaucratic intrigue, told me not to worry, since the worst that could happen probably would, and that would simply be me being quietly fired from my position and moved into some nice sinecure abroad!

Michael Wernick was, in spite of his legacy with the Charlottetown Accord disaster, a competent and thoughtful officer, and effectively evolved his group into our legal and policy team, although Michael himself remained a thoughtful advisor to me on a broader range of issues. His group took on the task of preparing policy pieces and pre-referendum material defending the federalist side and arguing against the separatist myths and propaganda. These "Argumentaires" were all very finely prepared and well thought-out pieces, but in the end they were probably most useful in giving active federalists material that they could use in debates. They were generally too high-brow to be useful in the actual mud-slinging and propaganda wars that the Parti Québécois was to unleash.

My first task was to begin assembling the operations and communications team that would be needed in the actual referendum battle, which we assumed could come as early as the late autumn of 1994, for it was clear that the Parti Québécois would win a substantial majority in the upcoming elections. Jacques Parizeau had been very explicit saying that his first order of business would be the calling of a sovereignty referendum. My principal advisor on personnel issues was Ron Bilodeau, always a source of support and someone who over time turned out to be a good friend. Ron had some ideas about people I might wish to bring onto the team, and we also called around to a number of other deputies for further thoughts. My team gradually began to take shape. Based on the 1980 experience, we anticipated having a team of well over a hundred but we did not want this to be commonly known or a source of political debate. One of our concerns was that a large federal team would imply too large a role for the federal government which the separatists would use in their propaganda, suggesting that the capability of the federalist forces in Québec were not up to the task of fighting a fair battle within the province, as stipulated by the Québec law on referenda passed by former Premier René Levesque prior to the first vote fourteen years earlier. We thus decided to keep all administrative matters relating to my team as invisible as possible, burying some of our expenditures in other budgets, asking departments and agencies to release personnel to us while continuing to keep them on their own books, and not even publishing the address of our principal offices.

One of the early new members of my team was Michelle d'Auray, a brilliantly talented, hard-working DG who came to us from Treasury Board. Michelle was always a breath of fresh air, irreverent and funny and never one to suffer fools gladly. She in turn brought in a team of very smart and creative professionals, including a young woman named Renée Brunet, who in the end were responsible for much of the public material used by the "No" side during the referendum. They of course were never given the credit they were due, since we had to pretend the source was the "Comité pour le Non", formally led by Daniel Johnson Jr., ex-Premier and leader of the Liberal Party of Québec (the "PLQ"), who were in fact closer at the federal level to the Progressive Conservative Party than the Liberal Party. Another team member who was to eventually go on to higher office in government was John Knubley. I also needed an executive assistant, and found William Georges in Ron Bilodeau's office enthusiastic to come and join me. He turned out to be a perfect "EA", a veritable "Radar" for me, always ahead of the curve and totally indefatigable. If I would get to the office at 0530, he would either be there in advance or I would I pick him up from his By-Town apartment, but even then he would have received the full analysis of the overnight news and the morning press and would be able to brief me before we started with anyone else. William left government shortly after the referendum, and moved back to Montreal as a Vice President at Domtar, eventually moving to the SAQ to run their investments and global operations. And supporting both myself and William was an unbelievable efficient secretary and administrative assistant, Giselle Scott. Another key player, Pierre Richard, came out of Defence, on his own recommendation that was passed through an in-law of his who was a personal friend of mine. Pierre had been a Major in the army, with tremendous planning and logistical skills, and he was to prove invaluable in making things happen around the province of Québec, a crucial contribution given the organizational weakness of the PLQ.

A further key member of my inner team was Marc Lafrenière, who joined my organization a little later than most others. Although initially the Assistant Secretary for Aboriginal Affairs, a secretariat outside of intergovernmental affairs, he was assigned to my team in late 1994 by the Clerk, Jocelyne Bourgon, with the instruction (intended to be hidden from me) to report directly to her. She was intending that he would serve to keep her better informed on what we were doing than I did, but Marc was not having any part in playing as an internal fifth columnist, and soon turned out to be a tremendous source of good advice, support and actually a foil which made managing the Clerk and her circle of close associates easier and not more difficult. In addition, Marc handled the relations with the First Nations and their leaders, and they were to play an important role in the final months leading up to the referendum.

The Political Setting and Ministerial Guidance

Another challenge that I faced as I took up my new responsibilities was that the world seemed to be divided into two groups of individuals. The first were Ministers and senior officials who felt they were either in charge of the unity file or had a particular responsibility for some dimension of it. The second was every other senior official of government, every federal and provincial politician and most senior business leaders, dozens of well-established journalists and a few million other Canadians, all of whom knew how best to win the referendum and were eager to offer advice.

Among the members of the first of these groups was Marcel Massé, the newly elected Member of Parliament for Hull-Aylmer and a former senior public servant, having been President of CIDA and then Under-Secretary of External Affairs when I was brought back from Prague in 1985 to help with the reorganization of the department following the integration of the trade function from the old Department of Industry Trade and Commerce. Massé was appointed by Chrétien as Minister for Intergovernmental Affairs, with Ron Bilodeau assigned as his Deputy, and he immediately saw himself as the point politician for Québec issues. Massé was a very smart guy, but not a politician at heart, and after a few meetings with Ron Bilodeau and me he gradually got the message that it would be the Prime Minister and not he who would run the political file on Québec issues. After that, he turned out to be a good trooper, always willing to do whatever we suggested might be politically helpful.

In fact, the Cabinet Ministers from Québec were collectively charged by Prime Minister Chrétien with ensuring that everything they did would be supportive of the federalist cause in the roiling political maelstrom that was to come. There was a weekly strategy meeting of Québec Ministers at breakfast on Tuesdays. Jean Pelletier would attend, and generally acted as informal chair, and both I and Ron Bilodeau would also be there, myself religiously and Ron about half the time. My attendance at this breakfast meeting began in the early summer of 1994 and continued whenever Parliament was in session until the referendum of 1995. The Québec ministers represented a relatively wide range of experience and influence, but there were in fact only a few of them. The most powerful of them was Finance Minister Paul Martin, but on Québec matters he was politically junior to André Ouellet, the Minister of Foreign Affairs and the Cabinet's informally designated "Québec Lieutenant". The breakfasts were usually held at Ouellet's office in the Centre Block on Parliament Hill. In addition there was Marcel Massé and Alfonso Gagliano, the latter being Minister of Public Works and a great link to Montreal's Italian and other "allophone" communities (meaning neither francophone nor the traditional anglophone communities of the relatively wealthy centre or the middle-class west island). Delightfully, there was also Sheila Finestone, MP for Mount Royal (Pierre Trudeau's traditional riding), appointed by Chrétien as Minister for Multiculturalism and the Status of Women. Sheila was a McGill graduate some years senior to me, but an intellectual at heart with a fabulous depth of understanding about almost everything. I lunched with Finestone on several occasions and found her a charming counterpart to the sharp-edged politicians of the cabinet. She had a wonderful sense of humour, but was always treated by other Ministers as being a political lightweight, and during our breakfast meetings her interventions, always in English in an otherwise French conversation, were graciously received but almost always substantively ignored. In early 1995, the composition of the breakfasts was changed with the arrival of the newly elected Lucienne Robillard, a former Québec provincial minister in the Johnson government who Chrétien had encouraged to run in a by-election. Upon her election, Chrétien immediately moved her into the Intergovernmental Affairs portfolio and shuffled Massé to the Treasury Board, implicitly recognizing Massé's inability to play more than a marginal political role on the unity issue.

At one of the Tuesday breakfasts, held in André Ouellet's Hill office, I had made some sort of comment about attitudes among the younger electorate, and Ouellet came at me like a freight train, dismissing my views not for their substance but because I was an anglophone and therefore could never really understand Québec. I was livid but held my tongue until everyone except the two of us were left. We then had a very heated exchange in which I basically told him that I was as emotionally committed to keeping Québec in Canada as was he and that if he saw me as an "outsider", then he should tell the PM to change the unity support team and replace me. Eventually we both calmed down, he apologized and somehow after that we had a much more cordial relationship. In fact, I think I earned his respect in part because of my willingness to stand up to him, for he was always a tough street fighter and liked a good confrontation.

The great advantage of the Québec ministers' breakfast was the fact that no single Minister could leave the breakfast with a belief that he or she was in charge of the unity issue or could "free-lance" politically. Jean Pelletier was a constant and firm reminder at these breakfasts that the Prime Minister himself was in charge of the Québec file, and even from mid-1994 reminded Ministers that any public statements made in Québec had to be reviewed in advance by PMO, preferably vetted first by me and my office. No Minister misunderstood the message that they were on a very short leash with respect to public statements that might have an impact on the volatile political situation inside Québec, where any comment could be misconstrued and no federal good deed left unpunished.

As a result of my participation in the Tuesday breakfasts of Québec Ministers, I developed a personal relationship with all of the Ministers, and with the encouragement of Jean Pelletier arranged to meet them one on one on an occasional basis to ensure that they felt their input was appreciated. This had one downside, which was that several of them saw me and my budget as an opportunity to deal with non-unity related political matters in Montreal. Both André Ouellet and Alfonso Gagliano asked me to try to find jobs for their friends at the Conseil pour l'Unité Canadien (CUC), the small federalist think tank and lobby group in Montreal. While we eventually ran a number of publicity programs through the CUC, including the published versions of our "Argumentaires" and some of the early advertising, anything we did with it was bound to undergo great public scrutiny and probably challenge from the Parti Québécois. Furthermore there was no way I was going to allow it to be abused for political ends. I did however agree to meet with various people, who sometimes seemed to be shady characters in fedoras and large Cadillacs with no discernable positive contribution to make. My general approach to these meetings was to downplay my own position and to make clear that I had no authority or budget to wield on my own.

Montreal Contacts and New Friends

In Montreal a series of federalist groups started to form well before the provincial election. I became involved in two such groups. The first was organized by former Minister Serge Joyal and was composed primarily of federal liberal stalwarts, such as Marc Lalonde, Bob Rabinovitch, Gerard Veilleux, John Rae and Eric Maldoff, along with one or two with deeper roots in the PLQ, such as Lise Bacon. André Ouellet was as member of this group, which met almost every week from June through December, although he almost always delegated Jacqueline Lanthier, his political assistant to attend in his place. Jean Pelletier and Eddie Goldenberg attended these meetings whenever they could, and Ron Bilodeau did on occasion, while I became a regular. Working with Marc Lalonde was a great pleasure; he was a former minister of several portfolios in the last government of Lester B. Pearson and in all successive Trudeau administrations and was an upbeat charming intellectual with a great sense of humour. John Rae, brother to Bobby Rae, then the sitting Ontario NDP Premier, had masterminded Jean Chrétien's election campaign and enjoyed the most complete confidence of the Prime Minister and his senior staff. A wily and brilliant political strategist who understood both provincial politics and the strengths and weaknesses of the PLQ, John Rae was a major player in the planning and execution of the federalist campaign, and a very regular participant in our deliberations on everything from regional organization to media advertising and polling. He also was one of the handful of non-PLQ people active in daily war-room deliberations later in the campaign. Eric Maldoff, who was also to become a good friend, was a lawyer from Montreal and one of the founders of Alliance Québec, the anglophone lobby group established shortly after the first referendum in the early 1980s. Eric was very close to Eddie Goldenberg and was a delightful character, fluently bilingual like most anglophone Montrealers of our generation, and very thoughtful. He understood deeply most of the political issues in which the separatist debate were imbedded, including the complex matter of the rights and interests of the First Nations, with whom he was deeply involved. But he was also a very astute political tactician, and over the months to come his views on how to position contentious arguments over territorial integrity and other matters would be very valuable. Eddie Goldenberg and I used him as a sounding board on many issues.

Most of the discussions of the Montreal group were "in-house" and covered both general views of developments and early planning for what the federalist side would need as the political temperature started to rise. On one or two occasions, someone from outside the group was invited, such as the economist André Renaud and the McGill sociologist Maurice Pinard. Many of the discussions were lively and interesting-especially to me as someone neither of the liberal cloth or experienced in all the past political battles represented around the table-and it evolved as an unseen advisory group to the federal government, a role encouraged by Jean Pelletier who encouraged us to develop ideas it generated and to occasionally use it as a sounding board for strategic ideas and policy alternatives.

The second group was organized around a nucleus of supporters of the Council for Canadian Unity that had been meeting on and off for some time even before the summer of 1994. Michel Vennat and Rémi Bujold took that nucleus and expanded it into a "Conseil Québec", which also met weekly, usually over breakfast in either the boardroom of former Clerk Paul Tellier, now CEO of Canadian National Railways, or that of Michel Vennat who had earlier in the year been appointed by Chrétien to be President and CEO of the Business Development Bank of Canada.

I was also fortunate to meet and spend time with former Prime Minister Pierre Trudeau, who was at that time still working from an office at Heenan Blaikie. The first time I had lunch with him the charming Roy Heenan joined us, but on three or four occasions we would have lunch on our own. Of course he had very strong views on a lot of unity-related issues, having not only been Prime Minister during the 1980 referendum and the repatriation of the Constitution, but also active behind the scenes during the Meech Lake debacle and, rather more quietly and incidentally during the debate on the Charlottetown Accord. Our conversations wandered rather far from the unity file, to his experiences as a young man, our shared interest in China and his early trips there, both as a student and as a journalist when he was editor of Cité Libre.

During my first few months as Deputy Secretary I focused on building out the staff of the unity team, developing my network in Montreal and doing some general work in preparation for the battle to come. I also went across the country to all provincial capitals outside Québec to meet with provincial Ministers of Intergovernmental Affairs, and usually with either Premiers or their chiefs of staff, to build relationships that could be drawn upon when needed later. One of our secondary themes in the lead up to the referendum was "Keep Canada Cool" since we knew that any anti-Québec activity would be welcomed and quickly propagandized by the separatist forces. In fact, later in the campaign, there was an attempt to burn a Québec flag in an Edmonton pub, and a local journalist had been alerted and invited in advance. It turned out that the instigator was unknown to the locals, spoke with a very slight but discernable Québécois accent, and when the flag was quickly extinguished, disappeared. Everyone, from the bartender in the pub to the journalist, believed this to be an intentional provocation by the PQ, and the journalist, when approached by an Alberta Intergovernmental Affairs official, consequently agreed not to report on the matter.

CHAPTER 14

THE SEPTEMBER ELECTION AND THE DECLARATION OF WAR

• • • • • • • • • • •

The election did not come in the spring of 1994 as we had initially anticipated, as Daniel Johnson, who had taken over the Premiership on the resignation of the ailing Robert Bourassa only on January 11ᵗʰ of that year, saw no downside to delaying until after the summer in the hope that he could build more support. We all hoped, but without much optimism, for at least enough of a dent in the PQ return to keep them in minority, but it was not to be. The Québec electorate was deeply tired of the Liberals, who had been in power since the last PQ government fell in 1985. It was somewhat ironic that the loser in the election of 1985 was Premier Pierre-Marc Johnson, brother to Daniel, after 70 short days in office following the resignation of René Levesque. In any case, the elections were finally called in August and on September 12ᵗʰ, 1994, Jacques Parizeau was elected with a majority government. And he came out swinging, making clear from the outset that his government would be focused virtually exclusively on his "grand projet" of forming an independent Québec and promising a referendum to that end within a year.

What followed, however, was what Prime Minister Chrétien would later call the "phoney war", an allusion to the period in the early part of World War II after the fall of Poland in 1939 and before Hitler sent his armies sweeping westward across Holland, Belgium and France. The Parti Québécois government, knowing that support for sovereignty was not sufficient for it to win a referendum immediately, promised the unveiling of a legislative bill on sovereignty, which was published in December, followed by a commission on sovereignty that was to tour the province and hold "États genéraux" to build support for separation and a sense of a great momentum throughout Québec.

.Shortly after the election, I was asked by Jean Pelletier to meet with a senior partner at the accounting firm of Samson Deloitte in Montreal. The board of the firm on the encouragement of its Chairman Claude Castonguay had prohibited its partners from engaging in any activity that could be construed as political or making any statements either for or against sovereignty. This was unacceptable to Pierre Pettigrew, an ardent and articulate federalist, who had served in the PMO during the Trudeau era and who felt he had no choice except to resign from the firm to retain his freedom to speak publicly on behalf of the federalist cause. Pettigrew's voice was welcome, but we had to find a way to support him since he would be giving up his salary. I met with him and promised that we would find a couple of federal contracts for him to work on as a private consultant, and in the end we did just that. I arranged one through Gordon Smith, then Deputy Minister of Foreign Affairs, for a research project relating to emerging trading arrangements and the implications for national sovereignty (or something along those lines) and I arranged another project directly with PCO. While Pettigrew really did complete the papers, I am not sure that anyone paid much attention to them, since the whole purpose was to get him out in the public eye, speaking at events or on television, arguing the case for Canada. He was very helpful to us and always available when we asked.

Another contract we entered into in late 1994 was one with a professor of constitutional politics at l'Université de Montréal who had challenged in op-ed pieces some of the myths being perpetrated by the separatists. We wanted him to do more of this, and to prepare for us publishable material debunking the preposterous assertions of the PQ. His name was Stéphane Dion, and his intellectual rigour, his concise and sabre-like style of writing were tremendous in exposing the fraudulent premises and faulty conclusions in the separatist arguments. Dion's contributions were very valuable, even if in mid-1995 the PQ discovered that he was under contract to the federal government and attempted to use that fact to undermine him publicly.

Much later, once the unity storm had passed and the referendum won, Pettigrew and Dion were in January 1996 appointed to the Cabinet as Ministers for International Cooperation and Intergovernmental Affairs respectively. Their appointments to cabinet pre-dated by two months their election to the House of Commons in by-elections for safe liberal seats vacated by André Ouellet and the back-bencher Shirley Maheu. Dion would eventually run for and win the Liberal leadership and serve for a period as leader of the opposition to a Harper minority government, and Pettigrew would eventually serve as Minister of International Trade during the last years of my time as Ambassador to China, but again I am getting ahead of my story. Both Pettigrew and Dion were both highly capable and extremely intelligent spokesmen for the federalist cause, and it was too bad they had not been already in Cabinet in 1994 and 1995.

The first two months after the provincial election were not too busy for our team. We spent these early months of the "phoney war" completing our policy papers and "Argumentaires", working with CUC on "soft" campaign material, consulting with business and other groups in Québec and elsewhere, and generally getting ready for the real battle to be engaged. This left me able to slip away for five days to participate in an East-West Foundation meeting in Hawaii of G-7 experts on China, a meeting I had committed to a year earlier and which I had my old department's full support to attend. It was a great meeting, with Michel Oksenberg, Damien Wilkinson, Stapleton Roy, Christopher Hum, Bernie Frolic and a few others, mostly friends from past encounters. We had a great discussion and were wonderfully hosted by the Commander of the US Pacific Fleet, a post not yet taken up by Admiral Joe Prueher (then Deputy Commander of Fleet Operations, who was to show up in Beijing as US Ambassador in 1999). It was during my few days in Hawaii that I received news from my staff in Ottawa that Bloc Québécois leader Lucien Bouchard was at death's door with necrotizing fasciitis, a flesh-eating disease. Given Bouchard's popularity and his determination to destroy the country I loved and served, I wondered what the consequences would be if he were to die and become a martyr to the separatist cause. However, after amputation of one of his legs, he recovered and was to live to become a most dangerous opponent a year later.

Watching what was happening outside the immediate political arena was also important. One of my media team came to me one day and said that the Bank of Montreal had just launched a nationwide advertising campaign to encourage consumer borrowing. The television advertisements had clips of a young family buying a house or a car, or a young couple vacationing somewhere, after meeting a local and smiling BMO banker, always ending with the theme "Yes, It's possible", and in francophone media "Oui, C'est possible!". This was simply too subliminally supportive of what would be the "Oui" campaign of the separatists, so I called the Vice President in charge of government relations at the Bank and asked if I could come and see him. George Bothwell was a man already in his 60s and a very nice man, but when I explained that we wanted the whole campaign pulled from the airways, he was quite resistant, arguing at first that no one would mix up messages between a consumer lending program and a political campaign for the sovereignty of Québec. I disagreed, and finally he said he would take the matter to his Chairman, Matt Barrett. After a certain amount of groaning and complaining, they pulled the program. When I met with Barrett later when briefing the Business Council on National Issues, he told me that the cancelling the program had cost the bank almost ten million dollars!

We knew from the beginning of our planning that all strategic and tactical decisions of the year to come would not be for the federal government or the national Liberal party to take on their own, and all would require the full support of Daniel Johnson, leader of the PLQ and leader of the Opposition in the National Assembly. Johnson would, according to the Québec referendum law, automatically become official leader of the "No" Committee when the referendum was formally called. As in 1980, the

PLQ saw itself as very much the primary federalist actor in the sovereignty debate, saw the federal parties and the federal government as secondary players, and intended to take all the principal decisions itself.

One of the autumn processes in which I personally was involved (but which did not involve my group) was an effort between the federal and provincial liberal parties to develop what we called "l'énoncé politique commun". This "common political statement" was intended to ensure that the principal federalist political allies would not trip each other up on sensitive issues, particularly those relating to constitutional questions and Quebec's traditional demands for greater recognition and more decentralization. The document was also intended to eventually constitute an agreed draft for the "manifesto" of the No Committee, required by law to be circulated to electors along with the manifesto of the Yes Committee during the formal referendum campaign. Representing the federal liberal party were Serge Joyal, Eric Maldoff and Jean-Claude Villiard, Vice President International of SNC-Lavalin and an old friend of mine from my Asia days. On the provincial side there was Pierre Anctil, John Parisella, Stephan Bertrand and a couple of other irregulars. I provided an initial draft to the group and was a "silent" drafter, and participated in some but not all of their meetings.

Discussions on the text of this common position paper were never concluded, running aground on the fine-tuning of words attempting to pretend there were no differences between the two main federalist parties on the need for constitutional change and devolution. There was in fact a very big divide, with the PLQ believing in the need for further devolution of powers while the DNA of the federal liberals had since the 1960s been fundamentally centralist. I made an effort to bridge differences and tried to pull Maldoff and Joyal, both firmly of the Pelletier view that constitutional references should be avoided, towards a middle ground, suggesting references in the text to eventual constitutional change, some limits to the federal spending power and some nodding in the direction of recognizing Québec as a distinct society, all hot buttons for the provincial party. I also met privately on a couple of occasions with Pierre Anctil, trying to see where he might be flexible. In the end neither side was willing to compromise so early in the game, and contented themselves with putting an "almost agreed" text on the shelf until later in the campaign, along with an annex of themes to highlight and issues to avoid.

The biggest benefits of the discussions on the "énoncé" were a higher level of interpersonal confidence between the two parties, and also between me and party representatives, and a heightened awareness of the politically problematic issues near which we would have to tread very carefully as the referendum approached. Although the "almost agreed" text should have also been useful as a draft for the eventual manifesto, in the end this did not turn out to be the case.

L'Avant-Projet de Loi

In early December, the PQ launched its first attack, a frontal assault which had all the textbook prerequisites of great strategy. With the unveiling of the "Avant-projet de Loi" (a draft bill) on the sovereignty of Quebec, Mr. Parizeau also announced a huge consultative process that was aimed at mobilizing Quebec public opinion over the upcoming months, permitting the adoption of the bill by the National Assembly in the early spring and a referendum before the summer. The preparation of the strategy was an extremely well-kept secret, and neither the PLQ nor the federal Government had anticipated the process that the PQ unleashed.

The tabling of the draft bill in he National Assembly proved to be the first test of the federalist coalition. Within two hours of the tabling, consultations among the PMO, ourselves and the PLQ had taken place and a consensus reached that there should be no federalist participation in the commissions. Sensitivities were also quickly evident, however. Marcel Massé was the first politician to publicly dismiss the idea of participation, irritating the office of Daniel Johnson who felt that the PLQ should have been left to speak for the federalist coalition.

To counter the "Avant-projet" we prepared an annotated version of the proposed bill in a pamplet entitled "A Critical Look at the Draft Bill on Sovereignty", which we called our "livret-critique", debunking all of the false assertions in the proposed law. It was a very well prepared piece in which we took issue with all the major assertions of the PQ, from the claim that Québec would be able to participate in all the international organizations and benefit from the trade agreements that Canada was party to, to the preposterous guarantee that following a "yes" vote and a declaration of sovereignty the citizens of a new Québec would still have the option of using Canadian passports and using the Canadian currency. We also addressed the thorny issue of the territory of an independent Québec, which the proposed law asserted would be guaranteed as the existing territory of the province. We simply pointed out that the principle of democratic choice should be consistently applied and asked the question: "If Canada could be divided up, as the separatists claim, why wouldn't the same apply to Québec?" The reaction of federal liberals and provincial liberals to our pamphlet was dramatically different. The Prime Minister, Jean Pelletier, John Rae and Eddie Goldenberg all thought it was a terrific document and wanted it to be distributed quickly, well before the touring commissions began their work. Initially we proposed that it include a letter signed jointly by the Prime Minister, Daniel Johnson and Jean Charest, the new leader of the federal Progressive Conservative Party following the resignation of the humiliated Kim Campbell. Charest's name was axed by PMO even before being proposed to the Prime Minister, perhaps because there were still three federal by-elections to be held and suspicions of the Conservatives were still very much in vogue.

The reaction of Daniel Johnson and Pierre Anctil to the "livret-critique" was quite negative. To see in print questions being raised on territorial integrity and other sensitive matters challenged a traditional PLQ effort to "butter its bread on both sides". The PLQ shared the PQ approach to territorial integrity and to "optionality' on economic association. So Johnson sat on the pamphlet for a week without taking a final decision, and Anctil suggested it would be better if it was distributed over the signature of Chrétien alone. We proceeded to print three million copies and prepared to distribute the pamphlet to provincial households, just as the draft bill had been.

Consultations with the PLQ on the "Livret-critique" were a harbinger of difficulties to come. Although a number of senior people in the PLQ (John Parisella and Richard Vigneault, in particular) found our document to be of very high quality and a "good idea", the fact that we had produced it and the idea of a joint signature were both in the end anathema to the provincial party. Initially, the Prime Minister was quite keen to distribute the document in any case, and we revised the letter to have his signature alone. There was a limited time window of relevance, since we could not distribute the document if the commissions had completed their work and begun the preparation of recommendations to the PQ government on changes to the draft bill. Given the long lead times necessary for printing, we proceeded to do so and signed a contract with Canada Post for distribution even before talks with the PLQ had been completed. However, Johnson become even more nervous about the plan and called the Prime Minister to ask it not be distributed, and Chrétien, not wishing to create discord in the federalist ranks, reluctantly agreed to at least wait until we had a sense of what sort of separatist momentum the PQ's roving commissions were generating.

What does one do with three million copies of a pamphlet, the existence of which is supposed to be completely secret? When the decision whether or not to distribute them was under consideration, they had been loaded into 17 large Canada Post trucks ready to roll towards distribution centres throughout the province. Canada Post needed their trucks back quickly for ongoing business. As usual, Pierre Richard solved our problem, and stuck the brochures, all 260 tons of them, in the back of an underutilized federal warehouse, where they languished until after the referendum, and from which they eventually were quietly removed for destruction in November of 1995.

A further component of our proposed attack on the draft bill was complementary to the "Livret-critique", but not reliant on its distribution. This was a series of full-page advertisements in Quebec daily newspapers and in regional weeklies, raising the same questions about the same assumptions that the "Livret-critique" had been aimed at demolishing. Once again, although these were not negotiations carried out at the level of the Prime Minister, the PLQ refused to agree with our plans. They argued that the commissions were not working to mobilize public opinion and that there was no need to attack the draft bill. Some of us argued otherwise, suggesting that a vigorous attack could further erode separatist support. In the end we set aside our plans and left unused some really terrific publicity that was all prepared and ready for use. This pattern was to repeat itself a dozen or more times before October 30th.

Having made the decision not to participate in the touring commission process, we were faced with the challenge of how to counter whatever impact it might have. The challenge was simply to monitor the commissions, a substantial task given that there were fifteen regional commissions and two roving commissions covering the elderly and youth. We decided that the only practical way to follow what was going on was to "be there", and this we did via the CUC. It was, in spite of CUC front, an operation largely conceived of and equipped by our group in Ottawa, and we received thrice daily reports from observers (generally young federalists, drawn from party ranks or from university groups) who attended every public meeting of every commission. About two and a half weeks into the commissions' operation, the presence of these observers was unearthed by the press and the PQ, the latter in many instances attacking the observers as spies or worse. We advised the CUC to admit their existence and to do so without apology. This firm position quickly blunted criticism, and in some cases caused the attacks on the observers to publicly rebound against the commissioners. I argued over the ensuing months that this experience demonstrated that we had a greater margin of public maneuver in being visibly active in putting the federalist case forward, but neither I nor others pushing for a "pre-campaign" were successful.

Although our attack strategy was blunted by the PLQ during this period, we did proceed with some "positive" activity. An early opportunity presented itself in the 30th anniversary of the Canadian flag, a February date which we used as an excuse to blanket Quebec with flags. Of course we did so in the context of a pan-Canadian campaign, one in which we could honestly say that 70% of space purchased was outside of Quebec. What we conveniently forgot to mention (not the last time) was that the concentration of exposure and therefore a much higher proportion than 30% of cost was in fact in Quebec. Even this campaign was greeted with some discomfort by our PLQ friends, and they even had Johnson suggest to the Prime Minister that we not proceed. When it was clear that the campaign was in fact pan-Canadian and that we had no intention of backing down, they accepted the campaign with a minimum of grumbling. And there was no way that Prime Minister Chrétien would have ever accepted downplaying the Canadian flag.

The Good Months and Policy Changes

The early months of the new year were good months for the federalist camp. Parizeau's touring commissions generated little interest, and it turned out to have been a very good strategic decision of the federalist coalition not to participate in what was clearly a biased process. For the most part, people outside the big cities of Montreal and Québec, even if nationalist at heart, seemed more worried about their day-to-day lives and the state of the economy that winter than the PQ's "grand projet".

Throughout the winter and spring our private polling, as well as the publicized polls of the major houses of Leger & Leger, Environics and others, showed little change in the support for separation, with the federal option constantly somewhere in the mid-50s. During these months we met frequently with McGill sociology professor Maurice Pinard, who probably understood attitudes and voting patterns in the province better than anyone else, anywhere. Pinard helped design the questions posed in our polls and knew how not to bias answers; he analyzed the polls of others and explained how undecided voters would likely swing, and was in short an extremely valuable advisor.

The early months of the year were also relatively policy rich. During its first year in office, the Chrétien government began its effort to reduce the federal deficit, which had grown to almost $46 billion by 1993. The 1994 budget did announce some reductions and aimed at cutting the deficit from 6% of GDP to 3% over three years, and promised significant savings in departmental operating budgets but did not yet seriously tackle transfer payments to the provinces or to individuals, the largest areas of government spending. It was only after several months in office that Minister of Finance Paul Martin realized that much more serious spending cuts, and some tax increases, would have to be implemented if the deficit dragon was to be slayed. At the beginning of the budget cutting exercise, every Minister had to develop a plan on how to reduce spending in his or her area of responsibility by a given target. As a Deputy Secretary to the Cabinet, and given the number of issues that theoretically could impact the national unity file, Jean Pelletier encouraged me to attend relevant Cabinet Committee meetings and sometimes full Cabinet. Jocelyne Bourgon was not happy when I did but could hardly object when it was clear I was there with PMO blessing. There was one meeting which I attended where the focus was on the budget cuts. Finance Minister Paul Martin introduced the issue in general terms, stressing the seriousness of the deficit problem, and then one Minister after another tried to defend their budgets, arguing directly to the Prime Minister why cuts simply could not be born in the area of transport or industry or fisheries. When the Minister of Employment and Immigration, Lloyd Axworthy, stated that cuts to social programs would violate the most treasured liberal traditions, Martin responded that his father had introduced the programs in the Pearson government in the 1960s, and he had no difficulty with rolling them back. Chrétien then intervened and said very firmly that Martin's program had his full support and that the next Minister to argue against cuts in his or her department would be allocated a "double cut". No one raised another objection.

It was in the preparation of the 1995 budget, the Chrétien government's second, that we saw an opportunity to piggy-back on the deficit reduction program with some policy changes that would be supportive of the federalist cause in the upcoming referendum. Originally mooted over a series of Thursday morning breakfasts with Québec Ministers, Paul Martin's idea was to reduce the restrictions on the main education and social transfers to take some of the sting out of reducing them, and to transfer the responsibility of some other programs, such as manpower training, to the provinces as well. Aside from helping reduce the federal deficit, such measures would remove from the separatists their argument about intrusive federal powers. While the Québec Ministers were all very supportive of these measures, others were not. Axworthy particularly fought the changes and many senior public servants also saw federal involvement in manpower training and the existing structure of the Established Programs Financing (EPF, covering education, hospital insurance and medicare) and the Canada Assistance Plan (the CAP, primarily covering welfare) as sacrosanct, and viewed the end of conditionality as being the end of national standards. In the end the Cabinet moved ahead with the removal of conditionality, and combined the EPT and the CAP into a single program, called the Canada Health and Social Transfer, allowing provinces full freedom to allocate the funds according to provincial priorities and policies. This change was warmly welcomed by the Québec liberals and other Québec federalists, even though the government held back on the transfer of manpower training, a politically charged issue since the failure of the Meech Lake Accord.

The Storm Delayed

By late March, it was clear that the separatist cause was languishing. The touring commissions, the "États genéraux", had failed. Still unable to move public opinion from the rough 55%-45% split against sovereignty Parizeau and the Parti Québécois were looking for some way to move the needle.

At the political level, Minister Lucienne Robillard, who had taken over the Intergovernmental Affairs portfolio from Marcel Massé (who was moved to the normally more powerful but less political position of President of the Treasury Board) when she was brought into Cabinet early in the year, was intended to be the voice and face of the federal government for the referendum. We kept her regularly briefed on developments. She was very active in giving speeches and appearing on television, and was clearly a better "media" presence than Massé ever was or could have been. I met with Robillard frequently, sometimes in her constituency office in Montreal since she was not expected to spend a lot of time in the House of Commons, and we developed a reasonably close and effective relationship.

It was following the PQ decision to delay the referendum, that the deception that they were to try to impose on the people of the province was to deepen. A Leger & Leger poll in May suggested that if assured of economic and political association with the rest of Canada, the people of Québec would be more supportive of a "Yes" vote and probably narrowly carry the day, perhaps as much as 54% to 47%. As if they were not already in cahoots, the Parti Québécois and the Bloc Québécois, reached out to the third party of Québec provincial politics, l"Action Démocratique du Québec, to propose a three-party agreement on an approach to the referendum. In order to bring Mario Dumont on board, the main focus of the agreement was to define the intended partnership with the rest of Canada that would follow a declaration of sovereignty. And in a well-televised ceremony, Jacques Parizeau of the Parti Québécois, Lucien Bouchard of the Bloc Québécois and Mario Dumont of the Action Démocratique signed their "entente". The document spoke of free trade with the rest of Canada, the free movement of people and capital, common institutions, shared responsibility for defense and postal services and shared institutions for financial regulation and many other matters. It painted a very attractive picture for soft nationalists, with Québec being an equal partner to Canada in the shared management of every imaginable dimension of governance. The image was more or less a two-country equivalent to the EU. The fact that no one outside of Québec, and indeed no one inside of the province other than the three leaders of separatist parties, had agreed to any such arrangement was to be fudged right up until voting day at the end of October.

Following the signing of this rather strange tripartite "entente" between Parizeau, Bouchard and Dumont on June 12th, we started moving into higher gear in preparation of the war that we no longer had any illusions of avoiding.

In many ways we were already quite well prepared, as we had spent the previous few months ensuring that we had a real capacity to reach into all the regions in Québec and to connect with local PLC, PLQ and other federalist groups throughout the province. This was not as easy as I had originally anticipated, largely because neither of the liberal parties was well organized in many of the eastern and central regions, and they continued to exhibit their traditional suspicions of each other. But Pierre Richard, my head of operations and a former military officer, had organized warehouses and depots that we could use for the distribution of campaign material, and our group had established our own quiet but trustworthy relationships with many of the PLQ activists.

We had also prepared a large amount of public material for potential use, and I continued to argue that we should use it even well in advance of the formal launching of the referendum campaign. In this I was constantly frustrated and got no support from anyone. By this time I was rather used to the minimalist approach, and had come to the personal conclusion that my penchant for attacking was probably not always the best strategy in any case. I was still not happy, and we stockpiled brochures and posters and all sorts of material, even fearing then much of it might never be used. After the shelving of our counter brochure to the "avant-projet de loi", we had become somewhat inured to having material ready and not used, but I remained of the view that it was better this way than needing material and having nothing in hand. Although Jean Pelletier and Eddie Goldenberg had been generally supportive of a more active campaign, the Prime Minister's calm confidence in the ongoing strength of federalist support and his unwillingness to counter Daniel Johnson absent a truly grave crisis, stayed our hand. In spite of our desire to hit back at the separatist camp for every silly statement that one of their leaders was to make, it was evident that an offensive strategy was not always the best.

We were active in a number of other "soft sell" campaigns. From the late winter we had been working on and then airing television advertisements for various federal departments on the services that Canadians across the country benefit from, from search and rescue services of the coast guard, to food safety programs to health care support. We worked with several advertising agencies and creative teams in Montreal to produce these commercials, particularly with the advertising agency where John Parisella worked, BCP. John Rae, Michelle d'Auray and I would go over to the BCP offices and to see and approve mock-ups of the programs, which began airing in the late spring and ran right through the autumn. To pretend that they were not simply aimed at the referendum campaign in Québec, they were produced in both official languages, and we purchased time on television outside of the province as well as inside, but we aimed our purchases at prime time, or close, inside Québec while letting them air with less frequency and in quiet and less expensive times elsewhere.

At the same time, we did not stop preparing more direct and aggressive material. We stockpiled ideas, themes, and some potential visual campaign material. I kept up with my efforts with Anctil directly, and of course with Goldenberg and Pelletier, to try to persuade them to be more publicly pro-active and aggressive, especially after the June 12th "entente", but the fact that the polling numbers were not moving against us was constantly dressed out as a justification for inaction. The other argument that was made was that no Québecker wanted to be bombarded with propaganda during the summer when everyone would prefer to be at the lake or the beach, with the political debates put as far away as possible from their minds. All we actually did get agreement to use during this time were the "argumentaires" that were distributed through the CUC and the ongoing general advertising that was trying to improve public appreciation for federal government programs and services.

I do not believe that the carefully argued pamphlets of the CUC or the TV commercials hyping our search and rescue services or the value of having federally-established safety standards for babies' cribs earned the federalist cause a single vote.

The Lobster Pot

Then in late June a friend of mine in the Department of Foreign Affairs and International Trade told me that Jacques Parizeau had said some very explosive things to a foreign diplomat about PQ intentions. With a little digging, I obtained a copy of a memorandum written by a senior departmental officer following a discussion with the Ambassador concerned, who turned out to be the Belgian, in which Parizeau compared the referendum process to a lobster pot, in which once the victim was inside, he could never get out. This frank admission of a one-way street and the crude and uncomplimentary comparison of the Québec people to a stupid crustacean was too good to let go by.

However, I had a real dilemma in deciding what to do with the "lobster" memorandum.

My relations with Jocelyne Bourgon, the Clerk of the Privy Council, had never recovered from the lows of a period six or so months earlier when my frustration with her approach to our work, and what she saw was my lack of respect for her authority, had resulted in her efforts to curtail my authority and independence and eventually her efforts to have me replaced. In fact, my dear friend Ronald Bilodeau, who was simultaneously Deputy Minister for Intergovernmental Affairs to Marcel Massé and Associate Clerk, and I used to laugh about this often, saying that any unity team was bound to be dismissed after only a few months and that then at least I, if not he, could go off to do something more fun like being named Ambassador to Botswana. Bourgon was never happy with any material that did not grow out of her own intellectual framework, all very Cartesian in logic, and always wished to have the final word in what was shown to or discussed with the Prime Minister. This, of course, was impossible in what was essentially a political process, and both the senior members of the PMO and sometimes the Prime Minister himself insisted on dealing with me on all sorts of matters, from polling plans to analyses to campaign material. This frustrated Bourgon, and at one point she told me categorically that I was to no longer attend preparatory meetings in Montreal with the PLQ and PLC, and that all material, even draft CUC "argumentaires" was to go through her office. The Prime Minister's Chief of Staff and the consummate gentleman, Jean Pelletier, gently over-rode her. I continued to go to Montreal and my role as primary governmental representative at political meetings, and eventually in the war-room during the referendum, was never undermined.

But, to return to the "lobster" story, I knew that there was no way that I could get Bourgon's agreement to do anything with a confidential memorandum. I also knew that Pierre Anctil and Daniel Johnson would also never agree to leaking the lobster story. I and some of the federal liberal party members of our coalition felt that Johnson was almost sleepwalking he was agreeing to so little, and both he and Anctil had shown themselves unwilling to challenge some of the traditional "have your cake and eat it too" positions of the PLQ. This was driven home to us hard when, based on polling done for us under the oversight of Maurice Pinard, we showed that we could immediately reduce by eight or nine percent the intention to vote "Yes" if we encouraged a public airing of the divisibility of Québec. If the democratic principle established that Canada was in theory divisible, the same principle should apply to Québec, and thus areas like the island of Montreal or the entire northern part of the province could opt to remain in Canada, if majorities there voted not to support separation. The argument was in part founded on the fact that the province of Québec in its modern form was in fact a creation of the federal parliament, which added in 1898 and 1912 large tracts of additional northern territory bought by the federal government from the Hudson's Bay Company to a previously quite small province. Matthew Coon Come, Grand Chief of the Cree Nation and a trained lawyer with a degree from McGill, was very firm on subordinating the divisibility principle to Québec since his people and other First Nations strongly opposed the sovereignty movement (Northern Québec eventually voted more than 98% "No" in the October referendum). In the end Matthew Coon Come was the only person who spoke publicly during 1995 about the divisibility of Québec because the PLQ was adamantly opposed to the issue being introduced into the campaign. The imbalanced possibility of multiple referenda on sovereignty as long as the "No" side continued to win, compared to the definitive and irreversible decision if the "Yes" side were ever to win, was another taboo theme.

So I took my "lobster" story to Eddie Goldenberg, and we agreed that I should take steps to ensure it became public but that we would not discuss it with anyone else on either the political or bureaucratic side of government. I ensured that copies were delivered to a number of journalists. I made one small error in doing this. I had the copies sent to media organizations in envelopes of my old department, thinking that journalists would assume that the leak was from some DFAIT official who had spoken to the Ambassador, but the envelopes I used were those of the "Department of External Affairs and International Trade" rather than its newer name of the "Department of Foreign Affairs and International Trade". After the story had broken, one journalist surmised that I was the source, and used the envelopes having had a stash of old envelopes lying around my house; this was absolutely true, but no one picked up the speculation to try to confirm the story! Even though I knew that the damning memorandum started to circulate among senior members of the French language TV network of Radio Canada, they did nothing with it until Chantal Hébert broke the story in La Presse. It was a great coup and Parizeau was publicly undermined when it appeared in early July.

For some reason, Jocelyne Bourgon was incensed over the leaking of the lobster memorandum and she decided to initiate an enquiry as to how it got into the public domain. She asked me to come to her office and grilled me about it, but I neither admitted to being its source nor lied directly. I think she probably concluded that I was in fact behind the caper, but could find no smoking gun and, as the PMO seemed rather pleased with the impact of the whole affair, she gradually if not gracefully let it drop.

My team was delighted by the lobster affair; it clearly embarrassed Parizeau and was unquestionably a goal for the federalist camp. My team even prepared bumper stickers with bright red lobsters on them that said "Si c'est Oui, On est Cuit" and tried to persuade our friends in the PLQ to distribute them. Some eventually filtered out into the public along with other creative bumper stickers Renée Brunet and others had come up with, and when I left the PCO in early 1996, Stéphane Dion and my team gave me a poster with a picture of me as a lobster as my going away present. There was "Si c'est Oui, On est Cuit" and the name "Homard Balloch" ("homard' being the French word for lobster) printed on it, with everyone's signatures and personal wishes on the borders and underneath. (Later it always hung on my office wall in China, first at the Embassy and then in my own company, and my Chinese visitors would look curiously at it but of course never understood what it was about.)

Strained Relations in the PCO

The lobster affair did not do anything to improve my relationship with Bourgon over the coming weeks, and I found it increasingly uncomfortable and rarely productive to attend the morning "Operations Committee" meeting she held of senior PCO officials. Whenever I could I got Marc

Lafrenière to attend on my behalf. Marc was a fine man and consummate professional who had been assigned to the unity team largely to "control" me on behalf of the Clerk, but who turned out to be a great and cooperative colleague. I could not always get away with this, however, and I still had to go to more of these morning meetings than I wanted to. I had taken a very brief and not very relaxed week-long vacation in early August (much to the frustration of my family, I had installed two extra lines and a secure telephone at our summer house in Jamestown, Rhode Island, and spent much of my time on the telephone to Ottawa or Montreal) and was back on the job by mid-month. Marc Lafrenière then took his holidays and I was thus more or less forced to attend the more morning meetings until he returned in early September.

On September 11th, Parizeau stated that the referendum would be held before the end of October, although the formal launch of the campaign did not happen until October 2nd. We had actually moved to a war footing on the day after Labour Day, September 5th. From that time forward, the Unity Group would meet every morning at 0600 to review overnight press and the day ahead, and would prepare reports for the Prime Minister and the War Room in Montreal, which had its own morning meeting which started around 0730. How we functioned during this time, when I was some mornings in Ottawa and some mornings in Montreal, I will describe in the following section on the referendum campaign itself.

There were a lot of other issues on the government's and therefore the PCO's agenda other than unity at this time, and luckily Bourgon did not seem too preoccupied with my files. Although the Damocles sword of the referendum was clearly hanging over everyone's head, there were a whole series of very important economic issues also under consideration, not the least of which was a reform of the national program of unemployment insurance, and there had been much internal bickering in government as a result of a big clash between Lloyd Axworthy and Brian Tobin which had begun at a Cabinet retreat in late June. There was also a Premiers' Meeting in the late summer, which of course Parizeau boycotted, to focus primarily on social security reform but which in fact also had a strong behind-the-scenes unity agenda. We had made a huge effort to ensure all the Premiers in provinces other than Québec were kept up-to-date with our strategy and our analysis and how they could help by dampening any anti-Québec sentiment in their own provinces as part of our "Keep Canada Cool" agenda, and they were all very supportive and as helpful as they could be.

It was during this late summer period that I first became aware of the infamous "Airbus" airfare, in which former Prime Minister Brian Mulroney was accused of receiving illegal kickbacks from an Air Canada purchase of aircraft from the European consortium, sometime in the late 1980s. Although I was never involved in the discussions on this matter, I remember at first wondering what was going on when Jocelyne Bourgon and Margaret Bloodworth, who as Deputy Secretary for Security and Intelligence covered RCMP matters, first started referring obliquely to an explosive matter that they were working on. I subsequently learned that it involved allegations against Prime Minister Mulroney, and there was much discussion about the preparation of a letter that either Justice or the RCMP was apparently working on. This was later to turn out to be the famous accusatory letter sent to the Swiss Government later in September, which asked their cooperation in searching for evidence that might implicate Mulroney and the former Newfoundland politician Frank Moores. Mary Dawson, Associate Deputy Minister at the Department of Justice, was clearly the bureaucrat running the file, and she was regularly present in the Langevin Block for meetings on this and other matters. By a certain point in this period, it became apparent that her Minister, Allan Rock, was well apprised of the file, and I presumed from the substantial attention that she was paying to the matter that, as Clerk, Jocelyne Bourgon must have been keeping the PMO aware of it as well. I remember being amazed and incredulous at the apparent allegations being made, but as I was never briefed about the details or the reasons for them, and mostly because my unity world was about to explode, I did not think much further about what I had observed until after the scandal broke late in the year, well after the referendum was over. What was then extraordinary to me was that Bourgon claimed that neither she nor any senior Justice Department officials were aware of the letter before it was sent.

It was during the summer that I made up my mind on a number of personal matters. I decided that I would of course continue doing everything I could to ensure that we won the referendum. I decided, however, that I would do so by making every decision that seemed helpful to our cause and ignore any potential impact my bureaucratic career. I had no idea at this point that I might be offered the position of Ambassador to China. When I moved to PCO, I had formally cut my ties with my old department, and my wife Liani and I had already come to the conclusion that getting into the diplomatic appointments sweepstakes and ending up in some mind-numbing quiet capital somewhere was not for us. Besides, although John Paynter was very ill with cancer, he was still the serving Ambassador, and I had spoken to him sometime in mid-summer to offer him moral support and my best wishes. He had sounded very upbeat and I concluded that he might just beat the devil and go back to Beijing where he would have done a great job.

In fact, what I decided I would do was pick up the threads that I had begun to weave in late 1993 and see if I could not land a good position in corporate Canada. I planned to call on Jacques Bougie of Alcan. He had reiterated his interest in talking to me in May when I saw him at a briefing of the BCNI, even if the specific job I had been considered for two years earlier was no longer available. During the referendum preparation and campaign, I had also met many other corporate leaders, so I thought my network was extensive enough to get a decent job search going.

What led me to conclude that the time had come to leave government was a growing disillusion with the process of decision-making in the government, and my realization that I could not work Jocelyne Bourgon and her lieutenants, some of who had appeared to do everything possible to undermine me during my early months at PCO. I had enormous respect for most of my PCO colleagues, like Ronald Bilodeau and Gary Breen, who was also to shortly leave government as well, and for most of the senior people in the Ottawa bureaucracy. But I was simply growing tired of the careerism and the pettiness which seemed to have infected the Bourgon regime, and I was tired of the intellectual dishonesty of the preoccupation with political correctness and appearance that I felt was taking over. I wondered what had happened to the great Clerks of the past, like Paul Tellier, Gordon Osbaldeston, and Michael Pitfield of my time in government, or the earlier and legendary Gordon Robertson and Arnold Heeney. These were individuals of tremendous intellect who had inspired a deep commitment to Canada and to public service, not just in the PCO but also more broadly across the public service. In their time, senior public servants were built up to be parallels to their political masters, as smart or smarter and committed to help the ministers in power to translate their vision for the country into a practical reality constructed in a fabric of policies and programs. Now it was clear that it was all about careerism, being sure that one could not be criticized, and at the same time trying always to be centre stage at the expense of subordinates. Bourgon's efforts to prevent other senior public servants establishing direct and strong relationships with the Prime Minister seemed almost paranoid to me. Meanwhile, I decided to give my all for the next few months and then get out, not knowing then how tough the referendum autumn would turn out to be or that it would be another six years before I finally made my way to the private sector. But I am getting ahead of myself, for there was still the formal campaign and the referendum to get through before I would have enough time to think for more than an occasional nano-second about my next job.

CHAPTER 15

THE BATTLE FOR CANADA

• • • • • • • • • • •

From Labour Day on we were in full war mode. A "War-Room" was formed in an office on Rue St. Denis in Montreal, where daily meetings and strategy sessions took place. Pierre Anctil would generally preside, although on occasion Daniel Johnson himself came. Martial Fillion was the PLQ person in charge of media and the preparation of daily "messages" and media lines, and we worked with him a lot. A mixed team of regional organizers from the PLQ and the regionally weaker federal liberals were regularly in attendance, as were representatives from both the federal conservatives. Denis Coderre, later to become a federal MP and Minister, ran the regional organization of the federal liberals and was in the war-room on a daily basis. Pierre-Claude Nolin was normally present on behalf of Jean Charest, leader of the Progressive Conservatives, and the federal liberals had a rotating representation from Jean Pelletier to Eddie Goldenberg and John Rae. I was the only non-political person permitted in the War-Room, and although Jocelyne Bourgon thought my involvement improper for an official, Jean Pelletier, who attended more often by telephone than in person, insisted on my involvement. When I attended by person, my driver Don would pick me up at 0430 at home and we would tear down to Montreal in time for the meeting, after which I would generally tear back to Ottawa. For us there was no speed limit on the 417.

Now no longer attending the Clerk's daily operations meetings, which Marc Lafrenière attended on the Unity Group's behalf, I was focused exclusively on the war in which we were engaged. The real daily kick-off meetings for me were an internal meeting of my group at 0600, attended in person or by telephone, followed by the Montreal War-Room meetings which began at either 0630 or 0700. I would attend one in person and the other by telephone, and if I was physically in Ottawa, I would generally be with Jean Pelletier and Eddie Goldberg in the PMO and the three of us would attend by telephone. Most mornings at 1000 or 1030, Eddie and I and Patrick Parisot, the Prime Minister's Press Secretary and speechwriter, would also meet to review the issues of the day and to prepare press lines for the PM, which in fact he really did not need, but as these guided the comments of any other Cabinet Minister approached by the press during the day, the meetings and press lines were useful.

Even before Parizeau kicked off the formal campaign, it was very evident that the preparation of campaign material by the PLQ would be hopelessly inadequate for the actual town-by-town battle that was to ensue. After consulting with John Ray and Jean Pelletier, I moved Michelle d'Auray and Renée Brunet to Montreal to take charge of material production, and I moved Pierre Richard down to effectively run the logistical support systems for federalist forces.

In the latter half of September, the Prime Minister travelled to New York to speak at the General Assembly of the United Nations, leaving he thought a relatively manageable national unity file for a few days. As the House was in session, Deputy Prime Minister Sheila Copps was Acting Prime Minister, which meant that I and other senior officials would brief her prior to Question Period. Copps was a tough, very self-confidant and experienced politician who had cut her teeth as part of the "Rat Pack" of aggressive liberal parliamentarians during the Mulroney years. Because she spoke reasonable French, she believed that her voice was credible in the strange ether of Québec politics, while in fact she came out almost unrecognized among federal ministers when we polled to measure which federalist voices were respected in the province. In the very first pre-QP briefing session after the PM had headed off to New York, she interrupted my suggestion as to how she should consider answering a potential question from Lucien Bouchard, who was it must be remembered the Leader of Her Majesty's Loyal Opposition and therefore had priority in challenging the government. She dismissed my suggestion that she should respond with a simple answer and avoid any confrontation, and simply said: "I am acting Prime Minister and I shall decide how to deal with Bouchard". Immediately after the briefing I called Jean Pelletier to warn him of my worry that Copps could create an incident in the House that could be used by the PQ to show that English Canada was moving into a confrontation mode. Pelletier intervened privately with Copps and she was duly circumspect during Question Period and caused none of us any anxiety in the days that the PM was away.

Throughout every day and all through every night, all Québec media was monitored and summaries were prepared by 0600 every day. Because our team in Ottawa was better equipped to monitor the media, we provided this service, sending daily reports to Montreal electronically in time for them to be printed. A year earlier we had established at our offices at 66 Slater Street a very sophisticated media monitoring capability, and even had a laser receiver on the roof to interconnect via line of sight with a re-broadcast unit in Hull that collected every television and radio station in the province. Our media team alone was 15 or 20 strong and was manned 24 hours a day.

For a while, everything seemed to be on track for a clear federalist victory. Parizeau did not seem to be able to electrify the province with his campaigning, and the polls remained a few points in our favour. On the hustings in Québec, Daniel Johnson, Liza Frulla and Lucienne Robillard were all very active, the Prime Minister gave a speech in Shawinigan, and all seemed well with the world.

At the beginning of the formal referendum campaign, the "Comité pour le Non" was supposed to submit to the Directeur général des Elections a "manifesto" that would be published along with the manifesto of the "Comité pour le Oui" and distributed to every household in Québec. The first draft was prepared by Pierre Anctil and a group of advisors to Daniel Johnson and then shared with Eric Maldoff, who had been named to represent the federal Liberal party in the drafting process. Eric sent copies to Eddie Goldenberg and to me. We were all aghast at the initial draft, which was dry and unemotional, and managed to avoid entirely any reference to Canada. We eventually managed to get the word "Canada" into the document in a couple of places, but it was an uninspiring manifesto at best, and showed clearly the equivocal attitude towards unity held by some of those around Daniel Johnson.

Family life throughout the autumn was not easy to keep in balance, but I tried my best. I would almost always be up and out of the house long before the children were awake, but I would try to take a break in the early evening to go home for supper. After a family meal and sometimes a little homework help or reading, I would head back into the office.

Right throughout September public support for the "Yes" option was stuck below the 50% level, and by early October the separatist camp was desperate. Apparently at the encouragement of his Chief of Staff Jean-François Lisée, on October 7th Parizeau agreed to name Lucien Bouchard as "Négociateur en Chef", in charge of negotiating the terms of economic and political association with the rest of Canada following a victory in the referendum. The result gave credibility to the concept that economic association would be easy to achieve following a successful declaration of independence, and there was an immediate surge in support for the "Yes" side, moving up to 53% in the space of two days.

The federalist camp basically went into panic mode. Every effort to attack the credibility of Bouchard and the tantalizing promise of independence with all the benefits of remaining in Canada seemed to fail. When Bouchard gave a speech lamenting the infertility of Québec women of the "white race", we thought he had opened a huge vulnerability. Both Liza Frulla and Lucienne Robillard responded publicly, condemning both the misogynous and racist implications of the remark. But their response had no impact, and support for the separatist cause continued to rise. Inside my group we brainstormed about all sorts of tactics that might change the dynamics of the campaign in a way that would permit the federalist forces to regain the momentum. Some were downright fanciful, such as the naming of Progressive Conservative leader Jean Charest to the federal cabinet as Minister for Constitutional Affairs. Charest was popular in Québec and the more I thought about it the more I thought the idea of bringing him into a sort of National Unity Cabinet might well short-circuit the Bouchard phenomenon. I took the idea to Jean Pelletier, complete with a draft press release that could be used to announce the appointment. Pelletier thought about it very carefully for several minutes before answering me, and instead of turning it down as idiotic simply put the draft in his drawer and said "peut-être, mais pas maintenant".

It was at this point that Prime Minister Chrétien decided that he could no longer play second fiddle to Daniel Johnson, and we moved to crisis mode to figure out what might be done to reverse the separatist surge. At a Cabinet meeting during the second week of the month, the populist Minister of Fisheries, Brian Tobin, presented a plan to garner coast-to-coast support for a giant federalist rally in Montreal just before the referendum, which quickly took on an unstoppable life of its own. I had no strong views on whether the concept was a good idea or not, but I was cautioned when I called John Rae to tell him of the proposal. John said to me that he would never embark on such an event only days before the referendum because the media treatment and the impact on the electorate was simply too unpredictable and therefore potentially dangerous. It was, however, an idea that appealed deeply to many in the Cabinet and Caucus, and indeed to citizenry from Newfoundland to British Columbia, all of whom had felt that their voices and their love for a Canada with Québec as an integral part, had been ignored in the referendum campaign and could only serve as a positive force for the "No" vote on October 30th.

With the "Canada Rally" fixed for Friday the 27th of October, we then focused on how the Prime Minister might engage more directly in the campaign to help stop the separatist tidal wave. It was decided that he would give a major speech at an already planned "No" campaign event in

Verdun on Tuesday, the 24th, focused on trying to underscore to Québécois that a vote opposing the referendum would not in fact be for the status quo and that real change was possible within the current federal structure. This would be followed by a speech to the nation on country-wide television on Wednesday night where the major focus would be a sobering message to Québécois on what they were putting at risk, and on the lies that they were being told by the separatist leaders.

As soon as it was decided to proceed with the "Canada Rally" on the 27th, it seemed as if the whole country was going to get in on the act. Brian Tobin was indefatigable, calling business leaders and provincial Premiers. Before we knew it, Canadian Airlines was offering a 90% discount on flights to Montreal from anywhere in the country, VIA Rail was offering half price fares, bus companies were offering free rides from all over Ontario and New Brunswick.

Once the general strategy for the last ten days of the campaign was set, all that was left was to implement it, a task of enormous dimensions. Apart from helping ensure that banners and other campaign material was available for the Verdun event, my team by necessity had to focus on the huge logistical challenges posed by the giant rally planned for Dominion Square at the centre of Montreal on the Friday. I personally had a chance to comment on drafts of the Prime Minister's speeches for the Verdun event and the televised address of Wednesday, both written by Eddie Goldenberg and Patrick Parisot, and was part of the PMO and war-room planning for the final ten days, but everyone else had to focus on the big rally on Friday.

Ten days before the vote, the United Nations held its fiftieth anniversary celebration in New York and the Prime Minister, partly in an effort to demonstrate confidence and draw attention to the important role Canada continued to play on the world stage, decided to participate. On Saturday, October 21st, we had a major meeting at the war-room on Rue St. Denis to refine the plan for the Verdun rally and other events. Eddie Goldenberg and Patrick Parisot were both there, while Jean Pelletier had gone to New

York with Chrétien. After the strategy session I headed back to Ottawa and Eddie and Patrick stayed behind to write the speeches that Chrétien would use on Tuesday and Wednesday. I listened to Radio Canada on the drive and heard in a news report something about Daniel Johnson commenting on constitutional change after the referendum. This was clearly off script, but I didn't think too much more about it. Unfortunately, a journalist in the Prime Minister's entourage in New York picked up on the remark and asked Chrétien if he was contemplating constitutional change following a "No" victory, and the Prime Minister answered instantly and definitively in the negative. So on Sunday all the Québec media were reporting that Chrétien had contradicted Johnson and that there was disagreement and disarray in the federalist camp.

On Sunday afternoon we had a conference call to assess the damage. Goldenberg said that he had met with Johnson, who had said that his remark about constitutional change was taken out of context and that he was sorry he had made it, but we all agreed that no further staking of the fire was smart and the best thing was to simply focus on the key messaging for the week ahead, recognizing that the rally in Verdun was a truly critical event.

The rally in Verdun turned out to be fabulous. It was held in an arena slightly too small for the crowd, so on television it looked like the level of support was overflowing what had been anticipated. We had organized lots of banners and both Québec and Canadian flags were everywhere, aimed at reinforcing the federalist message that a proud Québécois could also be a proud Canadian. The Prime Minister's speech was nothing short of brilliant, and it was delivered with confidence, commitment and a style that was uniquely Chrétien's. It promised a recognition of Québec as a distinct society, since the failure of the Meech Lake Accord a deeply emotive issue across the province, and contained a commitment to make no constitutional changes affecting Québec without the agreement of Québec, and to continue bringing decisions and services closer to the people, implying a sustained movement to delegate more powers to the provincial level. The speech was not appreciated among Ottawa centralists, but it was very well received in Québec and it seemed to act as a needle pricking the balloon of support for the "Yes" forces. Overnight polling conducted for us privately finally had the federalist option again in the majority. Bouchard and other separatist spokespeople fumed and accused Chrétien of misleading the people, but the tide had been reversed, and for the first time in weeks we started to feel that victory might well be within our reach.

Given the success of the Verdun speech, the Prime Minister's live television speech to the nation the following night turned out to be rather anti-climactic. Textually it was a deeply thoughtful appeal to Québécois and others on the real risks being posed to their future and to their country, and it was very well written. It was a vintage Parisot piece of work, repeating key messages very clearly, and underscoring the seriousness of the issue at hand. In delivery, Chrétien spoke to Canadians right across the country while posing a series of questions directly to the people of Québec, the last one being "Do you really think it makes any sense, any sense at all, to break up Canada?" The Prime Minister was quite tired by Wednesday and had been persuaded to use a teleprompter so that he could be seen to be looking directly at his audience as he posed these critical questions. In our pre-briefing session someone had recommended that Chrétien keep the text of the speech in front of him, and change pages from time to time as he proceeded through the speech, in order to calm his continuously busy hands. (I remember briefing him on all kinds of matters when the only sign that he was listening was him constantly rubbing his thumb and his forefinger together.) On this Wednesday night, the result (bad advice on our behalf) was a wooden presentation, with him changing and reshuffling the written text at illogical moments. But no harm was done, and Lucien Bouchard's response, for which he had a right as Leader of the Opposition, did not have much of an impact either. Our polling simply suggested that the slim majority won from the Verdun speech was still secure.

On to Friday.

On Wednesday afternoon I received a call from Jocelyn Beaudoin of the Conseil pour l'Unité Canadienne that the organizers of the Friday rally could not find any more Québec flags, and that he was concerned that if the only flags visible during the rally were Canadian flags the public impression in Québec could be that it was simply a massive anglophone event, trying to tell Québécois how to vote. I called Pierre Richard and Michelle d'Auray and put them to work to find more flags, and was assured that there would be no problem. A flag maker in North Bay, Ontario, was found and agreed to keep his production line open non-stop to produce 5,000 Québec flags that we could distribute in advance of the rally, thus ensuring a sea of blue and red and not just a sea of red. The flags would be delivered, we were promised, on Thursday evening. Problem solved. Or so we thought.

Late on Thursday evening, our organizers in Montreal were telling us that the flags had not arrived. We could not reach the North Bay manufacturer, who had apparently left at some point during the day to drive his truck full of flags himself to Montreal. As the hours went by, we became more and more worried until at about two o'clock in the morning he finally arrived. What had happened was that as he crossed into Québec from Ontario, he suddenly realized that every flag had his company's small label with "Made in Ontario" sewn into the seam. Realizing that the provenance of the flags could be politically damaging, he stopped the truck by the side of the road and with his driving companion removed by hand the label from each of the 5000 flags!

From Thursday afternoon onwards, people poured into Montreal. And the rally itself turned out to be fantastic, with tens of thousands of people from outside the province joining hundreds of thousands local Montrealers and other Québécois in Dominion Square. The day was a beautiful late autumn day with a clear blue sky and a light wind. A giant Canadian flag, maybe 40 metres by 20 metres and brought from Windsor, was passed from hand to hand over the heads of the crowd. Daniel Johnson, Jean Chrétien and Jean Charest gave the keynote speeches, and stood hand-in-hand on the podium. (I still have a signed photograph of the three of them that Chrétien gave to me a month or two later.) And then it ended with the entire crowd singing the national anthem.

No one really knows exactly how many people attended the rally. We did our best (with some expert help) to analyze the television shots of the crowd and also the transportation statistics. In the end we estimated that some 35,000 had probably come in from outside the province, and that there were at least 250,000 people in the square. People who attended all felt that the rally had been a tremendous success, some compare the experience as generationally uplifting, as iconic for them as Woodstock was for the young of the 1960s.

The sad thing about the Canada Rally is that it really did not help the federalist cause. Overnight polling (we were polling virtually around the clock at this stage) showed support for "Oui" back on top. We figured that this was probably because of the very biased way French language television covered the rally, most presenting it as English speaking Canadians telling Québécois what to do. Even Radio Canada, which was full of not very quiet separatists, under-reported the number of locals at the rally, and spent more than half its evening coverage on an almost certainly staged confrontation between a separatist and a federalist. John Rae had been correct; the event was too late in the campaign to be without risk. Newspaper and radio coverage of the rally was more balanced than that of television, and by late Saturday afternoon the polls were back in balance, but unfortunately there was another rally planned for Sunday, this one in Hull. We were all very worried, but there was at this stage not much we could do except to ensure that the rally looked as francophone and as "blue" as possible.

Sunday was another beautiful day in Ottawa, and I decided to take our children with me across the river to the rally in Hull. For them it was quite an experience and a lot of fun. The event got the same sort of coverage on Québec television as had Friday's Canada Rally, however, and by the evening the polls were looking grim again. This was the only time in my entire governmental career that I lied outright to a Prime Minister. Chrétien called me late that evening and asked me how the polls were looking, and I told him that we had no results, as we had stopped polling due to high levels of refusals to participate and uninterpretable data as we were simply too close to the vote the next day. While we had not stopped polling, some of what I told Chretien was probably true. We were seeing a substantial resurgence in "Oui" support, which the actual results the following day showed was either not real or not sustained. But I saw no benefit in telling Chrétien that the outlook on that Sunday night was as gloomy as it was. I saw only downside in adding to his existing anxiety and having him ending up looking rattled when the media focused on him the following morning, referendum day.

The actual day of voting was quite quiet for my Ottawa team. But the waiting was itself enormously stressful, and I could feel the tension in my back all day. The main focus of the Montreal team was to ensure at the local level throughout the province that federalists went out and voted. Unlike a national or provincial election, which are won riding by riding, the referendum would be won on the basis of total province-wide votes, so every federalist vote counted whether or not it was a lonely vote in a very separatist area in Saint-Jean or one of a large majority in suburban Montreal or Northern Québec. In the end the turnout was very high. The results began to be counted after eight in the evening and I watched the televised results come in first from our office on Slater Street to be with my team, and then moved over to the Langevin Block to watch it with friends in the PMO. The early results from the eastern part of the province were not as bad as we had feared and by about nine o'clock we were beginning to fell that things were OK. The results from the island of Montreal were closer than we had hoped for, and it really was not clear which way the vote would end, but by ten o'clock we realized that we would win. The relief was enormous. That it was very close was a disappointment, but it was a win nonetheless. We were to learn over the coming days that had it not been for extensive electoral fraud in Chomedey and two other ridings, we probably would have won by at least another two or three percent.

A day or two after the referendum, Prime Minister Chrétien asked me to come and see him, and when I went to his office he received me alone, which was rare. We chatted for a little while about the referendum and the unity issue, and then he turned the conversation to my future. He asked me whether I would like to continue working in the PCO on unity matters, as there was now a long agenda of issues to deal with following the promises made during the campaign, and a new Cabinet Committee to support to deal with them. Before I could answer he added that he was also considering nominating me as Ambassador to China.

The offer of China was not a complete surprise, although it had been such a long shot I had parked it well back in the recesses of my mind. Sometime in the late summer, my friend Senator Jack Austin, President of the Canada China Business Council, had invited me out to lunch. I was very busy and agreed to meet him for a quick bite. We talked about China and Jack asked me almost in passing whether I would ever be interested in serving as Ambassador to China. He told me that there was another name in play, with the support of Foreign Minister André Ouellet, but the business community was not happy with the candidate being proposed as he was viewed as being quite uninterested in business interests. I told Jack that of course I would be honoured to be considered, but that I thought it quite unlikely that the Prime Minister would turn down a recommendation from Ouellet, and that in any case there was no way I could think about my next move until after the referendum. During the autumn, the Ottawa rumour mill had more or less confirmed that the Ouellet nominee was about to be named Ambassador, which meant that I had simply stopped idly speculating about a return to diplomacy.

To Chrétien's offer of the ambassadorial nomination, I responded immediately and without hesitation that I would be honoured to go to China, and that in no case did I see myself remaining in the PCO. He then said to me that I had better go and speak with André Ouellet, who was not very happy at having his preferred candidate passed over. The following morning I did so, and Ouellet, with whom I had spent an enormous amount of time over the past many months, was in fact gracious and encouraging, but did say that he thought my lack of Chinese would be a handicap, and that I should make a huge effort me to get as much language training under my belt as I could before I moved to Beijing.

It was in fact a full two months more before the PCO chapter in my life was to come to an end, for there was the new Cabinet Committee to support, my team to wind down and a lot of loose ends to tie up, like disposing of the three million copies of the unused brochure on the "avant-projet de loi' from a year earlier. But the pressure was gone, and soon so too was I.

HRB talking with President Jiang Zemin after presenting credentials,
April 1996

The Mongolian Guard of Honour prior to presenting credentials in the Great
Khural in Ulaan Baatar, 1996

HRB with Foreign Minister Qian Qichen, 1996

HRB with President Jiang Zemin and Qian Qichen looking on, at departure
for 1997 State Visit to Canada

Premier Lucien Bouchard and Trade Minister Wu Yi during the controversial
Mission Québec in late 1997

Front Row: Vice Foreign Minister Li Zhaoxing, HRB,
Bank of China Chairman Wang Xuebing (later jailed for corruption)
Pierre Trudeau and President Jiang Zemin

Last visit to China of Pierre Trudeau, with law partner Roy Heenan and
George Bothwell of the Bank of Montreal

The Balloch boys with then General Manager, later Chairman,
Lu Youmei, of the Three Gorges project

At artisan cooperative, which made traditional boots and blankets,
in Gyantse, Tibet, summer 1997

The Prime Minister thanking Embassy staff for their support for his visit

Prime Minister at Fengdeng village in desperately poor Gansu,
site of Canada Fund water project

Jean Chrétien and the Balloch family, without daughter Cynthia who was
away at boarding school, November 1998

With long-time friend Bo Xilai
long before his fall from power

With family in chilly
Harbin, winter 1999

Caleb on board HMCS Vancouver as we
approach the military dock in Shanghai

Liani and other Ambassadorial
spouses singing at 1999 CCTV
Chinese New Year Gala Concert

PLA missile battalion during the
parade for the 50th anniversary of
the founding of the PRC

HRB and counterpart Ambassador Mei Ping signing agreements
in front of not-very-happy Zhu Rongji and Jean Chrétien

With Zhu Rongji and wife Lao An at Banff National Park during
1999 state visit

At the fabulous Forbidden City performance of
Turandot with Paul and Jackie Desmarais

BOOK V:

AMBASSADOR
TO CHINA

CHAPTER 16

BACK TO DIPLOMACY

• • • • • • • • • • •

We celebrated Christmas in Ottawa in 1995 with all our usual traditions, but there was a little different atmosphere hanging over the family, part interested anticipation and part worry about the impending move to China, especially among the children who now were counting the weeks before leaving their friends. Knowing that they were going to need new pastimes to replace some of what they were leaving behind, I gave them the start of a model railway, something which had always fascinated me. I had had a very limited large-scale clockwork train when I was small, but it was a simple figure-8 track and was too big to either leave out or to build into a miniature world. The present I gave the children was an HO-gauge starter set with a locomotive and a few carriages, some track and a 4X8 piece of thick plywood to begin a railroad. By the time we packed up for Beijing our first rudimentary circuit was built and affixed to the board.

After Christmas I spent a month supporting the new Cabinet Committee on Unity, charged with both following up the promises made by Prime Minister Chrétien in the speech he gave during the Verdun rally the Tuesday before the referendum, and beginning to map out the reference to the Supreme Court on the constitutionality of a provincially-held referendum on separation. This latter initiative would precipitate a ruling that the government would use as the basis for the Clarity Act. By the beginning of February I was concentrating on my Chinese full time, driving every morning to the Foreign Service Institute in Gatineau where I would spend all morning with one tutor and all afternoon with another, cramming in as much Chinese as I possibly could. It is, of course, a very complex language and very difficult to learn quickly, and my head felt as if it would explode with all I was trying to learn.

When an Ambassador is appointed it is a long-standing and required diplomatic practice that "Agrément", the concurrence of the receiving country, is sought before any announcement is made. Although I had little doubt that my nomination would be welcomed by the Chinese given my long involvement in Canada-China relations, it was not until late February that Agrément was received and my appointment made public. This also meant that my concentration on learning Chinese was no longer as focused, as I began to receive requests to meet with the wide range of Canadian groups with interests in China. The China Division organized for me visits to Toronto, Montreal, Calgary and Vancouver. In Ottawa I appeared before House Standing Committee on Foreign Affairs and met with Ministers whose departments were directly engaged in China.

In January, Prime Minister Chrétien shuffled the federal cabinet, bringing in as ministers Stéphane Dion as Minister of Intergovernmental Affairs and Pierre Pettigrew as Minister for International Cooperation. Both had been under contract to me during my time in the Privy Council Office and I had a chance to meet with both in their new roles before I left for China. I would never again have much to do with Dion, but I would interact with Pettigrew for most of the next year, since he was responsible for CIDA, which then had a rapidly expanding program in China, until the Prime Minister moved him to the Human Resources portfolio. Towards the end of my time as Ambassador, he became Minister of International Trade and I would again have a lot to do with him.

A more impactful change in the cabinet was the appointment of Lloyd Axworthy as Minister of Foreign Affairs, replacing André Ouellet who left the cabinet to become Chairman of Canada Post. Axworthy had always been interested in international affairs but was never fundamentally in tune with Chrétien on the core direction of Canadian foreign policy, which Chrétien saw above all as promoting fundamental Canadian economic and commercial interests and protecting and expanding Canadian global influence where and whenever possible. Chrétien was also very realistic about the weight Canada could bring to bear on internal change in other countries. Shortly after coming to power in 1993 he had been asked whether he was going to push Li Peng on human rights in China and he said, "I cannot even tell the Premier of Saskatchewan what to do; why do you think I can tell the Premier of China what to do?" Axworthy came from an older less nationally-grounded school, wanting to structure the core of foreign policy around key Canadian values rather than interests, and to "make a difference" wherever we could. With respect to China, this meant that from the very beginning of his time as Foreign Minister, Axworthy would be out of step with the Prime Minister, wanting to take a firmer line on human rights and on Tibet. In early March, I met with Axworthy for a discussion about my mandate and it was evident to me that I was going to have some juggling to do, for he was quite emphatic that he expected me to be more forceful on "soft" issues. He wanted to ensure that I was not only getting our human rights message across to the Chinese, but doing so in a way that would be audible to the NGO community back in Canada which he, but not the Prime Minister, saw as one of our principal constituencies.

Although I had initially planned to head to China in early April, it was decided to delay my departure by a couple of weeks to be in Ottawa for the visit of Qiao Shi, Chairman of the National People's Congress and one of the members of the Standing Committee of the Politburo. Qiao Shi was a leading proponent of building out a strong legal system in China and gradually making the PRC "Fazhi", a country ruled by law. Although he was in 1996 no longer as powerful as he had once been, given that he had opposed Jiang Zemin who had been made both General Secretary to the Party and President during the fallout of the Tiananmen crisis in 1989, he was still the leader of a strong reformist faction within the party. Officially the third highest-ranking official behind only the President and the Prime Minister, Qiao Shi was an open and very interesting interlocutor. In Ottawa, I joined his meetings with the Governor General Roméo Leblanc, Prime Minister Chrétien and Lloyd Axworthy, and briefer sessions with the Speakers of both the House and the Senate. While the call on Leblanc was really just for courtesy and the exchange relatively superficial, both the meetings with Chrétien and Axworthy were substantial. Chrétien used the meeting to talk about the progress made in the relationship since his first meeting with Jiang Zemin in November of 1993 and the government's desire to strengthen the trade and economic relationship, including the sale of the CANDU reactors, and Axworthy followed the brief that I had proposed and focused almost entirely on the possibility of Canada doing more to support China as it tried to strengthen the rule of law. Qiao Shi responded very positively and went away entirely satisfied with his visit.

As I was doing all the easy work of simply getting my brain re-engaged in China-related files, Liani was doing all the harder logistical work in preparing to move. She found tenants (the Ambassador of Myanmar, former Minister of Health and a Fulbright scholar, and his charming wife) for our home, organized with the children's schools to ensure they would be granted full credit for their year, and took charge of the physical packing and move. A lot of our personal effects would go into storage since we, like other Ambassadorial families, would be moving into a house not only fully furnished but with all the silverware and household acoutrements that come with an Official Residence. It was a busy time and before we knew it April had arrived and we were on our way to China.

CHAPTER 17

FIRST DAYS IN BEIJING AND PRESENTATION OF CREDENTIALS

• • • • • • • • • • •

We arrived in Beijing at the old airport, which is recognizable today as the refurbished Terminal 1 of the modern airport, which after our arrival was expanded first for the 50th anniversary of the PRC in 1999 and then again for the Olympic Games in 2008. We were met by a delegation of dark-suited Embassy section heads, well-dressed spouses, dark-suited representatives from the Ministry of Foreign Affairs, dark-suited representatives from the airport and the airlines, and one jean-clad, sandal-shod longhaired nephew. The latter was Nat Ahrens, son of sister Joy and Chip, who had been studying and working in China for some time. The first sign of our new status was that someone else cleared us through all the entry procedures while we lounged in a VIP room, and then someone else collected our 19 bags and boxes and brought them to the Residence. I recalled being one of those "someone elses" twenty years earlier and a few thousand miles to the south when Glenn Shortliffe arrived to take up his assignment as Ambassador to Indonesia.

As we pulled up at the Embassy, the gates were swung open by a combination of blue-suited Chinese guards and our khaki Canadian Military Police. Residence staff all dressed in white stood outside awaiting our arrival and welcomed us into the house, where the children went off instantly in all directions at once, hunting down bedrooms and new excitements. For them it was wonderful having cousin Nat there, and he stayed for a family dinner that evening and with his perfect Mandarin helped us with both organization and communication. Nat told us that our major domo,

Lao Jiang, had a strong Shandong accent and might be a touch hard to comprehend, giving us an excuse to cover the fact that we found everyone difficult to understand. The Residence was fine, with large reception rooms and a long dining room on the main floor with a walled garden outside for receptions. At the back was a large family living room where we would have our family meals, given that sitting at a table for 22 was not exactly our family style. Upstairs were the family quarters with bedrooms enough for the children and ourselves, set around a balcony that surrounded the large atrium above the central hall and an indoor fountain, which leaked so constantly that we soon turned it into an indoor rock garden. The boys' rooms were on the south side of the balcony and they could be seen from the hall or dining room below whenever they left their rooms, even to go to their bathroom. At the beginning of our time there I was a little embarrassed at having semi-naked or pajama-clad little boys running around during official dinners, but then I relaxed and realized than most of our Chinese guests loved children and very much liked the family atmosphere of our residence. It quickly became common practice for the twins to come and meet our guests, even if barefooted and all ready for bed.

The Residence was in the southwest corner of a larger embassy compound, with the Chancery in the Southeastern corner, where my office, the Political, Trade, Defense and Security offices were, along with all the secure communications and registry facilities. On the northeast corner of the compound, separated from the Chancery by a garden and a community swimming pool and tennis court, was another office building (which I shortly thereafter named the Paynter Building in memory of my recently deceased predecessor John Paynter) housing the Immigration, Consular, Administration and Development Divisions. Finally, in the northwest corner were eleven town houses, considered sufficient in number to house all the Canadian-based staff when the embassy was designed in the late 1970s, but which by the mid-1990s only supported a small proportion of our some 60 Canada-based staff and their families. Underneath the Chancery were two basement floors housing workshops and all the major mechanical systems, and doors to a network of tunnels that connected all the buildings. During our first evening in the Residence, Caleb and I went exploring in the tunnels, unaware that we were setting off an alarm as we opened the door from the Residence basement into the first passage, but after winding our way about 50 meters to the east we were confronted by a military policeman who was responding to the breach! Luckily the standing orders were not to shoot intruders, or else it would have been the shortest Ambassadorial tenure in global history.

The following morning I again tested both embassy security and the limits of my authority. I woke up early with jet-lag and decided to go out on the streets of Beijing for a run. At the back gate I was stopped by the guard on duty and told I was not supposed to leave the compound unaccompanied. I pointed out that I was the Ambassador and if that was an embassy rule, it was from that instant rescinded. Out I went. It became my habit to run in the early mornings, and about a week after my arrival I was joined by a young Chinese fellow runner whose English was surprisingly good. He told me that he worked for a small high-tech company, and for several weeks he was a charming companion, running wherever I chose to run and keeping easy pace with me. Unfortunately there came a morning when he was no longer there and I never saw him again. I concluded sadly that whichever part of the Chinese security apparatus had been nervous about my early morning forays was now satisfied that I was not heading out to meet with dissident monks or student revolutionaries.

The first few days were a total blur of staff meetings with division heads and then with all Canada-based staff, calls on the Ministry of Foreign Affairs and the Dean of the Diplomatic Corps (the Ambassador of Sierre Leone who had apparently been left forgotten in Beijing by his government a couple of decades earlier), speeches at a Canada-China Business Council lunch and at the opening of a Canadian art exhibit, and receiving the constant stream of visiting Canadian business delegations. The following Monday we had an important set of negotiations underway with a group from Ottawa, which meant our first formal dinner only five days after arriving. It was not too large an affair, only 16 guests, until a couple of Vice Ministers were added with three hours to go and then a Minister just turned up at the door with a couple of assistants in tow, all of whom had to be included in the seating plan as we had drinks in the terrace garden. So Liani and the staff calmly rearranged things, the dining table got magically longer and all was fine.

During our first few days we did an equal amount of family juggling as well. The four children had school placement tests and interviews, and tryouts for sports teams for the last semester of the school year. The twins turned seven on the day after we arrived, so we had a family birthday party for them, having had a party with their friends before we left Ottawa. Cynthia headed off to Datong on day seven for a four-day school "China Studies" trip. We also lived through our first sandstorm, watching the great yellow clouds sweep down the streets of the city, leaving a thin layer of gritty loess on everything.

On a Monday twelve days after our arrival in Beijing, I presented my credentials to the President of China, Jiang Zemin. Just after lunch, a big black Chinese protocol Mercedes pulled up at the Residence. Then with a lead police car complete with flashing lights and sirens and a fleet of Embassy vehicles following behind, we were whisked through traffic to the Great Hall of the People. Down the second ring road and along the great boulevard of Chang'an our motorcade snaked, drawing lots of stares and a few waves. Chang'an is the grand and perfectly straight east-west artery that bisects Beijing, separating the Forbidden City from Tiananmen, on which great military parades are held on key anniversaries and on which the tanks rolled in the 1989 crack-down. We turned off Chang'an in front of the Great Hall, down a lane reserved for high-level Pooh-Bahs, and swung up a great raised entrance to the Great Hall's South Gate.

Almost before the car stopped, my door was opened by a white-gloved attendant, embassy staff jumped out of the following cars and lined up behind me and up the half-dozen stone steps we walked. Just outside the huge open door, there was a small honour guard of perhaps sixteen or twenty soldiers, who snapped a salute in perfect unison as I passed by into a small ante-room and then straight into a large reception hall, perhaps fifty meters long. The President of China, the world's most populous country and a rising economic and political power, was standing in the very centre at the end of a long and ornate carpet, waiting for me just in front of Chinese and Canadian flags.

Suppressing a thought about a little kid from Newfoundland, I reminded myself to stand straight and not trip, and I led my legation north until I was directly in front of the President. I bowed slightly, handed him the vellum envelope with a great seal of Canada across its opening that contained my "Letter of Credence", asking the Government of the People's Republic of China to accept Howard Robert Balloch as Canada's Ambassador Extraordinary and Plenipotentiary and to afford him all requisite respect and appropriate courtesies. As I handed him the envelope I said in Chinese (a short spiel I had worked on with my tutor that morning) that I had the honour to present my credentials along with best wishes to him and the people of China from the Government and people of Canada. The President received the envelope, placed it on a silver platter held by a staff member and then asked me to introduce my staff. We had been limited to ten people and so I had brought my heads of section and my Defence Attaché, a couple of other senior officers and my executive assistant. I proceeded to introduce each one, remembering everyone's name except a senior Immigration Officer whose name completely eluded me as I got to him. The fellow's real given name, Sidney, completely eluded me, so I leapt at "Irving", which of course was immaterial to everyone except him. After a quick formal photograph with the President and the senior Foreign Ministry officials, we retired to a small side room for tea and an informal agenda-less discussion. President Jiang surprised me by his warmth and the degree to which he was well briefed. He knew that my nephew Nat was studying in Beijing (I wondered how many foreign students had been brought to the attention of the President of China) and the fact that Liani's family was originally from southern Fujian.

Jiang Zemin remembered, at least so he said, meeting me in Seattle at the first APEC Summit in November, 1993, and I offered him Prime Minister Chrétien's personal greetings, and then we chatted for about fifteen minutes about the relationship and what we collectively trying to accomplish. My Chinese was not good enough to continue from my formal presentation in the larger hall, so we spoke through an interpreter, but at one point the president waived off the interpretation of a point I had just made and said "For some reason I always find it easy to understand when Canadians speak." I responded by saying that this was perhaps a little because of our pronunciation and a little because Chinese and Canadians usually find that we begin with mutual respect before we form our words, even when we disagree. This delighted him and he agreed, suggesting that he wished all of Chinese partners took the same approach.

As our fifteen minutes came to an end, protocol officials started to fidget and signal and the President realized he was being told the conversation should end. We stood up and exchanged a last pleasantry, and then it was out the door and passed the honour guard for a final salute, before getting into my own official vehicle with the Canadian flag flying off the right front fender for the first time. I sensed then that a page had turned on a new and hopefully fascinating chapter of my life.

My credentials ceremony finished in the mid-afternoon of what was in any case a very busy day, with a Junior Minister's visit in full swing, so rather than head back to the Residence for a champagne celebration, I headed out with a couple of my staff to the Diaoyutai State Guest House for a meeting with the Foreign Minister and a dinner hosted for our visitor. On the way there I used the car telephone to call Sidney Frank who was en route somewhere else in another embassy car, and explained that having introduced him to the President of China as Irving I was faced with a choice between asking him to change his name, which would leave both me and the President entirely without inconvenience, or to apologize which would leave me humiliated and the President forever ill-informed. After great and due consideration, I explained, I was going to make my first plenipotentiary decision and simply apologize.

The rest of the week went by in a blur of activity which I was to learn was quite typical of the months to come – a whirlwind of meetings and calls and signing ceremonies. The week ended with a Friday night "gala opening" of the Beijing TV International Week, featuring performers from China and from around the world. Included was a Canadian "singing policeman", who of course only Cynthia had ever heard of. In normal fashion we did the unthinkable and requested and obtained four extra tickets so our children could come along. Liani and I had originally planned to split, with her sitting with three of the children and I with one, but the local organizers would have nothing of this and insisted that Liani join me in the VIP seats in the front row, which left the four children two rows back. In the intervening row were some senior officials, including a senior Communist Party leader and the Mayor of Beijing. The former of these was an elderly bald fellow who offered a most tempting pate for children's humour. A sharp parent's ear could pick up, just before the show began a "I bet you wouldn't pour some of your water on it . . ." and the like. Then at the beginning of the program, televised across Asia to a mere billion or so people, the producers spent a goodly amount of time filming the audience. Two big multi-panel screens on either side of the stage showed actually what was being broadcast. We could see ourselves every time the cameras panned across the VIPs, and we could also see four small terrorists two rows back, who of course were entertained that they could see themselves, planning events that would result in the instant rupture of Chinese-Canadian relations. Luckily the only transgression actually caught on camera was an ear-wiggling, cross-eyed weird-expression contest, then the real performance soon started and peace thereafter reigned.

One of my first objectives during my first few days in Beijing was to get to know the Embassy staff and particularly the senior management team. My first impression was that it was very strong, led by two particularly competent officers, Ken Sunquist as Commercial Minister and Guy Saint-Jacques as Political Minister.

At Canada's largest embassies, and Beijing was (as it is today, and always likely to be) our second largest mission after Washington, the next two or three positions are filled by professionals of a level equivalent to our ambassadors at medium sized posts. Both Ken Sunquist and Guy Saint-Jacques were already at the same level as our ambassadors in most Southeast Asian capitals.

Guy and I had served together for a year or so in the Science, Environment and Transportation Policy Division in the early 1980s, and he and his wife Sylvie had developed into good friends of Liani's and mine. Guy was deeply knowledgeable about China, always thoughtful and completely unflappable in a crisis, and was a tremendous support for me for the three and a half years he stayed in Beijing after my arrival. Guy later became Deputy High Commissioner to the UK, ran for several years the Personnel Branch of DFAIT (which is a very tough position), and then became Canada's Chief Negotiator and Ambassador Climate Change before returning to China as Ambassador thirteen years after serving there with me. When Guy, who had arrived about seven months before I did, departed in 1999, he left a big hole. I asked Ted Lipman, Consul General in Shanghai, to come to Beijing to replace him, and Ted stayed with me as Political Minister until I left the Embassy and the Foreign Service in 2001.

Ken Sunquist was already contemplating moving on when I arrived in Beijing, but agreed to stay for one more year. An archetypical Trade Commissioner, Ken had developed an excellent reputation among the leaders of Canadian businesses, both large and small, as always going the extra mile to support their efforts to penetrate the China market or to protect their interests once established. When he left in the summer of 1997, Ken went back to Ottawa for a year or two and then was appointed Ambassador to Indonesia. His replacement, recommended to me by Personnel Branch in Ottawa, was Robert Collette, who was originally a CIDA officer and who had transferred to the Trade Commissioner service in the mid-1980s. He stayed three years and was then appointed Ambassador to the Philippines. As Robert's successor in 2000, I brought in Rob Mackenzie, a Trade Commissioner without China experience but who, like Ken Sunquist, was very well liked by the business community. Rob had served both as Consul General in Buffalo and subsequently as the Chairman of a US-Canada Regional Development Authority in the transborder area from Buffalo through the Niagara region to Hamilton. I knew Rob personally having served with him for about six months in Prague, and he remained in Beijing for three years before moving to Shanghai as Consul General. He and his wife Sandy had, just like us, a daughter and three boys, much the same age as ours, and although they were not with us for very long before I left the service, we took one very memorable family vacation together to Dali and Lijiang in Yunnan. This was before the great onslaught of tourism to this UNESCO-protected corner of old China, and we stayed in the best hotel there was in Lijiang during that time, professing more stars than it deserved, but it was a very good time and we climbed mountains together and explored the old Naxi towns during the day and the children stayed up late at night playing euchre.

The Development Section was run by Bob Hamilton when I arrived, but he too would leave at the end of his normal posting in the summer of 1997, to be replaced by Henri-Paul Normandin. Henri-Paul was an outstanding officer who later transferred from CIDA to DFAIT and served both in headquarters as a senior Director General and then in our mission to the UN in New York as second-in-command, which carries an ambassadorial rank, before moving on to become Ambassador to Haiti. Henri-Paul and his wife Carole were somewhat younger than we, and had two young boys, the eldest of whom, Antoine, was the same age as our twins, and who became a life-long friend of theirs. They formed a little inseparable foursome along with another young lad, Michael Howard, son of Agriculture Counselor Bruce Howard who also arrived at the mission in 1997, replacing a fellow named Jim Booth who returned earlier than planned to Canada with Lou Gehrig's disease.

The fourth major section of the Embassy, and its largest in terms of staff numbers, was the immigration division, run when I arrived by an old Asia hand, Dennis Scown, who had served in many other missions in the region and would go on from Beijing to manage the large immigration program in the Philippines and return again, long after I had left, to run the China program for a second time. Dennis was a very experienced immigration professional who ran his shop in almost military fashion but was generally not very interested in matters outside his orbit, and left the mission in 1997. Susan Gregson replaced him and turned out to be a real gem, thoughtful and interested in the broader agenda we were pursuing in China. Susan had studied at Fudan University in Shanghai in the 1970s, where she had met a fellow student, Eugenio Clini, from Italy. Eugenio became a published expert on modern China and eventually became a professor of modern China at the University of Naples, which as Susan's career took off, became an alternating commitment for him with a teaching position at Carleton University in Ottawa. After I left the service, one of the companies I joined as an independent director was Methanex, where I met a long-serving fellow board member named Brian Gregson, who had been Chairman of Price Waterhouse Canada, and who turned out to be Susan's father. Susan, like Henri-Paul Normandin, found the challenges of broader foreign policy attractive and left the immigration service after her time in Beijing and was appointed a Director in Foreign Affairs. She eventually returned to China as Consul General in Shanghai (replacing Rob Mackenzie), and then became Assistant Deputy Minister for Human Resources at DFAIT headquarters.

Now back to the beginning of things . . .

CHAPTER 18

FINDING MY STRIDE

• • • • • • • • • • •

Once the children were settled down in school and I was formally in position, life began to settle into a rhythm, a frenetic one, but my staff was excellent and were eager to get the Embassy back to full steam after the long inter-regnum without an Ambassador in residence. Ken Sunquist and Guy Saint-Jacques had done an excellent job managing the post since the previous May when John Paynter had left for the last time. Ken had already been at the mission for almost three years, and Guy, a seasoned China-expert, had arrived shortly after Paynter returned to Canada. Ken and Guy were both extremely strong officers and had alternated as Chargé d'Affaires once it became evident that Paynter would never return, but it had been like running a company with a temporary CEO or an orchestra with an interim conductor. Access, political influence and strategic direction were all inevitably under-weighted until a full-time and formal Ambassador was in place.

Being a modern Canadian Ambassador really has four essential and generally accepted components. The first is to represent Canada and to intervene with the local government as required on matters of bilateral and international importance. The second is to interpret trends and developments in one's host country, and to accordingly advise the Canadian Government on its policies and programs. The third is to promote Canadian private-sector businesses and other non-governmental interests. The fourth is to be the centre of the Canadian community and to ensure the protection of Canadians when and if necessary. There are two other less public responsibilities. The first of these is to manage the Embassy, its personnel and budgets and buildings and fleets of cars, all comprising a substantial operation in Canada's second largest mission.

The final responsibility was to be host to the unending flow of politicians and business leaders arriving from Canada, serving on average five or six lunches or dinners every week for between 12 and 30 people. And this last responsibility made Liani a restaurateur, doing the bulk of the organization and work.

One of the first social events for Liani and I outside the hosting of dinners and lunches at the Official Residence, was as formal hosts for the Canadian Charity Ball, in 1996 the only charity event of the diplomatic community in Beijing (other would emerge in the years that followed). The proceeds of the event went to the Canada-China Child Health Foundation, a private group founded by pediatrician John Tse of the University of British Columbia with the blessing of both governments. The Foundation had by 1996 already opened almost one hundred rural children's clinics since its founding in the mid-1980s. As patrons of the event, Liani and I hosted the head table and were the first to dance, and because the Ball brought not only Canadians in Beijing together, but Americans, Australians, Britons and other foreign residents of the capital, we ended up meeting literally hundreds of people. We quickly learned (or at least I did, given Liani's superior memory for names) to master the neutral greeting of "Nice to see you" leaving unstated whether or not this was the first time or not. And dropped completely from the Ambassador's lexicon was the phrase "Have we met?", just in case the answer was "Yes, four times"!

When I arrived in Beijing, the ambassadorial car (called the "Official Vehicle" with diplomatic licence plate 123-001, the first three digits designating Canada) was an old dark blue Crown Victoria, almost six years old. My administrative officer told me that it should be replaced and that I could choose what to replace it with. He showed me a list of vehicles, which included quite a long list of North American, Japanese and European brands. I told him that I would insist on a Canadian-made vehicle and we chose a Buick Park Avenue Ultra, which was then probably the fanciest of the GM brands other than the Cadillac. But, I said, I wanted it to be bright red, the national colour of Canada. This, he told me a day later, had been refused by the procurement people at DFAIT headquarters, since ambassadorial cars were supposed to either black or dark blue. I was not to be deterred, and after four or five exchanges with ever more senior people at headquarters, I finally got my way, and the order for a bright red car was placed. After it arrived a number of months later, everyone thought it was great. Prime Minister Chrétien thought it was a terrific statement, Premier Zhu Rongji admired it (red of course was also the national colour of China), and all my diplomatic colleagues were jealous. Whenever we left a huge reception at the Great Hall of the People, we would come out the eastern gate to see a sea of dark blue and black cars of two hundred ambassadors and many more senior Chinese officials. In that sea of black and blue, there was one red car! Shortly after my car entered service, my Australian counterpart ordered a white official car, and my New Zealand counterpart a green one. As an epilogue to this story, when my successor arrived late in 2001, he refused to use it and ordered a dark blue car, believing I suppose that it was somehow not fitting for a serious ambassador to be seen running about in a bright red car.

My first full Ministerial visit was Anne McClellan, Minister of Natural Resources, and after meetings in Beijing we headed up to Harbin, capital of China's most northern province, Heilongjiang. Heilongjiang had been "twinned" with Alberta some years before, and there were a lot of climatic and agricultural similarities and many exchanges between the two provinces. Their capitals, Harbin and Edmonton, were also twinned, and we drove into the city from the Harbin airport along "Edmonton Avenue", which delighted McClellan, a rare Albertan in the federal Liberal Party. Harbin had largely been built as a Russian city when Tsar Nicolas I built the Trans-Siberian Railway and its southern spur that connected the east-west line, which ran straight out to Vladivostok, to Port Arthur, present-day Dalian. The Russian influence was greatest in the 1920s after the White Russians had taken refuge there as the Bolsheviks pushed them eastward, but was still physically evident in the 1990s with cupolas and orthodox churches and bits and pieces of Russo-European architecture scattered throughout the city. There were also plenty of Russians on the streets of Harbin, but these were border traders and not descendents of the earlier settlers who had all fled when the Japanese "liberated" Manchukuo in 1932. After our meeting and lunch with the Provincial governor we were taken on a tour of the city, which still had its Stalin Square, above the banks of the Songhua River where there were rowboats for hire. I had known Anne McClellan reasonably well in Ottawa and suggested that we take out a rowboat just for fun, so we scrambled down to the water's edge, jumped into a rowboat and headed out into the main part of the slow-flowing river. Her Chinese local handlers went a little nuts, and three of them jumped into a rowboat to follow us, but as an old Newfoundlander I could outpace them. We had a very pleasant row upriver, working off my lunch, and then turned around and went back to meet up with our unhappy local friends. Imagine, an Ambassador escaping with a visiting Minister!

One of my objectives after presenting credentials was to call on every Minister in the Chinese government, which some in the Embassy (as they had to prepare notes and accompany me) thought was a waste of time. This was an effort that extended up to the summer break, and was picked up afterwards, and I believed it to be very worthwhile, for even the Ministers of obscure departments, like the Ministry of Coal, or the Ministry of Light Industry No 2, had views about Canada or past relationships that could be relevant in the future. Some of these departments would disappear during one phase or another of governmental reorganization during the ensuing decade, but we built a reputation of being engaged and deeply interested in what was going on in the Chinese government, and found it easier to intervene on matters of Canadian interest later on when we needed to.

In early June I also had my first formal call on Premier Li Peng, who I had briefly met in Montreal the previous October when I was focused on domestic Canadian matters and only somewhat capriciously invited by the Prime Minister to join the dinner he hosted for his visiting Chinese counterpart. An introductory meeting for newly arrived ambassadors with either the premier or a vice-premier was normal in those days, and they tended to be quite short and formalistic. I was determined that mine would be less so, and began with recalling our meeting in Montreal and then launched directly into our hope that Prime Minister Chrétien would be able to come to China before the year was out, possibly en route to or from the APEC Summit in Manila. The Foreign Ministry had been indicating to us that this might not be possible because of other visitors planned for the end of the year, so I suggested to the Premier that it would be a good time for the two countries to sign our planned bilateral agreement on CANDU nuclear reactors. He perked up at this suggestion and turned to an accompanying aide and said that he would like to see if this could be worked into the diplomatic schedule. When he asked me what I hoped to accomplish during my time as Ambassador, I told him that I hoped to see a Canadian nuclear reactor already integrated into the Chinese grid, a doubling of our trade, a tripling of two-way investment flows between the two countries, and a quadrupling of the flow of tourists and students.

My meeting with Li Peng had me on Chinese national television for the fourth time since our arrival, which made me think that with its reach of 500 million viewers, I should have renegotiated my Ambassadorial emolument to be based on a per-viewer fee, standard in the marketing world but regrettably not in diplomacy!

I had also set an objective of getting to as many of China's provincial capitals as I possibly could, and for this I decided to let my schedule be set initially by opportunity, an early version of which presented itself in the form of a signing ceremony in Shenyang, capital of Liaoning province. The signing was for a Canadian-Chinese joint venture in a clean-coal thermal power project, bringing high technology coal processing to the old heavy-industry heartland of China's northeast. Shenyang needed this particular environmental technology badly, for this part of China was among the dirtiest of all, with great huge blast furnaces of Soviet-era heavy iron-works, locomotive and heavy-vehicle factories, chemical plants and ancient pulp and paper mills all churning out filthy water and filthier air. The visit was only for one working day and a night, and consisted of officiating at the commercial signing ceremony, a meeting with provincial Governor Wen Shizhen for both me and the CEO of the Ontario company that signed the agreement, and then a meeting for me alone with the Governor and Provincial Party Secretary Gu Jinchi. Wen Shizhen was a tall, large man with a very jolly countenance and a good sense of humour. He would become Party Secretary himself the following year and became quite a good friend over the years, even beyond my Ambassadorial time. But this first visit to Liaoning did not include any other part of the province, which was disappointing as I wanted to go to Dalian, which people were beginning to rave about as one of the prettiest and most dynamic cities of the northeast. I had visited Dalian once before, during a bleak January in the mid-1980s, when a flight I was on from Beijing to Tokyo developed mechanical trouble and stranded us there for two days. My memory of the city was like a scene from an Ingmar Bergman film, with grey people dragging grey carts through a grey and sooty city, with great grey factories spewing blackness that fell back to the city in a mockery of snow.

The spring and early summer of 1996 also allowed us to get to know a few more of our diplomatic colleagues. Chris Elder, the New Zealand Ambassador and his wife hosted a welcoming dinner for Liani and me and for my Australian counterpart Rick Smith, who had presented credentials on the same day as I, and his wife. I had known Rick from a past life when he was a senior official in Australia's Department of Foreign Affairs and Trade, and Chris was a thoughtful and well-informed sinologist. Included in the dinner were Len and Lady Appleyard of Britain, Igor Rogachev and his (third) wife Danya of Russia, and the Americans Jim and Mary Sasser. Len Appleyard was an old China hand, having served in the Embassy as First Secretary when it was sacked in the early years of the Cultural Revolution, and had interesting stories to tell. Igor Rogachev's relationship with China went back even further, to the first Beijing meeting between Mao Zedong and Nikita Khrushchev, at which Igor was a young interpreter on the Soviet side. I had met Rogachev during the Cambodian peace process when he was a senior official in the Soviet Foreign Ministry, and was soon to establish a very close relationship with him, built in part around an organized hockey program I started for Chinese and Canadian children, and into which we invited Russian youngsters as well as those of other nationalities.

Over the next year, Liani and I got to know American Ambassador Jim Sasser and his wife Mary quite well. They were a delightful down-to earth couple with a disarming southern charm that came half from their Tennessee roots and half from more than a decade as Senator on Capitol Hill. Jim was not having an easy time in Beijing given the bumpy nature of Sino-American relations, and he seemed to spend at least half his time in Washington trying to control the congressional crazies. He and Mary told us that they found the jobs of Ambassador and Senator quite similar; he spent half his time lobbying for that which was sensible and half his time being nice to people who were lobbying for that which was not.

On the family front, the children all seemed to be settling in reasonably well, although as an older child with a deeper commitment to her Canadian curriculum and a harder time pulling herself away from longer friendships, the move was hardest on Cynthia. But she was ever a trooper and simply worked harder at her studies and spent more time helping "her" twins adapt to their new schoolwork than with the cliquish girls of her seventh grade classroom. Before the summer had even begun, we also started to have family visitors, the first being a two-week visit of my sister Joy and her husband Chip and daughter Diana. Their son Nat was of course already in Beijing as a student, and together we spent time touring new stretches of the Great Wall at Simitai, and took a boat trip up through the Longjing Gorge up near the northwest municipal border between Beijing and the province of Hebei.

In June I went back to Ottawa for a few days to participate in a strategic policy meeting of top officials and senior Ambassadors that Foreign Minister Lloyd Axworthy was hosting, and also to appear before the House Standing Committee on Foreign Affairs to be grilled on human rights in China and our China policy. My presentation to the Standing Committee went fine, as neither the Reform Party nor the Bloc Québécois, the major opposition parties since the decimation of the Progressive Conservatives, paid much attention to the Government's China policy. I tabled a statement that tried to balance sustained concerns about the abuse of political and religious rights and a recognition of the enormous progress being made both in general personal freedoms and in the socio-economic situation in which the average Chinese found themselves, and set out all that we were doing in engaging the Chinese Government on human rights issues and in encouraging the development of the Chinese legal system.

It was at this time that I had my first Ambassadorial taste of serious negotiations. We had two sets in the May to July period of 1996, one being a special export credit facility that would assist Bombardier in setting up a major joint venture for the design and production of intercity railroad cars, a joint venture that turned out over the ensuing years to be a most successful one. It was this joint venture that Bombardier would use to bring in its European technology to build the high quality cars for China's high-speed trains. The second and more important of the two negotiations was the final and successful round of talks culminating in the basic project agreement for the sale of two CANDU heavy-water nuclear reactors. Our nuclear discussions had begun during the visit to Canada of Vice Premier Zou Jiahua some years earlier, when I had taken him secretly off to see the Darlington Nuclear Generating Station east of Toronto, so I felt a personal ownership of the file, and indeed the negotiating team from Atomic Energy of Canada Limited (AECL, a crown corporation), relied heavily on the Embassy for both advice in how to deal with their Chinese counterparts and intervention with the Chinese government agencies that were involved in the deal. The agreement reached in the early summer of 1996 did not deal with the financing, but instead dealt with the detailed delineation of responsibilities and a separation of the project into the nuclear core of the plant which would be under the control of AECL, and the "balance of plant" for which an engineering contract would be entered into with an international commercial firm and a Chinese partner.

Before our family summer vacation, I had also more or less completed as many of my introductory diplomatic calls as I would ever make. In spite of the tradition of calling on all heads of mission more senior to oneself, I limited my list to the major G-7 players, APEC countries, India, Pakistan and Russia. Similarly we started very quickly to politely decline most of the invitations we received for diplomatic dinners. We were fully consumed with entertaining Canadians with interests in China and their Chinese contacts, and Chinese Ministers or other senior people en route to or returning from Canada. We neither had the inclination nor the time to get on the diplomatic merry-go-round. I also took a decision that we would not host an external Canada Day reception for the diplomatic community and our local counterparts. There was one of these national day events almost every day and a less useful waste of taxpayers' money I could not have imagined. Years earlier, when I was running the Asia Branch in Ottawa, I had hated but could not avoid going to National Day Receptions, but had generally avoided staying for more than a very few minutes (I would go through the reception line to be seen by the hosting Ambassador and then sneak out the first door I could find), and I knew that no one senior in the Chinese government would care if they were not invited. Instead, we started the tradition of hosting an outdoor Canadian party, funded by the community itself rather than the taxpayer, and aimed primarily at children. We had our first version of the community Canada Day party on June 29th, which was the Saturday before July 1, and it was a big hit in the community, and on July 1st itself we were back to our work as restaurateurs, hosting both a big dinner for the visiting Bombardier CEO, followed by a recital by the Newstead Trio, which comprised a Canadian cellist, an American violinist and a Chinese pianist, which was delightful and left us determined to host more musical events in the Residence.

Before our summer break and annual sojourn to Jamestown, something Liani and I felt was very important to keep constant in our children's lives given all the tumult they were being put through, I also went north to Mongolia to present my credentials as Canada's Ambassador there; the Mongolian thread in my story is woven in a separate chapter.

Just after returning from North America, I made my first official visit to Guangdong. The day of our flight south was brilliantly clear and we had a great view of the country unfolding below. With mountains constantly to the west we watched the squared and clustered villages of the northern plain gradually give way to the less symmetrical patterns of habitation built along the waterways of central China, just as the endless wheat fields of Hebei gave way to the rice of Henan and Hubei, gold more dominant than green in the early autumn. We crossed the Yellow River and passed over tens of cities dotting the landscape at every confluence of rivers, some murky mud-brown with their west-east carriage of loess and others just light tan ribbons of dry riverbeds. Most of the cities were too insignificant for the pilot to bring to our attention, although he did point out the capital cities of Shijiazhuang, Zhengzhou and after an hour or so called our attention to the approach of the great Yangtze and the huge tripartite metropolis of Wuhan, once Wuchang, Hangkou and Hanyang. After the dusty dry north, the winding Yangtze with its tributaries to the west and its flood plains to the east appeared like a great artery with many veins and countless capillaries, and the sense even from many thousands of feet up was of almost endless fertility.

As we began our descent into Guangzhou, I recalled my only other landing in Guangzhou more than a dozen years before. I was then on a trans-Pacific Singapore Airlines flight heading to Hong Kong that was diverted due to a huge local storm. Although it was very stormy, visibility had been reasonable and as we circled around the cluster of Islands west of Hong Kong in the early morning light we could see the lightening and rain lashing the peaks of Victoria and the New Territories alike. After circling for almost an hour waiting for approval for a run at Kai Tak, our fuel started to run out and we were directed up the Pearl River to Guangzhou, then still not an open airport for international flights. After landing, our big Boeing 747 was parked off the end of the runway, much shorter in the mid-80s, for a couple of hours while the crew negotiated refueling. While stairs were brought to the forward cabin door, passengers were not permitted to de-plane, and with the engines off and the heat of the day building, the inside of the aircraft started to get very hot. Finally, several old rusty fuel trucks lumbered out and men on A-frame ladders started refueling our huge airliner. After about twenty minutes, one of the pilots ran down the stairs madly waving at the men handling the fuel bowsers. It turned out that they had over-fueled the plane, making it too heavy to take off on the short runway, and of course the under-equipped Chinese airport had no equipment to de-fuel a 747. And so we sat there on the hot tarmac until a special pump arrived to unload half the fuel. Because no one on board had visas for the PRC, all the passengers had had to stay on board, sweltering in the hot and humid air of the deep south for more than seven hours, with the open cabin doors providing little relief. That had been my inauspicious and unintended first visit to the great Guangzhou.

This time, of course, Guangzhou was our intended destination, and once on the ground we were whisked through the airport by the local Canadian Consul, Mary Boyd, and the protocol officials of Guangdong province, and taken through the clogged streets of the city, much more congested than Beijing, to the huge and very modern China Hotel. Being an older and riverside commercial center, Guangzhou was never the focus of imperial or subsequent planners, and lacked the great access boulevards and ring roads of the northern capital. In addition, half the city seemed dug up with its first subway line under construction. As the city was built on silt, the only way to build a subway was to dig huge trenches under the streets and subsequently construct waterproof concrete tunnels with tops. The China Hotel, which housed both the hotel in which I stayed and the Canadian Consulate (soon to be upgraded to a Consulate General) was a giant complex with a glitzy upmarket shopping arcade where later that day I gave a speech at the opening banquet of a "Canadian Food Week". In cooperation with exporters, we were flogging everything from smoked salmon to high-grade beef to ice wine, and all the upscale restaurant owners, hoteliers, chefs, supermarket owners and local pooh-bahs attended. I was interviewed in front of a promotion teepee, which in my remarks opening the event, I jokingly suggested was in fact my Consul's residence.

Of course the joke did not work in Chinese and I reminded myself again not to try to be funny in someone else's language.

The next morning was the normal provincial visit routine: calls on the Governor of Guangdong, the mayor of Guangzhou and a luncheon banquet with the heads of various provincial departments and agencies. Everyone spouted the same line originally laid down by Deng Xiaoping in his famous 1992 southern tour: "To be rich is glorious!" By the mid-90s it was evident that in every corner of the south that message had gotten through to everyone. There were deals to be done, investments to be made, new corporate subsidiaries of every Ministry emerging and experimentation of all kinds, from BOT ("build, operate and transfer") infrastructure projects to complex "shadow" joint ventures with local provincial companies to get around central government limitations in telecommunications or leasing or other restricted sectors. I gave a luncheon speech at the inaugural meeting of the local "Canadian Business Forum", comprised of just short of one hundred Canadian businesspeople resident in the region. The Governor of Guangdong, Lu Ruihua, hosted a dinner for me that evening, and I was reminded about the growing human links between the two countries when he told me of cousins of his who lived in Vancouver and a niece who was studying in Toronto.

The remainder of my trip in Guangdong was both interesting and enjoyable. We slowly worked our way out of the city by car the following morning, through a seemingly endless sprawl of industrial parks, inside of which millions of workers toiled away at making the toys and trinkets and cheap electronics and clothing and shoes and tools and ornaments that were already flooding the global marketplace. The level of industrial development was well ahead of the level of infrastructure, and the still narrow roads were bumper to bumper with over-loaded trucks heading downstream to the ports or to Hong Kong. We reached the electronic factory town of Shunde, and visited Nortel's latest factory making line cards for sophisticated telephone switching equipment, feeding the then early stages of the great Chinese telephone acquisition frenzy. Near the executive offices there were photographs of various events in Nortel's recent history, including a poster-size photograph of Jean Monty, then CEO of Nortel, myself and Zou Jiahua during the latter's visit to Canada a few years earlier. After the Nortel tour and lunch with the Shunde mayor we headed out to another Canadian venture, a housing complex developed by a small Alberta firm. We drove in the gates to find suburban Canada, with modern single family dwellings and nice lawns, flower gardens and picket fences. In a model home we found microwaves with English-French instruction panels and fireplace inserts made in Canada, countertops and kitchen cabinets from British Columbia, and even central vacuum systems. The homes were almost all sold, at prices that I then found extraordinarily high, at over 10,000 Renminbi per square meter. Fifteen years later they would be worth seven or eight times that amount, but of course this was before housing reform and the great Chinese home-building and home-buying boom.

As the autumn progressed we gradually started getting accustomed to the endless flow of official visitors from Canada, almost all of who expected me to attend whatever events they were involved in, and for us to host a formal meal in their honour in the residence. It would take about a year before I established an unpublished, but clearly understood, set of service standards which would see us pulling out all the stops for key federal Ministers and provincial Premiers, hosting modest but effective events for key federal deputy ministers (most of whom were friends and were careful not to abuse my time or the Embassy's resources) as well as important business leaders, while generally pawning off to my senior officers the steady torture of provincial ministers, members of parliament and others on vague junkets of one type or another.

One among the great wave of visitors that autumn was Sylvain Simard, the Minister of International Relations of Québec, a rather grand title for a provincial government that has no constitutional authority for international affairs. The Chinese, always extremely sensitive to separatist movements in other countries due to their own worries about Tibet and Taiwan, received him at an "appropriate" level of Director General in the Ministry of Foreign Affairs, not letting him close to even an Assistant Minister, much less a Vice Minister or the Minister himself. The visit, which was largely purposeless except to show supporters of the Parti Québécois that their government was out on the international hustings promoting Québec internationally, was reported in English-language Canadian newspapers in part because of the fact that I was the new Ambassador. The Globe and Mail carried a quote from Simard, saying "We know Mr. Balloch very well. He is no friend of the Québec Government". At one point during his visit the French Ambassador and I jointly officiated at the awarding of prizes to the best Chinese students of French, chosen through a national speech contest organized by two professors from Montreal and funded by both the Canadian Government and the Alliance Française. I invited Simard along and in my speech gave plenty of credit to successive Québec generations and governments for promoting and protecting the French fact in North America. The Chinese university hosting the event of course gave the French Ambassador and me the places of honour. I have never seen a politician so quietly angry as our dear M. Simard, not only not treated as the foreign minister of a sovereign state, but unable to find anything objectionable in the entirely French speech of an anglophone from Newfoundland!

We also had the 96th Conference of the Inter-Parliamentary Union, which brought a Canadian delegation to a meeting of some 3000 parliamentarians from around the world. Given that the membership included countries of all political forms and not simply democracies, this was a boondoggle without any real substance, and the Canadians were a multi-party group from so far up the backbenches that I had never met any of them before. We of course gave them a reception, and some poor junior sod from my political division had to pretend to take them seriously enough to work with them on their individual speeches, and just as importantly ensure that they did not get into any trouble touring around the city, which is what they really wanted to do. The head of the Canadian delegation was Senator Boza, a very nice older man with a sense of humour, and who said he was sure MacKenzie King was turning over in his grave with Canada represented at an IPU by two Canadians of Italian birth, one of Greek birth, one of Croatian birth, one of Bengali birth, with the sole Canadian-born representative being a Bloc Québécois MP who was representing Canada abroad while advocating its break-up at home.

The President of CIDA, Huguette Labelle, and the Minister of International Cooperation, newly-appointed Don Boudria, paid separate visits during the autumn of 1996, which gave me a double opportunity to push my case for a faster re-engineering of our development relationship with China, away from infrastructure and increasingly towards the directions we had initially adopted in the immediate post-Tiananmen period. I had a very good relationship with Huguette – about three years later she tried to persuade me to come back to Ottawa as Executive Vice President of CIDA and position myself as her replacement – and I had worked with Don Boudria when he had been government whip during my 1994-95 national unity days. By this time we had already begun programs in China to support criminal law reform and the training of judges and lawyers, and I wanted to see if we could do more and get a little closer to the edge of political acceptability with programs in democratic village governance and the establishment of legal aid systems for victims of government abuse at local levels. CIDA had an in-bred and institution-wide complex about having our aid program being used as a foreign policy tool and generally resisted any initiative that started in Foreign Affairs, but in this case both Huguette and the Minister were quite supportive and so we managed to start programs in these new areas over the next few years. They were also both sympathetic to my pleas for an increase in the aid program's allocation to the "Canada Fund", a budget controlled at the level of the mission for small projects that could be quickly implemented without reference to CIDA headquarters or subject to its enormously bureaucratic project review and approval process. Earlier known as the "Ambassador's Fund" in deference to the final approving authority, these small projects were in my view the most effective way of making a difference to people's lives at a local level. Our budget then was about a million dollars a year, and it was gradually doubled over the next two years and allowed us to rebuild village health clinics all over Tibet, begin experimental micro-financing projects in three provinces, and help really poor farmers in Guizhou set up small businesses. For as long as I was Ambassador I derived tremendous satisfaction from these projects and from working with my Canada Fund team.

As time passed and the sheer volume of my Beijing-based responsibilities became clear, with endless incoming ministerial visits being punctuated with the need to meet with outgoing Chinese delegations heading to Canada, I realized I would have to become more creative in figuring out ways to get to provincial capitals. Simply getting out of Beijing was a challenge. At this time most provincial governments worked on Saturdays and did not seem to mind organizing weekend visits and so we adopted a practice of going to provincial capitals and other important cities by overnight train on Friday nights, meeting with the appropriate governors and mayors on Saturday and also spending some time seeing interesting places. And of course we took all our four children along, sometimes timing the trips to coincide with a long weekend or school holiday, allowing an extra day or two to get to know another corner of China. We started this practice during our first autumn, and went by rail to Shenyang and Taiyuan and Nanjing on short weekend visits before the winter, and over our first few years in China were to end up going to more than fifteen provinces this way. The trains were very similar to older European trains, and were divided in two classes, with "hard seats" and "soft seats" for day trips and sleeping compartments similarly divided for longer overnight or multi-day travel. We would generally take two "soft sleeper" compartments, put the four children in one and take an adjacent one for ourselves, sometimes on our own and occasionally sharing with two random travelers. This was a great way to see the countryside and brought us into contact with normal people, which we all enjoyed. We could all put our growing capacity in Chinese to the test and the children had a riotous time horsing around in their own little cabin. We would hear them through the thin cabin walls and would intervene only if we started to hear things getting broken or a noise level that would disturb other travelers, almost all of whom seemed to be delighted to find a foreign family with four young children travelling as normal people in their midst.

Although we would eventually travel *en famille* to both Shanghai and Hangzhou by train, my first Ambassadorial visit to Shanghai was with Liani alone for a short two days, leaving the children in the care of themselves and a junior officer, Rachael Bedlington, who our children found tyrannical in her application of the lights-out and other rules that we had laid down. I had very much wanted to get to meet the mayor and visit the city before a planned Prime Ministerial visit there later in the autumn, when Prime Minister Chrétien would come through following his participation in the fourth APEC Summit in Manila. I was stunned by how much Pudong had changed since my previous visit in early 1994, when I was still ADM Asia accompanying Trade Minister Roy McClaren on a trade mission to China. What had been a giant construction site thirty months earlier was now taking shape as a modern city. The rather grotesque Pearl Tower, with its huge tripod base of oblique columns, was now complete, along with more than eighty skyscrapers, many designed by Canadian architects, and a central park about half the size of New York's Central Park was being excavated where marshland and a little hamlet had been. Visiting with the city planners we were told of plans for vast new subway networks and new tunnels and bridges across the Huangpu River. While in most places in the world these would be twenty-year dreams, in Shanghai I knew that in just a few years the new rapid transit system would not only be operating but would be overflowing.

My meeting and official lunch with Mayor Xu Kuangdi were delightful. Xu was an intellectual and had come from a well-educated family. An engineer by training, after a tough time in the countryside during the Cultural Revolution, Xu had spent time abroad, including a one-year stint in Canada lecturing first at l'École Polytechnique in Montreal and then at the University of Waterloo. In addition to his mayorial duties, Xu was also Party Secretary for the Pudong Development Area, was justifiably proud in describing the progress this city of the future was making, and seemed to me to be as capitalist a promoter as one could find anywhere in the world. I gave a speech to a gathering of the local Canadian Business Forum, already numbering in the hundreds, and Liani and I had a lunch hosted by our Consul General, Ted Lipman, with the British, American and Australian Consuls General and their wives. All four of the consuls general, including Ted, were real China experts, all fluent in mandarin and all having lived in the country for ten years or more during the different swings of the Chinese political pendulum. Their positive perspectives on where China was going were very interesting and very close to my still rather inchoate thoughts. They all believed that while there would likely be occasional bumps along the road, the direction of increasing openness and increasing personal freedoms was effectively unstoppable.

Among our many autumnal visitors was one non-politician, Rick Hansen, the "Man in Motion" who in the mid-1980s had wheeled his wheelchair around the world, 27,000 kilometres, in segments designed to touch all continents. In 1986 he had wheeled from Beijing to Shanghai, prior to flying to Australia where he had wheeled from east to west across the entire country. In Shanghai there had been a welcome ceremony organized for his arrival, with a number of local wheelchair athletes in attendance. The ceremony, which had been attended by Guy Saint-Jacques during his first assignment to China, had ended in scandal when a reporter from the Globe and Mail caught the some of the Chinese athletes folding up their wheelchairs and walking away after the event was over and the stadium all but empty. The article in the Globe and Mail was entitled "Miracle in Shanghai" and was deeply embarrassing to both the Chinese and to Rick Hansen, who asserted that even though they were ambulatory, the Chinese players were sufficiently disabled to be considered wheelchair athletes. In any case, in 1996, Hansen was back for the tenth anniversary of his "Man in Motion" tour at the invitation of Deng Pufeng, Chairman of the Chinese Disabled People's Federation and son of Deng Xiaoping. Deng Pufeng had been defenestrated during the Cultural Revolution and had spent a year in rehabilitation in Ottawa in the early 1980s. We took advantage of Hansen's presence to host our annual "Terry Fox Run", an event held to raise money for cancer research and named after a young Canadian who had lost a leg to cancer, and who had in 1981 bravely run from St. John's to past Thunder Bay in a planned run across the country. Terry's cancer had unfortunately spread and he collapsed with only half his run complete, but became a legend and the inspiration for the Terry Fox Runs held still to this day all around the world. Hansen had been a close friend of Terry Fox before the latter died, and was very happy to participate in our run. It was held on a clear and cool beautiful autumn day. Deng Pufeng came for the start, and Rick Hansen and I led off several hundred participants for the ten kilometre run in front of television cameras and press. All the Embassy children joined in, some running but most on roller-blades or bicycles, and they all got Rick Hansen to autograph a poster or a T-shirt or something else and a chance to speak to someone who was famous and inspirational to young Canadians, so it was a terrific day.

Running a large Embassy is like running a business with many different and not always connected parts. Below the layer of protocol and high-level visits and lunches and dinners, we had senior officers running very active trade, aid, immigration, defence relations, law enforcement and consular programs, as well as a hard-working team of political and economic analysts trying to keep their fingers on the pulse of change in China. In the consular area, I was beginning to understand why my consular officer felt that she was stuck deep in a morass of often impenetrable thickness. Consular cases fell into three categories, simple, sad and serious. The simple were the loss of passports or money, the sad involved injuries in accidents or deaths. Almost all serious consular cases involved Canadians who had gained their citizenship after emigrating from China, and, once armed with a Canadian passport returned to do business. One particular case involved a man intent on building a portfolio of more than profits. Originally Shanghainese, he had returned with the aim of collecting wives, something he had done with reasonable success for some time. Each of three such unsuspecting brides, all in the Shanghai region, he had managed to persuade of his fidelity, rushing around the city attending to each at least enough to keep them content for a year or two. Unfortunately, a friend of Wife Number Two happened to meet Wife Number Three and found their stories alarmingly alike, got them together and the ruse was exposed. Wife Number One emerged when the story was reported in the newspaper, as did a divorced wife back in Canada who was owed unpaid alimony and who claims our polygamous businessman had also nicked her bank card and absconded with her savings. The theft, not the polygamy, landed the fellow in jail. Needless to say our efforts at consular assistance were modest, and the end result was a reasonably long invitation to be the guest of the Shanghai correctional facilities. The view in the Embassy was that we had probably simply deferred a death penalty, carried out by four jilted and angry women the moment he was released from prison!

At the beginning of November I learned that there had never been a Remembrance Day Ceremony in Beijing, and there was no appropriate monument or cemetery where the allied community was tempted to hold one. In discussion with my Defence Attaché, Colonel Bill Trimble, I decided to take the bull by the horns and start a local variant of a long-held Canadian tradition. So we invited all those Commonwealth and NATO countries that recognized Armistice Day, as well as China and Russia, the latter because I never believed that one could talk about sacrifice during the wars of the twentieth century without recognizing the terrible price paid in Russian lives before Hitler's armies were driven back from the gates of Moscow. The Colonel and his staff did the organizing, I approved a format and Liani planned a post-ceremony reception. Flags from all the participating countries were collected and a bugler arranged.

November 11th was a beautiful but very windy day, and when I headed out to the Embassy green to check on the preparations an hour or so before the ceremony, I found military policemen and a bunch of local staff working to reinforce the flagstaffs of the fifteen or so nations to be represented, for the strong southwesterly breeze kept knocking them over like dominoes. More or less stabilized and definitely beautified with pots of flowers sitting on the base of each ten-foot flagstaff, the setting looked very appropriate, with all fifteen flags rippling proudly in the strong breeze.

Just before the ceremony was to begin, Colonel Trimble rushed up to me in the Residence garden looking as if he had just directed the Light Brigade to charge into the valley of death, and asked me whether one of our children might have the music the "The Last Post" and "Reveille", the two traditional laments of November 11th. Apparently the bugler who had been arranged and furnished with the scores had sent a friend instead and neglected to pass along the music earlier furnished by the Colonel's Warrant Officer. And no, neither our children nor I had the music. Luckily the alternate bugler was a very talented musician, and after I hummed "The Last Post", he recognized it and played it beautifully. But "Reveille" defeated me, for it had slipped out of my memory entirely. So a quick survey was taken of all the military attachés. American General Byrnes (whose wife was our twin boys' second grade teacher) was tone deaf, and neither Colonel Bouchet of the ever-victorious French nor the diplomatic community's great vinophile Generalisimo Franco of the Italian Marines could help. Luckily Wing Commander Kim Stevenson of the Royal Air Force came to my side and said that he would give it a go, borrowed the bugler's trumpet and played a beautiful rendition. The bugler instantly retained the simple music and we rushed out of the Residence garden to the Embassy green where Ambassadors, military attachés and their staff, a small contingent from the PLA, and about a hundred people and a circle of fifteen flags awaited us.

I began with a short address in the middle of which the Indian flag fell forward into the middle of the semicircle of flags in response to a particularly strong gust of wind. Had it been a more appropriate Italian or French flag, I think at this stage I would have collapsed in hysterics, but India has a noble military tradition. A Canadian corporal quickly righted the flag, and the rest of the ceremony went very smoothly. It turned out to be the beginning of a tradition that lasted at least as long as I remained

Ambassador, and subsequent years the UK, Australia, New Zealand, and India all took turns as host.

The flow of business visitors was simply non-stop. The volume was simply too great for me to host every CEO at the Residence, but I tried to offer something whenever the importance of the company or the nature of the business so merited. One of the most interesting was when Nortel's CEO Jean Monty, who I had known for years, brought to town his International Advisory Committee, the members of which included Reagan's former Defence Secretary Frank Carlucci, Britain's Sir Antony Pinington and the peripatetic financier and Enron board member Ronnie Chan. The lunch I gave to them was one of the most interesting I had hosted to date, for although it was billed as me giving my analysis of what was happening in China, the perspectives that Carlucci and others brought to the discussion were insightful and very interesting. None of them was without strong views on any subject that arose, but I did conclude after the lunch that some of the most senior among them had stopped listening and learning some time before.

Another group that came to Beijing was a delegation from the Canadian Pulp and Paper Association, the CPPA, in which my father had been very involved as President of Bowater Canada. I went to a reception hosted by the Ministry of Forestry and met Lise Lachapelle, who had just replaced Howard Hart as President of the CPPA, and she and many of the group had fond memories of my father, Tony Balloch. One executive there was Stuart Lang, who had grown up in Corner Brook, Newfoundland, next door to us at 7 Marcelle Avenue before we moved to the big house on Cobb Lane. I reminded him that his sister Mary had thrown my sister Pat's favourite porcelain doll across a room and smashed it, and told him that I had had to glue it back together. Stuart had entered the pulp and paper industry after university and moved away from Newfoundland, setting off on grand adventures which included ten years up the Amazon in Brazil on a floating mill, and eventually ended up as CEO of Crestwood, a mid-size but profitable BC firm.

The governmental visitors just rolled in and rolled out at such a pace that sometimes I would be in the middle of a toast at the start of a dinner and I would blank out, trying to remember whether the Parliamentary Secretary was responsible for Human resources or for Penitentiaries. The Chinese invited virtually everyone, wanting to learn about our national medical insurance and unemployment systems, pension plans, federal-provincial equalization programs, virtually all aspects of governance. It was a time when reform was beginning to result in serious changes in both the role and structure of government, and the Chinese government saw Canada as a good example of a capitalist country with socialist characteristics, as they built out their own form of capitalism called "socialism with Chinese characteristics".

It was not all business and government, however. Artist Sandra Safdie, sister of the great architect Moshe Safdie of Habitat and National Gallery fame, came on tour with a collection of her works, and I gave a speech at the opening which in those days was still a rare enough event in Beijing to merit television coverage. Then it was off to a black tie dinner at the Palace Hotel, a glitzy five-star hotel owned by the Public Security Ministry just off Wangfujing and soon to become part of the Peninsula chain. The manager there was Peter Finnamore, a Canadian and son of a very well known Montreal hotelier who ran both the Chateau Champlain when it opened and then the Queen Elizabeth Hotel for almost twenty years. The hotel was hosting a play called "Alone Together", a delightful farce about a couple with three boys who had grown up and moved away, only to keep rebounding back home to ruin their parents' hope for an idyllic empty-nest freedom. Liani and I wondered if this would eventually be our lot in life, in part hoped it would be, and found being on the receiving end of a performance a rather pleasant respite.

In early November I was asked by a young Beijing-born entrepreneur, Edward Zeng, who had gone to Canada in the 1980s and like so many became a Canadian citizen after studying and working there, to be the guest of honour at the opening of China's first Internet Café, a chain of which he was planning. As usual, the event was squeezed into a day of many other meetings, and I pulled up at the café, which was in Haidian District, I was a minute or two late. I was immediately rushed into the café and sat down in front of a computer and told by Edward to "surf the net", all the while being televised as this opening would be broadcast on the evening news. Following instructions, I first drew down a recent satellite image from the Canadian Space Agency of a city in southern China, zooming in to see images a small as ten meters wide taken as part of Canada's Radarsat program. This wowed me and a few other grey hairs, but the hundreds of younger people there all were more interested in my ability to "net shop", and I was encouraged to electronically interconnect with a large department store – the Lufthansa Centre – to browse through Chinese artifacts. Again, doing what I was told, I looked at and was encouraged to purchase a gold and green dragon and phoenix cloisonné sculpture. Not having been fully briefed, I passed on the opportunity, only to be told that the whole event had been carefully planned and that the sculpture was already en route in a taxi. So I quickly backed up and pretended to buy it. A few minutes later a taxi rolled up and the sculpture was delivered, and I gave a short speech on the wonders of internet shopping and modern technology. The dragon and phoenix sculpture still graces our home today.

CHAPTER 19

FIRST PRIME
MINISTERIAL VISIT

• • • • • • • • • • •

My discussion with Li Peng in June about the possibility of a visit by Prime Minister Chrétien before the end of the year had been a seed that bore fruit. In late November of 1996 Chrétien stopped over for a very short visit in Shanghai en route from the annual APEC Summit hosted that year by the Philippines. Liani joined me for the actual visit since Aline Chrétien would be joining her husband, although I went down in advance both to ensure the preparations were all in order and to welcome Art Eggleton, Minister of International Trade, who came a couple of days in advance. As I arrived a few hours before Eggleton was due, we held our planning meeting with the visits operations team, composed of a large number of officers drawn from all our missions in the greater China region, at the airport VIP lounge. After the operations team left, our Consul General Ted Lipman and I went out to the gate to meet the Minister's plane with trade and protocol officials from the Shanghai government. The plane pulled up to the gate, the protocol officials combed their hair, the passengers disembarked, but no Minister. Frantic calls were made to Hong Kong and confirmation received that the Minister had been seen boarding, when someone noticed that there were 400 names on the manifest of a Boeing 737. Another plane arrived a few minutes later with exactly the same flight number and Minister Eggleton appeared. Air China had overbooked its flight by such a margin that it had added an extra plane in Hong Kong, routing its passengers to the same busses but different aircraft on the apron at Kai Tak Airport.

Our first event with Eggleton was the opening of a Canada-China ceramics exhibit at a small and trendy gallery at the edge of the French Concession. The event was sponsored by Manulife. During the Prime Minister's visit two days later, Manulife would be given its formal licence to operate in Shanghai as the third foreign insurance firm licenced in China, and the first joint venture to offer life insurance in the retail market. Manulife had been active in Shanghai from the 1890s through 1949, with a hiatus during the Japanese occupation, but was closed when the communist revolutionary committee took over the city. At the ceramics exhibit there were a dozen Canadian ceramicists on show along with a like number of Chinese, and the mixture worked well. The opening was one day in advance of a visit to the show by Aline Chrétien, who would come with Liani while the Prime Minister and I were in formal talks with Li Peng, and the setting was a beautifully restored old-style Shanghainese teahouse. The building had beautifully carved crown moldings and cornices and interior balconies, with lovely old Chinese screens used as exhibit dividers. The show was opened by a VP of Manulife, for although CEO Dominic D'Allessandro was in town his luggage had been lost en route and he was scouring the city for clothes prior to his licence-granting ceremony forty-eight hours later.

The highlight of the visit of Minister Eggleton was the opening of a Canadian Food and Fashion Show at the Oriental Department Store, which was kicked off with a fashion show featuring Canadian furs. Eggleton and I were greeted on the steps of the store and escorted from our limousine by the most famous of China's then current crop of supermodels, dressed in beautiful fur coats. With one gorgeous model on each arm we were taken around the show, and the photographs taken would show us both of us with big smiles plastered on our face, nestled as we were between beautiful ladies in beaver and fox.

That evening, the day before the arrival of Prime Minister Chrétien, saw the opening of the annual general meeting of the Canada China Business Council with about three hundred Canadian business representatives present. The opening event was a panel billed as "The Three Ambassadors" with former Ambassador Earl Drake, outgoing Chinese Ambassador Zhang Yijun and myself all giving speeches about the progress and prospects for the relationship. Liani had arrived in Shanghai just before the event and she joined me in time to hear my speech, which she said was "OK"; Liani's views were always my best measure, since everyone else was always too fawning to give me anything but very positive feedback. Then it was off to the Hard Rock Café, rented in whole by a Canadian advertising agency for the night, for an evening show MC-ed by Da Shan, the stage name of Mark Rowswell, a young Canadian who was then just at the beginning of an enormously successful stage career in China. His popularity was built around his extraordinarily fluent Chinese and his capabilities as a comedian, and he was particularly loved for his "cross-talk" shows, a traditional quick-wit-and-retort genre of Beijing humour. Mark had just finished working at the Embassy as a locally-engaged assistant in our Cultural and Education Division assistant when I arrived as Ambassador, and he was to go on to become more famous across the country than any other Canadian, except perhaps for Norman Bethune.

Liani and I slipped away from the noisy Hard Rock Café as soon as we could and took a quiet walk on the Bund before retreating to our hotel. Immediately after arriving in our room, I was called away to a meeting room to join the Canadian negotiating team haggling with their Chinese counterparts over the financing arrangements for the sale of the two CANDU nuclear reactors. As it seemed with all Chinese negotiations, the talks were drawn out to the very end and intentionally made as tense as possible prior to the arrival of the Prime Minister. At one point the Chinese side threatened to break off the talks and took a thirty-minute break to confer with the Chairman of the State Planning Commission (soon to be renamed the National Development and Reform Commission). While we all knew that it was part theatre, it had to be played out until the final curtain, and we finally reached agreement at 0330. I was learning that no deal was ever done in China ahead of a deadline, since to do so would be to imply, particularly to one's bosses, that the best possible deal had not been squeezed out of the other side. But the deal was done and it was a big one, worth more than $3 billion, and for me a particular pleasure having been involved at the very beginning of the exchanges on the possibility of a nuclear relationship.

The following morning started early, and Liani and I skipped a big CCBC breakfast and headed out to the airport to greet the Prime Minister and his delegation. The arrival was smooth, and as the big grey Airbus (call number Canada One) came to a stop on the apron, the red carpets were unrolled and the hundred Chinese children with two flags each were deployed, and Jean and Aline Chrétien descended for the normal greetings and into the waiting limousines. I travelled with the Prime Minister, Liani with Aline in another car, neither with Chinese officials present since the Premier of China and his wife were awaiting us at the state guesthouse twenty minutes away.

En route to the meeting, the Prime Minister and I chatted very informally about how much had changed since I took him to the first APEC Summit in Seattle three years earlier, about the calming of the national unity storm, and about my impressions of China. I told Chrétien that he could forget about his large briefing books and gave him a wallet-size booklet that contained everything he would need for the trip, with not only his schedule but very brief bullet points touching on all the issues he would need to raise with Premier Li Peng and at every other event he would attend. I had gotten to know him well during my time in the Privy Council Office, and I knew that he would have ensured that he was up to speed on all major issues during the flight, and all he would need would be the briefest of reminders. He found the booklet a great innovation and a vast improvement over the massive briefing books the Department of Foreign Affairs and International Trade traditionally provided, and we eventually adopted them for all visiting ministers. In fact, the Prime Minister liked them so much that he asked for similar booklets to be prepared for his visits to all other countries, and our little innovation became a model for a new style of briefing adopted by missions around the world, although not always appreciated in posts where old-style ambassadors preferred the traditional and massive briefing books.

When we arrived at the Xijiao Guesthouse, Li Peng and his wife and about 400 journalists were waiting, and after the normal crush and set of semi-posed photos of the two leaders and their wives, Mme Chrétien, Mme Li Peng and Liani headed off for their separate program and we went inside the guesthouse for our formal bilateral meetings. The talks themselves covered, as they had to, all major international and bilateral matters, including the mandatory subject of Canadian concerns about human rights in China. Chrétien normally disliked raising human rights issues since it was a bit like tilting at windmills, but now we were starting up programs in the area of legal reform and the training of judges. Chrétien could thus put a positive and cooperative spin on the subject, which did not elicit the normal, very stiff response about unacceptable interference in domestic affairs that was Li Peng's normal defence. Li Peng was in fact more relaxed than I had seen him before, less strident and seemingly at ease both with the substantive issues and with Chrétien, perhaps because of his trip a year earlier to Canada. At the beginning of the talks he congratulated Chrétien on the referendum victory, and Chrétien responded that he would never let it happen again and told Li Peng that I had been a very important part of the federalist victory.

Following the meeting we had a formal signing ceremony for the nuclear reactor deal, just before which the Prime Minister asked me whether or not the rumour he had heard about a late night negotiating crisis was true. I assured him that the deal had always been "in the bag" and that we all had had plenty of sleep!

Following the government-to-government talks and the signing ceremony for the CANDU project, there was a formal signing of the Manulife life insurance licence and a ribbon cutting for the opening of Manulife's Shanghai office, after which Chrétien playfully offered to put one of the big bows from the cut ribbon on Li Peng's head as a hat, which was of course widely photographed and precipitated among opponents of our China policy criticism of Chrétien's closeness with the butcher of Tiananmen.

The rest of the day was a whirlwind, with a state lunch with seven hundred guests before which there were some more commercial signings that Chrétien and Li Peng witnessed, and following which I gave a press conference on behalf of the Prime Minister. The only real interest among the journalists was in the nuclear deal, with a few questions about whether human rights had been discussed. Nothing that could not be easily fielded, and then it was back in the Prime Ministerial limousine to head out to the airport. As we rode together in the car, I pointed out to Chrétien that his time in Shanghai could be characterized as earning some $600 million per hour for the Canadian taxpayer on the basis of the contracts signed during the eight-hour visit! I then watched the PM's great grey bird take off (an early lesson in the foreign service was never to assume a visitor had left until the plane could be seen leaving the airspace – there were terrible stories of planes not taking off or re-landing, with embassy staff already headed back to town with no means of being contacted) and then I started to relax. Liani headed directly back to Beijing and I went back into the city to participate in the remaining CCBC events.

CHAPTER 20

END OF THE YEAR

• • • • • • • • • • •

Shortly after the Prime Minister's stopover in Shanghai, I made my first official visit to Hong Kong, where I spoke publicly at a Canadian Chamber of Commerce luncheon, and privately at a gathering of all our trade commissioners from the greater China region. My Chamber of Commerce speech received good press coverage as being quite upbeat about Chinese growth and about stability through the Hong Kong retrocession now less than a year away. I also spent an hour with Governor Chris Patten who was interested in my views on Zhu Rongji, soon to become Premier, and his likely attitude towards Beijing-Hong Kong relations, and then another session with Zhou Nan, Beijing's senior representative in the territory. Since the People's Republic of China claimed that Hong Kong was an integral part of China, Zhou Nan and his predecessors could not be assigned there as ambassadors, and instead were named as "Heads" of the New China News Agency, the state propaganda arm. Zhou Nan was very sophisticated and thoughtful, and was clearly pushing the "kid glove" approach to both the handover process and to post-handover relations. He expressed to me some worries about Patten's tendency to speak publicly about sensitive issues and said that he sometimes was not sure that Patten's own image was not more important to him than the interests of the Hong Kong people. He was, as most senior Chinese were in private, quite dismissive of Britain's new-found interest in territorial democracy, having done nothing to advance it in the hundred years of colonial rule.

I also had dinner with my old friend Vincent Cheng, who I had known as a mid-level policy advisor to earlier Governors Ford and Wilson some years earlier. Vincent had then been on loan to the colonial government by HSBC and was one of the most senior Hong Kong natives in the territorial government, but by 1996 he was back in the HSBC system where he would eventually rise to Chairman of their local Hang Seng subsidiary and a senior executive of the parent bank itself. Vincent's take on the danger points of the months leading to the handover and the years that would follow were very thoughtful. He felt that the biggest danger would lie more in Hong Kong than in Beijing, and that there was a risk that the post-handover Chief Executive would be pressured to over-think Beijing's reaction to issues that the local government should simply move forward with managing on its own. On balance, however, he was very optimistic.

One of my calls during my three days in Hong Kong was on David Eldon, President and CEO of the Hong Kong and Shanghai Banking Corporation. HSBC had during the previous decade become much more active in Canada, having swallowed both the Bank of British Columbia and the Midland Bank of Canada. I began the meeting by complaining about a recent financial statement of the bank that had come to my attention and then handed him an annual report from 1911, signed by my grandfather, Gideon Balloch. Eldon was delightfully entertained by the fact that my grandfather had been Chairman, and we talked about the history of the bank and he promised to have someone in their archives do some research on Gideon's role. He later sent me a four-volume history of the bank, and told me that Gideon Balloch had in fact served as Chairman three times, the first in 1903 just a year or so after moving down from Fuzhou. The position was in those days always a non-executive position, and Gideon shared a rotating board seat with a Mr. Scarfe, who was a colleague of his at Gilman and Co., their merchant bank. The last time Gideon served as Chairman was in 1913. The bank records unfortunately do not reveal much in terms of home addresses or other personal details, but at least his role with HSBC became clearer, and I could fill in my father and other family members on a little more family history.

A busy few days back in Beijing followed, which included hosting a lunch for Bank of Montreal Chairman Matt Barrett, in town to receive the bank's Beijing branch licence, which would allow the bank to formally open its branch in 1997. I had gotten to know Barrett both as ADM Asia and during my consultations with business leaders during my national unity job, so it was pleasant to be reconnecting now in a new role. He would return regularly over the next couple of years.

Then it was off to another provincial visit, this time to Hubei where the timing was determined by the opening of a Canadian built water treatment plant in Erzhou, an eastern industrial suburb of Wuhan with a population of about one and a half million. Both Wuhan and Erzhou carried the scars of frightful environmental degradation, with huge steel factories and building materials plants spewing out frightful mixtures of noxious oxides and stone dust, as the centrality of the Wuhan area made it a key hub of old-style metal-bashing communist China. But the signs of the future were already visible, with vast tracts of new cityscape under construction and the beginnings of some light and higher technology industry also appearing.

My meetings with the Hubei Party Secretary, Jia Zhijie and Governor Jia Zhuping were both very pro-forma. They had both come up through the local party structure and neither struck me as ready for the challenges that a very populous province and a huge metropolis in a modernizing China would face, but they were requirements of the visit and the impressions I formed would later serve as a good base from which I could measure the truly extraordinary changes that would eventually come to Wuhan and the province.

The two highlights of my Erzhou trip were the opening of the water treatment plant and time I spent with the Erzhou Party Secretary. The former was a very grand affair, outdoors in a huge field near the plant with a stage and stands specially-built for the occasion, and with more than a thousand people in attendance and speeches by the Provincial Governor and others, and of course by me. The best part was the music, provided by a traditional Chinese drum band, all dressed in flashy reds and oranges, and wielding their drums with a panache that any Tang Emperor would have approved of. But they were not alone, for this was modern and not just traditional China. Just as the drummers started their performance before the speeches began, around the corner came the Erzhou Marching Band, with banners announcing its name in Chinese and English, and its performers all dressed in blue and white and looking every bit like the marching band of an American high school and playing exactly the same music, including American military marches, and completely ignoring the rhythm of the drummers. The cacophonic duet was outrageous and was repeated again at the end of the ceremony. I thought then that it was a good metaphor for the Hubei of the time, uncertain whether it was stuck in dynastic China or en route to becoming a little America!

Half-way through the formal banquet on the evening after the water treatment plant opening, and well into the Mao-tai, the Erzhou Party Secretary told me he was a keen tennis player and invited me to play with him the following afternoon. Given that my plans would no longer have me in the city, I proposed six in the morning, which was too early for him so we compromised and agreed to play at 11pm that very evening. The Party Secretary's enthusiasm outpaced his talent so we ended up playing doubles, with he and I playing against a local ringer and the CEO of the Canadian water treatment company. I kept score, trying to gently correct some of the atrocious line calls of my partner while using French to warn my opponent and compatriot that one never argues with a Party Secretary. As we played, there was a troop of lovely young ball-girls in short shorts and skimpy T-shirts not only gathering balls for us but constantly bringing us hot towels and water. What with Mao-tai circulating in my system from dinner and the pretty young women waiting on us, it was rather difficult to keep my mind on the game . . .

The closing two weeks of the calendar year saw me give a speech at the Great Hall of the People at the sixth annual Zhu Fuk Tong Awards for excellence in medical achievement, an award partially funded by Canada in memory of Dr. Norman Bethune, and a return by Trade Minister Art Eggleton to Beijing, his time in Shanghai with the CCBC the month before not having been an official visit. This meant formal bilateral economic and trade talks with Minister Wu Yi, which focused as always in those days on both the WTO accession issue for China and a number of bilateral irritants, of which there were then not many. The granting of China's first joint-venture insurance licence to Manulife, the granting of the Bank of Montreal's Beijing Branch licence and the signing of the nuclear agreement had together created a very positive atmosphere in the bilateral economic relationship. Eggleton also presided over the opening of a non-permanent Canadian wing of the Chinese Museum of National History on the eastern side of Tiananmen Square, funded by the Canadian Foundation for the Preservation of Chinese Artifacts, led by the irrepressible Nelly Ng of Toronto. The foundation was just beginning to become active in the preservation of treasures found during the clearing of land and the removal of temples in the middle reaches of the Yangtze River as preparatory work for the Three Gorges Dam advanced.

Eggleton's visit was the last formal event of the year, and with his departure I could put the whole Embassy into a stand-down mode and let the community focus on families and Christmas. We ourselves brought a twelve-foot Christmas tree inside the residence and began to decorate, daughter Cynthia organized a Christmas pageant in the Alvin Hamilton room of the Chancery, and we all took a deep breath.

A family Christmas followed, with all of our decorations and traditions transported to the Middle Kingdom from Ottawa, helping secure in everyone's mind that China was now home. Among the presents were lots of bits and pieces for the Balloch railroad, now growing in a dedicated and otherwise unused storage room in the basement of the Official Residence. And winter was real in Beijing, with little snow but sub-zero temperatures, and we skated for the first time in the open air on the moat of the Forbidden City at Zhongshan Park, and also on the lake at Houhai.

After Christmas I had sensibly organized a formal provincial visit to Hainan, and we flew as a family to Haikou for meetings with senior officials and then drove south to Xinlong, where we stayed overnight at the hot springs and walked along the old plantation's narrow-gauge railway and through the botanical gardens. Then it was southeast from Xinlong to Sanya, where we stayed at the newly opened Gloria Resort Hotel, the very first hotel built on the beach in Yalong Bay. The bay there had been a military district until the year before, and thus closed to the public and devoid of development. Our hotel stood alone on the southern edge of the sandy-white beach, which stretched northward for about four kilometers without another building, open and very beautiful. We returned for another family vacation three years later and already there were a dozen more hotels, and I was to return again after more than another decade of development to find Yalong Wan hopelessly over-built, with resort hotels cheek-by-jowl and covering every inch of waterfront from south of the Gloria Hotel to the rocks at the northern end of the bay.

We were among few guests at the Gloria Resort Hotel as it had only just opened and was not yet really actively marketing. The President of COFCO, China's state-owned trading company for grains and oilseeds, had told me about it. COFCO had a real-estate arm that was building out hotels under the Gloria brand (Kai Lai in Chinese) as well as residential housing projects. Much later we would buy our post-government home in a COFCO-financed Gloria development complex, but of course we did not know that in 1996.

On our second day of our stay in Sanya, we were advised by hotel staff that one part of the hotel, including a handsome villa set on the northeastern corner of the property, would be closed to regular guests for a few days due to the arrival of a senior Chinese leader. The leader turned out to be NPC Chairman and Politburo member Qiao Shi, taking a break from the pressures of politics in Beijing as the intra-party struggles deepened in advance of the 15th Party Congress scheduled for the following autumn. I had spent time with Qiao Shi during his official visit to Canada just before our move to China early in 1996, and so I passed a note to his staff requesting a chance to pay my respects. This was granted and I had a cup of tea and a very pleasant personal discussion with Qiao Shi at a table near the beach, allowing my four children all to come up and be introduced. We had a lovely chat about families and life and at his request I told him about my childhood in Newfoundland. It was, however, clearly a chance for him to get away from the pressures of Chinese political life at the pinnacle of power, and I of course avoided broaching any political subject.

And so 1996 came to a close, a big year of change for me and for the family, a very busy one with lots of new experiences, and as we left the heat and sandy beaches of Sanya to return to icy Beijing, we felt that our China lives, both personal and professional, were truly launched.

CHAPTER 21

DEATH OF DENG XIAOPING

• • • • • • • • • • •

On the morning of February 19ᵗʰ, 1997, all Chinese radio and television stations interrupted their regular programming to announce that Deng Xiaoping had died.

While Deng's death had been long expected and frequently rumoured over the previous two or three years, there had been no recent announcements of setbacks in hic condition or other indications of his impending demise. We would learn later that the inner-most leadership of the Communist Party and Deng's immediate family had known for some weeks that the end had come, and had made substantial preparations for his death prior to having his life support systems disconnected.

As soon as we heard the news, we sent a message to Ottawa recommending that the Prime Minister issue a statement and make a press comment. Our recommendation was to recognize the extraordinary contribution Deng had made to the modernization of China, but not to be excessively effusive give his role in authorizing the use of force in the Tiananmen crisis in 1989. Jean Chrétien found just the right balance, emphasizing the "pivotal role" Deng had played in turning China around after the Cultural Revolution, but also pointing out in answer to a journalist's question that some Canadians had "mixed feelings" about Deng's record in 1989, and that, he said, was "why, whenever we meet with the leaders of China, we always mention the rule of law".

In keeping with Deng's own wishes, the state limited the efforts to eulogize him, and referred to him simply as "Comrade", in contrast to the titles of "Great Leader" and "Teacher" that always accompanied references to

Mao Zedong. Similarly, there was to be no state funeral with foreign leaders, and the nightly broadcasts that followed his death for the next ten days told a factual story, concentrating mostly on his contributions to the modernization of China after 1987. Flags were flown at half mast for a week, but no holiday was pronounced and the largest impact on people's daily lives was probably that all centers of entertainment, such as movie theatres and KTV restaurants and bars were closed for three days.

In the days that followed Deng's death I was in Canada for an already scheduled five-city speaking tour, and the relevance of his passing immediately became the central issue both for my speeches and of the many press interviews I gave over those days. In the US press, there had been a flurry of articles immediately following Deng's death about the growing China threat and I tried to counter that theme and to add some perspective on Deng and his legacy. In addition to my speeches in Vancouver, Calgary, Toronto, Ottawa and Montreal, I was interviewed both on English and French CBC television. I argued that Deng's demise was the passing into history of an extraordinary man who had fought both next to Mao Zedong against the Japanese and the Kuomintang, and against Mao on many hugely important domestic policy issues. Since 1949 no one had had the steadying influence that Deng Xiaoping had exercised; like a seasoned pilot called to the bridge of a great ship every time it appeared close to foundering, he was responsible for the re-establishment of common sense after the Great Leap Forward, and later brought to an end the deeply destructive chaos of the Cultural Revolution. His decision to shift China from an ideologically-determined course to one of pragmatism was not at all understood at the end of the 1970s when he took control from Hua Guofeng; it was evident by the late 1990s that his policy of economic reform and the opening up of China was as profound and earth-tilting a course adjustment as any in modern world history. But I also argued that his death, however moving as the turning of a historical page, was not in itself very significant in the context of governance or direction for the modern China he was so critical in building. Indeed, it was his own reforms that resulted in the marginal relevance of his passing.

That Deng Xiaoping himself forbade a lengthy mourning period or a lying-in-state, and insisted that his ashes be simply scattered at sea, was an indication of his belief that the period of personality cults was and should forever remain buried as a relic of past errors, and the mistake of allowing too much power to be collected in the hands of a single leader should never be repeated.

CHAPTER 22

VISITS, VISITS AND MORE VISITS

• • • • • • • • • • •

During our break in Hainan, which bridged into January of 1997, I did some thinking about the organization of the Embassy and the use of my time. Looking back over the year that had just come to a close, I realized that I was being pulled in many directions that did not always justify the use of Ambassadorial time and attention, and that senior officers of the mission were also almost drowning in the organization of ministerial and other high-level visits. The prospects for 1997 were for an even more intense level of exchanges, and I was worried that we could end up losing sight of a number of our important analytical and influence-building objectives in simply managing the unending waves of visits.

I decided that what we needed was a small professional unit that could take over management of all the logistics related to visits, including hotels, motorcades, inter-city transportation, banquets and even the preparation of our new style of visit booklets, containing both scheduling and briefing material in pocket-size format. As soon as I got back to Beijing I discussed this with Guy Saint-Jacques and Ken Sunquist, my two ministers, and they were both strongly in favour of the idea, since it would provide great support to them and real relief for their officers. We sought and obtained in the then just-beginning departmental annual resource allocation exercise the requisite positions and funding, and hired a young mandarin-speaking Canadian named Owen Teo who was finishing up a degree at a local university to head up the effort. After adding a couple of administrative staff, Owen created a very professional Visits Unit, the efficiency of which made an enormous difference to our lives over the next few years. Owen would eventually write the Foreign Service exam and become a Trade Commissioner, and return to China as a diplomat.

And the visits kept rolling in.

The new year was lead off by the Secretary of State for Asia Pacific Raymond Chan, leading a group of small and medium size companies, stopping in Beijing and then moving on to Wuhan, Chongqing, Chengdu and Kunming. A counselor from the trade division accompanied them for the whole tour, while I simply gave the delegation a briefing and hosted a lunch before they set out. At virtually the same time Gil Molgat, speaker of the Senate brought a small parliamentary delegation and was received by Qiao Shi, giving me another chance to spend a little time with him. Even though Qiao Shi was still Chairman of the National People's Congress, his star was clearly waning. Dr. Arnold Bishop, the head of Canada's regulatory agency overseeing all nuclear reactors and the handling of fissile material, the Atomic Energy Control Board (AECB) was in town in late January for regulatory talks on the management of material to be transferred as part of the sale of the CANDU reactors. While this sort of visit would not necessarily require much involvement from an Ambassador, given my close involvement in the nuclear relationship I took advantage of Bishop's visit to reinforce my relationships with key players in China's nuclear hierarchy and both attended a couple of Bishop's meetings, including with Vice Premier Zhu Rongji, and hosted an evening reception for him.

As soon as we had packed off the AECB group for Shanghai and the Qinshan nuclear reactor site, we held a set of consular negotiations, led for us by my old friend Gar Pardy, a native of Gander, Newfoundland, who had been Director of South Asia when I was Director of North Asia some years earlier and who was now Director General for Consular Affairs. By this time consular affairs between Canada and China were becoming increasingly complex for two main reasons. The first was more and more of the large number of Chinese who had immigrated to Canada and obtained Canadian citizenship were coming back to China to do business and often to live. Many would bury their Canadian citizenship and hold themselves out locally as Chinese nationals, until they got into some kind of trouble, when they would pull out their Canadian citizenship and seek the help of the Embassy or one of our consulates. The second and increasingly pressing problem was the status of the more than one hundred thousand Canadian citizens in Hong Kong, which was now only a half year away from losing its British colonial status and becoming part of China. With Britain having refused to grant UK citizenship to more than a very small handful of people from Hong Kong, the local government had begun issuing Hong Kong local identity cards to all long-term residents of the territory, regardless of citizenship, and those identity cards were being treated by China as proof of being natives of the Hong Kong "Special Administrative region" and thus citizens of China. This could effectively result in many Canadian passport holders being de facto dual citizens, while under Chinese law dual citizenship was not permitted. Gar Pardy was to work his way through this field of nettles and come up with the reasonable compromise that any Canadian entering China with a Canadian passport and visa and holding himself out as a Canadian would be accepted as such by the Chinese authorities, while anyone using their Chinese documentation would not be. The new Hong Kong identity card complicated matters, but eventually the Chinese agreed to accept that Canadian citizens entering China using the card would still be treated as Canadians if their passport was Canadian and they had properly renounced Chinese citizenship if born in China. While this was completely logical and legal, it certainly did not stop citizenship-of-the-moment practices by Chinese Canadians, resulting in cries for consular assistance even in cases where people had clearly been holding themselves out as Chinese until the moment they were arrested or got into some sort of business difficulty.

The next three years were a constant flow of inward visits from cabinet ministers, provincial politicians, business leaders, cultural performers and academics, an amazing cross-section of a Canadian "Who's Who". Some were memorable, others less so. For the key ones, those of federal ministers and provincial premiers, I would have to be in Beijing and attend to them, accompanying them on calls on their Chinese counterparts and hosting meals or receptions. For others I could pass the responsibility of care and feeding to one of my senior staff. Most of the visits by federal cabinet ministers were in the end rather unmemorable, and there were lunches or dinners that I hosted where, standing at my seat with a glass in my hand at the beginning of the meal, I sometimes almost forgot who and what event I was toasting. A few, however, stand out, especially that of former Prime Minister Pierre Trudeau, some of the visits by provincial premiers, a visit by Lloyd Axworthy in 1998, and, not surprisingly, the virtually annual state visits in both directions.

At least as interesting as any visit by incoming political leaders, however, were my own trips inside China. To many of the northern and eastern provincial capitals and major cities, including Harbin, Changchun, Shenyang, Xi'an, Taiyuan, Jinan, Qingdao, Zhengzhou and Nanjing, I traveled by train and usually took the family along to allow them to get to see a bit of China outside Beijing. We would generally leave on either a Thursday or Friday evening, travel overnight and then return on the Sunday by plane, having met the provincial leadership and any Canadian businesses operating in the vicinity as well as interesting local sites. We travelled to Harbin in January in two different years to attend the annual Snow and Ice Festival, which gathered ice sculptors from around the world for the largest ice sculpture competition anywhere. The first time I went I had not been warned that I was to be a judge, and I ended up spending hours in the freezing cold without proper boots. Of course as the Canadian Ambassador I could not even intimate that all my toes were completely frozen! In Shandong after our official visit to Jinan, we went to Qufu where Confucius was born and climber Taishan, and elsewhere we did similar things. Going by train was a wonderful way to get a sense of the land and its people and the subsistence level of life through which the vast majority of Chinese still struggled.

CHAPTER 23

FIRST TRIP TO TIBET

• • • • • • • • • • •

In May of 1997 I paid my first visit to Tibet, which is officially the "Tibet Autonomous Region" (TAR) rather than simply a province, but it has since the 1950s always been governed with less rather than more autonomy than an average province.

There were four main purposes in my ten-day visit to Tibet: to observe and publicly demonstrate an interest in developments there; to visit with officials of the Office of Religious and Minority Affairs as well as with leaders of Tibetan Buddhist organizations and monasteries; to meet with regional justice officials and visit at least one prison to explore the conditions of incarceration; and to visit a series of Canada Fund projects, both those already underway or completed and those which could, subject to my approval, begin soon. The visit was quite political and the Canadian and international press very interested in it, and I had been actively encouraged to organize such a visit by our new Minister of Foreign Affairs, Lloyd Axworthy.

My delegation included our Development Counselor and senior CIDA representative at the Embassy, Bob Hamilton, Rachael Bedlington from the Political Section, Canada Fund Coordinator Lucie McNeil, and a "Special Advisor" from the Canadian Council of Churches, Cynthia McLean. In negotiating the arrangements for my visit, I had asked to bring both Canadian journalists and one or two representatives of non-governmental organizations with me, and argued with the Ministry of Foreign Affairs that permitting this would be a clear demonstration that China was becoming more transparent and had nothing to hide. The Ministry, which itself really had no say in the matter as the real decisions were made in the Ministry of State Security and the Office of Religious and Minority Affairs, both of which would be taking direction from the State Council, told me that taking journalists would be "inconvenient" but that I could bring members of Canadian NGOs. We invited the Canadian Council of Churches and the Canadian chapter of Amnesty International, but the latter decided that being included in an official group would leave it open to criticisms of being manipulated and decided to turn down the invitation. We were not at all surprised at being refused permission to bring journalists. As an alternative, with Minister Axworthy's blessing, we told both the Globe and Mail and Toronto Star correspondents that after the visit I would brief them and release a public report on what we had seen as well.

In those days, the only flights into Lhasa were from Chengdu, so on an early Tuesday morning we left behind the sweltering Sichuan heat and headed west for two hours, watching the land come up towards us. Mountains gave way to the high Tibetan Plateau two thousand metres above sea level, making the mountains that we could see northeast of Lhasa as we landed seem rather squat, rising only another eight hundred or a thousand metres above the grasslands.

As we landed, I thought while Tibet might well be part of China, it was as distant from Beijing and the great metropolises of the coast as the Northwest Territories were from Toronto and New York. The first most striking difference was simply the smaller number of people. Lhasa, Tibet's capital, had less than two hundred thousand people, and the entire autonomous region, an area the size of France, had less than three million people. At the airport, the usual jostling crowds of China's airports were missing, and as we awaited our luggage at the sole carrousel, we could look around and see other differences.

The waiting passengers were divisible into three distinct groups, four if you include the visiting western Ambassador and his delegation, surrounded now by local officials. The first group was a small band of tourists from

Taiwan, mostly Buddhist nuns and other adherents, trying to measure how they felt at two thousand metres of elevation and nervously chatting to themselves, and listening to a couple of officious local tour guides who were keeping them together and organizing their transportation. Tibet was a sufficiently untrammelled destination in those days that we would see this group several times again at monasteries and small town guesthouses, including at higher altitudes where one of the nuns was so debilitated from the thin air that one of our handlers intervened with their group leader to recommend immediate evacuation. The second group was clearly Tibetan, locals returning home from studies or business in larger Chinese cities. These Tibetans, including both civilians and monks, were surrounded by friends and family and create a high cacophony of too many people talking at once. The Tibetan language rang clear, as distant from Mandarin as Russian, consonantal and non-tonal. Without any evidence of distaste, they simply kept their distance from the third and largest group, all Han. These were the business people and the carpetbaggers, the hotel owners and shopkeepers, the officials and the army officers stationed in what they probably viewed as the back of beyond for three or four years. They were clearly the quietest and least happy, appearing ill at ease and talking in low voices, as if they were as foreign as we.

It was a long drive in from the airport, for the valley in which Lhasa sits is surrounded by hills too sharp for the long approaches of modern jetliners. Our car, like the vast majority of those found in this high and rugged land, was a big jeep with high clearance and a four-wheel drive. Outside was Tibet of the storybooks. The black shaggy yaks pulling ploughs, women in colourful headdresses seeding the barley fields, sun darkened children everywhere. There was no one-child policy in this minority area, and the authorities would only intervene to discourage too many children in the poorest of rural Tibet, and then only after the birth of a fourth child. The little hamlets we passed were all made of mud brick or stuccoed concrete, on the walls of which were drying pressed pads of yak dung, a principal source of household fuel. The hamlets were generally composed of a series of one-story houses, with little towers on each of their four corners, set inside a warren of walled courtyards, used for livestock, laundry and sometimes latrines.

It took us about an hour and a half to reach Lhasa, whose outskirts were definable by a large and filthy cement plant, spewing an awful green-grey smoke into the otherwise crisp and clean and brilliantly blue sky. Then Lhasa itself appeared, with the Potala Palace high on its rocky promontory right in the centre of the valley. The Potala Palace dominated the city, with its high white walls and deep red central buildings the image of Tibet itself. This, of course, was the very centre of both Tibetan Buddhism as a religion and of the theocratic state that existed for centuries, sometimes inside and sometimes outside of Chinese suzerainty, with the Dalai Lama and his court ensconced high above the impoverished town and their scattered domain, ruling on all matters and receiving homage from foreign powers and distant Buddhist sects, involving themselves deeply in questions both spiritual and political.

The first two days of my visit were all official and limited to Lhasa. During meetings with regional government officials, the state of Canada-China relations and the past and ongoing Canada Fund activities in the TAR served as a positive backdrop for both explanations by officials of the current economic and political conditions of the region and requests for further Canadian development assistance in a number of areas. From the Canadian standpoint, the meetings served to make clear Canada's policy towards Tibetan issues, which included not challenging its constitutional status as an integral part of the People's Republic of China, and our overall interest in contributing to the improvement of services that satisfy basic human needs in the region.

I had a very cordial meeting and lunch with Gyaincain Norbu, the native Tibetan Chairman of the TAR, who theoretically, but only theoretically, outranked the Party Secretary, a position always filled by a Han Chinese. I explained that we understood the complexity of balancing the need for development with the respect for the religion and traditions of a largely theocratic society, and said that we were pleased to be rebuilding village health clinics and supporting local artisanal industry. Rather than proceeding with the expected review of bilateral matters and the raising of human rights issues, I instead talked a little about the centuries long path the west had taken to separate church and state, and how I personally thought that this principle could well be the key to the long-term resolution, both for the Chinese government and for the Buddhist hierarchy, of the Tibetan question. I suggested that it would indeed be very much in China's interest to argue that the Tibetan Buddhist leadership should limit themselves to spiritual matters, and if the cost to the Chinese government was a complete retreat from interference in temple affairs, this would seem a small price to pay. Chairman Gyaincain seemed very interested in the concept, but I could see from the furious scribblings of a low-level staffer from the Waiban (the local government's division responsible for managing all foreign relations and visitors) that lots of skeptical eyes would peruse this concept before anyone commented officially. I also explained that Canadians generally, in part because so many of them came from families that had fled persecution, were concerned about religious freedoms and the treatment of religious minorities all around the world, and that I hoped my visit would give me a clear picture of the situation in Tibet. I thanked him for allowing us the chance to meet with judicial authorities and visit a prison as well.

My meeting with Chen Kuiyuan, successor to Hu Jintao as TAR Party Secretary and a reputed "hard-liner", was less warm and more formalistic. He welcomed Canada's recent decision not to "join the anti-China plot" of some western countries at a UNHCR meeting that had taken place in April in Geneva, which had been a resolution challenging China's treatment of Tibetans. I pointed out that Canada had not viewed the resolution as a plot and that we had refrained from co-sponsoring it on the basis of the significant progress we had perceived in Chinese legal reform and our belief that it was better to work cooperatively with China in such areas as judicial training and the development of legal aid and other institutions that would strengthen China as a civil society. I did point out that we remained concerned about religious freedoms in Tibet and elsewhere in China but I hoped that my visit would allow me and my delegation a better understanding of the progress that was being made.

We were then taken to Drapchi Prison, which was impressive to the point that we were tempted to conclude that we were being treated to at least a partially Potemkin experience. The prison was clean and well-appointed with mattressed bunks and switchable lights, twelve prisoner cells, clean and ample open areas both indoors and out, a very clean working environment in a carpet-making workshop. We were told the prisoners were given three warm meals a day with meat at least once, prepared by a democratically-elected kitchen team of prisoners, and that the prisoners all attended classes for two days a week in Tibetan and Chinese language studies, commercial studies and "good citizenry".

At Drapchi, we were given a tour of the carpet-making workshop, where prisoners were allegedly being trained in carpet-making skills that would allow them to integrate into the local workforce once released. Given that we were told that the average length of the training course was three months, and already knew that the average sentence being served at the prison was ten years or more, it was evident that the "training" was a thin cover for an economic activity aimed at bringing in revenue. Nonetheless, the working conditions were nothing short of excellent, with good ventilation and clean floors, and adequate if not mechanized stand-up looms. Prison officials assured us that carpets were woven on specific order, and indeed reference on tags indicated that they were destined to be identified as having come from specific factories, and that they would not find their way into the export market. We also visited a large and modern "teaching building" with some fifteen classrooms, each with a capacity for more than forty students. We presumed, but did not see, that some of the classrooms must have had other purposes, for the capacity of the building was clearly greater than justified by the 360 inmates who we were told would be on their "educational rotation" at any given time. We visited two classes in session, one a Chinese literature class for male inmates and the second a Tibetan language class for women. The former appeared in all detail a real class, the latter somewhat staged, but the desks and chairs in all the classrooms showed signs of real use and we saw teachers drawn from the more educated prisoners in preparation for classes yet to be held.

In the end we concluded that we had been shown the very best in a well-appointed and well run prison, and that even with a fair amount of discounting we had no reason to judge the facility to be only a Potemkin front for an otherwise brutal system. It really did seem that real efforts were being made to apply published national prison standards and to provide a humane and reasonably rehabilitative environment for those incarcerated. We of course could not evaluate whether the prisoners had been treated fairly by the judicial system in incarcerating them in the first place, and were given very evasive answers when we asked about how many were serving under "reform through labour" sentences, generally dispensed directly by police authorities without due process. We also were unable to see any evidence of prisoners being permitted to exercise their religious beliefs, or any prayer books or Tibetan prayer flags or other religious symbols, in spite of assertions to the contrary that inmates were given complete freedom to worship as they saw fit as long as they "did not disturb other prisoners". And we only saw a single prison, so generalities drawn from our visit had to be made very cautiously.

As we travelled further in Tibet, we were able to probe a little further into the experiences that religious communities and others had with the criminal justice system. Although we did hear evidence to corroborate some of the positive that we had seen and heard at Drapchi Prison, we also heard anecdotal stories of prison guards beating inmates who flaunted their religious belief and other police heavy-handedness during pre-sentence incarceration and interrogation. In the end, however, none of these stories, nor our doubts about the representational nature of the almost too-perfect Drapchi Prison, undermined our overall conclusion that, measured against either practices in other countries and just as importantly against what was known of the history of China's own brutal prison system, the authorities were making efforts not only to show progress but to actually implement real improvements.

Another major focus of our trip, indeed a requirement to satisfy public and parliamentary interest back in Canada, was the question of religious freedom and the treatment of the Buddhist sects that continued to treat the Dalai Lama as both their spiritual and political leader.

Both in Lhasa and in other towns and cities we visited temples and met with monks and the "Democratic Management Committees" that were approved as the governing entities of temples and religious orders. These committees were composed mostly of monks but also had representatives from the Office of Religious and Minority Affairs. Our visit coincided with the efforts of the Chinese government to find a new *modus operandi* with the Tibetan Buddhists that would permit an expanded zone of acceptable activity, including the recruitment of new and younger novitiates, increased interchange with Buddhist groups outside of China, and the expansion of the orders in revenue-generating activities. The counter-balancing concession was an acceptance of "political education" for all monks and nuns, which seemed focused primarily on undermining reverence for the Dalai Lama and an acceptance that his role and image in monastic teachings and displays be eliminated. While it was clear to us that the Buddhist leaders understood that their freedom to continue to exist as religious and economic actors in Tibet was dependent on accepting this new *modus operandi*, and to set aside and discourage all public adulation of the Dalai Lama, it was also evident that this acceptance was not heartfelt. Everywhere we went, once we were alone with a monk, we would hear reverent references to, or be shown hidden pictures of, the Dalai Lama. And in public places, like in the small stalls and busy turmoil of the Bharkor market area of the capital, images of the Dalai Lama were very easy to find, always in a place of reverence.

On the positive side it was clear that the secular authorities were more relaxed than in the past in permitting exchanges between the religious orders and outsiders. We were told by the monks themselves of exchanges with both India and Nepal and met with some who had participated in such activities. There was also a growing religious-based tourism, with groups of Buddhists from Taiwan, Korea, Japan and South Asia visiting Tibet and touring monasteries. There was no evidence of any impediments to full and open communications between these groups and local monks, and we saw on several occasions local and foreign groups in active discussion.

After three days of official meetings and temple visits in Lhasa, we shifted our focus to our development activities and the projects of the Canada Fund. The first project we went to was a small school for poor and handicapped children, where we were funding the teaching of artisanal Tibetan papermaking. The paper was coarse and made from the mix of the pulpy stem of a small flowering bush, native to Tibet, and ground up recycled paper. In almost all respect the method was the same that my siblings and I had used as children, when we would bring handfuls of pulp home from the mill in Corner Brook and make paper on screens. The children were being taught to shred the fibrous stems and blend them into the torn up recycled paper, cooking it all slowly into a fine porridge that could be spread on screens to dry. The papermaking at the handicapped school was under the direction of a very old teacher, who was one of the last artisans to have the knowledge passed on to him fifty years earlier. The paper he produced was very fine, with the appearance of a coated linen paper, and his aim was to gradually develop the children's skills until their product would be just as consistent and fine. The paper had been used for hundreds of years for the printing of Buddhist sutras, and a local monastery purchased all the paper the little school produced.

The children at the school were all very poor, but at least there was enough for them to eat and older people to look after them. The floors were plain concrete and their beds just hard wooden mats, but the place was clean and there was running water. They were all extremely polite, although were being taught only Tibetan so we could not converse directly with them, and they were being taught other basic skills as well as paper-making.

Given the hopelessness from which they had emerged, the school appeared more a source of joy than despair, but one could not leave without carrying a little of the overall sadness away.

On the Friday we headed north and east to a series of small medical clinics supported for several years by the Canada Fund. After the first forty-five minutes out of the city the tarmac disappeared from under us, and for the next ten hours we bumped up and down on dry country tracks barely visible across the valleys and nestled tight to the cliffs between them. The road was washed away in many places, and we learned quickly the advantage of our jeeps with its high clearance and four-wheel drive.

The little villages we passed through were very poor and very distant, even one from another. In most valleys there was a single county town of a few hundred people, and it was there that the scattered rural folk had to travel many hours on foot or by horse for more than the most rudimentary of services. During the 1960s, the Chinese authorities had brought the concept of its "barefoot doctors" to Tibet, and in each county town there was one such person, trained for a total of four or five months and capable of administering a minimal level of health care. These barefoot doctors were also farmers and only worked in their medical role when required, generally operating out of their own homes. What we were doing in our Canada Fund project was, in partnership with a local Tibet organization and the international group Médecins sans Frontières, building very small clinics in each of twenty-eight towns. We provided the funds for the buildings and some basic new equipment, such as stethoscopes and syringes and forceps and an initial supply of medicines that the doctors would replace through the local government. Médecins sans Frontières provided the medical training, and our local partner handled construction oversight and financial training. The clinics were wonderful, had been designed very simply but were clean and bright, and all the barefoot doctors we met, more women than men, were proud as punch of their new facilities, capabilities and their newfound community status. The only problem I had was with the signs outside the clinics, which said, in

Tibetan and English, "Canadian International Development Agency", so I ordered them all removed and replaced with bilingual signs that said "Gift of the People of Canada".

In every village we visited, the children poured around us, entranced and nervous and delighted at seeing a convoy of cars and fancy strangers. When we arrived a village leader would greet us by draping a traditional white scarf, a "hadad" around our necks and serve us yak butter tea in silver bowls. We were served this traditional tea everywhere we went, and as soon as even one little sip was taken our cups would be refilled to the brim. This I could have done without, for the drink was very rich and peculiar, but it was as unavoidable as the potholes, especially for me as the most important visitor. By the end of each day, even the thought of yak butter tea would make my stomach roil, and indeed by the time our entire Tibetan trip was over, I think all my clothes and hair and even skin reeked of the stuff.

After our tour of the northeastern villages where our clinics had been built, we returned to Lhasa for just a night before heading out of the city again, this time south and west towards the Himalayas. About an hour out of Lhasa we took a sharp turn to the south and, leaving tarmac behind for the next few days, headed up a tightly switch-backing road to the first of two major mountain passes we would cross. We climbed from the valley floor at about four thousand metres to the pass at well over five, where we could look south to the most beautiful emerald lake, Lake Landrop, a scorpion shaped body of water maybe twenty kilometres long, with many winding arms fed entirely by the mountain rain and snow. At the pass we stopped, not just to stretch our legs but also to allow the Tibetans among us to hang prayer flags and light small brush fires in the cairns that others had built. Then they tossed small "paper horses" into the wind, strong up in the mountain pass, and watched them swirl and twist their way down the mountainside. Our driver was particularly religious, a fact we commented on positively over the next few days, trusting that his deity would protect us all as he roared down the narrow bumpy roads, passing trucks on tight mountain curves. Someone on my staff suggested that if we did go off the edge, our driver was bound to be reincarnated as a Mario Andretti or a Jacques Villeneuve!

It took us two hours to work our way down from the pass to the edge of Lake Landrop, and we skirted around its northwestern flank before heading westward out of the high valley into still higher mountains. This time the climb was straighter and more gradual, but the mountains were more imposing, with heavy snow caps and glaciers. We climbed all the way to the Kaerola Pass, some fifty-eight hundred metres above sea level and directly under the glaciers. There we stopped again and repeated the same religious rituals, in which our Tibetan friends got us to good-heartedly participate. No one had a lot of energy for the air was very thin, and even the smallest climb left chests heaving and hearts pumping wildly. One of us, an interpreter from Beijing, was affected to the point of immobility, so she stayed in the car and moaned that she wished she had never come. The Tibetans smiled snidely at the wimpy Han Chinese but said nothing.

The Kaerola Pass was a very beautiful place, with two streams, one from the east and one from the west, joining to form a north-flowing river that we would follow for the next few hours. Before we did that, however, we stopped just over the pass for a picnic lunch, and I decided that a climb to the glacier's edge was a good idea. What I saw as two or three hundred metres turned out to be much further, perhaps a kilometre and the gradual shale slope turned into a slippery climb of almost forty degrees. Although a couple of our local companions started out with me, they both fell away before we reached our objective, but there was no way I was going to be defeated. I almost did not make it, and as I got higher the shortness of my breath warned me to sit down several times to take my pulse and wait until enough strength had returned for the next seventy or eighty metres. But I did make it, and with the rest of my team nothing more than little black spots off on the tundra-like meadow below. I scooped up a handful of snow and raised my arms to the magnificent deep blue of the mountain sky. When I and my violently trembling legs got back to the group, where I could drink some water and have what was left over from the picnic, the

Tibetans had clearly come to believe that I was both crazy and a good man. I had said that I wanted to touch the summer snow of the Himalayas and they were clearly impressed that I had been tenacious enough to actually do it.

We spent the better part of that afternoon following our little river first northward and then westward again through another valley, watching as it gradually picked up tributaries and grew in size and strength. At the end of the valley we came into a massive work site of a Chinese army engineering corps building a dam and a large hydroelectric power station. The scene could have been somewhere up in the Rocky Mountains of western Canada, except for the thousands of swarming green shirted workers.

It was late in the afternoon when we arrived at our destination, the town of Gyantse, where the local mayor greeted us by draping us with Hadads and offering us yak butter tea, and then took us around town to see a truly beautiful monastery and a traditional "Dzong" or old rural fort. After the requisite welcoming banquet, which was a dreadful affair with the local mayor chain-smoking and lecturing us on the wonderful plans he had to pave and industrialize his city, the following day we toured another of our local projects, this a traditional weaving factory, where the local coarse yak hair is died and woven into blankets, and finer sheep wool into homespun cloth. Again the little we had been able to do, in terms of training and the provision of basic looms and other equipment, seemed to be making an enormous difference in people's lives, reviving a local industry that had been snuffed out by collectivization and the imposed uniformity of the Cultural Revolution. The workshop we visited had about ten weavers and we watched as their shuttles flew back and forth and their homespun cloth grew longer and longer. Their gratitude to Canada was deep, and we were showered with gifts of blankets and cloth.

The day of our visit to the weavers was International Children's Day, and just after leaving the workshop we heard drums and singing, and then saw two streams of children converging on the crossroads where we were standing. At the front of the first stream of red and yellow bedecked Young Pioneers, came two ten-year old children, a boy and a girl, carrying a huge portrait of Mao Zedong. It was like being in a time warp, but I could not help thinking of all the damage his excesses had done to this beautiful land and hardy people.

From Gyantse we left the Himalayas behind us and turned north for the town of Shigatse, and traveled through a beautiful and fertile valley being sown with barley and corn. The farmers worked in unison, singing and bending as they hoed in an almost choreographed rhythm. The air was crisp and the atmosphere as clear and clean as the little streams that tumbled down the hillsides. I thought that the valley could well serve as a perfect image of Shangri-La, pastoral and peaceful.

Shigatse, a prefectural town and the second largest city in Tibet, was home to a beautiful monastery, the Tashilhunpo temple, and a pile of huge stones and shattered walls that constituted the ruins of a great Dzong that had been dismantled at the beginning of the 1960s and thoroughly destroyed during the Cultural Revolution. The Dzong, which is on a rocky promontory at the centre of the city, was completely rebuilt in the years following my visit, partly to attract tourists and partly as one of the projects in the temple reconstruction program the government points to as a demonstration of their tolerance of Buddhism. It now stands over the town much as the Potala Palace dominates the valley of Lhasa. In Shigatse, our hosts were much more sophisticated than those in the smaller Gyantse, and at our official dinner we engaged in a lengthy and thoughtful exchange on the complexities of separating church and state in Tibet. The local mayor argued that while this was a good objective, Tibetan Buddhism so integrated its religious teachings into social and civil matters that backing the religious out of matters more properly those of the state was virtually impossible. I found local attitudes far less propagandist than those in Lhasa, and our interlocutors, one of whom was a young vice mayor who had studied at the prestigious Fudan University in Shanghai, were all intelligent and deeply committed to improving the lives of the Tibetan people without destroying their culture.

After dinner that evening, the young vice-mayor took us on a long walk through the older parts of town, and even in the darkness we found the people boisterous and charming. Canada Fund Coordinator Lucie McNeil, stopped a young boy and tried to have a chat with him, coaxing him to tell her what he had hidden behind his back. The five-year old smiled, pulled out a plastic water pistol and squirted her, reminding us that children, all over the world, including Tibet, had more in common with each other than we usually recognized.

When we got back to Lhasa, only a five-hour drive on paved roads from Shigatse through rugged countryside and increasingly summer-like valleys with fields of winter buckwheat and barley emerging from their winter hibernation, we had a final set of meetings with the Tibetan leadership, this time represented by Chairman Raidi of the local People's Congress. We then hosted a reception for all our governmental contacts, our Canada Fund intermediaries and partners, Tibetans who had studied or been trained in Canada, and the handful of Canadians working or teaching in the Tibetan capital. On the advice of one of our local partners we arranged a traditional Tibetan orchestra, complete with a troop of singers and dancers, to perform during the reception. Our Tibetan guests were truly complimented by our interest and the respect that our choice of entertainment showed.

Back in Beijing, I prepared a report on what we had done and seen in Tibet, and our impressions on sensitive issues such as religious freedoms, the judicial system as seen through the prism of a single prison and the impact of Chinese development and other programs. Rachael Bedlington and Lucie McNeil helped me with the draft and in the end we were all quite satisfied that it portrayed a properly balanced view of what we had seen and done. This was the report that prior to the visit we had promised would be released publicly. We sent it off to Ottawa for comments from the China specialists in the Asia Branch, and they in turn shared it with Minister Axworthy's staff. A day or two later we received a redraft from Axworthy's staff, substantially changing the tone of the report to be much more critical and in my view much less balanced about what we had seen and our impressions of the impact of Chinese policies in the territory. I sent back a message saying that I was not willing to change the report because it reflected accurately what we had seen and what I believed to be the complex interplay of positive governmental policies bringing real benefit to an impoverished region and a negative ideological intolerance of sustained public reverence for the Dalai Lama. I also had made clear that I believed that western history and our own liberal traditions gave us a credible and balanced stance from which to both praise progress and criticize oppression at the same time, and that was the seven-hundred year tortuous march towards the separation of church and state. Axworthy's people, who even wanted to leave an implication that we did not accept that Tibet was an integral part of China, which was fundamental to our recognition of China, saw human rights issues in black and white and I did not, and I simply would not have my report rewritten. This exchange went back and forth and I was at one point told that the Minister himself wanted my report changed, or else it could not be released. Ministerial authority to prevent the report's release I accepted, and so I told our journalist friends that Ottawa had decided against a public release. However, as I had not classified the document, the Globe and Mail eventually sought and obtained it through a formal "Access to Information" request. As it was a balanced report that reflected the views for which I was known and had in fact expressed orally to journalists upon my return from Tibet, the whole matter ended more with a whimper than a bang. But Minister Axworthy, and certainly his staff, were not very happy with me.

At poor mountain village in southern Qinghai, with EA Weldon Epp, Canada Fund team, local villagers, and Liani and twins

Being greeted in Qinghai village with traditional Tibetan drink of fermented mare's milk

After presenting credentials in North Korea, scrimmaging with women's national team (photo courtesy of Toronto Star)

Joshua and Gideon with Jim Boutillier of Canadian Navy during call at Qingdao of HMCS Winnipeg

Running with PLA platoon during the 2000 Terry Fox Run in Tiananmen Square

Second visit to Tibet, this time with whole Balloch family, at Potala Palace

With Tibetan monks

Chatting with old friends Vice Premier Zeng Peiyan and Liaoning Party
Secretary Wen Shizhen

Liani and Aline Chrétien
touring the Forbidden City in
Beijing, February, 2001

Aline Chrétien and Liani at
children's clinic in Shanxi, 2001

Prime Minister with the children of the Canada-China Hockey League

Prime Minister Chrétien, premiers and territorial leaders fooling around before children's hockey game

HRB and Liani in the pit at the Terracotta Warrior museum in Xi'an

Vice Foreign Minister (later Minister, and a friend for decades)
Yang Jiechi and our wives

Toasting with Zhu Rongji to another successful visit, 2001

As President of Canada China Business Council,
with President Hu Jintao and businessman Henry Wang

Zhu Rongji, HRB and André Desmarais during 2001 Team Canada Gala

HRB, Premier Wen Jiabao, Jean Chrétien and Peter Kruyt of Power Corporation during CCBC 2003 AGM

With State Councillor (former Minister of Foreign Affairs)
Tang Jiaxuan in 2003

HRB speaking at Asia
Pacific Foundation's
2004 "China Summit",
Vancouver

Chatting with Premier
Wen Jiabao in 2007,
now simply as a
businessman

Discussion with Li Keqiang, in mid 2000s Party Secretary of Henan then Part Secretary of Liaoning, later Premier of China

Meeting future President Xi Jinping during a conference in Beijing, 2010. CCPIT Chairman and old friend Wan Jifei is to the left of Xi

CHAPTER 24

LAST VISIT OF PIERRE TRUDEAU

• • • • • • • • • • •

On the evening of a cool late September day, I slipped out of a dinner hosted by the Minister of Water Resources, a dinner called at the last minute in aid of the big contracts being let for the Three Gorges project. As we were on the way to the airport, political officer Rachael Bedlington called to say that the private Bank of Montreal plane we were planning to meet was twenty minutes early, so Lao Ji, my trusty driver, ramped up the official red rocket to about 140 kilometres per hour and we arrived at the airport just in time to join a long motorcade of Mercedes and police cars out onto the apron where a Challenger was just stopping. This was a mixed motorcade, organized in part by the Bank of China for Matt Barrett, Chairman and CEO of the Bank of Montreal, and partly by the Ministry of Foreign Affairs in honour of Barrett's much more important guest, former Prime Minister Pierre Elliot Trudeau. Barrett had invited Trudeau to join celebrations surrounding the opening of the bank's new branch in Beijing, then one of the very few foreign bank branches in China, and it was an inspired idea because it guaranteed highest-level access and huge media attention. With Barrett were his entire Board of Directors and their spouses, as well as former board members and the senior management of both the Canadian bank and its US and Mexican subsidiaries, Harris Bank and Bancomer. All told the group was about 150 strong, although only Trudeau, his friend and law partner Roy Heenan, Matt Barrett and the latter's new wife, Anne-Marie Sten, were on the Challenger. Anne-Marie Sten had been a super-model and mistress to the Saudi arms dealer Adnan Khashoggi, and her marriage to Matt Barrett earlier in the year had generated huge media attention.

Among other BMO board members were Peter Bentley, Chairman and CEO of the forest products company Canfor, who I had known since my first involvement with the BC business community when I was running the Asia branch, and who had also been a friend of my father's, having worked together on what turned out to be a technologically flawed paper mill in the Buckley Valley in the BC interior. Peter was from a Jewish family who had escaped by foot to Switzerland from their native Vienna in 1938 after the Nazi takeover both of Austria and his family's sugar mill. His father was one of the founders of Canfor, and on his retirement returned to Vienna with Peter's mother, who became deeply involved in the promotion of the Vienna Riding School. In another example of the "small world department", the week before the Bank of Montreal events in Beijing, Peter and his wife Sheila had bumped into my sister Pat and her husband Tim at a dinner in San Francisco. Also on the BMO board were other business contacts of mine, including Chairman Jack Fraser of Air Canada, CBC Chair Guylaine Saucier (who had been very helpful during the 1995 referendum) and Eric Molson, Chairman of the eponymous brewer and cousin to my McGill classmate Mark Molson.

The main dinner for the BMO branch opening was hosted in one of the larger Diaoyutai State Guest House villas. The seating plan for the dinner had many tables and the Bank of Montreal organizers had initially put their key people and the most senior Chinese alone at the head table, relegating Pierre Trudeau to table number 3. When Guy Saint-Jacques saw this he explained to the bank's representatives that this would be an impossible slight to Trudeau, who was seen by the Chinese Government as a great friend and was really the only reason most of the senior guests had accepted the invitation. After far more argument than should have been necessary, the bank finally relented and placed Trudeau at the head table next to Matt Barrett. On Barrett's right was Vice Premier Zhu Rongji, and I was next to him.

At the 15th Party Congress just a week earlier, Zhu Rongji had been elevated to be the second most senior member of the Standing Committee of the Politburo of the CCP, thus assuring his appointment as premier at the National People's Congress the following spring. I had travelled with Zhu across Canada almost five years earlier, and met him only in larger groups since becoming Ambassador, so sitting next to him immediately after the Party Congress was a great chance to engage directly. He was his usual affable self with me as he was with other foreign "friends", but I also found that he had gained a new aura of determined confidence. He spoke about how tough were some of the issues confronting China, especially reforming the financial sector and solving the massive burden of the old and inefficient state-owned sector. He explained that the course upon which the leadership had embarked could become a virtuous cycle if managed with determination, but that there would for a long time be very big risks should growth or reform start to falter.

The best part of the Bank of Montreal extravaganza was the time I spent with Trudeau. He asked to be taken around the city to see how much it had changed since his last visit, which had been four or five years earlier, so I of course offered to take him. He also had asked to see a doctor of traditional Chinese medicine to see if there was any particular program that could be recommended for some aging-related conditions, and so we organized that as well. As we drove around the city, either between meetings or just on our excursion, I encouraged Trudeau to tell me of his earlier impressions of the ever-changing China. He recounted that he had not made it all the way to Beijing when he came a student in 1949 during the last days of the revolution, but in 1960, during his trip as editor of *Cité Libre*, he spent a fair amount of time in the capital during the October 1st National Day celebrations. The People's Republic of China had been eleven years old at the time, and outwardly proud of its achievements. But the leadership had been shaken by a countrywide famine, the US-led trade embargo was still in place, although a little tattered with the Canadian and Australian and French decisions to provide massive amounts of food aid, and Trudeau had been invited along with other western journalists to see for themselves what China was like. Mao Zedong had received Trudeau on the balcony of the Gate of Heavenly Peace overlooking the massive Tiananmen Square as the massed legions of the PLA and China's latest weaponry marched past. Mao, Trudeau told me, had been in an expansive and confident mood. Trudeau and his friend Jacques Hébert (later a senator), then spent more than a month traveling through other parts of China, and they concluded that even with the food shortage and the failure of the Great Leap Forward, most people were still caught up in the enthusiasm of the new country. They wrote a little book about their experiences and impressions entitled *Deux Innocents en Chine Rouge*.

Trudeau was not to return to China after his 1960 trip until he had become Prime Minister and Canada had formally recognized the communist regime, and then he was received as a "great friend of China", an epithet he was never to lose. That first official visit was during the Cultural Revolution, the next after its end. Between that time and 1997, he had visited Beijing somewhat regularly, and he compared his reminiscences to snapshots of a modernizing China, glimpses caught every few years as China lurched left or right, and more recently as it finally started down a steadier, more productive path. Before his visit, Trudeau had asked us to see if we could arrange a private and un-publicized meeting with his old friend and former Premier Zhao Ziyang, under house arrest since the Tiananmen incident of 1989, and we had made a formal request to the protocol office of the Foreign Ministry. I had buttressed this official with an informal plea to the Vice Minister of Foreign Affairs, but we had had no response, so I sadly told Trudeau that I thought Chinese agreement was unlikely.

At one point during the program, Rachael Bedlington was escorting Trudeau down from his suite in the hotel and mustered enough nerve to ask him why all those many years before, he had pirouetted behind Queen Elizabeth's back during a G-7 meeting in London, only to cause a great scandal when the pirouette appeared on the front pages of the next day's newspapers. He explained to Rachael that he had meant no disrespect for the Queen, but was instead so amused by the fawning over her by the other leaders present that could not resist mocking them. And so, he said to Rachael "I just did this", and he stepped out of the elevator into the majestic lobby of the China World Hotel and did a pirouette, much to the astonishment of all of us waiting in the lobby, including a rather stunned protocol official!

I took advantage of a free evening in the BMO program to invite Trudeau and a few others to an informal dinner at the Residence. In addition to Trudeau and his law partner Roy Heenan, I had invited several senior Chinese guests including Vice Minister Li Zhaoxing and Michael Davies, a charming private investor and Chairman of a high tech financial services firm, and like Heenan a graduate of TCS, where our daughter Cynthia was then studying. Li Zhaoxing, who I had placed next to Trudeau, was a charming and gracious dinner companion, and took Trudeau aside after the dinner to pass personal wishes to him from Zhao Ziyang, who he explained had been too ill to receive Trudeau. Whether this was true or not, and whether Zhao was ever told about Trudeau's request to see him, I was never to know, but whether or not a diplomatic lie it made Trudeau feel a little better, and he gave Li a brief handwritten note to pass along to his old friend. Li also told us that President Jiang Zemin had invited Trudeau for tea and a private discussion at Zhongnanhai, the inner sanctum of the Chinese leadership, and Premier Li Peng wanted him included in the annual National Day banquet at the Great Hall of the People. As neither of these events was on the planned program, Trudeau naturally received the invitations with a little pride in the knowledge that he was still considered the great friend of China he had always been.

The next evening Matt Barrett and I co-hosted a large reception (at BMO expense) at Diaoyutai for several hundred people, including Huang Hua, former Vice Premier and the first Chinese Ambassador to Canada and later to the UN. Huang and Trudeau were old friends and had lots to chat about as we put them side-by-side at the head table along with a few current Chinese ministers. Spouses were included in the event, and Anne-Marie Sten at one point took me aside and asked me to encourage her husband to give her a helicopter for her upcoming birthday! We had arranged background music during the meal by a small traditional Chinese chamber group, and a performance of the National Children's Choir before the dinner. The children, aged between eight and sixteen, sang both Chinese and Canadian songs with their absolutely wonderful and well trained voices; they had in fact toured all over the world.

The tea with Jiang Zemin was very special, for the President had chosen to receive Trudeau with only his Ambassador present, at the old Yantai Ting, a beautiful set of very traditional buildings set up on the rocky hillock of the little peninsula that sticks out into the most southwestern corner of the Zhongnanhai lake. It was a beautiful day and the setting was simply breathtaking. Jiang Zemin was relaxed and very chatty, and extremely warm towards Trudeau and Canada. After an exchange of pleasantries and a discussion about the future of China that I found quite extraordinary for its openness, the President invited Trudeau and me to wander with him through the enchanting old complex, stepping out on a lookout for a view of the lake. The view seemed almost impossible in the middle of a huge and busy city, but it was real nonetheless, a lovely lake with willow and fruit trees, a small red and yellow pavilion with a traditional curved Chinese roof where newly-weds of the imperial household were said to spend their evenings, and where the President told us he gathered with other senior leaders on spring and summer evenings under a "no-business" rule as they tried to set aside the worries of their working days. The President used almost as much English as Chinese as we walked, speaking the former much better than I had been led to believe he could. He fell back on Chinese to tell little jokes and to quote Chinese proverbs, and it was all in all a most human and delightful experience. As we left, I told the President that I looked forward to travelling with him in little more than a month during his first state visit to Canada.

The final event of Trudeau's visit was the state banquet hosted by Premier Li Peng on the eve of China's National Day. Like every year, this was a grand affair for almost five thousand guests, each seated according to a very strict protocol of seniority. The protocol division of the Ministry of Foreign Affairs had called my local protocol secretary Wang Jine the day before in some agitation, asking if she could explain to me that they could not seat me at the same table as Trudeau, since if I were seated at a position higher than all those ambassadors who had presented their credentials before me, the entire diplomatic community would be in an uproar. Worse, they explained, in following years every ambassador would try to bring along a former leader so that they too could jump the line. I said that as long as Prime Minister Trudeau was treated with honour I would take my rightful place at table number eighty-two. (This was up from table number ninety-six the previous year, and I would eventually make it to the exalted table number five before I retired.) Li Peng made special reference to Trudeau's presence in his toast, and I took Trudeau on a round of introductions at the head table, so all was well in the end, which came mercifully soon with the Chief of State Protocol standing up and intoning in three languages that the dinner was over and "you may all please go home". And so we did, stopping for a final nightcap with Trudeau at his hotel on the way. Liani had a chance to have a good chat of her own with him at the end of the day, and they hit it off well, and as we left he gave her a big embrace. Always a gallant man.

I was to see Trudeau only one more time, during a visit to Montreal in 1999, before he died in 2000. In the intervening two years he had aged terribly, broken it seemed by the death of his youngest son Michel, lost in a 1998 avalanche while skiing in the Rocky Mountains. But I still treasure the exchanges we had, for he had been a seminal leader and an inspiration to me as a young Canadian when I was coming of age in the 1960s.

CHAPTER 25

PROVINCIAL PREMIERS

• • • • • • • • • • •

The first provincial premier to come to China during my time as Ambassador was Brian Tobin of Newfoundland and Labrador, who came to China in the spring of 1997. I had known Tobin very well when he was Minister of Fisheries in the early Chrétien cabinet when I was Deputy Secretary in the PCO dealing with national unity. Tobin and I had always gotten on well in spite of an occasional disagreement (such as on the impact on public support for the "No" cause of the famous Canada Rally three days before the 1995 referendum), and I was delighted to have him and a small group of Newfoundland business representatives in town.

Tobin was well received by the Chinese in part because he had been a federal Minister, and he had meetings with MOFTEC Minister Wu Yi and was received by her polished and multilingual predecessor Vice Premier Li Lanqing. On the day of his arrival, I hosted a welcoming dinner for the Newfoundland delegation, which included Vic Young, Chairman and CEO of Fishery Products International, Newfoundland's largest processor of seafood and a multi-billion dollar listed company. Vic was a lovely man and very down to earth. Unfortunately, his luggage had been lost on the trip over and he had no suit to wear for the dinner. I offered him one of mine but he declined, and he wore an old sweater and informal trousers instead. I had invited about thirty people in total, which meant that we could not all fit at our single dining room table, so were divided in three, with Premier Tobin, MOFTEC Vice Minister Sun Jenyu and a few other senior governmental types at the head table with me and the business representatives distributed with logical local Canadian and Chinese business people at the other two tables. I had placed Vic Young at the table with the China representative of the Royal Bank of Canada because I knew that Vic was on the RBC Board and I thought that this would give them a sensible thread from which to weave a conversation. The RBC representative, a polished and rather smarmy fellow from Chicago, took one look at this middle-aged wiry guy in an old sweater and decided that he must have been the premier's valet or bodyguard and spent the entire meal monopolizing the conversation and cutting Vic off every time he tried to intervene. Vic was a patient fellow and simply let it happen, and at the end of the meal turned to the RBC representative and said, in a strong and almost exaggerated Newfoundland accent, "I will give your regards to John Cleghorn when I see him at our RBC board meeting next month". According to Vic, the local representative's face turned ashen, but Vic simply turned on his heel and walked away. Cleghorn was then Chairman and CEO of RBC and a man of few airs. When Vic Young took him side at the next RBC board meeting to recount his experience with the bank's China representative, he had the latter fired the very next day. Cleghorn was a fellow McGill alumnus (he had been quarterback on the football team) and, as Chairman of the Conference Board of Canada, he tried later to recruit me as the Conference Board's President. When he retired in 2004 or so, and journalists asked him what he intended to next do in life, his response was that he simply wanted to improve his banjo-playing skills.

The second provincial premier to visit China during my time as Ambassador was Ralph Klein of Alberta, coming to Beijing in early October for the 15th World Petroleum Congress with a substantial business delegation from the Canadian oil patch in tow. The next World Petroleum Congress was scheduled for 2000 in Calgary. As a future host, one of the objectives of Klein and his delegation was to try to ensure that all the attendees at the 1997 event would commit to coming to Calgary, and to get Chinese support for that event. Klein also brought his Minister of Agriculture and a group of business leaders from Alberta's agriculture sector as well, so it was a large and complex group.

Premier Klein was very well received in Beijing, and it seemed that the entire hierarchy of Heilongjiang leaders came down to Beijing as well. Party Secretary Yue Qifeng happened to be in Beijing at the same time and invited Klein to a dinner at the Beijing Hotel, with Governor Tian Fengshan (who I was later to get to know better as Minister of Land and Resources in the central government, bridging between my time as Ambassador and as President of TBG) was the leader of the Heilongjiang delegation to the petroleum congress. Tian graciously accepted my invitation to the Residence for a dinner in honour of Premier Klein and the two-decade old "Sister-Province" relationship between Heilongjiang and Alberta. At that time, before a modern divided highway was built between the airport in Harbin and the city centre, anyone driving into town from the airport would drive along "Edmonton Road", just as there was (and still is) a Harbin Gate in downtown Edmonton. The Chinese Government also arranged Premier Klein to be received by Vice-Premier Zhu Rongji, and this was a very friendly meeting during which Zhu noted that President Jiang Zemin would begin his formal bilateral state visit to Canada later that same autumn in Calgary, leading to a tongue-in-cheek response from Klein that this was an appropriate place to begin a state visit to Canada given that it was really the new economic centre of our country.

The third provincial premier to come to China during my time as Ambassador was Lucien Bouchard of Québec. Unlike other provinces, Québec treated their premier like a national leader and had sent advance teams to China to work out the logistical and program details of the visit. This visit was being billed as "Mission Québec", clearly modeled on Chrétien's "Team Canada", with a very large delegation of Québec's political and business elite, all arriving on the same chartered aircraft.

It was a cool and smoggy November evening when Bouchard and his delegation landed, and as the plane was a charter, the backdrop for his arrival was not modern glass and chrome and fancy terminal gantries, but the ochre-brown wedding-cake building that served as China's first modern airport in the 1950s. Even in 1997 this old terminal seemed out of place, and at that time the only modern part of the airport was the small terminal which had been built in the 1980s and which, after the second and third terminals had been built and opened in 1999 and 2008 in time respectively for the 50th Anniversary of the PRC and for the Beijing Olympics, was refurbished and became Terminal 1. The old building where we awaited Bouchard had known history, however, and consequently seemed a little special. It was there that Mao Zedong or Zhou Enlai greeted foreign leaders, and I could see in my mind's eye the honour guard of young peasant soldiers, rigid and proud, as their leaders led visiting Soviet or Polish or Indian leaders to the waiting motorcade of Red Flag limousines. During the 1950s and 1960s, Beijing was one of the great pilgrimages for the third world and for the communist block, until Trudeau and Nixon and other early western leaders came and opened the floodgates from the first world as well.

But I was not at the airport to reminisce about history. As we waited for the chartered aircraft to arrive, Guy Saint-Jacques wandered over to me to warn me of an incoming request from the Québec team, and sure enough a minute later Québec's Chef du Protocol, a Mme Latulippe, came to me and suggested that to avoid any "interpretation of provocation", we remove the Canadian flag from the front fender of my car. I responded, sweetly and in French of course, that to avoid controversy I would not insist on flying the flag if and when I was in the car rented for Premier Bouchard, which of course was my right as the Ambassador of Canada, but could hardly be expected to have the flag removed from my own vehicle. A moment later the big chartered Canadian Airlines 767 turned into the apron and stopped. Steps were brought up to both the front and rear doors, but there were no red carpets, welcoming flags or Chinese protocol officials there. The Chinese were nervous and very proper about receiving a separatist premier. The journalists spilled out the aft door first and rushed forward to film the arrival; they were the first to note the lack of any trappings that could give this arrival the image of grandeur, and the first to write home that the only flag visible anywhere was the red and white one on the Ambassador's car.

I drove in to Beijing with Premier Bouchard in his rented limousine, with my car, flag and all just behind with Guy Saint-Jacques and a couple of provincial ministers. Busloads of business representatives and journalists followed. The "Mission Québec" was a huge affair, pushed hard by the Parti Québécois government to prove that Bouchard could go abroad and promote and protect Québec's interests every bit as well, if not better, than Canadian leaders could. There had been a significant amount of arm-twisting to ensure a very substantial business participation, and more than a hundred Québec-based firms had come along. Half of them were regular clients of the Embassy and already doing business in China, and the other half were being introduced to the China market for the first time. Along with the business people there were twenty journalists and no fewer than sixty provincial officials, a governmental entourage that was larger than ever attended a visit by Prime Minister Chrétien, even for the huge "Team Canada" delegations.

Both Prime Minister Chrétien and I had publicly welcomed the trip, saying that the federal government was always ready to work with Premier Bouchard, as we were with other Premiers, in the pursuit of economic objectives and of business deals that would bring jobs to Québec. We had also quietly ensured that there a lot of companies present that had also been on the Prime Minister's "Team Canada" trip two years earlier, and even representatives of federal financing agencies like the Export Development Corporation and the Business Development Bank of Canada. The big unanswered questions were about images; would there be friction between the Québec team and the Embassy, and how would the visit be played in the media back at home in Canada.

Bouchard and I were, inevitably, formal and proper with each other, even when no one else was around, and from the moment of his arrival until he left I was to be virtually omnipresent, more than I had been with Premier Klein. The first scheduled official event of the visit was a breakfast briefing for the delegation, and the scenario set up by the Québec people was already politically loaded. Although both the premier and I were to give speeches, his arrival in the hall was scheduled to coincide with the winding up of my welcoming remarks, with him entering with a large coterie of security and protocol officials and with the natural applause that would accompany the arrival of a state leader. So I gave a somewhat short and extemporaneous speech, entirely in French of course, and used up less time than planned. Then I came down from the podium and wandered among the business delegates, meeting old contacts and greeting new ones. When Bouchard arrived, the whole room was wandering about, and it took some time for everyone to notice that he was there at the podium, and then to find their seats again.

Later that morning, Bouchard and a Vice-Minister of Energy (most Ministers were curiously all "away" or otherwise unavailable for this sensitive visit, even though they were in fact generally accessible for Canadian visitors) gave speeches to open a series of business seminars during which business representatives gave short presentations and then mingled with invited Chinese officials and business people. The two speeches were from different, and not even parallel, universes. Bouchard's avoided any mention of Canada and extolled only the virtues of Québec and its industrial capabilities, while the Vice Minister gave an enormously positive overview of the China-Canada relationship generally with particular mention of hydro-electric and nuclear energy cooperation, and in the space of twenty minutes never mentioned once the word "Québec". This was a story repeated several times over the next few days, and the fifth estate took notice. Part of the reason was that Bouchard had been to Paris earlier in the year and his efforts to promote sovereignty there had caused a public furour, and the public controversy over that visit were still reverberating. In China, however, there was a profound determination in the Chinese Government not to allow the visit to be abused for domestic political purposes by the Parti Québécois, and although Bouchard avoided saying anything positive about Canada in public, in private he was gracious about our cooperation and the Embassy's professionalism, and even managed to say to the CBC station chief that he was travelling "comme un citoyen canadien". At other times he wore the mantle of a provincial premier less happily, and in answer to one journalist's question about the dearth of high-level meetings, he suggested that when he returned later to China as the leader of a sovereign Québec, he would be able to meet with more senior leaders.

When Lucien Bouchard replaced Jacques Parizeau as Québec's premier after the 1995 referendum, he kept Parizeau's chief of staff, Jean-François Lisée, as his own and also made him his official press secretary. Lisée was always an ardent separatist and was the mastermind behind the Parti Québécois' planning of all foreign visits for the premier and international events to ensure that they supported the separatist cause as much as possible. On the second day of the visit, the Québec Government announced that as a result of the visit, Québec would be opening a diplomatic mission in Beijing to serve the interests of Québec, and that its delegates would be afforded diplomatic privileges. The press release was made to sound as if some breakthrough agreement had been reached with the Chinese on the matter, and that Québec would be permitted to open a version of the "Maison du Québec" that it had long had in Paris, when in fact all that had transpired was that the Canadian Government had agreed that Québec could assign an officer to the Embassy to look after provincial interests, especially in the areas of tourism and investment promotion. This had been agreed weeks before the visit, and in fact the same arrangement was being put into place with Alberta. When I saw the provocative press release that Québec had issued, I decided that I needed to publicly clarify the situation and I called Jean Pelletier, the Prime Minister's Chief of Staff, and got his immediate and unreserved approval. So I called a half dozen of the key journalists and told them that the Québec Government was exaggerating what was a simple administrative arrangement, not yet fully in place between the two levels of government, wherein the Embassy would welcome, on a cost-recovery basis, the assignment of provincial representatives, the first two being from Alberta and Québec. The journalists were thrilled to finally have a story about friction, and Montreal's La Presse ran a front page piece under the headline "Dérapage Politique à Pékin", not only reporting on the story but drawing attention to the fact that Bouchard and I were old combatants from the national unity war of a few years earlier. The best bit of press coverage came in a political cartoon in the Journal de Montréal, a tabloid with the largest circulation in the province. The image was of a very happy Canadian Ambassador, holding a flag in one hand and a grumpy Bouchard by the other, with Bouchard saying in a small voice how satisfied he was with the support from the Canadian Embassy. Jean Pelletier called to tease me that he couldn't see Bouchard in the press coverage because I had wrapped him up in so many Canadian flags. The only unhappy federalists were our children who did not like the un-bearded caricature of their father the Ambassador in the Journal de Montréal's cartoon.

I actually thought that the Chinese Government was bending over too far in denying allowing Bouchard access to senior level people, especially as it had been common practice for Chinese ministers to meet with provincial premiers and to arrange a call during a premier's visit on a Vice Premier. The only minister to meet with Bouchard was the Minister of Water Resources because of the extent of Chinese interest in Canadian hydro-electric power experience. The Québec delegation knew that Klein had been received by Senior Vice Premier Zhu Rongji only a few weeks earlier, and they were absolutely incensed when they learned that on the third morning of Bouchard's visit, Zhu Rongji received Chairman Jean Monty and CEO John Roth of Nortel, who wanted nothing to do with the Québec mission and were in Beijing to celebrate Nortel's 25th anniversary of doing business in China. (Nortel had set up all the communications arrangements between China and the United States for the 1972 Nixon visit; the Chinese would not allow a US firm to do so, and the Americans had understandably refused to permit their President's communications to be managed by the Chinese.) I had not mentioned the Nortel visit to Bouchard, although it was very much in the press. In fact, I had arranged for my new Commercial Minister Robert Collette to attend in my stead a Tuesday night dinner hosted for the Québec delegation by Minister of Water Resources Niu, since I was attending a higher-level banquet for Nortel hosted at the Great Hall of the People. Concerned that the Chinese were being too restrictive with Bouchard, I asked my friend Vice Minister

Sun Jenyu to arrange a meeting with MOFTEC Minister Wu Yi, which he did, and Guy Saint-Jacques called his contacts at the Foreign Ministry to ask for at least one senior-level meeting. The Chinese finally relented and had the most junior of the Vice Premiers, outgoing Jiang Chunyun, receive Bouchard just before his departure.

I spent a fair amount of private time with Lucien Bouchard in cars going to and from meetings and events, and we gradually grew a little more relaxed with each other. I found him in many ways an attractive man, and he shared with me his frustration at having a job that kept him away from his two young children as much as it did. But there were issues that were harder to broach, and an unbridgeable gap in some perspectives. He told me how much he had enjoyed being Canadian Ambassador to France during the early Mulroney years, and he said what a high opinion he had of the professional Foreign Service. At one point he suggested that he would like to stop by the Embassy and meet the staff and perhaps their families, to which I brought him back to reality by saying that I hardly thought that would be popular among his delegation and that in any case not all the Embassy staff would welcome his presence, since Foreign Service staff tended to be a rather patriotic lot who saw him representing a force bent on destroying the country they held dear. While this chilled our immediate exchange, I kept getting the sense that Bouchard the man was not as fervent a separatist as Bouchard the politician, and that what he really wanted to achieve was the illusive autonomy of the comedian Yvon Deschamps, who called for "un Québec indépendant dans un Canada fort et uni"! And during his visit, while he avoided positive public references to Canada, he also avoided any public reference to his party's avowed independence agenda. His Minister of Natural Resources, Guy Chevrette, was less complicated and more direct, and at one dinner spent so much time bemoaning the heavy yoke of Canadian federalism and the role of non-francophones in the modern Québec economy, that both the Chinese and Québec business representatives at the table found early excuses to leave his table.

At the closing banquet of "Mission Québec", attended by a large number of local business people as well as the whole Québec delegation, my good friend Vice Minister Sun Jenyu of the Ministry of Trade and Economic Cooperation (MOFTEC), gave a wonderful speech full of praise for Canada, and did so almost entirely in French. This was a big hit and he drew a standing ovation for his effort. The following morning brought the Beijing leg of the mission to a close and Bouchard and a smaller group, with Robert Collette and Commercial First Secretary David Murphy as Embassy escorts, headed off to Shenyang and Dalian in Liaoning, while I hosted a lunch for a group of senior executives of all the Canadian firms involved in the Three Gorges power project, including the engineering consortium CCPI, Canadian GE (who were eventually to make three of the massive turbines for the project), Agra-Monenco, whose CEO Alex Taylor came from the Balloch Docks area of Glasgow, and CAE, in charge of power station controls and system simulators. They were all in China to participate in the ceremonies being held as the final concrete and ballast were poured to close the south channel of the Yangtze River, at the turn in the river where the first phase of the huge project was scheduled to begin generating electricity five years later.

On the afternoon of the very day that Bouchard left Beijing, I was back at the airport to greet the much more modest delegation of Glen Clark, Premier of British Columbia, who had begun a visit to China a few days earlier. He had wanted to start his visit in Beijing, but two provincial premiers at one time was too much to handle, so he had agreed to cycle his visit as Shanghai, Beijing and Hong Kong, while Bouchard went from Beijing to Liaoning to Shanghai.

Clark's visit was delightfully relaxed and informal after the politicized and much more formal Bouchard visit. Vice Minister Sun Jenyu of MOFTEC again received the group and gave a speech, this one mostly in English, to a dinner banquet of some 120 BC business representatives and their Chinese contacts and as many of the Chinese participants at the upcoming Vancouver APEC events as I could gather. Along with the fifth APEC

Summit, Vancouver would be hosting a meeting of APEC business leaders, billed as an "APEC CEO Summit" intended to make suggestions to political leaders on the trade and economic agenda that APEC should pursue over the next five years. Clark was also promoting international involvement and participation in the 1998 "GLOBE" environmental equipment show and its parallel environmental conference, so we invited both governmental officials and Chinese firms involved in environmental matters. At the actual APEC events, the role of the Premier of the province would be minimal and ceremonial, but the interest in attending the banquet for Clark was high because of the focus on Canada and on Vancouver, and Clark was pleased with the profile he and the province were given. Unlike in the case of Bouchard, the Chinese offered a call on a Vice Premier without being asked, and Clark was very graciously received by Li Lanqing, who was by this time being rumoured to replace Zhu Rongji as Senior Vice Premier when Zhu took over as Premier the following March.

In the middle of the second day of the Clark visit, I slipped away from the BC group and headed off to the Great Hall of the People to sign on behalf of Canada an international agreement bringing into being INBAR, a global research network for bamboo and rattan, to be headquartered in China and financed substantially by Canada's International Development Research Council (IDRC). Both Premier Li Peng and Vice premier Qian Qichen attended the signing, as did the Chinese representative to the new research network, Jiang Zehui, younger sister to President Jiang Zemin. While Jiang Zehui was truly a recognized expert in forestry and had earned her position through hard work and merit, her personal connection brought out a level of attendance more than commensurate with the importance of the relatively minor agreement being signed. The result for me was that I seemed to be all over Chinese television that week, with the calls of two provincial premiers on Vice Premiers (always televised in those days), the NORTEL anniversary meeting with Zhu Rongji and the signing of the INBAR agreement in front of Premier Li Peng. When I saw Prime Minister Chrétien the following month in Canada, I told him that my media exposure was outstripping his given I was being shown regularly on television to more than a billion people, to which he suggested that I should sell advertising on my forehead.

As the following years unfolded, almost all the other provincial premiers also visited, with both Mike Harris of Ontario, who was received by both Zhu Rongji and Li Peng, and Gary Filmon of Manitoba coming in 1998, and the long serving Roy Romonow of Saskatchewan in 1999. Bernard Lord of New Brunswick came in 2000 and we hosted a lovely evening with his brother, concert pianist Roger Lord entertaining our guests at the Residence. None, however, were as memorable as Mission Québec. And then in 2001, all thirteen provincial and territorial leaders would return with Prime Minister Chrétien for the second Team Canada visit to China, which will be the focus of another chapter of these anecdotes.

CHAPTER 26

STATE VISIT OF PRESIDENT JIANG ZEMIN, NOVEMBER 1997

• • • • • • • • • • •

When APEC meetings started at the end of the 1980s, it was envisaged that hosting the annual Ministerial Meetings would rotate between an ASEAN member state and a developed country. In the early 1990s, when the idea of having an annual summit meeting of heads of state or heads of government, there was fierce competition between Canada and Japan to host the third summit in 1995, following the first two in Seattle and Bogor, Indonesia. In spite of my efforts, we lost the competition to Japan, and ended up hosting the fifth summit instead. For me this actually turned out very well, since in the autumn of 1995 I was up to my neck in national unity matters and not involved in Asian issues. By 1997 I was back, this time as Ambassador to one of APEC's key economies, and given the state visit of its President that would follow the APEC Summit, I flew into Vancouver as the Summit was taking place. (The difference between an "official visit" and a "state visit" was the degree of protocol involved, with the former having less fanfare. Visits of leaders between Canada and China, however, were almost always characterized as state visits, with lots of pomp and ceremony, which the Chinese liked for internal propaganda reasons.)

It was a fabulously clear mid-November day, Vancouver at its best, as my flight from Beijing touched down. A few fluffy white cumulus clouds appeared above Grouse Mountain to the city's northwest, and a few more down near Mount Baker in Washington many miles to the southeast, but otherwise there was not the slightest blemish in the sky. Between the two principal runways sat a formidable array of big and fancy airplanes. Two great JAL 747s sat along side single versions of the same aircraft in Chinese, Korean, Indonesian and Philippine livery, with smaller DC-10s, A310s and even an older 707 belonging to the leaders of more modest APEC members, and of course, set somewhat apart, the Air Force One and Air Force Two 747s of the US President.

Before flying to Calgary, where I was to greet Jiang Zemin on his formal arrival, I met in Vancouver with the team organizing the trip's logistics, who were already involved in the APEC meeting. The team was composed of headquarters officers from both the Asia Branch and protocol, supplemented by two or three from my Embassy and other missions in the region. The task was enormous, organizing the movements of seventeen foreign leaders many of whom would use the occasion to meet each other as well as attend the APEC meetings, and the China sub-team also had to ensure that all the necessary arrangements were in place for the following visit of the President of China. APEC was an extravaganza, and Vancouver was a mess. There were many protests both along the roads and out at the University of British Columbia where the summit itself was held, and in the twenty-four hours before the leaders' meeting, it seemed that motorcades for all eighteen leaders were crisscrossing the city from one dedicated delegation hotel to another where more than a hundred bilateral meetings were to take place. The best story I later heard of all the APEC comings and goings, was from a young officer assigned from our Jakarta Embassy to act as liaison with the Suharto delegation. Upon leaving Vancouver three or four days after the meeting, the young staffer was in a taxi. The driver had a thick highland brogue, having only recently arrived from Scotland, and asked her whether she had been in town during all the kerfuffle of the previous week. Before she had a chance to answer, the driver told her that there had been a big movie being shot in the city, with the plot being an assassination of the President of the United States. When she politely suggested that he might have been referring to an actual APEC Summit, he dismissed her silliness, and said that he himself had seen all the extras dressed up as RCMP outriders and plainclothes policemen hanging around with little to do, and that there had even been a mock-up of Air Force One at the airport.

I flew up to Calgary twenty-four hours before the President and his delegation to brief the Governor General, Roméo Leblanc, who had agreed to come out west for the formal state greeting, and also to give a speech at the Petroleum Club the night before the visit. Interest in China was high, and there were more than 200 people at my speech, which got good coverage in both the electronic and written press. I also managed to squeeze in a get-together with Tim Kerrigan, a classmate from McGill who I had not seen since graduation. When we were students, Tim had come down to our summer home in Rhode Island a couple of times, and had been on the inaugural cruise of the 20-foot "Silver Moon" with my mother and brother Hugh when we delivered her from Marianopolis to Jamestown in 1971. Tim had become a lawyer in Calgary after finishing law school, had a family about the same age as mine, and it was fun catching up and sharing stories of our times as misbehaving youths.

I had a breakfast briefing with the Governor General and his wife Mme Fowler-Leblanc at their suite at the Palliser Hotel, before being escorted to the VIP holding area at the airport to await President Jiang. Both the Governor General and his wife were charming, and were interested in my views not only on China but also on national unity.

The big Chinese Boeing touched down mid-morning of an unseasonably Chinook-warmed day, and rolled to a stop along side a brilliant sidebar of red and white with scores of Canadian and Chinese flags fluttering perfectly in the western breeze. The door opened, the Canadian Chief of Protocol and the Chinese Ambassador went up the steps to greet the Chinese Head of State. After a brief delay to allow the rolling out of a red carpet and to give time for sixty Chinese journalists to disembark from the aft door and join their Canadian counterparts to record the official beginning of the first bilateral visit of a Chinese President to Canada in twenty years. From a diplomatic standpoint, Jiang's visit to Vancouver had been characterized as attending an APEC meeting and neither he nor other leaders were treated as paying formal visits to Canada.

Once we had lined up along the red carpet, Jiang Zemin and his wife, Wang Yeping, came down the steps onto Canadian soil for the formal beginning of the state visit. Second in his entourage was Vice Premier Qian Qichen, who I had known a decade earlier when he was a stately grey-haired Vice Minister nearing sixty, but who now had the mandatory jet-black hair of an ageless and youthful Vice Premier. Next in line was my pin-up lady, Madam Wu Yi, the testy MOFTEC Minister who had earlier taken great pleasure in demolishing US Trade Representative Mickey Kantor and who had become a friend of Roy McLaren, our Trade Minister from 1993 to 1996. (By this time McLaren had left politics to become our High Commissioner in London.) The Leblancs took Jiang Zemin and his wife to a small anti-room, with interpreters, while the rest of us took our places for the formal military honours.

The Honour Guard were of the storied Princess Patricia's Canadian Light Infantry, known as the *Princess Pats* or the *Patricias*, and they were very impressive. All about six-foot-six, with a ramrod straight female Sergeant of the Guard who led the President of China and the Governor General down the line of the rigidly immobile force and then two impressively precise presentations of arms. Beautiful renditions of the two national anthems were played by the Patricias Band, and a twenty-one gun salute from three big 155mm howitzers situated across the airfield provided percussive background as the President reviewed the honour guard.

Then we were whisked away in a great motorcade, past our very first set of protesters just outside the airport. Some were carrying signs saying "Free Tibet" or "Down with Dictators" (signs and protesters also having moved up to Calgary from the APEC meeting in Vancouver), but others carried signs irrelevant to China. In fact, just outside the gates of the airport was a Canada Post sorting centre, and all the postal workers were on strike and protesting as well. The anti-China protesters had mingled with the CUPW

(Canadian Union of Postal Workers) members and even had managed to get some of the latter to carry both sets of signs. The Governor General, riding in the same limousine as Jiang Zemin and myself, tried to distract the President's attention as the motorcade passed the demonstrators. Jiang, with an openness that was to mark his whole visit, patted Roméo Leblanc on the arm and told him not to worry, as he too had protested as a young man.

The first major event of the visit was a formal state lunch, the welcoming meal for the President. Hosted by the Governor General, who was warm and informal, the lunch included Alberta Premier Ralph Klein and Anne McLellan, then our Minister of Justice and a good friend of mine. Klein told the President of his successful visit to China of only a month or so earlier, and Anne recounted her own visit as Minister of Natural Resources, escaping on a rowboat with me and leaving our handlers stranded on the shore of the Songhua River in Harbin. Anne then described to the President the beauty of Banff National Park and told him that he should squeeze in the time for a visit. The President responded that he would like to, and I signaled to my First Secretary Julia Bentley, who was travelling with us across the country, to come over to the table and I told her to see if a visit could be arranged. She returned a few minutes later and whispered to me that both Security and Protocol had nixed the idea, given that it had not been prepared and that the RCMP had not swept the route. When I gently suggested that this was not the answer we were looking for, she told me that it was actually the Chinese head of security, a PLA General, who had dug in his heels. I then turned to the President and told him directly that it was his security chief who was preventing a tour of Banff. Jiang called over the General, spoke to him in a rapid Chinese I could not understand and all of a sudden the visit was on. The end of the lunch was advanced, although there was still enough time for a brief ceremony to "White-Hat" Jiang Zemin by Calgary Mayor Al Duerr (a traditional Calgary gift to visiting foreign leaders, although in this case it created a lot of criticism from the Canadian Tibetan community, substantial in Calgary, as well as human rights organizations). Planned downtime for the president and his wife was also cancelled, and Ralph Klein agreed to delay by an hour the dinner he was hosting that evening for three hundred leading citizens of Alberta. (In the end, most of the guests did not receive the notice of the delay and so ended up sitting around drinking at the Premier's expense for an extra sixty minutes.)

The trip to Banff was flawless. As an alternative to downtime at the Palliser Hotel, we suggested that the President and his wife ride alone in their limousine to permit them to rest or sleep if they wished, and I rode in a second car with Gary Mar, then Alberta's Minister of Education, representing the Alberta Government. The RCMP had in an incredibly short time secured the route, and the motorcade reached the edge of the national park in record time of about an hour, every interchange and cross-road sealed off by "leap-frogging" motorcycle outriders. As we entered the park and headed along back roads to the Banff Springs Hotel behind the Banff Centre a welcoming party of several huge great western elk was there to greet us. The President's car came to a screeching halt, causing the RCMP officers in the security car ahead to leap out of their vehicle, guns ready, in fear that something had gone wrong. No, it had just been Jiang Zemin and Wang Yeping who wanted to take some pictures of the magnificent animals, and the photographs would show the President of China approaching a young elk, with a great antlered buck and a few dams in the background.

The Banff Springs Hotel had, in spite of the short notice, literally rolled out a red carpet and had welcoming banners and flags flying as we arrived, and half of the hotel staff lined up to applaud as President Jiang and his wife got out of their car. There was not a lot of time to do much other than have a tea on the balcony and look at the wonderful view across the valley and up into the mountains. We arrived about forty-five minutes before the sun slipped below the pass. As we had our tea, the great mountain wall at the head of the valley turned from white and grey to pink, and the elk and the mountain goats on the golf course below and in the lower foothills were gradually gathered into the darkness. The scene was, as always, one of the great panoramas of the world, rivaling the Matterhorn or the Himalayas, and both Jiang Zemin and Wang Yeping were entranced and insisted on staying longer than the forty-five minutes protocol had allotted.

Our tea gave me my first chance for an informal one-on-one chat with Jiang Zemin, and I told him of my time as a young man working across the mountains at Windermere, and how some of my university classmates, one now a fellow ambassador, had worked as bus-boys or chambermaids at this hotel. I also told him of a peak not far from Banff, high in the Rockies, that had had its name changed in 1996 from Chinaman's Peak to Tung Peak. The highest mountain visible from Roger's Pass, it had been climbed by and named for a young navvy from southern China, brought in as one of the thousands of railway workers by Van Horne, president of the CPR. Premier Klein, I told the President, had found the earlier name impersonal and insulting, and just a few years earlier had commissioned a team of researchers to dig out the climber's actual name, and rechristened the peak. Jiang loved this story and was in a thoughtful and expansive mood, and said that he admired greatly modern Canada for its multiculturalism. I assured him that Canadians had not always been open to non-Europeans, and had a particularly shameful period of race-based immigration and ill-treatment of Chinese settlers, to which he answered in a quite intense tone that historically no country had ill-treated Chinese as thoroughly as China itself, and the worst excesses had been in living memory. He was obviously referring to the Cultural Revolution, expressing a private thought he could never have uttered publicly.

As the light faded from grey to black we rushed back to Calgary for Klein's dinner, which started a full hour late due to our dallying at Banff. The guests were Alberta's "everybody who was anybody", and of course I bumped into dozens of people whom I knew, from university classmates to academics to businessmen active in China. One of the latter was Executive VP of CP Rail, Hugh McDiarmid, who had lived with his wife Anne and two children just down the street from us in Ottawa. After the dinner, I headed over to their Calgary home for a drink and a pleasant interlude of not being an ambassador.

The following day we visited a large Nortel wireless communications equipment plant just north of the city. As they usually did for a visiting dignitary, Nortel had gathered all their senior executives, draped the plant in the banners and flags of the two countries, and toured Jiang Zemin around the multiple engineering stations, at each of which there was a Chinese-speaking Nortel engineer to brief the group. Before we left, the President inscribed a special memorial scroll in very handsome calligraphy, and was given a huge sendoff by workers arrayed on a balcony stretching three-quarters the way around the main foyer of the plant. As the President waved, the workers broke out in loud cheering and whistling, and I thought the scene could have been right out of an old 1950s newsreel entitled "The Party Secretary Visits Factory to the Heroic Applause of the Valiant Workers". The President was absolutely beaming as we left, and he laughed when, back in the car together, I suggested that when his term was up in China perhaps he should consider coming to Canada to run for election and take advantage of his evident popularity.

A final stop in the Calgary program was at a ranch north of the city not too far from the airport, where Jiang was taken around a breeding centre for high quality Hereford dairy cows, and given a baby breeding bull named "Long" (meaning "dragon") as a gift of Premier Klein of Alberta. Jiang seemed to be very content touring around the ranch and happy with his bull, which was, well after the visit was over, transferred to a breeding farm in Heilongjiang. (Fifteen years later I was at that farm at Beidahuang and was introduced to several generations of bred and cloned descendants of Long, among whom were the most productive milk cows in the entire country.) After the breeding centre it was up in the air in the President's 747, and off to Ottawa.

The Ottawa airport arrival was all ceremony again, with both the Governor General and Deputy Prime Minister Herb Grey in attendance and a very flashy honour guard from the famous Van Doos (Royal Vingt-Deuzième Régiment). Then we swept into town up the Colonel By Drive, entering after nightfall with a light sheen of ice on the canal and snow lightly falling, a perfect Ottawa setting. The Governor General hosted a dinner at Rideau Hall, where he had invited the President and his wife to stay. I was pleased to find among the 120 carefully chosen guests five of my predecessors, John Small, Arthur Menzies, Michel Gauvin, Earl Drake and Fred Bild. Dick Gorham, who had been Ambassador in the mid 1980s between Gauvin and Drake, had been invited as well, but was not well enough to accept. John Small and Arthur Menzies, our second and third post-recognition Ambassadors, had both spoken Chinese all their lives, having learned the language as children in China of missionary parents. Menzies' father had also been a renowned archeologist who discovered one of the most famous collections of oracle bones which his son returned to China and which are now in a museum in Jinan.

Drinks before dinner were held in the Chinese Room of Rideau Hall, adorned with artifacts given by benefactors over almost a century. Ramon Hnatyshyn, Leblanc's predecessor as Governor General, who in a curious twist of protocol was invited to the dinner, had arranged the Chinese Room to be refurbished to ensure that window pediments, tapestries and fittings were all done in chinoiserie to improve the setting for the well-displayed Chinese treasures, and the Chinese guests were duly impressed. At the dinner, Minister Wu Yi told me that she was simply stunned to find an elegant Chinese reception room and collection in the official residence of Canada's Governor General.

At the dinner, the President was placed across from the Governor General and between Prime Minister Chrétien and Mme Fowler-Leblanc, which permitted Chrétien and Jiang Zemin to begin what would amount by the end of the visit to more than eight hours of informal and formal discussion. The Prime Minister and President talked of their own personal history, with the former explaining how the rough and tumble of political opposition had made him tough, and the President talked of learning from his time as a worker in an automobile factory. From there it was on to other topics, and it was clear to me that the two got along very well and had, since their first meeting in Seattle four years earlier, developed an easy and surprisingly close relationship. When I checked after the dinner, it was confirmed that this had actually been their seventh meeting.

I had a private breakfast the following morning with John Manley, Minister of Industry, at a restaurant south of the city. Afterwards and after a mad drive in my RCMP-driven car through a building snowstorm, I arrived barely on time for a one-on-one briefing of Chrétien at his Centre Block office on Parliament Hill. The Prime Minister was in a very good mood and really did not want to talk about the issues about which I was supposed to be briefing him and he asked me how I was finding life in China and how long I wanted to remain Ambassador. I told him that I was finally feeling that I was getting my feet under me, that the Chinese had little time for heads of mission who didn't stay long, and so I hoped I could have a good long posting. He told me that he thought I was doing a great job even if Foreign Minister Axworthy did not seem to like me much, and said that I could stay as long as I wanted. As an aide stuck his head in the door to say that the President's motorcade was arriving on the Hill, I managed to mentioned a couple of issues that he really should not leave unmentioned during the talks to follow.

After a brief but very friendly tête-à-tête between the two leaders in Chrétien's office, with only the two ambassadors and interpreters present, we held the formal full bilateral talks in the Cabinet Room next to the Prime Minister's office. For me it was the first time back in the Cabinet Room since my time on the national unity file, and I felt no nostalgia whatsoever. Five Canadian Ministers participated in the morning's talks, including Foreign Minister Lloyd Axworthy, Trade Minister Sergio Marchi, Industry Minister John Manley (who arrived a little late, having had a tougher drive from our breakfast than I had had), CIDA Minister Diane Marleau and Minister of Environment David Anderson, who Chrétien had invited because he spoke Chinese. On the Chinese side there was Qian Qichen and Wu Yi and four or five vice ministers. After the relaxed dinner the night before and the tête-à-tête, the bilateral talks were almost a letdown, as the two leaders ground through the agreed agenda, almost as a necessary process so that they (and we as ambassadors) could subsequently refer to the various issues covered. Following the talks there was a signing ceremony in the Railroad Room of a bilateral Consular Agreement, three Memoranda of Understanding on new development projects, and an agreement permitting each country to open more offices in the other. This last agreement allowed China to move quickly to open its Consulate General in Calgary and Canada its new mission in Chongqing. After the signings Chrétien and Jiang held a joint press conference, a first for a visiting Chinese leader, who handled easily the predictable questions about human rights, saying that this had been a matter he had discussed with Chrétien, and that China valued both the bilateral dialogue on human rights and Canadian involvement in Chinese efforts at becoming a society based on law.

Lunch was at the Prime Minister's residence at 24 Sussex Drive and was a small affair with only six per side. It was a friendly and relaxed two hours, beginning with Chrétien taking Jiang for a walk in the snow in the garden overlooking the Ottawa River, and full of very open and interesting conversation following on from the morning's more formal sessions. Late in the luncheon, the two leaders got into a hopeless discussion in which they tried to describe the foundations of verbal humour in their respective cultures and languages. Each told a couple of jokes to the other and then attempted to explain them. It did not really work, of course, because humour is really non-translatable, but our fabulous interpreter Jean Duval ("Lao Du" as the Chinese called him) did his best to make the crosswalk and there was a lot of laughter and a further erosion of barriers.

Off to Toronto after lunch, I traveled in Jiang Zemin's 747, which had been parked outside and which took almost an hour to get de-iced, while we watched the Prime Minister's plane sneak out of its hangar and take off without a moment's delay. The evening was centred around the Canada China Business Council's Annual General Meeting and its gala dinner, the fourth year in a row that leaders of the two countries would speak at the event. This time it was particularly grand, with an intimate pre-dinner reception for the most exclusive 200 guests and the main dinner for about 1600. It was such a big event that the pre-dinner speeches of the two leaders had to be broadcast on two huge screens. But in spite of its size and the inevitable security, it was a very good dinner. The President and Prime Minister had two more hours side-by-side, and as seemed normal for CCBC events, as soon as the speeches were over and the meal served, the guests started to mingle from table to table until it seemed to be less of a dinner than a cross between a Jewish wedding and a church social. I did my own fair share of wandering, meeting far too many people and having my picture taken by future "friends" who might well seek the Embassy's recognition of our "friendship" in seeking visa assistance for family and friends, but all in all it was good networking.

The last morning, a Saturday, was a small breakfast hosted by Premier Mike Harris of Ontario and a session with senior representatives of the Toronto community of Chinese Canadians, during which Jiang Zemin was very good, telling them that he welcomed their contributions to the bilateral relationship but that they must remember to be good citizens of their adopted home. Then off to the airport and the state visit was done. As I watched the great 747 veer southward for a low pass over Niagara Falls, clearance for which was granted as a parting gift to the President, I breathed a great sigh of relief and asked my RCMP driver, a charming young tough-as-nails woman, to drop me at the Avis booth in Terminal 3, so I could do my inverted superman act and turn from an Ambassador into a normal human being, and head off to Port Hope to spend the rest of the weekend with daughter Cynthia, which was as always wonderful, ending only on Monday morning with a talk on China with her fellow students and teachers.

CHAPTER 27

VISIT OF LLOYD AXWORTHY

• • • • • • • • • • •

In the spring of 1998, Lloyd Axworthy paid his only visit to Beijing as Canada's Foreign Minister, even though he held the position for almost four years. He was clearly uncomfortable with the close relationship that Prime Minister Chrétien had established with the Chinese leadership and the priority that was given to Canada-China relations in our foreign policy. While he never actively opposed Chrétien or argued against the very rapid warming of our relationship, he spent most of his efforts elsewhere, pushing successfully for a global treaty banning land mines and other multilateral endeavours. He could not, however, completely avoid such an important bilateral partner as China, so he routed through Beijing on his way to the annual ASEAN dialogue meeting, held in 1998 in Vietnam.

Axworthy's trip to China was short and primarily consisted of a formal bilateral meeting and a state dinner with his counterpart Tang Jiaxuan, who had just replaced Qian Qichen, and a relatively brief meeting with Premier Li Peng. The bilateral meeting was fine, focusing substantially on multilateral matters given that there were very few irritants in the bilateral relationship at the time. Tang Jiaxuan, who had served as Chinese Ambassador to Japan and was a skilled and smooth diplomat, responded without rancor when Axworthy raised Canada's concerns about China's human rights record, assured Axworthy that China valued the formal human rights dialogue that we had established the year before between the two countries, and encouraged a broader bilateral engagement on such matters as legal reform.

The meeting with Premier Li Peng was not at all so smooth, amounting to what used to be known in the world of diplomacy as a "full and frank" exchange of views. Back in the cold war era, whenever a meeting was characterized as being "frank" it generally meant that the two interlocutors had agreed on nothing and sometimes almost come to blows.

Almost at the beginning of the meeting, after Li welcomed Axworthy to China for his first visit as Foreign Minister, Axworthy told Li that Canada and Canadians were concerned about the human rights situation in China, and continued to look for an honest accounting of the 1989 Tiananmen incident. This was not how we had suggested the human rights issue be raised and the frontal approach and the reference to Tiananmen certainly caught the Chinese by surprise. Li immediately reddened and lashed out at Axworthy, asking him if he had discussed his plan to raise this issue with Prime Minister Chrétien before he left Ottawa. He asked, "Why do you not follow your boss's orders?" Axworthy of course was stunned and thrown completely off balance, and when he seemed to have no response whatsoever to Li's tirade I intervened to explain that what the Minister was saying was that the entire Canadian Government, including Prime Minister Chrétien, valued the human rights dialogue as part of our broader and very healthy bilateral relationship. Li then answered me and said bluntly "Well, you had better tell your Minister that!" The Chinese interpreter simply translated that as "Thank you for the clarification", and then Axworthy then turned to a request for Chinese support for some international issue or other. Li was uninterested in further dialogue, the meeting wound up earlier than scheduled but luckily without further rancor, but the traditional post-meeting photograph did not take place.

In keeping with normal practice, Guy Saint-Jacques also attended the meeting between Axworthy and Li Peng. A few days earlier Guy had broken a bone in his foot while playing hockey, and was on crutches. At the end of the frosty meeting, as we were trying to exit the meeting room as fast as possible, Li Peng turned to Guy, who he had met on many occasions and knew as a deeply knowledgeable old China hand, and asked what had happened to his leg. Guy explained, in Chinese of course, and he and the Premier had a very friendly and informal exchange. It was a conversation radically different in tone than that between Li Peng and Axworthy, but luckily the latter, who would continue fuming for hours, did not notice.

Axworthy came away from the meeting offended by Li's outburst, and furious with having been set back on his heels and left without a rational riposte to the Premier's aggressiveness. He clearly saw the Embassy as excessively sympathetic to the Chinese and was no happier with me than he had been after my Tibet report of the year before. He seemed quite content to leave Beijing and as far as I know he never returned again, certainly not as Foreign Minister.

CHAPTER 28

CALM IN THE ASIAN STORM

• • • • • • • • • • •

Affecting me personally less than the big visits and the negotiations and the occasional bilateral arguments were substantial changes and events taking place in China's external environment and in the larger global setting. The long anticipated handover of Hong Kong took place on July 1st, 1997 and was managed with extraordinary deftness by the Chinese, with the PLA contingent replacing the departing British forces in a smooth and almost invisible manner. I and the other Beijing-based Ambassadors from major countries did not go to Hong Kong for the handover ceremonies, leaving our countries to be represented by our local Consuls General as a signal that although we might be theoretically henceforth responsible for Hong Kong, the "one-country two-systems" assured the territory by its Basic Law meant that it really was an autonomous territory and we would treat it as such.

Early in my time in China I called on the Governor of the People's Bank of China as part of my extensive round of introductory meetings. Dai Xianglong had been in the position for less than a year, having taken over the position from Zhu Rongji, who had formally held the position along with his vice premiership for two short years. Dai was the first professional Governor, with a strong banking background from the Agricultural bank of China and with sufficient economic training to manage the complex issues, both internal and external, with which the central bank was then dealing.

In my first discussion with Dai, I asked him when he anticipated the renminbi would be fully convertible on the capital as well as the current account. Economic and financial reforms were moving rapidly ahead at this stage, and the IMF and most observers were calling for China to move quickly to full convertibility. Being a good central banker, Dai hedged his answer, saying that China had to be sure that its banking system and broader financial system were sufficiently robust and ready before doing so, but that he thought it most probable that full convertibility would come before the end of the decade, meaning of course by the year 2000. What Dai did not foresee was the Asian Financial Crisis, spread to and undermining global markets in a cascade of national crises over the next two years.

It began with a speculative run on the Thai baht in May, 1997, and by the middle of that summer, the baht, the Malaysian ringgit and the Philippine peso had already been devalued. The Singaporean and Indonesian currencies then came under pressure, with the latter collapsing more than 30% in value, and by the autumn the infection had spread to the Hong Kong Stock market. Both the South Korean won and the Indonesian rupiah fell to record lows against the US dollar. On October 27th, the Dow Jones Industrial Average lost 554 points, its biggest drop ever, and shortly thereafter Japan announced that its economy was in a recession for the first time in 24 years. The IMF and US President Clinton continued to preach tough austerity measures but sustained openness, but not all countries listened. Malaysia ignored IMF advice and closed trading in its currency, making the ringgit unconvertible. As the crisis rolled forward through the first half of 1998, currency markets around the world became increasingly risk averse, and investors fled emerging markets. The Russian economy collapsed in a confused political environment, eventually forcing a massive devaluation of the ruble. The US and European markets continued to gyrate, and all eyes turned to China to see how it would react.

The Chinese government was extremely worried about being infected by the virus-like disease to which so many other economies were falling prey. But it studied carefully what various governments were doing, what the IMF was continuing to preach and what was actually happening. The Malaysian situation was particularly informative. In making the ringgit unconvertible, it closed off its economy from the free flow of capital. The IMF had warned that such a move would cause internal instability and a significant employment loss, and would likely take decades to recover from. Instead, the Malaysian economy stabilized with domestic investment and exports recovering quickly. I learned that Zhu Rongji himself was chairing a State Council committee to analyze the implications of both the crisis and the policy responses of various countries for their implications for China. Malaysia's decision to swim against the IMF orthodoxy was seen as an intelligent alternative to some other countries continuing to flounder, and the conclusion Zhu and his committee reached was unequivocal. First, everything that could be done to sustain the attractiveness of the Chinese economy for inward investment should be done, and any thought of relaxing controls on the outflow of capital should be set aside. And the reputation of the IMF as a source of good policy advice was in the gutter. China would follow its own path.

Throughout the crisis, China was very sensitive to any implication that the Chinese was being affected by the storm outside its borders. In the early autumn of 1998, the Royal Bank of Canada announced that it was, in reaction to the Asian Financial Crisis, closing most of its branches in Asia, including those in Shanghai, Taipei and Hong Kong.

I was sitting in my office in the Embassy one early autumn morning in 1998 with a couple of staff members discussing some upcoming event, when my secretary stuck her head in the door and said that the Premier's office was on the line and wished to speak with me. I picked up the receiver and identified myself, and was told by a male voice, in English, to please wait a moment. About a minute later, the same voice said, "Ambassador Balloch, Premier Zhu Rongji is on the line", and indeed he was. Zhu, with his assistant translating everything he said, told me that he had been surprised and disappointed to hear the news that the Royal Bank of Canada was closing its Shanghai branch, and that he would like me to intervene with the current CEO and Chairman to reverse the decision. He said that it was particularly disappointing given the friendship that he had built up over the years with Alan Taylor, the RBC's Chairman and CEO for many years, and that he was worried that the outside world might interpret RBC's decision as a loss of confidence in the Chinese economy, lumping it in with the other economies that were being buffeted by the roiling international crisis. I told Premier Zhu that I would call the current Chairman and see what I could do.

Late that evening, which was early morning Toronto, I reached RBC's John Cleghorn, who had replaced Alan Taylor about three years earlier. When I told Cleghorn that I had received a personal plea from the Premier of China asking me to try to prevent RBC from closing its Shanghai branch, he said that he would look into it and get back to me. I cautioned him that if the bank proceeded with the closure they might find it very difficult some years hence to re-open. It took Cleghorn a full thirty-six hours to get back to me, and when he did the news was not good. He explained the corporate strategic rational behind the decision and said that Shanghai was not being singled out, and that he could not override the decision of the commercial banking division that had made the decision as part of a much broader re-alignment of focus and resources. I was stunned that a direct plea from the Premier of China did not move them into some sort of face-saving compromise, and I pleaded with him to at least keep a skeleton branch open, but Cleghorn was unmovable. When I called back the Premier's office with the bad news, I was asked whether I thought we could find an alternative Canadian bank to replace RBC as the only Canadian bank with a branch in Shanghai, and I said I would try, but from neither Bank of Montreal nor Scotiabank did we elicit much interest and so the matter died. Many years later, just as I predicted, RBC would decide that it indeed needed a branch in Shanghai, and then found it very difficult and slow getting all the approvals required to re-open.

Inside China there were not many tangible indications of the turbulent economic waters roiling outside, but there were some. Since the end of the Soviet Union and the capitalist transformation of the Russian economy, Russian traders had been hugely present in the Beijing wholesale and informal markets. Individuals would come down from Irkutsk, Khabarovsk or Vladivostok and buy as much clothing and inexpensive household goods as they could, and bring it all back to Russia to sell in the open markets there. The still-outdoor Silk Market near the US Embassy, and the markets of Hongqiao and Sanlitun were always full of big Russian men buying goods in quantity and trying to drive prices as low as possible. Because of this large itinerant trade, there were Russian stores and restaurants scattered about certain areas of the city, particularly around Ritan Park, just north of the old diplomatic district. When the Ruble devalued in the autumn of 1998, virtually all the Russian traders disappeared overnight; the collapse in the value of their currency had instantly priced Chinese goods out of their market and ruined their individual businesses.

In September of 1998, Liani and I were invited by Paul and Jackie Desmarais to join their family and friends at the opening of Turandot, Puccini's opera about a mythical Chinese princess, being performed at the Forbidden City. The event was outrageously expensive, with tickets starting at $1800 a seat. But the prices did not matter, for the event became one of the "must-attend" events of the year for the world's wealthiest opera-loving jet set. I had been on business in the south and arrived back in Beijing the morning of the concert, and saw dozens of private jets with North American and European registration numbers parked near the old terminal at Beijing's airport. Mao, I thought, must have been rolling over in his grave.

The opening concert took place on a lovely cool autumn evening, with the moon playing hide and seek with clouds that vaguely threatened but did not deliver rain. This was fortunate for the performance was set outdoors on the front steps and balconies of a beautiful red-walled and golden-roofed temple in the palace's southeast corner between its outer and inner walls. Since the revolution, the temple had been known at the Worker's Cultural Palace, but with Turandot being performed it had regained its old name as the Imperial Ancestral Temple. Produced by *enfant terrible* and sometimes regime critic Zhang Yimou, with Zubin Mehta directing the Maggio Musicale Fiorentino and the principal singers all from La Scala, the opera was grand and stunning. Scene-setting soldiers, many of them, were drawn from the performing arts troupe of the PLA, and the drumming and percussion was at decibels that could be heard right across the city. This and the staging were vintage Zhang Yimou, who had arranged to have built a false front to the temple, perfectly in harmony with the real building, that could slide open and shut to allow shifts of scenes. The lighting and sound were truly magical in the open air. Allowing such a performance, and allowing it to be promoted as a huge coming-of-age of music in China, was seen a big gamble for the Chinese government at the time, and a mark of the openness of the Jiang-Zhu regime, and it probably helped pave the way for Beijing being awarded the 2008 Olympics. It was certainly a coup for Zhang Yimou, who was also chosen later to produce the opening and closing ceremonies of the Olympics. I came away from Turandot thinking that China was indeed turning a huge corner, internationalizing faster than any of us had really thought possible. While the portrait of Mao Zedong was still hanging on the Gate of Heavenly Peace, his successors had thoroughly repudiated virtually every dimension of his dogma, from condemnations of traditional Chinese and Western culture to the basic organization of a communist state.

The late 1990s also saw an increase in the flow back to China of the diaspora of overseas Chinese. After the smooth handover of Hong Kong from British to Chinese sovereignty on July 1st, 1997, confidence in the Chinese regime had moved to a new level. The numbers of business people moving to the mainland from Hong Kong and Taiwan, and from the communities of ethnic Chinese in North America as well, increased substantially. Former students who had stayed behind in Canada and the US at the time of the Tiananmen crisis in 1989 now started to come back to China to support North American business ventures or to start their own entrepreneurial ones. There was in 1998 a poignant exhibition shown at the National Art Museum entitled Beyond Golden Mountain, which showed through the eyes of overseas Chinese artists how they had seen their adopted homes in North America, and now it seemed they were coming back to a China they barely recognized.

Throughout the autumn of 1998, much of life went on as normal. We held bilateral Joint Economic and Trade Committee meetings in Beijing, led on our side by Rob Wright, Deputy Minister of International Trade who would eventually become Ambassador to China following my immediate successor, Joseph Caron. These were normal processes in the bilateral agenda, without much lasting significance, as were the regular Ministerial and technical exchanges that were the manifestations of the Canada-China relationship visible to the press and the business and academic communities. But what was less visible was the constant interaction that a big embassy needed to have with its principal interlocutors in the main ministries with which we dealt. None were more key than the Ministry of Foreign Affairs and MOFTEC, the trade ministry.

In the early autumn of 1998, the Assistant Minister of Foreign Affairs, Yang Jiechi, invited the senior Canadian diplomatic staff and their spouses and children to an informal and very special day at a small resort east of Beijing that was normally reserved for the Ministry's internal use. On the Chinese side were all the MFA staff that dealt with Canadians, as well as a few others that had served in the Chinese Embassy in Ottawa and were now assigned elsewhere in the Foreign Ministry. It was a wonderful, relaxed day, with a ban on business discussions. We bowled against each other, played ping pong and billiards, and Canadians and Chinese diplomats and their spouses wandered around the handsome gardens together chatting about life and children. Yang Jiechi and I racked up just about the lowest scores in bowling, leading us to agree that we would report our results as golf scores, as those we would have been proud of! It was a thoughtful invitation and a very enjoyable time, and it was an indication of how much we respected each other and how closely we were working together to forge a strong relationship between the two countries.

About a year later, Vice Minister Sun Jenyu of MOFTEC invited all the trade and commercial officers and me to a day at a MOFTEC entertainment centre, and this too was a friendly and very pleasant interlude in our regular lives. Forming friendships that transcended working relationships was one of the great satisfactions of diplomatic life.

CHAPTER 29

STATE VISIT OF JEAN CHRÉTIEN, NOVEMBER 1998

• • • • • • • • • • • •

During the last exchange between President Jiang Zemin and the Prime Minister in Toronto in November of 1997, Jiang had formally invited Chrétien to pay a full state visit to China, and in the months that followed we had nailed down the timing to be immediately following the APEC Summit in Kuala Lumpur. The Chinese Foreign Ministry told us that it had been a decision of Premier Zhu Rongji that the timeslot be given to Canada and not to Japan, which had also been seeking an immediate post-APEC visit.

In 1997, the Government of China announced a major economic development strategy for the poorer western provinces of the country ("Xibu Kaifa Zhanlue"). Our development efforts had since 1989 been focused on two broad objectives, the first to assist China's reform efforts especially in the field of law, and the second to help with poverty alleviation in the most destitute areas of the country. When the initial planning of the visit began, I suggested that we vary the normal Beijing-Shanghai agenda and go deep into China, not only seeing another side of the country but also to make the point that Canada was engaged well beyond the business and government centres of the east. Our Prime Minister's Office thought this was a good idea, and when we presented it to the Foreign Ministry in Beijing we received an extremely positive reaction. So the visit was set up to bring Chrétien to Beijing for the normal governmental meetings and a speech at the CCBC Annual General Meeting, and then to exit China after a visit to Gansu, selected because it was among the poorest provinces and because we had been engaged in a number of development projects there through the Canada Fund, the small fund for supporting local initiatives that was under my authority rather than subject to the enormously bureaucratic project approval processes of the bureaucracy at CIDA headquarters in Ottawa.

Chrétien arrived on his big Airbus direct from Malaysia, accompanied by thirty or so officials from PMO and DFAIT, thirty journalists, the Prime Ministerial security detail and Secretary of State for Asia Raymond Chan. Sergio Marchi, Minister of International Trade and Huguette Labelle, President of CIDA, also members of the prime Minister's delegation, came in separately. Marchi had been in Malaysia at the Trade Ministers' meeting which preceded the APEC Leaders' meeting by a few days and had planned to come to China early to lead a CCBC mission to Dalian in Liaoning. Marchi missed his connecting flight from Hong Kong to Beijing, and André Desmarais, then Chairman of CCBC, sent his Challenger down from Dalian to pick Marchi up so that the latter could still participate in the Dalian program. At my suggestion to avoid any press or opposition criticism of a potential conflict of interest, Desmarais formally requested Marchi to accept the offer of a private flight as a favour to the businesses represented in Dalian. The two days in Dalian were very interesting and productive. As usual Mayor Bo Xilai had laid on a terrific welcome and the entire city was bedecked with posters and banners welcoming the Canadian Minister and his business delegation. This was early in a strong relationship between Bo Xilai and the CCBC, and between Bo and Desmarais and indeed between Bo and myself. Whatever may have transpired many years later when he was Party Secretary in Chongqing and an aspiring member of the Standing Committee of the Politburo, in Dalian as Mayor, in Shenyang as the Governor of Liaoning and in Beijing as Minister of Commerce, he demonstrated himself to be a progressive reformer, a take-charge political leader and a good friend to Canada.

The formal airport greeting for Chrétien in Beijing was relatively low-key, with Vice Minister of Foreign Affairs Yang Jiechi, Ambassador to Canada Mei Ping and Chief of Protocol Zhang Yesui the official greeting party, and scores of brightly-dressed Chinese children, to which we had added almost as many from our local Canadian community, all waving little Canadian and Chinese flags. Yang was soon to become Ambassador to the US and would later return to Beijing as Foreign Minister and then State Councilor and grew over time to be a good friend.

One very sad back-note to the visit was that Aline Chrétien had been impelled to withdraw from accompanying her husband at the last minute due to the crisis that had just shattered the family of Pierre Trudeau, that being the loss of the former Prime Minister's son Michel in an avalanche in the mountains of British Columbia. Aline had rushed back from Southeast Asia to be with Pierre Trudeau and to attend a memorial service held in Montreal.

On the way into town, and in fact throughout the whole trip, I rode alone with the Prime Minister in his limousine, which gave me plenty of time to brief him. I had learned in the past that the best way to help Chrétien be ready for meetings was to give him a general overview of the people and issues at play during the formal briefing sessions, always attended by Ministers and senior officials as well. Then just before each meeting, usually in the car when I was alone with him, I would go through the key points he should make on each specific agenda item and give him a set of little cards with nothing more than a few memory-jogging lines on each. Chrétien was deeply committed to building a very strong relationship between the two countries, and personally with China's leaders, and he remembered issues from meeting to meeting very effectively, so he was a joy to work with. In this instance, we had pretty well covered all the general issues by the time we arrived at the China World Hotel, where a formal briefing with others present had been organized in a conference room next to Chrétien's suite, so the larger session lasted less long than planned and the Prime Minister asked me to share with the group my impressions of Zhu Rongji and how he was doing since he had formally taken over as Premier the previous March. My views were very positive and I said that I thought we were in for five years of very aggressive and important reform.

November weather in Beijing was always a little unpredictable, so it had been decided to have the formal welcoming ceremony inside the Great Hall of the People rather than outside on Tiananmen Square. We were happier with this in any case as it was less likely to cause journalists to draw people's attention to the events that had happened on the square eight and a half years earlier. While the honour guard was an impressive phalanx of young Chinese military men, in the event it seemed palpable that neither Jean Chrétien nor Zhu Rongji put that much value on the pomp of a state visit. Once the two national anthems had been played, they walked as fast as permitted by their escort past the battalion as a 19-gun salute echoed from the ceremonial artillery outside the Great Hall of the People. We then proceeded directly into a two-hour formal bilateral meeting in the Dongdating (Great Eastern Hall) in the Great Hall of the People, with journalists allowed for a brief "photo op" before being escorted out, permitting the two leaders and their principal delegations to get down to work. (Inside the Great Hall of the People there are, in addition to the huge amphitheatre used for meetings of the National People's congress, receiving rooms named for every one of China's provinces, including Taiwan, and a few grander rooms like the Dongdating and its western counterpart, the Xidating.)

With Premier Zhu on the Chinese side of the table were Minister of Land and Resources Zhou Yongkang, State Administrators for Environment Protection and Forestry Xie Zhenhua and Wang Zhibao and a slew of Vice Ministers, including Yang Jiechi and Sun Zhenyu from MFA and MOFTEC. After a brief stint as Party Secretary in Sichuan, Zhou Yongkang would later become the Party's heavyweight security chief and Minister of Public Security and finally slip from influence only after the 2012-13 generational handover. I had had Zhou to dinner at the Residence when he was still President of the oil and gas giant CNPC, and over the years got to know him reasonably well, and he was always well disposed to Canadians. MFA and MOFTEC were represented by their Vice Ministers since both of their Ministers had travelled on from the APEC meeting with President Jiang Zemin to other countries in Southeast Asia and would only return to Beijing halfway through Chrétien's visit. The absence of Foreign Minister Li Zhaoxing had given Lloyd Axworthy a welcomed excuse not to accompany Chrétien to China, something he successfully avoided all but once during his four years as Foreign Minister.

The talks themselves were very straightforward and there were few serious disagreements to address. At this time Canada and China were in the midst of a series of bilateral discussions on WTO-related matters, trying to reach agreement on them as part of the multiple agreements China needed to conclude as part of its WTO accession steps. Chrétien pushed for better access to the Chinese market for processed foods and more licenses for Canadian financial institutions, and Zhu responded positively on both fronts, giving the Prime Minister early warning that China would shortly grant a second Canadian life insurer, which we knew would be SunLife, the right to establish in China. Some of the time was focused on a slew of new bilateral projects in environmental protection, agriculture and public sector and legislative reform, key new areas of focus that I had been encouraging for our development assistance program. After the formal talks, there was a public signing ceremony where bilateral agreements on these matters were signed, and a brief press scrum by Prime Minister Chrétien, the Chinese having politely turned down our suggestion for a repeat of the bilateral press conference that we had held in Ottawa during Jiang Zemin's visit the previous year. The day ended with a formal state dinner for about 200 guests, mostly officials, in the ornate Xidating of the Great Hall of the People.

After the state dinner, which ended reasonably early, Liani and I took Chrétien back to a reception room at the China World Hotel where he could meet and mingle with Embassy staff and their families. This was originally planned for both the Prime Minister and his wife, and Aline's absence made it a little less engaging than it might have been since she always added a warm and personal touch to events like these, but it was still a big hit in the Embassy community. The Prime Minister made some remarks about how he valued the dedication of both Foreign Service employees and their families who contributed and sacrificed so much for their country, which made everyone feel good, and then had pictures taken with families.

The next day was a very heavy day. It began with a speech of the Prime Minister at Qinghua University, by reputation the MIT of China and the alma mater of Zhu Rongji, who had officially been, until just before his elevation to the premiership, the Dean of the economics faculty. When we arrived at the university, we began with a small meeting for Chrétien with Presidents Chen Jia'er of Beijing University, Hou Zixin of Nankai University in Tianjin, and Wang Dazhong of Qinghai, to discuss the "Three-by-Three Partnership" between these three prestigious universities and McGill, University of Toronto and UBC, which the government had been supporting for some years. The speech, which I had played a part in drafting, talked about the importance in modern societies of free expression and of balanced progress towards both a more developed economy and a society in which fundamental precepts of human rights were respected and protected in law and in practice. It was not an accusatory approach but the message was clear, and the press grudgingly gave Chrétien credit for broaching the issues publicly. Not surprisingly, the coverage in the Chinese media, which was fulsome, did not cover the more contentious components.

From the speech it was off to the opening of a little food kiosk, brightly painted to look like a Canadian flag, owned and operated by a small Vancouver company in a joint venture with the Beijing Bus Trolley Company, offering imported Canadian products in a fast food setting. Chrétien of course loved the setting and turned it into a great photo opportunity, capturing Chrétien ordering a chicken leg and French fries. The business idea was to build dozens of these street-side kiosks at bus depots around Beijing, but in the end the concept did not fit well with the city's self-image as a modern capital, and the only two kiosks actually built had to be removed as part of a massive city ban on street vendors some years later. By that time the owners, our friends Annie Chong-Hill and Lawrence Hill of Global Foods, were finding doing business in China very frustrating and not very profitable, so they turned down the city's offer to help them find space inside bus stations and malls for their outlets and simply pulled out of China. Theirs was, and regrettably remains, a very common experience for small businesses trying to break into the Chinese market.

A week or two before the visit, the Ministry of Foreign Affairs had advised us that Li Peng, now Chairman of the Standing Committee of the National People's Congress wanted to invite his "old friend", Prime Minister Chrétien for a meal during the visit. When we had advised PMO of this they had resisted, knowing that the press saw Li Peng as a hardliner still wearing a portion of responsibility for the Tiananmen crackdown, while Zhu Rongji and Jiang Zemin carried none of the same baggage. I had pointed out that an invitation so made could not really be turned down, and so we squeezed it down as much as possible, limiting the Canadian side so the Chinese would be forced to a similarly small number, and reduced the time to less than ninety minutes for both the meeting and the lunch. In the end we need not to have worried much; the day was so full of newsworthy events that the lunch with Li Peng went virtually unrecorded, and was in fact a perfectly personable and pleasant affair.

President Jiang Zemin had only just arrived back in the Chinese capital after visiting other Southeast Asian capitals following the APEC Summit in Kuala Lumpur, where he had already had a bilateral meeting with Chrétien. Nonetheless, according to Vice Minister Yang Jiechi, the President wanted to make a public statement about the importance of the relationship with Canada and had accordingly insisted on publicly receiving the Prime Minister even though they had just been together in Malaysia. The meeting turned out to be very friendly and quite short, more of a photo-opportunity for the press than anything else, and then it was back to a focus on CCBC events. The first of these was a joint meeting of Chrétien and Zhu Rongji with twenty senior business leaders from both countries, which turned out to be mostly an exchange between the Chinese

Premier and Canadian business leaders. Zhu was in his element, and was direct and forthright in his answers to the questions they posed, and he was as often as not quite critical of the Chinese bureaucracy for resisting reform or thwarting changes already announced, and he seemed always determined to find a solution to any problem raised. It was at the huge CCBC gala dinner, with almost eight hundred people in attendance, that we were to get our surprise of the day.

Just before the dinner, the two leaders were taken through an area outside the large banquet hall where we had arranged to be hung an exhibition entitled "Canada Through Chinese Eyes", a collection of forty paintings by ten well-known Chinese artists who had individually toured through part of Canada and painted landscapes in their own styles. The project had been blessed as part of our bilateral cultural exchange program, and the paintings were very beautiful. The collection had been unveiled by then Minister of Canadian Heritage Sheila Copps during a visit to Shanghai two months earlier, and we used the Prime Minister's visit to give it publicity for its arrival in the Chinese capital.

It was a tradition at CCBC annual events to invite the leaders of both countries to give speeches, with the local leader speaking last. Chrétien gave a fine but not terribly memorable speech, for his speech at Qinghua University in the morning had covered everything we wished to say publicly about the relationship and our hopes for sustained change in China, and then turned the podium over to his Chinese counterpart. As he had done almost five years earlier when visiting Canada as Vice Premier, Zhu Rongji paid scant attention to his prepared text and spoke extemporaneously. Highly complementary of the Chrétien government and of the long and steadfast friendship between the two countries, he concluded one part of his remarks by saying very directly that "Canada is China's best friend". This was a very well attended event, with no fewer than six Chinese Ministers present, including Tang Jiaxuan (MFA), Zhou Yongkang, Fu Zhihuan (Railways), Shi Guangsheng (Trade), Xie Zhenhua (Environment), Liu Huaqui (State Council) as well as Party Secretary Wen

Shizhen of Liaoning and literally dozens of Vice Ministers and scores of Chairmen and Presidents of state-owned enterprises. Zhu's message was clearly received, and there was no question that the operating environment for Canadian businesses in China was from this moment forward to pass into its happiest historical period. Eight or nine years later, when Prime Minister Harper intentionally put a big chill on the relationship and frozen senior level visits, I and many others looked wistfully back on the Zhu speech and the good times that followed.

Winter came early in the autumn of 1998, and when we woke for an early departure the following morning it was snowing quite heavily. The Prime Minister's motorcade was smaller than usual, with some of the staff heading to the airport early and a much smaller accompanying delegation going with him to Lanzhou in any case. I was in the Prime Minister's limousine and we were about fourth car in line, following both Chinese and Canadian Security and one car with protocol officials. Throughout the visit we had traveled with motorcycle outriders, and this morning was no different. There were six People's Armed Police motorcycles surrounding our car, with two parallel riders in front, two in back, and one rider on each side of the limousine, almost immediately astride the Prime Minister on the right and me on the left. As we roared towards the airport in the very early morning light, the snow continued to fall, and Chrétien said to me that he thought the Chinese were crazy to use high-speed motorcycle escorts in the snow. Almost as soon as the words were out of his mouth, I noticed the rider outside my side of the limousine was starting to wobble. I pointed him out to Chrétien and said that I thought he was going to fall, and then our driver started to brake heavily, drawing our attention forward. As if in slow motion, we watched the Chinese security car directly ahead skid sideways on the ice. The two motorcyclists between that car and our limousine tried to stop but could not, and both went over on their sides and slammed, luckily at a greatly reduced speed, into the side of the security car. Our driver brought our limousine to a stop only a few feet from the fallen riders, soon numbering four as one of the riders behind us also lost his balance. Immediately behind us, a second limousine with a senior Chinese official from the Ministry of Foreign Affairs and my Political Minister, Guy Saint-Jacques, also skidded as its driver saw the confusion ahead and they went into a complete 360 degree spin, luckily colliding with no one. Within no more than twenty seconds, both security cars had emptied and the Prime Minister's limousine was surrounded by a mix of People's Armed Police and RCMP, all facing outwards, clearly implementing a well-rehearsed emergency reaction to a potential attack on the motorcade. There was, of course, no attack, and within a few minutes someone had taken charge, the fallen motorcyclists and their riders moved out of the way, a reserve security car brought forward and the motorcade went back on its way, without motorcycles and at a more measured pace. We were later to be told that none of the riders suffered more than superficial injuries, but as we took off in the Prime Minister's Airbus we joked that the security official who had not changed motorcade plans when the snow began would probably spend the remainder of his career guarding a border crossing with Russia north of Qiqihar.

At the airport's VIP terminal, all seemed relatively calm, although I noticed that Guy Saint-Jacques was clearly unhappy about something. He signaled me over and told me that Charles Reeves, the Embassy Officer who had been assigned responsibility for part of the logistics of the Gansu trip, had missed the motorcade. Apparently he had been out bar-hopping the night before with members of the Prime Minister's delegation and had overslept, and consequently had failed to bring to the airport all the tickets for officials returning from Lanzhou to Beijing by commercial flights. In those days nothing was electronic or computerized, so Guy had to arrange the purchase of new tickets for fifteen or so staff members, and the double ticketing fiasco was left to later to resolve. Guy, who was one of the most thorough and efficient Foreign Service officers I ever worked with, was clearly not happy with Charles Reeves, and although I was not present to hear their subsequent conversation, I was rather glad I was not Charles. His next assignment, I believe, was processing visas in Shanghai.

With the early winter storm thickening, we were very lucky to be able to travel to Gansu at all. After a rudimentary de-icing, the Prime Minister's aircraft was the last to be permitted to take off before the airport was closed until the storm abated.

As we flew west the 1,500 kilometres to Lanzhou, capital of Gansu province where the Silk Road begins and the Great Wall ends, I pointed out to the Prime Minister that he was going deeper into China than any western leader had ever gone, and as the weather cleared and we looked down on the arid loess plateau, with its endless array of windswept ridges and little valleys, in which small and isolated villages could be seen, I think we all got a good sense of how far the province of Gansu was from the bustling metropolises of the east. We had chosen Gansu for the Prime Minister's western China visit because it was one of the poorest provinces in China, poorer than its neighbours Qinghai and Xinjiang. It had been and was continuing as the focus of many of our poverty alleviation projects, particularly the small projects funded through the Embassy-controlled Canada Fund.

Immediately upon landing and being officially greeted by Gansu Vice Governor Guo Kun, we drove northward away from Lanzhou to a very small village named Fengdeng in the county of Gaolan. After leaving the paved regional road we turned off on a gravel spur, which my development staff told me had been freshly graded for the visit, but even so was far from level or smooth. As we pulled into the village we could see and hear hundreds of children, all brightly dressed in the clear morning, banging on drums and making a wonderful racket to greet the only national leader from any country, including their own, to have ever visited. Along with provincial Governor Song Zhaosu and dozens of provincial officials, the entire county and village hierarchies had not surprisingly turned out to welcome us, along with all the sun-darkened and leathery-faced villagers and all their children. With flags and banners everywhere on a crystal clear November day, it was a fantastic setting for the Prime Minister and for the busloads of Canadian and Chinese cameramen and journalists.

Fengdeng, a clay and straw village of about 1,400 people, had been selected by the Embassy and the Gansu provincial poverty alleviation office as the beneficiary of a project to capture and store rainwater. This part of China received a reasonable rainfall (up to 500mm) annually, but it was concentrated in a very short and intense summer rainy season, and the vast amount of the water simply passed over the hard and unabsorbing land and ran off into a tributary of the Yellow River. For most of the year the villagers of Fengdeng would have to trek five kilometres to a well over a distant hill to get water for household use, the only local source being a stagnant pond that filled up with the summer rains and then was gradually depleted, becoming increasingly unhealthy as the year progressed. Our project would build concrete collection channels and clean underground cisterns, allowing the village to become self-sufficient in water, and permitting their outdoor pond to be used for irrigation as opposed to household use. Villagers would no longer need to travel to the distant well, giving them more time to attend to their fields, to animal husbandry and to income earning pursuits. Fengdeng was one of four poor and barren Gansu villages where we would be installing these catchment and storage systems, and the village leaders from the other three were in Fengdeng for the visit.

After a visit to the village centre and a tour through the homes of two local families, the Prime Minister departed from the prepared script and asked to be shown the local pond, so one of the village leaders led us there, where a Canadian Press photographer caught a fabulous picture of Chrétien with a local peasant and a donkey, making the front page of most newspapers the following morning in Canada. Then we entered a walled schoolyard, around the walls of which a photographic exhibition of all the other Canada Fund projects we had done in the province over the years, with representatives from each of the beneficiary villages beside the photos of their village to explain to the Prime Minister and the accompanying Governor how the Canada Fund had improved their lives. It was all very moving, and a wonderful backdrop to a signing ceremony for three more Canada Fund projects, with a provincial official and me as the signatories.

After our visit to the village, we drove into the capital for meetings with provincial leaders and other events. In the car, the Prime Minister was ebullient about his visit to Fengdeng and the impact we were making on real people's lives. I told him that the average all-in cost of each of our some fifty Canada Fund projects around the country was about $20,000, and that in this case we were putting in four water catchment and storage systems like the one in Fengdeng for less than $40,000. I said that I believed there was no better return on our investment in terms of both real impact and Canada's reputation. Chrétien responded that he agreed completely, and said that if he could have his own way he would trash most of the CIDA-funded development aid, through which the development community of Canadian consultants and academics and engineers seemed to be the real beneficiaries of most of Canada's aid, and simply do small Canada Fund projects around the world.

Lanzhou itself had a storied past, being a key city along the northern Silk Road trading route and a prefectural headquarters even in the time of the Qin dynasty. In the early 1920s the Soviet Union had established a significant presence in Lanzhou, allegedly in agreement with the Republican Government, and during the Japanese invasion and occupation it was used as a depot for the supply of Soviet support for the anti-Japanese war. After the war it was chosen by Mao Zedong to be a major industrial hub, far from the coast and thus safe from American invasion, and close enough to the Soviet Union to be a major recipient of Soviet industrial aid. It was not a handsome city, and it was on the day of our visit also heavily polluted, with thick and acrid smoke from its refineries and factories hanging over the city. During a separate visit I was once told of a plan to solve the pollution by cutting a vast hole in the mountain north of the city to allow the prevailing northerly wind to blow away the horrible air. Luckily, sanity intervened at some level and more rational pollution abatement measures would over time be imposed.

The rest of our visit to Lanzhou was the predictable mix of a formal meal hosted by Governor Song, a meeting with beneficiaries of China-Canada educational exchange programs, and a visit to Lanzhou University which was working on a series of CIDA-funded projects with the University of Manitoba in crop selection and material science, and with other Canadian universities on projects as varied as transportation planning, women's studies and medical trauma care. But all seemed somewhat bland after the fabulous visit to Fengdeng, and many years later Jean Chrétien was to tell me that his visit to that poor village and to see the impact Canada was having was one of the highlights of all his many trips abroad as Prime Minister. And I was also told that in Fengdeng village, the visit of the great western leader Jean Chrétien gradually became part of regional lore, with people from neighbouring counties visiting the village to see both its transformative water systems and mounted photographs from the visit, proving an old proverb quoted by Governor Song Zhaosu during the formal banquet: "When drinking water, one should never forget the one who sunk the well".

Some weeks after this third visit in four years of Prime Minister Chrétien, I had the occasion to be at an event with Zhu Rongji, who told me that he knew that it had been at my suggestion that Chrétien had gone to Gansu to support the Chinese government's western development efforts. When he thanked me, I told him that we were all very satisfied that we had gone there, none more than the Prime Minister, and that he could return the favour by visiting a poorer part of Canada when he next visited. When he asked where would I suggest, I said that there would be no better choice than the province of my childhood, Newfoundland.

CHAPTER 30

INTO THE HINTERLANDS

• • • • • • • • • • • •

Whenever there were not pressing negotiations or high-level visitors requiring my presence in Beijing, I tried to head out to another part of the country, especially to the poorer regions where we had bilateral projects. Three of my most memorable visits were to the Three Gorges project on the Yangtze River in Hubei which was followed by a family trip by ship up the river to Chongqing, another to the very poor province of Guizhou, and a third to the Muslim region of Hetian in Xinjiang south of the Taklamakhan Desert.

Since the mid-1980s, the Chinese had been interested in adapting Canadian experience and know-how in large hydroelectric projects in their own generations-long dream to harness the flow of the mighty Yangtze. Even in the early years of the young Republic of China in the second decade of the century, there had been talk of building a dam and power plant just downriver from a narrow part of the river called the Three Gorges, close to the city of Yicheng. In the late 1980s, as Director of North Asia, I myself had travelled with Chinese leaders to James Bay in Northern Québec to see what was then the largest hydroelectric complex in the world. Through CIDA, Canada had financed a feasibility study, luckily complete before the Tiananmen crisis of 1989, and Canadian firms were deeply involved in the massive project, from building generators to providing the computerized management information and control systems. There were a lot of critics of the project, arguing that the human cost of relocating almost two million inhabitants from the 650-kilometre long reservoir flood area, or the risks of catastrophe in the event of the dam's failure, or the problem of silting behind the dam, individually or collectively made the project inadvisable. The World Bank and many bilateral aid agencies had taken a position that they would not be involved and the public in most western countries opposed the project either on alleged environmental or humanitarian grounds. Others, usually without any science to substantiate their assertions, argued that the dam was too large and complicated to be safely engineered and risked catastrophic failure in the event of an earthquake. I felt very differently on the basis of many discussions with professional engineers who had in one way or another been involved in the project's planning. I believed that the Chinese were well aware of the risks and were determined to address them thoroughly, and I thought that the benefits of hydropower over other forms of generation were so significant that the project made all the sense in the world. And, after all, large-scale Canadian hydroelectric projects had faced significant challenges as well, making opposition in principle to the Three Gorges Dam very sanctimonious and in my view self-righteous. I had worked hard over more than ten years, first at the Director level, then as ADM for Asia, and finally as Ambassador, to keep Canada supportive of the project.

For my first visit to the Three Gorges site in 1997, I brought Liani and the children both to see the project and to then travel up the Yangtze River by boat. When we visited the project site, the main cofferdams were already in place to divert the main flow of the river away from the principal channel so that construction could begin, and significant progress had already been made in building the first half of the huge permanent dam.

We were greeted very warmly by the project's General Manager, Lu Youmei, who had been to Canada literally dozens of time to learn everything he could from Canadian experiences. I had met him during one of those trips some five years earlier. In deference to the support Canada had consistently offered, Lu gave us a "deep-dive" half-day tour of the project that would normally only be given to senior leaders. The sheer size of the earthworks was humbling, and to see the beginnings of what would eventually be a 200 metre tall dam made one feel like a Lilliputian. We could see the preliminary cutaway for the huge ship locks for major sea-going freighters and the site of a smaller ship-lift for river craft, although no excavation work had yet begun on the latter. For the children, all interested in engineering, wandering around such a massive project in full construction mode was nothing short of fantastic. I returned a couple of more times during my years as Ambassador, and stayed in touch over the years with Lu Youmei who went from being project manager to Chairman of the Three Gorges Corporation after the dam and power plant were fully functional.

After our day at the dam site, we boarded a modest cruise boat to go up the river from Yicheng to Chongqing, a four-day trip. Our co-passengers were mostly Chinese, with a few from Taiwan and Hong Kong, and it was a very interesting trip. Part of the entertainment for all the other passengers was watching our four young children competently and competitively playing Mazhong together. As we worked our way upriver against the endless flow of the great brown river, sometimes in tits narrows moving at a speed that created standing waves but mostly just aimlessly and steadily washing by, we saw the changes coming to this ancient river scene. Some of the towns along the banks of the river were already being evacuated in anticipation of the rising water, which would measure 175 metres above its natural level at the dam and even 35 metres at Chongqing, 650 winding kilometres inland. We went up the "Little Three Gorges" in small sampans, which the children loved, and climbed along the riverbanks of clear streams and brooks that fed the mighty Yangtze, and we walked through Fengdu, the old "city of devils" where the haunting statuary and improbably carvings of the underworld would all eventually be moved to a new town constructed for tourists on higher ground tens of kilometres away.

My visit to Guizhou, China's poorest province in the late 1990s, was like travelling back to a China of another era. I travelled with Henri-Paul Normandin, our Head of Aid, and a couple of staff from the Canada Fund team. We started with a required visit to the provincial capital of Guiyang, and a dinner with long-serving Party Secretary Liu Fangren, who seemed determined to prove that the local Maotai was China'a only real baijiu and that it should always be drunk in great quantities, and then a more thoughtful meeting with Governor Qian Yunlu. Qian was deeply gripped with the question of rural poverty, especially among the many ethnic minorities in the province, and was very interested in the impact that we were achieving with a joint Canada-World Bank project in micro-financing of locally-established businesses. After Guiyang we went out into distant Miao and Zhuang counties where we were implementing some of these projects, and saw two agricultural cooperatives that had been established, the first growing and marketing mushrooms and the second raising pigs and processing the meat for markets in the city. The mushroom cooperative was particularly interesting. Using loans as small as several hundred renminbi, or less than $100, local peasant families of a very poor local village had, along with their normal subsistence farming, begun cultivating mushrooms in dark pits designed and dug for this purpose. Young men and women then collected the mushrooms and took them to market towns and to Guiyang for sale, and as they learned more about the market were able to adjust their supply and their pricing to ensure a steady if small profit stream. The cooperative then distributed some of this profit to members of the cooperative and used some for the building of a new local school and other community facilities. The project was turning out to be very successful, and the cooperative had already been able to buy a small and inexpensive van for delivering its produce to the markets, and the income being earned was substantially improving the lot of local farmers. One of the young men who was helping run the cooperative had also become head of one of the local village committees, effectively the mayor, and when we were travelling with him it was clear that he had become a very popular leader of his community. Guizhou was one of the three provinces where we were working with the World Bank to experiment with micro-lending schemes, the others being Shaanxi and Xinjiang.

The site of our micro-finance project in western Xinjiang was south of the Taklamakhan Desert in the prefecture of Hotan on the old southern Silk Road. Four thousand kilometres west of Beijing, this was a different world. Hotan represented an oasis on the long trek from Kashgar on the borders with Tajikistan and Kyrgyzstan to Bayingolin at the edge of Qinghai, blessed by rivers and aquifers fed from the northern slopes of the Kunlun Mountains. The prefecture seat was Hetian, a busy and noisy market town, almost entirely Uyghur. Most of the men wore patterned, or occasionally traditional white, Muslim caps, and the women were all very brightly dressed with their heads covered in vividly coloured scarfs. Faces were more Turkic than Han, noses more prominent, eyes more inset and eyebrows thicker. The streets were an open market, busy and noisy and full of the smell of roasted lamb and spices. This was clearly well on the way to Central Asia. It was in the outlying villages of the prefecture that our micro-financing project was being implemented, and the local Party Secretary, a Uyghur, spent a day touring with us around these villages. In the evening he invited us to his own home, a big traditional Uyghur home with a large central room with high benches around three sides of the room, which served both as beds at night and sitting places during meals. It was evident that the Party Secretary's home was more communal than personal, with people wandering in and out all evening without any evidence of a plan. He had arranged local dancers and musicians to entertain us, including a traditional belly dance by very beautiful local young women with raven hair and open midriffs. Some of the older men danced as well, and encouraged us to learn the steps and the elaborate arm movements that complemented the movements of the young women. The food was heavy, slabs of fatty mutton and a local flatbread, but very delicious. And while all Muslim, the men drank heavily and were delighted that we drank along with them glass for glass.

The project in Hetian seemed to have been very successful, like other micro-finance schemes in Guizhou and Shaanxi, and was effectively self-financing after less than three years of operation. At that time there had been a lot of debate in the international development community as to what made some micro-finance programs successful and others less so. In China there had been an argument whether these tiny loans should carry commercial rates of interest or be made interest-free given the relative poverty of the recipients. Interestingly, the Chinese poverty alleviation and civil affairs ministries had argued for interest-free loans, while we and the World Bank had believed that the impact of interest was less monetary than disciplinary, and over time the Chinese authorities came around to our point of view. In fact, in Hetian and elsewhere, we learned that the first golden rule of micro-finance programs was to charge reasonable rates of interest, since this motivated borrowers to get their loans paid off quickly and become eligible for more and often larger loans. The second rule was to put the local women in charge of the administration and collection, since the men would be ashamed not to pay back their loans when village women all knew everyone's record in doing so. Where the men were left in charge, the social pressure to make side deals on deferments or other relationship-based arrangements inhibited effective decision-making and fund management. Wherever these two golden rules were followed, rates of default were effectively zero.

CHAPTER 31

STATE VISIT TO CANADA OF PREMIER ZHU RONGJI, APRIL 1999

• • • • • • • • • • •

In the early winter of 1999, the Chinese Foreign Ministry advised us that Premier Zhu Rongji would accept Prime Minister Chrétien's invitation to pay a state visit to Canada in the spring, either before or after a visit to the United States. As we began to discuss the itinerary, we suggested that the visit include Newfoundland, picking up on my exchange with Zhu following Chrétien's visit to Lanzhou. The Foreign Ministry thought that the Premier's office would be highly unlikely to agree, and we were reasonably sure that they recommended against it, but to their surprise word came back that the Premier himself had decided that he would begin the visit in Canada's eastern most province.

President Clinton had visited China in mid-1998 for a very successful visit that included a televised and uncensored speech and a very warm welcome, and it was expected that Zhu's visit to the United States would be similarly warm. The US and China had been in very intensive and far too public negotiations on their bilateral agreement on China's WTO accession, and China had, under Zhu's instruction, prepared a very attractive package of concessions which the Americans had indicated would be sufficient to allow Zhu and Clinton to sign an agreement in Washington. However, facing substantial opposition from Congress, Clinton reversed himself and withdrew US agreement to the deal during the visit, angering and embarrassing Zhu, who left Washington and publicly was heard to say that Clinton "lacked courage". When Clinton realized the damage that had ben done, he called Zhu, by this time in New York being fêted by the business community, to suggest he return to Washington to finish the negotiations. Zhu turned him down, and after a speech in Boston, left the United States and headed up to Newfoundland.

While the messy drama over the bilateral US-China WTO deal was publicly visible south of the border, we had our own drama unfolding in St. John's. Two days before the Zhu visit was scheduled to begin, Andy Wells, the Mayor of St. John's, had the Free Tibet flag hoisted on the flagpole in front of City Hall. The Chinese advance team, already in St. John's, advised their Embassy in Ottawa. Ambassador Mei Ping went apoplectic and immediately threatened to have the visit cancelled if the flag was not removed. An official from the Protocol Division of DFAIT in Ottawa called the Mayor's office to request that the offending flag be taken down, by which time the press had gotten hold of the issue, so Andy Wells, always seeking the spotlight, predictably and publicly stated that Canada was a free country and he could fly any flag he wished at his city hall as a peaceful protest to Chinese brutality. I was already in Canada and decided to fly to St. John's a day early, and met with my friend Premier Brian Tobin to figure out how to resolve the matter. Brian, both a consummate politician and tough as nails, knew Andy Wells very well and knew that the more we asked him to do one thing the more likely he was to do the reverse. But Brian also knew exactly where the mayor's financial backing came from. So, with the help of Vic Young, the CEO of Fishery Products International, a key leader of the Newfoundland business community and a mutual friend of ours, we sat in the Premier's office and called as many of Wells' supporters as we could, getting them to call him and threaten political purgatory and financial penury. After about two hours, a secretary stuck her head in the door and told Premier Tobin that Andy Wells was on the line. Brian answered on speakerphone and we listened as Andy Wells angrily and with many expletives said he was taking down the flag, but that he would some day get his revenge on Tobin and the "lily-livered, kowtowing feds". Crisis averted.

April evenings in Newfoundland are often foggy, but we were not worried because Premier Zhu's arrival was scheduled for mid-afternoon. Unfortunately, just after noon we received a call from Boston with the news that the Premier had stayed longer at an event at Harvard than planned, and that his arrival would be delayed until the early evening, and as the hour approached we watched with growing trepidation as the fog banks rolled in. By the time we got to the airport the fog was as thick as pea soup, and we began to worry that the visit would start with a most inauspicious diversion to Gander or Goose Bay. We could hear the big 747 as it approached, but as it came in to land its engines roared and it aborted not just its first but also its second attempt. By this time protocol and security officials were madly calling the airport authorities at Gander and trying to round up RCMP support for an arrival there. Luckily, on the third attempt, the plane landed, and we all breathed a big sigh of relief. When Zhu Rongji and his wife Lao An descended the steps the fog was so thick that we could barely see the plane's fuselage, but we could see a Premier who, in spite of an attempt to be pleasant during the welcoming ceremony, was clearly looking tired and unhappy, probably thinking that the entire North American trip had been a major mistake.

The twenty-four hour visit to St. John's had intended to be a light visit to permit the Premier to recharge his batteries after a long visit in the US and a busy official program over the next week in Canada. The official program contained only a brief meeting with the Premier and a meal with the provincial business community, with the remainder of the time left for rest and sightseeing. After the business lunch Zhu Rongji answered a few questions by the press, and when asked what he thought about the mayor (who was not invited to the meal) flying the Free Tibet flag, he answered simply that perhaps the mayor should have "been better educated". In the end, the fog remained heavy the morning after the Premier's arrival, and Zhu decided not to participate in the sightseeing. I took the other members of the delegation, including my old friend Zeng Peiyan, now a Vice Premier, and Trade Minister Shi Guangsheng up to Signal Hill and then on a walk along the docks, but the fog really did make the visit less enjoyable than we had all hoped. When we got on the Premier's plane for the flight to Ottawa, a visibly rested Zhu Rongji turned to me and said in a jocular tone that he had accepted my invitation to see Newfoundland, and that I had let him down by not taking care of the fog!

The program that followed the light St. John's visit was indeed a heavy one, with stops in Ottawa, Toronto, Calgary, Vancouver and Victoria, a six-city tour that Zhu would later correctly claim was more extensive than any other foreign leader took during the time Jean Chrétien was Prime Minister. It was also a larger number of cities in a single country than Zhu himself ever visited on any other foreign tour.

The Ottawa program was laid out as a full state visit, with the Prime Minister on hand to greet Premier Zhu at the airport and inspect an honour guard in the ceremonial hangar. The meetings began with a tête-à-tête in the Prime Minister's office on the Hill, with only interpreters, Ambassador Mei Ping and me in attendance. Chrétien asked Zhu about the difficult meetings he had had in Washington and Zhu was completely forthright, saying that Clinton reversed himself on the WTO agreement and had put him (Zhu) in an impossible situation. When Clinton had called him just before his departure for Canada, no one on the Chinese side believed that Clinton would be able to agree to an arrangement fair to China. Zhu said that getting everyone in Beijing to agree to what was to have been codified in the proposed agreement had taken an enormous effort, and he was now quite pessimistic that an agreement could be quickly concluded. He asked Chrétien for his views on Clinton and why he seemed unable to deliver as promised. Chrétien's response was that Congress was in a very negative mood with a Republican Senate Leader, Trent Lott, both anti-Clinton and very opposed to allowing China in the WTO, and that Clinton had been weakened by the Lewinsky scandal and was unable to build the consensus he needed. The two leaders then agreed that it would be good to conclude the Canada-China agreement on WTO accession, and that by doing so it would make it internationally clear that it was the failure in Washington was more due to a US inability to get its act together than to Chinese inflexibility. When Chrétien suggested that they should try to sign and announce the bilateral deal that very morning, Zhu immediately concurred, and Chrétien turned to me and asked me to "fix it with Sergio".

In parallel with the tête-à-tête between Chrétien and Zhu Rongji, the two Trade Ministers, Sergio Marchi and Shi Guangsheng, had held an early morning meeting with their officials to hammer out the last few elements of our bilateral agreement on China's access to the world trade body, and agreement that was at this stage virtually complete with only a very few minor issues left unsettled. The complexity of China's entry into the WTO was that every major trading partner to China had its own list of priorities, and by the spring of 1999, China needed the agreement of not just the US, but the EU and Canada, having already reached agreement with Japan and a number of smaller countries. In the final accession agreement, any concession to a single country would be open to all of China's trading partners under the MFN principle (requiring the granting of access to any partner the same access granted to the "Most Favoured Nation"). The bilateral negotiations were partly about the rules that would apply once China was in the WTO, and partly (and particularly in the case of the US) about granting specific concessions or licenses to foreign firms in advance of WTO entry.

Following the small meeting in the Prime Minister's office, Chrétien and Zhu and their two Ambassadors moved across the second floor atrium of the western tower of Centre Block to the Cabinet Room where the larger delegations had already gathered. As we entered, I went immediately to Sergio Marchi to tell him that Zhu and Chrétien had agreed to sign and announce our bilateral WTO agreement later in the day. Sergio responded that he had gotten a completely different message from Shi Guangsheng during their meeting, and he believed that China would be wary of announcing concessions to Canada, even if already agreed, for fear of encouraging the Americans to seek greater concessions in their bilateral agreement than China was prepared to offer. At the beginning of the full bilateral meeting chaired by the two Prime Ministers with phalanxes of Ministers and Deputy Ministers on either side of the long cabinet table, Chrétien proposed explicitly that the two sides sign and announce the bilateral understanding on China's WTO accession. What happened next I never saw happen before or since in a negotiation with the Chinese. Shi Guangsheng, who was sitting several places away from Zhu Rongji, got up from his seat and went to Zhu, and whispered something to him. Zhu, looking rather angry, asked Chrétien if he could have a moment to consult with his Minister, and the two of them stood and retreated to the edge of the room for a one-on-one exchange. When he returned to the table, Zhu said that he had just been informed by his Trade Minister that there were still a few minor matters separating us on the agreement and that, while none were major, it might not be possible to conclude the agreement that day. This was a substantial disappointment and let some of the positive air out of the subsequent exchanges, but we managed to conclude and sign some other agreements, including the first framework on bilateral cooperation in combatting crime, and an agreement on market access to China for Canadian beef and other animal products.

The remainder of the visit was a variant of the state visit of President Jiang Zemin eighteen months earlier, with a call on Governor General Roméo Leblanc and a small lunch at 24 Sussex Drive with the Prime Minister, then off to Toronto for a gala hosted by the CCBC, where he and Chrétien were keynote speakers. For those of us involved in writing speeches for Chrétien, it was getting increasingly difficult to come up with anything new for him to say. He had spoken at five previous CCBC galas since being elected, and not much had changed in the relationship or in the world since his last speech just five months earlier. Zhu on the other hand spent some time talking about changes in the Chinese economy and how well it had weathered the Asian financial crisis, and remained very upbeat about the relationship with Canada, saying publicly, to our surprise, that Canada and China had basically reached agreement on China's WTO entry and that China was deeply appreciative of Canada's backing of its accession efforts. Following the speeches it was the usual milling around at the dinner, and finally the RCMP had to put a ring of officers around the head table so that the leaders could eat even a small amount of their meal.

In Calgary, after a "White Hat" greeting by Mayor Al Duerr at the airport, giving Zhu Rongji the handsome white Stetson all famous visitors to Calgary receive, we headed downtown to the Palliser Hotel. There we were greeted by warring groups of slogan chanters directly across the street, with Free Tibet and Falun Gong protesters wielding protest placards and competing with a pro-Chinese crowd, all with long welcome banners. As Zhu got out of our limousine he turned and waived to the pro-Chinese people, looking like he was waiving to everyone. Once in the hotel, we all went up to our various rooms to change for an evening banquet, but as soon as I reached my room there was an urgent message asking me to come back down, for the Premier was stuck in an elevator. As he was being taken up to his suite, more of his security and staff had gotten in the elevator than should have and the elevator decided to stop between the 6th and 7th floors. The fire department was called and between them and the hotel's mechanical staff, the elevator was freed after about 15 minutes, but between this incident and the constant noise from the protesters, amplified by the canyon-like space between the Palliser and the facing buildings, the Chinese delegation started to get very upset. Ambassador Mei Ping, fearful for the impact on his own career, asked to see me to register a protest and to insist that the street be cleared of all protesters. I told him that peaceful protest was part of public life in Canada, and that the RCMP would ensure that the security of the Premier and his delegation would not be in any way jeopardized. The remainder of the Calgary visit, which included the formal opening of the new Chinese Consulate General, was fine and generally unremarkable, with Anne McLellan, now Justice Minister, as the accompanying federal minister with Premier Ralph Klein hosting a dinner for several hundred.

The next day was quiet, with Zhu allowing his delegation to go to an animal genetics research centre without him, and then three hours wandering through Banff National Park, just awakening from the winter. Zhu was evidently fatigued, as if his seventy years were catching up with him, and his wife Lao An clearly wanted him to slow down. Nonetheless, he was a delightful companion when I was together with him, asking questions about how average people live and what they saw as their greatest challenges. I asked him how his daughter, Zhu Yanlei was doing, reminding him that I had met her when we were traveling together in 1993 during his trip to Canada as Vice Premier. He said that she was fine and doing well in Hong Kong, and then said that when he became Premier he had insisted that his two children return to China and work in positions where no one could accuse them of abusing their links to him. I wondered whether this was a vague reference to Li Peng's family, but of course I dared not ask.

The final two days of Zhu's cross-Canada trip were mostly sightseeing, except for a tour of the Ballard fuel-cell plant in Burnaby and a meeting in Vancouver with Premier Glen Clark, then under media siege following a televised RCMP raid four weeks earlier on his home on allegations of corruption (he eventually resigned in August, but was cleared of all charges by the BC Supreme Court the following year). I then took Zhu on a boat tour of Vancouver harbour, which started with some rather unpleasant and completely inexcusable jostling by protesters who were allowed to get far too close to the Premier as we were boarding the luxury yacht *Hotei II*. This was the only time in my career that I had cause to complain about the quality of security being provided a visiting leader, and I called the RCMP officer in charge from the yacht and explained what had happened. He was quite chagrinned, and from the time we returned to the dock until Zhu left Canada, the security cordon was kept substantially wider. The boat trip itself was very pleasant; Zhu was interested in the fact that most of the large container cranes on the False Creek docks had been sourced in Shanghai, and seemed to slough off the security breach.

In Victoria, our only official event was a meal hosted by federal Minister of Environment David Anderson, who had been a Foreign Service officer and learned mandarin before entering politics, and Zhu was impressed that a federal cabinet minister spoke Chinese. In Victoria, we visited the

Butchart Gardens, which were in full spring flower. As we were walking through the Gardens, we came across a tour group of Chinese, and Zhu suggested to me that we walk over to chat with them, which we did, although given the incident the day before it took me a few minutes to persuade our security handlers to let us do so, and even then we had two strapping RCMP plainclothes officers beside the Premier. It turned out the tour group was from Taiwan, and Zhu had a very pleasant exchange with several of its members, and then turned to the whole group and wished them a very pleasant stay in Canada, and welcomed them to visit the mainland at any time. As we turned back to join our own delegation, the tour group spontaneously broke into applause. The Premier was beaming when we got back to the others, and he turned to Zeng Peiyan and said that he had just made a positive contribution to cross-straits relations.

As Zhu Rongji left Canada on this last official visit, at the airport in Vancouver he said to me and David Anderson, who was there on behalf of the Prime Minister to say good-bye, that he had felt very relaxed in Canada, and that he appreciated all that we had done for him. He said that he was very glad he had gone to the United States first, as now he was able to go home relaxed and ready to re-engage in his heavy official duties. And up into his 747 and back to China he went.

CHAPTER 32

SPRING 1999 – AN UNHAPPY INTERLUDE

• • • • • • • • • • •

On the afternoon of May 7, I gave a speech at Beijing University on Canadian foreign policy, and built on the theme of Canadian use of multilateral institutions and alliances to increase Canadian influence. I talked about Canada's role in the UN and particularly in UN peacekeeping, how our influence had helped ensure that the coalition in the Gulf War of 1991 had acted strictly with the authority of the UN. I talked also about the ongoing war in Kosovo and why NATO had intervened, citing the principle of humanitarian intervention.

Less than twenty-four hours later, I watched CNN's footage of this humanitarian intervention when the broadcaster filmed the aftermath of the bombing of the Chinese Embassy in Belgrade by American B-2 bombers.

China went ballistic, understandably so. No one could believe that the mighty United States, with the greatest intelligence services in the world and the most sophisticated weaponry, had mistaken the Chinese Embassy, unchanged in its same address for three years, for some Yugoslav military building. Within hours the streets surrounding the US Embassy and most other major NATO Embassies were surrounded by huge crowds of protesters, throwing rocks and chanting anti-NATO and anti-US slogans. We were all effectively under siege. At the US Embassy, the crowds were particularly violent and the police not particularly interested in keeping them under control. The consequence was that many windows were broken and the US Embassy staff had to retreat to internal rooms. In Chengdu, crowds broke into the US Consulate General and did a huge amount of damage, and set fire to the Consul General's residence, a fire that was luckily put out before anyone was hurt.

The crowds outside our Embassy were kept in better check by the police, who for the most part kept them away from our walls and main gate. It was only during the first day of protests, a Saturday, that we could not leave the compound by the front gate. However, because the protesters had not been permitted down the small street between our main compound (where both the Chancery and Residence are located) and our secondary compound, then still under construction, we could slip quietly in and out of the Embassy. I did so, not using my official vehicle or flying the Canadian flag, but using a non-descript van from the embassy vehicle pool, and was driven down to the area where the US and British Embassies were located to get a sense for myself of the virulence of the protests. There was no question that the crowds were truly angry, and that while the government was in favour of letting that anger be seen it was not necessary for the authorities to incite it, even though a number of western journalists portrayed the protests as entirely government-organized. For the next few days, we encouraged Canada-based staff to maintain the lowest possible profile, to remain in their staff quarters unless there was a compelling need to leave it, and to cancel or postpone whatever obligations they might have had outside the Embassy.

On the second day after the bombing, NATO Ambassadors in Beijing received an instruction from their respective headquarters that, following a NATO meeting in Brussels, it had been decided that an apology should be made to the Chinese on behalf of the alliance. The two most senior NATO Ambassadors were to seek a meeting with the Foreign Ministry to present the apology. Unfortunately, given that diplomatic seniority is established by the date of an Ambassador's presentation of credentials, the two most senior NATO Ambassadors in China at the time were from Poland, which had just become a member of the western alliance, and from Denmark, and neither Poland nor Denmark had any forces whatsoever involved in the Kosovo campaign. To have the formal apology presented by a Pole and a Dane was nothing short of ludicrous, and angered the Chinese Government further. It also angered me and some of my other NATO colleagues, including the German and French Ambassadors. Even Jim Sasser, the US Ambassador, who was completely unable to leave his Residence, agreed privately that the way the NATO apology was offered simply rubbed salt into the Chinese wound. We were all regularly speaking with each other by telephone, organizing "care packages" to be passed over the fence at the back of the US Embassy for Jim and Mary Sasser, and meeting at missions not under siege. Finally President Clinton took control and set aside the mealy-mouthed explanations of his military and State Department spokesmen, and made a clear and unequivocal apology, both in a call with President Jiang Zemin and publicly.

A most dangerous situation developed late in the second day, when Chinese police allowed protestors to reach the fences and walls of the US Embassy compound. A few protestors started climbing over the wall, and were summarily pushed back over by American Marines, who could handle the odd penetration but would have been clearly unable to handle hundreds of protestors climbing over the walls simultaneously. And that is what the crowd outside the US Embassy seemed to be intent on doing. The US Deputy Chief of Mission called Guy Saint-Jacques, his Canadian equivalent, described the rapidly deteriorating situation and asked Canada to intervene with the Chinese authorities. He told Guy that the US Marines had orders to shoot intruders, and that the Chinese authorities should be under no delusion that these orders would be remanded. He felt that a warning from another country would emphasize the seriousness of the situation to the Chinese, who were not paying much attention to calls or complaints from the Americans themselves. Guy called the Director General in charge of US and Canadian affairs at the Foreign Ministry and told them that if any more protestors came over the wall, they would be shot and a much more serious crisis would start to unfold, and that the Chinese authorities would be seen as accountable. Within less than thirty minutes, several busloads of police arrived and backed the protestors away from the immediate perimeter of the American Embassy. The most acute moment in the crisis had passed.

By the third day, even the occasional protestors near our Embassy had departed and the more regular phalanxes near the UK mission had begun to thin. Although there was still an occasional march-by of university students or others, the pressure and the palpable sense of danger had lifted. We generally believed that the Chinese Government had welcomed and assisted in the organization of a sustained presence outside the American Embassy and the general public outcry, but had not encouraged violence, and as soon as it was seen that the large crowds might create incidents that could result in shootings and death, or start to demonize other than the perfidious Americans, then the word went out to the universities to tone down and eventually turn off the flow of protestors.

I thought the whole incident was terribly miss-handled from the diplomatic end, but there was little I could do or say. Canada was part of NATO and was militarily active in the Kosovo campaign, even if neither we nor any country other than the US was involved in the targeting of American bombers. To express my personal regret and disagreement with the approach taken by the alliance, I encouraged our twin boys to organize a delegation of children from the International School of Beijing to lay flowers at a memorial that had been set up downtown to the three Chinese Embassy staff members killed in the bombing. They both organized the group and led it, and there were pictures in the Chinese press of these young westerners laying flowers at the "Martyrs' Memorial". Senior people in the Foreign Ministry knew that the twin boys in the photo were mine, and understood my message.

The crisis eventually passed, the US ended up paying $4.5 million to the families of the victims and $28 million for the damage to the Chinese Embassy in Belgrade, and the Chinese paid $2.8 million to the US for the damage to American diplomatic buildings in Chengdu and Beijing. Clinton and Jiang Zemin and Zhu Rongji, conscious of the enormous importance of not letting the US-China relationship disintegrate completely, made a great effort over the next six months to get things back on an even keel, and before the end of the year the two countries had concluded their bilateral pact on China's entry to the WTO, an agreement on almost exactly the terms that Zhu had offered to Clinton during the failed April negotiations. But even though the incident was put behind us, no Chinese official with whom ever I discussed the Belgrade bombing believed that it was a targeting error. Two of the "journalists" killed had actually been employees of a branch of the Ministry of State Security and one of the bombs wiped out the Embassy's communications centre, which the Chinese had allowed to be used for rebroadcasts by the Serb para-military forces. As Canadian Ambassador I subsequently saw a lot of classified material on what had happened, and I came away completely convinced that senior members of the US Administration had no knowledge of, nor role in, the targeting, but I was never completely convinced that some excessively smart CIA desk officer did not know exactly what he was doing.

CHAPTER 33

SUMMER AND AUTUMN, 1999

• • • • • • • • • • •

At least for a while the Belgrade bombing took much of the wind out of the positive momentum generated by the April Zhu Rongji visit, but there was still a lot going on in the bilateral relationship. By the end of the summer the bombing was remembered and publicly characterized only as a US action rather than a broader NATO transgression. In late May I went off to Kunming in the southern province of Yunnan to open a Canadian Garden at the World Horticultural Exhibition, with both junior environmental minister Christine Stewart and the peripatetic Montreal Mayor, Pierre Bourque, in attendance, and spent some time meeting both municipal and provincial leaders.

Shortly after we arrived in 1996, Liani and I had presided over the 9th annual Canadian Charity Ball, which was then and for all the time I remained Ambassador organized by the Embassy. In the spring of 1999 we had held the 12th version of the event, the fourth with Liani and I as hosts. Since arriving we had shifted the recipients of the money we raised away from international organizations and NGOs to local recipients where we could really see the results of our contributions. The ball in 1999 was a tremendous success and with the money we raised we built a new school in Yanqing County, a very poor district in Beijing's distant northeast corner, well beyond the Great Wall. To ensure that the money was well spent and local needs met, Liani engaged the local branch of the All China Women's Federation to work with us, and they were dedicated and wonderful to work with. By the end of the summer the school was built, and so we led a group of Embassy and community representatives out to the school for an opening ceremony. The school was made up of a series of one-story buildings, simple but with electricity and heating for the frigid winters, and the school planners had erected two huge relief maps in a central square, one of China and one of Canada. Our twins came with us, along with some of their embassy friends, and they chatted with the younger Chinese pupils and could sense a bit what it would have been like to be them. Seeing the new school and all its reasonably modern supplies and books, all of which had been purchased from our donation, and the scene with all the happy children and parents was very heart warming. We concluded that this was a far better focus of our charitable efforts than some distant organization with a headquarters in Toronto or Geneva or even Beijing.

September saw a couple of interesting visits. The first was a tandem trip by former Foreign Minister and now Chairman of Canada Post, André Ouellet with the minister responsible for the post office, the Minister of Public Works Alphonso Gagliano. The purpose was the biannual meeting of the Universal Postal Union, hosted by China in 1999 and due next to be hosted by Canada. I had worked with both ministers in my national unity days, and so naturally we spent a lot of time chatting about political issues. I attended only two of their events, one was a huge reception which we hosted for all the UPU delegations, which was thoroughly boring, and the second was with the Chinese Minister of Construction for the signing of a bilateral agreement on cooperation in construction technology. We were trying to get the Chinese to adjust their building codes to make them more friendly to the use of wood, an effort that would be successful and would lead to a vast expansion of the export to China of western lumber. The Chinese Minister, Yu Zhengsheng, then gave a dinner for us. I had met Yu first when he was Party Secretary in Qingdao during one of my first provincial visits and found him a very open and thoughtful man, I also saw him later, after my retirement as Ambassador when he was Party Secretary of Hubei and then of Shanghai (after Xi Jinping). What I knew about his background, but avoided sharing with Ouellet and Gagliano since I couldn't trust them not to abuse it, was that Yu was very close to the family of Deng Xiaoping, and particularly his disabled son Deng Pufeng. After the death of Deng Xiaoping in 1997, Yu Zhengsheng served to represent the family's interests whenever needed in the upper echelons of power. Even more amazing was that his career was never damaged by a younger brother's defection to the United States in the early 1980s, and he would end up in 2012 being chosen as one of the seven leaders of Central Committee of the Politburo.

The second visitor in September was Premier Ralph Klein of Alberta, who was a delightful man, and because I enjoyed him so much I broke my own rule about not travelling outside of Beijing with provincial premiers and went with him to Harbin, capital of Heilongjiang, China's northernmost province and Alberta's twin. Provincial Governor Tian Fengshan threw a fabulous dinner for Klein, with music and dancers and a great deal of baijiu, but the best part of the trip was simply walking and chatting with Klein, who I had seen a lot of over the years, but this time together allowed us to develop a more personal relationship. As for Tian, he would later serve as Minister of Land and Resources, and was a principal reason the Ministry agreed to allow my company in 2003 to take over the hosting of the annual China Mining conference and exhibition, a permission we received about a week before Tian was removed from his post for corruption!

By the middle of 1999, the city of Beijing was going through a visible transformation. First, the city passed an ordinance banning all outdoor billboards and building-top advertisements within the second ring road. Parks were cleaned up and sidewalks rebuilt with new interlocking and coloured brick. Those responsible for Li Ka-shing's huge Oriental Plaza construction site on the corner of Chang'an Jie and Wangfujing were ordered to hang the project's glass curtain wall before the end of August so that it would at least look finished, even if by doing so they would make actual completion more complicated. The undersides of underpasses and the facades of old buildings facing major thoroughfares were repainted. Grass verges beside the main roads were wither re-sodded or, in cases where this was impractical, simply painted with a green paint. Everything was made to look spic-and-span, preparing for the 50th Anniversary of the People's Republic of China.

And it was quite the anniversary. As Ambassador I was invited every year to the Premier's National Day Banquet, and this year was a huge event on the last day of September, with many international leaders from all corners of the earth present, even though there had not been a general invitation issued as there would be many years later for the Olympics. This banquet was my fourth National Day and we had therefore gradually worked our way up in precedence to a more prestigious table nearer the Premier's and by this time I was sufficiently at ease with my contacts that I could wander even up to the head table to greet senior members of the government, many of whom had been to Canada or hosted their Canadian counterparts since I had been in office.

On the 10th and 25th and 40th anniversaries of the founding of modern China, the parades in front of the Forbidden City had been led by China's "Paramount Leader" standing in a Red Flag Limousine with a special cut-out in its roof. The first two of these events had Mao Zedong in the car and the last had Deng Xiaoping. Jiang Zemin followed their tradition to the "T", dressed in a dark Mao suit and stood waist-high out of the specially built limousine, driving slowly passed an honour guard of soldiers and sailors and then moved to the central platform of the Gate of Heavenly Peace to watch wave after wave of military units march by. We were in the VIP viewing stands just below the Chinese leaders and for five hours we watched the parade, which began with regiments of the men and women of the People's Liberation Army. Some of the women's units were composed of fit and handsome short-skirted young women in what appeared to be designer uniforms, leading us to believe that if they were ever sent into battle, all the opposing male soldiers would simply lay down their weapons and ask the Chinese soldiers out for dinner: a truly debilitating force indeed. Following the soldiers there were artillery units and air-to-ground missile squadrons and nuclear ballistic missiles (or at least mock-ups) on huge mobile launch platforms. And after the core military had gone by, there were units of police and firemen a float for every province and city and territory, including one for Taiwan, whose leaders clearly had no role in its preparation. It was clearly a huge propaganda exercise no doubt, but quite a tremendous show in any case. And as the night drew near, there were tremendous fireworks lasting for more than an hour in Tiananmen Square, and then the fireworks and revelry continued all over the city until the wee hours of October 2nd.

One of the most delightful Canadians to visit during my time as Ambassador was Beverly McLachlin, Chief Justice of the Supreme Court of Canada, who came to Beijing twice, once in early 1999 and then again in mid 2000, a year before I left the service. She came both times as part of our efforts to promote the rule of law in China and both times spoke at the National Judges College, which we had helped finance and had supported very substantially with exchanges of law professors and active professionals from our criminal justice system. During her first visit, we had excellent meetings with Minister of Justice Zhang Fusen, President of the Supreme Court Xiao Yang and Vice President Cao Jianming. Cao was a good friend of mine and was a huge champion of legal reform and of our bilateral cooperation in the field.

But the best meeting McLachlin had was a call on Premier Zhu Rongji during her second visit. The Premier received us in a traditional Chinese reception room at Zhongnanhai, a gorgeous red and yellow room with lacquered squares in the ceiling and a lovely view of the central part of the lake. Premier Zhu told McLachlin that when the emperors who had built this little pavilion were ruling China there was no concept of the rule of law, and that it was simply power and magisterial judgment that determined right and wrong. He said that legal reform and turning China into a "Fazhi" or a "country of law" was a very high priority for his government. He added however that doing so was a huge task, pointing out "There are 180 thousand judges in China, of whom maybe ten percent understand the law. How do we change that overnight?"

In late November of 1999, Foreign Minister Lloyd Axworthy called a meeting of about twenty of Canada's most senior Heads of Mission for a policy retreat, which was held at Wilson House on the bluff above Meech

Lake in the Gatineau. Aside from an enjoyable chance to get together and compare notes with other sernior colleagues, the trip also gave me the chance to drop in and see the Prime Minister, who told me to get ready for a return Team Canada to China late the following year, and to see other political and public service friends. At his request I had lunch with Mel Cappe, the Clerk of the Privy Council, who asked me whether I was interested in returning to Ottawa soon as a Deputy Minister somewhere. My answer was instantaneous and unambiguous; I told him I would be happy to come back for a senior and interesting job, but I would not be keen on any one of a dozen of the minor domestic departments. I said that I loved my job, the PM thought I was doing well in Beijing, and that I would be happy to stay in China until the right position came up. In fact it was only a month later that Mel called and said that my name could well be in play as a candidate for Deputy Minister of Foreign Affairs, and I responded that that was a position I would absolutely accept. It would be four or five more months before I would hear another word about this.

We had one last Ministerial visit before the end of the year. With US-China relations back on an even keel after a difficult first half of the year, and no longer any significant impediments in place to full Chinese accession to the World Trade Organization, the path was cleared for the signing of the bilateral Canada-China agreement, virtually unchanged from the draft accord that had been ready for signature at the time of the Zhu Rongji visit. This we arranged to take place during formal bilateral economic and trade talks in Beijing, led on the Canadian side by Pierre Pettigrew, who had been moved by Chrétien to the position as Minister for International Trade in August, replacing Sergio Marchi. I had known Pettigrew very well during my time as Deputy Secretary to the Cabinet, before he ran for election when working with us as a federalist spokesperson at public events and on television. It was a delight to have him in Beijing for the talks, which were rather unsubstantive given that all major bilateral issues had been pushed as far as they could be pushed in the WTO talks, but it was still a highlight of the year end to get the formal agreement signed.

Just before Christmas, I and the rest of the Beijing-based Ambassadors from the APEC member economies were invited to a reception hosted by Premier Zhu Rongji to quietly celebrate the return to Chinese sovereignty of Macau. The Chinese had decided to celebrate with a group of countries which included none of the former European colonial powers, and most of which had themselves been colonies at one time or another. I was sure that there were of course wonderful celebrations going on in Macau, where President Jiang Zemin was present for the handover, but from the Beijing perspective one could really sense that this was the final step in correcting more than a century and a half of egregious behavior by the West, aided and abetted of course by Chinese weakness, but thoroughly immoral internationalism nonetheless. Zhu was very reflective that evening, and I had some time one-on-one with him. We chatted about his trip to Canada earlier in the year and he asked me to send his best wish to his friend Jean Chrétien, which of course I did.

CHAPTER 34

A NEW CENTURY IN AN OLD PROFESSION

• • • • • • • • • • •

The Canadian Department of Foreign Affairs and Trade, like many organizations around the world, had been completely spooked by the implications of computer confusion and electronic chaos as the new millennium dawned. Supposedly, with many computers and electronic systems set up since the beginning of the computer age to recognize years only by their last two digits, when the world rolled to 00/00/00 there would be massive outages of electrical grids and computerized systems from banking back offices to telephone networks. For two years, the world had been trying to reprogram everything in a massive effort in advance of Y2K, as the Armageddon of midnight on December 31st approached. Anticipating at least some sort of shut-down in the brightly lit night-time Beijing, I and our twins went up on the roof of the Residence to watch the city lights. Alas, nothing at all happened . . .

By the beginning of the year 2000, I was starting to become a relative old-timer in Beijing's diplomatic community. Most Ambassadorial assignments were for three years, and by this time I had been longer in Beijing than any other G-8 Head of Mission except Igor Rogachev of Russia. My Australian colleague, neighbour and friend, Rick Smith and his wife Jan had arrived at the same time as we had and in January we gave a dinner for them on their departure, and shortly thereafter a welcoming dinner for his successor, David Irvine. Admiral Joe Prueher, former Commander of the US Pacific Fleet also arrived early in the year to replace Jim Sasser as US Ambassador, and again we hosted the G-8 Ambassadors and spouses to welcome him and his charming wife Suzanne. Although not a career diplomat, Joe was to do a very good job as Ambassador, steering the relationship smoothly through some fairly choppy waters in 2001, ably supported by his Deputy Chief of Mission, Bill McCahill, an experienced sinologist and very professional diplomat. Being higher in the pecking order in the diplomatic corps had virtually no advantages beyond sitting closer to powerful people at Chinese-hosted functions. What it did mean was an almost endless stream of calls by newly arrived Ambassadors, especially from Commonwealth countries and members of La Francophonie, as well as APEC, since I was, once Rick Smith had left, the senior Ambassador of all three organizations. I found the diplomatic community full of very nice people, a few of whom understood a little bit about China, and a very small number of professionals whose views and insights I actively sought out. And I did not have the time or the interest to partake in the diplomatic circus of dining with each other. Unfortunately for my senior officers, this meant that when it was *de rigeur* for Canada to be represented at some Commonwealth function or Fête de la Francophonie, someone else was dispatched in my place.

And the bilateral agenda was in any case quite unforgiving in those days. Shortly after the world had not collapsed or fallen back a thousand years through a massive Y2K wormhole, Ralph Goodale, Minister of Natural Resources and Minister responsible for the Wheat Board came to China. He had been moved from the full agriculture portfolio in the cabinet shuffle of the year before, and had retained the Wheat Board file because the new Minister of Agriculture, Lyle Vanclief, was from Ontario, a real farmer but not familiar with the particularities of the prairie wheat world, in which Goodale had grown up. With Goodale were three provincial ministers, Tim Hudak from Ontario (he would much later become leader of the Ontario Conservative Party), David Zimelt from British Columbia, and my old friend Gary Mar from Alberta, as well as almost eighty business representatives. It was almost as complex and rich a program as a Prime Ministerial program, and the Chinese, perhaps emphasizing how much they valued their agricultural relationship with Canada, pulled out all the stops. I think we saw no less than four Ministers, including Tian Fengshan of MLR, Chen Yaobang of Agriculture and Yu Zhengsheng of the Ministry of Construction. Vice Premier Wen Jiabao, a geologist by training and a big supporter of closer bilateral relations in the mining and geoscience areas, spent more than an hour with us. By this time there was already lots of political speculation about the makeup of the next leadership team, following Jiang Zemin and Zhu Rongji, and Wen Jiabao was clearly a front-runner to become Premier. I therefore found the meetings that Canadian ministers and I had with him to be of greater interest than simply his views on the issues at hand. He was always very focused and very well briefed, and seemed to be more than simply repeating a briefing note. The Chinese were always excellent at briefing their ministers and senior leaders, and kept excellent records of what had already been exchanged at lower or higher levels on any given file. Wen Jiabao was also attentive, with a habit of looking directly at his interlocutor even when seating in the traditional inverted "U" arrangement of many formal meetings, rather than looking out into the assembled guests. But his habit of almost always smiling, even when dealing with difficult or contentious issues was almost off-putting, as if he was saying that either the matter was really not of much merit or that we should simply accept the Chinese position as given. Zhu Rongji, on the other hand, rarely smiled when in serious discussion, and you were never left in any doubt when the Chinese position was inflexible and why, and whether there was room for further discussion or compromise. Zhu also had a practice of directly assigning an issue to a minister or senior official to deal with even with a foreigner present, or of criticizing someone if an issue that should have been dealt with had dragged on, while Wen, at least in the many meetings that I attended, never gave any indication of displeasure or impatience with his own people.

One of the purposes of the Goodale visit was to support AECL, then half way through building the two CANDU reactors in northeast Zhejiang between Shanghai and Hangzhou, and to encourage the Chinese to consider adding to their stable of heavy water reactors following the commissioning of the first two. China's civilian nuclear energy program was then managed by the State Commission of Science, Technology and Industry for National

Defence (COSTIND), which really answered to the Chinese PLA, and we spent a half day meeting and eating with Chairman Liu Jibin and then, when the Beijing program was finished, went with COSTIND Vice-Chairman Zheng Hanzhu to Shanghai and Qinshan to visit the CANDU construction site. At this time the calandra containment buildings were being built using a novel technology. The concrete pouring was continuous, with the forms being raised at a speed of about 45 centimetres a day. The site was a beehive of activity, with most of the non-critical project buildings almost complete, and one of the two massive calandra already having arrived from Canada. Al Kilpatrick, a former colleague of mine, had just the previous summer become CEO of AECL and he was there with us and it was a delight to catch up with him. We also took Goodale to "Canada Village" where all the expatriate managers, engineers and technicians were living. This was a perfect little Canadian town with almost two hundred families, a little school, wonderful playgrounds and sporting facilities, and a communal dining facility structured in the form of a club. All the employees, some of whom had worked on CANDU projects in Korea and Romania, seemed very well adjusted to this rather strange completely Canadian island in a Chinese sea, and Goodale, being a born politician, clearly loved his interaction with the families.

CHAPTER 35

THE CHINESE INVASION

• • • • • • • • • • •

Over a six-week period during the late summer of 1999, several small ships loaded with Chinese illegal immigrants were intercepted off the British Columbia coast by Canadian authorities. The ships were small rust-buckets, either converted trawlers or small coastal tramps, and when intercepted the conditions on board were quite horrible. Although in total there were less than five hundred people involved, mostly from Fujian province, this became a huge media story and quickly a major political issue. Rumours of more ships on the way circulated widely, and there was talk of an almost unstoppable flood of people landing all along Canada's sparsely inhabited west coast. Many Canadians wanted the would-be refugees turned around and sent home, others felt that they should be offered succour since if sent home they would be punished, possibly harshly, both for illegally leaving China and for embarrassing their motherland in the western media. The people were all removed to Esquimalt Navy Base for processing. Immigration officials and the RCMP interviewed every migrant, separated out about thirty-five who were charged with human smuggling and jailed, and removed the remainder at a west coast armed forces base, where a hastily erected compound was used as a camp, with sufficient security to prevent anyone from quietly slipping away. The community of immigration lawyers was all over the issue, hired by various groups to claim refugee status on behalf of any migrant they could sign up.

For us in Beijing, the task was to get the Chinese authorities to cooperate in cracking down on those engaged in human smuggling, the ring leaders who sold passage and arranged the boats, and in trying through public campaigns to dissuade people from falling victim to the smugglers' schemes. Susan Gregson, my Minister-Counselor in charge of our large immigration and visa section, and I went to see both an Assistant Minister in the Foreign Ministry and a Vice Minister in the Ministry of Public Security, Zhu Entao, who both stated that the Chinese government in Beijing shared our objectives and promised support for any public campaign we might have wished to mount. Zhu Entao furthermore assured us that any migrants returned to China would be treated lightly and subsequently monitored, but would not be jailed or heavily fined unless they tried to leave illegally a second time. He encouraged us, however, to go directly to the authorities in Fujian and underscore what an important issue this was and why local cooperation at all levels would be needed to start to squeeze the flow at its source, and told us that regional public security leaders would support us in our local campaign. And so, supported by Susan Gregson and a couple of her staff responsible for managing our illegal migration interdiction efforts, and in particular a very industrious and effective young officer named Tom Meadows, off we went to Fujian.

This was my third trip to Fujian, but the first to the provincial capital since Xi Jinping had become Governor in mid-1999. The Fujian officials were careful to separate my visit into a working-level engagement to deal with the illegal migration issue, and a political visit by a senior Ambassador from a western country. Because of this, all of our meetings except one were with officials in the provincial government responsible for public security and civil affairs, and only I and a single assistant were received by Governor Xi. It was a short meeting, but I found him well informed about Canada. He greeted me initially in English and said that he had lived in America for a time, and he seemed very open and affable. I would not meet him again for more than ten years, at which point he had become Vice President of the country and heir apparent to Hu Jintao. At that time I was in business and moderating a panel at an international conference on Chinese investment. He remembered meeting me as Ambassador and laughed when I told him that I had switched from being Ambassador of Canada to being a roving Ambassador for China.

After our meetings in Fujian, Susan Gregson and her team took me out towards the coast through the coastal towns and fishing villages in the Minjiang estuary and south of Fuzhou between Fujin and Pintai. These were the primary provenance of the rusty little vessels that were being used by the migrant smugglers. This was not a wealthy area, and the small towns were built around the main streets, with one or two story homes built out of local brick and clearly locally-made and often ill-fitting windows, street-facing and extremely close together. And then, in each town there would be perhaps one or two well-finished three-story homes, tiled on the outside with a little tower and a side-lot that clearly indicated relative wealth. These homes, we were told, were the homes built by the families of the émigrés who had made it to New York or Toronto and worked as cooks or plasterers, remitting much of their savings home. In some villages there were absolute castles of homes, and these were of those who had really made it, having left their semi-indentured servitude of the illegal migrant and actually started businesses of their own. As we travelled through the little towns in the hard-to-patrol bays and inlets of this rocky coast, I realized that the deep cultural traditions of the people of Fujian made emigration a natural and honoured goal, both in the northern and the southern regions of the province (quite distinct due to language separation between Fukienese in the north and Mingnanhua in the south). It was, after all, from Quanzhou that Zheng He's great fleets sailed in the fifteenth century as China began exploring not only Southeast Asia but the Indian Ocean and Arabia and East Africa and (if one accepts even a little of what the British submariner and amateur archaeologist Gavin Menzies argues) perhaps even beyond.

As we travelled from town to town, the local officials were all very solicitous and assured us, as indeed the provincial officials had, that they were all doing everything they could to prevent the rings of human smugglers from operating. We did not find this very believable, but hoped that our visit and the pressures created from above might make it so. Our last Ministerial visitor to raise the issue at a high level was Elinor Caplan, who had become Minister of Citizenship and Immigration in 1999, and when she visited in the late winter she was received not only by the Minister of Public Security Jia Chunwang, but by the senior party leader and security "heavy" Luo Gan. Philip Murray, Commissioner of the RCMP also came to China and formalized an agreement with the Ministry of Public Security which permitted us to add an RCMP liaison officer to the Embassy, and this turned out to be very well received by the Chinese security world. We henceforth found cooperation with them much improved on all sorts of issues, from commercial crime to human smuggling to combined efforts to stem the flow of illegal drugs.

In the end, the flow of sea-borne illegal migrants dried up quite quickly and by the summer of 2000 there were no more rusty trawlers arriving in Canada. To me it was clear that the smuggling rings had been paying off local officials and border authorities to turn a blind eye when the boats were preparing to leave, and that the embarrassing publicity China received in the international press encouraged a crackdown on the corruption involved. Also, as the smugglers found on the first few boats were found guilty and jailed, and hundreds of the would-be migrants were found not to be real refugees and sent home, the whole venture seemed a lot less attractive both to the organizers and the victims.

CHAPTER 36

LIFE IN MID-STRIDE

• • • • • • • • • • •

With the onset of the 1999-2000 school year, our Beijing-based family was reduced once again, now with Caleb joining his sister Cynthia at Trinity College School in Port Hope. This, along with a busy sports and extra-curricular schedule for Joshua and Gideon, meant fewer trips to the provinces, except during school vacations. At Christmas of that year with the whole family together again, we returned to Sanya in Hainan, repeating our visit of three years earlier. It was astounding how much the place had changed. During our first visit, the Gloria Hotel had been the only hotel on the long white beach of Yalong Bay. Now there were hotels all the way along, perhaps twenty of them, and the beach was full of people from dawn to dusk. And dozens more hotels were being built. While it was a lovely family time together, the crowds made it a little less special than before, and we were never particularly attracted to return for a third time. I went back more than a decade later on business, and was quite horrified to find what was once a lovely pristine stretch of five or six white sandy kilometres then divided into long seigneurial-like resort strips perpendicular to the beach where every hotel brand in the world was limited to a narrow beachfront.

Shortly after Christmas of that year, Prescott and Betty Lou Bush visited us for the last time, and this time they came to dinner at the Residence. Prescott Bush Jr. was the older brother of President George H. Bush and the uncle of George W., and had served as the President of the US China Chamber of Commerce. My mother and Betty Lou Kaufman, both daughters of US Admirals, had been childhood friends, and they had stayed in touch after Betty Lou married into the Bush family. Their daughter Kelsey was a good friend of my sister Pat, who as a teen had stayed occasionally at the Bush compound in Kennebunkport. As a ten or twelve year old I had found the slightly older Kelsey very beautiful, and remember singing songs from South Pacific with my sisters and her. When my parents moved to Connecticut in the early 1970s, they saw the Bushes from time to time, and I once dined at their home while visiting during my early diplomatic career. Press had noticed my appointment as Ambassador and got back in touch shortly after we arrived in China, and would drop in to see me almost every time he visited, and we would try to find a free evening to dine together as couples when Betty Lou accompanied him. Although Press only made one stab at the family business of elected politics, running for Republican nomination for a Connecticut senate seat in the early 1980s before withdrawing at the last minute, he had been politically involved in the China file since George Senior had served as head of the US Liaison Office in the mid-1970s.

In March, with Cynthia and Caleb home for spring vacation from boarding school, I combined an official visit to Shaanxi, in part to scout out the possibility of bringing the Prime Minister there on his next visit, with a family trip. As was our practice, not only did we visit the famous historical and archaeological sites around Xi'an, we also visited a children's hospital and a poor village where we were setting up a micro-finance program in cooperation with the All China Women's Federation. The Governor, Cheng Andong, gave a dinner for me and included the children, which made the event much more relaxed than without, and he reacted extremely positively when I told him that I was trying to get our Prime Minister to Xi'an later in the year not just to see the terracotta warriors but to promote our rural development activities as well. Cheng was a delightful and friendly man, coming close to the end of a working life spent entirely in Shaanxi, first as a mining engineer then climbing his way up as a town mayor then to the county level and finally to the provincial government. He had not joined the Communist Party until after the Cultural Revolution and had nothing good to say about Mao and the early leaders, simply telling me that he was glad as he approached his retirement that the party was now in the hands of engineers!

The spring was the usual turnstile of visits in the two directions, with Agriculture Minister Lyle Vanclief and two other Canadian Ministers inbound, and three or four Chinese Ministers outbound, which always meant a dinner at the Residence. Another outbound visitor was the mayor of Dalian, Bo Xilai, son of the revolutionary general Bo Yibo, who had hosted me several times and our whole family once as well. Shortly after his visit that spring to Canada I saw him again in Dalian for the fifth anniversary of the founding of the Maple Leaf School, a private school started by a Canadian citizen of Chinese origin, Sherman Jen, which offered kindergarten through high school and gave graduates both a Chinese diploma and a Canadian diploma, monitored and certified by the British Columbia Ministry of Education. Bo would later go on to be Governor of Liaoning and then Minister of Commerce, and finally Party Secretary of Chongqing. We sustained a very good relationship as he moved up that ladder and as I moved out of my Ambassadorial role. He was widely touted as a probably Politburo Central Committee member as the final year of the Hu-Wen decade began, which I was very happy about since I would have then had a real friend at the pinnacle of Chinese power. It was only a few weeks before his dizzying fall from grace in 2012 that I had a final meal with him in Chongqing. His wife was convicted of the murder of a British businessman and Bo himself of being both complicit in his wife's crime and personally guilty of corruption. But back in 2000, he was a princeling on the rise, a wonderfully charismatic leader who had transformed Dalian from a miserable grey industrial city to a clean and modern city that became a national model for urban development. And he was a delightfully charming man and a wonderful dinner companion.

In May of that year, we had the second visit of the Canadian Navy, this time by the Algonquin, a refitted tribal class guided missile destroyer, and the Winnipeg, a city-class frigate. As I had done in 1998 in Shanghai with son Caleb, I arranged with the Chinese Navy to be taken by the pilot boat out to meet the ships about ten miles offshore, this time with twin sons Joshua and Gideon who climbed up a Jacob's Ladder with me so that we could sail in on board the Winnipeg. The commander of the visiting fleet was a Rear Admiral named Ron Buck, a tough fireplug of a Newfoundlander, who was delighted to learn that I had grown up in Corner Brook. Once he learned that we all associated with the Rock, even if removed by a generation in the case of the twins, he ensured that the boys were taken on a very through tour of the ship, including into the Command and Control Centre, where they were thrilled to learn all about the vessel's systems and speed and weaponry. The young officers briefing them told them that what they were kearning was highly classified, so they ended up feeling very privileged and never divulged to anybody the secret details of the ship's capabilities.

Most of the next few months were just a rolling continuance of ambassadorial life. Hosting incoming business delegations for lunch, outgoing Chinese officials for dinner. One particular evening I recall from this time was a private invitation, for Liani and I and the children, to the home of Zhang Hanzhi, the charming widow of former foreign minister Qiao Guanhua. Zhang had briefly been Mao's English tutor in the early 1970s and she had become a diplomat and served as the interpreter for the secret 1971 meetings between Zhou Enlai and Henry Kissinger. We had been together at many events and dinners with her, and had her to our Residence on a few occasions, but this was the first time we were invited en famille to her home. Her daughter Hong Huang, a publisher of note and media star, was there with her baby boy. Their home was a beautiful courtyard home between Chaoyangmen and Jianguomen Streets, in an area of the city that was once full of courtyard homes and hutongs, which were being gradually torn down and replaced with tall modern buildings. Zhang told us that she was constantly fighting the city planners to protect her home as well as the few other homes like it that remained in the neighbourhood. She had no tolerance for the corruption that she said was rife in the city government, and her daughter, who had studied at Vassar in the United States, was even more scathing about some of the leaders involved. Hong would later become one of the country's most prolific bloggers and a regular commentator on political matters including corruption. The home had initially been in the family of Zhang's adopted father, Zhang Shizhao, once President of the Central Research Institute of Culture and History and a revolutionary supporter of Mao, and when Zhang Shizhao died in the middle of the Cultural Revolution, it was formally assigned to then Foreign Minister Qiao Guanhua, who had been encouraged to marry the then young Zhang Hanzhi. It was a large but not princely traditional home with one outer and two inner courtyards and a perimeter wall with a door from the street that was not lined up with the entry gate into the outer courtyard. Once inside it was as if the modern city had disappeared. Plum trees grew in the larger of the inner courtyards around which the family sleeping quarters and reception areas were arrayed, with the kitchens and utility areas set off the courtyards by a side row of semi-detached little buildings. Zhang was in a very expansive mood and told us how she was intensely nervous when she started tutoring Mao, who she said was a terrible student as he kept wanting to hear more about the outside word than really applying himself to the study of English. Her tutoring lasted less than six months in the mid-1960s, but out of it came her appointment to the Foreign Ministry and eventually her marriage to Qiao Guanhua, who was later accused of being too close to Jiang Qing and the Gang-of-Four. Zhang Hanzhi and Qiao were both placed under house arrest for a period following the Cultural Revolution, but were rehabilitated over time, and Qiao's moderating influence on Chinese foreign policy in Mao's final years was recognized.

The summer was spent in part preparing for the upcoming Team Canada visit, and I toured eastern Canada to meet with the Premiers who would be coming, as well with prospective business representatives at lunches hosted by local chambers of commerce or boards of trade. When we were back in Beijing from our summer family holidays, an old acquaintance named Tongsun Park came through town en route to North Korea with Maurice Strong. Tongsun Park had been introduced to me many years earlier by our Consul General in New York, Alan Sullivan (who had interviewed me for entry into the Foreign Service in the mid-1970s) and had dropped by to see me from time to time over the years. I was always a little cautious about Park, who had in the 1970s been indicted (but never found guilty) for bribing US Congressmen on behalf of the South Korean government (the case was known as "Koreagate"), but he was a very pleasant and interesting fellow. Originally from North Korea, he had always been interested in working to reduce the isolation of the Pyongyang regime, and this time had obtained with Maurice Strong some sort of loose mandate from Secretary General Kofi Annan to help de-escalate tensions on the Korean peninsula. Responsible for our relations with the DPRK, I was a little surprised that I had not heard anything about the mission, and when we asked our Embassy at the UN to check, staffers in the UN Secretariat also drew a blank, so I wrote it off as a somewhat personal venture, possibly with a light blessing by Annan given that Tongsun Park always seemed to have direct access to the Secretary General. Nothing was to come of this trip in any case, and when I was in Pyongyang later, no one had seemed to have heard about it. Tongsun Park was to surface twice more in the years that followed, once shortly after I had retired as Ambassador when he wanted to see if I was interested in getting involved in setting up a firm that could facilitate the purchase of European technology to permit the construction of nuclear submarines for Taiwan, a promise of President George W. Bush that was proving very difficult to deliver. I politely declined any involvement in that venture, and then did not see him for ten years, after he had served three years in a US minimum security prison for his role in siphoning off funds from the UN's "Oil for Food" program which allowed Saddam Hussein's Iraq to bypass sanctions and sell enough oil to pay for imported wheat and other basic foodstuffs. Tongsun Park was found guilty of bribing UN officials to permit more than basic foodstuffs be imported into Iraq. Maurice Strong was also implicated in that disaster, allegedly receiving a one million dollar check directly from Park, although he was never formally indicted. The last time Tongsun Park came by he was getting on in years and was simply a charming older fellow, and he told us that he was no longer involved in business dealings.

In the middle of the autumn I was back in Canada for celebrations on the 30th anniversary of the establishment of Canada-China diplomatic relations, and for an annual "Asia Pacific Summit" hosted by the Asia

Pacific Foundation of Canada. I gave a speech at the conference on the Chinese economy, and I also had invited my friend Liu Mingkang, then President of the Bank of China to give a talk on the state of the Chinese banking industry. Liu gave the most extraordinarily honest speech, in which he laid bare all the weaknesses of the banking sector, eexplicitly listing non-performing loans, weak risk management and too much government interference. To say this publicly in the west was unheard of in those days. Liu Mingkang would shortly thereafter be named Chairman of the China Banking Regulatory Commission, and over the next decade stickhandle a very substantial reform of the banking sector, so it was clear that his outspoken views helped rather than hurt his future.

CHAPTER 37

QINGHAI AND THE END OF YEAR FIVE

• • • • • • • • • • •

In November of 2000, I made my first official visit to the western province of Qinghai, and planned a full week traveling around the Xining area and south and southeast up into the Tibetan Plateau (which in Chinese is called the Qinghai-Tibet Plateau). Liani and the twins were able to come, and I brought with me both Weldon Epp, my executive assistant at the time (twelve years later he had advanced so fast in the system that he was appointed Consul General in Guangzhou), and some of the development assistance team. Zhao Leji was Governor of Qinghai at the time and put on a sumptuous banquet our first night. Zhao was Han Chinese but had been born and grown up in Xining and seemed very attuned to the challenges of governing a poor and ethnically diverse province, among the most diverse in China. At that time the youngest governor in the whole country, he was later to become Party Secretary of Qinghai and then Shaanxi before moving to Beijing where he was to rise eventually to the Politburo and be appointed in charge of the powerful Central Organization Bureau at the 18th Party Congress. Back in 2000 he was vitally interested in development economics, and we spent most of the evening discussing the importance of local business and how micro-finance programs were as important as infrastructure development.

From Xining we went first out into the countryside nearby to see a small scale solar energy project that was financed by CIDA and run by a Canadian company called ATS for the local manufacture of micro-solar systems that could be used on roof-tops to provide light and a tiny amount of additional electricity for a single country home. The fellow running the project was an electrical engineering graduate of the University of Waterloo, Shawn Qu. Shawn was very enthusiastic about the future of solar power and would shortly leave ATS to start his own firm, Canadian Solar International, which eventually became a major producer of solar components from cells to wafers to full modules and ended up listing on NASDAQ, at one point with a market cap of almost two billion dollars. In my post-diplomatic life I helped him arrange a couple of financing rounds, assisted in his IPO and then much later helped his firm acquire a three hundred million dollar solar project operator in Canada. In Qinghai, he had a little workshop with two rooms and maybe ten workers, putting together tiny systems that would make a huge difference in the lives of the poorest peasants. When we went to a home, made of clay brick, with one of these micro-solar systems already installed, the couple who lived there showed us proudly how this permitted their daughter to continue to read and study after the end of natural light, thus giving her a much greater chance to succeed at school.

Then we headed south and east and up onto the Tibetan plain to a little village called Xiazelong, which was on top of a steep and rocky hill that could only be reached by tractor or donkey cart. We had built a school in Xiazelong and funded the acquisition of textbooks and other school materials. The village leaders met us at the bottom of the hill with two tractors, each pulling a cart, into which we piled for the bumpy and twisting ascent to the village square. As we entered there were lines of children all dressed in their best and brightest clothes, waving and cheering. The entire population of the village had come out to greet us, and the local village head held a ceremony and led a performance of dancers and singers, all to thank us for their school. Following the ceremony, we had lunch with a local family in their home. We sat on a "kang", a built-in bed platform that bordered two of the walls, and were served goat meat and a form of local bread by the village women. It was extremely touching and convinced me for the thousandth time that the best development aid by far was the most local and smallest scale, where you could be certain that every dollar spent was spent on something that made a difference.

From Xiazelong we headed further into the Tibetan region of southern Qinghai and, after a drive of many hours on the winding dust roads, we climbed up to a tiny little corner of civilization called Mountain Edge Pass Village, at almost four thousand metres above sea level. We could see the village from eight or ten kilometres away, perched on a hill at the confluence of two valleys. As we approached the little town we realized that it was actually walled, and what had looked like steep parts of a distant hill were in fact clay walls. We parked perhaps eight hundred metres short of the village gate, and as we walked some of the villagers appeared on the walls while others and hundreds of children, lined the sides of the dusty track which led to the village's gate. Many of the women had covered heads, others were bareheaded but adorned with colourful scarfs. This people of this little village were half Tibetan and half Muslim Hui, and they had lived side by side for generations in apparent harmony. The village leaders greeted us by giving us a local form of fermented mare's milk and the Tibetan hadas, the white scarf of welcome. Then we were taken to two small projects which we had financed through the Canada Fund, one a potable water cistern and filtration system and the other a small solar energy installation. As we walked through the village, the children delighted in chattering away at our twins in a mixture of their local language and mandarin, migrating to the latter when they realized that our boys could speak it almost as well as they could. The locals had of course only been learning mandarin since they began their state schooling. At the end of our tour, we were offered lunch in the home of one of the village leaders, with others sitting with us and the women serving heavy local wheat cakes and strips of roasted goat.

After our time in Mountain Edge Pass Village, which ended with the necessary photographs of us with as many village children as could crowd into the frame, we headed down to the town of Tongren, where we visited both the old Longwu Monastery of the Yellow Hat sect of Tibetan Buddhism, set at the base of Xishan mountain. Before we arrived in Tongren, it had started to snow, and by the time we arrived at the monastery there was a good four or five centimetres on the ground. Our twins, much more excited about the snow than the architecture, started a snowball fight in the big open square in the centre of temple and even managed to get a few of the young monks playfully involved. We also visited the Wutong Monastery in Sangkeshan, just north of Tongren, and watched the monks painting Tibetan Thankas, many using centuries old styles but some also quite modern. We ended up buying two, which have graced the walls of our home ever since.

Our last stop before returning to Xining was another extraordinary cultural find for us, at a town called Camel Springs in Xunhua County, home to the Salar people, one of China's more than fifty ethnic minorities. As we approached the town, we could see the visible differences from the Han regions or even the predominantly Tibetan and Hui towns of southern Qinghai. The roofs and statuary looked very Turkic, and there were stone camels and Arabic arches shaped like inverted wine glasses. Even the people looked less Chinese and more Middle Eastern than the similarly Muslim Hui with whom they shared a religious core. How the Salar people ended up in a little corner of Qinghai has been much debated, but the theory I found the most attractive was that they had come from Samarkand and had migrated in the 13th century all the way to the Pacific coast near Shanghai before deciding to return, and ended up settling in Qinghai, for unknown reasons, in the middle of their return voyage. An anthropologist friend of mine even speculated that they were actually part of the lost tribe of Israel, having found their way first to Samarkand hundreds of years before moving further east. We had assisted, again with a Canada Fund project, in establishing a micro-finance program for local sheep breeding, allowing poor Salar villagers to borrow funds to expand their breeding stock and to take training programs, gradually enlarging their flocks to a size where they could be run as real businesses rather than just as subsistence husbandry. It was a very successful program, and the local leaders were very grateful for our support, and gave us a roast-lamb lunch in the homes of one of the local teachers, who we had also used as the trainer for those taking out the stock breeding loans.

Back in Beijing, I officiated over the last of the Terry Fox Runs I was to be involved in as Ambassador. From the first small school and Embassy based run in 1996 when we had had a few hundred participants, I had gradually pushed and harassed my staff to expand the participation to include many Chinese organizations. The following year we had Deng Pufeng, son of Deng Xiaoping, and Rick Hansen, lead us off in wheelchairs, and every year we had expanded the local involvement. In 1999, we obtained the blessing of the Chinese Ministry of Health and the China Cancer Society, largely because we had obtained the prior agreement of the Terry Fox Foundation that we could dedicate the funds we raised to Chinese cancer research. That year we had run from the Embassy to the China Cancer Hospital at the southwestern corner of the Second Ring Road and had persuaded the Beijing Government to close the ring road for the Sunday morning of our run. In 2000, I had set my sights even higher, and had lobbied with a Vice-Mayor of the city to allow us to run a multi-lap course around Tiananmen Square. Not only did he agree, he also joined the run, along with more than thirty Chinese companies or state danweis, and even a platoon from the PLA. I started the run alongside the Vice Mayor, and ended up crossing the finish line three or four times so that I could have my picture taken with the various groups that had joined the run, including the PLA platoon, who had stayed together as they ran their circuits. After I left the Embassy, the run retreated to its foreign community habitat, which I thought was great pity, but my successor was not a runner and it would have been hard to beat the Terry Fox Tiananmen Square run of 2000.

The year-end and holiday season began with a pre-Christmas visit to Yunnan, combining as we often tried to do an official visit with a family visit. After my required sessions in Kunming with Canadian firms and the government, and a very gracious meal hosted by Governor Li Jiating, who was removed from power and arrested for corruption just six months later. Nonetheless he was a delightful dinner companion and entertained not just me and our family but my Commercial Minister Rob Mackenzie and his family as well. Then we and the Mackenzies flew northwest to the old towns of Dali and Lijiang, the latter nestled up at the edge of the foothills of the Himalayas and home to the Naxi people and their lilting traditional music. Lijiang's restoration as a UNESCO historical site had just been completed and it was a wonderful place to spend a few days, wandering both through the town and also up around Heilongtang (Black Dragon Pond), one of the most perfectly proportioned temple lakes I have ever seen, and even climbing up to edge of the glaciers. The children were very happy in the mountain air and, as the elder two of both our family and the Mackenzies had just arrived back from boarding school for the Christmas break, had lots of fun being together, climbing hills or exploring Lijiang during the day and playing euchre together in the evenings after dinner.

Christmas itself was back in Beijing, then there was a senior Heads of Mission meeting back in Ottawa, hosted for the first time by our new Foreign Minister John Manley, who I found to be much easier to deal with than Lloyd Axworthy. Manley was focused, recognized how important China was and saw our foreign policy as very much supporting Canadian economic objectives. Much of my Ottawa time was not spent with my Ambassadorial colleagues but with the PMO as the final preparations for the largest ever Prime Ministerial Team Canada visit were being put to bed.

As soon as I was back in Beijing from my trip to Ottawa, the Clerk of the Privy Council, Mel Cappe, called me and told me that the Government wanted me to come back to Ottawa to be Deputy Minister of International Trade. I thanked him for the offer and told him that I would think about it, but that I was also thinking hard about leaving the public service and going into business, an option that would become increasingly difficult for me if I waited too much longer. I agreed to give him a firm answer after the February Team Canada visit.

CHAPTER 38

TEAM CANADA, FEBRUARY 2001

• • • • • • • • • • •

The Team Canada concept was dreamt up first when the Prime Minister Chrétien, André Desmarais, Jack Austin, Chairman and President of the Canada China Business Council respectively, and I were together in Seattle just after the Liberal victory in 1993. The original idea was simply to invite some provincial premiers and business leaders along on a state visit to demonstrate that Prime Ministerial travel was directly supportive of increased exports, reflecting the "jobs and growth" agenda that had been the theme of the Liberal's election campaign. During the early months of 1994 it was decided that it was politically impossible to only invite a select number of provinces to come, and so the Prime Minister wrote to all premiers and, to demonstrate the value of such a trip to the Canadian economy, told them that our objective was to invite firms from across the country and to collectively witness as large commercial signing ceremony. Once it was decided in early 1994 that the first Team Canada trip would be in November in combination with the first state visit of Prime Minister Chrétien to China, André Desmarais and I set a target of having one billion dollars worth of agreements signed. In early March André called me and told me that he thought our target was too low and that he was getting a great response from CCBC member companies. In the end, almost eight billion dollars worth of deals were signed, but given my move to the Privy Council Office six months before that 1994 visit, I had not participated in any part of the visit except the earliest planning phase. Given the 1994 success in China, Team Canada visits had been organized to many other countries, and in late 2000 the Prime Minister agreed that it was time to do a return visit to China, he himself having had very successful visits with smaller delegations in 1996 and 1998.

For an Embassy, even a big one like Beijing, organizing a Team Canada was almost exponentially more complex than simply a state visit. With provincial and territorial leaders and literally hundreds of senior business leaders all used to being treated as VIPs and expecting personalized programs and special treatment, the risk of having someone ending up feeling overlooked or inadequately respected was high, and we started planning more than a year in advance of the actual visit. Initially the idea had been to have the event take place in the traditional autumn Asia-visit slot, presumably on one of the shoulders of the APEC leaders meeting in Brunei, scheduled for the middle of November. I put Ted Lipman, our former Consul General in Shanghai and now Political Minister in Beijing, in charge of the logistics for the official delegation, and Robert Collette, Commercial Minister, in charge of the business program. The first advance team from the PMO came in May, and in the summer Rob Mackenzie, who had arrived to replace Collette, took over the overall responsibility for the business program, but given that he was new to the China scene a great deal of the work was taken up by the indomitable and ever-reliable Counselor Ron Hoffmann. Stuart Beck, who had replaced Lipman as Consul General in Shanghai, and long-serving Consul General in Hong Kong Colin Russel were each given oversight responsibility for the planning of the stops in their respective cities.

In late July I received a telephone call from the Prime Minister's Chief of Staff, Jean Pelletier, to ask me to confidentially approach the Chinese and forewarn them of a potential delay in the visit. At this time, it was clear that, in spite of efforts by influential backers of both parties, the Alliance Party under Stockwell Day and the Progressive Conservative Party under Joe Clark would not be able to come together under a single right-of-centre banner. Jean Chrétien, ever the wily politician, sensed that a continuation of disarray in his opposing ranks and a relatively strong economy combined to create an ideal political environment for an early election even though it had only been three years since the last one. Pelletier stressed that no decision had been made and that I was to treat this initial probe as very confidential. I went to see Vice Minister Yang Jiechi who had travelled with us during the Chrétien visit to Gansu in 1998, and who was a good friend. Yang, who was shortly to be posted to Washington as Ambassador, was very understanding and said that he was sure that some alternative dates could be worked out sometime in early 2001. When the official election call came some weeks later, the Chinese were all ready with a slot in February, a little less than three months after the election, which was announced for November 27th. In the end, Chrétien sent Foreign Affairs Minister John Manley to the APEC Summit that year in his stead, staying at home himself to campaign. The Liberals ended up not only winning the election but actually increasing their parliamentary majority, Chrétien's third in a row.

While the Prime Minister continued to believe that the Team Canada model was a terrific one, and while the general Canadian public seemed to like the image of federal and provincial and business leaders going abroad together to promote Canadian exports and investment, we were well aware that many business leaders had tired of being dragged around the world on missions that were so large that no real attention would be paid to their specific interests, and during which they would spend a large proportion of their time either waiting for some event to start or as apparent "extras" to political ceremonies that afforded them no particular benefit. We decided from the earliest planning meetings that we would try to limit the discontent among the business delegates as much as possible, which meant tailoring sectoral or in some cases company-specific programs to absorb their time when official meetings were taking place. This we set out to do, which meant bringing in extra staff from headquarters and from other regional missions to buttress the Embassy team.

As the visit approached, it was clear that the overall delegation would be huge. Two provincial premiers backed out of the delayed trip due to provincial elections, Ralph Klein of Alberta, and Roger Grimes of Newfoundland. Roy Romonow of Saskatchewan came as planned although by the time of the actual mission he was no longer Premier, having retired ten days earlier, but in deference to his long tenure, the new Premier Lorne Calvert, a Romonow protégé and his chosen successor, asked Roy to attend on behalf of the province. All provincial leaders except Lucien Bouchard of Quebec came on the Team Canada plane, a specially chartered 747 painted in "Team Canada 2001" livery, with Bouchard claiming that his obligations elsewhere prevented him from joining the group for the Vancouver departure, and he arrived in Beijing the day after the formal program had begun. Prime Minister Chrétien had also invited 90-year-old Mitchell Sharp to join the delegation. Sharp had been Trudeau's Secretary of State for External Affairs in 1970 when Canada recognized China, and although no longer spry physically was still very competent mentally. I had gotten to know him a bit when I was in the Privy Council Office and he was serving as a personal advisor to Chrétien for the vast salary of one dollar a year, and working out of an office next to my frequent collaborator Eddie Goldenberg in the Langevin Block. I would occasionally drop in and chat with him when visiting with Eddie, generally talking about China and his years as SSEA. The Chinese, who have good records, long memories and great respect for the aged, treated Sharp like royalty throughout the visit. From the federal government, Trade Minister Pierre Pettigrew and Secretary of State for Asia Pacific Ray Pagtakhan were with the Prime Minister and on the plane, and thankfully this time there were no added Members of Parliament. The leaders of the Yukon, Northwest Territories and Nunavut all came in person, as did more than five hundred businessmen and women, making the overall delegation a whopping 832 people. The Chinese told us that this was the largest foreign delegation ever to visit China, and it made a huge media splash, with front page news stories in every Chinese paper and leading coverage on all television stations. Coming in from the formal welcome at the airport, where Vice Foreign Minister (soon to be named Minister) Li Zhaoxing led the welcoming party, the motorcade was more than 20 limousines long, followed by some 25 buses.

It was well into the evening when we arrived at the China World Hotel, and there was no program planned for that evening, but the Prime Minister invited Liani and me to join him and his wife Aline, along with Jean

Pelletier and Eddie Goldenberg for a drink and a brief chat in his suite, and we had a very pleasant informal conversation about the days ahead of us. The Chrétiens were very relaxed, and the PM was in a very humorous mood, joking about how far we had gone in the more than seven years since we were all together for the first APEC Summit in 1993. We also used the time for a discussion with the Prime Minister of some of the sensitive issues that would be dealt with in the coming days, some of which would be raised only in the smallest of meetings, which would not include the provincial and territorial representatives.

Early the following morning we held a general briefing for the official delegation, which included all the provincial and territorial leaders, Mr. Sharp, Pettigrew and Pagtakhan. I gave an overview of trends in China and of the bilateral relationship, and then Stewart Beck, who I was determined to give as much profile as I could during the visit, talked about economic change in Shanghai and the Yangtze River delta and the extent to which Canadian interests were engaged there. Then it was off to a hydroponic farm in Shunyi that had been established by a Montreal company, successfully producing lettuces and tomatoes and other vegetables for the restaurant and high-end retail market in Beijing. Inside these huge glass greenhouses, as large as rugby fields, were a series of winding serpentine tanks carrying styrofoam flats that allowed plant roots to be in the water and the leaves in the bright sunlight. At the beginning of each serpentine the seedlings began their voyage, and by the time the growing flats reached the end of these little rivers at the far end of the greenhouse the lettuces and other vegetables were perfectly formed and ready for harvesting. It was a great "photo op" for the Prime Minister and the premiers, but unfortunately not for the leader from Québec, where the company was headquartered. We had set this as part of the program weeks before and in complete ignorance that Premier Bouchard of Québec would not yet be in Beijing, and journalists pointed out his absence, trying to suggest that either the feds had planned to have the Prime Minister visit with a successful Québec company without the Québec premier to emphasize that it was the federal level of government that was the principal player on the international stage,

623

or that Bouchard had stayed away to avoid being upstaged. In reality it was just a fluke of scheduling, this day being a Sunday and there being no other free time left to arrange such a visit.

Given the presence of all our provincial and territorial leaders, we had suggested to the Chinese MFA that we have a special event that would bring them together with Chinese provincial leaders. The ministry basically said that we were free to issue any invitations we wished, especially as the official visit would not yet have started, so we invited all the western and poorer provincial governments to join us for lunch on Sunday. The lunch included Party Secretary Wen Shizhen from Liaoning, who never missed a Canadian event and had been made an "Honorary Director" of the CCBC, as well as Governors or Vice Governors of almost all of China's western provinces, as well as a few from provinces twinned with Canadian counterparts. Prime Minister Chrétien was the official host, and the media gave it great coverage as further Canadian support for development in western China, and after a brief speech by me and toasts by both Prime Minister and Zeng Peiyan, Chairman of the State Development Planning Commission (shortly to be renamed the National Development and Reform Commission, which Zeng was to leave in 2002 to become Vice Premier), the event disintegrated into another great milling around social event, the best indication of a successful networking event that one could have. And the formal program had not yet even begun.

The formal bilateral state visit began in the afternoon in the Beidating (North Hall) of the Great Hall of the People, with Zhu Rongji and his wife Lao An greeting the Chrétiens and a score of beautifully dressed Chinese children waving flags and a few of them presenting flowers. Then there were the formal introductions of the delegation, National Anthems, inspection of the Guard of Honour and a 19-gun salute, an almost exact replica of the 1998 welcome ceremony.

Then followed the largest formal bilateral meeting I experienced in my professional career, with all provincial and territorial leaders at the table along with the normal battery of federal ministers and officials, although in reality only Prime Minister Chrétien spoke for Canada, and with me on one side of him and his interpreter on the other we were like a little command centre for the long Canadian delegation arrayed some fifteen strong on either side of us. The agenda was, with one exception, a standard review of bilateral and multilateral issues and bilateral programs, and specific trade matters (Chinese entry into the WTO was now simply a formality that was scheduled to take place later in the year) and the one or two commercial issues that we had deemed worthy of being raised at this level. Before every visit, we would receive dozens, if not more, of requests by companies to push their licensing applications, challenge Chinese treatment of their investments, appeal some sort of treatment or other by Chinese provincial or central authorities, or support their effort to sell their products or services to some entity – like an airline or the railways – controlled by the Chinese Government. We took all these requests seriously, for as long as I was Ambassador no one in the Embassy had any doubt that among our most important constituencies was the Canadian business community. But few merited being raised individually by the Prime Minister with his Chinese counterpart.

The one issue that was on the leaders' agenda for the first time was that of Lai Changxing, a man from Xiamen in southern Fujian who had fled to Canada after being accused of running a smuggling ring worth billions of dollars, corrupting scores of local officials to protect his business through bribes and providing access to luxury goods and beautiful women in his famous "Red Mansion" hotel in downtown Fujian. In November of 1999, as the police were preparing to arrest him, he was tipped off and fled by speedboat to Hong Kong, where he had obtained a passport a few years earlier. Less than two weeks later he was in Vancouver without having to have gone through any visa vetting process, since Hong Kong passport holders do not need visas to visit Canada. Once his presence became known and his time as a visitor approached its expiry, he filed with the Canadian immigration authorities a request for political asylum. I had been called into the Foreign Ministry during the autumn of 2000 to receive a request that Canada extradite Lai. I had explained that under Canadian law he had the right of due process and that while his request for political asylum had been turned down by an initial refugee determination panel, he had appealed and that such an appeal, and subsequent appeals, could drag the case out for some time.

I had hoped to keep the Lai case off the official agenda of the prime ministerial talks, but I had not succeeded. Almost at the start of the discussions, Zhu Rongji raised the issue and made clear China's position that Lai should be extradited quickly. While he did not dwell on it, probably because of such a large audience of provincial and territorial leaders and officials, he was clearly not satisfied with Chrétien's response about Canadian legal processes. So the discussion moved on to other issues. Zhu raised the Lai matter again privately during the dinner, and this time did so in a very intense tone, saying that it was inexcusable to allow the Canadian legal system to be abused to protect such a filthy criminal and that we should just send him back. When the interpreter, Jean Duval, repeated what he had said in English but in a more diplomatic way, Zhu corrected him and said, in English, "that is Not what I said. Please do your job and translate exactly what I said." Duval reddened, since it was a rather terrible thing for a great interpreter to be challenged, but repeated a more direct and severe version of Zhu's words. Zhu then said that this was a very important issue that could damage the otherwise extraordinarily good relationship and added, pointing at me, that Chrétien should ask his Ambassador to explain privately why this case was so important. In fact, Zhu seemed to care more about it than any other leader, and I and others had concluded that Lai's eventual testimony could have power-tilting fallout. Certain other national figures, including Li Peng, former Premier, and particularly Jia Qinglin, former Party Secretary of Fujian and by 2001 Party Secretary in Beijing, had family members implicated in the scandal. Chrétien told Zhu that there was an additional dimension to the case that had to be understood in addition to the fact that until Lai had exhausted his legal rights in Canada the government could not take action to deport him. The second dimension was that Canadian law prohibited the extradition of prisoners to any place if they faced a serious risk of the death penalty. Zhu said that he was sure an assurance that Lai would not be put to death could be arranged, but unfortunately responded to a journalist's question later by saying, "If Lai were to be put to death three times, that would not be enough"! Given the importance of the extradition to the Chinese Government, and because I was convinced that we could rely on their assurance that the man would not be put to death, I subsequently suggested to the Prime Minister that we should be prepared, as soon as Lai lost a court case and before his lawyers had a chance to file an appeal, to bundle him into a chartered aircraft and deport him. Chrétien said that while he agreed, he feared that such a move would create simply too big a controversy.

In the end, the Lai case was to drag on for another decade and serve as a constant irritant in the bilateral relationship. It was made more complicated by the Chinese themselves, who at one point sent Lai's brother and a group of officers from the Ministry of Public Security to Canada, disguised as a business delegation (a ruse we discovered) to try to strong-arm Lai back to China, and by many public statements that made clear that the Chinese authorities presumed him guilty with an eventual trial and verdict clearly already set in stone. Lai's final legal appeal was turned down in 2011 in the Canadian Federal Court system and he was extradited to China, where he was later convicted and sentenced to life imprisonment. While there may have been no presumption of innocence, the Chinese at least respected their promise to exclude capital punishment as a potential sentence. And by the time he was extradited, tried and sentenced, some of the Chinese political figures whose careers his testimony might have affected had retired or died, so we will probably never know what the impact might have been had he been sent home ten years earlier.

The formal bilateral meeting of Chrétien's 2001 state visit was followed by a signing ceremony for bilateral agreements, none of which were particularly earth-shaking given that it had only been fifteen months since Zhu's own state visit to Canada. Before every state visit, right at the start of the planning stage, a call would go out from the senior person managing the China relationship at headquarters to the Embassy and to other government departments for proposals on "deliverables", and we had year after year scrounged for new ones. In 2001 they were very run-of-the-mill: a few development projects in the areas of environmental technology and legal reform (really just extending our support for the National Judges College, an agreement I might have, absent a state visit, signed in my office), and one or two others. Immediately on the heels of the formal bilateral meeting, and still at the Great Hall of the People, was the formal Chinese banquet, and all the spouses we had dispatched to the hotel after the welcoming ceremony were motorcaded back to join us. Given the size of our delegation, some 60 strong, there was a single long head table for the most senior federal representatives and a series of smaller round tables for the provincial and territorial leaders, each hosted by a Chinese Minister or equivalent. Without the business community, there was none of the usual milling around, and only two short toasts by Zhu as host and Chrétien as guest, and largely due to the close relationship the two Prime Ministers had forged over may meetings, the evening was very pleasant and surprisingly relaxed. The Chinese had arranged an extremely fine chamber group from the National Philharmonic Orchestra to play a medley of Canadian and Chinese music during the dinner, and it was evident that the state of the bilateral relationship simply could not have been better.

Looking back at these visits, it seems extraordinary how we filled the time with non-stop movement and events. Monday was a rushed visit out to Xi'an, a thousand kilometers to the west and then back to Beijing at nightfall. Trade Minister Pierre Pettigrew and the business delegation remained in Beijing, with seminars and business meetings arranged jointly be the Embassy and the CCBC, and we had given the provinces the choice of having their premiers stay with their companies or come to Xi'an, and they collectively decided to come to Xian. The flights to and from were like Federal-Provincial First Ministers meetings, with Chrétien and the premiers wandering around the big plane chatting in small groups or one-on-one, dealing with matters that sometimes were far from China or trade issues. The PMO had been fully supportive of the idea of a visit to Xi'an, both to pick up on the successful themes we had built up with the trip to Gansu in 1998 and also to visit the terracotta warriors, but had wanted us to avoid as much as possible formal ceremonies and meals. This was simply not possible without offending our provincial hosts.

After an airport greeting by the Executive Vice Governor Jia Zhibang, who had rushed back to Xi'an after attending our Western China lunch the day before in Beijing and who later would become Governor of Shaanxi and eventually Minister of Forestry in the Central Government, the visit began with a meeting with Governor Cheng Andong. This meeting was little more than a staged "photo op" for journalists and television cameras to record the meeting for the evening news, and was followed by a signing ceremony for some Canada Fund projects that we were carrying out in Shaanxi, including one supporting the modernization of rudimentary health clinics in rural areas, and another setting up micro-finance programs in minority communities. As these were local programs, the signatories to the agreements were senior local officials and the Ambassador, which of course meant that our children could see me on television if they watched the evening news, although I think by this time seeing their father on the news had rather lost its excitement. Then a mercifully short formal lunch and we headed off to one of the "Child Friendly Centres" supported by the Canada Fund, and this was a terrific visit, allowing not just the politicians but their spouses to wander through the attractive clinic with much modern equipment and incredibly appreciative staff. Liani and Aline Chrétien, and several of the premiers' wives, were given a demonstration of a training program where nurses were teaching girls how to take care of infants so that they could be helpers to their families and to their villages.

We then piled back into the cars and buses and set off for the Terracotta Warriors Museum, where Prime Minister Chrétien and Aline, and therefore the rest of us, were given the honour of being only the second foreign visitors to be allowed deep into the restoration area where the warriors were actually standing. The first such visit had been by President

Clinton the year before, and most foreign visitors were kept on the viewing platform above the warriors. Being right down in the pit in the middle of the Terracotta Army, able to see the warriors up close, one got a real sense of another time, twenty-three hundred years earlier, when the Qin dynasty had unified China for the first time. It was also a great setting for photographs, and pictures of the Prime Minister and Aline Chrétien in the midst of the warriors were all over Chinese and Canadian newspapers and television the next day.

We flew back to Beijing that evening too late for anything to be squeezed into the program, which began again in earnest the following morning with a speech on the rule of law by the Prime Minister at the National Judges College, an event which did not include provincial premiers or spouses. The speech was excellent and the audience, which included the staff and students at the college and a few special invitees that we had asked to be included from the law faculties of mainland universities, and it was given reasonable press, but of course the more contentious elements, such as the importance of even the government and party being subject to the law and how vital an independent judiciary is to a modern society were not replayed in the Chinese media.

On the drive from the National Judges College to Zhongnanhai, with the Prime Minister and I riding together as was normal in all official motorcades, Chrétien asked me what I was going to do next, saying that he had heard I was being asked to return to Ottawa as Deputy Minister of International Trade. I told him that I was honoured by the offer, that I was seriously considering it, but that I also thought the time was coming when I might wish to leave the public service. I said that I had invested much in China and I was reasonably sure, after more than five years as Ambassador, I could make a success of a business built around my knowledge and relationships. Chrétien responded that he thought I was doing a great job as Ambassador and I could stay as long as I liked, but that he understood if I wished to leave the government "at least for a little while". He said that he had spent some time outside of government and that they had been good years and had allowed him to earn some money, and that he was sure I could be successful. He then told me that I could always come back and run for parliament.

As we drove back from the Judges College, the provincial and territorial leaders were taken by a separate motorcade and met us just outside Zhongnanhai so we could enter as a single delegation for a lunch hosted by Jiang Zemin. By this time the President and Chrétien had met so many times over the past eight years that they really were personal friends, had met each other's families and knew a lot about each other. So after a gracious toast to the whole delegation, the luncheon discussion between the two leaders was just that, between them, while everyone else at the table chatted with neighbours. The afternoon began with a big signing ceremony for commercial deals, allegedly almost six billion dollars worth, presided over by the Prime Minister and Zeng Peiyan, and then a meeting with Embassy staff and families was scheduled, and for which I had organized a special event.

Since shortly after arriving in China as Ambassador, I and a couple of friends had been running a children's hockey league for foreign and Chinese children, and it had become quite successful. As the event at which our visiting Team Canada delegation could meet Embassy staff and children, we had organized a hockey game, at the rink in the centre of the China World shopping centre, between two teams of Canadian and Chinese children from the league, all dressed in Team Canada jerseys, naturally half in red jerseys and half in white. At the beginning of the event, I asked Prime Minister Chrétien to drop the puck, but only after donning a Team Canada jersey of his own, with his name across the back. I had jerseys for him and for every premier and territorial leader, and for myself of course, and even had a jersey made up for Zhu Rongji that the Premier Minister could give to him later. Chrétien loved the event, the jerseys and the kids, and he mocked a face off with Premier Mike Harris, a large photo of which appeared on the front of Canada's Globe and Mail newspaper the following morning. All the premiers and territorial leaders had a good time watching the children play hockey and it was very good for the Embassy staff to realize that their efforts and contributions were appreciated by those they served.

The day wrapped up with a thirty-minute meeting with NPC Chairman Li Peng at the Nandating (South Hall) of the Great Hall of the People, after which we climbed back into the motorcade and drove all the way around to the eastern entrance of the same building for the evening event. During the planning stage of the visit, the advance team had suggested to the Chinese that the Prime Minister and his delegation could walk either inside or outside the Great Hall from the side of the Li Peng meeting to the dinner, but this was ruled impossible for protocol reasons, since it might make the meeting with Li Peng seem like an add-on to a more important evening event which Premier Zhu Rongji would attend, which of course it was. The dinner was formally a CCBC dinner to which the two prime ministers were invited, along with all the provincial and territorial leaders and another two thousand guests. As was standard for these sorts of events, we started with a VIP reception for about a hundred, allowing senior-most business leaders meet briefly with Chrétien and Zhu, and then the gala itself for the twenty-seven hundred people present. CCBC had produced a great slide presentation of past events in honour of the thirtieth anniversary of the establishment of diplomatic relations then just past, and the two leaders gave their usual extremely upbeat speeches about the Canada-China relationship.

It was a trimmed down business delegation that accompanied us to Shanghai early the following morning, bringing the overall group to just below six hundred from the eight hundred plus in Beijing. As we landed in Shanghai we were joined by Mayor Pierre Bourque of Montreal, a city twinned with Shanghai. Bourque had worked hard at the relationship between the two cities, had installed a Montreal Pavilion in Pudong's Central Park, and had, given his own background as a botanist, established Montreal city planning and landscaping firms as the "go-to" firms as

Shanghai proceeded with its modernization and park and green-space development plans.

At the airport we stopped long enough for the Prime Minister to kick off a promotional event for Bombardier, with a new Regional Jet just delivered to Shanghai Airlines. Then it was into the city in our motorcade, although I had insisted that Consul General Stewart Beck ride with the Prime Minister instead of me, and I took Pierre Bourque in a separate car. The PMO had earlier suggested that I ride with Chrétien throughout, since he was very familiar with me, but I really wanted Stewart to get some exposure. I had advised him on how to brief the PM, and the signs to watch for that indicated disinterest or impatience, and warned him against raising any matter related to the service. Years earlier, a Commissioner (in the pre-retrocession days) in Hong Kong had taken advantage of time with a visiting Prime Minister to bend his ear on the need for a new Official Residence, with the result being that the Official Residence received a new resident shortly thereafter. Stewart did a good job, however, and had also organized a very good Shanghai leg of the visit, and it all went as smoothly as clockwork.

Mayor Xu Kuangdi was then in his sixth and last year as mayor of Shanghai and was coming close to retiring from an active political role. But he was as ebullient and charming as ever, and was a great friend to Canada, having taught briefly in the 1980s both at École Polytechnique in Montreal and at the University of Waterloo. He opened the meeting with the Prime Minister by asking how the Montréal Canadiens were doing, and they then sent most of their time together chatting about personal things and shared interests. Mayors Xu and Bourque then signed a Shanghai-Montreal partnership agreement on environmental management exchanges, and then Xu hosted a lunch in the gorgeous Grand Hall of the old Jinjiang complex, built in the 1920s in art deco style. We then went to Pudong to attend the ribbon cutting ceremony for the Montreal Pavilion, a very modern showcase for Montreal IT companies. We took an early evening cruise on the Huangpu River, during which I had arranged for Tess Johnston to give a talk on the history of Shanghai. Tess was an American friend of mine who had been assigned to the US Consulate General in Shanghai years earlier, fallen in love with the city and stayed, dedicating herself to architectural preservation and historical research. Her talk generated substantial interest and we arranged for Aline Chrétien and several others who were so inclined to meet again with Tess the following day in the French Concession, and upon departure from Shanghai I gave each provincial leader and their spouse a book on Shanghai architecture that she and a local photographer friend had written.

The last day of the Shanghai leg opened with a speech by the Prime Minister at the East China University of Politics and Law, virtually the same speech he had given at the National Judges College in Beijing. Cao Jianming, then Vice-President (and later President) of the Chinese Supreme Court and the most determined supporter of the National Judges College, had been President of the University before moving to Beijing and was also one of its graduates. Prior to the visit, when I discussed with Cao the possibility of the Prime Minister speaking at the National Judges College, Cao had encouraged me to have the Prime Minister also speak at his alma mater, and thus reach a larger and more diverse audience for the messages he would give at the NJC. The Consulate had also gathered a number of elderly graduates of St. John's University now living in Canada to attend the speech. Saint John's was a pre-revolutionary English-language college on the same campus, and although there was no real academic lineage between the two, the alumnae of Saint John's, many of whom went on to successful careers in the US and Canada, had established themselves as friends of the new and newly liberalizing East China University. The speech was very well received, and the students had lots of questions, appearing very well informed about the rule of law in Canada and western countries.

Then it was back downtown for the business program, a Team Canada Business Lunch at the Pudong Shangri-La, with hundreds of local business representatives from Shanghai and surrounding cities networking with their Canadian business counterparts, and another ceremony at the Grand Hyatt where the Prime Minister and Mayor Xu witnessed the signing of commercial agreements. As the day wound down, we piled again into our long motorcade and headed out to the airport, re-boarded our Team Canada 747 and took off for Hong Kong.

The two-day Hong Kong program included a greatly reduced business delegation and less emphasis on commercial signings, with the business delegation staying at hotels on the island side of the harbour and the official delegation staying at the Peninsula Hotel in Kowloon. A particular problem had arisen when the visit was being organized over the issue of rooms for the provincial premiers. In theoretical constitutional terms, all the provinces are equal, and by formal protocol, the seniority of premiers is determined by the date they assumed office. This meant that Premier Binns of PEI, with a population roughly equal to a borough of Toronto, had to be treated the same as Premier Harris of Ontario. The Peninsula simply did not have very many big suites, and so it was decided by the PMO advance team, after assigning the beautiful Presidential Suite in the new tower to the Prime Minister, that each premier and territorial leader would get one of the identical junior suites, of which there were enough. This left the finest suite in the old part of the hotel, the Xanadu Suite, which occupied the whole eastern front of the top floor, available for Ambassador and Mme Balloch, and it was truly one of the nicest suites in which we have ever stayed. The shelves and china cabinets were filled with Ming Dynasty porcelain and other beautiful pieces, and the walls with 19th century paintings. There was a large dressing room and a small dining room as well as a very beautiful living room facing Hong Kong Harbour, and it seemed to Liani and me a great pity that the Prime Minister's program would leave us little time to enjoy such a lovely setting.

Following the transfer of sovereignty from Britain to China in 1997, the leader of the Hong Kong Government was called the Chief Executive, and the first Chief Executive, Tung Chee-Hwa, who had been the CEO of a successful shipping company, was still in power in 2001. Tung and his entire cabinet were all in attendance for most of the official functions during the Team Canada visit, for Canada was a major player in Hong Kong, with many of its senior business leaders and more than two hundred thousand of its citizens holding Canadian passports. Tung hosted the Prime Minister and the official delegation for a formal meeting and an official lunch on the first day of the visit, and then also hosted a dinner on the second day to which he invited a very interesting and eclectic group of the Hong Kong elite, from the nonagenarian media patriarch Run-Run Shaw to Li Ka-shing to the multi-billionaire and very eccentric Nina Wang, then Asia's richest woman. Wang, then in her mid-sixties and made up and dressed like a 16-year old, controlled Chinachem, the chemical empire built by her husband Teddy, who had disappeared after being kidnapped eleven years earlier. Liani and I had met her once before at the opening of the Dalian International Fashion show in 1998, and she remembered meeting us with then mayor Bo Xilai.

The Hong Kong program also contained a commercial signing ceremony and a business lunch, which Tung Chee-hwa attended along with what seemed to be half of the Hong Kong business community, a huge number of whom had studied in Canada or had homes and family there. As I listened to the speeches I realized one huge difference between that event and the events in Beijing and Shanghai, and that was that everything was in English and there was no translation or interpretation of anything. What with that and the huge number of Canadians, I felt that we were already at least half way across the Pacific.

A visit to the Canadian International School of Hong Kong, founded ten years earlier, was a final and high point of the Hong Kong visit. Built on a series of terraces down a steep and rocky hillside on the coast in Aberdeen, at this time it was already rapidly emerging as one of the finest schools in the territory, offering both an Ontario degree and an International Baccalaureate. The school had gone all-out for the visit, and as soon as we arrived children in crisply ironed uniforms escorted us on a tour of the school. We ended in an open space on the lowest floor for a presentation and the singing by the children of *O Canada*. Whether the children who could sing well were told to lip-synch, or the entire school had practiced for hundreds of hours, it was hauntingly well sung and a tremendous closing event for our week-long Team Canada visit. Jean and Aline Chrétien were clearly touched, but they were not alone. As I stood listening, I looked quietly around at each of the premiers, all clearly caught in the emotion of the moment, and I noticed separatist premier Lucien Bouchard, standing straight and firm in spite of his artificial leg, with a tear running down his cheek. There, I thought, is a complicated man.

The next morning, eight days after meeting the Team Canada 747 as it landed in Beijing, I watched it take off from Hong Kong. As the big aircraft mounted into the sky, pulled up its landing gear, veered off slightly to the north to pick up its assigned route to Canada, and grew smaller and smaller in the sky, I breathed a big sigh of relief and realized that this was almost certainly the last high-level hurrah for Ambassador Howard Balloch.

Liani and I went back to the Peninsula and began to pack up our things in the elegant Xanadu Suite. It was time to come back to reality and move across to the Shangri-La and a perfectly ordinary room, where we had planned to spend a couple of more days relaxing before heading back to Beijing. There was a knock on the door and the hotel manager was there to thank us for the visit. When he offered us a complementary ride to the airport we told him that we were actually moving across the harbor for a few days of private time in somewhat more modest digs. He would hear nothing of that and invited us to stay for two more nights, free of charge, and so we remained in the Xanadu Suite and invited friends to join us for drinks, luxuriating in a style to which we had not, and probably never would, become truly accustomed.

CHAPTER 39

FINAL MONTHS

. . . .

Returning to Beijing after the Team Canada visit was like a holiday after a grueling championship playoffs. Those involved in the planning and implementation of the largest delegation in the history of Canadian diplomacy felt as if we had achieved what we had set out to achieve, and we could all relax until the tempo built up again. One of the results of the visit was that there were no more ministerial or high-level provincial visits scheduled for some time, since they had been vacuumed into the Team Canada colossus.

As I had promised, I called Mel Cappe to discuss my future, and told him that I had decided definitively to leave the public service in the summer, and I supplemented the call with a formal letter. Mel completely understood and said that while I would be missed, he wished me well. A few days later, the Prime Minister's Chief of Staff, Jean Pelletier, called me to try to persuade me to change my mind. At one point in the conversation he asked whether I did not think I had a responsibility to the country to take on the position being offered. Holding a little bit of steam in check, I asked him whether he did not think what I had done over my twenty-five year career, including my contributions to national unity and to the pursuit of Canadian interests in China, did not represent an account of service fully paid. He backed down and said that he completely understood, and then graciously added that the public service would be a lesser place without me.

In March of 2001 I paid my last official visit to Tibet, mixing both business and pleasure and bringing my family with me. Liani and I wanted our four children to see Tibet for themselves and understand both the poverty and the beauty of the place. En route we stopped in Chengdu, where the Governor of Sichuan hosted a dinner for our whole family. A special "Chuancai" fish dish was served, in which a live fish is fried very quickly by dipping it tail first in extremely hot and spicy oil and keeping the head above the surface. It is then served while still alive, while deep-fried flesh is peeled off its sides. When it was brought to the table during our banquet, I could see the eyes of our four children almost pop out of their faces as they looked at the spectacle of a fish held vertical on a spit and the mouth opening and closing. "Grossed-out" and ignoring my half-hearted effort to suggest that the fish was not really still alive and the opening and closing mouth simply caused by steam rising, the four of them rose from the table in unison and retreated to the ante-room, only to return when the offending dish was removed from our presence.

During this second visit to Tibet we spent a week in the Lhasa area, toured through the Potala Palace and other sites in the city area. The children all found the altitude a little difficult at first, noting that it not only made climbing stairs and running around more tiring, but that it also made normal foods taste different and strange. Once my official meetings were completed, we visited development projects and toured the nearby countryside. We went back to the paper-making school for handicapped children that I had visited in 1997 and I was pleased to find it physically in good shape and apparently doing very well. The old teacher was still in charge and had brought in an apprentice who was now doing a lot of the teaching of the children. Our own children tried their hands at paper-making and we took away both home-made paper and a good feeling that everything that could be done for these poor handicapped children was in fact being done. We also visited the Dode Orphanage for young children that had been rebuilt with a small Canada Fund donation, and our children had fun playing on the swings and trying to communicate with the young orphans, who were all delighted to have foreign children in their midst. The following day we went upcountry to Zayu Village in Drannang County where we were implementing a training program for rural healthcare workers, some of whom were teenage girls younger than our Cynthia. Then we went to the little town of Namseling, where our children wandered around the mud-brick town and found very interesting the programs we were running to help local women establish a commercial sewing business and another to provide solar energy for both water-heating and local electricity. In the end it was a good idea to bring the children, for I think they all came away with a much better appreciation of how poor Tibet was, and how important sustained economic development was for the lives of ordinary Tibetans.

One byproduct of our family visit to Tibet was produced when Caleb decided to join the Amnesty International club at Trinity College School the following autumn. When the discussion turned to China and Tibet, he tried to explain the local situation as he had seen it through his own eyes, suggesting that a balance had to be found between traditional religious life, which was a far-from-free theocratic existence, and modern development. Other students were completely uninterested in hearing a first hand account of things and preferred to accept only the completely one-sided versions of China's liberal critics. Caleb found this very narrow-minded and simplistic, and immediately quit the club.

In April, it looked like we were going to have another repeat of the frenzied anti-American protests that we had seen years earlier following the US bombing of the Chinese Embassy in Belgrade. A Chinese J-8 fighter jet collided with an American EP-3 naval intelligence aircraft between the coast of Hainan and the Paracel Islands, resulting in the loss of the Chinese plane and its pilot. The EP-3 was crippled and almost crashed, but the pilots managed to make an emergency landing, without clearance from Chinese military air traffic control, at a Chinese military base near Haikou. At first the US Government wanted to place all the blame on the "cowboy" tactics of the dead Chinese fighter pilot and to insist publicly that the spy-plane had been in international airspace, which the Chinese contested. I and my British counterpart, Tony Galsworthy, both spoke to Joe Prueher, the American Ambassador, and encouraged him to argue for a softer line since renewed anti-western sentiment was something none of us wanted. Prueher, a military man himself, persuaded the Pentagon to agree to a US apology of sorts, which was done by sending a letter saying that the American Government was sorry about the death of the pilot and sorry that clearance had not been received before the EP-3 made its emergency landing. It was not a very robust apology, but enough to get the crew released and the dismantled aircraft flown back to the US in the belly of a chartered Russian cargo plane.

As the summer approached so did the end of many postings. We hosted farewell dinners for both Joe Prueher and EU Ambassador Endymion Wilkinson before having similar dinners hosted for us. We had to turn down many kind offers from other diplomats as more than a dozen Chinese Ministers, Vice Ministers, and provincial leaders also wanted to host meals to bid a formal farewell, and my priority as always was to play on the Canada-China field rather than in the diplomatic sandbox. This round of goodbyes and the seeking of agrément for my successor Joseph Caron seemed all part of a somewhat surreal fog, but it gradually sunk home that my time as Ambassador to China was really coming to an end. In my last week at the end of July, I paid final farewell calls on Foreign Minister Tang Jiaxuan and my old friend and former Trade Minister, State Counselor Wu Yi, both of whom were very gracious in their comments on my contribution to the relationship. When I told Wu Yi that I was leaving the Canadian Government and would return to China to set up my own firm, she gave me two thumbs up and said "Fa Cai", which basically means "get rich"! My final formal good-bye dinner was hosted at Diaoyutai Guest House by Vice Minister and soon to be Minister Li Zhaoxing, and then before we knew it the packers had come and we were on our way.

Well before our departure, Liani had done a thorough job researching the local real estate market and we had committed to but our home in Beijing's northern suburb of Shunyi. All of our personal goods from the Official Residence were thus shipped not to Canada, but a mere 18 kilometres to our new house. Unfortunately, the day before our departure, there was a massive summer rainstorm and the basement of the house, where hundreds of cardboard boxes had been placed waiting our eventual return later in the summer, flooded with a half metre of water. A quick change of plans was put into effect, and only I and our twins actually left Beijing, and Liani bore the brunt of the disaster and stayed behind to clean up the mess and empty all the boxes, and to agree with the developer and contractors on a plan to waterproof the outside of the basement and refinish the ruined rooms.

BOOK VI:

PERIPHERAL POSTS

CHAPTER 40

MONGOLIA

. . . .

Until the collapse of the USSR and the dismantlement of the Soviet empire, Mongolia was a satrapy of Moscow, different in form but effectively not in freedom to act from the Soviet western republics. Mongolia sent its own representatives to international organizations and maintained few embassies beyond those in the capitals of its immediate neighbours. The Canadian Ambassador to the USSR was also accredited to Mongolia, and most would travel there once or twice in their mandate, since there were no Canadian firms engaged there and the voice one heard in Ulaan Baatar was simply that of a Moscow ventriloquist. As elsewhere, communism and Soviet control ended in 1990, and by 1992 the country had a new constitution based on a multi-party system and the rule of law. Canada shifted its representation from Moscow to Beijing, and in the summer of 1996 I would be the second Beijing-based envoy to present my credentials in Ulaan Baatar.

I knew we had slipped off the plate of modern Asia as soon as the old and slightly rickety MIAT 727 landed on the one runway of the Ulaan Baatar International Airport. Off to the left as we taxied toward the terminal was a graveyard of a dozen or so cannibalized Soviet helicopters, old MIL Mi-4s and Mi-17s, and half as many Antonov An-2 bi-planes, most with their wings in tatters but a couple clearly in service with the fuselages brightly painted in local livery. We deplaned down an old mobile stairway and were met on the tarmac by Mongolia's Chief of Protocol, and were taken to a VIP room in the terminal to await our luggage. We watched three men unload the plane, one tossing the bags out of the plane to a second man below who more or less caught them, or at least softened somewhat the impact of them hitting the ground, and a third who heaved them back up onto the open back of an old Russian half-ton truck. Three trips by the three men later, we could see our luggage finally on the truck, so we went outside, pointed it out and it was tossed down, put in our jeeps and off we set to the centre of the city. The road was macadam but in frightful shape, with huge potholes and edging broken away, so our progress was slow, but I didn't mind since it allowed a better appreciation of what was around us.

As we left the airport area heading east into the city there were dusty hills to the south with a few scattered pines and a hint of coming green cover on the earth, but generally quite barren, while to our left the undulating land led to a small river valley before climbing again. On this northern side of the road we soon came to one of the many shantytowns that surrounded Ulaan Baatar, with hundreds of tiny wood-slat homes interspersed with an almost equal number of traditional gher homes. The gher is a round, hide-wrapped dwelling, about two metres in height at its centre and between four and eight metres in diameter, with a slightly conical roof, either a wooden or leather door, and a stove pipe sticking through. While there were cart paths visible in the dirt between the main road and the shantytown, there were no real roads evident and no sign of any motorized vehicles within it. As we proceeded I saw slightly ahead of us to the southeast a young Mongol clad in cap and red cape astride a beautiful small black horse, galloping at an astounding pace away from the road towards steep pine-clad hills. The images of the young horseman and the traditional ghers might have completed a bucolic if rugged first impression of Mongolia had not we crested a small hill and turned towards the valley in which the capital lay. Then on our left was an instant counterpoint to the scenes of the nomadic life. A huge thermal power plant sat belching filthy smoke skyward from hundred-metre tall smokestacks, with four giant cooling tanks and gangly transmission towers, all rusty, taking power lines off in a half dozen directions. Both were fair images, I was to learn, of modern Mongolia.

On my first visit I found the country a strange mixture, not quite Asia, not quite Europe. After only a few days, it was evident to me that many

Mongolians felt a greater affinity to their neighbours to the North than to the Chinese, and the way they approached a lot of questions and issues was closer to Moscow than Beijing. I was told that a month earlier, the Mongolian military had held a celebration to which both Chinese and Russian representatives were invited. Generals from each country gave speeches full of platitudes about good neighbourliness. The Chinese general received lukewarm applause, the Russian a standing ovation. Suspicion and fear of the Chinese was palpable, and in spite of extraordinarily brutal subjugation during the Stalinist era (in 1937 more than 30,000 Mongolian intellectuals and monks were murdered under Moscow's orders), the Soviet help in successfully defending Mongolia against the Japanese 1939 invasion, and the Soviet post-war role in building infrastructure and industry dominated the bilateral narrative. And the hasty removal of almost 100,000 troops and 50,000 civilians at the time of the collapse of the Soviet Union in 1990 and 1991 left a very big hole in the Mongolian economy.

The city of Ulaan Baatar also did not appear to be an Asian city. Having only come into being as a city after the 1921 revolution, during which it broke clearly away from China and allied itself with the Soviet Union, it was in the mid-1990s an un-modernized jumble of periodic Russian architectural styles. Near the grand central Sukhbaatar Square and the Great Khural, Mongolia's crumbling pillared parliament, could be seen an amalgam of yellow or ochre pseudo-classical Italianate buildings with false Doric columns and plastered stonework veneer on wooden frames (like much of Moscow), Stalinist imperial wedding-cake rococo, and a sort of Brezhnevian constructionalism in a few large buildings with great sway-back roofs and oblique columns like the great Soviet pavilion at Expo67 in Montreal. There were very handsome Buddhist monasteries, very reminiscent of Tibet or Nepal, but in the city itself there seemed very little that was typically Mongolian. The city was also clearly well past whatever prime it might have known during the communist era, with the roads full of potholes and gardens and boulevards completely unkempt. Sukhbaatar Square in front of the parliament, once a grand setting for military parades and great socialist rallies, was a sea of weeds and broken concrete.

Outside downtown, which was not large given that the metropolitan area only contained about 600,000 of the then national population of 2.5 million, dozens of grey factory buildings stood deserted, and kilometres of boring five-floor apartment blocks boasting crumbling concrete exteriors, coloured only by washing hanging from balconies. Beyond these and behind corrugated iron fences lay more shantytowns of one room homes made of whatever scrap material could be found and little alleys like that we had seen near the airport. Goats and cows could be seen wandering between the wood and iron shacks and the occasional gher, with lots of little children in colourful but tattered clothes running about. Strangely perhaps, the shantytowns reminded me of poor Newfoundland when I was growing up.

The people we met, however, seemed charming and straightforward, and both interesting and interested in the world beyond. And in spite of the evident fact that a blond and bearded foreigner in a flag-flying car is not a regular everyday sight (there were then few westerners and a tiny handful of resident western embassies in Ulaan Baatar), there was not the intrusive in-your-face curiosity that one encountered in those days in secondary Chinese cities.

Although Canada did not have a resident mission, we did have a small office headed by an Honorary Consul, Chris Johnstone, who we had contracted to serve part-time for both consular and development work and to oversee a staff of two local Mongolians. Chris, who was son of an Ottawa colleague, former Deputy Minister Bob Johnstone, was married to a beautiful and charming local Mongolian, with whom he had two children, and his principal job was serving as the representative of a small Canadian gold exploration company. Chris had organized a reception and several dinners for my visit, and in this way I was able to meet foreign diplomats, the twenty or so Canadians resident in the city (mostly geologists, with a few teachers and a missionary or two), and a very interesting group of relatively internationalized Mongolians.

The ceremony for my presentation of credentials was a wonderful contrast to the rundown state of the physical plant of the Mongolian capital. I was met at my hotel by the Chief of Protocol and escorted in a large Mercedes Benz to the Great Khural, which housed the Presidential offices as well as the parliament. It was a cloudless and crisp morning, and the sky was deep blue (due to the city's 1300 metres of elevation) and all the colours were very vivid. We arrived in the columned courtyard of this imposing if somewhat dilapidated building to be met by a brilliantly dressed military band and honour guard, all reds and blues. After an excellent rendition of *O Canada*, and I could only presume a similarly fine Mongolian national anthem, the sergeant-major of the guard of honour, who stood about six-three and wielded a very long and sharp-looking sabre, marched up to me, evidently decided not to remove my head with a single swipe of his glistening sword, and invited me to inspect the guard, which numbered about twenty of the tallest and broadest soldiers imaginable, in dress uniforms and as rigid and polished as the finest Canadian or American honour guard. I marched their length, turn and return to the middle where I stopped and saluted them, as I had been instructed to do. To my salute they responded with a blood-curdling shout which I took to be a personal compliment, quickly calculating that to interpret as anything else could be bad for my health.

After the honour guard, I was escorted inside for a very simple presentation ceremony, handing my credentials to President Orchibat in a grand hall bedecked with Mongolian flags and huge paintings of the Mongolian steppes. The President then invited me to sit for the normal post-presentation discussion, which went on not for the scheduled thirty minutes but for more than an hour. Orchibat, who was a man about ten years my senior, had been President since the democratic revolution of 1990, first as the chosen leader of the parliament and then as the country's first popularly elected president. A Soviet-trained mining engineer, Orchibat was quite well informed about Canada, and told me that he wished to model Mongolia's resource extraction regime on Canada's and attract both Canadian and other foreign miners to help lift his country from its poverty. He also encouraged me to have the Canadian Government enlarge its development program, to this point limited to programs of the International Development Research Centre and Canada Fund projects, and to open a resident mission in Ulaan Baatar. This I was to do throughout my time in Beijing, since with the importance of the Canada-China relationship I simply did not have the time to visit Mongolia often enough to establish the sort of personal knowledge and relationships that an ambassador should have, but it was more than a decade later before Canada opened its Embassy in Ulaan Baatar.

The evening after my credentials presentation we were taken by the Deputy Foreign Minister to a performance of Mongolian music and dance, in anticipation of which I simply hoped I would not fall asleep. I was stunningly surprised. I had never before heard traditional Mongolian music, played on local two-string instruments similar to the Chinese *erhu*, but tuned to a western scale, and traditional flutes and reeded horns closer to clarinets than trumpets. The music was a lilting western-style orchestration of traditional songs and laments of the nomadic Mongolian people. I also was introduced to "throat singing", where men sang by vibrating their vocal chords so deeply in the throats that their mouths served only as a sound box, producing a deeply haunting sound, which had I not seen the singers would have thought was some unknown string instrument with a range slightly lower than the cello. The dancing was brilliant, with a mix of acrobatic dancing by young women to Cossack-like leather-booted squat dancing.

The rest of my three days in Ulaan Baatar was composed of virtually non-stop meetings with Prime Minister Enkhsaikhan and his Ministers. Enkhsaikhan and his Mongolian Democratic Union had only ten days before my visit defeated the Mongolian People's Revolutionary Party in the national parliamentary elections, which were held one year before

Presidential elections. This had been the first time a coalition of parties had defeated the MPRP, which had reformed itself from a quisling communist party into a democratic party in 1990 and had won both democratic election held since that time. Enkhsaikhan and his Ministers were very inexperienced and quite young, with an average age well short of forty years old, and were rather desperate for outside assistance, having proved that Mongolian democracy was working and now planning a tremendous program of shock therapy to move the country rapidly to a fully liberalized free market. As Canadian Ambassador I received a tremendous amount of supplication for enanced aid and for the establishment of a resident mission, and my diplomatically worded deflections about fiscal restraint at home and gradualism in the relationship went largely unheard. Irrespective of my own inclinations and sympathies, I knew that I had little hope of getting much attention in Ottawa for enhanced engagement with Mongolia, at least until our mining community was better established there, so I encouraged Enkhsaikhan to create an investment regime for natural resource extraction that would be attractive and stable, and offered to set up exchanges with the Canadian Department of Natural Resources and Canadian academics who had done work on comparative investment regimes. I did not know at this time that this would be a theme that would be replayed almost endlessly, and become very important to me well beyond my time as Ambassador.

After all my official meetings were finished I stayed an extra day, and we headed out of the city towards the east. What an extraordinary difference! After a few miles, the shantytowns gave way to a rolling steppe, with rugged hills on either side of a huge valley. The hills were mostly treeless, and curiously reminiscent for me of some of the geography of part of western Newfoundland or the highlands of Scotland. The people of the steppe, while evidently not that numerous, were everywhere visible, horseborne shepherds and travelers on the small Mongolian horses, even little children galloping across the valley heading perhaps home or to a neighbour's gher. And here we saw the ghers in the proper setting, scattered across the plain or up on the hillsides, generally in clusters of five or more, but occasionally alone. We ended up in the picturesque valley of Terelj, about an hour and a half out of Ulaan Baatar. There we found the clearest little river that I had ever seen in Asia, set at the centre of the valley in a mixed woods of birch and pine, very like many places in Canada. Trout were visible in the shadows of quiet pools, and the water was numbingly cold to cross which we did once on fallen logs and by taking off our footwear and rolling up our trousers and wading knee deep across fords of rounded stones in the shallows. Above the central river and woods rose Alpine-like meadows, with herds of sheep and goats being tended by hardy and sun-darkened Mongols on their beautiful small horses. Higher still were pine-clad hilltops, perhaps three or four hundred meters above the valley floor, themselves foothills to the more distant mountains of the Hinta range. We spent the afternoon walking and riding, and I was reminded what James Baker, Secretary of State under George H. W. Bush, confided in Gareth Evans and me when asked at a Manila ASEAN meeting why he visited Mongolia so often. Having publicly given the geo-strategic answer, he said quietly to us that he really came for the fine trout fishing and the hunting and the natural beauty of the Mongolian countryside. I now understood what he had been saying.

I went back to Mongolia about once a year as Ambassador, always a little frustrated because I could not dedicate more time and attention to the place, and constantly arguing with Ottawa for more political attention and for an eventual resident mission. In 1997, I made an autumn trip, which allowed me to meet the new President, Bagabandi, who had won the Presidential election that year, and spend some time with a more ensconced Enkhsaikhan. During that year and the next, an increasing number of Canadian mining companies were setting up shop, and there were more than a dozen active Canadian geologists in country, some employees of specific firms and some contracting their services of firms needing either expertise or independent resource reports for public filings. It was either during my 1997 or my 1998 visit that our Honourary Consul Chris Johnstone arrange a dinner for me to host any of the geologists in Ulaan Baatar at that time, during which I met a fellow called André Beaulieu, a tough back-country guy well into his sixties who was as entertaining a character as I had ever met, regaling us with amusing stories from a life spent in northern Canada and South Africa and the Congo. In 2000, the Embassy in Beijing received an emergency call from the locally-engaged consular clerk at our little office in Ulaan Baatar with the news that André had died of a massive heart attack. There was an additional problem in that when he died he was in the arms of a beautiful young Mongolian, who claimed that she was short a fee, substantial in local terms, for a full weekend's worth of services agreed upon in advance by the unfortunate André. In order to avoid embarrassment to the family, we quietly authorized a payment to the young woman, for somewhat less than she was requesting, from the consular division's budget for "incidental costs" and did not include it in the costs associated with shipping the remains back to Canada, which were in the normal course of things recovered from the family.

On my trip to Mongolia in the autumn of 1999, I brought Liani and our twin boys, Caleb having left that summer to join his sister at Trinity College School in Canada. Once my usual meetings with government ministers and officials were completed, including one with the then new Prime Minister, Amarjargal, who was the fifth incumbent of the position since I had become Ambassador three and a half years earlier, we travelled out to the National Park in Terelj, which the boys loved. They had a wonderful day riding horses with local children riding alongside, and climbing the huge and famous "Turtle Rock", a great granite about twenty metres high and fifty across that was shaped like the back of a turtle. We also walked along the streams of the birch forest, and had a traditional Mongolian lunch in a local gher.

In Ulaan Baatar we visited with Chris Johnstone a number of our Canada Fund projects, including a soup kitchen for the homeless run by the only Catholic order in the country, the nuns of the Sisters of Mercy. At the time, Ulaan Baatar was having a major problem with homeless children and youth, who had left their homes in the countryside or in smaller towns and come to Ulaan Baatar in the hopes of finding a better life. During the brutal winters of the coldest capital city in the world, with nighttime temperatures frequently below -35 degrees Celsius, the street children would sneak underground where they could sleep near the hot water pipes from the central power stations that were used to heat buildings and provide hot water throughout the city. This led to many accidents and ill-health, and the capacity of the city's rudimentary social service infrastructure was hopelessly insufficient to deal with the problem. In addition to funding the soup kitchens run by the Sisters of Mercy, we also funded a project brought to us by Montreal-based *Cirque du Soleil*, which was sourcing many of its young acrobats in Mongolia. The project was to fund the creation of small groups of child performers and a travelling school. The children were trained in juggling and acrobatics, and would travel from district to district performing for money, usually little more than enough to provide subsistence, but a far better life than sleeping in the underground tunnels. In addition, our funds were sufficient to have a couple of young twenty or twenty-five year olds stay with the little circus band and see to their basic needs and provide as much rudimentary teaching as they could. The band put on a performance just for us, and it was quite heart-warming to see how these young lives had been improved, although I wondered what they would end up doing once they reached adulthood. I later learned that at least a few made it into the real *Cirque du Soleil* troupe, and I can only hope that the others at least found some sort of sustainable employment.

CHAPTER 41

THE DEMOCRATIC PEOPLE'S REPUBLIC OF KOREA

• • • • • • • • • • •

While the Embassy in Beijing had been responsible for monitoring issues related to North Korea for some time, Canada along with most western countries had never formally recognized the regime in Pyongyang. In 1988, when Joe Clark was Secretary of State for External Affairs, Canada had made an effort to create a multilateral dialogue on Korean issues in much the same form as the Helsinki accords had broadened the East-West dialogue, with multiple tracks or "baskets" covering exchanges on everything from security to cultural exchanges and human rights. This was the North Pacific Cooperative Security Dialogue which was initially welcomed by South Koreans, the Chinese and the Soviets, but when the US Department of Defence determined that the Soviets might use such a dialogue to limit US naval dominance in the western Pacific, the US came firmly down against our proposal, the Japanese followed suit and the initiative was punted off onto an academic channel and effectively buried. Nonetheless, I and other Asianists in the Canadian Foreign Service had continued to argue that engaging Pyongyang on as many tracks as possible was strategically more likely to lead to a more open DPRK than continuing to treat it as a diplomatic pariah. We were not alone in our views or actions, as Britain, Australia and Italy all established diplomatic relations with North Korea at about the same time as we did.

Our collective shift in policy was welcomed by the South Korean Government, then led by President Kim Dae-jung, a dissident during the years of military government, and the first South Korean leader to visit Pyongyang, which he did in the summer of 2000. Kim's efforts to reduce tensions on the peninsula earned him the Nobel Peace Prize, and most western countries were keen to be supportive. Even the United States, long a hawk on Korean matters, supported Kim, with Ambassador Stephen Bosworth and Assistant Secretary of State Wendy Sherman responsible for what looked to be a fundamental redesign of American policy of substantially reduced troop levels in South Korea and food and other assistance for the North.

Throughout the 1990s and in spite of the lack of diplomatic relations, Canada had continually contributed wheat and other foodstuffs to quite regular campaigns of the World Food Program of the UN aimed at alleviating shortages in North Korea. In the early part of the decade I had met Catherine Bertini, head of the WFP, during a visit she made to Ottawa to drum up support for one such campaign, and since being appointed Ambassador in Beijing with responsibility for the DPRK, I had received her several times before and after her trips into the hermit kingdom. I was very sympathetic to the plight of the children in North Korea, and with the firm support of my Head of Aid, Henri-Paul Normandin, we had argued successfully with Ottawa for generous Canadian contribution to WFP appeals.

With the support of allies in departmental headquarters, and in the company of a number of likeminded countries like Britain, we decided during the first half of 2000 to establish diplomatic relations with North Korea. I held talks with the latter's ambassador to China to agree on the principle of establishing formal relations, paralleled by talks between our respective missions to the UN in New York, and once agreed we sent Political Counselor Sven Jurschewsky to Pyongyang to work out the modalities and timing for my trip and the formal presentation of credentials. I had originally hoped to go to Pyongyang before the end of the year, but the delay in the Prime Minister's big Team Canada trip to February resulted in it being deferred until after that visit. With me I brought both Sven Jurschewsky and Development Counselor Henri-Paul Normandin, as well as an accompanying journalist, Martin Cohen of the

Toronto Star. We also arranged to have a representative of the WFP meet us there as one of our objectives was to see where and how Canadian food aid was being distributed.

We flew from Beijing to Pyongyang on Air China, deplaned by old-fashioned stairway and were whisked into the city by a little band of foreign affairs officials. Contrary to what we had been told, we did not have our mobile telephones confiscated for the duration of our stay, but as we could discern no carrier nor receive a signal, we decided the oversight was probably not a particularly dangerous breach of North Korean security.

The drive into town was like going back in time to China or Eastern Europe of decades earlier. Aside from a few buses, there were almost no vehicles on the roads, and certainly no private cars. The architecture of the city was, on the other hand, quite handsome, with many of the government buildings finished on a European quasi-classical style. Some reminded me a bit of Ceausescu's florid style in Bucharest. In the distance we could see an enormous and very steep pyramid of a building, the more than 100-storey Ryugyong Hotel that the state had started to build in the mid-1980s. Construction had stopped just after the steel and concrete structure was topped-off, when financial support from the Soviet Union came to an abrupt end in 1990, and there were no windows or cladding on the building's skeleton whatsoever. It was supposed to have been the tallest hotel in the world, but now stood as a strange and rusting monument to North Korean hubris, a decrepit crane still towering from its more than 300 metre height.

There were also lots of real monuments, from the flame-topped Juche Tower (*juche* being the official ideology of the DPRK, a curious amalgam of self-reliance, militarism and glorification of Kim Il-Sung), to a great Arch of Triumph memorializing victory over the imperialists in the Korean War and, of course, a Reunification Arch memorializing an event to come. There were a lot of people on the streets, mostly walking or waiting for busses, and the quality of clothing and the lack of any evident levity or joy in the small groups gathered reminded me of a bleak Ingmar Bergman film. Walking around our hotel later in the day, with watchers always in tow, when we nodded in greeting at a passerby, we would elicit only averted eyes and sometimes a slight increase in pace to get further way from us quickly.

We stayed at the two-towered Koryo Hotel, built in the 1970s with perfectly adequate if outdated rooms and allegedly very up-to-date listening devices. On the evening of our arrival, a Vice Minister from the Foreign Ministry hosted a dinner for me in a state guesthouse, where the privations and shortages facing the country at large were absolutely not in evidence.

The following morning I met with the Chinese Ambassador to the DPRK, Wang Guozhang, whom I had known prior to his appointment when we were both dealing with APEC issues for our respective governments. I had always found him an open and cooperative diplomat, and so I had, prior to my trip, passed through the Chinese Ministry of Foreign Affairs a message that I would very much like to see him again and to benefit from his perspective on what was evolving in Pyongyang. He very kindly invited me to breakfast and gave me almost two hours of his time, accompanied by one of his senior officers. The picture they painted was not a pretty one. They described a leadership incapable of serious reform, paranoid about outside influences yet addicted to outside support, most of which of course came from China. He told me that he was very pleased countries like Britain and Canada were establishing diplomatic relations with the country, and said he concurred completely that the effort to broaden North Korea's engagement with western countries away from strictly North-South and DPRK-US axes should be pursued. He warned me, however, to anticipate frustration. The Chinese government, he explained, had made multiple and very high-level efforts to encourage Kim Jong Il to open up and begin the process of reform and had almost nothing to show for their efforts. Even Zhu Rongji had tried his best, touring Kim Jong Il around Shanghai, showing him the modern Pudong as an example of what reform and opening up could bring. He himself, Wang told me, tried constantly to persuade North Korean leaders to embark more bravely on a path of change, but that without a fundamental change of attitude at the very top, we could all expect the status quo, and the country to continue not only to slip relatively but absolutely as it became less self-sufficient in food. Ambassador Wang told me that he was quite frustrated but that he would be shortly going back to China for a month of home leave. He said he could not wait to put his feet back down on the soil of personal freedoms and real progress. This was the Ambassador of China speaking!

I presented my credentials later that morning to Kim Yong Nam, the President of the Presidium of the Supreme People's Assembly, who acted as the DPRK's Head of State for all formal functions. The formal Head of State was still President Kim Il Sung, who had been made "Eternal President" upon his death in 1994. When I became Ambassador, the Supreme Leader was Kim Il Sung's son, Kim Jong Il, (who was to become "Eternal General Secretary" of the Korean Workers Party upon his death in 2011). When it was emphasized to me by the Chief of Protocol that Kim Il Sung was still President, and that Kim Yong Nam would receive me "on behalf of the President", I was terribly tempted to ask which of Kim Yong Nam or Kim Jong Il was the better conversationalist or to suggest that Kim Il Sung's ongoing incumbency could well explain the current dynamism of the local economy, but my diplomatic side got the better of me and I refrained from saying anything. The actual ceremony for presenting my credentials was thus graced by neither a conversation with a real leader, as had been the case five years earlier with Jiang Zemin of China, nor the panache of the special Guard of Honour in Ulaan Baatar, as when I presented my credentials to President Orchibat of Mongolia. And the discussion that followed was not a conversation at all, with Kim Yong Nam simply spouting platitudes of North Korean ideology to the extent to which I was not sure he was in fact more than a mechanized dummy with a speaker inside. And he certainly gave no indication that he had any idea where Canada was.

The credentials ceremony left me in a very bad mood, and I was simply determined not to be abused by my diplomatic handlers. Nonetheless, they controlled my schedule and the next event was already set to be a visit to the Memorial Palace, where I was expected to pay my respects to The Great Leader, Kim Il Sung, still the President of the DPRK in spite of his unfortunate demise seven years earlier.

The Memorial Palace was a fantastic, grotesque statement about the country and its priorities. A huge, layered building of three levels in a Stalinist style bearing some similarity in form to Beijing's Great Hall of the People, it was perhaps four hundred metres long, colonnaded and clad in white marble. We parked outside the northeast corner of the huge square in front of the building, and were taken into an underground reception area, where we went through metal scanners and left keys and passports and non-functioning mobile phones in security bins to be picked up later. We then rode on long mechanized underground walkways to the building itself, and went up an elevator to start our tour. Before we entered the exhibits, we passed through a small airlock where jets of air blew dust off our clothes. Then we went from room to room, each dedicated to the life of the Great Leader. One room had the elongated Mercedes limousine in which he normally travelled up on a pedestal, another held his railway car through the window of which one could see the little desk at which he sat and wrote extraordinary works while touring his blessed country. As we passed from chamber to chamber I was reminded of the Christian twelve stations of the cross, and how extraordinarily like the worship of a monotheistic god or a millennial prophet this all was. One room held all of Kim Il Sung's medals and awards, some given by Stalin and all the merry band of communist dictators, quisling or otherwise. Husak, Honecker, Tito, Ceausescu, Castro, and a host of tin-pot dictators long forgotten, had all awarded Kim with medals, displayed alongside photographs of their meetings either in North Korea or abroad. And finally we were brought to the central hall where Kim Il Sung's preserved body lay. Before we entered this sacred chamber we went into a small ante-room which served as a point where museum officials could carefully control the numbers of people inside the memorial hall. There we were reminded not to speak when inside, and offered bunches of slightly off-colour plastic flowers to lay on the steps surrounding the elevated glass sarcophagus. Normal visitors could be seen paying for these rental flowers, which were occasionally gathered up and recycled back to the ante-room to be bought again and again. And around the pickled body there were weeping and a few kneeling visitors, distraught or overwhelmed in the presence of their god-like leader.

Just before we left the Memorial Palace, I was asked to sit at a desk and write and sign, not in a simple Visitor's Book, but in a very ornate and beautiful leather "Book of Condolences". As I sat, I asked myself what on earth could I possibly say that would not create a diplomatic incident and still keep my dignity after touring this outrageous monstrosity. With my North Korean handlers behind me, I wrote: "An extraordinary palace. I now finally understand the relationship between the leader Kim Il Sung and his people". The protocol officials all nodded gravely at this pithy comment, not of course understanding its possible double meaning.

The only really substantive and thoughtful meeting I had during my time in Pyongyang was with Foreign Minister Paek Nam Sun, who had been the face of a more engaged DPRK as it had made an effort to improve its relations with southeast Asian countries by becoming a dialogue partner with ASEAN, and as Canada and a few other western countries entered into formal diplomatic relations. Paek was reasonably well informed about Canadian strengths and said that the DPRK would welcome more Canadian activity in his country. He suggested in particular that his government would like support in the area of agricultural technology to adapt strains of Canadian hard wheat to the climate of the country, and he had been briefed to know that such a program would likely be carried out through IDRC. He also said that investment by Canadian mining firms would be welcome, and that special government-to-government agreements could be negotiated to ensure that their investments would be both secure and profitable.

In keeping with part of our mission's objectives, we spent more than a day visiting beneficiaries of the World Food Program's activities to which Canada had contributed quite generously. The first such visit was to a biscuit factory, which made wheat biscuits for distribution through the North Korean school system. The factory was completely legitimate, with great long mixing and processing machines, imported second hand from Europe, clearly doing what they were intended to do which was to make nutritious biscuits from high quality wheat with an array of vitamins and essential minerals added. It was run by an Italian expatriate who told us that he was receiving the supplies he needed, and that he was confident that the biscuits were indeed being widely distributed throughout the country's school system, as well as to hospitals. We were then taken to a primary school where we saw the biscuits being distributed, but it was clearly far from typical. The children were well dressed and clearly very well fed, and greeted us politely in Korean and a few words of English. The teachers were pretty young women, again well fed and well-dressed. When we asked to go to other, randomly selected schools, we were told that this would not be convenient, so we were left with not much to conclude about how deep into a society clearly in need our food aid was reaching. One member of our group was taken to a port some distance away to watch wheat being unloaded, but again that did not tell us very much. Most importantly, however, the WFP representative who came with us on these visits, told us that she had been able to visit many towns and villages which their program was intended to reach and she was reasonably certain the bulk of the food aid was in fact reaching the intended recipients.

At one point during our visit, after a particularly useless and propaganda laden meeting with a friendship group from the People's Assembly, the DPRK's pretence of a parliament, as we were being taken off to see another museum I decided I would try to wrest control of my schedule away from the protocol officials squiring us around. I said to them that I had heard that Pyongyang had a world-class hockey rink and I wanted to go and see it. At first they resisted with the usual phrase of "not convenient", at which point I dug in my heels and said that without such a visit, the remainder of their planned day would be "not convenient" to me, and I would spend the rest of the day walking around the city on my own. So they bent and took me to the ice skating centre, where we found the North Korean Women's national team in the middle of a practice. The young women had all the latest CCM hockey equipment and fine skates, and appeared reasonably talented. I asked my handlers to find me the largest pair of men's skates they could, and they produced a pair only a size or two too small. I squeezed my feet into them, having to take off my socks to have any chance of doing so, and went out on the ice with the national women's team, taking shots on their goalie and participating in passing drills. Once the players saw their coach, who spoke some English, chat with me and welcome me to participate, they were very good-natured and included me in their passing and shooting drills. Martin Cohen of the Toronto Star took pictures of me on the ice, still wearing my bow tie, and the front page of the following day's edition of his newspaper carried a photograph of me with one of the national team players.

We did of course get together with the handful of resident western diplomats, such as the Swedish and Czech Ambassadors, all of whom had useful perspectives on trends and developments a little different from the insights Ambassador Wang had shared with me, but on balance no one at all, not even a senior Chinese diplomat with years of effort, really saw deeply into the workings of the Korean Worker's Party or into the mind of Kim Jong Il.

I left Pyongyang with few regrets that I had not had more time there, and left the now established formal relationship, as relatively empty of substance as it was, for my successors to pursue. But I did feel as if we had taken a step forward towards some form of engagement, always in my view to be preferred to "shunning" the regimes we did not approve, and I felt that becoming an accredited Ambassador to Pyongyang completed a path I had started down almost fifteen years earlier when I encouraged Joe Clark to launch the effort to multilateralize our collective effort to bring North Korea out of its hostile isolation. Unfortunately, after the terrorist attack on the World Trade Center the following September, President George W. Bush included the DPRK in its famous speech on the "Axis of Evil", American policy switched from being supportive of South Korea's "Sunshine Policy" of cooperative engagement to opposing any aid or investment. The shift was to help snuff out the small flames of openness in Pyongyang and drive the regime back into sullen hostility. I spoke at a conference on North Korea at a conference at Cambridge University in Britain a year after I retired, well after 9/11 and the shift back to hawkishness by the US. Both Stephen Bosworth, who had left his post as Ambassador in Seoul and was now Principal of the Fletcher School of Law and Diplomacy at Tufts University, and Wendy Sherman, now an academic, also spoke at the conference, but neither criticized the Bush administration for torpedoing the Sunshine Policy. Privately I upbraided them and asked how they could remain silent when they work that they had done was being undone with such potentially dangerous long-term consequences. Their only answer was that following the World Trade Center attacks, America had to rally around its President. What a pity, I thought, and what a disappointment from intellectuals of a country with the greatest tradition in the world of free speech and open debate.

BOOK VII:

LIFE AFTER DIPLOMACY

CHAPTER 42

JUMPING INTO THE SEA

· · · · · · · · · · ·

In Japan, when a senior public servant retires from government and moves into the private sector, it is said that this is a "Descent into Heaven", implying both the high esteem in which bureaucrats are held and the much better life-style and income of business. In China, once officials have reached even a modestly senior level, such as Assistant Minister (equivalent to Assistant Secretary in the US or ADM in Canada), they are simply not permitted to leave the state system, although many of course end up shifting back and forth between government positions and executive positions in the big state-owned companies. For the few who do leave completely when they still can, they are said to "Xia Hai" or "Jump into the Sea". And that, in the summer of 2001, was exactly what I did.

The public service of Canada is not a very flexible working environment, and federal public service pensions are governed by a fairly strict set of rules. When I researched what it would mean for my pension to leave at the age of fifty, with twenty-five years of service, I discovered that I could defer the receipt of my pension until the age of sixty-five, following which I would be able to draw an annual stipend equal to a very small proportion of my final service salary. And if I left government after June 6th, 2001, I would have no choice except this, since pensions became "locked-in" on one's fiftieth birthday. I decided, therefore to withdraw my pension entirely and I retired officially on June 5th, the day before. The problem in doing so was that Government did not want the post of Ambassador vacant as early as the beginning of June, and so asked me to stay on as Ambassador through most of the summer, which I did, being paid under a special "Order-In-Council" which effectively meant that there was a new person, a non-public servant and no longer a member of the professional Foreign

Service, serving as Ambassador in Beijing. Chinese officials, my staff in the Embassy and diplomatic colleagues, even my family, somehow did not notice that there was an imposter in place, finding the bow-tied diplomat uncommonly similar to the professional Foreign Service type that had been serving as Canadian Head of Mission over the past five and a half years!

The plan I had worked out for the beginning of my time in the private sector was to establish a financial and market access consultancy with an American friend, Bill Krueger, who had been in Beijing for a few years and was CEO of XinDe, a joint venture between Siemens and CITIC focused on mobile communications. Bill wanted to broaden his interests and we set up a local firm which we called White Birch International, owned half by one of Bill's companies and half by a firm I had just established in the BVI called The Balloch Group. Bill was to be co-owner, operationally largely passive beyond helping to drum up clients and sharing in the financing, and I would build out the consultancy.

A year or two before my involvement with him, Bill Krueger had built out an office for XinDe in the China World complex on Jianguomenwai Dajie and had spared no expense in doing so. His designer had found extremely beautiful old Chinese doors for the main entrance, and lots of old Chinese furniture and ornamentation for the interior. He had taken a whole floor of the building but clearly did not need it, so we carved out an area, with a separate and far less fancy entrance, for White Birch. Initially the only formal employee I had was Wang Jine, who had served as my protocol assistant in the Embassy. She was terrific for maintaining my contacts with government officials, both at the central and provincial levels, as this is what she had been doing for me as Ambassador.

My biggest worry in starting off in business for the first time was whether I could actually find any clients. Through contacts and friends I spread the word about what I was doing, and after a month or so I received a call from a friend of a friend, whose Texas-based company felt that they needed to thoroughly rethink their China strategy and to strengthen their knowledge of what was going on in sectors of the Chinese economy of importance to them. After a number of calls and e-mail messages and my first formal proposal, the firm accepted the terms I offered and I had my very first client. I went home to Liani, pleased as punch, and told her not only did we have our first client but that it was a large reputable American firm that would help build our reputation. Unfortunately, this first client was ENRON, and just a very few months after they engaged us they blew up, leaving us with eighty-seven thousand dollars in unpaid fees. I was sent by the bankruptcy court the mandatory notification that all unsecured creditors received, and since I did believe I would ever get any money back, I personally filled out the claim forms rather than hiring a lawyer to do it. And then I sent it off to United States Bankruptcy Court #1, 1 Bowling Green, New York, New York, where it undoubtedly still sits at the bottom of a very large pile of contested claims, and will likely do so until my grandchildren are retired.

The two other significant engagements that I undertook under the White Birch umbrella were with a Canadian steel fabricator, ADF, which was looking to enter the Chinese market and build out a high quality fabrication facility, and with CIBC. The latter hired us to help them secure syndicate positions in the listing of major Chinese state-owned enterprises, then just beginning to list in Hong Kong with secondary listings (through what are called American Depository Receipts) in New York. The ADF contract allowed me to bring in my first professional staff member, Wang Jun (or Tanso as he called himself in English), and was an enjoyable file, since we had to travel around the country meeting potential partners and visiting steel fabricating shops. The CIBC file was my first direct experience with corruption in China. We made a strong and successful case for CIBC to be included in the syndicate listing the huge China Telecom, arguing that none of the lead banks had any Canadian distribution, and we secured a very small co-manager role with about a half of one percent of the syndicate's economics. When I pushed for a bigger role, I was visited in my office by someone who claimed to be advising the Chairman of China Telecom, and he said that there was a very simple way to increase the CIBC role and the commensurate economics, and that was to engage him on a commission basis, such that for every extra half-percent of the economics we would pay him one hundred thousand dollars, which he in turn use to "take care of" key decision makers inside the company. Neither I nor Warren Gilman, who had just taken over as head of CIBC in Asia, had any intention of engaging an agent on such terms, so CIBC ended up with a formal but virtually worthless position in the syndicate. This was the first time but far from the last that my refusal to pay bribes, usually requested through middlemen holding themselves out as agents, was to cost me business and revenues, and I learned much later that my reputation for "not understanding how to take care of people" meant that many people in the state-owned sector argued against my firm being hired.

By the spring of 2002 I began to feel that White Birch was not the right platform for me. My partner, Bill Krueger, was completely preoccupied with XinDe business and was contributing neither capital nor sweat to our shared firm, and he had a very different vision about how the company should evolve and the types of businesses it should get into. I took the family back to North America for our regular summer vacation, with the twins in hockey camp and the older children with summer jobs before family time in Jamestown, and I spent a lot of time just thinking through how to move forward, concluding in the end to dissolve my partnership with Krueger.

Once back in China I was courted by a number of would-be partners, including a couple of small New York based investment banks, but after meeting the principals involved and doing some due diligence, I decided to set up entirely on my own. In this I received huge encouragement from Liani, who pointed out that it was in fact my reputation and my execution that had led to our early engagements and successes. I also received support from Nereida Flannery, a young woman who had been running the local office of the Canada China Business Council, who said that she would like to come and work with me to help build out a business. In the autumn of 2002, we established a wholly-owned subsidiary of The Balloch Group and to use that name in our business, with four salaried employees (Nereida, who also became an equity-owning partner, Tanso Wang, Wang Jine and driver Liu Dong) with Liani serving as accountant and comptroller.

Shortly after "jumping into the sea" I also started being involved in the business world beyond starting my own firm. I was approached by André Desmarais and the board of the Canada China Business Council, and I was pleased to agree to a five year term as its President, replacing the long-serving Jack Austin. I also joined a couple of public company boards. The first of these was a mobile software company with a proprietary input system for Chinese and other ideographic languages called Zi Corporation, founded by a Calgary entrepreneur named Michael Lobsinger. Then in early 2002 Robert Friedland asked me to join the board of his newly created energy company, Ivanhoe Energy and I did so. My CCBC work and my board participation gave me additional interaction with the business community, and helped me start to weave a network of business professionals who over the years were to provide much good advice and support as I built out my own business.

CHAPTER 43

THE BALLOCH GROUP

• • • • • • • • • • •

Once we had decided to go it alone, we developed a medium term vision for The Balloch Group (quickly known as TBG) which was to use transactional market entry contracts to begin building out a proper financial consultancy that would help with the financing of incoming businesses and joint ventures, and then gradually develop the capacity to help Chinese firms with their international objectives, from listing on North American stock exchanges to investing abroad.

One of TBG's first new engagements as an independent firm grew out of a discussion that I had with Robert Friedland. Robert had bought the exploration rights to a tract of land in the southern Gobi Desert from Rio Tinto some years earlier, believing a local geologist that Rio was wrong in concluding that a surface outcropping of oxidized copper ore was a stranded deposit of little value. Rio had drilled a few exploration holes in the vicinity of the outcropping, found little of interest and abandoned the project. Robert, always determined, had believed the local lore and had organized a very intensive drilling program. By 2002 it was already firmly established and independently confirmed that Ivanhoe Mines' Oyu Tolgoi (Turquoise Hill) deposit was significant enough to be commercially exploited on a large scale. (Continued work over the next few years would confirm it as the world's largest as yet undeveloped copper deposit.) I suggested to Robert that he should consider using Chinese contractors and sourcing a maximum amount of goods and services from China to reduce the eventual costs of building the mine. Earlier in the year I had been to the large Jinchuan nickel mine in Gansu, and had been enormously impressed with a brand new flotation plant that had been built by a local contractor at less than half the cost of a similar plant in Canada or

Australia. Robert then engaged us to do a study of the potential impact on capital costs of what we called the "China Discount Factor". To carry out the study, I brought on staff Tim Sun, a young professional with a mining engineering degree from Queen's University in Canada. Tim did such a good job that one of the Ivanhoe directors, Gordon Toll, approached me and asked if I would object if Ivanhoe offered Tim a full-time position. He said that the company still wished to engage our services, but as they moved the sourcing work in-house they would like me to concentrate on relations with the Mongolian government and parliament. The major focus of this work was the negotiations of what was called a "Stability Agreement", which was intended to be an agreement between the company and the government on the long-term fiscal and royalty regime that would govern the mine's operation. Parliament would be involved because the company needed the agreement to be passed as a law over-riding existing statutes or exempting the company from them in key areas, and making more difficult the predictable future efforts to modify the terms of the agreement. This work brought me back to Mongolia again on a very regular basis, and also justified the hiring of a young Mongolian woman, Ariunaa Batbold, a graduate of Dartmouth College who had been working for Bain Consulting in Texas prior to moving to Beijing to be with her Chinese husband.

As I spent more time in Ulaan Baatar I began to see other opportunities for financial advisory work, particularly in the mining sector, and I found that one of the small Mongolian Banks, Anod Bank, had been trying to build out an investment banking team with only marginal success. I approached them and proposed that they allow me to take that team and create an independent investment bank, jointly owned by Anod and a newly layered-in parent company of TBG, which we called The Balloch Investment Group, or TBIG. The name we chose for the bank was Mongolian International Capital Corporation, or MICC, a name shamelessly modeled after CICC, China's first domestic investment bank established a decade earlier by CITIC and Morgan Stanley. I became MICC's Chairman and we hired the team leader of Anod's investment banking group as President. Achit

Erdene had studied in the US at Middlebury and Tufts and was a very smart young man, and most importantly seemed to have a high degree of integrity, a quality somewhat rare in Mongolian business. I would eventually transfer Ariunaa to MICC as Vice President where she stayed for a couple of years before heading back to the US to complete her immigration and start a family.

I had visited Ulaan Baatar about once a year as Ambassador, but working there in business was very different, and gave me a much broader exposure to the local business and political community. It was a very tough environment, in which business sometimes turned violent as would-be oligarchs tangled with each other, some the beneficiaries of buying state assets cheaply in the privatization process that had been rushed through in the early 1990s just as in Russia and most of the former Soviet republics. One weekend I was staying over in Mongolia and went out with the Chairman of Anod Bank and his family to climb a small mountain and have a picnic. It was a beautiful early summer day and the pine woods were full of blossoms and lovely little streams. When we got to the top of the mountain, the Chairman collapsed on a blanket, exhausted from the long walk, and out of his pocket fell a huge pistol. The drivers of our two cars were also carrying weapons, and walked up the hill with us as bodyguards.

The politicians of Mongolia, whose support Ivanhoe needed for its Stability Agreement, were as tough and difficult as the businessmen, and in fact were often the same people. There was absolutely no concept of conflict of interest in Mongolia, and as soon as anyone held any power they seemed to use it to further their own business interests. All the studies Ivanhoe had conducted suggested that the cost of developing the Oyu Tolgoi copper-gold deposit would be very high, somewhere between six and ten billion dollars. Mongolian politicians tended to ignore the fact that this money would have to come from the international capital markets where reasonable returns and manageable risk would be key to opening wallets. Instead, they argued alternatively that the majority of the project should be owned by the Mongolian Government through a "free carry" and that the project should raise funds through a listing on the local Mongolian stock exchange, whose total liquidity only measured in the tens of millions. The four-year Mongolian election cycle had parliamentary and presidential elections offset by a year, which meant that there was effectively at best a two year period when an election campaign was not underway. Worse, in the elections during much of the first decade of this century, no single party won a majority, leading to fragile coalition governments in which one or another party would always be trying to play a populist card of national ownership. With the Oyu Tolgoi project being by far the largest project in the country, the fact that it alone would drive a double-digit increase in the GDP of the country for many years was overlooked in constant cries that foreigners were walking away with resources that belonged to the Mongolian people.

In the early autumn of 2003 I was in Ulaan Baatar with Ivanhoe Chairman Robert Friedland, and during one of our meetings State Secretary of Finance Khurelbaatar asked for Ivanhoe's assistance in raising funds to help Mongolia pay off its Soviet-era Ruble-denominated date. Two years earlier, the Russian Government of Prime Minister Mikhail Kasyonov had offered Mongolia a very generous deal, in which more than 90% of the debt built up over decades of Soviet domination could be retired for a one-time payment of about $250 million. The term of the deal would expire at the end of the year, and Vladimir Putin had made it clear that he was not a supporter of such a generous arrangement. The risk was that Russia would exact a much higher payment, possible in the form of access to Mongolian mineral resources if the agreement expired without settlement. Khurelbaatar made the request almost in passing, and Robert simply responded that we would do what we could, and the conversation went on to other matters. However, in late November when I was in Ulaan Baatar on my own, Khurelbaatar approached me directly and said that the government could see its way to coming up with about $150 million but that it would be short the amount required by the Russians, who had made clear that there would be no extension. He asked whether Ivanhoe could lend Mongolia the remainder, which was roughly $100 million. I immediately called Robert and told him that the request made several months earlier was now a very serious plea for help. A sovereign state borrowing from a private corporation was virtually unheard of, but Robert realized that Ivanhoe really had no choice but to help. He asked me to push back with Khurelbaatar on the amount, which I did, reducing the request to $50 million by squeezing more from government reserves. Robert then arranged a small equity raise in the capital markets and obtained his board's agreement for a $50 million facility, which I spent much of December in Mongolia negotiating in the form of a special bond, bearing a 3% interest rate, with a three-year maturity. This was a thrilling success, and the Mongolian Government was deeply appreciative, since the Soviet-era debt was paid off at extremely beneficial terms, and Mongolia could approach the future without a heavy albatross around its neck. Even this good will, however, did not last long, and soon half the politicians in Mongolia were accusing Ivanhoe of "bribing" Mongolia for the purpose of obtaining concessions in the stability agreement negotiations. In Mongolia, no good deed ever seemed to go unpunished!

Shortly after negotiating the $50 million bond, Robert asked me to join the board of Ivanhoe Mines, which I was happy to do, even though it meant that Ivanhoe could no longer be a client of TBG. Nonetheless, that began a most interesting seven year stint as an Ivanhoe Mines director, which ended only as Rio Tinto began its takeover of the firm in 2011. The board was a terrific one and I was to develop friendships with some fascinating people with whom I remained connected for years thereafter.

The relationship between TBG and CIBC began with a finder's agreement under which we had secured CIBC's participation in the listings of China Telecom, Air China and a few other transactions, and then in 2004 it moved to a new level. The then Chairman and CEO of the bank, John Hunkin, and Don Lindsay, the CEO of CIBC World Markets, the investment banking division, were planning a trip to China and Hong Kong as part of a strategic review of the bank's approach to China, and Warren Gilman asked me to prepare an analysis of options. We produced a four-volume review of the opportunities and choices in all areas of financial services, from straight commercial banking through a minority investment in a Chinese bank to fund management and trust company joint ventures. Although CIBC decided in the end not to take up any of our recommendations to make a significant investment in a partnership with a Chinese institution, Don and I hit it off well and he asked if I would consider letting CIBC take a small interest in TBG in return for acting as their agent and corporate finance arm in China. We concluded an agreement several months later, and Nereida and I hired a few more staff and organized a small capital markets group under Wen Bo, an MBA from the Richard Ivey Business School, to focus on supporting CIBC in its efforts to win listings business for its New York and Toronto operations.

During John Hunkin's visit to Beijing, during which I was trying to persuade him and the senior CIBC team to take China more seriously and consider establishing a substantial presence, I arranged for Hunkin to be received by my old friend Zeng Peiyan, who was by this time a Vice Premier. We had an excellent meeting with Zeng, who was asked by Hunkin how the Chinese government could cope financially with its huge obligations to its people in the areas of medical care and free education. Zeng thought for a moment and then responded, "We would love to be as socialist as Canada, but we cannot afford it".

Between the beginning of our formal relationship with CIBC and the financial crisis in 2008, our listings business blossomed. Although we obtained a lead banker position in only a few deals, we participated in roughly forty syndicates, mostly for NSDAQ listings, and positioned CIBC as one of the leading mid-market China players on Wall Street. This was a very busy time for Chinese firms in the US market, and the activity attracted a lot of competition. At one end were the bulge bracket banks, like Goldman Sachs and Deutsche Bank and JPMorgan, who initially eschewed the smaller listings, but as the flow of large Chinese state-owned listings started to thin, they started to come down into smaller territory and compete with us. At the other end of the market were the smaller and very aggressive firms, like Roth, Piper Jaffray, and Rodman and Renshaw. Some of them would take Chinese firms public through back-door listings, using US shell companies and reverse takeovers, sometimes first to the OTC market before graduating to a major exchange. This generally meant that the thorough vetting and due diligence process that was required for a full IPO was avoided, and the result of course was that many firms turned out to be shadows of what their public documents claimed, with falsified financial and other records. We were approached by many firms that wanted to go down this back-door route, but I established a very firm policy in TBG that we would not work with any firm in which we did not have complete confidence in their financials and their management.

In the early years the work we did with the CIBC US capital markets group was very good for TBG. It helped establish us in the market and gave us credibility that would have taken us longer to build by ourselves. But as time went by and the CIBC team in Hong Kong grew stronger, the inevitable stresses of an unevenly aligned relationship started to show. Investment bankers from the CIBC offices in Hong Kong and Singapore would come into China and try to source deals that did not involve TBG so that they would not have to share fees with us. In addition, the interest in China at the senior most levels in CIBC dissipated very quickly after Don Lindsay left to become CEO of Teck Mining, and Gerry McGaughey, a skeptic about sustained growth in China, replaced John Hunkin as Chairman and CEO. Initiatives that Don and I had planned, such as a TBG-CIBC co-branded monthly China newsletter, went nowhere, although I was still invited to participate in CIBC conferences and CEO roundtables and other events from time to time. But there was no doubt in my mind that the relationship between us would either have to move in the direction of greater integration or be broken off.

From our very beginning in TBG we had a plan to position ourselves in the natural resource sector. It was clear to me that Chinese growth was going to require vast amounts of virtually every mineral, from iron ore and metallurgical coal, to copper and nickel, to precious metals and rare earths.

We did an internal study on the amounts of various metals China would likely consume over the coming quarter century and what percentage of this demand it could supply itself. Our conclusion was that the world had not yet realized how large China's import requirements would likely become, and that in many commodities these requirements would seriously stress global supply. I also believed that China would begin to invest abroad in a very major way to secure the strategic resources it would need to feed its growth, and that platitudes from senior executives of international mining and trading firms about secure supplies being available on the international commodity market would carry no weight with the Chinese. In order to position ourselves in the mining sector, we teamed up with a German-Chinese joint-venture exhibition company and offered the Chinese Ministry of Land and Resources (MLR) to internationalize a very small mining conference that they hosted every year. In the early years of the decade it had been held in Kunming, which we knew was not an ideal place to attract substantive international attendance, so the offer we made late in 2003 included a move to Beijing. MLR agreed to our proposal, and we took over the conference, rebranding the China International Mining Conference and Exhibition as "China Mining" and holding our first such event in 2004. TBG was responsible for the conference and all the international marketing, while our German partners were in charge of the exhibition.

We built China Mining into a truly first class event, growing from the 300 or so mostly Chinese attendees at the 2003 conference before we took it over to over 3000 attendees, the majority being foreign, in 2008, the last year we organized it. It became a very large undertaking, requiring a full time team that would swell in the autumn as the conference approached. Marketing it around the world involved building partnerships with other major mining conferences, particularly the annual Prospectors and Developers Conference in Toronto and the Diggers And Dealers conference held every August in Kalgourlie, Western Australia. I and other staff members, generally Nereida or Peter Fritz, who joined us in 2005, would attend these events both to market our own services and to promote China

Mining. As the event itself approached each year, we would draw in dozens of young volunteer hosts and hostesses from local universities or mining institutes, since managing the registration and handling of thousands of attendees was a huge task. We made a little money from China Mining in the first year, and did a little better in each subsequent year, but more importantly it played a tremendous role in branding TBG in the mining space, both domestically and internationally. In 2009 the government decided to move China Mining to Tianjin as part of the efforts being made to bring more international events to that city, and the city itself took over the organizational responsibilities. MLR offered us a subcontracting role, but by this time I felt that we had exacted all the benefit we were likely to derive from the conference and I also believed the move to Tianjin would reduce its draw to foreign participants, so I declined the offer. Furthermore, by this time we had had a falling out with our German partner, whose local Chinese general manager appeared to have been evading taxes and possibly engaging in other highly questionable practices, so we gently closed that chapter in our corporate story.

As the TBG team became stronger, and I myself became more at ease in my new investment banking skin, we also found that we were capable of executing substantial deals on our own, without the involvement of CIBC. Nereida Flannery led a series of small acquisitions in central Asia for Zijin Mining, a private company based in Xiamen, and I became quite close to the management of state-owned Wuhan Iron and Steel (WISCO), one of China's largest steel-makers. The first transaction we did with WISCO was acting for Wire Rope Corporation of America, who hired us to help them establish in the Chinese market. Their original idea was to find a small wire rope factory to buy, but I persuaded them that teaming up with a large upstream supplier with a China-wide reach might make more sense. We finally selected WISCO as the best partner for what turned out to be a $100 million joint venture that became the most advanced wire rope manufacturer in Asia.

Success in getting the wire rope joint venture launched resulted in WISCO's Chairman, Deng Qilin, asking me to help them find new sources of iron ore. We looked at opportunities in many countries and finally ended up looking more closely at various projects in the Labrador trough that runs north of Sept Isles along the Québec-Labrador border. The most exciting near-production project was owned by Consolidated Thompson, whose Chairman was my old friend Brian Tobin, former federal minister and Premier of Newfoundland. I approached Brian and their CEO, Richard Quesnel, and we began a lengthy negotiations that culminated in a complicated deal in which WISCO became a 20% shareholder in Consolidated Thompson as well as the co-owner of a project company developing the Bloom Lake deposit, initially scheduled to begin producing eight million tons of ore annually by 2009. In addition, WISCO had options on future expansion and other projects, and an off-take right to a larger proportion of the iron ore produced than their shareholding would suggest. The negotiations were very difficult because of the structure and a complicated pricing formula, but mostly because of the cultural chasm between the two firms, and there were several times when I thought they were doomed to fail. On Christmas Eve of 2005, the lead negotiator for WISCO, a senior Vice President, agreed to a deal with Richard Quesnel and we went to meet Chairman Deng for more or less a celebratory meeting. Deng walked into the meeting and said that his Vice President had had no authority to agree to the price we had settled on, and that his final offer was some twenty million dollars less. Everyone was speechless, and when Consolidated Thompson's financial advisor tried to engage Deng in negotiating, the latter stood up and left the room, never to return. It was almost two months later before I was able get the two sides together again, and this time had them negotiate by video conference, with me sometimes on the Wuhan end of the conference and sometimes on the Canada end, nudging and cajoling the two sides to a final deal. We finally got there, after one marathon 26-hour session with a video link open between Montreal and Wuhan, over which Brian Tobin and others could see a half dozen WISCO representatives sprawled on tables and the floor, sound asleep. But we go to where we needed to get and the deal turned out to be a great deal for both sides. When Consolidated Thompson was taken over by Cliffs Resources some years later, WICO made a $600 million profit on its shareholding in the listed company, and still kept its ownership at the project level and all its off-take rights. China's powerful National Development and Reform Commission was to publicly hold out the investment as the most successful overseas investment of any state-owned enterprise for that year, which of course had a wonderful impact on our reputation.

The most enjoyable part of the CIBC relationship was working on larger natural resource deals with Warren Gilman in Hong Kong and Neil Johnson in Sydney. Some time after our successful Consolidated Thompson deal, which had irritated CIBC headquarters because we had not brought their Toronto team into the deal, Neil called me suggesting that we take a look at a very large metallurgical coal opportunity in Mozambique, owned by Riversdale Mining of Australia. WISCO was at the time quite desperate for high quality coking coal and were very interested, so signed TBG up to assist them in a transaction that was to be structured quite like the one we had negotiated for them in Canada. Neil represented Riversdale. This resulted in a wonderful trip with our respective clients to Maputo and some five hundred kilometres up the Zambezi River to Tete, where Riversdale's huge holdings were. The biggest challenge of the project was going to be not the mining, which was a quite straightforward open pit, but the logistics of getting the coal to the coast. Our due diligence had us flying a small plane along an old colonial rail line from Tete across the southern finger of Malawi to Nacala, Mozambique's northern deep-water port. Seeing this arid and terribly poor part of Africa from only a few hundred metres up was fantastic, but left a deep impression of how far back in time economic development in this part of Africa was. Near the big coal deposits there were lots of little villages, with mud huts less than two metres tall as the standard dwellings, lots of poorly dressed children playing in the sandy soil, and toothless older people of absolutely indeterminable age lounging on old chairs or squatting at the edge of tiny gardens. At the end of our visit, Neil and I flew back together on a private plane to Johannesburg, a first time in South Africa for me, and I found the rolling countryside around the city to be fabulously beautiful. I could see why the early Dutch and later English settlers had been so attracted to the place.

The WISCO-Riversdale negotiations were even more difficult than the Consolidated Thompson ones, with Michael O'Keefe, Chairman of the Australian company as mercurial and obdurate as Chairman Deng Qilin. But Neil and I kept grinding in sessions in Wuhan, Sydney, Shanghai and Hong Kong, and finally were a hairs-breadth from a final deal when Rio Tinto made an unsolicited offer (something we had constantly been warning WISCO about) for one hundred percent of Riversdale at an attractive premium to its market price. Although I tried to persuade Deng Qilin that we could work out he same deal with Rio that we had negotiated with Riversdale, the notion of being in partnership with arch-enemy Rio was unthinkable for him and the deal died.

WISCO, like all major state-owned enterprises with headquarters elsewhere in the country, maintained a representative office in Beijing. In WISCO's case this was a beautiful courtyard home, renovated such that the central courtyard was excavated to an extra sub-ground level, allowing a two floor atrium around offices built in very traditional Beijing architecture. In November of 2007 I was having dinner there with Chairman Deng Qilin and Vice President Liu Xinquan immediately after receiving an e-mail from Neil Johnson advising me that BHP was about to announce a friendly takeover of rival Rio Tinto. I told Deng and Liu the impending news and said that I thought Chinese reaction would be very negative to more than 40% of global seaborne iron ore and a similar percentage of traded metallurgical coal being in the hands of a single firm. Deng, who at the time was serving as Chairman of the China Iron and Steel Association, sprung from his seat and called first the chairman of BaoSteel and then the chairman of Anshan Steel, the two other giant steel groups. They were all close to apoplectic and would translate their worries over the oligopolistic control over vital inputs for Chinese growth into vehement Chinese government opposition to the deal. The deal eventually died in the middle of the financial crisis, by which time the aluminium firm Chalco had purchased on the open market a small minority stake in Rio in the mistaken belief that China could use that stake to influence the deal, losing tens of millions of dollars in the process.

Beginning in the early days of TBG, one of the sidelines to our transactional business I pursued, largely to compensate for the lumpy and somewhat unpredictable flow of advisory fees, were personal briefings of North American corporate boards of management teams. In late 2003 I was approached by the Vancouver-based Methanex and asked to brief their global Executive Leadership Team at its annual retreat, being held that year at the Boulders Resort in Arizona. Several months after doing so, I was approached by the Methanex Board and asked if I would consider joining as a director. I did so, and began an association that was to become one of the real pleasures of my post-government life. The firm was blessed with visionary leadership, a great management team, which worked phenomenally well together, and a delightful group of fellow board members.

As the decade progressed so did TBG. Our capital markets work, pursued in cooperation with CIBC, was complemented by a growing business in international mergers and acquisitions and private placements. We arranged funding for a growing Beijing manufacturer of modern aluminium doors and windows, riding the crest of the exploding construction market. We funded a Wuhan based maker of biodegradable plastics and a Nanjing biotechnology firm, among others. I was too busy to participate in all deals, but I would try to make myself available for critical inflection points of deal acquisition or when needed in negotiations. By the end of 2007 we were really firing on all cylinders, and had opened offices in Shanghai and New York, as well as Wuhan to handle the relationship with WISCO and our other clients in central China. In 2008, and again in 2009, TBG was ranked by China Venture, a research consultancy, as the Top Boutique Investment Bank in China, having ranked in the top five in the previous two years.

In 2005 we were doing a fundraising for a Chinese ski resort and I was introduced to Jamie Dingman of the Shipston Group, who was clearly uninterested in what we were pitching but who expressed an interest in learning more about what we were doing in China. Shipston was a private investment office, active in many parts of the world, investing for Mike Dingman and his family. Mike had been a very successful American banker and then industrialist, had been a member of the boards of both the Ford Motor Company and Time Warner, and then an active investor in the early years of the post-Soviet Russia and eastern Europe. At the time we met he was very interested in expanding his investments in China, and he and his long-time investment partner Frank Mosier of the Moscow-based Kazimir Group, offered in 2006 to take a small stake in TBIG, which I accepted. Their purpose was to find opportunities in which Shipston could invest, either alongside us or on their own, and over the ensuing five years made a number of such investments. Mike and his wife Betsy were delightful hosts to Liani and me, and to several of our Chinese friends and would-be partners, both at their home in the Bahamas and in their summer home in New Hampshire.

Several years into our relationship with Shipston, one very large project on which I worked with them, and with Jamie in particular, was an effort to buy Volvo from Ford when the latter put Volvo up for sale during the global financial crisis. Shipston assembled a great team of financial and industry specialists, including Paul Meister of Fischer Scientific in the first category, and the former head of Ford's global production team, Shamel Rushwin, in the latter. My role initially was to manage the China angle since it was clear to us all that a successful future for Volvo had to include a vastly expanded production in China and annual sales there in multiples of their paltry ten or fifteen thousand units that they were achieving at the time, but I gradually became involved in pretty well all of the consortium's efforts. The concept we had was not to sell Volvo to a Chinese group but to buy it as a global consortium and then to work out a very substantial production arrangement in China with a local partner. We travelled back and forth to Gothenburg and Stockholm, we met with Swedish pension funds and investment houses, we met with Ford in London and Detroit, and we worked out potential post-purchase partnerships with Chinese automakers. Mike Dingman and Paul Meister brought in a team from Goldman Sachs with whom they had worked closely in the past, as our key financial advisor, and we made a full and formal offer for the company. It was, unfortunately, several hundred million dollars less than offered by Geely Automobile of Hangzhou, who offered a price that our consortium simply could not justify. I found it particularly galling that the Geely offer was partially financed by our financial advisor Goldman Sachs, who explained away this seemingly stunning conflict of interest as the investment banking and the direct investment arms of Goldmans being quite separate from each other. Geely closed their deal with Ford in March of 2010, and we retreated from the field. And as we did, I was reminded on the old 1950s song that ended with the line: "We may be fighting a losing battle, but having one hell of a time trying to win".

In late 2006 I hosted a dinner in Beijing for a visiting delegation from the Canadian Council of Chief Executives (formerly the Business Council on National Issues, with which I had dealt extensively both in my last two Ottawa-based jobs and as Ambassador). Included in the twenty-five or so visiting CEOs was a sub-group of top executives from the oil patch, which provided my a great opportunity to get to know some of the oil and gas elite in Calgary and to strengthen my relationships with the heads of the major Chinese SOEs. Also included in the group were some CEOs from domestic Canadian sectors I had had very little familiarity with, including retail and real estate. From the latter sector, Gary Whitelaw of Bentall Capital and I got into a conversation about the Chinese real estate market, about which I was very bullish. This led over the following months to an agreement to set up a $200 million Chinese residential real estate fund, in which Bentall and TBIG would be majority and minority partners respectively in the General Partnership. SunLife of Canada, Canada Pension Plan Investment Board and SITQ, one of the real estate subsidiaries of the Caisse de Dépot et Placement du Québec (CDP) came in as limited partners. Unfortunately, in negotiating the entry of the three large limited partners, Gary had felt he had to agree to give each of them a veto over any final investment decision. We put together a local fund management team composed of Canadian professionals sent over from Bentall Capital, and a local GM who had worked in part of the Li Kashing real estate empire. The team spent the next two years looking for projects and made only one substantial investment, in Jilin City in the northeastern province of the same name, before the global financial crisis and a substantial retreat from risk caused both our principal limited partners and Gary Whitelaw himself to decide to withdraw their commitments and to wind up the fund. Neither Bentall nor our LPs ever really had the risk appetite needed for real estate investment in China, and their veto power turned out to be a fatal flaw for the fund's success. The LPs could not reach unanimous agreement on, and therefore turned down, two particularly attractive opportunities for which I had argued strenuously. The first was in Dalian with Yida, a large real estate developer run by a very close friend of mine, Sun Yinhuan, who was willing, largely because of our friendship, to allow us to invest alongside him in a beautiful high-end development. The project eventually went ahead without a contribution from our fund (Yida was by no means short of funds itself), and produced more than a 40% rate of return. The second project that I could not get approved by our investors was in Wuhan, again in a residential project developed by another friend of mine, You Shouben, which in a mirror of the Dalian case went on to earn fabulous returns. My friendships with both Sun Yinhuan and You Shouben survived the failed courtships, however, and I would go on to continue helping the former with some of his investments and to invest myself in projects of the latter.

Not all TBG's investment banking deals were successful, of course, some ending with a whimper and one or two with a big bang. The biggest bang was a mining deal which began in the spring of 2008 and played out as the global financial crisis unfolded in the late summer and autumn. We were hired by a Chinese investment group called Tinpo Holdings, put together for the purpose, to acquire a Canadian listed company named Western Prospectors, which had rights to a very rich uranium deposit in

Mongolia. The Chinese group was composed of several businessmen and a former Deutsche Bank investment banker, named Chen Yunfei, who was now acting as a principal. I represented Tinpo and relied heavily on the credentials of Chen with respect to the group's *bona fides*, although I did ensure through bank references that the investors behind Tinpo had sufficient funds to make such an acquisition. I approached both the CEO and the Chairman of Western Prospectors, and began a negotiation which concluded with a Board supported agreement to acquire the entire firm for $75 million. As it was a public company, the offer had to be put to shareholders, who were asked to tender their shares by a certain date in the early autumn, at which point Tinpo was obligated to "take up and pay". About a week before the take-up and pay date, Chen Yunfei called me to say that his partners were getting cold feet and that they wanted to find an excuse to withdraw the offer, suggesting that we claim that a statement made a Mongolian cabinet minister on the possible nationalization of all uranium holdings as a "Material Adverse Change", known as a "MAC". I told Chen that this would not wash, and checked with legal counsel in Toronto who unequivocally confirmed my views. Chen and his partners insisted, however, and on the day of closing we had the group's counsel file a withdrawal on the basis of the questionable MAC. What had really happened was that two of the partners behind Tinpo had withdrawn their funds and the company simply no longer had enough money to buy the shares. Over the next few weeks, we tried to put the deal back together through seeking participation from investment funds, but it was a time of great turmoil in the financial markets and we were unable to do so. The upshot was that the board of Western Prospectors filed a lawsuit against Tinpo and its investors, and against TBG and me personally, for the full amount of the $75 million plus damages. This was not the best day in my investment-banking career. I hired a superb litigator from Toronto, Clifford Lax, to represent me and he eventually managed to get the claims against me withdrawn, and a year later Western Prospectors was bought be the Chinese National Nuclear Corporation. As an epilogue to this sorry story, the Mongolian Government did eventually initiate steps to nationalize the deposit, along a nearby deposit owned by a Canadian-Russian joint venture named Khan Resources, and the whole dispute moved to highest level in the unending Mongolia-China hate-love relationship.

The global financial crisis also produced opportunities for TBG that would have never come our way in more stable times. In early October of 2008, I received a call from Gislain Parent, the CFO of the Caisse de Dépot et Placement du Québec (CDP). I had spent a day with the Executive Management Committee and Board of Directors of CDP three years earlier to discuss opportunities in China. Through that, through CDP's investment in the Bentall-Balloch real estate fund, and through studies that TBG had done for them, I had established a very good relationship with CDP's CEO Henri-Paul Rousseau and his senior management team. Parent told me that Rousseau wanted to know whether I thought there might be some way to approach Chinese lenders to provide some short-term financing to cover a liquidity problem that they were facing given a huge fall in market value of its portfolio. When I asked how large the problem was and how much was needed to fix it, Parent said that the minimum needed was $3 billion although a somewhat larger cushion would be welcome. I told him I would call him back. I called two or three friends in Chinese financial institutions, including Gao Xiqing at China Investment Corp (CIC). Gao was the only one who understood the need. When I suggested that the CDP portfolio of corporate bonds was actually worth far more than its current market value, pointing to the sustained good credit ratings of the vast majority of the holdings, Gao was completely dismissive, saying that ratings no longer meant anything and that the rating agencies were all useless. However, he said he would try to help and assigned a team to work with us to see if we could come up with a solution. I called Parent back, less than two hours after he had called me and told him that I might be able to do something. Over the next three days we worked developing a framework deal that eventually turned into a $3.5 billion facility, structured as a repurchase agreement in which CDP used its highest quality holdings as security for a loan from CIC. Completing and closing the deal was a huge task, since CIC insisted that ever asset included in the repurchase facility be analyzed and approved and this work was led by Mark Davis, an experienced banker who headed up our New York office, but once the overall agreement was reached, the rest was just hard work and success a foregone conclusion. The result was that CDP did not have to sell down its holdings and ended up weathering the financial crisis in much better shape than other pension funds which had to unwind assets in a very distressed market and take huge portfolio losses. This was the very first such facility arranged out of China to a western financial institution. Although the deal was never publicly announced, it became well enough known to very substantially enhance the reputation of our little firm.

The global financial crisis was as tough on the day-to-day investment banking work of TBG as on most small financial advisory firms, and resulted in the drying up of both our capital markets business and our private placement business, given that many of the investment partners we had been working with prior to the crisis had retreated from the field. We stayed alive through our CIC-CDP deal, and through merger and acquisition work, primarily working with Chinese natural resource firms investing offshore. We acted as advisor to Sinochem Petroleum in their acquisition of Emerald Energy, and we continued to support a number of Chinese mining firms as they expanded their footprints abroad, but this was a more specialist focus than I or my senior team had intended for the next stage of TBG.

In addition, I became worried about how well we would be positioned once the financial crisis past and the global economy returned to some semblance of normalcy. Early in the crisis, CIBC had sold its US investment bank to Oppenheimer, which left us without an active partner in the largest capital market in the world, something we would need if we were to regain our momentum once the crisis abated. When the sale was announced, I had gone quickly to New York to meet with Bud Lowenthal, CEO of Oppenheimer, who made it clear to me that he was not interested enough in the China market to establish anything more than an opportunity-based arms-length relationship. I started to look actively for a new North

American partner who could replace CIBC. Mark Davis and I analyzed at and met with a half dozen mid-size and specialized firms, but none met the four criteria we had established, which were: to be interested but not too well-established in China; active in the natural resource space; have capital markets operations in both the United States and Canada; and finally be willing to look at an equity-based relationship to ensure an alignment of interests.

Half way through 2010, when our partnership conversations were continuing with a couple of mid-sized US investment banks, we were approached by Canaccord Genuity of Canada, who offered to buy TBG and integrate it into its growing international presence as Canaccord Genuity Asia. Canaccord Genuity itself was the result of a 2008-2009 merger between the brokerage-focused Canaccord and the M&A-focused Genuity, the latter having been created by a number of senior bankers who left CIBC in the middle of the previous decade, just as my relationship with CIBC was getting underway. After several months of negotiations, we signed an agreement on November 22, 2010 and closed the deal at the end of January 2011. TBG was independent no more.

As part of the agreement to sell TBG to Canaccord, I agreed to remain as Chairman of the renamed Canaccord Genuity Asia for up to five years, during which time I would continue to earn equity in the publicly listed Canaccord Financial. During the first two years we had some very real successes. We advised on the $3 billion Sinopec purchase of Daylight Energy of Calgary, we negotiated the purchase of Ontario's largest solar power project company to CSI, a long-time client of TBG whose Chairman and CEO I had first met when he was working on a CIDA-financed micro-solar project in Qinghai in the late 1990s. We negotiated a major new private equity investment relationship between a large Canadian pension fund and an Asian partner. And we did some very successful smaller deals between China and the US.

Shortly before the Canaccord acquisition of TBG, I was approached by Sol Kerzner, founder of the Kerzner Group and a friend of Mike Dingman, to see if I could help them in his efforts to bring the Atlantis and One&Only hotel brands to Asia. They had been approached by many would-be partners and wanted support in selecting which might be worthwhile pursuing. At the same time, the Kerzner Group was going through an agonizing restructuring, trying to extract itself from a huge debt burden entered into as it bought itself back from the public markets. Unfortunately, their "going private" buy-back took place not too long before the global financial crisis, a part of which was the crippling of US consumer spending, which meant that just when Kerzner needed robust revenues from its key Atlantis Bahamas resort, tourism fell through the floor and the group could not meet its debt obligations. While the short term crisis had to be dealt with immediately, Sol Kerzner and his board believed that having resorts in China, seemingly immune to global downturns than the Caribbean or the middle east, would both allow it to benefit from rapidly growing Chinese tourism but also put the group in a cyclically less vulnerable position going forward. Sol Kerzner was not interested in engaging Canaccord as a firm; he and his senior team wanted my personal support. As I was now part of Canaccord, however, the engagement had to be corporately established, although Kerzner forced Canaccord to agree to what the latter claimed they never accepted, which was a "key man" provision under which, if I were not available for carrying out the mandate, Kerzner could immediately cancel the contract.

As we proceeded with our first major discussions with a Chinese owner on a potential luxury One&Only hotel at Tufu Bay in Hainan, the final restructuring of the Kerzner Group was taking place half a world away. The local partner was a state-owned firm with no real estate experience, the investment arm of the Gezhouba Hydroelectric Power Company. We chose a luxury hotel at Yalong Bay (where we had first stayed as a family at Christmas time in 1996) as the setting for the negotiations on the Kerzner side were led by Alan Leibman, acting CEO and on the Chinese side by He Jingang, a charming man but completely new to the world of hotel or resort management, which are largely all about the management and other fees paid by the hotel owner to the management company and how the two share the profits, as well as the role of each in choosing and overseeing the local team that will run the resort. Leibman was tough and very direct, He Jingang was very indirect and elliptical, and at one point it was clear to me that the two could never agree to a deal negotiating across the table. I pulled out an old trick and suggested we take a break, and with the Gezhouba team in the conference room and Alan on a terrace some distance away, I shuttled between the two and brokered a final deal, cajoling each of the two principals into compromises without having to lose face in front of the large groups gathered from the two firms. Although I had offered the involvement and support of a debt restructuring team from Canaccord, the Kerzner Group was well advised by a number of New York and London banks, and some months after we reached agreement on the new One&Only, the restructuring was completed, Alan Leibman became CEO and Sol Kerzner retreated to the role of Chairman.

The second Kerzner project was a much larger one, and it was really the major objective that initially brought Sol Kerzner to China in the first place. This was to be an Atlantis, the third in the World, a unique kind of seaside resort with aquaria, a huge waterpark and dolphin shows and rides. The problem in seaside China is that the government tends to maximize density. The beautiful pristine beach that we stayed on in 1996 at Yalong Bay, with its single hotel, had over the following ten years been transformed into a crowded stack of hotel resorts, each with a small waterfront and a long landward extension, very like the seigneurial land division in colonial French Canada. The Atlantis resorts in Bahamas and Dubai, which were to be emulated in the planning for the one in Sanya, each had great long stretches of beachfront, with the resort laid out front to the beach. Every hotel plot planned for the big new resort beaches in Hainan was set out in the perpendicular mode, not amenable for an Atlantis. The Atlantis resorts were famous, however, and there were lots of potential partners offering sites. We looked at half-built resorts up the western coast from Sanya, we looked at undeveloped rocky bays, we were even shown a lot of land that had a major road between it and the beachfront, to be soved according to the local land-use office by simply building a massive bridge across the road. Believing that success in China is almost always about choosing the right local partner, I advised to concentrate our partnership and requirements discussions with one particular partner, Fosun. I had worked with Fosun on a number of cross-border deals and was very impressed with them. They had also just brought on board a terrific new head of a strategic investment group, Qian Jiannong, who had been CEO of the US-listed China Napstar and had spent almost eleven years in Germany. Qian and the Chairman of Fosun, Guo Guangsheng went to visit Atlantis The Palm in Dubai and suggested that we invite Sanya's Party Secretary and the Vice Governor of Hainan Province, Zhang Sixian to stop by and see the resort on the way to Europe, which he did. I had known Zhang when he had been the Deputy Party Secretary of Shanghai, and I toured with him around Atlantis and all the accompanying facilities. In the waterpark I challenged him to go down the steep one hundred meter main slide. He said he would if I led the way, so I did and he followed, as did a few but no all of the visiting Hainan delegation. With his support, the beach area at Haitang Bay was re-zoned in a way that an Atlantis would work, Fosun obtained the land and we concluded a very good agreement for both sides. Qian was always a delight to work with, focused and very smart, qualities that ran right through the Fosun organization.

For the most part, the traditional investment banking work between my China-based team and the Canadian and US investment banking teams of Canaccord Genuity was fine and interesting for my former TBG bankers. And I personally derived much enjoyment from my time working with the head of the Calgary Oil and Gas team, Bruce McDonald, as well as with Phil Evershed, the firm's Global Head of Investment Banking whose senior team was based primarily in Toronto. But the post-sale relationship with Canaccord was not all good, and I found that there were people in the larger corporate family, some in the firm for a long time and some newly hired, with whom I was simply not comfortable working, either due to their approach to deal-making or their attitudes towards China. And no longer being master of my own ship was simply not so much fun any more. So after slightly more than two full years as Chairman of Canaccord Genuity Asia, I resigned from the firm on April 1st, 2013. Liani took my pictures off the wall, we recovered our TBG logo, the stylized boat from the Balloch family coat of arms, and we closed another chapter in my life.

CHAPTER 44

LIFE AFTER LIFE AFTER
DIPLOMACY
AN AFTERWORD

· · · · · · · · · · ·

When Canaccord Genuity purchased TBG, they did not buy the direct investment side of the TBIG company, just the investment bank. Thus the direct investments that we made in education and real estate and medical services survived through the Canaccord period and remain a focus for me going forward. There were also a few relationships that I brought into Canaccord that came out with me, such as my role supporting the Kerzner Group in its efforts to expand in Asia, and on which there was still work to do.

Several years before putting these anecdotes down on paper, I was being interviewed by a Chinese journalist when she asked me to explain the strange phenomenon of a senior diplomat ending up as a businessman. I answered that I had not always been a diplomat, and that I saw my life divided into four major chapters. The first chapter, I said, was a quarter century of growing up and fooling around. The second was a quarter century of being a public servant, moving from being a very junior bureaucrat to culminating in a great five and a half years as Ambassador to one of the world's most important countries. The third quarter century, during which I was currently living, I said would be about business and making a little money. And the fourth quarter century would be growing old and fooling around. Then, I said, I might start it all over again!

Whether I have now closed, or partly closed, that third chapter of my life, only half way through its planned quarter century, and moved on early to the fourth chapter, I simply do not yet know. But the path of life, always uncertain and foggy from a distance, has a curious way of unveiling itself as we move forward, as long as we keep putting one foot in front of the other.

As our family motto reminds me: *Non progredi est regredi.*